THE

TREE OF CULTURE

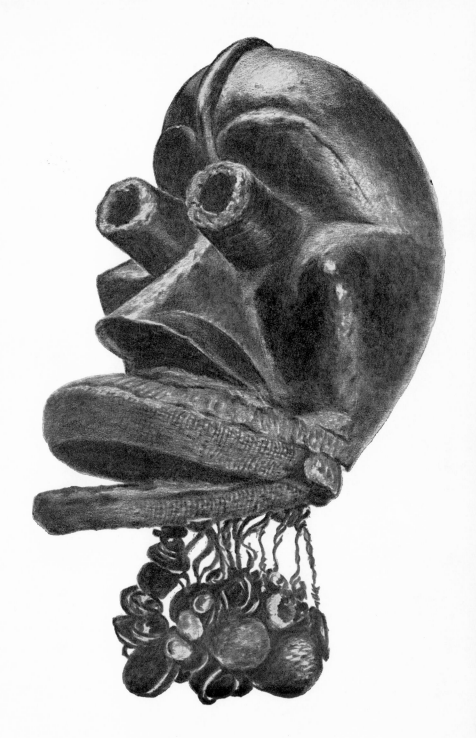

WEST AFRICAN CEREMONIAL MASK

THE

Tree of Culture

RALPH LINTON

NEW YORK: ALFRED A. KNOPF

1956

L. C. Catalog card number: 55-5173

© *Alfred A. Knopf, Inc., 1955*

THIS IS A BORZOI BOOK
PUBLISHED BY ALFRED A. KNOPF, INC.

PUBLISHED APRIL 18, 1955
SECOND PRINTING, AUGUST 1956

PREFACE

DR. RALPH LINTON devoted four years of the spare time salvaged from a busy life in the writing of this book. However, the concepts were evolved and the data accumulated during forty years of work in the varied fields of anthropology: archeology, ethnology, and studies in anthropological theory and personality and culture. This book is an attempt to synthesize the experience, the reading and thinking of a lifetime into one volume which traces the evolution of culture from its multiple beginnings at the sub-human level through its divergent lines of development. The purpose of the book was to make a factual presentation of the most significant data now available. This was a project which required not only broad knowledge but considerable temerity. Anthropological data has been accumulating with such amazing speed in recent years that few scientists venture to deal with the material except as specialists in particular areas or periods. However, Dr. Linton felt that the vast body of information which is available should make possible differentiation of the main divergent lines of cultural development and the assignment of culture elements to their points of origin. This could be accomplished only by a wide over-all presentation, which precludes definitive treatment of the many eras and areas covered. Dr. Linton felt that it was important to assemble this material in compact and intelligible order.

The title of the book refers, not to the familiar evolutionary tree with a single trunk and spreading branches, but to the banyan tree of the tropics. The branches of the banyan tree cross and fuse and send down adventitious, aerial roots which turn into supporting trunks. Although the banyan tree spreads and grows until it becomes a miniature jungle, it remains a single plant and its various branches are traceable to the parent trunk. So cultural evolution, in spite of diffusion and borrowing and divergent development, can be traced to its prehistoric origins.

The first half of the book deals with the general development of culture: the change from food-gathering to food-raising and the other discoveries and inventions which have given man constantly improving control over his environment. Another consistent trend has been the tribal organization of local groups sharing a common language and culture. There has also been a tendency toward increasing large social aggregates formed through the domination of one group over another (empires) or through voluntary association of originally independent groups (confederacies). These have everywhere resulted in increased efficiency in maintaining order and coordinating effort. City living has been an outgrowth of these patterns, although the city emerged so late in human history that our species is still not perfectly adjusted to this phenomenon.

These common directional trends correspond to the first growth of the banyan tree when it sends forth trunk and branches from its original roots. The second half of the book deals with the growth of civilizations, and the comparison here is with the branches which send down roots which find favorable ground and turn into sturdy independent trunks.

All cultures grow irregularly. They have certain foci of interest which have induced them to develop to a high degree those elements which seem important to them and to lag behind in the development of others or to reject them completely. In borrowing from other cultures, which is one of the most important processes of culture growth, they select only those elements which fit into their interest patterns. All the great civilizations of the world have developed along such specialized lines, elaborating and integrating the processes in which their interest centered. This trait has served to increase the richness and variety of world culture, for the successful achievements of one civilization are sooner or later taken over by others.

The Chinese, from the first, have had a practical interest in government and very early evolved a system for the control of large populations in both city and rural areas. Their government has endured for a longer continuous period than that of any other civilization and has contributed many patterns to the political systems of other countries. India's primary contribution has been in the fields of religion and philosophy, but the Indians have exhibited a decided cultural lag in technology. Disharmonic development in cultures is prevented from going too far by the fact that eventually the disharmony will produce conditions which prove too hampering for essential processes of the culture, making adjustments imperative. A case in point is the American preoccupation with technology and our lack of interest in social and political change, which has created a situation in which our institutions and distribution system have failed to keep up with technological advances.

The area in which evolutionary development is least clearly recognizable is that involving the satisfaction of the psychological needs of individuals. The most urgent of these needs is for favorable response from other members of society, but since this is usually expressed through symbolic behavior, its expression may assume a great variety of forms, any one of which is satisfying to those who have been taught to value it. Needs for some sort of aesthetic expression and for escapes from reality also seem universal, and each of the various cultural lines has developed its own solutions and has set its own goals.

The development of techniques for adjusting individuals to their social and cultural environment also fails to show any general evolutionary trend. Apparently the attention of societies has not been consciously directed toward the shaping of individual personalities, perhaps because knowledge of the factors involved and the techniques required are even now so incomplete. Most significant of all, in view of the present world situation, is the fact that no society so far has developed adequate techniques for adjusting the individual for life in a rapidly changing cultural milieu.

This book is not history in the usual sense. In an agricultural society (and most societies were agricultural until a few hundred years ago, and a large proportion of them still are), the invention of a new type of plow is of much more importance than a victory on the battlefield. To a historian it may seem strange that more space is allotted to the Australian aborigines than to the Roman Empire, but to the anthropologist the Australians represent a laboratory where one can see the operation of many elements of culture which otherwise can be surmised only from archeological findings. However, the religion, the social organization, the focus of interest of culture do affect the lives of all the people in the society, and an attempt has been made to show how such elements and processes grow and what has determined the characteristics of the great civilizations of the world.

The Tree of Culture was nearing completion when Dr. Linton died on December 24, 1953. In 1948 a grant from the Wenner-Gren Foundation for Anthropological Research made possible the transcription of the lecture course on which the book is based. Although Dr. Linton himself made use of these transcripts only as a guide and outline, they have proved invaluable for the completion of the book, which I have undertaken, but which would have been impossible without these manuscripts. That this is not the book it might have been had Dr. Linton been given time to complete and edit it himself is undeniable. I have done my best to make it as nearly as possible what he had planned and hoped to make it.

I am grateful for the valuable advice and help which Dr. Linton's friends have generously given me. I especially wish to thank LeRoy and Martha Davidson, Melville Herskovits, Floyd Lounsbury, Sidney Mintz, George P. Murdock, Irving Rouse, Ralph Turner, and Martin Yang. A special note of thanks is due to Will Huntington, not only for doing the excellent drawings in this book, but for his understanding cooperation with Dr. Linton. Claire Vernick, to whom Dr. Linton dictated most of this book and who had worked with him on it since its inception, has also been of inestimable help, and I am grateful to Yale University for making it possible for me to retain her services for the completion of this volume. Special acknowledgements are due the Axel Wenner-Gren Foundation for Anthropological Research, not only for making the lecture transcriptions available, but also for providing the means for travel and research in connection with this book.

ADELIN LINTON

New Haven, Connecticut
June, 1954

Contents

PART SEVEN: *MEDITERRANEAN COMPLEX*

PART EIGHT: *AFRICA*

PART NINE: *THE ORIENT*

PART TEN: *THE NEW WORLD*

CONCLUSION   661

Illustrations

[BY WILL HUNTINGTON]

Maps

[BY THEODORE R. MILLER]

PART ONE

In the Beginning

Chapter I

On the Way to Homo Sapiens

THE PRIMARY purpose of this book is to set down what we know about the origins and growth of what the anthropologist calls culture: the mass of behavior that human beings in any society learn from their elders and pass on to the younger generation. However, before going into this, it is worthwhile to say a little about the origins and qualities of the animal responsible for this curious behavior. This is the more necessary because there is, as always, a lag between what the scientist knows and what the non-scientist believes. The battle between the anthropologists and the anti-evolutionists, which in any case was mainly shadow-boxing on the part of the anti-evolutionists, has long since been fought and won. Outside of a few geographical or intellectual back districts, no one questions today that we are descended from some sort of animal. The main problems are what sort of animal, and what line human evolution has followed. We can dispose of one popular misunderstanding immediately. It is certain that man is not descended from any anthropoid ape now extant. These apes are not our ancestors but are cousins whose line of descent branched off from our own at least a million years ago.

In the attempt to reconstruct human ancestry we have to rely on the evidence of a few fossils, eked out by what we know of the processes of evolution, and by the fairly clear picture which we have of the pattern of primate development in general. It would be nice if we had more early human and semi-human fossils, but it is unlikely that the supply will ever be very large. Until very recent times, in fact, until man learned to raise his own food, he was a comparatively rare species. Our semi-human ancestors were even rarer since they were not as well equipped for exploiting their environment as the first true men. Fifty square miles to support each individual would be a conservative estimate even in favorable territory. Moreover, fossilization requires special conditions. A body which lies out in the open becomes one more item in the economy

3

of nature by way of buzzards, jackals, and all sorts of other carrion eaters down to the bacteria that consume the blood and marrow in the bones, and the rodents that finally gnaw these bones for the gelatin and lime in them. If a skeleton is to be preserved, it must be covered up. Most of the fossils of land animals that we have are the remains of individuals who were caught in bogs or quicksands or were drowned in rivers and carried down to still pools where the bones sank to the bottom and were covered. Even our semi-human ancestors presumably got caught in bogs and quicksands less frequently than their larger and stupider animal compatriots, while primates in general show a strong disinclination for bathing. A comparatively small number of mammalian fossils come from caves, but caves are found in only a few localities and at the time man was evolving they tended to be occupied by large and inhospitable carnivores.

In spite of these difficulties, a moderate number of human and subhuman fossils have been found. There is no point in trying to describe these in detail, since new finds are being made every few months; a list drawn up now would probably be incomplete by the time this book appears. The main significance of these fossils is that they indicate the line of human development. They are points along an evolutionary trajectory, and by sighting from one to another we can extend this evolutionary trajectory from ourselves back into the remote past. When it comes to extending it from ourselves forward, the problem becomes more difficult. During the last half-million years or so, our species has done most of its adjustment by using its brains instead of its genes, a switch which introduces so many new variables into the picture that predictions become little better than guesswork.

From everything that we now know, it seems that our remote ancestors were monkeys. Those who are annoyed by this may take comfort from the fact that at least the founders of our family line were educated in the higher branches. They probably were fairly small beasts who trotted along branches on all fours in the fashion of most modern monkeys and jumped from limb to limb spread-eagled, ready to grab hold with any one of their four corners. Although they probably had tails, it is highly unlikely that they were able to swing by them. Tail-swinging seems to be a special development of the New World monkeys, who are far from the human family line. Any time you read a travel book in which the author mentions seeing African or Asiatic monkeys behaving in that way, you can transfer the volume from *Travel* to *Fiction*.

The first step in the direction of man came when these little beasts took to a new method of travel. Instead of jumping from branch to branch, they began to swing from one branch to another in very much the fashion of an athlete on the flying rings. This brought about important changes in structure which really laid the groundwork for most of the later and more specific features of man's bodily development. In branch-swinging, the body hangs from the arms and is thus brought into a quite different position from that which it has in animals that travel on all fours.

This resulted in a series of structural adaptations. The body became shorter and more compact so that it could be swung for long distances from the arms like a weight on the end of a string. The pelvis took over the task of supporting the viscera, which had formerly been held up by the sling-like abdominal muscles, and became deeper and more bowl-shaped. The shoulder joints, which had previously had only a moderately free rotation, as in modern monkeys, were loosened until they developed the sort of articulation which makes it possible for man today to throw a baseball. This was a tremendously important development since, among other things, it extended the range of man's aggression through the thrown rock and spear and the swung club. The front feet, now completely released from supporting the weight of the body, had its toes elongated into sky hooks, while on each foot one of these toes became increasingly set off from the rest to serve as a thumb. Lastly, the frequent elimination of individuals who could not judge distances when jumping or grab branches successfully led to a steady development of patterns of stereoscopic vision and of neuro-muscular coordination. In other words, most of the things which made the modern man physically the sort of animal that he is today got their start in this branch-swinging adaptation.

At some time during this branch-swinging period the human and anthropoid lines separated. The ancestors of the anthropoids stayed in the trees long enough for their arms to become elongated and to perfect mechanisms for free travel. Later, when some of them became too large for tree living, they had already evolved so far in this direction that even when they came to the ground they were unable to adapt very successfully. The long period of progressive adjustment to branch-swinging had left them overweighted forward and weak in the hind legs. When modern anthropoids travel on the ground, they normally travel on all fours. At the same time, their adaptation to tree living has gone so far that their hands and feet are by no means as well adapted to ground travel as those of their monkey ancestors. Anthropoids walk on the outer edges of their feet and the knuckles of their hands.

While the ancestors of the anthropoids were following the tree road, our ancestors took to the ground. We have no way of telling why they did this, but we do know that during the Miocene geological period, which was probably the time when the human and the anthropoid lines separated, there were very extensive climatic changes in many parts of the world. It is possible that rather than our ancestors leaving the trees, the trees left them. However, the one thing that we can be sure of is that our ancestors came to the ground after their arms and eyes had become fairly well adjusted to tree-swinging but before their bodies had become so well adjusted to it that they could not start out handily on another tack. Even the earliest semi-human fossils which we have show the modern human style of leg and foot fully developed, while such ancient forms as the Neanderthal man had arms which were relatively shorter than those of modern man.

Our type of head seems to have been the last modern characteristic to appear in human evolution. The earliest human ancestors, such as the Java man and the Peking man and the recent African finds, must have looked very much like the animal headed humans figured in medieval bestiaries. These ancestors had human bodies but heads which were essentially ape-like except for one striking difference. Even the earliest semi-humans lacked the large canines of the ape and had teeth which were strikingly like our own. This is especially significant since it indicates that even these remote ancestors probably enjoyed both meat and vegetable foods. Although the brains of these semi-humans were relatively larger than those of any living ape, they nevertheless were very small by modern human standards. The change in this respect seems to

SUB-HUMAN FAMILY

have come with a rush, since the earliest skulls of our own species have a brain capacity quite up to or even larger than the modern average. There is a gap in the record here that is still waiting to be bridged.

From the physical point of view man is merely another large terrestrial primate. He is actually not as far evolved in terms of structural specialization as his cousins the anthropoids. He is set off from the other members of his order, and indeed from other mammals in general, by his tremendous ability to learn, to think, and to communicate to others what he has learned and thought. In such matters, just as in his physical structure, it is possible to see him as the end product of certain generalized evolutionary trends, but here the record is even more incomplete. The break which separates man from the nearest animals in all these respects is so enormous that the differences become not simply quantitative but qualitative.

In rating these special human abilities most people today would probably put intelligence first. This is a direct reflection of our current cultural values with their stress on reasoning ability, as shown in I.Q. tests. Actually, the two most important human qualities are probably superlative learning ability and language. It is wonderful to be able to solve problems by reason rather than trial and error, but we tend to forget that the results of thinking can be no more valid than the premises with which the process starts. These premises have to be learned, usually from other people.

The ability to learn is by no means limited to human beings. Its high development in our species is the culmination of a recognizable evolutionary trend. All living forms respond to their environment with either instinctual or learned behavior. In instinctual responses the circuit of receptor to effector is built into the nervous system. A particular stimulus automatically produces a particular response. The most extreme examples of this are to be found in the insect world where exceedingly elaborate behavior, such as that of the mud wasp or trap-door spider, is carried on quite automatically. In learned behavior, on the other hand, the response is established through practice and experience. If the behavior is rewarded and is repeated often enough, it becomes automatized, i.e., is developed into what we call a habit. Habits are carried on without involving the conscious mind and superficially may look very much like instincts. The great difference is that any habit which has been learned can be extinguished and another more effective habit acquired in its place. This makes for much greater flexibility in the individual's adjustment to his environment.

At the lower levels of evolution, most behavior is controlled by instinct, although even such lowly forms as earth worms and cockroaches can learn a little. As animals increase in the complexity of their nervous

systems, there is a progressive shift from instinct to learning as the dominant factor in their behavior. Instincts practically disappear by the time
one reaches primates in the evolutionary scale. When we get to humans,
who are the ultimate products of the evolutionary trends toward more
and more complex neurological organization, automatic unlearned responses seem to be limited to reactions controlled by the autonomic
nervous system. These would include such things as the digestive processes, adaptation of the eye to light intensity, and similar involuntary
responses. The fewer instincts a species possesses, the greater the range
of behaviors it can develop, and this fact, coupled with the enormous
capacity for learning which characterizes humans, has resulted in a richness and variety of learned behavior which is completely without parallel in other species.

Thanks to the works of modern psychologists, we understand the
processes involved in learning fairly well. Unfortunately, we know considerably less about thinking. This process seems to represent a reorganization of previously learned responses to meet an unfamiliar situation.
The same end can be accomplished by trial and error but much more
slowly and clumsily. The rudiments of thinking ability are found in
many mammalian species other than man. Primates, and especially anthropoids, are better at it than most other animals, but here again the
gap which separates even a stupid human from the most intelligent anthropoid is tremendous. Anthropoid reasoning reaches at best the level
of that of a three to four year old human child.

The use of language is very closely associated with the superior
thinking ability of humans. In his ability to communicate man differs
even more from other animals than he does in his learning or thinking.
Most mammals make sounds or have movements expressive of such emotional states as hunger, anger, fear, pleasure or pain. These are recognized by other individuals of the same species and serve for communication, as anyone who has kept pets can testify. However, man is the
only species which has developed communication to the point where he
can transmit abstract ideas. The symbols which we use are normally verbal, and we usually think of speech and language as synonymous, but
the same sort of communication can be achieved in other ways. It is only
necessary that the symbols used should have the same value for both
communicating parties. Thus, the sign language of the Plains Indians
can be used for such complicated purposes as giving geographic information, preaching a sermon, or making a proposal of marriage with suitable financial guarantees. However, such developments in communication are atypical. Most human language is based on speech. Although
research has shown that speech begins with the shaping up and fixing of
particular phonetic patterns which fall within the range of chance varia-

tion in the sounds made by the child, most of speech has to be learned by imitation. It is a curious fact that there is no mammalian species other than man which imitates sounds. The almost insurmountable difficulties which have attended all efforts to teach apes to talk seem to be due largely to the impossibility of getting them to imitate sounds. An anthropoid can learn readily enough to associate particular objects or acts with particular words just as horses or dogs can, but the idea of trying to imitate these words cannot be gotten over to them. In this respect, humans are truly unique.

We know absolutely nothing about the early stages in the development of language, although this has not prevented philologists from putting forward a number of more or less ingenious theories with which we need not concern ourselves here. There is also at least one experiment on record. The Emperor Akbar, having been told that Hebrew was the original language of mankind and that children who had been taught no other would speak it automatically, had a group of infants isolated with deaf mutes as nurses to see what would happen. When they were presented to him a few years later he found that they communicated by gestures, like their nurses.

It is safe to conclude that the use of language is exceedingly old, but unwritten languages disappear without leaving a trace. By the time that writing first appeared, in Egypt and the Near East, about 4000 B.C., the evolution of language was complete. The earliest languages which have left a record were as complex in their grammar and as adequate for the conveyance of ideas as any modern ones. Moreover, everything indicates that during the early part of human history there were far more languages spoken than there are at present. Each of the little, strictly local groups in which early man must have lived probably had its own.

The so-called primitive languages can throw no light on language origins, since most of them are actually more complicated in grammar than the tongues spoken by civilized peoples. They present a truly bewildering array of concepts expressed in grammatical form, such things as gender based on shape or consistency; singular, dual, and plural pronouns inclusive and exclusive; and a host of other forms. One suspects that in the development of many languages grammar must reach a point where it becomes so unwieldy that the people cease to bother with it, like an American soldier abroad. After all, a surprising amount of communication is possible without the correct use of irregular verbs. Such breakdowns result in almost grammarless languages such as Chinese or English, the latter a crystallized survival of the patois which the Norman man-at-arms used with the Saxon bar-maid. However, in the absence of grammar, with its possibilities for expressing multiple ideas by slight modifications of a few roots, a larger vocabulary becomes necessary. The enormous vocabulary of English is a necessity if the language is to be used to convey precise ideas. Equally grammarless Chinese, with a much more limited vocabulary, has the brevity and uncertainty of meaning of a cablegram.

In spite of such differences, we have abundant evidence that any idea can be conveyed in any language. The differences lie in whether the society has been familiar enough with the idea, or sufficiently interested, to coin a single term for it. Thus, to convey the idea of an airplane in an aboriginal Australian dialect would require several hundred words, while in English a single word would do it. However, it would take quite as long to convey in English the idea of Alchuringa ancestor which could be conveyed by a single Australian word.

The symbolic system created by language is a tremendous aid to the individual in thinking, although the concepts embodied in the structure of the language in which he thinks are likely to have their effects on the outcome. This is a field which is just beginning to be explored by the emergent science of semantics. Thus, the fact that there is no inanimate gender in Indo-European languages makes all their speakers animistic in their approach to abstractions. If our grammar divided the contents of the universe into animate and inanimate, as do the Algonquin languages, our philosophers would have been saved from wandering into many logical bypaths.

Most of our thinking is done in words, although other symbols can also be used. Thus the artist or musician operates with a different, nonverbal, set of symbols and has corresponding difficulty in describing his creative processes. With the aid of symbols it is possible for the individual to solve problems and arrive at results without going through the slow and clumsy process of overt trial and error. The use of words in thinking is very much like the use of mathematical symbols in calculation. Mathematical symbols make it possible to solve all sorts of problems without weighing or counting actual objects. Word symbols make it possible to determine the results of particular actions without actually performing them.

The human combination of extreme learning ability and language has made it possible for our species to accumulate and transmit from generation to generation a wealth of knowledge and tested behavior patterns which no other species can even approach. In other mammalian species, offspring can and do learn a few simple forms of behavior by imitating their parents, but the possibilities are limited both by the parents' inability to transmit abstract ideas and by the relatively short time that parents and young are together. In humans, the child's dependence on and consequent association with parents must continue for 10 to 12 years as a minimum. Before the first third of this period has passed, the child has acquired language and the parent can thus transmit to him the proper responses not only for situations which arise while they are together but for those which may arise in the future. Parents can tell children about all sorts of things which can happen and what to do when they do.

Since humans are the most intelligent and also the most easily taught of animals, one would expect them to be the most highly individuated. No two persons are exactly alike in their physical and mental potentialities, and certainly no two individuals, even identical twins reared in the same family, have the same experiences. Human beings are thus potentially less alike than the individuals of any other species. It is most surprising therefore, that they have chosen to live in closely organized groups whose members carry on a variety of specialized activities but are mutually interdependent for the satisfaction of practically all their fundamental needs. Many other mammalian species live in herds or packs, but the organization in these is minimal. The only division of activities is that devolving upon the two sexes by their different roles in connection with reproduction, while social control is a simple matter of the poorer fighters giving precedence to the better ones. To find anything which even remotely resembles the complexity of human societies, one must go to the social insects, such as the ants and the bees. Here the cooperation which is necessary for the survival of the community is assured by the physical specialization of the various groups of workers, fighters, and so forth, and by a high development of instincts. Since humans lack such instincts, it becomes necessary to subject them to an extraordinarily long and elaborate training if they are to function successfully as members of a society. We are, in fact, anthropoid apes trying to live like termites, and, as any philosophical observer can attest, not doing too well at it.

Chapter II

The Pleistocene Age

WE DO NOT KNOW where the first recognizable representatives of our species appeared, but we can be fairly sure that it was not in some small, clearly delimited area. There was no Garden of Eden. Subhuman fossils which might be in our line of ancestry have been found as far apart as China, Western Europe and South Africa, and we can be fairly sure that various subhuman species occupied all the temperate and tropical parts of Eurasia and Africa. We do not know which of these is our ancestor or whether two or more subhuman species may not have contributed to the making of modern man. It seems that when any two primates of opposite sex and of the same or similar species meet, their normal reaction is to make a pass at each other, and if the various species of semi-humans did not mix their genes, it was probably not for lack of trying.

As has been said before, the fossil record is exceedingly fragmentary, but the earliest remains of our own species which have been discovered show them to have been like modern men in every respect. Apparently, these first representatives of homo sapiens were like ourselves even to the extent of having the same psychological potentialities. The great difference between their way of life and ours was due to the difference in the amount of knowledge which was available for them to learn and transmit.

Since our species emerged, it seems to have made most of its environmental adjustment by way of changes in its learned, transmitted behavior. It has, to be sure, produced physical varieties partly in response to environmental factors which it could not handle in any other way, partly, it seems, by chance, but none of these changes have been very far reaching. Their results are to be seen in what we call the races of mankind.

Before undertaking a discussion of these human varieties and how

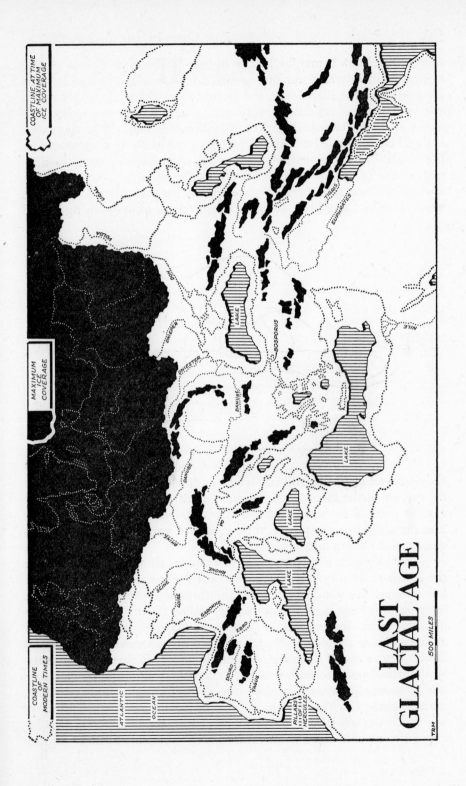

LAST GLACIAL AGE

500 MILES

COASTLINE AT TIME
OF MAXIMUM
ICE COVERAGE

MAXIMUM
ICE
COVERAGE

COASTLINE OF
MODERN TIMES

ATLANTIC

OCEAN

PILLARS
((OF))
HERCULES

TAGUS

DOURO

EBRO

GARONNE

LOIRE

SEINE

RHONE

RHINE

DANUBE

DANUBE

DNIESTER

DNIEPER

DON

VOLGA

URAL

LAKE

LAKE

LAKE

LAKE

LAKE

LAKE

BOSPORUS

TIGRIS

EUPHRATES

NILE

TRM

they came about, it may be best to digress briefly to give some picture
of the world in which our first human ancestors found themselves. By
the middle of the Pleistocene, the earliest date which we can assign for
our own species, conditions were very much as they are today. The
mammals had established world domination long before. The dinosaurs,
beloved of the comic book artists, had been out of the way for many million years. Birds were entirely as they are now. Even the same families
and genera of birds were living much as they do today. The mammals
also had evolved into species very much like the present ones. Although,
when men first appeared, such bizarre forms as saber-tooth tigers and

BRONTOSAURUS

shovel-jawed elephants still survived in a few out of the way places, by
the middle of the Pleistocene the general character of animal life in the
various parts of the world was not very different from what it is today.
The main differences were in the location of various ecological aggregates rather than in their content.

The Pleistocene was a period of extreme climatic fluctuations. In
the Northern Hemisphere, there were at least four extended periods of
low temperature with ice advance, and three intervening periods when
temperatures were higher than they are today. During the second interglacial period, for instance, hippopotami sported in the Rhine and
Thames. These periods of glacial advance and recession were tremendously long, some of them running into hundreds of thousands of years.
Within these periods there were also minor fluctuations in temperature
like those which have taken place during the historic period and which
are still going on. Thus, we know that in the Bronze Age Scandinavia
was much warmer than it is now and that this favorable period was followed by one of lowered temperature which gave place again to warmer

weather around 1000 A.D. This warmer period made it possible for the Norse to settle in Greenland and to raise barley in Iceland. By the 14th century temperatures had gone down again, while at the present writing they seem to be going up everywhere. During the last few years, the glaciers have been retreating on all fronts and in Iceland have uncovered fields which were farmed by the Vikings.

The reasons for these temperature fluctuations are still very imperfectly understood, and, after all, have little to do with our present discussion. Suffice it to say that earliest man, like any other animal, was in very close adjustment with his natural environment and unquestionably shifted with the changing climate, as did the plants and the animals on which he was accustomed to live. It seems highly probable that this is responsible for much of the confusion that archeologists find in some of the earliest European sites. We know that until 20 or 30 thousand years ago cultures developed very slowly. Periods longer than the whole of recorded history might go by without any recognizable changes. It is quite possible that the climate changed faster than culture and that the mixture of cultures which is found in such sites reflects the ebb and flow of peoples across Europe in response to its changing ecologies.

During the Pleistocene period, although the general arrangement of the world's land masses was much as it is today, there were differences in the details. Some of these must have been important for early man. We will only deal with the Old World at this point since what went on in the New World had no bearing on human beginnings. Man did not manage to reach the Americas until a mere 20 to 30 thousand years ago at the earliest, and possibly not before 15 thousand years ago. By this time, he was physically indistinguishable from some of the historic American Indians and had a culture more advanced than that of some of the food gathering peoples living today. We also need not concern ourselves with the outer islands of the Pacific, whose settlement came even later. Only people who had already learned how to build good seagoing vessels could reach Polynesia, which probably was not populated much before the beginning of the Christian era.

It should be remembered that even at the peak of the glacial advances ice never covered the whole of the Eurasiatic continent. Its distribution was always irregular, with different centers for the different glaciations. As such periods developed, ice moved out from the various Asiatic and European mountain ranges, but except at the very height of a glacial advance even the interiors of the continents were never completely covered. Thus, far Northeastern Asia seems to have never been glaciated, although the temperatures there must have been exceedingly low at the time of the glacial advances. Probably, the snowfall in this region was too light to form glacial ice. Across Southern Eurasia and

Africa there were no glaciers. Here the equivalents of the glacial periods were the so-called Pluvials. These were times of comparatively cool, rainy weather which made many regions which are now desert desirable for human occupation.

During and immediately after each glacial advance, there was a marked drop in sea level, varying from 100 to as much as 250 feet. It is generally believed that this was due to the locking up of great quantities of water in the continental glaciers. Whatever the cause, it had the effect of making all of the world's land masses more extensive than they are at present. Eastern Asia extended south to take in Java, Sumatra, Borneo and most of the other Indonesian Islands. To the south of this enlarged Asiatic continent, and separated from it by a strip of deep sea much older than the Pleistocene, there was another continent in which Australia, Tasmania, New Guinea and most of the Melanesian Islands were linked together. The strait which separated these two continents was narrow enough so that man was able to cross into the Southern continent in fairly early times. He brought with him his first animal friend, the dog, who thus became the only other mammal of modern placental type to gain a foothold in Australia. The native fauna there are still archaic marsupials such as kangaroos and opossums.

To the westward, the Eurasian continent was much more closely linked with Africa than it is today. Northeast Africa and Southwest Asia, if they were not actually joined, were separated only by an easily passable strait at the mouth of the Red Sea, while the Isthmus of Suez was there then as it is now. Perhaps more important than the actual distribution of land at this point is the fact that during the Pluvials the territory on both sides of the Red Sea, which is now some of the toughest desert in the world, was well-watered park country with abundant game. The only barrier which migrants had to pass was, therefore, a narrow waterway. That man did go back and forth here from very early times is proved by the practical identity of the older cultural remains on the two sides of the Red Sea.

Farther to the west, the present site of the Mediterranean seems to have been occupied by two lakes divided by a ridge running from Sicily to Africa and cut off from the Atlantic by another ridge at Gibraltar. The archeological remains show no indications of people going back and forth between Italy and North Africa until relatively late times when they were able to travel by sea, but there is abundant evidence that there was travel back and forth between North Africa and Spain by way of the Gibraltar land bridge.

Much of what is now the Mediterranean Sea bottom was probably well suited for occupation during the Pluvials. In these periods what is now the desert of Sahara was also well watered and teeming with game.

In spite of the Pluvial and Interpluvial variation in rainfall, most of Africa south of the Sahara seems to have had very much the same range of climates as are found there at present. This accounts for the survival in that continent of such archaic beasts as the elephant, rhinoceros, and giraffe.

To sum up, when modern man appeared Eurasia and Africa were much more closely tied together than they are at present, and great areas which are now undesirable were well suited for human occupation. During the warm interglacial periods, it would have been possible for a family to wander from North China to the Cape of Good Hope, or from Sumatra to Scandinavia, without encountering any insurmountable natural barriers. Needless to say, any family would have encountered many different environments in the course of such wandering, and it is against the background of such environmental differences that we must look at human varieties and their origins.

PART TWO

Evolutionary Processes

Chapter III

Race

PROBLEMS OF RACE, and particularly of race relations, absorb so much of
our interest at the present time that a discussion of human history which
did not involve some mention of this subject would be incomplete. There
is a tremendous amount of literature on racial origins and a number of
ideas have become generally accepted in spite of the fact that there is
very little direct evidence on which to base conclusions. Even the field
of human genetics is still very imperfectly understood. Unfortunately,
human beings do not lend themselves to genetic experiments, while an
even greater difficulty arises from the fact that subject and observer
have the same life span. No scientist is likely to see even four generations of a single human family line.

As was said in an earlier chapter, there seems to be good evidence
that during the Pliocene and Pleistocene there were a number of subhuman species scattered throughout the tropical and warmer temperate regions of the Old World. While none of these species were fully
human from the anatomical point of view, several of them behaved like
humans to the extent of using tools and fire. It is interesting to note that
most of them also seem to have been addicted to the exceedingly human
practice of cannibalism, rare in other mammalian species. We do not
know whether our own species, homo sapiens, evolved from a single one
of these prehuman species or whether it began as a hybrid between two
or more. However, it may be said authoritatively that the various great
divisions, i.e., racial stocks, commonly used in classifying modern human
varieties, are not descendants of different subhuman ancestors. The old
idea, once held by physical anthropologists, was that there were original
clearly differentiated Negro, Caucasoid and Mongoloid groups and that
the innumerable intermediate types which now link the extreme examples of each stock came about as a result of crossing. As a matter of fact,
the earliest finds of true humans do not substantiate this idea in any

way. The earliest representatives of homo sapiens show a striking diversity in all the physical characteristics used as a basis for racial classification and none of them are readily assignable to any one of the great stocks. This may be due in part to the fact that we lack data on their skin color, hair texture, shape of nose and lips, and similar superficial characteristics on which current racial classification is so largely based. Nevertheless, the variability of these early forms is truly amazing. Thus, in the upper cave at Chukutien in Northern China, three skulls of approximately the same age have been identified as being respectively North Chinese of modern type, an Eskimo and a Melanesian. Since it is highly improbable that Chukutien was the center of an antediluvian United Nations, the only answer would seem to be that even within this one locality the population was exceedingly variable. If we take the whole range of known upper Paleolithic skeletons, we find that very few, even of those from neighboring localities, are alike.

It would seem very desirable to review the problem of racial differentiation in the light not only of fossil evidence, but also of what we know of early human patterns of settlement and their possible effects on racial differentiation. Early man seems to have spread over the Old World rather rapidly until he occupied all but the Circumpolar and most inhospitable desert regions. However, if we may judge from the situation in those parts of the world where the inhabitants were still following a simple food gathering economy when first encountered by Europeans, the distribution of the species was by no means uniform. As with any other wild species, the population density of early man varied from one region to another in direct relation to the food supply. We have every reason to believe that even the earliest men lived in bands, i.e., units composed of several families. The members of such a unit normally camped and traveled together. The possible size of the bands in any locality was set by the number of individuals who could be supported by hunters and food gatherers working out from a central camping place. It is improbable that any of the early human bands exceeded 200 to 300 individuals, while most of them were certainly much smaller. Modern food gathering peoples without domestic animals other than the dog rarely live in groups of over 50 or 60 persons.

As long as unoccupied territory is available, populations spread by a sort of budding process. When the membership of a band becomes too large for advantageous exploitation of local resources, the group splits and a new band is formed. Under normal circumstances, bands are not free-wandering units. Each band normally occupies a definite territory within which it makes regular annual circuits, coming back to the same camp sites year after year at the same seasons to exploit the local food resources. Several bands usually form a larger unit, a tribe, whose members have a vague feeling of unity based upon common language and customs, but in the absence of formal patterns of government such tribal units cannot grow to any great size. In general, trespassing on another band's territory is resented and punished. However, it is a significant fact that none of the really primitive food gathering groups indulge in anything which can be called systematic warfare. Rather than one group attempting to drive another out of its territory to provide room for increasing numbers, the pattern seems to be for the population to stabilize in relation to its food supply. Although there may be considerable fluctuation from time to time in accordance with good or bad years, the general population levels remain very much the same. It is highly probable that this was also the situation with early man.

The members of a tribe normally marry among themselves and even bands are frequently endogamous. Observation of many different species has shown that the situation of small, highly inbred groups is ideal for the fixation of mutations and consequent speeding up of the evolutionary process. In general, the smaller the inbreeding group, the more significant any mutation becomes for the formation of a new variety. In large populations, single mutations tend to be swamped out and lost; while in small ones, single mutations, especially if they are of an advantageous sort, will be propagated to more and more individuals in each generation, the mutant genes reaching them through a large percentage of their ancestors instead of through only a few. In this way the new characteristics can spread rapidly to the entire group, resulting in a permanent change. When the pattern of small, inbreeding groups is combined with occasional contacts with other groups, resulting in transfers of the locally fixed mutations, one has the most favorable situation for adaptive evolution.

We can picture the early human population as consisting of a great number of small groups, the members of each of which showed what might be called a family resemblance. There would be occasional transfers of genes as a result of sporadic contact occurring between different bands or tribes. Since genes are transmitted either individually or in small linked groups, the tendency would be for each mutant character to show a continuous geographic distribution, but to vary in its frequency of occurrence from high frequency near its center to low frequency at the outer limits of its occurrence. Since different mutations would arise at different points, their spreads would overlap, producing a wide range of different combinations of physical characteristics. Thus, to take a hypothetical case, the epicanthic fold, i.e., slant eyes, might be distributed across Eurasia from its presumably Far Eastern point of origin, becoming less frequent within various populations as one went westward and combining in various groups with such unmongoloid characteristics as curly hair, gray eyes, and so forth. These other characteristics in turn would have their own geographic centers of distribution, diminishing in frequency from these centers toward the peripheries of the area in which they were found. Very much this situation is revealed by the current studies of blood types which show fairly systematic distributions but do not coincide with other racial criteria. This picture is greatly simplified and could be modified in various ways, especially as a result of large scale migrations, but there is good reason to believe that large scale migrations were rare in pre-food-raising times.

Since the very beginnings, human beings have been able to do most of their adjustment to their environment by way of learned behavior, i.e., culture. Thus, a lake or a river people would meet their problems of travel on the water by the development of canoes and paddles rather than by the progressive selection of the individuals who were best adapted structurally to swimming. However, there are certain aspects of environment which cannot be dealt with culturally, or at least can only be dealt with by elaborate devices which lay beyond the capacity of early man. Among these are temperature and light intensity.

Although our information is still very inadequate, it seems that certain types of body build are better adapted to certain temperatures. The human body is an engine and, like any other engine, must dispose of the surplus heat generated in its operation. Tall, rangy individuals provide more radiating surface than do short, chunky ones of the same weight. As a result, natural selection would give tall, skinny individuals a better chance in high temperature areas and short, chunky ones a better chance in the Arctic. While this sort of selection would not show results at once, its effects would be cumulative. Thus in some of the hottest regions in the world we have the Nilotic Negroes, many of whom are well over six feet with a build reminiscent of a stork, and in the Arctic, the Eskimos, whose build is reminiscent of that of a granite boulder. Unfortunately for these generalizations there are also exceptions. The tallest, although by no means slenderest, human variety known to science is the Scottish lowlander, who occupies a far from tropical climate, while the Congo Pygmy, not to be confused with the Oceanic Negrito, is almost as chunky as the Eskimo. However, the generalization holds in enough cases to suggest that natural selection really has been at work here.

Another area in which natural selection has certainly occurred is that of skin color in relation to light. It can be said with certainty that there is nowhere in the world where very dark skinned groups are to be found in regions deficient in sunlight, such as Scandinavia, or in which blonde groups have survived for any length of time in regions of intense sunlight. Unfortunately, the selective mechanisms involved are still imperfectly understood, but it seems that there is an optimum amount of sunlight for human beings and that either too much or too little has to be balanced off by pigment changes. Too much actinic ray apparently results in damage to the nervous system and also, if the experience of whites in the tropics is to be trusted, in injuries to the female reproductive system. Where sunlight is insufficient, on the other hand, the ray screen provided by heavy pigment is definitely disadvantageous. The dark members of a community will be more subject to rickets than the lighter members. Needless to say, these difficulties are not immediately fatal, but in any group whose members varied in the depth of their skin color, they would eventually shift the group norm in the direction of the depth of pigment which was most advantageous under the local conditions. It is certainly significant that it is not only in Northwestern Europe that we have the emergence of lightly pigmented types. A tendency toward light pigmentation can be traced clear across the circumpolar areas of the Old World and even to the Indians of British Columbia. In this far northern Pacific region, where the skies are almost as cloudy as those over Scandinavia, individuals of unmixed Indian ancestry often show pale skins, green or gray eyes, and red hair.

There are probably other and subtler human adjustments to natural environment for which we are still unable to trace the connections. Also, as a factor in the establishment of distinctive local types one must take into account the purely social matter of the preferences which certain groups feel for certain physical characteristics. Thus, there are many African tribes who prefer the black that shines, while others regard feminine avoirdupois with reverence and carefully fatten their women before marriage. The Maya combined with their keen aesthetic sense a preference for such characteristics as big noses, retreating foreheads, weak chins and cross eyes. The extraordinary profiles to be seen on Maya monuments are not caricatures but represent the classic type of Maya beauty, as thoroughly approved socially and probably no farther from reality than the classical type of Greek beauty. It has been urged that social selection is of no great significance at the primitive level since all members of a primitive group get married. However, they do not all marry the same people. The most beautiful girls, whatever this means in local terms, can marry the best hunters and their children have that much better chance for survival. As for the handsome male, his opportunity for propagating his genes in or out of wedlock is always considerably better than that of the ugly man.

There is one other aspect of evolutionary adaptation which has been exceedingly important in determining the spread of various racial groups. Unfortunately, little attention has been paid to this factor in the past, since it is not immediately obvious, but one may predict that it will become of increasing importance as population movements in the modern world become freer. This is the acquisition by different human groups of tolerance for different diseases. We know that when any human group is subjected to the attacks of a particular disease for several generations, those who survive will develop a certain degree of tolerance. The disease will be much less destructive to them than it will be to a group who have never been exposed to it previously. Since the members of the tolerant group are very frequently carriers of the disease, they are able to wage a type of bacterial warfare which is none the less deadly because it is unconscious. All students of early American history will be familiar with the terrific ravages of smallpox when it was introduced into the New World by Europeans, while students of European history will be equally familiar with the far reaching political and social consequences of syphilis, which the American Indians graciously gave to the Europeans in exchange. Fortunately for Western Europe, this introduction was not followed by the invasion of a swarm of syphilis-tolerant individuals of a different race and culture, but even without this its influence can be traced in such diverse phenomena as the defeat of a French army in Italy, the elimination of bathing as a North European custom and the introduction of wigs as necessary adjuncts to aristocratic male costume.

One of the most interesting cases of disease tolerance in its relation to racial distributions is provided by malaria. Most Negro groups appear to be much more tolerant of the malignant variety of malaria than Europeans or Asiatics. Europeans, on the other hand, have a higher tolerance for the variety of malaria known as benign tertian than do Negroes. In Oceania we find that a fairly clear-cut line can be drawn between the areas in which two racial types occur. Polynesians, brown skinned people of Southeast Asiatic origin, are to be found in practically all areas where there are no anopheles mosquitoes and consequently no malaria. Melanesians, dark skinned people of Negroid type, are to be found wherever there are anopheles mosquitoes and malaria. The only exception to the rule seems to be in Fiji, where a Negroid population is to be found in the absence of anopheles, a quite understandable situation since the absence of malaria would not affect settlers tolerant to it.

In Madagascar, brown people of Southeast Asiatic origin occupy the central plateau of the island where there were no anopheles mosquitoes until they were introduced by the building of a railroad from the coast. Completely surrounding this island of Asiatics was a belt of Negroid peoples who occupy all the fever infected coastal lowlands. One of the most interesting aspects of this situation was that the Negroid people all speak Malayo-Polynesian languages and have cultures which show a strong Asiatic tinge. There can be little doubt that they arrived on the island after the Malayo-Polynesians by a process of gradual infiltration rather than mass settlement. They presumably brought malaria with them from Africa, with the result that the Asiatic racial type was eliminated in all areas where there were fever carrying mosquitoes, although not before the Asiatics had transmitted much of their culture to the Negro immigrants.

In the New World also, Negro slaves introduced malignant malaria into many tropical regions, leading to the practical extinction of the local Indian population. Even in Europe, Negro slaves who were brought in by the Portugese were responsible for the depopulation of the Tagus valley by malignant malaria. We cannot say how often such situations have arisen in early human history, but disease tolerances and susceptibilities must certainly have played a considerable role in establishing racial distributions.

In summary, we can imagine a long period during which there was a great multiplicity of human types, each of which had very limited geographic distribution and was represented by only a small group of individuals. This situation probably persisted for many thousands of years, at least during the whole of the Old Stone age. An abrupt change must have occurred with the invention of food raising. As has been said before, food gathering populations tend to stabilize on the basis of the existing wild food supply. With agriculture, the productive potential of land is tremendously increased. In the presence of an assured food supply populations can double every twenty-five years. Thus, to cite a current example, the Navajo Indians, who were supposed to number between twenty- and twenty-five thousand when I first encountered them in 1912, now number over sixty thousand. Groups who for any reason had acquired food raising were thus at a great advantage, the more so since with the new technique they could utilize the territories of tribes who were still on a food gathering economy.

The result was a rapid expansion of the food-raising peoples. There is abundant evidence for great migrations having taken place from the Southwestern Asiatic center of Old World agriculture early in the food-raising period. Both the Alpine and Mediterranean physical types, dominant in historic Europe, can be traced back to this general region. Such migrations not only increased the numbers of the racial groups who practiced food-raising, but also automatically decreased the number of hunters and food gatherers. Even if the migrants did not kill off the earlier populations of territories they invaded, they reduced their numbers by destroying the supply of wild foods. Actually, the migrants do not seem to have exterminated the old food-gathering populations of Europe, but simply absorbed them, as the occasional appearance of Paleolithic physical types in the present European population shows.

In spite of the fact that the world's population has increased enormously since the invention of food-raising, there are probably fewer human varieties, i.e., races, extant today than there were at the end of the Old Stone age. Although the processes leading to production of new human varieties are still operative, they have not had time to differentiate such great, rapidly expanded groups as the Mediterranean Caucasians or Malays into any large number of distinctive sub-types.

Aside from their relation to disease tolerance and adaptation to climate, racial differences seem to have had little or no effect on human history. Their present significance is almost entirely social; i.e., the individual's physical characteristics are significant only in so far as they mark him as a member of a particular social group. In spite of numerous investigations and a great mass of literature on the subject, the existence of significant psychological differences between various races has never been proved. Apparently, the members of any racial group can assume any culture in which they are reared and we know that members of all the great racial stocks have made important additions to culture at one time or another. The only significant effect that race can have on culture, so far as we can determine at present, is that the size, strength and agility characteristic of a particular group's members is likely to influence the type of tools and weapons they prefer and their methods of using them. Thus, it has been found that Malay workmen, most of whom are small and lightly muscled, have difficulty in operating machines which have been designed for large and physically powerful Europeans.

It is quite possible that there may have been actual hereditary differences in intelligence between some of the original small racial enclaves into which early man was divided, but contact and competition between various racial types has been going on for so long that any innately deficient groups, if they ever existed, seem to have been eliminated. For the purposes of the study of cultural history and development, all human groups may be taken as equivalent. This does not mean that all have made an equal contribution to the growth of culture, but everything indicates that the differences which exist are due to historic accident rather than to any innate qualities of the groups in question.

Chapter IV

Society, Culture, and the Individual

MOST OF human existence revolves about the interrelations and interactions of society, culture, and the individual. These entities are so closely interdependent that investigators are likely to become confused when they try to differentiate them. In particular, the terms culture and society are often used interchangeably. Nevertheless, each of the three is a phenomenon of a different order and each has its own special characteristics and its special role in the dynamic configuration formed by all three together. A society is an organized group of individuals. A culture is an organized group of learned responses characteristic of a particular society. The individual is a living organism capable of independent thought, feeling, and action, but with his independence limited and all his responses profoundly modified by contact with the society and culture in which he develops.

The individual has a limited life span. Societies and cultures, on the other hand, are continua with no predetermined duration. They normally persist far beyond the life span of any of their individual members and there seem to be no inherent factors which might prevent them from surviving indefinitely. Certain philosophic historians to the contrary, we have no evidence that societies and cultures ever die of old age. They frequently succumb to violence or economic poverty, but the cultural mechanism is so flexible that, as long as the personnel of a society can be maintained either by physical reproduction or recruitment, the society can survive. It may have to modify most of its structure and change its methods of life profoundly, but it will still persist as an organized functioning group.

Why human beings have a tendency to form aggregates is a question for which we have no final answer. It is a fact that most primates are gregarious and the social scientist of two or three generations ago blithely took care of this universal human pattern by positing the existence of a gregarious instinct. Unfortunately for such an attractive theory, it is very questionable whether human beings have any instincts in the sense that this term is commonly used by students of animal behavior. However, all human beings have certain experiences which predispose them to group living. Thus, human infants are always exceedingly dependent little animals who cannot survive without the care and aid of adults. As a result, an unconscious association is established between comfort and security and the presence of other individuals.

A further contribution toward this predisposition for group living is made by the difference between the breeding interval in our own species and the time required for the individual to reach a point where he can take care of himself. Evidence from many societies indicates that where there is no artificial spacing of births, a woman will produce offspring every 18 months on an average, while even in the simplest societies where economic factors are least significant, children cannot very well become independent before the age of twelve. This means that during several of the most formative years of his life the child is in close and constant association not only with parents but with brothers and sisters older and younger than himself. In this way he obtains an intensive training in cooperation and social adjustment and a reinforcement of the psychological effects of his infantile dependency.

The human tendency to form aggregates is linked with an equally strong tendency to transform these aggregates into societies through organization. This process can be seen in operation in summer camps, work crews, offices, and, in fact, wherever groups of individuals remain in contact for any length of time. Perhaps it would be better to call such units subsocieties, since they usually are part of a larger social whole. The interactions of the individuals who form the group are reduced to habitual, predictable terms; leadership emerges and tasks are allotted. The organization of new subsocieties is facilitated by the fact that the individuals who compose them have all had experiences of social living. Very often the culture will include patterns for the organization of such new or temporary units. For example, the 18th century British culture provided crews who mutinied and "went on the account" (turned pirate) with a conventional pattern of organization developed by generations of free-booters.

Although new societies can be formed readily enough, a society of what may be considered the normal type usually has a lengthy existence. It includes individuals of both sexes and all ages and insures its survival by producing children and training them to fill places in its system of organization. The nucleus of such societies is composed of its adult and able-bodied members. Children are able to make some contribution toward its operation, but their role is primarily that of replacements. Like the members of a second team, they are in training, learning to perform the functions and preparing to occupy the positions currently associated with their elders. Old people in most societies make their social contribution mainly by acting as repositories of experience and by offering advice, a role which, as anyone can testify, they usually find congenial.

There has been a tendency on the part of some of the more formalistic social scientists to picture any society as groups of individuals trying to hold themselves together by more or less ingenious devices. Such devices may be needed where aggregates of adults are organizing themselves into new societies or under conditions like those in a modern city with its anonymous population. However, the small, long continuing, localized aggregates which form the basis for most societies certainly require no such devices. The members of such a community are held together not only by economic interdependence but even more strongly by emotional ties based upon affection and habitual association. Above all, as sharers of a common culture, the members of such a group are able to understand each other better and to feel more at ease with each other than they can with persons having a different cultural background. Note the behavior of Americans meeting in a French village. Even in those cases where the structure of a society has collapsed under the impact of a stronger alien society and culture so that the group can no longer function adequately, it is an observed fact that its members will continue to stay together simply because they share a common language and have common understandings.

A continuing group of individuals such as that provided by the normal society can be organized in several different ways simultaneously. To understand this, one need only think of the multiplicity of organizational systems which exist in such a group as a college community. Here one can observe the organization of the entire group for educational purposes into units whose membership is determined by academic progress. At the same time, the same aggregate will be organized along quite different lines in response to considerations of social prestige and for the carrying on of social activities in the popular sense of that term. There will be numerous fraternities and sororities and a non-fraternity student group, not to speak of various scientific and literary clubs, membership in which is based on interest in particular subjects.

Human societies of the usual self-perpetuating type always have the following simultaneous patterns of organization as a minimum. First, the group's members are classified according to age and sex and, strictly on this basis, are assigned certain patterns of behavior. Thus, at the primitive level, men are universally expected to do the hunting and fighting, women to collect vegetable foods and care for small children. Second, the society's members are divided into smaller organized units, i.e., families. Unfortunately, the English term "family" fails to differentiate between what is frequently referred to as the nuclear family, consisting of a couple and their children, and the various groupings based upon blood relationship, either real or assumed. The individual's membership in a family unit immediately establishes for him a series of reciprocal rights and obligations toward a whole series of other persons who are members of the same unit. Third, all societies recognize the existence of formal, culturally patterned relationships which individuals enter into voluntarily. The distinction between these and the unavoidable relationships based on kin ties is neatly summed up in our own proverb, "God gives us our relatives, but thank God we can choose our friends." The functional importance of this type of organization differs greatly from one society to another. There are certain societies in which the great majority of personal relationships are prescribed for the individual on a kin basis, others in which most personal relationships are of a voluntary type. However, relationships of both types are always present.

Last, in every society both individuals and the categories of individuals established by the various simultaneous systems of organization will be rated in a prestige series. Every group whose existence is recognized by a society, whether age category, family, or athletic club, is regarded as inferior or superior relative to some other group of the same type. Thus, in practically all societies, men will rank women socially, and adults will rank children. The relative ranking of adults and the old is less constant. However, it seems to be a fact that even in those societies in which the old are theoretically dominant, only those old people who have attained high individual prestige while active adults exercise real power in old age. Similarly, families within a society are always ranked in a prestige series. Such differences appear most clearly when marriages are projected, each family wanting its member to marry up when possible. In spite of the numerous variations in systems of prestige rating in different societies, it is important to note that there are no genuinely equalitarian human societies. The so-called equalitarian societies are simply those in which the individual is given a minimum of social handicap and allowed to find his own level.

Most societies have other patterns of organization in addition to the minimal set just cited. In most cases, a series of local groups with similar cultures and patterns of organization are united into larger units such as the tribe or state. The division of an entire society into social classes differing in prestige and normally in social functions is also a common phenomenon. In both these cases the units which have combined to form the larger society will be found to differ culturally at certain points and to possess a feeling of internal solidarity and a degree of organization greater than those existing across group lines. In other words, the classes or local groups which compose a society are really sub-societies with their own distinct sub-cultures. Contrast the behavior of the English gentleman and the English cockney or the values of Hollywood and Richmond, Virginia.

Although a culture and a society are always associated, they are phenomena of different orders. The relation between them is established through the medium of the individuals who compose the society and express the culture in their behavior. However, each individual expresses only part of the culture, never the whole. No one person is ever familiar with the entire culture of his society, yet the organized group of individuals who compose the society are jointly able to know and practice the whole culture. They have enough common knowledge to understand and predict each others' responses, but the fact that they are members of a society makes it possible for them to be specialists. Knowledge or skills vital for the group may be confined to a very small percentage of its members. Thus, the knowledge and practice of medicine in our society is delegated to only a few individuals, often to only one in a community; yet all the community's members can still benefit. Moreover, medical knowledge and practice will be interrelated with a number of other patterns within the community's culture, influencing the form and operation of these and being influenced in turn. For example, neither the doctor nor the sanitary engineer in a modern community will be familiar with more than a small area of the other's field, yet they will strongly influence each other's technical practices.

Perhaps the best expression of the relation between a culture and a society is to say that the culture bears very much the same relation to the society as the total knowledge and habitual response patterns of an individual bear to him as a living organism. Like the knowledge and habitual responses of the individual, the culture represents an integration of past experience, in this case that of the society throughout its duration. It also forms a configuration all of whose parts are to some degree interrelated, although the interdependence between the various elements which compose a culture is even looser than that between the various elements which make up the personality of an individual.

Discussions of culture content are hampered at present by a hopelessly confused terminology, but I will refer to the distinguishable internally coherent responses or groups of closely interrelated responses which make up a culture as *culture elements*. This term, although far from precise, would seem to be the most nearly neutral among those now in use. The presence of a culture element is assumed if the response

of a society's members to a repetitive situation is also repetitive. However, culture elements are by no means as definite or clearly delimited
as they have been assumed to be by many writers on the subject. As
we know from modern semantics, no two things or acts are ever identical: they are merely more or less similar. Although a culture element is
usually treated as though it were a single prescribed response, every
culture element is essentially a range of variation. Responses which
fall within this range are effective; those which fall outside the range
are not. In discussing cultural phenomena, it is customary to take the
mode of the varying behaviors which fall within the effective range
and to treat this as if it were an invariable pattern of response. However, this must be regarded as primarily a descriptive device. It gives
only an approximation of the actual situation. The fact that every real
culture element is a range and not a point contributes very considerably
to the flexibility of cultures and their capacity for undergoing numerous
changes and stresses without actual disruption.

The interrelations between various culture elements are often exceedingly loose, so much so that certain elements can be eliminated from
the culture or added to it with no recognizable effect on certain other
elements already present. Thus, for example, if bridge were relinquished
by Americans in favor of canasta, the effect on our patterns of air travel
would be imperceptible. Even when much closer interrelations are present, they are often by no means obvious. In many cases, they become
evident only in change situations where the introduction of new culture
elements or the elimination of old ones result in unanticipated malad-
justments. For example, the changes resultant on the introduction of
money into a society which had previously had a barter economy may
reveal previously unsuspected relations between family structure and
agricultural techniques.

Although it is the individuals composing a society who transmit and
implement its culture, any culture involves the participation of so many
individuals, especially if one recognizes its persistence in time, that the
differences between its participants largely cancel out. It is possible
to study and compare cultures without reference to the particular persons who have implemented them and on this basis to arrive at certain
valid conclusions regarding the functions of cultures, their normal content and structure, and the processes involved in their growth and
change. The function of any culture as a whole is to assure the survival
and well-being of the society with which it is associated. It does this
by providing the society's members with tested techniques for meeting
various problems which arise. The most immediate and pressing of these
problems are those of providing food and shelter and of obtaining and
processing raw materials. These are immediately related to physical

survival and unless they can be solved adequately, the society is doomed to extinction.

The techniques developed in this connection are always basic to the organization and functioning of much of the rest of the culture. At the same time, there seems to be little justification for the position of the more extreme economic determinists who regard all other aspects of culture as by-products of the technology. Comparative studies show that the technological equipment of any society sets limits to the range within which many of the other elements composing its culture can be developed and elaborated, but this range is wide enough to permit several alternatives. Cultures which are closely similar in their technology may differ profoundly in their formal social structure, religion and art.

Problems of physical survival are only a few among the many for which a culture must offer adequate solutions. It must also provide the members of a society with techniques for living together with a minimum of friction and engaging in cooperative activities. The whole organized configuration of such techniques constitutes the social system in the oldest and longest established meaning of that term. A social system is that part of a culture which provides solutions to the problems of group living in the same way that another part of the culture provides the solution to the problems of physical survival. The culture must further provide techniques for the training of individuals, so that they can function as members of society, and for the control or elimination of individuals whose training has not been successful.

Lastly, culture must make allowance for the psychological needs of individuals. It must provide them with harmless escapes from boredom, as in games, story telling, and aesthetic activities, and provide them with reassurance in crisis situations. This last is normally taken care of by those elements of culture which we subsume under the terms magic and religion. In connection with these, the culture must also provide a series of pronouncements on the nature of the universe and on the origins of things in so far as the curiosity of the society's members requires satisfaction.

A culture as a whole provides answers to all the needs of a society and of the average individual member of it. However, any attempt to establish direct and complete correlations between particular needs and particular cultural elements is foredoomed to failure. Every element of culture appears to have multiple functions, and the same element may bear a significant relation to several different needs. The most that can be said in any case is that the primary function of a particular culture element seems to be related to this social or individual need and its secondary functions are related to such and such other needs. For example, the configuration of culture elements involved in making a bow might be said to have its main function in connection with food getting, since a bow is a hunting appliance, but at the same time, a well made bow may serve to confer prestige upon its maker, to satisfy his aesthetic urge, and even, because of the inclusion in the procedure of manufacture of certain magical elements, contribute to the reassurance of the individual who uses the bow in situations of doubtful outcome, such as hunting or war expeditions.

Every culture is elaborated far beyond the point which would suffice to insure the survival of the society. Moreover, one is constantly impressed by the disharmony resulting from such elaborations. Thus, the Australian aborigines have developed social organization to a fantastic degree while paying little attention to technology. The Pueblo Indians devote a large part of their time to making religious paraphernalia and performing elaborate rituals, while the realistic techniques for the agriculture on which they depend for their food supply are exceedingly simple. We ourselves have developed our technology to an extreme degree while allowing our political system to become archaic and inefficient.

These elaborations can only be explained in terms of the various societies' hierarchies of interest, i.e., of the relative value which they attach to various activities. Those activities which a society considers important serve as nuclear points for the organization of numerous culture elements. These may contribute little to the performance in practical terms, but they meet the psychological needs of individuals, especially their desire for prestige and for favorable response from others. Activities which carry high value will naturally result in greater rewards to the individual who is successful in them or invents new elaborations connected with them.

In the internal structuring of culture also, wide areas of culture content tend to be oriented about the dominant interests of the society. A good example of this is afforded by the contrast in the roles of sports in modern England and in France. The relative importance attached to these activities by each country may be judged by the space devoted to them in newspapers, the time which the average individual spends either in sports or as a spectator, the amount of land devoted to playing fields, the amount of money expended on sporting appliances, and so forth.

The elements which compose a culture are of several different orders. The most readily accessible to direct observation and record are those associated with the technology and the artifacts which it produces. Early in the development of anthropological studies the term *material culture* was coined to refer to such artifacts. However, the present tendency among anthropologists is to exclude the objects themselves from the culture concept but to include what might be termed the patterns for objects. Thus, a stone axe itself is not regarded as a culture element, but the shape, size, finish, materials, and so forth characteristic of the axes made and used by a particular society are considered culture elements.

Somewhat less readily ascertainable than the culture elements of these first two orders are the behaviors which control the social relations of individuals. Although these can frequently be observed in action, the fact that so many different individuals with different personality characteristics are in close interaction leads to a heightened degree of variation in practice. The investigator's difficulties are also increased by the existence in many cases of ideal patterns: conscious statements as to the way in which individuals in different social positions should behave. In comparing such statements with the real culture patterns, one often finds striking inconsistencies. Still less accessible to the investigator are those generalized patterns of response which may be termed value-attitude systems. In many cases these systems are actually unconscious and unverbalized, but like the content of the subconscious mind of the individual, they exercise tremendous emotional effect and are reflected in numerous patterns of overt behavior. The study of this level of culture is the most difficult of all, since it involves constantly making subjective judgments in which the investigator's own past experiences and personality are likely to influence the outcome.

The third component in the human trilogy, the individual, might seem at first sight the easiest to deal with. The individual is after all a living being: a distinct biological entity with inborn capacities for thought, feeling and action. However, the individual, as he exists at any point in time, is a product of a very complex interaction between his genetically determined physical and psychological potentialities and his environment. The individual's patterns of overt behavior and, even more, that subtle thing which we term his personality, represent an integration of his past experiences. Most of these experiences can be phrased in terms of culture. They derive mainly from contacts with other members of his society, whose behaviors fall within the ranges established by its culture, i.e., its real culture patterns. Because of the very multiplicity of these individuals, the differences in their interpretation of the culture patterns will tend to cancel out, so that the ultimate result will be very much the same as if the individual had been exposed to repetitive experience with the mode of the pattern range.

The influence of culture upon the individual is exerted in two quite different ways. On the one hand, the developing individual is given an opportunity to learn a great deal of his society's culture directly and objectively. All societies have conscious techniques for educating the rising generation and it may be said at once that for the transmission of knowledge and concrete patterns of behavior these techniques are always adequate. If they were not, the society could not survive the passing of the founding generation. The individual can learn anything within reason on the basis of anticipated rewards for success or punishment for failure. Even in those areas of culture where there is no conscious education, a great variety of patterns are transmitted through imitation. As any parent can testify, children tend to model their behavior upon that of older associates, thus not infrequently acquiring habits which are congruous with the actual culture patterns of their society rather than with its ideal verbalized patterns.

On the other hand, societies have not yet developed effective conscious techniques for the transmission of many of their values and attitudes. These are normally assumed by the developing individual quite unconsciously as a part of his acquisition of the total culture. They are implicit in numerous mutually consistent patterns of behavior within the culture. The individual derives them for himself, generalizing from such patterns, while his own performance of the patterns reinforces the values and attitudes in his own mind. In a period of cultural confusion such as our own, the values and attitudes actually incorporated in our culture and those which are ideally prescribed by it may and often do differ widely. The unfortunate modern educator finds that parents expect him to inculcate in their children the ideal value-attitude systems to which they do not adhere in their own conduct and that they blame him if he fails in what is certainly an almost impossible task. The attempt to transmit value-attitude systems verbally usually results in nothing more nor less than verbal transmission. The individual learns what he should say about the correct values and attitudes and can produce this verbal statement on demand, but the statement is not charged with emotional effect and bears very little relation to his actual conduct.

In addition to the transmission of concrete behavior patterns and knowledge, culture also exercises its influence in another and more subtle fashion. It shapes the individual by what a society's members, acting in accordance with their culture, do to the children. Thus, every society has its own culturally prescribed patterns of care for infants. In some societies they will be swaddled or bound rigidly on a cradle board; in other societies, they will be left unhampered by clothing of any sort. In some, they will be kept in almost constant physical contact with another person, carried astride the mother's hip or on the back of another child; in others they will have practically no direct physical contact with other individuals. In some societies, they will be fed whenever they cry; in others, they will be fed on a rigid schedule or simply at the convenience of the mother. From what we know of the effects of early experience on the development of personality in our own society, each possible combination of these techniques might be expected to have certain more or less enduring results. The adult is quite incapable of remembering the treatment he received as an infant, but at the same time, this treatment will leave its mark in the deep levels of his personality. From the degree to which the first few years of life are secure and comfortable, and particularly from the degree to which the child is able to elicit favorable response from his elders, will come the picture of the world which he will carry with him subconsciously in later years.

This picture will influence his interpretation of all sorts of situations as they arise and, through this, his responses. If his earliest experiences leave him with an anticipation of hostility, he will act on this assumption and approach adult relationships with a "chip on his shoulder." If, on the other hand, his earliest experiences have convinced him of his adequacy to meet situations and of the general friendliness of the world in which he finds himself, he will face new situations without anxiety and be able to evaluate them and meet them realistically. If his early environment is neither hostile nor friendly, but indifferent, the type of environment which is created by most institutions which have to care for small children *en masse*, he is likely to develop a subconscious anticipation of futility based on his failure to elicit any sort of a response when he was a small child, and to have his energies sapped by constant anticipation of failure. Research on the personality characteristics of individuals in different societies, which is one of the newest developments in the anthropological field, indicates that these are by no means empty speculations. The personality norms for members of different societies do differ, and the normal type for each society, in the sense of that which is of most frequent occurrence, is of the sort which one would expect the particular society's techniques of child care to produce.

No matter what the method by which the individual receives the elements of culture characteristic of his society, he is sure to internalize most of them. This process is called *enculturation*. Even the most deliberately unconventional person is unable to escape his culture to any significant degree. Thus, anyone who has become acquainted with the free spirits of Greenwich Village must recognize that their unconventionality is almost as thoroughly patterned as the conventionality of Park Ave. Their revolt against bourgeois culture has merely produced another subculture within the general American pattern. The individual imagination cannot be sufficiently divorced from its culturally dominated experience to permit any really profound originality. Cultural influences are so deep that even the behavior of the insane reflects them strongly. Thus, Napoleon and Julius Caesar are rarely to be found in asylums today, having given place to Hitler or Franklin D. Roosevelt. Hysterias, which may legitimately be regarded as manifestations of the unconscious, are so thoroughly conditioned by culture that the distribution of the various types can be mapped in time and space as accurately as those of fashions in dress. Thus, the fainting lady of the eighteen-fifties is as extinct today as the Model T Ford, and demonic possession ended when witchcraft vanished from law codes.

In spite of the thorough enculturation of the individual, he still retains the capacity to think and to devise new forms of behavior in response to situations for which the patterns of his culture are inadequate. Enculturation merely limits the conceptual tools with which he can operate and the directions in which he will think. The individual is the irreducible variable in every social and cultural situation. He is the yeast in the cultural brew, and every new element of culture can be traced back ultimately to some individual's mind.

Chapter V

Processes of Culture Change

ALL CULTURES, even the simplest, seem to be in a continuous state of change. The earlier anthropologists assumed that cultures with relatively simple technology and political structure represented only slightly modified survivals of the ancient conditions of our own ancestors and for that reason dubbed them primitive. Also, largely as a device for simplifying their own theoretical studies, they assumed that such cultures were static or nearly so, persisting unchanged over long time periods. Actually, we have plenty of evidence that this is not the case. Not only do all archeological records, fragmentary as they are, show change through time, but wherever explorers have visited a "primitive" tribe at intervals of a generation or more, their reports show that changes have taken place. Since there is always the possibility that these changes may have been set in motion by the first explorer's visit or by contacts with other Europeans during the interval, the archeological evidence is more reliable. From this it appears that changes in technology, the only part of culture on which it provides conclusive evidence, were exceedingly slow during the first nine-tenths of human existence. Thousands of years seem to have gone by without the introduction of any new tool or appliance. However, during the last twenty-five or thirty thousand years, there has been a progressive speeding up of cultural change. Certain curious features of this speeding up process will be discussed later.

In their operation, the processes of culture change fall into a definite sequence. The first step is the presentation to the society of a potential addition to its culture. This is followed by the new element's acceptance or rejection. If accepted, there are further processes of modification and integration by which the new element and the pre-existing culture are brought into adjustment. Lastly, there is usually, but not always, the elimination of an older culture element or elements whose functions have been taken over by the new element.

A potential element of culture may be invented or borrowed. In either case, the new idea or appliance originates with some individual, or at most with a small series of individuals who have either pooled their ingenuity to solve a problem or contributed improving details during the development of the invention. There can be no invention without an inventor. The main difference between invention and borrowing is that if the new thing originates within the setting provided by the society and its culture, we refer to it as an invention, while if it has originated in some other society and has been taken from another culture by the group under consideration, we speak of the process as culture borrowing or as the diffusion of the particular trait. The actual processes of acceptance or rejection and of integration will be the same in either case, although the attitude of the receiving society toward the one in which the potential element originated may influence acceptance.

One of the problems which has intrigued philosophers for many years and which is still debated today, largely because of its involvement with totalitarian doctrines, is whether the inventor is a free intellect operating on his own initiative or whether he is merely an agent of society. In support of the latter position, totalitarians point to the fact that inventions seem to appear at the times when societies need them. Thus, again and again, mechanical devices designed for the same purpose and very often employing the same principle have been invented at approximately the same time by several different men working independently. Also, when any element of culture fails to perform its functions adequately, new elements which will meet the need usually seem to be invented or borrowed. If only this evidence is considered, the conclusion that the inventor functions simply as an agent of his society is almost inevitable. However, there are other factors which make this conclusion much less probable. In the first place, a successful invention is not simply one which will work and fulfill the purposes for which it was designed; it must also be one which will be accepted by the society and integrated into the culture. Unless this second step occurs, the invention is still-born. In non-literate societies or, before the days of patent offices, even in literate ones, the invention which was not accepted was permanently lost. The phenomenon of inventors responding to the needs of their societies is thus in most cases more apparent than real. If the inventor were merely a social agent, he would scarcely produce devices for which his society had no need and in which they took no interest. Nevertheless, we know that innumerable inventions of this sort have been made. The famous notebooks of Leonardo da Vinci are a case in point. Here he amused himself by sketching devices, most of which were unquestionably workable, but most of which in turn were never even constructed until the recent fascist Italian regime built them for prestige and exhibition purposes.

In summary, the inventor is quite capable of operating as a free agent and may invent without reference to his society's needs. At the same time, any deficiency in his society's culture will be recognized by him and by others and will therefore give direction to the exercise of his inventive ability. Moreover, if the deficiency is a significant one, both the financial and prestige rewards for the individual who remedies it are likely to be more considerable than those for one who devotes his attention to some problem in which the society is not particularly interested. Consider, for example, the rewards which would accrue in our own society to an individual who, in time of increasing gas shortage, produced a carburetor which would double mileage to the gallon, with the rewards for the inventor of a new technique in non-objective painting.

In the case of either inventions or borrowings, an important role in acceptance is usually played by an individual whom we may call the innovator. Inventors themselves are rarely good salesmen. They tend to be too heavily involved with problems other than those of publicity. The innovator sees in the invention or in the borrowed element an opportunity for personal prestige or profit or for those disinterested good works so deeply suspected by the modern student of personality. In any society, the innovator who is of high social rank has a great initial advantage. This fact is reflected in our own advertising campaigns, where

THE INEFFICIENT GUN

the products are always described as being used by young society matrons or men of distinction rather than by waitresses or boiler makers.

Although we belong to a society whose culture has been undergoing changes unparalleled in extent and rapidity for the past 200 years, we actually know surprisingly little about the various factors involved in the acceptance or rejection of new culture elements. Very few case studies have been made. We are accustomed to think of the utility of a potential culture element as the most important factor effecting its acceptance, but this is certainly an oversimplification. Utility is a highly relative matter. The potential effectiveness of any new appliance depends upon the ability of members of the society to operate it, or at least upon the difficulty involved in learning to operate it. Thus, a gun in the hands of a native who usually fires with his eyes shut is considerably less efficient than a bow and arrow. Similarly, such a culture element as the parliamentary system is likely to be much less effective than a dictatorship among a people who have been accustomed to authoritarian control within each social unit from the family up.

One thing which we can be sure of is that a new culture element which is congruous with the preexisting value system of the society will be accepted much more readily than one which is not. Again and again one finds that the acceptance of institutions or devices which would seem superior on a purely utilitarian level are blocked because the new thing controverts some existing values. Thus, during the Crimean war, military ethics were enough to insure the rejection of Captain Dunready's highly practical suggestion that the Malakoff could be taken without loss by using a few tons of coal and a few hundred-weight of sulphur when the wind would blow the fumes into the fortress. Again, during a post-war period when most European nations suffer from a marked shortage of males, a simple and effective answer would seem to be to legalize the institution of polygyny. There are abundant examples of this institution to be observed in contemporary societies, in most of which it seems to function efficiently, yet certain values of our own culture preclude its acceptance.

The importance of the innovator's social status in determining a society's acceptance or rejection of new things has already been mentioned. In the case of borrowed elements, similar considerations extend to the society with which the new element originated. Every society looks up to some other society for its real or presumed superiority along certain lines and at the same time regards it as inferior along others. Thus, women's fashions, with the possible exception of those in the sports field, are presumably better designed by the French than by anyone else. Men's fashions, on the other hand, are presumed to be best designed by the English. Germans are, or were until recently, regarded as pre-eminent in the field of chemical inventions. Even before World War II, no one would have tried to popularize either men's or women's fashions in the United States by announcing that they were of German origin, still less to launch a new chemical product as a French invention. The initial prestige which attaches to an object because of its place of origin or the social level of the innovators who accept it first will have profound effects on the willingness of the society to incorporate it into its culture.

One of the most important factors in connection with the diffusion of cultural elements is that they transfer from one society to another almost exclusively in terms of their form. In other words, the borrowing society copies particular patterns of behavior as it apprehends them, usually without understanding their original culture context. The new element is thus transferred at the objective level and comes into the receiving culture stripped of most of the meanings and associations which it carried in its original context. The assignment of new meanings is one of the most important aspects of the integrative process. In this way, new elements can be made intelligible to the members of the receiving society and can be adjusted to its existing values. Thus, in British Columbia, the Eagle and Beaver trade-marks of the Astor and Hudson Bay Companies were used as crests by leading families trading with them. Excellent examples of this sort of reinterpretation can be seen not only in connection with the transfer of techniques but also and particularly in the effects of the transfer of religions from one society to another. To understand the way in which forms may be reworked to become congruous with preexisting attitudes, one need only study the history of Christianity and its progressive modifications as it passed from a Jewish sect, to a proletarian secret society with mutual aid aspects, to the state religion of Imperial Rome, and ultimately to the warlike barbarians beyond the Roman borders. Surely, in spite of a similarity in outward forms, it would be hard to find a greater contrast than that between primitive Christianity and the doctrines taught by its founder and the elaborate ritualistic religion which sired the Crusades.

The last process involved in culture change is that of the elimination of older culture elements. This elimination is much less complete than one might anticipate because of the factors of multiple function which have been discussed elsewhere. It is very rare for a new culture element, even after its integration into the culture, to be able to take over all the functions of the element whose main function it is assuming. For example, although the rifle and pistol have long since replaced the sword in its original weapon functions, the sword still survives as a piece of ceremonial paraphernalia, carrying with it associations of aristocracy and military command. In the introduction of new non-material elements we find a somewhat similar situation. The sacred myth of an old religion survives as folklore when the former worshipers have become apostate. The deities of the older faith fuse with the new gods, and in due course of time one finds them with their names changed, perhaps, but with most of their old attributes intact.

One of the most interesting aspects of culture change is the variable rate at which it proceeds. The pattern, as revealed to us by history and archeology, indicates that in many cultures long periods of slow change and relative quiescence have alternated with periods of exceedingly rapid change and development. The most significant of these periods of rapid change have been associated with the introduction of new technological processes such as agriculture or, on a smaller scale, iron working, which opened up obvious new culture possibilities which the society was quick to exploit. However, there have been numerous periods of rapid cultural development which are not correlated with any such fundamental technological changes. All educated Europeans will recognize such examples in the Great Age of Athens or the Italian Renaissance in our own culture line, but everything indicates that these were not isolated instances but rather examples of a general tendency. The causes of such periods are still very imperfectly understood. In the southwestern United States the use of tree ring dating has made possible an accurate reconstruction of the chronology. In this region there seems to have been a long period during which, in spite of the presence of corn and rather casual agriculture, the culture remained at a low level with a sparse population occupying small settlements. Technological development was minimal; such appliances as pottery, the loom, and the bow were lacking. Suddenly, in about 750 A.D., the culture began an extraordinarily rapid development which, by the year 1000 A.D., had carried it to a cultural level equivalent to that of the historic Pueblo Indians.

In Egypt we have indications of such a period of extraordinarily rapid development at the beginning of the dynastic period. For two or three centuries the rapidity of change was almost comparable to that in our own society at the present time. For instance, the largest and most skillfully constructed of the pyramids was built within 150 years of the time that the Egyptians first began to use stone in any form of construction. Coupled with these technological advances went the invention of elaborate techniques for the exploitation of the peasantry and the diversion of their economic surplus into religious channels. Apparently these techniques became too effective, resulting in widespread hardship and, finally, social revolt, and a period of confusion followed from which Egyptian culture emerged in very much the form it kept for the next thousand years.

The reasons for these sudden upswings in culture seem to be highly varied, but in each situation one can detect the presence of factors which resulted in a sudden release of energy. In the Anasazi culture of the Southwest, the only new factor which appears at the beginning of the period of rapid advance, is the cultivation of beans. One is tempted to believe that this crop, by providing a large source of proteins, established the local food economy on a sound basis. Corn and beans provide a nearly balanced ration on which any population can live with a few supplements from wild plants and small game. This, in common with unexploited soils and a rainfall possibly somewhat heavier than at present, resulted in a more ample food supply, a rapid increase in population, and corresponding energy release. In Egypt, the sources may be sought partly in an Asiatic invasion shortly before the beginning of the dynastic period which seems to have introduced new ideas. However, this in itself would not have resulted in the marked increase in energy necessary to exploit these ideas. Since there was no change in the basic economy as far as we know, it seems probable that the establishment of centralized government and the elimination of the constant wastage involved in the wars between the Nomes was the significant factor.

Between these periods of rapid growth there is always a slow tide of change going on. Because of the phenomenon of fixation of interest during a growth period, there is a tendency for the culture to concentrate on one or a few lines of development while paying little attention to the rest. This results in increasing disharmony within the culture, which in turn has a braking effect on the speed of cultural growth. As the disharmonies within the culture become increasingly pronounced, more and more of the society's energy and resources have to be expended on makeshift adjustments until the period of rapid change gradually grinds to a halt. Our own society would seem to be in such a period at the present time. Its tremendous and still accelerating development of science and technology has not been accompanied by an equal development in social, economic, and political patterns. If nothing else, our unwillingness to deal realistically with the problem of war, even in the face of modern atomic developments, is likely to bring this period of rapid scientific advance to a close simply by the destruction of the economic surpluses upon which the leisure required for scientific investigation and the funds required for laboratory apparatus depend.

In the past, these periods of rapid advance have been followed by much longer periods in which the main energies of the society have been devoted to sorting and integrating the new culture elements which have been developed or borrowed during the period of rapid advance. Part of this process consists in the elimination from the culture of many of the alternative patterns and, in some cases, the dropping of new culture elements which experience shows cannot be successfully integrated.

While one hesitates to evaluate the importance of culture elements of different orders, it must be admitted that a combination of technology and natural environment seems to set the frame within which other elements of culture have to be integrated. While technology does not indicate any single line of cultural development or any form of institution as the only possible one, it nevertheless establishes a condition of limited possibilities. So long as there is no fundamental change in technology, variations in other elements of the culture will be limited in both their direction of growth and their scope. It is interesting to note in this connection that the Greek concept of the cyclical nature of history was thoroughly justified in terms of the time span for which they had information. As long as Greek culture depended upon rather crude techniques of hand manufacture, with the additional handicap of slave artisans and their indifference, the cycle from monarchy to democracy to oligarchy to tyranny to monarchy again would almost inevitably repeat itself time after time. On the other hand, by opening up possibilities for further development, a basic invention or series of inventions in the technological field may result in exceedingly rapid and far-reaching changes outside technology. Note the startling changes in many areas of our own culture set in motion by the development of mechanical transportation from railroads to airplanes.

If one observes the development of culture as a whole, three really revolutionary technological advances can be recognized. First, the epoch-making potentialities opened up with the first human departure from the animal condition, the use of tools and the domestication of fire. Second, the domestication of plants and animals followed in various places in both the Old and New World by exceedingly rapid cultural advances leading eventually to the development of the city, one of the most revolutionary social inventions in the whole of human history. Third, what may be termed the domestication of power based upon the ability of man to produce power at will and, with few exceptions, wherever he needed it, as distinct from the earlier use of the wild power of wind or water at the points where it was available. Intimately linked with this has been the invention of the scientific method, which promises increasing control of many other aspects of nature. We are now in the early phases of this third period and are only beginning to explore the potentialities which it offers for developments in our culture outside technology, particularly in the social, political, and economic fields. It is safe to predict that even two or three centuries from now, such social inventions as modern-type Capitalism, Fascism, and Communism will be regarded as primitive experiments directed toward the adjustment of modern society to modern technology.

Chapter VI

Cultural Evolution

SINCE THE DISCOVERY of the principles of biological evolution, there have been repeated attempts to apply a similar concept to the development of culture. It is obvious that there has been a vast amount of cultural change and enrichment throughout human history. The problem is whether this change and enrichment shows any consistent direction or sequences of events which have been repeated in numerous cultural lines. If it can be shown that such is the case, we can say that the development of culture follows evolutionary principles, and it should be possible to extrapolate from the direction of past developments to future developments.

Early anthropologists were firmly convinced of the existence of such principles and believed that all cultures had passed through much the same successive stages in their development. They even attempted to classify all cultures according to the system they had set up, and they regarded the so-called primitive cultures as examples of development arrested at various stages. The work of later anthropologists has definitely disproved the theory of arrestment. All existing cultures have an equally long history and, as far as we know, no culture ever reaches a state of complete stasis. The so-called primitive cultures merely represent the terminal points of divergent lines of cultural development. The one point at which certain of the "primitive" cultures of today can be said to resemble early stages in the development of our own is in their technology and its social consequences. As we have noted, the state of technological advance in a society, particularly the techniques it employs for getting food and shelter and manufacturing necessary objects, do seem to set certain broad limits to the forms which some other elements of the culture may assume. For example, it is obvious that no people who live by hunting and food gathering can support a divine king with his accompanying court and ritual trappings. This type of political structure has as a prerequisite a settled population with a considerable economic surplus. Again, we find that organized city life has as a prerequisite the development of agriculture and of techniques for the transportation of goods in bulk. In the absence of these no large concentration of population can be victualed. In other words, the technological basis of any society does not indicate a single form for each of the other associated institutions, but limits the number of possible forms and rules out certain forms altogether.

Much of the confusion with regard to the application of evolutionary theories to culture phenomena stems from the failure to realize that human culture as a whole is made up of many *cultures.* The situation is closely similar to that found in living forms, where there are a tremendous variety of Species, Genera, Families, and Orders. In the case of cultures, the resemblances of even the most diverse forms so far outweigh the differences that they should be regarded as comparable to the Species and Genera of a single biological Family. We know that in the evolution of life certain fundamental principles have been at work, but that the end results of the operation of these principles have been profoundly different. Thus, the mechanisms of chance mutations and natural selection, operating through different gene aggregates and environments, have produced such divergent forms as the elephant, the ostrich, and the bee. Each of these can be shown to have evolved from simpler forms, but in order to find any organism ancestral to all of them, one would have to go back to the level of the annelid worms.

The actual processes of cultural evolution are those already described in the discussion of culture change given in the previous chapter. They can be regarded as evolutionary only insofar as the changes which have gone on in culture show some definite, fairly consistent direction. In the evolution of cultures, as in that of living beings, the change processes have been, in general, directed toward a better adjustment of the social organism to its environment. This holds for a large majority of cases, although in cultural, as in biological evolution, there are examples of degeneration, of non-functional elaborations in response to previously established trends, and of hypertrophies.

In the normal course of cultural evolution adjustment has involved, first of all, an increasing control of the natural environment through technology. Concurrent with this has been the adjustment of the non-technological aspects of the culture to the conditions created by the interaction of the environment and the technology. In this, cultural evolution is quite comparable to that of living organisms. However, it is one of the puzzling aspects of evolution in both culture and living forms that certain trends appear for which no practical explanation can be found, and that these trends may continue until this results in hypertrophy. At the biological level, there appear to be a number of examples of species which actually developed certain features of their structure to a point where they were deleterious to the survival of the species in any environment. The enormous horns of the Irish elk have been cited as an example. This feature of hypertrophy seems to be associated with the closing phases in the evolutionary development of Families and Orders. After such animal groupings have reached the climax of their development, they tend to proliferate odd and often apparently non-functional characteristics. It has recently been suggested by one scientist that our own species represents an example of this same phenomenon. The long established anthropoids, whose great period was the Miocene, in the Pleistocene produced a species, *homo sapiens*, characterized by cerebral hypertrophy. In plain English, man is an ape with a brain too active for his own good. Anyone observing the developments in the field of modern warfare will probably agree that, as has so often been the case, this particular type of hypertrophy threatens the existence of the species.

IRISH ELK

In the development of culture also, we have numerous examples of hypertrophy. In our discussion of the organization of cultures we mentioned that each society has certain dominant interests about which it tends to elaborate behavior. Such interests and elaborations may be carried to the point where they become authentically non-functional and where they even interfere with the successful operation of other and more necessary aspects of the culture. Our own society would be an excellent case in point, since our preoccupation with technological development has led to a neglect of social invention which may well prove catastrophic. For example, our tremendous interest in mechanics has resulted in an exceedingly rapid increase in production potential, while at the same time we have failed to devise any adequate technique for the distribution of the products of this potential. At the present moment, war or the preparation for war seems to be the only way by which we can keep our industrial machine operating at full production capacity. Although a considerable part of our population is still badly clothed, housed, and fed, our distributional techniques are still so faulty that running the industrial plant at full blast in peace time results in overproduction, unemployment and economic paralysis.

Turning to less advanced cultures, we find similar examples of hypertrophy. The Southwestern Indians had developed ritualism and ceremonial observances to the point where they actually took up most of the time and energy not employed in the business of food-getting. Among the Indians of the Northwest Coast, the struggle for wealth to be used for purposes of ostentatious waste and prestige enhancement overshadowed all other considerations, so that all activities came to be evaluated in economic terms. Among the Kwakiutl, even marriages were regarded as forced loans. Theoretically, the bridegroom forced the bride price upon his wife's father as a loan to be repaid with interest and the wife was given as the first installment of repayment. If the marriage was congenial, the son-in-law took care to force other gifts upon his father-in-law from time to time, thus keeping him in his debt. If he failed to do this, the marriage was not necessarily dissolved, but a woman who did not return to her own family under these circumstances was referred to contemptuously as one who "stayed for nothing."

Like living forms, cultures seem to have begun with a few differentiated lines. If there was ever a time when all humans shared a single culture or even a group of closely similar cultures, no traces of this period have so far been discovered. The nearest approximation to it would be the widely distributed pebble and flake cultures of the first inter-glacial, and even these show numerous local variations. At the very beginning of implement design, different traditions of stone working were followed in different parts of the world. Unfortunately, technological development is the only part of the cultural record which is available for most of human history and even in this the record is exceedingly incomplete, since all groups make many of the things which they use out of perishable materials. One can draw only a few conclusions as to the social and intellectual life of a people from the archeological record alone. One may, for example, conclude from the finding of several hearths at the same level in a cave that several families probably occupied it simultaneously. This in turn would suggest that there must have been some sort of social organization and some in-group larger than the family itself, but it is quite impossible to say what the actual structuring of either the families or the larger society was. In the same way, when we find a Neanderthal skeleton buried in the sleeping position with weapons and the bones from a supply of meat laid beside him, we may conclude that the Neanderthal people had some belief in survival after death, but it would be quite impossible to conjecture what their picture of heaven might be.

It is only when we reach the level of recorded history, beginning at the earliest about 4000 B.C. in Egypt and the Near East, that we can begin to fill in the larger part of the picture. Even here, unfortunately, several millennia passed before the things which the modern anthropologist would like most to know about were written down. Writing in its inception was a tool for the glorification of gods and kings. It was only when, in the hands of the clever Semites, it was proletarianized through the invention of the alphabet and applied to everyday business, that we get records of what people actually thought and felt.

In spite of its innumerable deficiencies, human history as a whole does show certain sequences as normal, though not universal. Thus, as far as we know, hunting and food-gathering preceded food-raising in every part of the world. This does not mean that in certain cultures there may not have been a reversion from food-raising to hunting and food-gathering. Thus, after the introduction of the horse, a number of Indian tribes, who had previously been agricultural, reverted to a purely hunting existence. Similarly, the development of agriculture and settled village life everywhere preceded the emergence of the city. In technology we find that the use of stone seems to have preceded that of metal in all cases, although here again there are isolated instances of reversion. Thus, on the islands of Matty and Dorour on the northeastern edge of Melanesia, there was no metal in use at the time of their discovery. Nevertheless, certain of their tools and particularly their weapons were accurate copies of metal prototypes, the metal forms being reproduced even down to such details as rivetheads carved on the handles of wooden swords. In the development of metal-working, in turn, there seems to have been a fairly uniform sequence beginning with the use of native metals, copper, gold and, rarely, silver and meteoric iron, which could be worked cold. This was followed by the development of forging, followed by smelting and casting, with the rapid invention of bronze and other alloys. Iron working normally came considerably later in the sequence. However, here again exceptions can be noted in particular cultures. In Melanesia, because of European contact, the population passed directly from stone-using to iron-using in the latter half of the 19th century. In Africa a similar sequence can be noted. There appears to have been no Bronze or Copper Age on the continent south of the Sahara.

In social organization and religion the sequences appear to be much less constant, although the development of certain forms must have been inhibited until the emergence of the necessary economic base. Thus it is safe to assume that the earliest human beings everywhere lived in small semi-nomadic units composed of several families. The size of such units would have been set by the available food supply. We may further conclude on the basis of patterns found among modern food-gathering peoples, as well as mammals in general, that each of these earliest human groups occupied a fairly definite territory, moving within it seasonally and according to the abundance or lack of food in various parts of the range. Both the high mobility of domestic animal-using nomads and the permanent settlement of agricultural villages must have succeeded this early semi-nomadic type of life, but it is impossible to place these two as constant stages in a general evolutionary series. They represent divergent developments from a common base.

The study of such developmental sequences in particular aspects of culture would correspond to the study of the evolution of particular organs in biology. No corresponding sequences can be shown for the development of cultures as wholes. Even in the evolution of technology two significantly different trends are evident. In one of these, technological advance centers upon perfection of the appliances used and involves a series of improving inventions often extending over many centuries. Thus, the development of European weaving involved the progressive improvement of the loom beginning with the simple weaving frame and terminating in the modern multiple heddle power-driven apparatus. In the other line of development technological advance rests primarily on the acquisition of manual skill by successive generations of workers. An outstanding example can be found in the case of Peruvian textiles, where both spinning and weaving remained mechanically primitive. The Peruvians never even invented the thrown spindle, but made their thread by a finger-twisting process, with the spindle serving primarily as a reel. In the same way, their loom remained of an exceedingly simple and primitive type from start to finish. However, without improving the appliances, they were able, through development of greater and greater manual skill, to produce thread as fine or even finer than that which can be produced by modern machinery, and to duplicate on their simple looms every type of weaving known anywhere in the world, plus a few unique local forms.

Of these two trends, that toward apparatus perfection leads to greater production with less labor. That toward perfection of manipulation may lead to a superior product but is prodigal of labor and soon reaches a developmental dead end. It is interesting to note that the first line of evolution seems to be characteristic of many Old World cultures, while the second is more characteristic of New World ones.

Another pattern which is frequently encountered in the evolution of technology is a tendency to increase the number of materials used while reducing the number of purposes for which each material is used. The culmination of this trend can be seen in modern plastics or alloys tailored to serve a single purpose. This multiplication of materials is frequently coupled with an actual loss of technical skills in working a particular material, since such skills are no longer required. An example of the last would be the progressive loss of skill in the making of chipped stone implements which characterized the late phase of stone implement making in Egypt at a time when stone tools had been replaced by metal for all except ritual purposes. This trend is well illustrated by the archeological record from western Europe. Here all but the last phases of the Old Stone Age (Paleolithic) witnessed a steady improvement in the utilization of flint and related stones. Throughout the whole period, up to and including the middle Paleolithic, such stones were chipped and flaked more and more skillfully, with a steady increase in the number and variety of specialized forms. At the close of the middle Paleolithic one flint working skill, the ability to produce long, slender blades, continued to develop, but skill in shaping small implements by percussion diminished as the demand for such implements declined. Stone now gave place at many points to bone, antler, and ivory, materials which combined toughness with hardness and were actually better suited than stone for such things as wedges, javelin points, and harpoons.

Still later, in the Mesolithic, the number and variety of chipped stone objects decreased still further, even the large, relatively slender blades and gravers of the Upper Paleolithic giving place to small straight edged flakes. This transformation in stone technique has led certain investigators to conclude that the Mesolithic was a technologically degenerate era. However, the occasional finds in peat bogs indicate that the declines in stone working and the reduction of the number and variety of bone and antler implements was actually the result of the invention of a new technique of tool making in which small flints were set into a wooden base in order to give a cutting edge. Such composite tools combined the toughness and ease of working of wood with the harder cutting edge of stone and as such were superior to either. There is good reason to believe that a parallel but different evolution took place in Southeastern Asia during the entire period from the first use

SOUTH SEA NATIVES WITH JEEP

of stone artifacts to the introduction of metal. This tropic region offered a variety of hardwoods, and especially bamboo. Bamboo is an invaluable material for knives and projectile points. Its hard, silicious coat gives an edge which cuts on the same principle as the edge of a highly sized piece of paper and is almost as effective as metal for cutting any soft material. Bamboo arrow and spear heads are fully the equals in effectiveness of either stone or antler ones. The stone implements from Southeastern Asia show a striking continuity for many thousands of years, remaining crudely shaped and relatively unspecialized. When well made chipped stone implements, such as knives and projectile points, do appear in the region toward the close of the Stone Age, they seem to have been introduced by migrants coming from the north or west. In this case, the presence of bamboo apparently precluded the development of the finer types of stone-working by either percussion or pressure flaking, and when chipped stone implements do appear in groups whose culture derives from the Southeast Asiatic area, they give every indication of having been reinvented locally or derived from simple originals.

While the linkage of certain culture elements is fairly common, the integration within cultures is loose enough so that some parts of a culture may be highly evolved while others have remained simple. The situation here is further complicated by the factor of diffusion, so that, as at present in some parts of the South Seas, groups who show a simple village-type of organization and a firm belief in the validity of magic are also good mechanics, repairing jeeps and motor boats. Even where outside contacts have not been significant, the tendency for disharmonic development within cultures interferes with any clear picture of universal evolutionary stages.

To cite a few examples of such disharmony, it is generally taken for granted that agriculture is a prerequisite for the development of settled life, elaborate craftsmanship carried on by professionals, and aristocratic patterns of social structure. Nevertheless, on the Northwest Coast, where the only domestic animal was the dog and where agriculture was never practiced, we find all these phenomena present in well-developed form. Here the food economy was based on a combination of annual salmon runs and berry harvests with techniques for food preservation. There was thus an adequate basis for permanent settlement. The housing in this region was more permanent than that of agricultural villages anywhere in America north of New Mexico. The art reached a development in both technique and conceptualization which has rarely been paralleled by uncivilized peoples, while the social patterns were highly complex, with not only a hereditary aristocracy, but with techniques for vertical mobility through the ostentatious expenditure of wealth.

METATE

In California, although the development of culture was not as high as on the Northwest Coast, we again find non-agricultural groups who were as thoroughly settled as any people in the world. Here the economy leaned heavily on a natural crop, acorns, which could be stored for considerable periods. The average California Indian spent his life in one small area which his tribal mythology informed him was the center of the world and the place where it was created. In fact, the old men could point out the spots at which each of the acts of creation had taken place. With this pattern of settled life went highly developed patterns of trade, property, and of social status based on wealth. In technology, the basketry of the region represented probably the highest point to which this product was developed anywhere in the world, but, for no recognizable reason, pottery was completely lacking in the area except at one point on its southern periphery where it could clearly be traced to fairly recent diffusion.

Turning to more elaborate cultures, we find the Inca in South America reaching an extraordinarily high development in technology, but even more in political organization. The Inca State was the first genuinely totalitarian state in history, with an absolute control and benevolent care for its subjects which might be envied even by a Stalin. The control was so complete that there was not even private trade or a monetary system, and the ruler's recognition of the old adage that "Satan finds some mischief still for idle hands to do" resulted in a tremendous production of structures and objects. It is also evident from the study of the Peruvian sequence of cultures that these techniques for the utilization of labor and for keeping the entire population occupied in all its waking hours had the result of stultifying individual creative ability. Throughout the reign of the Incas, the same things were done with greater and greater technical skill and on a larger and larger scale, but with a progressive diminution of artistic merit and originality.

The same influences worked to stultify intellectual activities. The Peruvians seem to have made no important advances in astronomy or mathematics, and the examples of Inca literature which have survived are far from inspiring. Most curious of all, in view of the amount of "paper work" inevitably involved in the administration of a large and highly centralized state, they never developed any system of writing. They did have a feeble substitute in knotted string records, "quipu," but these seem to have been simply appliances for keeping accounts and aids to the memories of a special class of officials whose brains constituted the national archives.

In contrast to this, the Maya, who produced the greatest civilization in Middle America, never developed anything like the Incas' technological skill. Even at the time of the Spanish conquest, they were only beginning a feeble use of metal, and their buildings, although they astonish by the elaboration of their decoration, showed a poor understanding of structural principles. Throughout their entire history, they were never able to develop patterns for enduring political organization on any basis larger than the tribe, and the energies of the civilization were wasted by constant internal wars. In spite of this, they developed an art of amazing beauty and originality, and a writing system, which at the time of conquest, seems to have been on the verge of emerging into a true syllabary. They also made amazing advances in mathematics and astronomy, among other things inventing independently for themselves the use of zero and of notation by position. Their calendar was extraordinarily elaborate and accurate, and the few books of theirs which have survived show a surprising understanding of the movements of the heavenly bodies.

These are only a few examples of many that might be cited, but they may suffice to show the difficulty of arranging cultures as wholes in anything like a coherent evolutionary series. It is almost as difficult to do this as it would be to arrange all modern species of animals in a similar order.

At the same time, the existence of a definite direction in the development of culture would seem to be fairly well demonstrated by the numerous parallels between the Old and the New World cultures. Similar parallels between Old World cultures can conceivably be explained on the basis of diffusion even when geographic distance and impossibility of direct contact would have made the transfer of culture elements from one society to another impossible without other societies' acting as intermediaries. However, the emergence of the New World civilizations was so widely separated from that of the Old World civilizations in both space and time that any interchange of culture elements would appear impossible. Thus, by the time the Maya civilization took definite shape, Egypt, which has frequently been suggested as its source, was already a Roman Province.

In spite of this lack of contact, the two sets of cultures do show striking parallels which, it would seem, can only be explained on the basis of some general trend in cultural development which we can describe as evolutionary. Thus we find the Maya at a certain point in their development producing a system of writing which even seems to have followed the same steps in its development as those which characterized the earliest writing systems in the Near East. Again we find that the sequence of metals used in the development of metallurgy in America parallels that in the Old World up to the point of iron working. The center of this development seems to have been in northern South America, from which it spread to Mexico and Peru. All the Old World techniques of metal working, except those involved in the use of iron, were developed independently with only slight differences. The Inca even carried their metallurgy to the point of being able to melt and work platinum. In view of these skills, one can scarcely doubt that if iron ore had been available in their territory, they would have carried America on into the iron age.

In social and political organization we see the emergence of theo-cratic rule among the Maya and of divine kingship among the Inca, both closely paralleling similar institutions in some of the Old World civiliza-tions. Even the concept of formal law, with judges and trial procedure, which is notably lacking in most American Indian cultures emerged in Mexico and Peru, probably as an unavoidable accompaniment of the development of urban life. This list of resemblances could be extended considerably.

In the study of the evolution of culture, it is necessary for us to substitute for any one evolutionary scheme a recognition of separate lines of culture evolving in various parts of the world but following somewhat the same developmental patterns. In spite of the complexities introduced into the picture by diffusion and by tribal movements, it is possible to place most historic cultures relative to one or another of these main lines of development. Some of the basic elements in these patterns will be examined in the chapters which follow.

PART THREE

Basic Inventions

Chapter VII

Fire and Tools

THE USE of fire and the making and using of tools are common to the whole of mankind and differentiate humans sharply from all other animals. Both of these go back to an exceedingly remote period in history. In fact, there is no evidence of the use of both fire and tools by subhuman species, presumably including our own ancestors, before *homo sapiens* had been evolved. Both fire using and tool using have enough in common, wherever found, so that unnecessary repetition can be avoided by treating them in general terms before going into their more specific manifestations in particular lines of cultural development.

The evidence for the use of fire by early man and even by various prehuman groups is conclusive. Charcoal, being pure carbon, is hard and indestructible. When buried, it will last indefinitely. Although in some cases it may be impossible to tell whether charcoal is a relic of a natural or a man-made fire, it has been found under conditions which leave no doubt that fire was actually used by prehuman species. Thus, the lower Chukutien cave from which Sinanthropus remains have been taken contains hearths, and some investigators believe that the South African caves in which the older and less human Australopithicus Prometheus have been found show traces of fire.

Fire is, of course, infinitely older than man. It may be started by volcanic action, by lightning, by spontaneous combustion, or even by the friction of two dry branches rubbing in the wind. Most animals are afraid of it. Man tamed it and utilized it for many millennia before he learned how to create it. While there have been repeated travelers' tales, first of tribes who did not know fire and second of those who did not know how to make it, none of these have proved true. At the same time, any of the technologically less advanced peoples found fire-making a difficult and laborious process. Fire, once kindled, was kept going for as long as possible, a practice which is still characteristic of peasant groups everywhere in the world. Fire is not difficult to preserve by the use of rotten wood, lichen, stems with pithy centers, such as the dry fennel stalk with which Prometheus stole fire for man, and other slow burning materials. Fire is regularly carried by such groups as the Australian aborigines or the Oceanic Negritos when they move camp, while among settled villagers the fire on the hearth, unless temporarily extinguished for ceremonial reasons, is kept going for as long as the house stands.

A: EOLITH   B: FLINT STRIKE-A-LIGHT WITH NODULE OF PYRITE

Even our prehuman ancestors made stone implements by percussion and must have been familiar with the sparks produced by striking two stones together. The resemblance between these and sparks from a fire may have led to the first experiments in fire-making, but most sparks produced by striking two stones together are not hot enough to kindle tinder. Prior to the use of iron the only materials which could be used for striking a light were flint and iron pyrite. The earliest indications that we have of fire making came from the upper Paleolithic period in Europe, probably not more than 25 to 30 thousand years ago. Here flints shaped for use as strike-a-lights and pieces of pyrite have been found together in charcoal deposits. Pyrite is available in only a few places and most of the "primitive" fire-making appliances depend upon the friction principle. This is employed in such diverse apparatus as the fire drill, fire saw, and the fire plow. However, it is easy to convince anyone who has attempted to make fire by any one of these methods that they could have been invented only after such techniques as drilling, sawing, polishing, etc. had been developed to a high degree. All these processes have to be carried on rapidly to generate enough heat to be noticed and all the friction methods of fire making require a type of skill and, particularly, muscular control which it is exceedingly hard for the amateur to attain.

At the same time, once the method of fire-making by friction has been learned, it can be carried out with surprising speed. One of my native friends in the Marquesas repeatedly made fire for me in 45 seconds with the fire plow, one of the simplest friction devices. Even under his careful tutelage I was never able to acquire the muscular control needed to make fire by this method. It depended upon rapid strokes with heavy pressure, but with every stroke except the last of exactly the same length so that wood dust could accumulate at the end of the slot. The last stroke had to be not more than $\frac{1}{8}$ of an inch longer than the preceding ones. If it was as much as $\frac{1}{4}$ of an inch longer, the dust on which the catching of the spark depended was lost and the whole procedure had to be gone through again.

Once fire had been tamed, it became man's most useful servant, and his collaborator in the earliest of chemical processes and in a whole series of manufactures. We are prone to think of the main utility of fire

FIRE SAW

to earliest man in terms of light and heat. However, these were probably less important than some other things. The earliest semi-human fire users were denisons of tropical or warm temperate regions, conditions under which heat was not too important, and like many of the simpler peoples today, they probably rose and lay down with the sun.

Fire may have assisted in giving protection against large carnivores, but its main value was certainly in connection with technology. Several European writers have expatiated on the value of cooking as an aid in the tenderizing of meat, an idea which reflects the troubles of modern man and his dental bridgework. Even today, such people as the Eskimo live largely on raw meat and find no difficulty in masticating it. Actually, any form of animal food which can be eaten cooked can be eaten raw, with the possible exception of a few sea foods. The difference is simply a matter of jaw muscles and taste preference. The real importance of fire to the food supply lay in its use in the preparation of vegetable foods, especially those which permitted of preservation. Fruits are practically the only plant foods which can be consumed without cooking, and this does not even hold for all of these. While fruits swell the sea-

FIRE DRILL

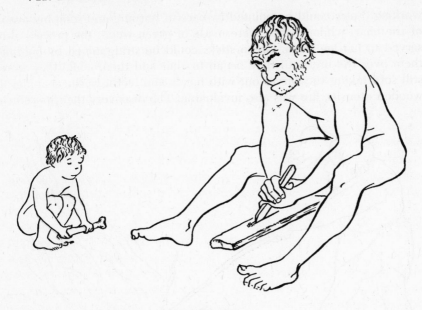

FIRE PLOW

sonal food supply, most of them cannot be preserved and are available throughout the year only in tropical regions.

Roots, which lend themselves better to storage, with very few exceptions require cooking to make them edible. Even such mild roots as sugar beets or potatoes can cause uncomfortable intestinal upsets if consumed raw. Taro, the great staple of the Polynesians, is filled with salicylic acid crystals which make it exceedingly irritating unless cooked, while manioc, the staple crop of the South American jungles, contains hydrocyanic acid, an exceedingly deadly poison which has to be destroyed by heat. The various seed crops such as grains and legumes are, with few exceptions, quite inedible without cooking. These are the crops which lend themselves most readily to long term preservation and storage and which, therefore, are a society's best insurance against famine. They are also forms which, first as wild plants and later as domesticated ones, range far north of the tropics. It was the use of fire which made it possible for our ancestors to change from the predominantly frugivorous diet of our anthropoid ancestors to the predominantly seed and root diet of our own species. By making many new food plants available, it increased the food supply and also extended the human range into more northern latitudes and into arid regions where the heavy starch supply characteristic of the seeds of many desert plants could become a human staple.

The earliest technological use of fire was in connection with woodworking. Poles could be pointed by careful burning and scraping away of the char, while, if they were made of green wood, the process also served to harden them. Green sticks could be straightened by holding them over the fire until they began to char and then, while they were still soft, taking the curves out with hands and teeth. In the shaping of wooden utensils, fire was also invaluable. The discovery that fire which

SHAPING A POLE

had once taken hold on a block of wood could be controlled and directed by blowing through a hollow reed seems to have been made independently in many places. With the use of this simple appliance and a flint flake or sharp shell for scraping away the char, it was possible to hollow bowls and canoes and shape articles of furniture. By this method an experienced workman could shape objects with surprising precision. Except for the length of time involved, it was fully as effective as the work that could be done with non-metal cutting tools.

In the clearing of land and the felling of timber for use, fire is also highly effective. Trees of any size can be brought down by kindling a fire at the root and then scraping away char and guiding the fire as it gradually eats into the trunk. Where a long stick of undamaged timber is desired, the upward spread of the fire can be controlled by plastering wet clay across the top of the scarf. Craftsmen skilled in this technique can even throw a log in the spot they want it to fall with almost the precision of a skilled axeman.

Needless to say, fire is the basis for most of the more elaborate later developments in technology. It has made possible first pottery, then metallurgy, and eventually a tremendous number of technological processes which depend on chemical reactions which take place in the presence of heat.

The use of tools or, more correctly, the making and saving of tools, reflects the peculiar qualities of the human mind much more directly than does the use of fire. The use of tools is not an exclusively human characteristic; the great apes employ sticks and stones which may come to hand for poking and pounding and some very curious examples of tool using have been recorded even among insects. However, as far as we know, there is no animal which ever shapes a natural object to adapt it for use as a tool or which saves an object which has been used once to use again. The human tool is one more manifestation of the curious quality of the human mind which makes us conscious of past and future and able to plan our behavior with an eye to both.

TREE CUTTING

Even the simplest tools require some little skill for their manufacture, as will be discovered by anyone who tries to duplicate even such a simple object as a properly balanced club or stone chopper. The wide range of tools and appliances which are made by the members of even the simplest human societies is made possible by the universal pattern of specialization. Even in those societies in which there are no professional or semi-professional artisans, all ordinary manufactures are delegated either to men or to women. Moreover, this sex division of labor is much the same wherever it occurs. Such universal patterns derive from universally present facts, such as the greater size and strength of the male, and his greater activity based on the differing roles of the two sexes in connection with the production and care of children. These factors unquestionably led to the earliest differentiation in food gathering activities. This must have begun at an extremely remote period. The males became the main providers of the animal foods, since they were able to run down their prey and engage it in combat. The females, being hampered throughout most of their adult lives by the presence of infants either *in utero* or in arms, were unable to engage in such active pursuits but were able to collect vegetable foods and shell fish. Their share of the food quest frequently required heavier and certainly more continuous labor than did that of the male, but it did not require the sudden spurts of unhampered activity. Although at a relatively late period in human history the involvement of men in agriculture somewhat shifted this original division, the ancient pattern is still reflected in many of our customs. Thus to this day in the American family dinner the meat is placed in front of the father to be served and the vegetables in front of the mother. This is a folk memory of the days when the father collected the meat with his spear and the mother the vegetables with her digging stick.

The division of manufacturies reflects both the differences in strength and activity and also the foci of interest of the two sexes. Thus, the manufacture of tools and weapons is everywhere a male occupation, even though such work as the making of stone implements, which can be carried on on a sedentary basis and most of which requires skill rather than strength, would seem quite as well adapted to female as well as male potentialities. Going a step further, woodworking is nearly always carried on by men. Men also make woven artifacts which require real strength in their manufacture, for example the mats of flattened bamboos which are used in many parts of the tropics for floors and house walls. Women everywhere make ordinary mats and baskets. Woman's universal association with basketry may stem from the fact that most of their collecting activities involved the transportation of numerous small objects such as fruit, seeds, and roots, while anyone who has attempted to transport a healthy nude infant will recognize that the transportation of such an active and slippery object can be greatly facilitated by any sort of container that will serve to immobilize it. A final relatively constant item of primitive women's equipment is the digging stick, made in a surprising variety of forms. Made by men, since it is of wood, it is wielded by women and serves them both as a tool and a weapon.

At more complex levels of culture, women also make pottery and weave, but since these culture elements are lacking in several lines of culture development, we will not attempt to deal with them here.

One who reads any of the numerous descriptions of the life of very ancient man must be struck by the importance attached to stone tools. In fact, the first of the great periods into which human history is usually divided is known as the Stone Age. This is not because early man used stone so much more than he did other materials. A glance at the cave man's actual equipment would probably have shown wooden clubs and spears, bark baskets, skin bags and fur clothing, with only an occasional stone knife, scraper, or chopper. However, everything except the knife, scraper, or chopper was made of perishable materials. Only stone, and later bone, has survived for the record. Early man's stone implements were mainly used for making other things. They were primary tools, like the modern axe, hammer, plane, and knife. Also, it is interesting to note

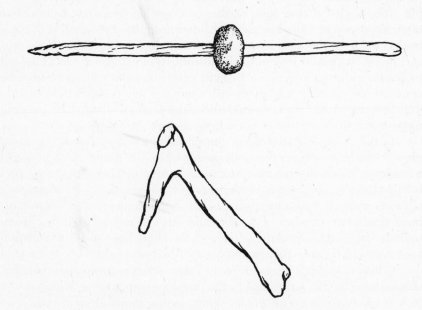

A: WEIGHTED DIGGING STICK   B: WOODEN HOE

that all our modern hand tools were developed long before the dawn of history, and that most of them have changed their original forms very little.

There are three main types of stone tools: grinding stones, so obvious that they are usually overlooked in listings, chipped tools, and pecked and ground tools. The first two go back to the very earliest period in human history, while the third appears much later. A grinding stone is simply any piece of rough surfaced stone which can be used to smooth and shape a piece of softer material. It was used much as we use sandpaper and did not have to be shaped. Such stones must have been employed at a very early time for wood working and later became the main instruments for bone working. Grinding stones are hard to detect in archeological deposits since the only shaping they get comes from use and most of the rocks which make good abrasives are soft and break up easily.

Chipped stone tools are made from rocks which, like glass, give a smooth, sharp edge on fracture. Actually, glass is the best material and when the first telegraph line was run across Australia it became a problem how to keep the natives, who were still living in a stone age, from stealing the insulators to chip into knives. This was solved by dumping a load of broken glass and crockery at the foot of each pole so that the native could get his raw material without having to climb for it. Obsidian, a volcanic glass, is the best natural material, and Stone Age people often traded it over long distances. Obsidian from the Yellowstone often shows up in Ohio mounds. Obsidian from the Island of Melos was traded all over the eastern Mediterranean during the New Stone Age and made the island rich until the introduction of bronze tools brought technological unemployment. In most cases the stone chipper had to be content with flint, jasper, or the still coarser grained cherts and quartzites. In general, the finer grained and more homogeneous the stone, the more perfectly implements made from it could be shaped.

In the simplest sort of stone chipping the workman takes a piece of glassy, brittle stone and a smooth pebble of dense, tough stone to use as a hammer. With the hammer stone he strikes off large chips from the brittle stone. Such chips have sharp edges and can be used as knives or scrapers without reworking. What is left of the stone after the chips have been struck off is known as the *core* and this also can be used as a heavy tool for chopping, especially if some of the chips have been struck off in such a way as to leave the core with a sharp edge or point.

While chips can be used "as is," they often come in inconvenient shapes. One of the early steps in the development of stone working was to learn how to strike off *blades*, long narrow strips of stone, sharp on both edges. In making these, one end of the piece of glassy stone was

AUSTRALIAN ABORIGINES ACQUIRING RAW MATERIALS

HAMMER STONE CHIPPING

broken across to get a flat surface, called a *striking platform.* The workman then struck down on this flat surface just back from the edge. Each
blow, if delivered at the right angle, would knock off a blade running
the length of the piece. With good material and "know how" such work
went very rapidly. Eight or ten blades could be struck off in a minute.
The core was thrown away when it got too small to give a good striking
surface. The blades could be used until dull, a matter of only a few
strokes, and then broken into lengths and shaped into arrowheads,
scrapers and so forth.

Surprisingly delicate shaping could be done by light blows with a
small hammer stone, but the high point in stone chipping technique
came with the invention of *pressure flaking.* This was the method used
in making all but the crudest American Indian knives and arrow heads.
The workman took a large flake or blade and held it in the palm of his
left hand, resting on a piece of buckskin. Then, with a bone about four
inches long, ground to a narrow chisel edge at one end, he pressed down
on the edge of the flake, forcing off a chip. When he had gone around the
edges of the flake on one side, he turned it over and treated the other
side in the same way.

The making of chipped stone implements is by no means a lost art,
as many curio collectors have discovered. In skilled hands the work goes
with surprising speed. Given good material, an excellent knife or arrow-

head can be made in half an hour and a serviceable one in half that time. When an Indian lost his arrow he grieved much more over the shaft and feathers than over the easily replaceable stone point.

While an Indian arrowhead is a good example of stone chipping, the ordinary Indian axe is an equally good example of pecking and grinding techniques. Although stone implements made by this method appear very late in human history, it requires much less skill than stone chipping. To make a stone axe, the workman takes a piece of stone which is hard and dense and will not break like flint. Granite is good, basalt better, and jade the best of all. Then with another stone he batters its surface, pulverizing it and knocking off little pieces until it has the shape he wants. Lastly, he grinds down the rough surface with sandstone or sand and water and sharpens the edge by rubbing on a flat rock. If he puts in a few extra hours of work polishing, it will not cut better but he may feel happier when he looks at it. A serviceable stone axe can be made in about eight hours.

Pecking and grinding stone go best when they can be handled like fancy work, and this may be the reason why the technique did not come into use until so late. A man who was always on the move would not want to carry an unfinished implement around with him for weeks so

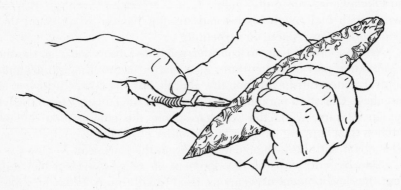

· PRESSURE FLAKING

that he could work on it in his spare time. Ground and polished stone go best with crops, cattle, and a house where one can keep the tool and bring it out to work on while one talks to a friend.

The slowest and most laborious type of stone working was deep drilling. Shallow holes could be drilled with a chipped stone point. This gives a conical depression quite different from the mark of a metal drill and such depressions are a good guide for determining whether stone objects are ancient or modern. Deeper holes were made by drilling from both sides, but even with this technique chipped drills were of little use when the stone was more than an inch thick. Deeper work was done with a tubular drill made from a reed. Sand and water were fed to the bottom of the drill and the shaft spun between the palms. Of course the soft reed wore away much more quickly than the stone, but reeds were plentiful. By this method the later stone age people of Europe pierced their axes for handles and the early Egyptians hollowed out stone bowls and jars.

The American continent played no part in the development of either stone tools or stone working techniques. By the time its first settlers arrived, some twenty to thirty thousand years ago, at the outside, all the basic inventions in this field had been made. The Americans developed a few improvements in axes, designed to make them easier to haft, and a fluted javelin point which had better penetration than the simple chipped type, but these seem to have exhausted their ingenuity.

Shapes of hand tools have a surprisingly long life. With every sort of tool there goes a collection of muscular habits adjusted to it. A new tool form requires the development of new habits. Even when the new tool is better made and more efficient than the old one, the trained worker finds it annoying and it takes him some time to adjust to it. A friend of mine who was an occupation officer on Okinawa reports that the Okinawans were quite unable to use American saws but with their own, which had rough blades and straight handles, they could do as good work as any American carpenter.

We are brought up to consider religious observances as the most conservative part of our culture. As a matter of fact the real centers of cultural conservatism are not the church but the kitchen-drawer and tool chest. Christian paraphernalia and ritual trace mainly from the later Roman Empire, while the wooden spoon, the combination hammer-hatchet, the chopping knife and many other objects of everyday use have come down with little change in form from the European Neolithic.

Side by side with the development of tools, used to make things, went the development of weapons, used to kill things. It has become an anthropological convention to speak of our subhuman and first human ancestors as helpless prey to carnivorous animals. Actually, these ancestors were themselves dangerous carnivores, more than a match for most of the animals they encountered. They had strength, intelligence and the characteristic primate love of destruction for its own sake. If reports of recent South African finds are to be trusted, some of the pre-humans used weapons even before they used tools. Cave deposits show thigh bones of big animals nicely suited for use as clubs, bashed in baboon skulls whose fractures fit the thigh bones, and horn points which would have made good daggers.

By the time our ancestors reached the human level they certainly had clubs and spears and knew how to throw stones. They were able to develop such aggressive extension of the personality partly because of their intelligence, partly because of their upright posture and free swinging shoulder joint. Only primates can throw, and only anthropoids and humans can throw really well. While the sword and axe are improvements over the stabbing spear and club, the real evolution of weapons has been along the lines of increased range. The harder, the straighter, and the farther a missile can be hurled, the more satisfactory it is for both offense and defense. Even the atom bomb speeding toward its target in a jet plane is only the most recent step in an unbroken developmental series which began with the cast spear and thrown stone.

One of the first additions to this primordial equipment was a contrivance known as a *bolas*. Remains of this weapon have been found in Middle Paleolithic sites and it still survives in use in far South America and among the Eskimo. It is made from a collection of weights, usually three, each of which is attached to a cord and all the cords tied together at their ends. In use, the thrower grasps the cords by the central knot, whirls the bolas around his head and lets drive. The weights spread

KILLING BIRDS WITH THE BOLAS

out as they fly through the air, like the spreading charge from a shotgun. When a cord or weight strikes anything, the flight is arrested and the whole apparatus wraps itself about whatever has been struck.

Another very ancient missile weapon was the sling. To the present younger generation the name suggests something made from a strip of inner tube and a forked stick, but the ancient weapon was even simpler. It was a strip of skin or woven fiber with a pocket near its middle in which a stone could be placed. One end of the sling was wrapped around the user's palm while the other end had a knot which was grasped between thumb and finger. In throwing, the sling was whirled around the head and the knot released when the stone reached the right point in its swing. The longer the sling, the greater its range and the less its accuracy. Some of the Melanesians who lived in fortified hilltop villages used slings six feet or more in length, whirling them over the edge of towers constructed for the purpose. Such weapons were effective for spraying an advancing force at long range but could not hit any particular target. In several parts of Oceania the natives had discovered that a cigar-shaped sling stone flew farther and straighter than an irregular stone and carried nets of prepared ammunition into battle with them.

It takes long training to become an expert slinger, but this simple contrivance can be a deadly weapon in the hands of a man who knows how to use it. Admiral Porter, who fought the Marquesan natives in the early eighteen hundreds says that their slung stones were almost as effective as musketry fire. The Antandroy of Madagascar are experts, and while in their territory I had the pleasure of hearing a native missionary preach of David and Goliath. After a round by round description of the fight which few radio announcers could have bettered, he concluded: "Now, my friends, what do we learn from this? Any one of us would have had better sense than to attack a slinger in the open when we were armed only with a helmet and breastplate and a sword, a shield and a spear. Goliath was an experienced warrior and yet he did this. My friends, this shows that God takes away the brains of his enemies."

The spear-thrower was a companion contrivance to the sling and one which employed the same arm-lengthening principle. The spear-thrower itself was a straight piece of wood with an inward pointed spur at the end. The javelin used with it had a depression in the butt end to fit this spur. In making a cast, the spear-thrower was swung up and over, pushing the javelin forward and approximately doubling the force and range of the same spear thrown by hand. This weapon was certainly older than the bow. It was used by the Upper Paleolithic people of Europe and by the ancestors of the American Indians and is still used by the Australians. Although replaced by the bow in most places, it has some advantages. A heavy javelin thrown with it at short range has greater penetration and shocking power than most arrows. The Aztec and their neighbors in the Mexican Plateau kept the spear-thrower for military use although they used bows for hunting. They wore heavy quilted armor which was largely arrow proof but could not stand up against javelins hurled with the *atlatl* (the Mexican name for spear-thrower). Even the Spaniards developed a healthy respect for this weapon, which could drive a javelin through a steel breastplate at point blank range.

The bow and arrow seems to have been invented later than the spear-thrower but its origin remains a mystery. No one has been able

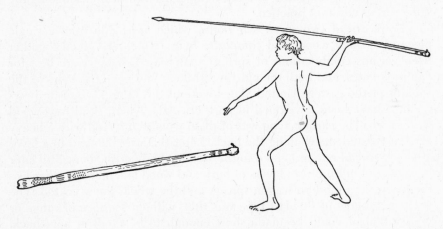

SPEAR THROWER (ATLATL)

to suggest any useful appliance from which it could have been developed. Its distribution strongly suggests that it was invented at some one place in the Old World, perhaps the work of some primitive Edison. It did not reach America until long after the first settlement and never did reach Australia. It was known everywhere in Southeast Asia and the islands of the Pacific, but in most places it failed to "take" as a weapon, being used in hunting and sport. This may have been due to the patterns of head hunting and, less universally, cannibalism which existed in these regions. When the real aim of the fighting was to get heads and meat, there was little point to picking off the enemy at long range.

It takes considerable skill and experience to make a good bow and arrow, and the first weapon of this sort must have been relatively inefficient. Unless the early archers used poison, like the modern Bushmen and African Pygmies, they could have done little damage to either big game or human enemies. However, as time went on the bow was de-

veloped into the most efficient weapon known prior to the modern repeating rifle and revolver. The bow lacked some of the range and penetration of the earlier firearms, but it had other advantages. A moderately
good archer could shoot a quarter of a mile and loose ten or more arrows a minute, while an expert could do much better. As late as the time
of the Spanish Armada, English longbowmen, some of whom still survived in the back districts, outranged the Spanish arquebus men as well
as blanketing them with the speed and accuracy of their fire. The real
reason that the bow went out of use in Europe seems to have been the
rise of military conscription. It takes only a short time to train a man to
load a gun and fire it toward the enemy, but a good archer takes as long
to develop as a good golfer and has to keep his bow-arm in shape by the
same sort of constant practice.

Bows are of two sorts: *self bows,* which are made from a single
piece of springy wood, and *composite bows,* which are glued together
from various combinations of springy materials. Self bows are best for
damp climates, and both the old English long bows and the bows of the
Indians of the eastern United States were of this type. Composite bows
seem to have been developed in northern Asia, where good bow-wood
was scarce. The earliest type was of plain wood reinforced with a heavy
cord of twisted sinew along the back. Later this was changed to a layer
of sinew spread out and glued to the wooden body of the bow. Still later
bows were built up from layers of horn and wood laid on each other like
the leaves in a modern wagon spring, and the whole sinew coated. The
great advantage of this last type was that, without sacrifice of range or
penetration, it could be made short enough to be used on horseback.

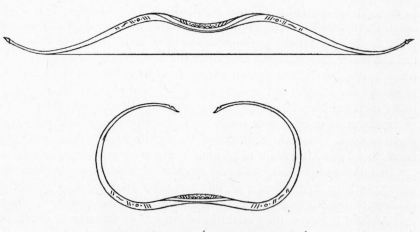

COMPOSITE BOW (WOOD AND HORN)

Such bows became the main weapons of the nomads of the Asiatic steppes and were largely responsible for the repeated victories of Huns, Turks, and Mongols over European armies. The longest flight shot on record, over eight hundred yards, was made with a Turkish bow of this type. The classical Greeks borrowed the composite bow from the Scythians, and its peculiar double curve when strung has been immortalized in the conventional picture of Cupid's bow.

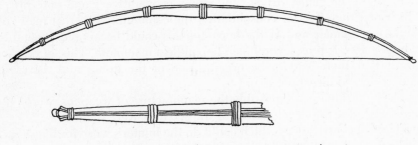

COMPOSITE BOW (WOOD AND RAWHIDE)

Even the club has had its developments as a missile weapon. These fall into two types: throwing clubs, which have a short, straight shaft and heavy head, and boomerangs, which are flat, curved blades, usually with sharpened edges. Throwing clubs turn slowly end over end in flight and the thrower must be expert at estimating the distance to his target. Boomerangs spin in flight like a propeller. If the two halves of the blade are given a slight twist so that their flat surfaces slope in opposite directions, the weapon will circle out when thrown and then come back to the thrower. Needless to say it will not return if it hits anything. Such return boomerangs were made by the ancient Egyptians and modern Australians and were used by both for hunting birds. The boomerang would be thrown across a flock of resting birds, flushing them, and would then come back through them as they rose. Throwing clubs of either sort are inferior weapons for most purposes and have continued in use mainly where better appliances were lacking.

With the development of tools and weapons there was an improvement in hunting techniques and an increase in the meat food supply comparable to the increase that came in vegetable food supply with the introduction of fire. In particular, with the spear thrower, the sling, and the like it became possible for our ancestors to handle bigger and bigger game. They developed, if we are to judge from modern so-called primitives, great skill in tracking and stalking and probably all sorts of ingenious contrivances for getting near game. We know, for instance, that such modern hunting people as the Bushmen used a most amusing lot of disguises of one sort or another to get in bow range of game. There is one very famous Bushman painting showing a herd of antelope and two or three ostriches; one ostrich looks just like the rest except that it has human legs. One of the Bushman's regular stalking tricks was to get in an ostrich skin with a stick up through the neck; and then, imitating the ostrich's movements, he could work up to the not too observant antelope from down wind. Also, very early, there must have been the surrounding of game, drives, and other cooperative game enterprises which had the effect of consolidating the community. A great many of the larger animals and of the herd animals could be hunted profitably only in packs. It took several men to handle a mammoth. This, of course, meant that there had to be organization of the group and therefore leadership and direction.

Tools, which made possible the manufacture of weapons, were also responsible for the development of traps. These were the first machines, mechanical contrivances which could do the hunter's work for him. How far back such appliances go is uncertain, but some of the cave paintings in France show what may be either traps or houses. An amazing variety of traps were invented in different parts of the world, but nearly all of them are based on one of the following principles or on some combination of these principles: *The Pitfall.* This is simply a pit, with or without a sharp stake set upright in the bottom. The opening of the pit is camouflaged with a layer of some light material. Anything that steps on this falls through. *The Deadfall.* This is a contrivance by which a weight is dropped on the game. The figure-four trap used by farm boys to catch rabbits is the most familiar example to Americans. *The Snare.* This is a running noose which tightens around the animal's neck or leg. Very often the noose is fastened to some sort of spring pole which will jerk the animal off the ground when it is caught.

To be effective, traps have to be designed for particular sorts of game and set with an understanding of their habits. A trap made and set to catch anything will usually catch nothing. Peculiarities of behavior in various species have resulted in the development of some special trap forms which do not fit any of the regular classifications. One of the most gruesome of these is the contrivance which the Eskimos use for killing wolves. They take a bright new knife, sharpen it to a razor edge, and freeze the hilt into a chunk of ice so that the blade will stand upright; then they lay this down beside the game trail where wolves come. The wolf will lick any bright object out of curiosity. The wolf licks the knife blade, gets his tongue cut, and tastes the blood. As a cut from a very sharp instrument is not particularly painful, the wolf will proceed to lick the knife until he cuts his tongue to pieces. Other wolves in the pack, infuriated by the blood, will turn on him and then turn on each other. A good many wolves can be disposed of in this way.

Another gruesome method is used by the Eskimo for killing bears. They take a double-pointed piece of springy whalebone, bend it double, and freeze it in a lump of fat. This is thrown out when the bears come and since they bolt their food, some bear will swallow it whole. When it is in his interior, the whalebone springs open as the fat melts and the pointed ends pierce the bear's stomach. In due course he dies of peritonitis.

GUINEA TRAP

One of the most amusing traps I ever encountered was in use in Madagascar; it is also used in many parts of Africa. I was traveling through the open veldt country in the southwestern part of Madagascar and saw a ring of clay about six to eight inches across and about one inch high, modeled on a flat rock. My native bearers explained that this was a trap for catching guinea fowl. Some ground nuts, which are like peanuts except that the kernels are larger, rounder, and harder, were put inside the circle, which served to keep them from rolling off the rock. The kernels were a little too big for the guinea fowl to actually pick up, but they would keep on trying. Every time a guinea hen pecked at one and missed, its beak came down on the rock. As guinea fowl are persistent creatures, they would keep this up until their heads swelled up and they went blind. Every day or so the owner of the trap would come and hunt through the brush near the trap and pick up the disabled birds. This may be hard to believe, but any poultry raiser knows that the same thing can happen to chickens when they are fed on a concrete floor.

The use of tools and modified weapons, such as the harpoon, also helped man to add fish to his supply. As far as we can discover, the earliest men did not use fish. There are no indications in Europe, where we have the most complete records because of cave living, of fishing having been of any interest to humans until the Upper Paleolithic, at most twenty to twenty-five thousand years ago. The use of fish probably began with shore scavenging: picking up the dead fish that had been washed in, gathering oysters and sea food at low tide, and now and then catching fish by hand. Later all sorts of fishing techniques were developed. Large fish were speared and shot with the bow and arrow. Both of these require a good deal of practice, because a fish is not where it appears to be when looked down upon through the water, and to be able to hit it the fisherman must learn to estimate the amount of refraction. Various contrivances such as fish hooks and gorges were developed. The gorge is older than the hook and a simpler device. It is simply a double pointed piece of wood or bone about an inch and a half long, around which the bait is wrapped. The fish swallows the whole thing. As soon as there is a pull on the line, the gorge turns crosswise and the fish is never able to get off. The only trouble is that the fish must be slit open in order to get the gorge to use again. This type of contrivance is still used in a good many places with set lines.

Nets and fish traps were probably somewhat later developments. Modern "primitives" have a great variety of both, the commonest net forms being dip nets and seines. Fish traps are usually based on the principle of making it easy for the fish to get into an enclosure or basket and exceedingly difficult for them to get out. When there is a considerable rise and fall of the tides, large stone walled enclosures which are under water when the tide is in, and dry or very shallow when it is out, are highly effective.

All this is important to the history of culture since, where people developed successful fishing techniques, it became possible for them to settle down. Fishermen ceased to be nomadic long before the discovery of food raising and the domestication of plants and animals. Fishing also opened up great areas for occupation, particularly in the interiors of the northern glaciated regions, which stretch all across Eurasia and also across northern North America. These regions have strings of glacial lakes set in forest or tundra. Until fairly late in human history, when people had developed snowshoes, skis, the toboggan, and so forth to cope with the heavy winter snow of this region, the only way in which men could survive here over the winter was to settle down around lakes or at spots in the river where the current was quiet so that the river would freeze over, and get their food by fishing through the ice.

The use of tools and fire gave man an incomparably greater control over his environment than any other mammal. This made possible an unparalleled extension of his range. There is no other warm blooded animal which is so widely distributed, unless we count man's friend, the dog, whom he took with him in his wanderings. In particular, the development of hunting equipment made it possible for him to penetrate into northern territory never reached by any of his vegetarian primate ancestors. Man is able to subsist on a meat diet, and such groups such as the Eskimo are able to thrive in a region where the only possible vegetable foods are berries, rock lichen, and reindeer moss. The last can only be eaten after it has been processed by partial digestion in the reindeer's stomach. This tremendously wide spatial spread has also enabled *homo sapiens* to convert itself from a decidedly rare species to an exceedingly numerous one. There is no other large mammal now extant which can approach him in numbers. In fact, with modern science operating to prevent the operation of the factors which once held human populations in balance with their food supply, the most serious problem which confronts man at this writing is how to keep his numbers down to the point where the earth's resources can provide the average individual with a good life.

Chapter VIII

Domestication of Plants
and Animals

THE INVENTION of food-raising ushered in the second great period in human history. It transformed *homo sapiens* from one of the rarest to the most numerous of mammalian species. It also resulted in a tremendous acceleration in the rate of cultural development. This was no doubt due in part to the surplus of time and economic resources which food-raising made available, but it may also have been linked with population increase.

Everything seems to indicate that the enrichment of culture depends primarily upon above-average minds which never form more than a small fraction of the population: perhaps one in 3,000 would be a fair estimate for most societies. These individuals seem to be mutants whose appearance is quite unpredictable. Their abilities are rarely inherited, and they may be born in any racial group and at any social level. Therefore, the larger the population, the greater the number of such mutants, and consequently, the greater the potential for culture growth.

Early students of the evolution of culture believed that the domestication of animals preceded agriculture. After man the hunter had tamed his prey, according to their somewhat romantic formulation, woman, the plant-gatherer and homemaker, gently diverted him from hunting and herding and persuaded him to settle down to planting and plowing. However, it seems fairly certain that, with very few exceptions, agriculture preceded animal domestication. It is almost impossible to tame animals and attach them to a human group as long as this group is continually on the move in search of food. It was not until humans had begun to raise crops and settle down that they tamed most of the domestic species which we have today.

The most notable exception to this rule is the dog. The association of man and the dog began in Mesolithic times and may well have been a symbiotic relationship. The dog, with his keen senses of hearing and smell, could track game and give warning of enemies and was rewarded for this by being thrown the scraps of the hunters' feast. At the same time, as any dog owner will recognize, the personality patterns of the two species were so similar that it was easy for them to come to understandings and form mutual attachments.

The early stages in this association were probably much like the situation which is found today among the Australian aborigines. Here there are both wild and tamed dogs of the same breed. When an Australian native wants a hunting dog, he goes out and catches a puppy which, as it grows up, is taught to help in tracking and finding wounded animals. When the dog becomes fully adult, it usually runs away and returns to its wild life. However, there are occasional dogs, especially bitches, who become so strongly attached to the human family that they will not run away. Such dogs and their puppies are highly valued and are treated very much as members of society. Native women will even nurse the young animals. Although fully domesticated strains of dogs could be developed in this way, the present arrangement must have existed for a long time. Since man and the dog were the only large placental mammals in Australia when Europeans arrived, the aborigines must have brought the dog with them when they came from Asia.

The other exception to the rule that agriculture precedes animal domestication is the reindeer. These animals provide a reliable food supply throughout most of far northern Eurasia in a region where agriculture is impossible. Because of the reindeer pattern of migration in dense herds, it was possible for human groups to attach themselves to these wild herds, protecting them from their natural enemies, the wolves, and killing from the herd with as little disturbance as possible when food was needed. Reindeer are not difficult to tame, although they never become completely reliable and have to be rebroken for use after a single season free on the range. Their utilization other than as a source of meat seems to have been developed in imitation of cattle- and horse-using nomad peoples to the south with whom the reindeer herders were in contact.

The domestication of other animal species did not occur until humans had established settled village life. There can be little question that domestication began with the keeping of pets, and that the original motives were not economic. Even today, there are many uncivilized peoples who keep a great variety of pet birds and animals simply for the amusement and emotional outlets which they provide. Young animals are cute and appealing. The hunter who has killed a mother animal for food often brings the cubs home for his children to play with. Young humans and young animals always have an affinity for each other. However, as animals of most species grow older they either run away or become troublesome and go into the pot at the first sign of food shortage.

Various species differ in their adaptability. In order to become domesticated the species has to be tough enough to survive abuse and neglect, and capable of forming sufficiently strong attachments to either people or places so that they will stay around the village even when unconfined. Not all species are capable of this sort of adjustment.

It is important to note that the real test of domestication is whether a species will breed in captivity. Many animals which can be tamed and even put to economic use cannot withstand this test. Thus, elephants have been tamed and used for at least five thousand years. In the Gilgamesh epic, a Mesopotamian religious poem which goes back to at least 3500 B.C., there is mention of what must have been a tame elephant "that shakes off its blanket." Although the taming and training of elephants are so ancient, until very recently it has been impossible to breed them in captivity. Even now in Nepal, Burma, and other regions where elephants are used as work animals, great areas are maintained as elephant preserves in which the animals live and breed wild. The young adult elephants can be trained easily when caught, and this holds even for African elephants, who were never tamed by the natives.

It is an interesting fact that no economically significant animal species was domesticated within historic times. As a matter of fact, a number of species which were domesticated at one time have been allowed to revert. For example, the Egyptians herded various species of gazelle and antelope with their cattle. However, these animals proved to be less productive of milk and meat than cattle and their domestication was dropped. The Egyptians also domesticated the hyena, which is quite dog-like in its behavior, and makes a good hunter and tracker. It is hard to say why the hyena was allowed to revert to a wild state unless its odor was too strong for even the olfactorally callous early Egyptians.

The process of domestication of any species involves the elimination of the wildest or most vicious individuals and the development of docile strains. The animal which became troublesome or dangerous would be killed and the docile ones allowed to live. By this process of selection relatively gentle breeds can be developed even in naturally ferocious species. Thus, the lions bred in California for Hollywood use are getting less ferocious in each generation and also, like other Hollywood stars, handsomer. No wild African lion can show the smooth coat and magnificent spread of mane of the Hollywood variety.

Early students of domestication were particularly impressed by the physiological changes which can be observed in domestic animals in contrast with wild ones. Domestic animals tend to show a persistence of juvenile characteristics, and their bony structure is lighter and the bone itself of softer and spongier texture. These differences are pronounced enough so that in archeological sites the bones of domestic and wild animals of the same species can readily be distinguished. Similar conditions were noted in the skeletons of wild animals kept in zoos, particularly of those born in captivity.

With the introduction of proper feeding, based on modern knowledge of nutrition, the differences between wild animals and zoo-bred ones tend to disappear. It seems highly probable that in the initial stages of the domestication process, plain malnutrition played a significant role. The tame animal, penned up and fed by its owner, or at least driven to the pastures which he selected, did not obtain all the necessary food elements in optimum amounts. It suffered from "hidden hunger" and the resulting diminution in vigor must have made it less aggressive and eas-

SOAY SHEEP

ier to handle up to the point where real domestic breeds were produced by selection for docility.

The fact that we always refer to early man as a hunter and food-gatherer reflects the importance which humans attach to meat, much as does the listing of meats as the principal dishes on any menu. Actually, early man was not primarily a hunter except in those fortunate localities where game was plentiful, or in the far north where vegetable food was scanty or lacking. In most parts of the world human beings have depended much more on seeds, roots, or fruits than on meat. The regions where food raising began were those in which the population was already heavily dependent upon wild vegetable foods and where they had become accustomed to the laborious processes involved in gathering roots and seeds. In places where game was plentiful even the taking over of agricultural techniques already developed elsewhere met with strong resistance, since hoeing is a much less entertaining occupation than hunting.

The full complex of plant domestication involves a whole series of techniques: planting, cultivation, the use of fertilizer or fallowing, and, in arid regions, irrigation. However, instead of a progressively logical evolution of agriculture in which people always began by planting, then learned to cultivate and fertilize, the distribution of these techniques among living primitives is irregular. Each technique is found alone in one group or another as an initial step in their emergence from simple food-gathering.

For instance, in Australia, the natives made the discovery that if they threw peelings and shoots scraped off in preparing wild yams in a place where the soil was black, they would find a yam patch growing there when they returned to the camp site the following year. They replanted tops deliberately, but they never cultivated or fertilized yam patches. This haphazard planting was their only agricultural achievement.

In British Columbia, on the other hand, the Indians did no planting except for the occasional scattering of tobacco seeds on burned-over ground by some of the southern tribes. However, they prized sweet clover and skunk cabbage as greens. The skunk cabbage is one of the first plants to appear in the spring and its shoots were in demand for cooking with dry salmon which had been kept since the previous spring run. It probably improved the flavor, and women who discovered a good patch of clover or cabbage would fence it, weed it, and put up various ingenious scarecrows to keep the deer away. Other women would respect the patch as her property. However, it never occurred to anyone to try to plant or fertilize such patches.

The use of fertilizer is one of the rarest agricultural techniques, yet it was used by the Indians of our own Atlantic coast. The New England tribes put a herring in each hill of corn when they planted, then went off to hunt, leaving the corn to its own devices until they returned to harvest any which had survived weeds and insect pests.

In the Rocky Mountain plateau the Paiutes neither planted nor cultivated, but they irrigated. They were fond of pig-weed, which they used as greens in the spring and as seeds in the autumn. The Paiutes built small dams at the heads of shallow valleys to impound the winter snow water. The pig-weed grew in the valleys below the dams and each band had an official irrigator who made the rounds of the pig-weed patches from time to time, and if they seemed to be getting too dry, would poke a hole in the dam, let some water run down over them, and then fill up the hole again.

It can be seen from the foregoing that there was no one neat pattern in the development of agriculture. Each crop and each climate presented its own problems which had to be solved.

Much study has been given to the question of where various plants and animals were domesticated. A highly ingenious theory has been worked out by the Russians in connection with the domestication of plants. This theory begins with the quite logical assumption that the region in which the greatest number of related species and genera of a particular plant is found is the center of its evolutionary differentiation. Similarly, the region in which the greatest number of varieties or related species of a domesticated plant are under cultivation will presumably be the place at which it was domesticated. In the diffusion of an already domesticated crop only a few of the many original varieties will be carried to each new territory. While this would scarcely hold in modern times, with experiment stations deliberately breeding new varieties, it is probably valid for ancient farmers. By plotting the distribution of various plants on this basis it has been possible to establish the probable points of domestication for most economically important crops. Unfortunately the Russian insistence that all science should be applied science has made them limit their researches to climates from which plants could be introduced into Russia. There is still little information on the origin of tropical crops.

It is highly significant that in the Old World large numbers of crops can be traced to a few areas which are also those significant for animal domestication. It is thus possible to speak of centers for the development of food-raising, with only a few outlying plant and animal species to be accounted for.

In the development of food-raising the region extending from Northwestern India across Asia Minor and south to the Red Sea and the Sinai desert was of outstanding importance. This region constitutes a single ecological area characterized by light seasonal rainfall and a continental climate with marked difference in winter and summer temperature. Fortunately for the spread of the type of culture developed here, such climates produced species which are highly adaptable and which can be acclimated to life even in far northern environments. The only climatic conditions which they cannot stand are those to be found in humid tropics.

Seven to eight thousand years ago this whole region seems to have been park country. Either the rainfall was considerably more than it is at present or run-off was less, for much of the land which is now desert was covered with grass and supported game. However, game was not plentiful and the population seems to have relied heavily on grass seeds for its food supply. The region contained a great variety of wild grasses, among which were the ancestors of our modern wheat, oats, rye and barley. There were a number of species of wild wheat, distinct enough to prevent hybridization.

The presence of polished sickle flints in Mesolithic sites shows that the people were reaping grain even before they began to cultivate it, although these grains are among the easiest domesticated plants to grow. At first the sowings were mixed, but as agricultural technique improved, and particularly as the grain growing population shifted out of Southwest Asia into other regions, the different kinds of grain were gradually sorted out. Barley seems to have been the favorite Southwestern Asiatic crop in early times, but as farmers moved northward they found that barley did not do as well as wheat and changed their staple crop accordingly. North of the zone where wheat did best, rye and oats, which had originally been weeds sown unintentionally with the wheat, could still produce good crops. Oats flourished the furthest north of all. There were, of course, further adaptations through the development of particular varieties suited to particular soils or local variations in climate.

All the later cultures which traced their origins to this Southwest Asiatic area were primarily grain-raisers. However, a few other plants were domesticated in the same general region. A number of plants of the beet-cabbage family were brought under domestication, as well as the onion and cucumber. Apples, pears, almonds, and a bit later, grapes, figs and dates were cultivated here, and also flax. There were two species of flax: one raised for its fiber, the other for its seed. Although the oil pressed from this seed (linseed oil) has now been relegated to industrial uses, it seems to have formed part of the diet of Neolithic man, whose food supply was notably short in fats.

Within the Southwestern Asiatic region the Russian botanists have distinguished two centers: one in northeastern Persia and western Afghanistan, the other in Asia Minor. However, the crops and cultures of these two were so much alike that we need not try to distinguish them. Presumably as a result of influences from Southwestern Asia, two other somewhat later centers of domestication were developed. One of these was in the highlands of Abyssinia, where a surprising number of local plants seem to have been brought under domestication, including several species of wheat and barley. However, the Abyssinian plateau is completely surrounded by deserts and drops away rapidly on the west and south to tropical lowlands unsuited for the growing of grain crops. As a center it seems to have had very little influence on the subsequent development of agriculture. In North Africa various species of hard (durum) wheats were domesticated. The olive, one of the most important sources of edible oil, was also domesticated either here or on the northern shores of the Mediterranean. However, the climatic conditions which it required were so specific that it could not be diffused much beyond the Mediterranean littoral.

Most of our familiar domestic animals seem to have been brought under control in this same Southwestern Asiatic region. Various breeds of cattle, sheep, goats, and donkeys were also developed here from the local wild species. The pig also may have been domesticated here although, if so, there was a second independent center of pig domestication in Southeastern Asia. In any case, the pig did not figure in Southwestern Asiatic economy to anything like the extent which it did in Southeastern Asia or in the forested regions of Western Europe. In the same region but at a much later time the dromedary camel was added to the local equipment.

Horses had been introduced into this region by 3000 B.C., but were still rare animals used for display or in war. Their first domestication was certainly not in this region. The backward trail seems to lead to the Central Asiatic Steppes, but horse-taming may have been an exceedingly ancient and widespread practice. Horses run in bands made up of mares and young animals, dominated by a single stallion. Since stallions are always anxious to add new mares to their harems, tame mares would be valuable to horse hunters as decoys, and domestication may have begun in this way.

The utilization of horses for anything but food or decoys seems to have been later than that of cattle, for the first pictures of horses in use show a type of harness obviously based on the ox yoke. This arrangement was by no means satisfactory, since the yoke or breast strap interferes with the horse's breathing, but it was not until the Middle Ages that the invention of the horse collar in Northern Europe made possible a really effective use of horse traction. Until fairly late in history horses were not ridden at all, and it was still later that an effective saddle suitable for military use was developed.

The ancient people of Southwestern Asia were also responsible for the invention of milking, one of the most revolutionary economic developments in human history. This invention seems to have been made only once. The American Indians failed to develop it in the regions where they had a potential milk animal, the llama, and even in South China and Japan the technique has been introduced only within the last century.

The first animal to be milked was probably the goat, since man was most evenly matched with it in size and weight. This is also suggested by the earliest pictures of milking which have come down to us. These show men milking cattle from directly behind, a position which would certainly have discouraged the practice if the first experiments had been made with cows. Later the milking technique was extended to take in practically all domestic animals standing higher than pigs, including such, to us, improbable species as horses and sheep. The economic potentialities of milking were enormous. As long as domestic animals were used only for meat, it was impossible for settled people to raise enough animal food per acre to dispense with other protein sources. With milking, on the other hand, herds of a size which could be pastured within walking distance of the village could provide a steady increment of necessary food elements and make the villagers independent of other protein sources. The main diet in the Southwestern Asiatic region consisted of grain hulled but not polished, so that the minerals and vitamins were retained, then cracked, boiled, and eaten with milk. This was to become the basic diet of all European and most Asiatic peoples from the Neolithic on. Until quite recently the Scottish peasant ate little else. One is reminded of Dr. Johnson's definition of oats as food for horses in England and for men in Scotland, and the Scot's response, "And where else will you find such horses and such men?"

Boiled grain and milk, with an occasional bit of fish or fresh meat and greens in season for roughage, provide a diet on which men can live and labor, and on which children can build good bones, sound teeth and strong muscles. The main shortage in such a diet is that of vitamins of the B complex, and this was early met by the grain-raising people through their discovery of how to brew beer.

In predynastic Egypt, as early as 4500 B.C., the farmers had learned how to malt their grain, i.e., sprout it before grinding so as to transform some of the starch into sugar, and obtain better fermentation and higher alcoholic content. In all cultures which stem from the Southwestern Asiatic center, beer has been a regular part of diet. The laws of Hammurabi, the world's earliest code of fair employment practices, specified how much beer and what kind of beer was to be given to workmen on what kind of jobs. Dark beer must be given to workmen for heavy labor, light beer for easier tasks. Since the ancient beer was soupy with yeast, much like that produced by amateurs during the American prohibition era, it provided not only vitamins but a fair amount of protein. It is interesting to note that the South African natives, who still live mainly on a mush and milk diet supplemented by beer, suffered from dietary deficiency and consequent lowering of disease resistance when missionaries stepped in and stopped their brewing.

From the Southwestern Asiatic center the culture configuration based on a milk and grain economy spread widely, taking certain basic elements with it. Since this culture was ancestral to all the higher civilizations of the Old World it will be described in detail elsewhere. As has already been said, the plants and animals on which the Southwestern Asiatic economy depended were temperate climate forms. The animals were hardier than the plants but even so, climate set a definite limit to the spread of the complex.

Given sufficient rainfall, both plants and animals could survive almost to the Arctic zone, and in regions which were too dry for raising grains, animals could still be pastured. Thus wheat was cultivated as far north as Archangel in Russia, although the season was so short that special barns like tobacco barns had to be built to ripen the grain after it was cut. Cattle were also raised, although hay had to be cured for them and barns built to shelter them in the winter.

Grain would not grow well in Africa outside the Abyssinian plateau, the Mediterranean coast, and the far southern tip of the continent. Cattle, on the other hand, were able to thrive in the African plateau and were in use all the way to the Cape of Good Hope. Throughout this region they provided the economic basis of a distinctive type of culture with well marked characteristics. However, as far as we can determine, not a single animal or plant of primary economic importance was domesticated in Africa south of the Sahara. A few plants, such as okra, some millets, and the oil palm, were brought under cultivation, but there were no native crops capable of supporting large populations. As we shall see later, the effects of this on the evolution of Negro culture were tremendous.

A second and quite independent center of plant and animal domestication occurred in Southeastern Asia. The dividing line between this and the Southwestern area of domestication apparently ran north and south through Central India and was directly related to differences in ecology. The climate of the Ganges Valley and of much of Southern India resembles that of the coastal regions of Southeastern Asia from Burma to Indochina and of the large Indonesian islands. Its outstanding features are heavy seasonal rainfall and constant heat. Most of this territory was covered with dense jungle in ancient times. Seed bearing grasses, which require plenty of sun and light, were scarce here, but the jungle provided numerous wild roots and fruits upon which the ancient food-gathering economy of the region depended heavily.

Throughout much of this region mountains run down fairly close to the coast and changes in altitude produce marked changes in environment. It seems highly probable that this led to the domestication of different crops in the lowlands and in the highlands. The Russian botanists believe that there was still another center of plant domestication in the mountainous regions of South China contiguous to this Southeast Asiatic center, but none of the crops which they refer to this region were adequate in themselves to provide for large populations or advanced cultures.

The staple lowland crops were yam, taro, and banana. Intensive study might show different centers of domestication for some of these, but all three were developed from wild plants of the Southeast Asiatic coastal region. Breadfruit may also have been domesticated here, although the evidence is less satisfactory. Wild varieties of breadfruit are still found in Melanesia.

The yam is frequently confused with the sweet potato, but it belongs to an entirely different botanical family. Although the roots look very much alike, the yam plant is a low bush rather than a vine. Some varieties reach huge size, single roots of a hundred pounds weight being on record. Yams will grow in poor ground and with little care, but they also provide poor food, high in bulk but low in nourishment.

Taro is a plant of the arum family, related to the calla lily. It has a large heart-shaped leaf and a root that resembles a long, rather warty, turnip. It is a swamp plant and most varieties do best with their roots under water. Plants can be left in the field for years and the roots dug as needed, although they grow larger and coarser textured with time. Old roots weighing 30 pounds or more are not unusual. Taro contains salicylic acid crystals which make it inedible when raw. It is usually prepared by baking in an earth oven and mashing to a paste, when it forms a palatable and nourishing food, one which contains considerable fat as well as starch. The Hawaiians increased the flavor by fermenting the pounded paste in pits, producing the famous *poi*.

The banana is too well known to require description.

Breadfruit grows on a large, handsome tree which provides good timber. The fruit ranges in size from as big as a man's fist to as big as his head. It is a bumpy, pale yellow-green sphere covered with a thin shell much like that of an avocado. There is a small seedless core surrounded by stiff white flesh which, like taro, is inedible until cooked. The common method of cooking is to throw the fruit into an open fire and turn it until the shell is charred on all sides. The native cook can tell when the fruit is done by its sound when tapped, much as one tests the ripeness of a watermelon. When done it is peeled, cracked open by a light blow, and the core lifted out. It can be eaten at once but tastes best when mixed with coconut cream and pounded to a smooth paste.

These four plants were all good sources of starch, but since they required a hot, humid climate neither their cultivation nor the Southeastern Asiatic patterns of culture associated with them could spread very far on the Asiatic mainland. Thus they could not be grown profitably in China north of the mountain barrier where the climate was continental, or in the semi-arid region extending west from India to the Mediterranean. On the other hand, the climate of the islands to the south and east of Asia was favorable, and the Southeastern Asiatic crops and culture spread into Indonesia and eventually into all the tropical islands of the Pacific.

The coconut also belongs to this region. Since it grows only near the sea and does best where there is a seepage of salt water around the roots, its range was too limited for it to be of great economic importance on the Southeastern Asiatic mainland. However, in the Pacific Islands it became a veritable staff of life. Coconut and pandanus were the only economically valuable plants which would grow on the low coral islands, and pandanus was of only minor value. The green coconuts provided drink, the ripe ones food and fiber for cordage; the leaves were woven into mats and baskets and used for thatching, while the bone-hard wood of the palm's outer shell was an excellent material for tools and weapons.

The paper mulberry was also domesticated in the Southeastern Asiatic region. This plant is still used for making Chinese rice paper. It was cultivated by the natives as a source of bark cloth, which in this region replaced the woven cloth of the Western agricultural peoples. Bark cloth was made by stripping off the bark of the mulberry tree, scraping off the coarse outer bark, soaking the inner bark for a few days, and then beating it out thin. New strips of bark were beaten on as needed and there was no limit to the possible size of a piece. A Fijian village once made a single strip eight feet wide and over a hundred yards long as a present for a visiting chief. Bark cloth was well adapted for tropical clothing since it was windproof but had no warmth. Its main disadvantage was that it disintegrated like paper when it got wet. When natives who wore it were caught in a shower, they stripped off their clothing and wrapped it in leaves until the rain stopped. At the same time bark cloth had the advantage of being plentiful and easily made. A woman could easily pound enough in a day to last an average family for a week. The natives never bothered to clean or repair it; when it became dirty or torn, it was simply thrown away. Since the natives had never learned to wash or mend clothes it took them a long time to adapt to European garments, which at first were worn until they fell to pieces. There was a great decline in cleanliness, with resulting skin diseases and other infections. The early missionaries' insistence that the natives keep their bodies constantly covered also contributed to this.

Most of the Southeastern Asiatic crops are so thoroughly domesticated that they have become seedless. Bananas, breadfruit, and paper mulberry all have to be propagated by cuttings. This, together with the great number of varieties which have been developed under cultivation, suggests that agriculture is exceedingly old in this region. Certainly its techniques are highly developed. Taro was probably the first plant to be grown in flooded beds, with all the preparatory labor this involved.

Two animals domesticated in Southeast Asia have become exceedingly important in world economy. These are the pig, also domesticated independently in the West, and the chicken. Both seem to have been domesticated for religious rather than economic reasons. Even today they contribute little to the local food supply. The people in Southeast Asia practiced what is called haruspication: divining from the entrails of animals. The Romans also used this method. Before the Senate opened, the priests would sacrifice an animal and examine its internal organs. The Roman substitute for a filibuster was for the die-hard minority to have the augur announce that the auspices were bad and the Senate should not meet that day.

The people of the Southeastern Asiatic region divined from pig livers and, in fact, still do in Borneo. White administrators there have had to become experts in the art since, when any important question arises such as leasing land for oil, the natives kill a pig and inspect the liver. The white administrator has to be able to convince them that the auspices for the project are good.

Pigs domesticate easily and pig keeping seems to have begun as a way of having one of the animals available whenever it was necessary to consult the auspices. Later, pigs came to occupy a peculiar position in many of the Oceanic cultures. They became a device for transforming an ordinary subsistence economy into an economy of luxury and display. In all these cultures pigs were kept tied up and were fed by hand, not driven out to pasture as they were in the West. Since the pig ate much the same food that humans did, every pig that was added to the establishment was the equivalent of taking on an extra family member to be supported. Since pigs were usually killed only at funeral feasts or at ceremonies in which the number and size of the pigs sacrificed was an important ritual matter, pig raising became a luxury occupation. It was really a form of ostentatious waste.

In the New Hebrides in particular, the natives seem to have gone hog wild. Some tribes here paid fantastic prices for hermaphrodite pigs; others knocked out the upper canines of young boars so that the tusks in the lower jaw would grow in a circle. It took six to eight years to produce a full-circle tusk, during all of which time the owner ran the risk of losing his entire investment through the pig's death. For two or three years, while the tusk was growing down into the lower jaw to complete the circle, the pig had to be fed soft food by hand. A really enthusiastic pig-raiser would usually take on a new wife to care for each pig when it reached this stage.

Pigs with full-circle tusks were sacrificed at various ceremonies and fixed numbers of them were required for promotion to each grade in the men's secret societies. By the time a boar had grown full-circle tusks he was so old and his meat so strong and stringy that he was almost inedible. Actually, only women and children ate the animals sacrificed at these times. To complete the picture of ostentatious waste, a particularly hardy boar might live until his tusks grew into two complete circles. Such a beast would confer prestige not only on his owner but on the entire district. Pig fanciers would come from many miles and pay a small pig for the privilege of looking at such a *chef d'œuvre*.

The chicken also seems to have been domesticated first for magical reasons. Its ancestor, the wild jungle fowl, also had the trick of crowing from time to time during the night and always just before dawn, at the time when all ghosts must hurry back to the earth.

Southeast Asiatic villagers kept chickens to frighten away ghosts and evil spirits. There may also have been a factor of aesthetic satisfaction, for the wild rooster is a beautiful bird, as colorful as many pheasants. Little economic use was made of them. Even today, many Southeast Asiatic peoples do not eat chicken eggs and rarely kill the birds except as sacrifices in minor rites. Although Western peoples put the chicken to more practical uses, it carried with it in its diffusion the old myth of the efficacy of the cocks in frightening away ghosts. Thus the old Scottish ballad, when the ghosts of the three sons of the Wife of Usher's Well return:

> *Up then crew the red, red cock,*
>   *And up and crew the gray;*
> *The eldest to the youngest said,*
>   *'Tis time we were away.'*

> *The cock he hadna craw'd but once,*
>   *And clapp'd his wings at a',*
> *When the youngest to the eldest said,*
>   *'Brother, we must awa'.*

'The cock doth craw, the day doth daw,
    The cannerin' work doth chide;
Gin we be miss'd out o' our place,
    A sair pain we maun bide.'

'Lie still, lie still but a little wee while,
    Lie still but if we may;
Gin my mother should miss us when she wakes,
    She'll go mad ere it be day.'

'Fare ye weel, my mother dear!
    Fareweel to barn and byre!
And fare ye weel, the bonny lass
    That kindles my mother's fire!'

The plants and animals just described seem to have originated in the tropical lowlands and were associated with a coastal and riverine culture which had fish as one of its most important resources. The resulting economy made for permanent settlement, since trees, once planted, continued bearing for many years and the irrigation systems required for taro involved too much labor and were too continuously productive to be abandoned. It was this coastal complex which was diffused eastward into Oceania to become the basis for the later Melanesian, Micronesian and Polynesian economies.

In the mountain regions of Southeastern Asia a different type of agricultural economy was developed. The jungle was cut and burned at the end of the dry season and seeds or cuttings planted among the ashes in holes made with a sharp pointed stick. The fields yielded a plentiful crop the first year, a moderate one the second, and a poor one the third, after which it was necessary to allow the land to lie fallow for ten to twenty years, depending on the length of time required for the jungle to grow up again. The rapid decline in production seems to have been due quite as much to weed growth in the cleared area as to soil exhaustion. In the absence of systematic cultivation, weeds seeded themselves and increased so rapidly year by year that the simplest way to deal with them was to allow the jungle regrowth cycle to smother them out, giving the first crop after a new burning a clear field.

This kind of agriculture necessitated a sort of slow motion nomadism in which a village settled in one place until the land within easy walking distance had been exhausted, then moved on. Where wooden houses were used they were often made so that they could be knocked down and reassembled at the new site. Such shifts took place every 15 to 25 years. The high proportion of land which had to be left lying fallow at any given time made it necessary for each village to keep control over a territory of many square miles. Another factor which must have contributed to setting a pattern of extensive holdings was the relative scarcity of certain necessary food elements. The use of animals for milk was foreign to the old Southeast Asiatic culture, game was not abundant, and none of the crops raised by the hill people before the introduction of American plants were good protein sources. In order to obtain a balanced ration every village had to have a large area in which to hunt and gather wild foods. Population pressure inevitably led to conflict, and in tribes with this type of economy every village was sporadically at war with all its neighbors.

The first crops raised by the hill people seem to have been yams and certain varieties of rice. There can be little doubt that rice was cultivated by the cutting and burning method some time before it began to be raised under irrigation. Even today "dry" rice is grown in various outlying regions to which the elaborate techniques of irrigated rice cultivation are only beginning to penetrate. The cultivation of wet rice involves a complicated series of techniques, some of which may very well have been taken over from the cultivation of taro. That the latter is the older crop would seem to be indicated by its wider geographic distribution. Thus rice will grow well in any of the Polynesian and Melanesian high islands into which taro has been introduced, and it is hard to believe that any people who were as expert and interested horticulturists as the Polynesians would have failed to carry rice with them on their migrations if they had been familiar with it.

The cultivation of dry rice is generally believed to have begun in Assam, the hill region lying between India and Burma at the head of the Bay of Bengal. Where the domestication of irrigated rice began is still unknown, but the fully irrigated rice complex involved the use of a domestic animal, the water buffalo. Tropical swamps are this animal's natural habitat. It can be used as a source of milk, meat and traction in regions where cattle cannot survive. Its domestication made it possible to extend the use of the plow and wheel into the Southeast Asiatic region. The combination of irrigated rice, the water buffalo, and the plow created an economic basis for dense population comparable to that provided by grain, oxen, and the plow in the West. In fact, it provided an even better basis, for rice is the most profitable of all crops. There are areas in Southeastern Asia where the population, living almost entirely on rice, reaches a density of over 2000 per square mile of land in cultivation. The plant has the additional advantage of having relatively light mineral and phosphorous requirements so that the same fields can be kept in use indefinitely by simple fallowing and the use of animal and human fertilizers. Lastly, and frequently overlooked in the descriptions of rice culture, the warm shallow water of the rice beds provides an ideal environment for the rapid growth of small fish and insect larvae. The dredging of the rice beds after harvest provides an important supply of protein food in a region where there is a notable protein shortage.

From Southeastern Asia, rice culture was carried northward into China and eventually to Korea and Japan. In all these regions it became the basis of a dense and stabilized population. Where the ancient growers of Western Asiatic grains were constantly stimulated to migration by soil exhaustion, the people who grew irrigated rice tended to be non-migratory. The upkeep of the rice beds required much labor but yielded rich returns. The spread of such groups was comparable to that of a lichen in that they expanded slowly, taking in more and more territory but covering it solidly. Where a wet rice economy had once been established it was rarely displaced. The spread of Western grain-growers, on the other hand, tended to be rapid and irregular, with shifting areas of cultivation and unstable frontiers between farmers and pastoral nomads.

Chapter IX

Metallurgy, Writing,
and Technological Inventions

THE ESTABLISHMENT of grain agriculture and dairying in the Near East was followed by an exceedingly rapid advance in culture. Most of the inventions basic to ancient civilization seem to have been made before 3500 B.C. One of the most important of these was the development of metallurgy. Native metals had been known in the Near East since very early times. They may even have been noticed and worked sporadically in the Mesolithic. However, the supplies of native metal were small and the discovery of the new substance had no noticeable effect on the culture. It was treated as an unusually tough and malleable stone and worked cold by hammering and grinding. True metallurgy did not begin until it became possible to reduce metals from their ores. Even then, for 2000 years or more metal of any sort remained so rare and so valuable that its use was largely limited to weapons and ornaments. Metal tools did not become common until the invention of iron-working.

The reduction of metal from ore began in the Near East somewhere between 4000 and 5000 B.C. Copper seems to have been the first metal to be smelted. The copper carbonate ores, malachite and azurite, were already being mined and ground for paint. They reduce to metallic copper at a relatively low temperature, and one is tempted to refer the beginnings of smelting to the experience of some unfortunate Near Eastern gentleman who dropped his paint bag into the fire on a night when there was a high wind. When the fire had died, he would have discovered in place of his vanity kit a small lump of copper, a material already known and valued much more than its ores. The initial discovery that stone could be turned into metal seems to have been followed by experimentation and by a fairly rapid invention of the basic metal working techniques. Pure copper is exceedingly difficult to cast in closed molds since

103

it bubbles and, unless the gasses can escape, ruins the casting. However, the presence of very small percentages of various impurities, especially arsensic, serves to deoxygenate it and make casting in closed molds possible. It is an interesting fact that the Sumerians appear to have used alloyed copper (bronze) at the very beginning of their metallurgical career, then changed to pure copper, and still later reverted to bronze again. The most probable explanation would seem to be that they began their metallurgy with the smelting of impure copper ores which gave an easily cast natural alloy. Later, when these ores were exhausted, they turned to other sources which gave them purer copper, and still later

OPEN STONE MOLD

they consciously alloyed their copper by mixing other metals, especially tin, with it.

The earliest casting process seems to have been to run the molten metal direct from the smelting furnace into shallow open molds having the general outline of the implements to be made. The blanks thus formed were finished by hammering and grinding, much as the native copper had been treated. Hammering hardens copper, and by pounding the edges of a knife or axe blade it was possible to get a metal which would cut as well as soft iron. At the same time, pounding makes copper brittle. At a fairly early time the metal workers learned how to compensate for this by annealing, i.e., heating the metal white hot and plunging it into water. This softens copper and its alloys and makes it possible to continue the pounding process.

The discovery that metal could be gotten from certain stones must have been an exciting one. Everything indicates that shortly after the first discovery of smelting, the metal workers experimented with every available sort of stone which might be a metallic ore. Most of such ores

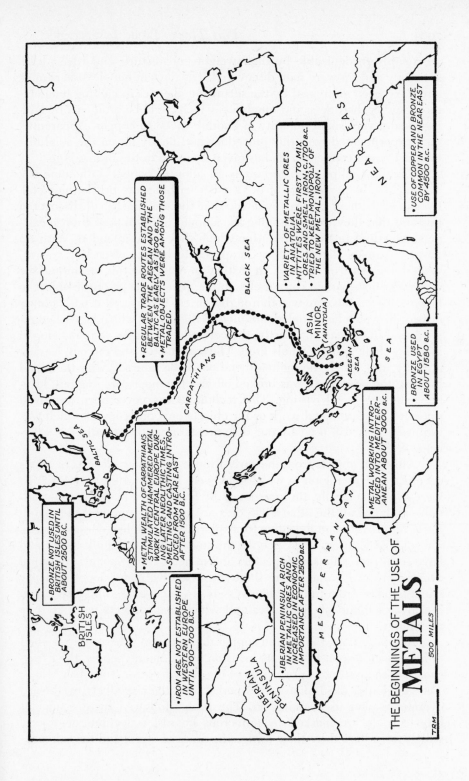

THE BEGINNINGS OF THE USE OF **METALS**

500 MILES

NEAR EAST

BLACK SEA

BALTIC SEA

CARPATHIANS

ASIA MINOR (ANATOLIA)

AEGEAN SEA

SEA

MEDITERRANEAN

IBERIAN PENINSULA

BRITISH ISLES

TRM

• USE OF COPPER AND BRONZE COMMON IN THE NEAR EAST BY 4500 B.C.

• VARIETY OF METALLIC ORES IN ANATOLIA.
• HITTITES WERE FIRST TO MIX ORES AND SMELT IRON, C. 1700 B.C.
• TRIED TO KEEP MONOPOLY OF THE NEW METAL, IRON.

• REGULAR TRADE ROUTES ESTABLISHED BETWEEN THE AEGEAN AND THE BALTIC AS EARLY AS 1500 B.C.
• METAL OBJECTS WERE AMONG THOSE TRADED.

• BRONZE USED IN EGYPT ABOUT 1580 B.C.

• METAL WORKING INTRO-DUCED INTO MEDITERR-ANEAN ABOUT 3000 B.C.

• METAL WEALTH OF CARPATHIANS STIMULATED HAMMERED METAL WORK IN CENTRAL EUROPE DUR-ING LATER NEOLITHIC TIMES.
• SMELTING AND CASTING INTRO-DUCED FROM NEAR EAST AFTER 1500 B.C.

• BRONZE NOT USED IN BRITISH ISLES UNTIL ABOUT 2500 B.C.

• IRON AGE NOT ESTABLISHED IN WESTERN EUROPE UNTIL 900-700 B.C.

• IBERIAN PENINSULA RICH IN METALLIC ORES AND INCREASED IN ECONOMIC IMPORTANCE AFTER 2500 B.C.

are readily recognizable by their weight and texture, and silver, lead, antimony and tin were soon discovered. The ancient metal workers must also have been impressed by the surprising changes in melting temperature, fluidity, hardness, and toughness which could be produced by adding even a very small quantity of another metal to copper. Apparently, they experimented with this procedure and finally hit on the combination of tin and copper which has given its name to the Bronze Age.

The best all-purpose bronze is an alloy of copper with some tin. The higher the percentage of tin, the harder but more brittle the metal. By 1500 B.C. there is clear evidence that the craftsmen had discovered this and that they were changing the amount of tin in their bronze castings according to the purpose for which they were intended. With tin bronze, or even slightly before, a special technique of casting was invented, the *lost wax* method. In casting an object by this technique, the craftsman first made a core of clay in the general shape of the object to be cast. When the core was thoroughly dried, he covered it with a layer of wax on which he modeled and incised the details which he wished reproduced in the casting. Lastly, the core and wax layer were enveloped in a clay shell, and the whole fired. The wax melted and ran out, leaving a cavity into which the molten metal could be poured. After the metal had set, the outer shell was broken off and the inner core dug out, leaving a hollow metal casting. This technique has never been improved upon for delicate metal work or for objects only one copy of which was required. It is still used by our own artists in casting small bronze figures.

Although objects from the early Bronze Age show all sorts of alloys according to the region in which they were made and the metals which were available locally, tin bronze was by far the best material and gradually replaced all the others. Tin ores are relatively rare and the search for them provided an incentive for exploration much like our own desire for gold. At least one early people, the so-called Beaker Folk, seemed to have been professional prospectors and miners. Their remains are found everywhere in Europe where there are extensive metal deposits. Their name is taken from tumbler-like vessels of coarse incised pottery which are always found on their sites and which one suspects were used as beer mugs.

At a later time, the tin and copper deposits of northern Italy seemed to have been responsible for its invasion by an Asiatic people, the Etruscans. These mysterious precursors of the Romans came from Asia Minor. They exploited the Italian mines and traded their products northward overland as far as Scandinavia. The routes followed by this ancient bronze trade are marked by numerous hoards, collections of objects which were buried by their owners in times of stress and never recovered. The variety of objects in these hoards and the fact that many of them are broken reflects the value of bronze in itself. As the techniques of metallurgy reached more and more parts of Europe, local styles developed, so that it is easy for the archeologist to tell when and where a particular bronze object was made. Although the Scandinavian peoples developed a rich and diverse bronze equipment, they seem never to have smelted the metal locally. They obtained it from the south in the form of scrap as well as finished objects, then melted it down and recast it in their own favorite forms.

The use of tin bronze marked a real transition from stone to metal in Eurasia. The possession of metal for weapons became a matter of deadly importance, and most of the new alloy went for military or ornamental uses. It was only in the closing phases of the Bronze Age, when the supply of bronze had been accumulated over centuries, that bronze tools became common. Even then, the use of stone lingered on among the villagers in the higher cultures and among peoples remote from civilization. Needless to say, bronze came to carry prestige, and bronze forms were frequently imitated in stone by those who could not afford the originals. Thus, in the closing phases of the Stone Age in Scandinavia, we find stone daggers and flint axes which are unquestionably modeled on bronze originals, and the hammer axe and the double-bladed battle axe in stone, which were the characteristic weapons of the people who made the first large-scale invasion of Western Europe from the Steppes, can be traced without a break from Sumerian originals in bronze.

Why iron came into use only toward the end of the Second Millennium B.C. must remain a puzzle. Iron ores are much commoner than those of any other metals, and the hematite iron ores in particular are readily recognizable by their weight and texture. It is hard to believe that the Near Eastern metallurgists did not experiment with iron ores as they did with the other ores in their territory. Also, the metal itself was known in Egypt from very early times in the form of meteoric iron. Interestingly enough, the Egyptians seem to have guessed its source, for the hieroglyphic for iron means "star metal." The best explanation for the early neglect of iron lies, I believe, in the sharp contrast between the techniques required for its successful working and those used in dealing with copper and its alloys.

In smelting copper, the molten metal collects in the bottom of the furnace while the slag floats on top. In iron-smelting, at least at the temperatures which could be produced by the ancient furnaces, the iron is never completely liquefied. It forms instead a gray, spongy mass technically known as the *bloom*. The interstices of this mass are filled with molten slag which must be forced out by pounding the metal while still white hot. The process is much like that of squeezing water from a sponge. Molten copper can be run into a mold directly from the smelting furnace. To melt iron requires a very high temperature and involved a second operation for the primitive smith. The more carbon in the iron, the lower the melting temperature and the greater its fluidity, but iron with a high carbon content is exceedingly hard and brittle. Our familiar cast iron is an alloy of this sort and is mainly useful for stoves and ornamental railings. Even in these the metal is so brittle that it can be shattered almost as readily as a glass casting of equal weight. If the early metallurgists had ever succeeded in casting iron they would have faced a further difficulty, since any attempt to soften it by the familiar technique for copper, annealing, would have produced a violent explosion. Even with wrought iron, the copper annealing technique would only result in tempering the metal, making it that much harder and more intractable. It seems exceedingly probable that the early smiths did at-

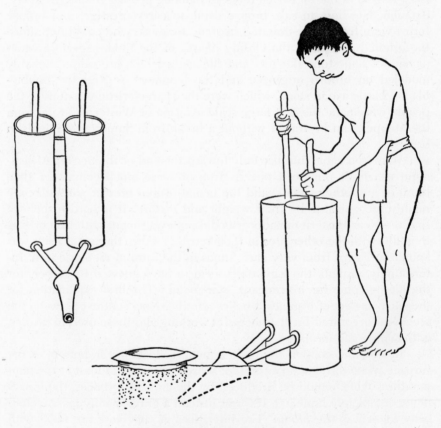

DOUBLE PISTON BELLOWS

tempt to smelt iron ores and work iron, but gave the metal up as a bad job.

Whatever the reason, we know that the regular use of iron for tools and weapons appears comparatively late and that it was first used extensively by Barbarians who were marginal to the main area of the Bronze Age cultures. Perhaps it was these Barbarians' lack of skill in the working of other metals which led them to try out new techniques and eventually to develop the methods for smelting and using the new metal.

Iron seems to have been successfully worked first in Turkestan or in Northern Asia Minor. It is possible that there was a second center of independent development in southern India; in any case, it was here that steel was invented. While a high carbon content makes iron both hard and brittle, a lower carbon content converts it into steel, hard but also tough. Some groups in southern India still make steel by a method so simple that it may well be the original one. The filings of relatively pure wrought iron obtained from the local ores are put in sealed clay vessels with grass and the whole heated in charcoal furnaces. The grass is charred to almost pure carbon, which combines with the molten iron to give steel.

Iron was little, if at all, superior to bronze for most of the purposes for which metal was employed by ancient soldiers and craftsmen. The great importance of iron lay in its abundance. The widespread occurrence of iron ores made it possible for all peoples who had become familiar with iron-working techniques to shift from stone to metal tools. When we speak of the abundance of iron it must be remembered that we are doing so in terms of hand industries. Even today, unmechanized cultures succeed in getting along with what are, from our point of view, amazingly small amounts of metal. Many tools and most farm implements are made of wood shod with iron only on the cutting edge, while such things as steel construction or even extensive use of iron for nails in buildings are unknown.

Although the Bronze Age is constantly referred to as a period in the development of culture, the use of bronze was by no means universal. It seems to have centered in the region about the eastern end of the Mediterranean and to have spread from there over to Europe, eastward to the Indus Valley, and, somewhat later, to China by way of Turkestan. Outside Egypt, the ancient use of bronze in Africa was confined to the Mediterranean littoral. The justly famous West African "bronze" castings are mostly brass or copper, and none of them is more than a few centuries old. There was no bronze age in eastern or southern India or southeastern Asia. A few bronze objects of the Dong-son culture have been found in Indo-China, but this culture is relatively late and iron was in use there at the same period.

The situation in Africa south of the Sahara presents interesting problems. There was unquestionably a direct transition here from stone-using to iron-using. This has been seized upon as an example of the fallacy of regarding Negroes as a backward race, and the statement has repeatedly been made that Negroes discovered iron-working independently and were using iron when Europeans were still in the Bronze or even the Stone Age. As a matter of fact we have no conclusive evidence as to the time at which the use of iron appeared in Africa. However, its use was still being diffused to new tribes in the 16th century A.D., which certainly suggests a late introduction. The African techniques of iron-working and the forms of many African tools and weapons differ from European ones but are strongly suggestive of those in use in Southeast Asia. In particular, the highly efficient Asiatic double cylinder piston bellows seems to be basic to African iron-working, with a few East African tribes using the genuine Indonesian apparatus while the rest have what could easily be interpreted as simplified and degenerate forms. It seems highly probable that iron-working was introduced into Negro Africa by migrants from Southeast Asia, perhaps by the same early Indonesian voyagers who settled the island of Madagascar. The absence of either stone or bronze implements on this island suggests that the first Indonesian settlers already had iron when they arrived.

Writing was also a Near Eastern invention and one whose contribution to civilization has been even greater than that of metal. Without techniques for recording and preserving the results of observations, science never could have come into existence. If the ancient priests who were the first astronomers had had to rely on their memories of the movements of the heavenly bodies, they would never have realized how exact and predictable these movements were over long time intervals. Neither would they have arrived at the concepts of natural laws and of a mechanistic universe which were the foundations of all later scientific research.

Writing appears almost simultaneously some 5000–6000 years ago in Egypt, Mesopotamia, and the Indus Valley. Another equally primitive form of writing appears in China some 2000 years later as part of a complex of culture elements of Southwestern Asiatic origin. Even the earliest written characters from these various areas are quite different, which suggests that there was no single origin point for writing. At the same time all these areas have a common remote cultural ancestry in the Southwestern Asiatic food-raising complex. Probably this ancestral culture had as one of its characteristics a tendency to record events with pictures. This tendency resulted in an independent development of pictographs in several localities within the area and the initial local differences were increased by the use of various materials and techniques.

Thus, in Egypt the form of the characters was influenced by their use in painting and low-relief carving, while in Mesopotamia their application to clay led to the development of the highly conventionalized cuneiform symbols. In China, the earliest writing technique seems to have been that of scratching characters on bone or bamboo. Later, they were painted and this in itself modified what had originally been recognizable pictures to the conventional Chinese characters.

In all these areas the first step in the development of writing seems to have been the use of pictographs, i.e., actual pictures of things. However, for these pictures to serve to communicate ideas or to have meaning for anyone except the artist himself, it was necessary for them to be both simplified and conventionalized. Certain characteristics of the thing represented had to be exaggerated in order to make it clearly recognizable. Thus, it would take an exceedingly good artist to draw naturalistic pictures of a dog and a wolf which would be immediately recognizable as different animals. However, if one figure had the tail curled over the back and the other the tail low, there could be no mistake. Dogs' tails curl up, which wolves' tails never do.

In course of time a series of conventional figures of this sort would come to be generally understood and could be used for communication. Some of the North American Indian tribes had reached this stage independently and were able to send simple messages scratched on birch bark. The main difficulties of the system lay in the tremendous number of pictures required for anything except the simplest sort of communication and in the impossibility of making pictures of many things. Thus, no one could draw wind or light, much less such a psychological state as happiness or an abstract concept like energy. At this point, two lines emerged for possible future development. One of them involved the attachment of purely conventional values to signs, as when a scroll represents speech, a series of wavy lines water, or a stone the abstract quality of hardness. Pictures used in this way are known as ideographs. The other was the attachment of phonetic values to pictures of things with monosyllabic names, and the use of these pictures to build up longer words. This technique, known as rebus writing, is sometimes used among ourselves in making puzzles for small children. The real transition from pictographs to true writing came when people speaking different languages took over rebus writing systems. For them each picture would have only one meaning: it would stand for the sound of a particular syllable and nothing else. The number of syllables employed in any language is limited, and most syllabaries, as writing of this sort is called, do not include more than 200 symbols. Such a syllabary makes it possible for anyone to learn to read and write without devoting a lifetime to the task. However, even the simplest syllabic system is fairly complicated and difficult to learn, and can become the basis of a profitable profession, that of scribe.

Against the advantages of greater simplification and wider distribution of literacy within the society, scribes weighed the possibilities of technological unemployment and were content with the status quo. In Egypt in particular, although the possibilities of writing were explored in very early times with the development of a syllabary, of ideographs, and even of true alphabetic symbols, all three forms were retained and mingled in the same inscriptions. Although the characters themselves were simplified for everyday use, the scribes, who dominated both learning and government administration, preferred to keep writing a mystery, and throughout the whole of Egyptian history the writer was a professional who devoted years to learning his craft. In Mesopotamia, writing was much simpler, and a knowledge of it seems to have been widespread among merchants and professionals. Nevertheless, it was still complicated enough so that most of the population remained illiterate and the letter-writer was a professional even as in many Eastern bazaars today.

The development of a true alphabet proletarianized learning much as the use of iron proletarianized metal. All alphabets now in use can be traced to a single point of origin in the Sinai peninsula. The Egyptians carried on extensive mining operations here and employed, in addition to criminals and prisoners of war, contingents of pastoral Semites who were forced to work for them when their regular food supplies failed. The sheiks of the Semites acted as mine foremen and were required to draw up reports on their output and payroll. Since the regular Egyptian system of writing was much too complicated for them to learn, they took the simple symbols representing single sounds which were a part of the Egyptian system, and thus developed the first alphabet.

This took place about 1800 B.C. The alphabet spread from Sinai to other Semitic regions and eventually reached those great ancient traders and sea-farers, the Phoenicians. As business men engaged in long-range ventures requiring contracts and correspondence, the Phoenicians were quick to realize the advantage of an easily learned and therefore widely diffusable system of writing. They carried it west to the Greeks, who, prehensile as always, promptly accepted it and developed a whole series of local variations. All of these differed from the original Phoenician alphabet in the use of vowel signs. Vowel signs were unnecessary in the gutteral Semitic tongues, but were all-important for recording the Indo-European languages. From Greece, the alphabet was carried westward to Italy, where it assumed the Roman form, and, by a much later movement, north into the Slavic countries, where it became the ancestor of the later Cyrillic alphabet, whose characters differ from the Latin ones, thus contributing considerably to the lack of understanding between Russia and the rest of Europe.

Chinese writing followed the same evolutionary pattern as the Western forms up to the point where a syllabary might have emerged, but here, for some reason, it took a divergent course. Instead of developing on into a true phonetic system, it evolved in the ideographic direction; i.e., the characters came to represent combinations of ideas rather than combinations of sounds. The reason for this may have been an early extension of political units in China beyond the limits of particular dialects, thus diminishing the value of phonetic writing; or it may have reflected the philosophic and analytical interests of the scholar class who controlled both education and government administration. Whatever the reason, this evolution produced a system of writing which could be learned as a separate language. On the credit side, this writing makes it possible for persons who cannot communicate at all in their spoken languages, Chinese, Japanese, Koreans and Annamese, for example, to write back and forth freely and with perfect understanding. On the debit side, it requires a vocabulary of characters comparable in numbers to the word vocabulary of any spoken language. Knowledge of several thousand characters is required for ordinary literacy, while the total number is supposed to be in the neighborhood of 25,000 or 30,000.

We know very little about the Indus Valley writing since the only examples of it which have been preserved are on seals and rarely consist of more than three or four characters. The number of these signs seems to indicate that it was a syllabary, but we do not even know the language for which the characters were used.

The Southwestern Asiatic center also contributed to the development of civilization three mechanical inventions secondary in their importance only to metallurgy and writing. These were the wheel, the plow, and the loom. Until a few years ago it was believed that the wheel was an exclusive Southwestern Asiatic invention. However, it is now known that the ancient Mexicans had discovered the wheel principle, but, curiously enough, used it only for children's toys. It is still safe to say that all wheels put to practical uses, whether for transportation or in mechanics, trace back to Southwestern Asia.

The early phases of the development of the wheel are obscure. Sledges were used before wheels and probably were drawn over rollers when heavy objects were transported. Apparently, the wheel was derived from a roller by the rather simple device of cutting away most of the wood from the roller's center so as to leave a solid one-piece pair of wheels and axle. A box body of some sort was then fastened on top of the axle by greased leather straps or hollowed wooden blocks within which the axle could turn freely. Simple carts of this sort are said to have continued in use in some parts of India until recent times. The oldest wheels known to us come from the royal tombs at Ur and already show rather complicated construction. Although wheel and axle were fastened together solidly and the wheels were disks, the wheels were made of several layers of thin wood glued together so that the grains in the different layers lay at an angle to each other. The whole was finished with a rawhide tire held on by closely spaced copper nails whose heads formed the tread. The axle fixed to the cart with a wheel separate appeared somewhat later in Sumer, but it was already known by 3000 B.C. Only shortly thereafter the spoked wheel appeared. Although carts were probably used for transporting freight, the Sumerian monuments indicate that one of the first uses of wheeled vehicles was in war. The Sumerian chariot was a clumsy affair, four-wheeled and with a solid plank body which protected the chariot crew to above the waist. Chariot tactics probably consisted in driving the chariot into the ranks of the enemy until it lost headway, then using it as a sort of fortified fighting platform from which the crew could throw javelins and strike down at the enemy.

The discovery of the wheel principle opened up great areas of technical development. Even today it is basic to most mechanical appliances. In the lathe it made possible the turning of wood and even stone to symmetrical cylindrical shapes. The same principle, applied to clay, became the potter's wheel. The potter's wheel, in its simplest and most universal form, is really an ancient style pair of disk cart wheels with axle attached. The axle is set vertically and the operator spins the lower wheel with his foot while with his hands he spreads and shapes the soft clay upon the upper wheel. This contrivance made it possible to mass produce and standardize pottery, the first technical product for which this can be said.

Fragile as the ancient wares were, they could still replace most other types of containers since the breaking of a bowl or jar was only a minor catastrophe. The potter could turn out another in a few minutes and a large supply would be available at any market at prices which even the poorest could afford. The ancient potter also rendered an unconscious service to the modern archeologist. Pottery can be broken, but pottery is difficult to destroy. The fragments will survive in rubbish heaps for thousands of years and still provide some of the best clues for the recognition of ancient cultures and periods.

The fact that the wheel began as a transportation appliance has had curious consequences which are recognizable even today. Transport in the ancient Near East involved the use of domestic animals, oxen or donkeys, and all work with domestic animals in these early cultures fell to the men. As a result, all appliances and types of manufacture in which wheels were involved were assigned to the masculine sphere of activity, and most of them have remained so. Thus, wherever in the Old World pottery is modeled by hand, it is a woman's product. Wherever the potter's wheel is used the potters are men. The widely held belief in our own society that women do not make good mechanics is a by-product of this same ancient situation. The lady machinist of war-time has long since disproved this idea in fact, but it survives as a relic of the original division of labor and the place the wheel occupied in it.

We do not know how the plow originated or whether it was evolved from a simpler device. However, the first plows were simple

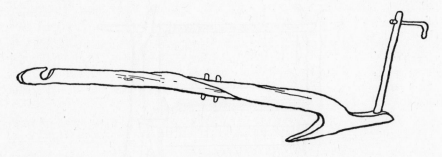

CROOK ARD

enough. They consisted of nothing more than a sapling with one lopped and pointed branch left protruding two-thirds of the way down the trunk. A pair of animals were yoked to the upper end of the trunk and the man steered the contrivance by its lower end, as the protruding branch was dragged through the earth. Since the branch wore away rapidly, one of the first improvements was to add a separate share made of the hardest wood obtainable or, in later times, shod with metal. Plows of this primitive type are still in use throughout most of Asia. They are not adapted for breaking prairie sod or for turning over subsoil. However, in the semi-arid Southwestern Asiatic region in which they were first developed, they are highly functional, since they break up the surface soil and provide a dust mulch which prevents the evaporation of moisture and gives seeds a chance to sprout.

The social effects of the plow and the loom were even more immediate and far-reaching than those of the wheel. In the Southwestern Asiatic Neolithic division of labor, women seem to have carried on the first agriculture, to have made pottery, mats, and baskets, and to have taken care of the cooking and baby-tending much as they do today. The men, on the other hand, hunted, fought, cared for the domestic animals (after animals had been domesticated) and worked in wood and stone.

With the development of the plow, which, like the wheel, required animal traction, men passed over into agriculture. This transformation was most complete in connection with crops that were mass produced. The plow is an uneconomic instrument for the small garden which, after the initial breaking of the soil, can be better taken care of with the hoe. Women retained a place in agriculture during the hurried periods of sowing and harvesting the major crops, and in the kitchen garden, which thrives best under close attention and loving care. Even today on many American farms, one finds that while the field work is done by the

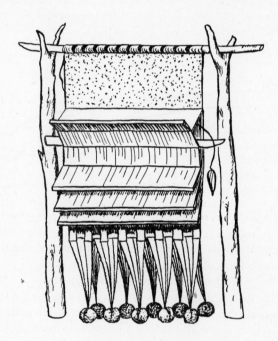

NEOLITHIC LOOM

men, the garden is the women's sphere and any surplus of "truck" coming from it can be sold for her profit.

With the coming of the plow and the potter's wheel, women found themselves with more leisure than they had ever had before, and the loom served to take up the slack. As with most other simple early appliances, the exact steps in the development of this machine can only be conjectured. Probably it began with some sort of simple vertical frame carrying a crossbar from which the warp threads were hung. Such a frame has advantages for both speed and evenness of weaving over the simple interlacing of loose strands which one finds in ordinary mat mak-

ing. The first steps in the improvement of the machine were the attachment of weights to the lower ends of the threads on the frame and the
introduction of heddles, i.e., crossbars, which were attached to alternate
warp threads, making it possible to lift a whole series of these threads
at the same time and throw a shuttle carrying a weft thread across the
fabric in a single movement. This speeded up matters and also, with the
development of multiple heddles, made possible the weaving of complicated designs.

The loom made possible a new level of both quantity and quality in
clothing. It also may have been responsible for the emergence of the first
ideas of personal cleanliness. The older skin clothing could not be
washed; cloth, whether woven from wool or vegetable fiber, could be.
Cloth could also be mass produced and provided an ideal method for
the busy housewife to contribute to the family exchequer in the brief intervals between spells of cooking and baby-tending. The loom could be
set up in the house or under some near-by shelter, and the woman could
repair to it and weave a few inches whenever there were no pressing
demands on her time. The product was sufficiently standardized, useful,
and indestructible so that it could serve as currency. Thus, we find in
the earliest Egyptian tax rolls that taxes might be collected in either
grain or linen, while as late as the 10th century A.D. wadmal, a coarse
woolen cloth, useful for many purposes, served as a medium of exchange
in Scandinavia.

Chapter X

Cities and States

ALL STUDENTS of culture recognize that there is more than a quantitative difference between the cultures of peasant communities and civilizations, but there is little agreement as to exactly where the line can be drawn. Perhaps the best criterion for differentiation is the presence or absence of cities. Even today there is little realization of how important and unique this form of human aggregate is. It represents a social invention which in its significance for the growth of culture is fully as important as any technological invention with the possible exception of food-raising.

Perhaps at this point it would be best to define what is meant by a city. It is a community which subsists by the exchange of manufactured products and services for food and raw materials. Its very existence depends upon this exchange. In this respect it differs from the village. The people of a village derive their food and most of their raw materials from the immediate neighborhood. In general, their zone of exploitation is limited by the distance to which a man can travel, work in the fields, and return on the same day. The size of the population which can exist at the village level will naturally vary with the environment, but rarely exceeds a few hundred persons. The city, on the other hand, has no known upper limit for its population size.

As with all definitions, that just given presents certain difficulties and one can recognize doubtful cases. Thus the village passes over into the city by imperceptible degrees. In many parts of the world there are villages which raise all or nearly all of their own food, but which also carry on one or more specialized manufactures, usually based on local materials, and then exchange their special products for the specialties of other village communities. Small villages may also be established for the exploitation of a particular natural resource, such as a mineral deposit, under conditions in which most of their food has to be obtained by trade. Mining camps in the Arctic would be a case in point. However, the definition of the city as a community which depends primarily upon trade and specialized services for its food and raw materials is still generally valid.

The rise of modern transportation techniques and of large, economically interdependent political aggregates has introduced some variations on the city pattern, but there are certain structural features of the pre-mechanized city which are universal. Its structure is much like that of a cell, with the city proper as its nucleus, the village-studded area surrounding it corresponding to the cell protoplasm, and with occasional pseudopods running out to contact sources of necessary raw materials.

There are certain prerequisites for the establishment of such an organism. First of all, there must be a relatively dense population in the area in order to create the surplus of food required to support the nuclear city group. This factor was most important in the early stages of city development. Even in unmechanized societies, cities can be set up in sparsely populated territory if they are located at crucial points for trade exchange. However, in early times the dense populations necessary to support cities were possible only in river valleys where the rich soil allowed permanent settlement and gave heavy returns for cultivation. Quite as important as dense population was the presence of effective techniques for the transportation of bulk goods. Luxury objects can be traded over great distances in periods or regions where such techniques are lacking. Thus, in North America, the Hopewell mound builders of Ohio received limited quantities of obsidian from the Yellowstone, copper from Lake Superior, mica from North Carolina, and shells from the Gulf of Mexico. However, the transportation of bulk goods presents a different problem. They can be moved more readily by water than by any other means and, failing this, must rely upon animal transport with or without the aid of wheeled vehicles. Human transport of such bulk goods, especially staple foods, is uneconomic since the human bearer must carry his own food, thus setting strict limits to the distance over which he can carry a payload. Even with the wheel, the victualing of cities presents a serious problem if water transport is not available.

All the great cities of the pre-mechanized era in the Near East, China and India were on rivers or the coast. In this connection, the presence of irrigation systems is also very important. The irrigated fields support a dense population, while the network of canals provides water transport. In America, where the wheel was completely lacking and pack animals were available only in a limited area in South America, there were very few true cities. Tenochtitlan, the ancient city of Mexico, may well have been the only real city north of the Isthmus. It stood on an island in a large lake surrounded by rich farm lands and could thus be fed by local produce brought by water. Its political dominance made it possible for it to ignore land transport costs and have luxury objects and the more valuable raw materials brought as tribute. Cuzco, the Inca capital, was also a real city, made possible by the use of pack animals and its position as administrative center for a great and highly organized empire.

It is an open question whether there were any other true cities in the New World when Europeans arrived. The coastal valleys of Peru, with their high development of irrigated agriculture, offered possibilities, but the pattern seems to have been one of several settlements to a valley, each surrounding a ceremonial center. The so-called cities of Meso-America were really tribal ceremonial centers. Great numbers of people from the surrounding countryside resorted to them from time to time, but the only permanent residents were small cadres of priests and caretakers. Thus, in the Maya territory, it is estimated that with the local cutting and burning agricultural techniques a family could produce its year's food supply with about two hundred days of labor. The balance of the time could be spent in celebrating religious festivals and in building the great ceremonial structures which still survive. Each contingent of the mass labor required for these probably brought its own food, worked for a few days, and returned to its village when the food was exhausted. A similar pattern existed in the Southeastern United States, where the sites of such ceremonial centers are still marked by great earthworks.

Wherever cities appeared they posed a whole series of new social problems. Many of these stemmed from the simple biological fact that our species even now has not adapted itself successfully to life in large aggregates. Until some five thousand years ago all human beings lived in relatively small communities which had only infrequent contacts with outsiders. Even today, a large part of the world's population follows this residence pattern. Under such conditions disease outbreaks are localized and communities rarely have to deal with the virulent strains which develop when bacteria pass rapidly through a great number of hosts. In the city there is much greater opportunity for the exchange of diseases and the emergence of virulent mutations. Not only are large numbers of people crowded together, but the far-flung trade on which the city depends for its existence brings constant increments of infection. Nearly all of the great epidemics which have ravaged Europe in historic times can be traced to particular cities into which they were introduced by foreign goods or travelers.

The mortality rate for adults in pre-mechanized cities was bad enough, but that for infants was even worse. It was quite out of the question for such cities to maintain their population by simple reproduction. Even now, when modern sanitary techniques have reduced the death rate to more reasonable size, it is doubtful whether any city maintains its population in this way. As disease diminishes, other factors come in to keep the population down. The city dweller, confronted by the difficulties of rearing children in crowded quarters and by the economic insecurity inseparable from city life, limits his offspring. That there may be a further sterility factor derived from high tension living seems probable, but whatever the complex causes, the results are the same. City populations do not and never have reproduced themselves.

It follows that city populations have always been kept up by a flow of individuals from the villages and farm lands within the city's zone of exploitation—the protoplasm of the city cell. These immigrants were the raw material from which the city shaped its urbanized inhabitants. In colloquial parlance, the village and farm fed yokels into the city along with other raw materials necessary to its existence and the city transformed the yokel into a specialized product, the city slicker.

The peasants who went to the pre-mechanized city were by no means a random sample of the rural population. They were mostly those who did not fit into village life. At the lower end of the scale were the local ne'er-do-wells and petty criminals whom the village, when its patience was exhausted, disposed of by the ancient and world-wide pattern of "running out of town." In the anonymity of the city such individuals could carry on their petty depredations with much less danger to themselves. More valuable material was provided by those peasants who, having lost their equity in village lands, flowed to the city in the hope of finding some type of employment. The natural increase of families and the working of laws of inheritance provided a constant stream of such unfortunates. If the society practiced primogeniture, the younger sons had to leave the village to fend for themselves. Even if joint family patterns were developed in the hope of holding property together for the kin group, few joint families lasted more than three generations. Successive divisions soon made the holdings too small to support a family and the less fortunate or less able men were forced to sell and to migrate. Such migrants provided the city with a mass of cheap unskilled labor which formed the earliest authentic proletariat. It was also the first labor which could be treated as a commodity, since it was not linked to the employer by ties of blood or familiar association.

Lastly, there must have been a fair number of individuals who went to the city of their own free will because they were conscious of the added opportunities for advancement and employment which the urban environment provided. In other words, the ancient city drew

most heavily from the dregs and, by our standards, from the cream of
the rural dwellers. This gave the city population a distinctive quality
from the start. It was heavily weighted on the side of the unstable individual, one who lacked the stolid contentment of the successful peasant.

The city dweller loses the security which comes from living among
neighbors or sharing the activities of an extended kin group, but at the
same time, his success is not hampered by poor relations. The breakdown of extended kin ties seems to be characteristic of city life in all
times and places. In general, city immigrants seem to find the possible
rewards worth the risk. It may be noted that once the peasant has moved
to the city, he is in almost all cases unwilling to return to rural life. The
leit motif of the old song, "How're you gonna keep 'em down on the
farm, after they've seen Paree?" seems to have been as valid in Sumerian
times as it is today.

Even today, the population of any city is composed largely of ,
strangers, and of socially difficult strangers. This sets new problems of
social control. The informal pressures of public opinion, which are effective in keeping the average individual in line in any small face-to-face
community, become largely inoperative. No one in the city cares what
you do, nor do you care what strangers think. The behavior of modern
conventioneers turned loose on the town might serve as a case in point.
It thus becomes necessary to develop new systems of control based on
formal patterns of coercion. The police force and the police court appeared exceedingly early in history in forms not very different from
those which they still retain.

A significant by-product of the earliest city life of which we have
record was the emergence of highly formal patterns of law and legal
procedure. The village may or may not recognize the existence of formal laws as distinct from simple taboos and folkways. However, even
in those cultures in which formal law exists, it is still possible to achieve
a fairly close approximation of justice in small face-to-face communities. Where everyone in the community knows everyone else, the possible number of offenders in any case is so limited that apprehension becomes almost certain, while in interpersonal disputes there can be very
little doubt as to who is in the right.

In the city, on the other hand, the number of possible offenders is
much greater and the chance of apprehending the wrong man is increased accordingly. In civil cases it is quite impossible for the judge,
who can know nothing of the personalities involved in a dispute or
their backgrounds of previous interaction, to administer real justice of
the sort which emerges more or less automatically in the village. It
seems highly probable that, when it first emerged, the whole concept of

formal law and legal procedure was actually a by-product of the urban situation. Confronted by the necessity of dealing with persons and disputes *en masse* and under circumstances where the judge's knowledge of the actual factors involved was minimal, there was an attempt to substitute for authentic knowledge what were, in effect, magical practices. Thus, it was loudly announced that the law was no respecter of persons, a fact which if adhered to would immediately remove its operation from the possibility of achieving justice. The operation of the law and its agents was surrounded by solemn ritual, both to impress the observer and as a part of the magical performance. Proceedings were carried on with rigid formality and in the solemn atmosphere appropriate to an approach to the supernatural. One finds that penalties for contempt of court are practically as old as courts themselves.

The lawyer and judge emerged as technologists who studied the wordings of laws with microscopic care. Precedents were cited, and the more ancient these were and the greater amount of research required to establish them, the greater their magical efficacy. Only in China, a civilization divergent in this as in many other respects, was precedent deliberately ignored in favor of the current situation.

Formal law codes and stereotyped legal procedures may exist in non-urbanized societies, as they do in most African tribes and in Indonesia, with its *adat* law. However, the small face-to-face community can function quite successfully without such patterns. The city definitely cannot. It is significant that, although American Indian cultures were notably lacking in legal concepts, both formal law codes and stereotyped legal procedures were developed in the few localities where city living occurred.

In return for raw materials and population, the city furnished the area which it dominated with specialized services. The most important of these were associated with religion, administration, and trade. The city was normally a religious center for the inhabitants of the surrounding territory, a center to which the peasantry resorted for impressive and therefore presumably hyper-effective appeals to the supernatural powers. The assemblies created by periodic religious ceremonies readily lend themselves to purposes of trade and exchange. The pious pilgrims brought with them surplus produce which they exchanged for goods which their own village could not provide. In this connection, the city also provided a distribution point for foreign products which could be much more economically handled in this way than through small sales to scattered villages.

Temple and market were central features of most ancient cities. Needless to say, the city was a place for the exchange of ideas as well as goods. Cities everywhere functioned as focal points in the diffusion

of culture. Not only did travelers and merchants come to them from a
distance, but there was also a strong tendency for such strangers to
establish foreign quarters within the city itself. This resulted in a close
and continuous association between groups of different cultures with
greatly increased opportunities for the exchange of ideas. In these ancient cities, as in our modern ones, there was a two-directional acculturation process whereby the settled stranger within the gates both gave
and received new things.

The importance of the early city as an administrative center has
frequently been overlooked. Every ancient city had its palace, which
was not only the ruler's residence but also the site of the various offices
required for the administration of the city's territory. In the ancient
city the relation between secular and religious rulers was always close,
if not always sympathetic, and one often finds the palaces and the administrative offices blending into the temple establishment.

The ancient city also supported a much more varied range of activities and specialists than was possible in the village. Skilled craftsmen, such as jewelers, or armorers, whose services would be needed
only intermittently in a small community, could become full-time operators in the city, thanks to the expanded market. The presence of
numerous fellow-craftsmen and imports of foreign objects provided
both a stimulus to the improvement of techniques and an understanding
audience who could appreciate and provide prestige rewards for superior workmanship. The cities were also able to offer continuous employment to doctors, lawyers, scribes, teachers, and so forth. Members
of these professions were actually attached to the temple establishment
and aided in maintaining its domination over the intellectual life of the
community. Much as in the case of the skilled craftsman, the presence
of numerous workers in the same field had a stimulating effect on the
development of ideas. In the city, for the first time, it became possible
for the philosopher or primitive scientist to meet others with common
interests and to whet his mind against theirs.

Lastly, the city was the real center for the development of the second oldest profession. (The oldest is that of medicine man.) The function of the prostitute is to care for strangers. There is little need for her
under village conditions where the sexes are usually fairly well balanced
in number and all adults automatically marry. In the ancient city, on
the other hand, there was a heavy surplus of males, since men could
leave their villages much more readily than women. Everywhere in the
Near East the temple prostitute was a regular part of the temple establishment. The city god, like any other male notable, was provided with
a large complement of women, but since he proved an inactive and
unjealous spouse, these women found substitutes for him elsewhere and

contributed their earnings to the temple upkeep. A society which was only emerging from village patterns also required some time to develop adequate techniques for the housing and feeding of city transients, and this gave an opportunity for prostitution of a different type. The secular prostitute was very frequently an innkeeper or had a small apartment in which she received successive travelers and provided them for a few days with a "home away from home."

Although the earliest political units were the tribe and city, larger political units, the precursors of the modern state, began to emerge very early in the Near East. Chronologically, and perhaps functionally, such states are an aftermath of city development. It was comparatively simple for the city, already accustomed to the control and exploitation of adjoining villages, to extend this rule over neighboring cities less powerful than itself. Still later, as the rising wealth of the cities provided increasing temptations for the Barbarians who hovered on the borders of civilization, a series of conquest states of progressively larger size emerged.

The organization of political units larger than the tribe or city, particularly of units involving a heterogeneous collection of groups of different language and culture, involved a whole series of new problems for which solutions had to be found. Patterns of empire as they exist today have a long background of development. All political units larger than the tribe or city belong to one or the other of two organizational types: federations or empires. As Robert Lowie has pointed out, both of these originate in war.

The federation may exist at any level of cultural complexity. It is based upon the voluntary cooperation of a group of previously independent political units. It begins with an offensive or defensive alliance, but offensive alliances rarely lead to federation. If successful in their immediate objective, they are almost certain to be followed by disputes over the distributions of loot and consequent collapse. The defensive alliance develops into a federation when the external pressures are strong and continuous. As the various groups in the alliance become more and more used to working together, cooperative patterns develop, and economic and political integration goes on to the point where the initial alliance is transformed first into a confederation and then into a federal organization with ever-increasing power delegated to a central authority. This process can be observed both in the history of the United States and in the process now going on in Western Europe, where a confederation is gradually emerging under the continuous Russian threat. The greatest weakness of this type of organization lies in the necessary give and take between the component members. Its successful functioning involves free discussion, acceptance of the will of the majority, and respect for minority rights. Groups who have not been accustomed to the operation of democratic institutions can rarely federate successfully. This is particularly true where political control is absolute, since rivalries between the rulers of the component states are almost certain to lead to war and the splitting of the group. For example, it would be difficult to imagine a federated Europe based on the cooperation of Hitler, Stalin, and Mussolini, however similar their totalitarian ideologies might have been or whatever the effectiveness of a temporary alliance between them.

Confederations seem to have been exceedingly rare in Eurasia, probably because of the autocratic patterns associated with the early civilizations there. The Hittites, an Indo-European speaking people who developed a large state in Asia Minor on the periphery of the region of ancient civilization, may have had some sort of confederacy, but information is lacking. The Greeks attempted it from time to time, but their institutions were far too democratic. Greek politicians were always poor losers, and the Greek institution of ostracism, which removed the defeated candidate from the city and from the possibility of a local *coup d'état,* was dictated by sound experience. The Greeks rarely got beyond the point of temporary offensive or defensive alliances, and even these were hampered by personal ambitions and mutual distrust.

In the New World, on the other hand, confederacies were frequent and patterns of confederate organization highly developed. In Meso-America and throughout the whole of eastern North America, this type of organization was the rule rather than the exception. The League of the Iroquois, with its center in what is now New York State, will be familiar to most readers, while even the Aztec "empire" was based upon the domination of a league of three cities of the Lake of Mexico. The great "New Empire" period of the Yucatan Maya was also based on a league of three cities, Uxmal, Mayapan, and Chichen Itza.

These American confederacies seemed to have realized that it was not enough to develop techniques for settling disputes between their component members. These members also needed an opportunity to work off their inevitable rivalries and hostilities in harmless action. There is an almost exact correlation in the distribution in America of confederacies and of organized inter-community ball games. Whether these games were the various forms of la crosse played in the eastern United States or the more elaborate and ceremonial basketball-like games played in the ball courts of Middle-America, they had certain features in common. In preparing for them, the magic used by the contenders seems to have been essentially the same as war magic. The winning community gained heavy profits as a result of the wagers placed on their team, or by formalized rights to loot. Thus, in the Mayan ball games, when one team made a goal, its members were entitled to seize any article of clothing or ornament from the rooters on the other side. One can imagine the rapid evacuation of the loser's grandstand which took place when a point was scored. To make the game still more interesting, it was customary in this area to treat the captain of the losing team as a prisoner of war, sacrificing him to the principle deity of the winners. The celebrated Greek games may well have had a similar initial purpose, but if so, they failed to compensate for Greek individualism and city patriotism.

Empires were characteristic of the Old World just as confederacies were of the New. The development of their organizational patterns can be traced from early times, thanks to the Near Eastern habit of writing on indestructible materials. Imperial patterns seem to have begun with the conquest of city by city in the Near East and to have received a new stimulus from the entry upon the scene of successive waves of Barbarian invaders.

Empire building began with simple looting. The armies of one Mesopotamian city would capture another city and carry off all portable valuables including, if possible, the city god. This last was a partial insurance against revolt since the city, deprived of its god, was deprived of supernatural assistance. From time to time the conquering city would demand tribute from the conquered under threat of re-invasion. It might also demand levies of troops to assist its own forces in the further extension of its conquests. Indeed, during the days of the Egyptian and later Babylonian Empires, it became almost a convention to enlist defeated foes and use them as the spearhead for future penetration into enemy territory.

This type of empire required no elaboration of governmental machinery. However, it had numerous disadvantages. The conquered groups enjoyed complete autonomy once the conquerors had retired out of immediate striking distance. They were held in subjugation by fear and sent tribute only as long as they felt that the conquerors were a serious threat. Any period of confusion within the conquering group resulted in the prompt collapse of the empire. The Assyrian Empire, for instance, regularly had to be reconquered by each new king as soon as he ascended the throne. Such a system was uneconomical not only because of the costs of successive punitive expeditions but also because of the time required for the conquered to recuperate after an invasion. Several years would pass before the flow of tribute could be resumed.

Always and everywhere, the real problem of the empire has been how to obtain the maximum return from the conquered with the minimum of cost and trouble to the conquerors. The conquered must have enough wealth left after paying taxes or tribute so that they will be

willing to keep on working; at the same time they must not be permitted to accumulate enough surplus to make war successfully. One of
the earliest methods of solving this problem was that of splitting the
conquered nation, moving part of its people into a distant region, while
part of another nation was brought in to take their place. This technique
was independently invented both in the Near East and by the Inca Empire, the only true empire developed in the New World. It reached its
highest Old World development in the Assyrian, Neo-Babylonian and
first Persian Empires. It seems to have been effective as a preventative
of revolt, since hostility between the survivors of the original local population and the newcomers was inevitable, and each could be relied upon
to watch the other and report to the central government any defection.

With the Barbarian invasion which began toward the close of the
Bronze Age, still other problems emerged. Lacking cities or patterns of
prolonged settlement, these invaders had no fixed base of operation.
When they moved down into the territory of the more civilized city
dwellers, they came to stay. At the same time, since their existing social
and political organization was relatively rudimentary, they had no patterns for governing the conquered and had to improvise rapidly.

Two possibilities presented themselves. The conquerors could break
up their forces after the initial conquest and spread out over the conquered territory, each chief with his followers holding a different part
of it. This pattern required no high development of governmental machinery, and the care and exploitation of the conquered peoples could
be carried on on a basis not very different from the care and exploitation of domestic animals, in which these Barbarians were already expert. This pattern was certainly present in most of Western Europe in
early times. It can be recognized in historic Ireland and in Scandinavia,
and even relatively late conquests such as that of Saxon England by the
Normans were followed by an occupation of very much this type. The
main disadvantages of this system lay in the difficulty which the conquerors had in rapid mobilization in case of revolt and in the relatively
rapid cultural absorption of the conquering group by the conquered.
Small isolated groups of conquerors surrounded by an alien population
soon learned the local language and acquired local customs. This process would be accelerated by the use of members of the subject group as
servants and especially as nurses for children. It seems to be a fact that
no aristocratic group is willing to take care of its own children if it can
find servants to perform the task. After the first generation the conquerors would feel themselves closer to the local inhabitants than to
distant representatives of their own nation. Rivalries between local
chiefs easily led to civil wars, the drafting of followers from the subject
group, and increasing consciousness of common interests. Within a few

generations conquerors and conquered would become one people.

The other possibility was to concentrate the conquerors in armed camps in a few strategic localities. Already existing cities might be taken over for this purpose, but the more usual practice seems to have been to form new settlements in which the conquerors could carry on some approximation of their pre-conquest way of life. This was the system favored by most conquerors in Asia. Under this system taxes had to be collected from the subject peoples by the central government and then disbursed downward from the ruler to the conquerors. This arrangement had the advantage that forces could be mustered rapidly to put down revolt. It also served to slow up the inevitable process of assimilation of the conquerors by the conquered. Its immediate and practical disadvantage was that the collection, handling, and redistribution of tribute required elaborate bureaucratic machinery and a professional civil service of a sort certain to be lacking in any Barbarian tribe. To maintain this system, the conquerors had to recruit a considerable force of minor officials from the conquered. As a matter of fact, where the conquest was one of an already established empire, as in the various nomad invasions of China, the lower levels of the existing bureaucracy were often able to survive with only a change of allegiance.

This arrangement had important repercussions upon the organization of the conquerors themselves. It inevitably enhanced the power of their ruler at the expense of his own tribesmen, who became dependent upon him for their share in the benefits of the conquest. At the same time, the alien ruler became to the conquered people a symbol of government and a potential protector as well as exploiter. There seems to have been a strong tendency for such rulers to recognize common interests with the conquered and to use them as a curb on the power of their own nobility. Especially in those civilizations in which the native ruler enjoyed personal divinity or other forms of extreme prestige and power, the Barbarian ruler would be encouraged by his native subjects to assume these perquisites of office. The gap separating chief and follower in the Barbarian cultures was far smaller than that separating king and subject in the ancient civilizations. The commoners of the conquering tribe inevitably resented their chief's assumptions while he in turn found support for his newly acquired honors among the old nobility and officialdom of the conquered.

Actually, the history of Eurasia is one of successive conquests of settled civilized groups by conquerors and the assimilation of these conquerors. Everywhere except in China, the earlier Barbarians belonged to what has been termed the Dairying Culture. These were followed in turn by the much better organized and militarily more efficient true nomads such as the Huns and Mongols.

PART FOUR

Hunters
and Food-Gatherers

Chapter XI

Paleolithic Cultures

ACCORDING TO the most recent estimates the beginnings of culture, as shown by tools and traces of fire, go back at least 600,000 years. Men of our own species have been in existence for at least 100,000 years and the earliest culture which can be positively ascribed to them already shows a greater variety of tools and weapons than are in use by some tribes still extant. For all but the last 7500 years of this enormous time span, all human beings have lived by hunting and food-gathering. The importance of this phase of man's economic development in setting the patterns for later lines of cultural evolution can hardly be overestimated, and it is regrettable that we still know so little about it.

One who has the temerity to plunge into the huge and highly technical literature dealing with the earlier stages of human history cannot fail to be struck by the contrast between some nine-tenths of the Old World, for which information is either entirely lacking or woefully inadequate, and a few small areas, France and England in particular, which have been studied in extreme detail. The material on these areas bristles with the names of local cultures, each beloved by its discoverer, whose interrelations are matters of vigorous dispute. The non-specialist cannot be blamed for feeling that he has wandered into a maze which has no exit.

That Europe should have been the part of the world whose early history was most intensively studied was a historic accident, a by-product of the invention there of the scientific method. However, it was in many respects a regrettable accident. One may question whether any other part of the world which was occupied by early man offers a poorer guide to the reconstruction of cultural evolution. It is fairly certain that man did not originate in Europe, and there is abundant evidence that throughout most of history the continent has functioned as a receiver rather than a donor of new cultural developments. The four glacial advances and three glacial retreats which alternately forced man out of and lured him back into Europe made the development of culture appear there as a series of discrete episodes rather than as a continuing process. To attempt to apply the typologies and chronological sequences derived from study of European materials to Central or Eastern Asia or Africa south of the Sahara can only lead, as it has led, to confusion. This is even more the case when one tries to apply European typologies to American materials.

The settlement of America occurred in such recent times and the cultural developments in the New World were so independent and in certain respects distinctive that it is best to postpone any discussion of American prehistory. Culture began and underwent most of its early development in the Old World. The most striking fact about this early Old World record is that even in the most ancient times of which we have knowledge there were already a number of cultures. These cultures existed not only in different areas but also, in some cases, within the same geographic area. In the same area varying cultures may have belonged to groups who exploited different environments, such as forest dwellers and prairie dwellers, or may represent occupations by different peoples at time intervals too brief to be revealed by the geological record.

Since stone tools are the only objects which have survived from man's remote past, the classifications of early cultures now in use are based exclusively on differences in the form and techniques of manufacture of such tools.[1] At the bottom of the cultural series lie the so-called Eoliths, implements so crude that it is questionable whether they were deliberately shaped. These go back to the very beginnings of the Pleistocene geological period and perhaps before. Next come cultures characterized by chopping tools made from large pebbles and by big irregular flakes. Most of the stone used was of coarse texture, and the work is so crude that it is hard to identify any consistent implement forms. Industries of this general type, but with numerous local variations, are found over much of Africa and in Southern Asia from Central India eastward. A few sites are also known from southern and western Europe, but this was the time of the first glaciation and most of the continent was uninhabitable.

In Europe and Africa the industries of this type disappeared early. In Southeastern Asia, on the other hand, they persisted until quite late, extending from the beginning of the Pleistocene into post-glacial times. The climate changed very little here, so that there was no great incentive to technological development, and the presence of plenty of bamboo

---

[1] A very few objects of wood and bone have survived from the Lower Paleolithic, but none of these are a help in cultural classification.

and hard tropical woods made elaborate stone-working unnecessary.

At the end of the first glacial period, roughly 500,000 years ago, two distinct types of culture established themselves in Europe. These are known from their characteristic methods of stone-working as the Core Cultures and the Flake Cultures. Both lasted until the beginning of the fourth glacial, or for about 400,000 years. This period as a whole is known as the Lower Paleolithic. There was a slow improvement in techniques and a diversification of implement forms from first to last. The various stages in this evolution have been given distinctive names and are treated as separate cultures by European archeologists, but they represent progress through time rather than new beginnings.

In the Core Culture line the main artifact was a heavy almond-shaped tool called a hand axe. The makers of these implements tried to shape them as symmetrically as possible and paid no attention to the size or shape of the flakes struck off in the process. Some of these flakes were no doubt used for cutting or scraping, but they were essentially a by-product. In the Flake Culture line, the worker tried to get flakes of a particular shape and size and threw away the core when no more good ones could be struck off. Toward the close of the Second Interglacial an important innovation in stone working occurred in this line. The core was dressed so as to give a flat striking surface at one end. This Levalloisian technique interposed another step between the raw material and the finished tool, indicating more foresight and purpose. It also made possible the production of much better flakes, which were retouched to produce specialized tools.

It seems probable that these two lines of development in stone-working were linked with other cultural differences. There has been much speculation as to how the hand axes were used. The earlier ones were often left smooth at the thick end to provide a grip, but the later ones were chipped to a sharp edge all round. If they were held in the hand as weapons they must have been padded with moss or hide to keep the wielder from getting cut. Actual experiments have shown that these implements are poorly adapted for killing large animals at close quarters, and most archeologists now believe that they were really used for grubbing roots. This would suggest a heavily vegetarian diet. It is also significant that the people responsible for the Core Cultures seem to have been allergic to cold weather. At each glacial advance they retreated from Europe, probably into Africa, where the remains show a long unbroken occupation and an uninterrupted evolution of their favorite implement.

The Flake Cultures began with the use of very large, irregular flakes. As time went on these assumed more definite shapes until in the Levalloisian various specialized tools are recognizable. Few of these

artifacts could have been used as weapons, but most of them are well
suited for woodworking. It has been suggested that the carriers of the
Flake Cultures were predominantly hunters well equipped with wooden
clubs and stabbing weapons. In any case, there are indications that they
could adapt to colder weather than the Core Culture people. Their
range seems to have lain north of that of the Core people, and they
seem to have been able to hang on in a few European localities through
the Third Glacial.

The long persistence of these two cultural traditions as distinct and
separate evolutionary lines makes it seem possible that they were the
work of different human species. If so, the Core Cultures were the work
of our own ancestors, *Homo sapiens* and his precursors, the Flake Cultures the work of the ancestors of Neanderthal. However, all this is pure
conjecture and of no great significance for the evolution of culture in
general. A species intelligent enough to make stone implements as elaborate as those produced by either the Core or Flake industries at the close
of the Third Glacial must have been intelligent enough to borrow the
forms and techniques used by another human group in its stone-working. During the Third Interglacial considerable cultural mixture seems
to have gone on in Europe. The Core Cultures disappear as a distinct
tradition, although not until some of their techniques had been transferred to the Flake Culture line, and a new culture, the Mousterian, appears. This period is called the Middle Paleolithic and was much shorter
than the Old Paleolithic, probably not more than 50,000 years.

Whether the Mousterian was developed in Europe or came into the
continent as a result of a migration from Central Asia is still in dispute.
The question cannot be settled until we know more of the early history
of Asia north of the great East-West mountain barrier. However, there
can be no doubt that Mousterian culture was the final flowering of the
long-lived Flake tradition and that it was largely the work of Neanderthal man. This gentleman is the best known of all early human varieties.
His slightly bent knees, forward thrust head, and massive chinless jaw
decorate innumerable museum walls, and his presumed habits are favorite material for writers of science fiction. His evolutionary position
is uncertain, but the last Neanderthalers are much less like ourselves
than the earlier ones. Except for a brief flyer into North Africa, Neanderthal seems to have kept fairly well to northern latitudes and he was able
to stay in Europe through the first half of the Fourth and last Glacial.
He was human enough to interbreed with our own direct ancestors in
Palestine, where the two varieties of man shared the Mousterian culture,
and the best explanation for his differences seems to be that he was a
sub-Arctic human variety in process of developing into a distinct species.
Most of the things that distinguish him from our own ancestors can be

paralleled in northeastern as contrasted with southwestern varieties of other Eurasian mammalian species of wide distribution.

In any case, the behavior of Neanderthal seems to have been thoroughly human. During the bitter weather of the Fourth Glacial he took to caves wherever these were available, and since his ideas on sanitation were rudimentary, to say the least, he has left considerable evidence of his living habits. Bones from his meals, ashes from his fires, and lost and broken implements were simply trodden into the floor of the cave, forming in time deposits several feet thick. The implements from these deposits include triangular flakes, smooth on one side, which could have been used as spear points or knives, and other flakes with a curved edge showing signs of use as scrapers. Several caves have yielded artificially shaped spherical stones, two or three of these of nearly the same size often found close together. There can be little doubt that these are the remains of *bolas* (see p. 77). Simple as this weapon was, its invention must have involved considerable observation and ingenuity. Such an appliance is a far cry from a simple implement like the hand axe.

It is safe to conclude that the Neanderthalers made many wooden objects and probably had containers made from bent bark or even crude basketry. Moreover, in view of the glacial climate of Europe during much of their stay, they probably wrapped themselves in animal skins. It may be noted in this connection that arthritis was common among the middle aged.

Only a few facts about their way of life can be deduced with any certainty. They must have had some sort of band organization like that of the most backward hunting peoples today. Several hearths are often found on the same level in a cave, indicating that several families lived together, and hunting the big game which was their favorite food must have required the cooperation of a number of men. It is idle to speculate on how the Neanderthal bands were organized or what their family groups were like, but frequent evidences of cannibalism suggest that anyone outside the band was considered, quite literally, as fair game.

Still other finds suggest that Neanderthal shared most of the psychological characteristics of modern man. He collected red ochre and presumably used it to paint himself and his possessions. It must have been a precious material, yet he placed it in the graves of his dead. That he believed in some sort of existence after death can hardly be doubted. He not only buried his dead but placed with them food and weapons. He also practiced magical rites. A recently opened cave at Monte Circeo in Italy contained the skull of a Neanderthal, its base broken out to remove the brain, lying in a shallow hole surrounded by an oval of small stones. This can only be explained as a relic of some ancient sacrifice or ritual. There is also evidence that the Neanderthals had some sort of magical practices associated with the Cave Bear. This animal was well suited to become the demonic deity of a Stone Age people since it was their most dangerous enemy. A full grown bear might stand twelve feet high on its hind legs, and, from its build, must have been fast as well as strong. Caches of carefully arranged bear skulls and thigh bones have been found in several caves, indicating that there was some sort of bear cult. It might also be noted that the bones are almost always those of young animals, suggesting that the full grown bears were more than a match for the hunters.

CAVE PAINTING

At the close of the last glacial, a new people entered Europe, bringing with them a new culture and ushering in a new archeological period, the Upper Paleolithic. The retreat of the ice had left the continent cold and comparatively dry. Most of it was park country, open plains with woods in the river bottoms and clumps of trees where depressions held the melting snow. Such territory is particularly favorable for grazing animals, and there were tremendous game herds comparable to those which covered the African highlands at the time the first modern European settlers arrived. It must have been a region of cold winters and hot summers, and much of the game probably moved north and south every year with the changing seasons. The newcomers were primarily hunters and had equipment which was a great improvement over that of their Mousterian predecessors. Their stone work was based on the use of long narrow flakes (blades) struck from a prepared core. For this reason the numerous related cultures of the Upper Paleolithic period in Europe, Western Asia, and Africa are known as the Blade Cultures. The blades, in turn, were worked up into many small, highly specialized tools. Their most important innovation in connection with these was a flat-backed knife or graver called a *burin*. This was made from a stone blade, one edge of which had been knocked off, leaving a flat surface so that the workman could lay his index finger along a blade and guide the edge or graver point when working.

Except for a brief interlude in Europe during the period which we call Solutrean, Upper Paleolithic stone tools were used merely for making other tools and weapons. The favorite materials of the period were bone, mammoth ivory, and antler. From these were made javelin points, wedges for splitting wood, arrow straighteners, and spear throwers. There were also bone whistles, perhaps used as an accompaniment to the ceremonial dances which we know these people performed.

Like their predecessors, the Europeans of this period lived in the mouths of caves when these were available, and had the indifference to garbage disposal which an arctic climate makes possible. However, there were by no means enough caves to go around, and there were many localities in which they were entirely lacking. Where the people could stay in one spot long enough to make it worth while, they built pit houses: roughly circular or oval holes in the ground about three to four feet deep, whose sides were lined with bark, mammoth shoulder blades or stone slabs. There are no traces of roofs, but these probably were made from skins or branches and bark piled over a crude frame of saplings. Since they had no tools suited to felling trees, construction must have been light. They made excellent bone and ivory needles with eyes, tools which are needed only for fine and careful sewing. This suggests that they wore tailored garments, but we have no clue to Upper Paleolithic fashions. Their painters and sculptors rarely represented human beings, and, with one exception, always showed their subjects in the nude. Perhaps, like the pre-missionary Eskimo, they followed the sensible procedure of stripping whenever they came into the warmth of a cave or a house. There is a famous cave painting showing a nude dancer wearing a deer's head mask with horns attached, and several drawings show what may be masked men. The one clothed picture which has come to light so far shows a man's head and shoulders in profile. The shoulders are covered with some sort of brown garment, presumably a fur robe or parka, but it shows no details of the style. Some of their footprints which have been preserved in the soft clay of cave floors show the widely spread great toe which is developed by climbing clay hills barefoot.

Although the Neanderthal people had camped in the mouths of caves, the Cro-Magnon people of the Upper Paleolithic were the first to penetrate their depths. They carried on ceremonies in the deep galleries for the increase of game and for success in hunting. Their artists often worked in places that were so inaccessible that it seems unlikely that they ever expected their work to be seen after they finished it. Probably, the drawing, as an act of creation, was supposed in some way to reinforce the creative powers of the species. In addition to these remote and hidden figures, which must have been the work of individual medicine men, there were veritable cave temples, chambers which were elaborately decorated with series of paintings, and even with animals modeled in clay.

Some twenty years ago one of these caves was discovered completely intact. A young man in the south of France, Casteret, who was an enthusiastic cave hunter, decided that there might be a cave inside a mountain from which a fair sized river issued. With more courage than caution he took matches and candles in a water-tight rubber case and swam upstream underwater until he came out in a cave which was exactly as the last visitors had left it many thousands of years before. The footprints of these ancient men were still plain in the clay of the cave floor. Back from the stream there was a sort of amphitheatre with a life-size clay figure of a bear. This had had a bear skin draped over it; the skull was still lying between the front paws of the image where it had fallen off when the skin rotted away. All around the figure the earth was trampled where the cave men had danced. They had finished off the ceremony by stabbing the bear figure with spears, the marks of which were still plain. Other figures of animals were painted on the walls of the cave and still others, smaller than the central bear figure, were modeled in the clay of the floor. At one place in the cave a stalagmite had formed a comfortable seat. This was worn and well greased from long use. A niche in one side a little below the seat contained bits of bone and antler and several half-finished and finished beads. This may have been the favorite seat of some guardian of the sacred place, a primitive verger who amused himself between services by beadmaking. Similar ceremonial sites, though rarely as well preserved, have been found in many other places in France and in northern Spain.

Archeologists have been much impressed by the extraordinary skill of these primitive artists. Almost all the drawings are of animals, and the great majority of them fall into two classes: pregnant females or animals which, from their poses, may well represent dead game brought home. There are occasional pictures of animals in vigorous motion but very few that show any narrative quality. This is another strong reason for assuming that the artist's intention was magical rather than decorative. Most carvings of animals were on implements, but there are a few small figures in the round, probably worn as amulets. There is also a very remarkable series of little figures of women, pregnant and with sex characteristics exaggerated. All these are grossly fat, apparently the ancient standard of beauty. These figures were probably used in some fertility cult, perhaps an early version of the worship of the Earth Goddess, widespread in the Old World in historic times.

Farther south in Spain a new type of cave art appears, one which is diametrically opposed in its spirit to that of the northern artists. In this we have numerous paintings of both men and animals, always doing something and usually in groups. One painting shows a crowd of women dressed in bell-bottomed skirts engaging in some sort of dance. Another shows a man climbing a bee tree with the bees swarming out of the hive entrance, and there are numerous pictures of running animals and charging bowmen whose vigor and simplification it would be difficult for any modern artist to equal.

Even the Spanish cave paintings rarely show men in combat, and it is improbable that these earliest Europeans carried on systematic warfare. There were certainly amicable contacts between the various local groups, perhaps somewhat like the get-togethers of the modern Australian aborigines, in which past offenses and jealousies are worked off by relatively harmless formalized fights. That they met and traded is proved by the finding of objects far from their source. Sea shells from the Mediterranean were treasured as ornaments and were traded as far as central Europe. There was also a trade in seal skins between some point on the French coast, perhaps Brittany, and Spain, since we find in the Spanish caves, far south of the range of this particular species, seal skulls with no other bones. Presumably the skins were traded with the heads attached.

NEOLITHIC ART, SPAIN

As in the case of Neanderthal man, we have no concrete knowledge on the social or political organization of these people. We may assume that, as in the modern hunting peoples of the Circumpolar zone who are certainly their cultural descendants, all adults were married. Since in a culture of this sort where the main food supply was big game there would certainly be more widows than widowers, it is probable that the best hunters provided for the surplus by taking care of several wives. As regards government, the obvious importance of magic in the culture suggests that, again as with the modern hunters of the north, the most important individual in the community and the nearest approach to a chief was a shaman. Such men were specialists in magic who knew how to make charms and cast spells, and could even, on occasion, send their souls out of their bodies to see what was happening far away.

In this description of the Blade Cultures we have treated Europe as though it were the center, simply because it is the territory for which we have the most information. There are caves there which have preserved an extensive inventory of objects and even paintings which would have long since been obliterated if they had been made in the open air. Also, more work on this period has been done in Europe than anywhere else. However, it is exceedingly improbable that Europe was the origin

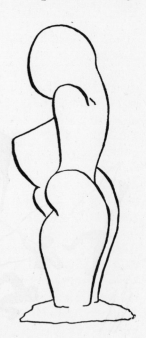

FEMALE FIGURINES, AURIGNACIAN

point of the Blade Cultures. Everything points toward some as yet unexplored region in central Asia as their birthplace. From this center they
were spread westward into Europe and southward through the Near
East, eventually reaching North Africa by way of Suez or by a traverse
farther east at the mouth of the Red Sea. The latter is pure conjecture
since, unfortunately, we know practically nothing of the prehistoric
archeology of Arabia or of the adjoining parts of Africa.

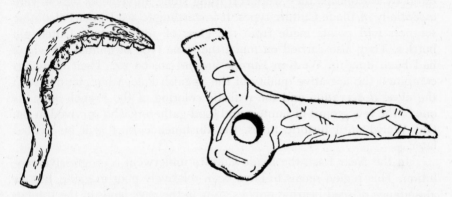

(A) WOOD AND STONE FLAKE SICKLE   (B) BONE ARROW STRAIGHTENER

In Africa, the Blade Cultures became somewhat simplified and the
elaboration of bone, horn and ivory implements which characterizes
them in Europe seems to have been lacking. This may be partly due to
the fact that the more ancient North African sites of this culture are
mainly rubbish heaps left at open camps. The climate of this region was
unquestionably more hospitable at the close of the glacial period than
it has been since. Many of the camps were in regions where it would be
quite impossible for a hunting, food-gathering people to live today. They
contain the remains of a fauna not unlike that of the African veldt, but
in contrast with the European remains, the rubbish heaps contain few
bones of large animals. The favorite game of these early North Africans
seems to have been an edible snail, and tremendous heaps of snail shells
remain to indicate their skill in capturing it. Like their European con-
frères, they made some naturalistic drawings of animals on rocks, but
they left no human figures. Even the little *Venus* figures which are widespread features of the European Upper Paleolithic are lacking. The few
human skeletons that have come from these North African sites are
definitely Caucasoid and show a race not unlike the later population
of the region.

Remains of this culture are found all down the African plateau.
Somewhere in its spread it was transmitted to the ancestors of the

Bushmen, a purely African variety of humans. We do not know whether this transmission was direct or through intermediaries, but the Bushmen, whose historic center is in far South Africa, once extended at least as far north as Kenya. During the late prehistoric period they were first driven southward and then forced into the more inhospitable areas by the invasions of Bantu-speaking people. In their southward flight they carried Upper Paleolithic culture with them almost unchanged. When encountered by Europeans they were still using stone implements which were essentially of Blade Culture types. It is startling to see Upper Paleolithic scrapers and points made from the glass of 18th century Dutch gin bottles. They also carried on much the same type of animal art which had been done in Western Europe around 20,000 B.C. Their drawings combined the narrative quality of the Spanish Paleolithic pictures with the close observation and the realistic coloring of the French ones. As one of the few groups of hunters and food-gatherers who survived in the Old World until historic times, the Bushmen culture will be treated later.

In the Near East, the Blade Culture underwent a progressive evolution. This region seems to have been relatively poor in game, but an abundance of seed-bearing grasses grew in the park lands of the Iranian plateau and around the eastern end of the Mediterranean. The people of the Blade Culture who moved into these regions gradually changed from main reliance on hunting to main reliance on reaping. Where vegetable foods are abundant and reliable, it becomes possible for food-gathering peoples to develop fairly permanent settlements, and this seems to have been the situation here. With time, the Blade Culture of this region differentiated into a great number of local forms, each of which differed from the rest in certain respects, but all of which were clearly in the blade tradition. There was a considerable use of bone and antler for artifacts, and although no cave paintings of the European sort have survived, carved tool handles and other small objects indicate that naturalistic animal art was present. The most important technical invention made here was that of the sickle, one of the basic Old World tools. The first sickles were made from bent pieces of wood, along the inner side of which a row of flint flakes were set to provide a cutting edge. With use, these flakes acquired a peculiar glassy polish which makes them easily recognizable in archeological collections. It was in this region and out of this dependency on wild seed grasses that the world's first agriculture developed.

We may anticipate that numerous remains of the Blade Cultures will be found throughout Central Asia. Not only is this presumably their point of origin, but there are hints that they survived here until comparatively late times. Some sites have already come to light on the Caspian, but this region is still largely archeological *terra incognita*. Such work as has been done here has been directed mainly toward the later cultures dating from the end of the New Stone Age on, and the finds have been so rich that it is only in the last few years that archeologists have attempted to reach the older levels.

In Europe, the climate began to change about 10,000 B.C. The ice continued its retreat northward, and the weather, particularly that along the Atlantic coast, became warmer and much wetter, resulting in heavy forest growth and, with this, in a change in the game. The great herds of bison and wild cattle which had frequented the earlier park lands drifted eastward and the stag became the mainstay of the hunters' economy. However, this drop in game was partly compensated for by the exploitation of a new food source. In ancient times rivers running into the Atlantic were rich sources of fish. Salmon in particular must have come in by thousands to spawn and the inhabitants became increasingly dependent upon them. It would be interesting to know whether, like the Indians of the Northwest Coast of America, they developed techniques for preserving the fish to provide them with a food reserve from one spawning season to the next, but on this we have no information.

The European population of this closing phase of the Paleolithic broke up into small groups, living along the streams where the fishing was good. The culture became fragmented into all sorts of local forms. It is generally said that the culture of this period was degenerate, since the remains which have come down to us from it show a deterioration in flint and antler working. The old animal art also disappears from the archeological record. However, an alternative explanation is possible. During the brief Mesolithic period which followed the Upper Paleolithic,

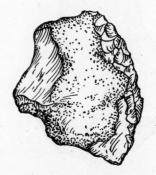

(A) MOUSTERIAN POINT   (B) MOUSTERIAN SIDE SCRAPER

craftsmen turned more and more toward composite tools, only the stone elements of which survived.

The Upper Paleolithic skill in striking blades was developed still further in the Mesolithic, making it possible to produce small, thin blades which were straight, flat, and sharp-edged. These blades were set in wooden implements to give a cutting edge. The changing ecology may have stimulated this development by providing an increased quantity of hard woods and a poorer quality of bone and antler. Thus, a dagger or spear point would be made from a hard wood spike grooved along the sides, with a series of slender flint flakes set in end-to-end. The whole was probably reinforced and streamlined with a layer of pitch. In this way, one could make an implement which had the sharp cutting edge of flint and at the same time the tensile strength of wood, bone, or ivory.

Back from the Atlantic, extending across Eastern Europe and Asia, the climatic changes following the last glacial retreat seem to have resulted in little more than a progressive northward movement of climatic and ecological zones. The park land conditions which had existed in Western Europe at the close of the last glacial advance lasted much longer in far Eastern Europe and Central Asia. As the ice retreated still farther, open grass lands (the *steppes*) appeared to the south and, to the north, wide belts of forests (the *tiega*). These forests extended from the Baltic practically to Bering Strait, with hard woods to the south and conifers to the north. North of the forest lay the tundra, a treeless zone where the ground was frozen to a great depth and where the surface alternately thawed and froze with the changing seasons. This was and still

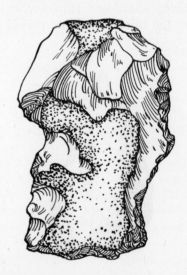

(A) CHELLEAN HAND AXE   (B) CLACTONIAN FLAKE TOOL

is an excessively inhospitable zone for human occupation. The summer thaw turns the surface to mud and the standing pools breed great hordes of mosquitoes and stinging flies. During the thaw, overland travel becomes impossible and all movement has to be by canoes on the rivers. North of the tundra lies the Arctic Coast, a region which offers a richer food supply than the tundra, but which requires a highly specialized

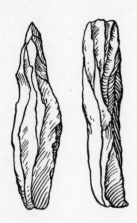 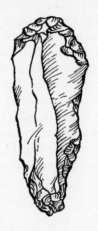

(A) LOWER AURIGNACIAN BURIN   (B) LOWER AURIGNACIAN END SCRAPER

culture for its successful exploitation. In the New World the final conquest of this region was accomplished by the Eskimo who, with their dog teams, sledges, snow houses and techniques for sealing through the ice, were able to wring an adequate living from it.

The Upper Paleolithic of Far Eastern Europe and Asia are still imperfectly known, especially to European and American scholars, since the results of most of the archeological work which has been done in this region have been published in Russian and are not readily available. However, it seems safe to assume that at least the park land and forest belts of northern Eurasia were occupied over a long period by people with cultures of the Blade type. The time of this occupation, depending as it did upon the progressively changing environment, must have been earliest in the southern and central regions. There are no indications that Upper Paleolithic peoples reached far northeastern Asia.

The northern Mesolithic cultures were by no means static and underwent a progressive development down to the historic period. Pottery seems to have been invented independently in this zone. Its use was limited to conical cooking pots of coarse grit tempered ware, poorly fired and decorated with incised designs if at all. One of the most significant developments, of which we have no indications in Europe, was that of the technique of fishing through the ice in winter. In this the fisherman cut a hole in the ice and covered the hole and himself with a small skin tent. From this darkened spot he could look down into the water, watch the fish moving about, and tempt them within reach of his spear by the use of a minnow-shaped lure of bone or stone let down on the end of a cord. Ice fishing could be carried on only at lakes or at those places in rivers where the water was quiet enough to permit the formation of thick ice. At these points people settled for the winter and protected themselves by building pit houses, the same type of structure known to the Upper Paleolithic peoples of western Europe. In summer they ranged widely in the forest, probably breaking up into small groups of at most two or three families. The entire band returned to the same winter camp year after year.

The Mesolithic cultures of far northeastern Asia are of particular interest to Americans since there can be little doubt that the first settlers of the New World had a cultural equipment of this sort. In spite of the claims of various enthusiasts, the presence of Old Paleolithic or even

WINTER FISHING

Upper Paleolithic cultures in America has never been proved, while the recently developed Carbon 14 dating technique sets the date of the earliest known American remains at somewhere around 12,000 B.C.

We still know comparatively little of the cultures and ecological conditions in Northeastern Asia at the close of the glacial period, but it can be said with certainty that when Asiatics had acquired the skills needed to hunt northern game, and shelter themselves in an Arctic environment, the way to the New World lay open. Even if Bering Strait had come into existence by the time that men reached this remote frontier, it would have formed no serious barrier for people who had canoes or who were accustomed to traveling on sea ice in winter. How successive waves of migrants reached the New World, how they spread over it, and how, in certain favored localities, they built civilizations curiously like and yet unlike those of the Old World is a fascinating story which must be left for a later section of this book.

The history of Southeast Asia during and immediately after the closing phases of the glacial period is still exceedingly obscure. As was pointed out in an earlier chapter, technological improvement here seems to have taken the form of an increasing use of wood and bamboo. Since these are perishable, the archeological record gives a false effect of cultural simplicity. One has only to contrast the stone inventory of modern Stone Age peoples such as the Melanesians or Polynesians (both with cultures stemming from Southeast Asia) with the total content of their material culture to realize how deceptive such a record may be. An extensive and elaborate equipment of basketry, matting, wooden utensils, bamboo tools and weapons, and even a complicated art may have existed in Southeast Asia in Upper Paleolithic and Mesolithic times and passed without leaving a trace.

Chapter XII

Historic Hunters and Food-Gatherers

THE EQUIPMENT of ancient hunters and food-gatherers, though crude by modern standards, enabled our species to occupy a much greater range of environment than any other mammal. People who were still at this technological level reached all parts of the world which did not require long ocean voyages and settled nearly all the regions which are inhabited today. In the process they encountered a wide range of climates and natural resources and adjusted to both. It is highly probable that by the end of the Mesolithic there were more distinct languages and cultures in existence than the world has seen since. However, all these cultures were subject to certain limitations inseparable from the hunting and food-gathering economy.

In the first place, the world's population must have been small. There probably were not a hundred thousand people on the entire continent of Europe at any time prior to the introduction of food-raising. The upper limit of human population was set, like that of any other wild species, by the supply of food available year in and year out. A series of good years might bring an increase but this would be cut back sooner or later by famine. In temperate regions the human population may very well have followed cycles of increase and abrupt decrease comparable to those which have been observed in game animals in various parts of the northern hemisphere.

Even more significant for cultural development was the small size of local groups. The number of individuals who can live together constantly is set by the amount of food which they can obtain by working out from a central camp. Even under the most favorable conditions the local groups of hunters and food-gatherers rarely reached 200 persons, while many of them must have been limited to four or five families. To judge from modern hunters and food-gatherers, several of such local groups would get together from time to time to hold ceremonies, exchange gifts and also, legitimately or otherwise, to exchange genes, but most of the year was spent in isolation. Day to day life offered no opportunity for the development of the more elaborate skills. All men had to know how to make their own tools and weapons and all women how to dress skins, weave baskets, and carry on similar domestic industries. There is much wisdom in the old proverb that "Jack of all trades is master of none." People who must change their occupations constantly to meet the needs of the moment have little opportunity to become master craftsmen and still less to explore the possibilities of their craft and play with their techniques, one of the most fertile sources of improving inventions.

Still another feature inherent in food-gathering and hunting economies is the limits which they set to the accumulation of property. Except for a very few favored localities, camps must be shifted often. To judge from modern examples, the normal pattern was probably one of seasonal movements within a clearly defined range. Each local group kept to a particular territory, much as most animal packs do, and trespass was a legitimate cause for war. Within its territory, the group moved from one familiar camp site to another following the times of various wild harvests and the shifts in game supply. All property had to be carried along at each move.

Women no doubt did most of the carrying, a pattern which may be offensive to our modern ideas of chivalry but had a sound basis in common sense. When the group was on the march the men might be called on at any moment to chase a deer or fight off an enemy attack, and they could not afford to be tangled up in baggage. Under these conditions, property over and above that actually needed for getting a living or for beautifying the wearer became mere excess baggage.

Such frequent moves also affected the development of technology from another direction. The unfinished object was a useless item of baggage. Any tool or implement which could not be completed during the few days the group stayed in any one camp became more trouble than it was worth. Needless to say, frequent moves also discouraged the development of architecture. There was no point in building an elaborate shelter when it would only be occupied for a few days.

Even more important than the technological limitations imposed by a hunting, food-gathering economy were the social and political limitations. Food-gatherers could establish kinship systems of extraordinary complexity, as among the modern Australian aborigines, but other types of organization were held to a minimum. Kin obligations and marriage taboos might confront the individual at every turn, but he would never encounter an organized system of social classes or an organized church. The sort of interpersonal relations existing in small face-to-face groups were not antithetical to the recognition of different levels of individual prestige, but they operated against the fixing of prestige levels on a hereditary basis. The development of organized religion was impossible until societies had enough economic surplus to support specialized workers with the supernatural on a full-time basis. All existing food-gathering societies have their shamans, but these function only incidentally and, as it were, in intervals between hunting expeditions. Lastly, organized government, formally designated rulers, and police were quite unknown at the hunting, food-gathering level. Governments are expensive, as even we are discovering, and food-gathering people could not support them. Actually, they were also unnecessary under the existing conditions. Each of the little groups controlled its own members through informal pressures of the sort familiar to anyone who has lived in a small town, while questions of policy or disputes between groups could be settled by discussion among high-prestige individuals.

These generalizations are valid for at least nine-tenths of the world's hunting, food-gathering peoples, past as well as present. However, there are some exceptions as there are, indeed, to any generalization regarding the behavior of human beings living as members of organized societies. In a few localities a combination of local abundance and special skills made it possible for groups who did not raise food to live much as though they did. Thus, in British Columbia, the fabulous runs of salmon in the spring, combined with techniques for preserving salmon and a year-round supply of sea fish and shell fish, gave leisure and a secure food supply. A rich and complex culture, richer than that of many agricultural villages, was developed here.

The Mesolithic period in the Old World was too short to permit of the development of such elaborations. We can imagine the Mesolithic ancestors of both Europeans and Asiatics as wanderers, scanty in numbers and impoverished in culture by later standards. Most of the hunting, food-gathering cultures of the Old World disappeared rapidly after the invention of food raising. Regions which provided an abundance of game or wild vegetable foods were, with very few exceptions, also good regions for herding or agriculture. People who knew the food-raising techniques were able to increase very rapidly and to spread over more and more territory, swamping out the sparse Mesolithic tribes whom they found in possession. That they absorbed rather than exterminated these tribes is shown by the sporadic reappearance of individuals with the physical characteristics of the local Mesolithic people in modern populations.

The spread of the food-raising peoples seems to have been very rapid. During the whole period for which we have written records the Old World food-gathering cultures have been limited to regions which were either unsuited to food-raising or so isolated that the food-raising peoples could not settle them. In the New World many more and decidedly more elaborate food-gathering cultures survived until the time of the European discovery. However, even in the Americas the main centers of high culture and, with few exceptions, of dense population, were agricultural. In the Old World food-gathering, hunting cultures survived in: (1) the subarctic zone of Eurasia; (2) the Congo Rain Forest; (3) arid South Africa; (4) various heavily forested areas in southern Asia and adjacent islands from India to the Philippines; (5) the Australian continent.

The subarctic Eurasians were the direct inheritors of the Mesolithic culture which developed in the northern forests some 10,000 years ago. This culture is best known to us from European sites, but it probably extended, with slight local variations, clear to the Pacific. The material equipment which the Mesolithic population bequeathed to their descendants and the improvements and additions to it which they made

EARLY SNOWSHOES

have already been discussed. Due to their long contact with culturally more advanced peoples to the south, such elements as metal working and animal domestication, based on reindeer, were also widely accepted. However, these do not seem to have greatly altered the regional way of life.

The local conditions were such as to prevent any large or enduring settlements. In general the pattern seems to have been that of bands whose members camped together for part of the year. In the earliest period, before the development of techniques for winter movement, the bands seem to have spent the winter at places where ice fishing was possible. After the development of the sled, snow shoe, and ski, and probably in part under the influence of a developing fur trade, families spent the winter scattered out looking after their trap lines and came together for a time in the Spring.

Each band recognized a head man whose powers were mainly advisory. There was a tendency for the office to become hereditary in a particular family and for band chiefs to be regarded as trustees of fishing places, desirable camp sites, and other communal property. There was no tribal organization but several bands who spoke a common language and intermarried would regard themselves as a tribe. Such a group would punish trespass on its territory, but true warfare was unknown, and such features as war honors, head trophies, and taking of captives were completely lacking.

Marriage was normally within the tribe but outside the band. Monogamy was normal, but widows and other surplus women were taken care of as plural wives. Descent was reckoned equally on both sides of the family, but no long genealogies were kept. As a result of the bilateral descent, every individual had recognized kinsmen in each of several bands and could take up residence with any one of these kinsmen. This provided insurance against starvation if game failed in the territory of one's own band, but it also had other implications. Under ordinary conditions the main problem confronting these northern tribes was not food but manpower. Band chiefs would do their best to attract able-bodied young men or even women to join their groups. The stingy or inefficient leader would see his band melt away until its numbers fell below those needed for survival, while the generous and able band chief could build his following to optimum size. This pattern may well have been ancestral to developments as diverse as the Norse chieftain, whose highest praise was that he was a "mighty ring giver," and the Northwest Coast Indian chief ostentatiously distributing his wealth at a potlatch.

Religion also took a distinctive form in this area. The supernatural world was as anarchic as the human tribe. There was no supreme being nor, in fact, any group of deities with clearly defined attributes. Instead, the world was populated by great numbers of spirits, some animal, who might appear in either their own or human form, some human with similar shape-changing abilities, while still others, among the most powerful and dangerous, were monsters with partly human, partly animal attributes.

These beings were conceived as thoroughly material but able to appear or disappear at will and to change their shapes in the twinkling of an eye. Any individual might, with good fortune, establish a friendly and profitable relation with one of the supernatural beings, but most dealings with them were left to the shamans, individuals who combined the offices of priest, magician, and doctor. These shamans were persons with hysteric tendencies who were able to work themselves into trance states by dancing and drumming until they fell unconscious. While unconscious they would be visited by their spirits who would speak with various voices from different parts of the lodge, transport objects, touch members of the awed audience, and in general produce effects strikingly similar to modern standard psychic phenomena. There can be little doubt that the darkened earth lodge of the Circumpolar peoples, with its unconscious shaman and its crowding supernaturals, is the ancestor and prototype of our own spiritualist séances.

This religion concerned itself mainly with two things, the search for game and the healing of the sick. It is interesting to note that there was a striking lack of fertility rites. Supernatural powers were used to locate game and elaborate taboos were directed toward keeping the good will of slain animals so that they would be willing to be reborn, but the matter of increase was left to the animals themselves. If hunting was bad the shaman, in the trance state, sent his soul to locate the game. He also sent it to see what was going on in the outside world or among the people on the moon. This must have been an important source of entertainment and interest to the little bands snowed-in at their fishing places through the long winters.

The shaman also diagnosed illnesses. There was very little fear of malevolent magic, and this was rarely given as a cause of sickness. Many maladies were thought to be due to the absence of the person's soul. Once again in the trance state, the shaman sent his soul to capture the fugitive and bring it back. In the course of the pursuit he might cross rivers, climb mountains and battle demons, all acted out while in his trance. In spite of this preoccupation with souls, ideas as to life after death were exceedingly vague. There was a life after death but no certainty how or where. A dead person's possessions were usually placed with him, less to provide for his comfort than to sever all ties and prevent him from coming back to annoy the living. As with other supernatural beings, the dead were not conceived of as thin ghosts but as material beings whose sudden appearances and disappearances were made possible by their being exceedingly quick on their feet. Corpses, as distinct from souls, might also possess a horrible life of their own and wander at night devouring men and animals, a belief which may have stemmed from the long preservation of bodies in Arctic cold. A similar belief, either transmitted to or shared by the nomadic peoples of the steppes, became the background of the later vampire beliefs of Europe.

While the Circumpolar culture has left its mark on at least two of the great civilizations, those of China and of Europe, as much cannot be said for the other surviving hunters and food-gatherers. In Africa, small groups of these people still live in two regions, the Congo forests and the arid parts of South Africa. The Congo food-gatherers are Pygmies of exaggerated Negroid type. They live as dependents of the large Negroes of the region, clothing themselves in cast-offs and obtaining most of their tools and weapons from their large neighbors. The relationship is commonly represented as one in which the settled agricultural Negroes exchange their vegetable foods for the Pygmies' game. Actually, the Negroes have their own professional hunters who take care of their need for meat, and the main service of the Pygmies is as scouts. Ranging widely through the forests as they do, they are able to give the villagers warning of enemy war parties and to assist them in laying ambushes. With the end of intertribal war, the usefulness of the Pygmies to their Negro overlords has come to an end, and, according to recent accounts,

EARLY SKIS

the overlords' willingness to provide them with food and needed tools has diminished accordingly.

In far South Africa another group, the Bushmen, have maintained a Paleolithic culture until recent times in the Kalahari Desert. Physically they are a divergent race of Negroid stock: small, slender, yellow-skinned individuals with slant eyes superficially like those of the Chinese or Japanese, but with Negroid features and exceedingly kinky hair. Their tools and implements represent a direct continuation of the old Blade Cultures of Western Europe and North Africa. The present poverty of their equipment is certainly due in part to the highly unfavorable environment in which they are now found. In earlier times they occupied a much larger area in South Africa and had a more elaborate technology which included pottery-making.

The most elaborate Bushman artifact is the bow and arrow. Bows are simple wooden staves, small and feeble; arrowheads have a transverse cutting edge, like a chisel; a bone barb, smeared with a particularly deadly poison, is thrust diagonally into the reed shaft just behind the head. The chisel edge of the arrow serves to cut veins and to get the poison into the animal's circulation more rapidly. The only other implement of importance is the woman's digging stick, a straight piece of hard wood weighted with a doughnut-shaped stone. This is used for collecting roots and small burrowing animals and also makes a handy club at close quarters.

Household equipment is limited to two or three mats and a few ostrich egg shells used as water bottles. Clothing consists of scanty aprons of soft tanned hide and of fur robes worn against the nightly cold.

Bushmen are organized in tribes, vague groupings based on the sense of unity which comes from speaking a common dialect and occasional contacts between the members. The tribe, in turn, is composed of bands which are the real units for social life. Each band roams within a particular territory. Where the resources are poorest even bands break down into single families which roam alone, coming together at long intervals.

Each band has a chief, an old man of strong personality but doubtful formal authority, who directs communal affairs, helps to settle disputes and, above all, is the keeper of a sacred fire. Although all adult Bushmen know how to make fire, this fire occupies a special position reminiscent of the days when primitive man had to keep constant guard over this gift of the gods to prevent it from being lost. All fires in the encampment of the bands must be kindled from the sacred fire. In the encampment each family has its own diminutive dome-shaped hut and its own cooking fire. Unmarried men have a hut of their own to which the boys repair immediately after puberty.

Families are usually monogamous, although widows and other unattached women are cared for by being taken as plural wives of the best hunters. Wives are always taken from another band within the same tribe.

Bushman religion is poorly known, but they seem to believe in a supreme being whose representation or vehicle on earth is, curiously enough, the praying mantis. Their folklore, consisting mainly of animal tales, is surprisingly rich, and they have carried over from their Paleolithic ancestors a quite extraordinary skill in drawing men and animals. Wherever the Bushmen have been, cave mouths and rock shelters are decorated with elaborate polychrome paintings executed with rare spirit and almost photographic fidelity. These paintings represent hunting scenes, dances and fights, but their purpose is unknown.

Several groups of hunters and food-gatherers have been able to survive until the present time in the inhospitable jungles of Southeast Asia and the adjoining islands. These groups show two quite distinct physical types, one Negroid, the other, called Veddoid, somewhat Caucasic. However, all of them have in common small stature and slight build, which may be related to many generations of underfeeding and intense moist heat.

In spite of their differences in physical type and language, all these groups depend on much the same sort of economy. Caves and rock shelters are used as dwellings where available. Failing this, houses are simply leaf-thatched lean-tos arranged in a circle about a central open space. Hunting is done with bow or blow gun, the latter appliance apparently having been invented in this region, although its time and place of origin are unknown. Blow guns are like gigantic pea shooters eight

ROCK PAINTING, AFRICA

feet or more in length. The simplest type of blow gun is nothing more than a single joint of a very long jointed species of bamboo which grows in this region. More elaborate forms with mouthpiece and sights are made of wood. The blow gun arrows, splints of bamboo feathered with cotton or thistle down, are much too light to form effective weapons in themselves but they are tipped with a deadly paralyzing poison made from the sap of the Upas tree. This has the double advantages of bringing down the prey before it can travel far and of being harmless when taken internally so that it does not injure the meat.

All have much the same rudimentary social institutions. They live in small bands which claim particular territories and punish trespass. Chiefs and formal political or tribal organization are lacking. In general they follow a pattern, also widespread among the more advanced peoples of this region, by which adolescent sex experimentation is permitted but marriage is monogamous and unfaithfulness by either party is severely punished.

Religion centers about a supreme being who expresses his disapproval by thunderstorms, violent enough in this region to be awe inspiring. Taboos are numerous and are directed toward placating him. There are medicine men who control disease and work against evil spirits and ghosts, of which the natives have a vigorous if not clearly rationalized fear. It is interesting to note that there is very little fear among any of these peoples of malevolent magic practiced by other persons.

Although none of these little people live in the sort of clientage which characterizes the African Pygmies, they are in general dominated by larger neighboring groups. The only exception to this is the Andamanese in the Bay of Bengal who, until about 100 years ago, maintained complete independence by killing any strangers who landed on their shore and burning their bodies and their equipment. This inhospitable conduct seems to have been motivated mainly by a great fear of disease. In spite of this iron curtain, the Andaman Islanders seem to have received certain elements of material culture, notably pottery and canoes, from their more advanced neighbors.

The last, and in many ways the most interesting of the Old World food-gathering groups, are the Australian aborigines. In this isolated continent, where many archaic forms of life have survived, we also find archaic humans. Intensive studies of the Australian physical type suggest that the island continent was reached by three waves of invaders, differing in race. However, the commonest Australian physical type appears to represent a very old, highly generalized human stock corresponding rather closely in its skeletal characteristics to the oldest remains of our own species which have so far come to light.

If there were successive waves of migration into Australia, each wave presumably brought with it a somewhat different culture, but it is quite impossible to reconstruct these cultures at the present time. Australian culture is by no means uniform, but it is characterized everywhere by a poor development of technology. Clothing is nonexistent except for decorative purposes or the occasional use of untanned, unsewn skins wrapped around the body haphazardly in cold weather. Housing is of the most rudimentary sort, consisting of simple open windbreaks in dry country or, in wet country, of low domed huts thrown together of any materials that might be available. In cold weather, fire is made to substitute for both clothing and housing. The traveling native carries a burning brand which he moves around his body from time to time to warm himself, and at night he sleeps between fires.

The principal weapons are the spear and spear thrower and a short knobbed club. The spear thrower is the most important single implement, so much so that in some of the Australian tribes the name for it is given the same grammatical form as that used in referring to parts of the individual's own body. A bit of sharp flint is often gummed to the lower end for use as a knife or scraper, and the shaft is often expanded to form an oval plate on which food can be cut up, colors for body painting pre-

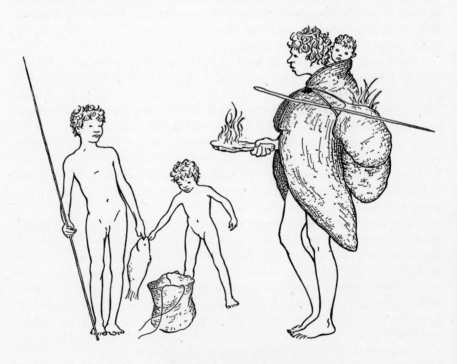

AUSTRALIAN COSTUMES

pared, and so forth. Spears differ considerably with the region and there is an extensive trade in various types.

Most stone implements are crudely made by percussion, but the natives of Worora seem to have invented the art of pressure flaking independently and in fairly recent times, using it for the manufacture of spearheads and knives. Crude ground and polished stone axes, hafted in a bent withe, provide the only exceptions to the general Paleolithic tone of the native stone work.

The boomerang, most advertised of Australian weapons, is actually present only in northern and central Australia. Those used by different

THROWING CLUB

tribes vary greatly in size, decoration and details of form. The return boomerang has a still more limited distribution and is primarily a toy or at most a bird-hunting appliance. It is said that the aborigines do not understand the principle involved and that a man never knows whether a new boomerang will return properly until he has thrown it.

Shields are used in northern and central Australia. They are made of solid wood and are, with few exceptions, so small that they must be regarded as fending weapons rather than cover.

Equipment other than tools and weapons is of the crudest sort. A few twined bags and baskets and occasional containers of bark or wood exhaust the inventory. Nevertheless, objects are frequently decorated with painted or incised designs which show unusual precision in execution. Large earth paintings symbolizing the outstanding characteristics of totem animals are made in central Australia as a part of rites for increase, while in far northeastern Australia, Arnhemland, there is an unusually vigorous art of painting on bark with representations of mythological characters and events. The art in general is characterized by great vigor and movement and the designs are for the most part abstract rather than naturalistic.

Neither pottery nor the bow were present in Australia in historic times, although archeological finds indicate that they had been introduced in the northern part of the continent but for some reason failed of acceptance.

The poverty of Australian technology is matched by an almost equal poverty of political organization. There are no real tribes, but only territorial divisions characterized by differences in language and culture. There are no chiefs, courts, or other formal agencies of government; conduct is controlled by an elaborate series of regulations based on kinship and by innumerable taboos, both sets of regulations being enforced by a combination of supernatural sanctions and public opinion. Any situations not covered by one or the other of these sets of regulations are settled by informal councils of old and respected men whose position might be thought of as a combination of Emily Post and a Holy Synod.

As with all food-gathering peoples, the Australians live in bands, groups of families who normally camp together and roam over a well-defined territory. From time to time adjoining bands come together to perform ceremonies, particularly the initiation of boys into manhood and rites for increase of game. These get-togethers are occasions of high emotional tension. The meeting begins with formalized fights in which all grudges resulting from trespass, failure to fulfill exchange obligations, and so forth, are worked off. Men of different bands throw spears at each other and the women often join in, belaboring each other with their digging sticks. There is much noise and excitement and a fair number of wounds are given and received. There are even occasional killings, and it is said that in some of the tribes the bodies of such casualties are welcomed as an addition to the food brought for the occasion. When the old men feel that the battle has gone on long enough, they call a halt and

BOOMERANG

hold a feast to which all contribute. The combatants are reconciled through a temporary exchange of women during which the usual rules of kin avoidance are suspended.

Australian social organization has a complexity which has made it the delight of students of primitive institutions. The distribution of various patterns of social organization on the continent is sufficiently sys-

AUSTRALIAN SHIELDS

tematic to make possible a fairly accurate reconstruction of the development of various institutions. The most complex social patterns are found in the north-central part of the continent, becoming increasingly simple and presumably older as one goes toward the margins. Patrilineal bands are present everywhere, and combined with these there is a twofold division of the tribe based on descent in the female line. The functions of these divisions, moieties as they are called, are primarily ceremonial. Each moiety initiates boys of the other moiety into manhood and also, in many cases, takes care for the other moiety's dead. Less peripheral and presumably somewhat later is a system in which the moieties are further subdivided into matrilineal clans. Lastly, in central and northern Australia, the clan organization is replaced by a division of the whole group into four sections, made by dividing each moiety in half. Under this arrangement children belong to a different section from either of their parents and have to marry someone belonging to the one section remaining when both their own and their parents' section have been ruled out. In the next generation, if it is a four-class system, the children revert to the section of one of the grandparents. Thus if a tribe is divided into four sections

A —— *B*

C —— *D*

a man from *A* has to marry a woman from *B*, and their children are in section *D*. A woman in *D* has to marry a man in *C* and their children will be *B*.

In the central part of the continent each of the four sections is further split in two, giving an eight-class system. In this case children belong to the class to which their great-grandmother belonged. An individual calls all persons of the same sex and generation included in a particular section by the same relationship term. Thus a man will call all his father's brothers "father," all his mother's sisters "mother," all the men of his own generation in his section "brother," and all the women of his wife's generation and section "wife."

Although this elaborate kinship system is ordinarily thought of as important mainly for the regulation of marriage, actually it governs all sorts of interpersonal relations. The hunters bringing in game, or the women returning from a day of root digging, have to divide their take with all their kin according to strict regulations. For instance, if a man kills a kangaroo, his wife's brothers are entitled to a certain part of the animal, his own brothers to another part, and so forth. He will, of course, receive a return in kind from each of his relatives when they kill game. Not only mutual aid and marriage but also avoidance are controlled by rules based on kin ties. The most rigid of these rules is that a man must

DIJALMOMG SPIRIT, ARNHEMLAND

never be alone with or even address his mother-in-law. He also must
maintain different degrees of social distance toward a whole series of
male and female relatives, talking to one category only with his back
turned, sitting so many paces from relatives of another, and so forth.
This regulation of kin behavior is carried so far that in one of the northern Queensland tribes, when a man sneezes, instead of saying *Gesund-
heit* all those in hearing slap themselves, the place on their bodies varying according to their relationship to the sneezer.

Because of the rules of band exogamy and the absence of any real
continuing warfare between bands, these kin ties cut across linguistic
and cultural lines. In some parts of Australia it is usual for young men to
take a sort of grand tour, in the course of which they are passed from
band to band and cared for in each by their hypothetical relatives until
they have made a circuit of several hundred miles. In spite of the differing kin terms and categories in different regions, the natives are exceedingly adroit in correlating the various systems. If the individual can find
a kin tie with even one person in the band, living or remembered, he can
be socially oriented immediately. His relatives in different degrees are
pointed out to him and he is told exactly how to behave toward each. It
is said that when a man meets a member of a strange band the first step
is to sit down, recite genealogies, and try to establish such a link. If one
can be found, all is well; if none can be found, the stranger may be
classed as a brother of any man willing to stand sponsor for him or, failing this, will be killed simply because there is no social technique by
which he can be fitted into the group.

The complexity of Australian kin organization is matched by that of
their ceremonial life. It seems amazing that so many diverse rites could
be performed with so little technological equipment. It has already been
said that the variations of physical type in Australia suggest a series of
migrations. If such occurred they must have taken place in some remote
time, for in no other part of the world is there so complete a linkage between the people and the land. The mythical period to which the beginnings of things are traced is known to the Australians by a term meaning
"the dream time," and the division between past and present seems to
be far from clear in their own minds: at least, it is always possible to re-
create this past and to strengthen its influences by ceremonial observances and for the medicine man to go back into the "dream time" and
participate in its events while in a trance state.

In the Australian mythology, creation did not take place in some remote Garden of Eden but in the very territory where each band lives.
The mysterious *alchuringa* ancestors, who were neither men nor animals
but partook of the qualities of both, wandered about performing casual

miracles at well remembered spots and leaving here and there caches of souls which could incarnate themselves in either humans or animals, as fancy dictated.

From the native point of view, membership in a band depends not upon biological descent but on the possession of a local soul. The knowledge of the ancestors' wanderings and of the sacred places which they have established is the most precious possession of the tribe and, in theory at least, is limited to adult males. The men of an Australian band really constitute a secret society, with the women and children providing the necessary audience of admiring outsiders. At puberty the boy is initiated into the secret society of adults by rites which are a dramatic representation of death and rebirth. He is carried off by members of the opposite moiety amid the lamentations of his relatives and taken to a camp in the bush where he is subjected to various taboos and to physical ill treatment which varies in violence with the region. As in the case of kinship regulations, patterns show a fairly consistent geographic dis-

MALIGNANT SPIRIT, ARNHEMLAND

tribution. Mutilations performed upon the novice vary from simple scarification, in the southern coastal regions, to a combination of scarification,
knocking out teeth, circumcision, and subincision, in central Australia.
While these mutilations are no doubt designed in part to test the courage of the initiate and to determine whether he is ready to perform the
necessary masculine role, they also serve, among a naked people, as visible signs that the boy has attained manhood and knows at least the necessary minimum of the secret lore.

The ceremonies of initiation usually end with the display to the initiates of the *churinga* of the band. Even Paleolithic man seems to have
discovered that if a thin slat of wood is attached to the end of a string
and whirled around the head, it will make a peculiar whistling and roaring sound. This appliance, called a bull-roarer, was used to frighten the
uninitiated away from places where ceremonies were going on in regions as diverse as California, far South America, Melanesia, and ancient
Europe, but the bull-roarer cult reached its maximum development in
Australia. The *churinga* is a glorified bull-roarer made from wood or,
more rarely, from stone, and carved with incised designs. In most cases
it copies the form of the original instrument but can no longer be used
for noise making. Each man is represented by one of these *churingas*
which has presumably been dropped by his soul when it entered his
mother's womb to be reincarnated. When the child is born his father
searches for the *churinga* until he finds it (presumably with the aid of
an older man, expert in *churinga*-making). It is then stored in some secret place with the *churingas* of all other band members and is kept here
even after the individual's death.

While all men undergo initiation and are given a glimpse of the esoteric lore, full knowledge of this is reserved for a selected group and it
is not transmitted even to these until they have reached late middle age.
According to the native statements, such higher initiates undergo another ceremony of death and resurrection in which their flesh and internal organs are magically removed, cleansed, and then put back with various objects, mostly small stones, which confer supernatural powers. The
process as described is modeled directly on that employed by many native groups in actual mummification. Individuals who have been sanctified in this way have power to work all sorts of magic: to bring rain, increase game, ascertain what is happening at a distance, and cure illness.
Their activities are generally benevolent although, as with any wielders
of supernatural power, they can also use their knowledge to cause injury. However they are sharply differentiated in the native mind from
the malevolent sorcerers who have acquired their knowledge in less legitimate ways and who use it for evil. These sorcerers kill their victims
magically by projecting malevolent objects into them or by stealing upon

them at night while they are asleep and removing their kidney fat or some of their vital organs and stuffing in grass in place of these. They then close the wound magically. The individual revives the next morning apparently none the worse for the experience, but inevitably dies within two or three days.

There is considerable fear of this black magic among the natives, but it is characteristic of their well-adjusted patterns of social life and social obligations that the sorcerer is never a member of the victim's own band. After a death a medicine man will be called in to divine the cause of the death and will accuse some individual from another band, usually one already suspected of sorcery. A punitive expedition will then be sent to kill him, and it is said that the members of his own band will not protect him under these circumstances.

Of all the curious patterns of Australian native life, the one which has attracted most attention is *totemism.* This is the belief that a special relationship exists between a particular species of animal or plant or natural phenomenon and a particular human group. In Australia every social grouping is related to a totem. The native idea is not that the human group is descended from the animal species but rather that the two share souls from a common repository in which these souls were left by the *alchuringa* ancestors during the "dream time." In general, the holders of a particular totem are forbidden to kill or eat their totem animal except on certain solemn occasions when the old men of the group may eat it as a sort of a sacrament, reminiscent of the practice of some Australians of eating their own dead. Although members of the group do not eat their own totem, they are responsible for its increase for the good of the entire community, and the most important native religious rites center about persuading the souls in the various soul caches to be reborn as animals. In these increase rites, events of the "dream time" are reenacted with the aid of ground paintings and theatrical costumes consisting of elaborate headdresses, body painting, or coats of downy feathers glued on with blood. One of the younger men of the totem group is selected to provide this adhesive.

In discussing the life of the Australian aborigines, the present tense has been used throughout as a matter of convenience. Actually, many tribes have become extinct, others are living under direct European domination with consequent changes in their original patterns of culture, and still others, especially in the desert regions, are carrying on their aboriginal culture with little change.

There can be no doubt that the Australian aborigines eventually will disappear as a distinct ethnic and cultural group. Their culture has had no influence on the main lines of developing civilization. It does not even throw much light upon the social and religious institutions of the earliest human societies, for the Australian systems are so elaborate and unique that they can only be explained as a result of independent evolution. At the same time, certain themes present in Australian culture can be recognized as present in the amazingly diverse local cultures of Melanesia. Thus, the Australian dependence upon kinship as a guide to social interaction is paralleled by the complexity and functional importance of Melanesian kinship systems. The Australian initiation rites and transmission of magical secrets to men is paralleled in the Melanesian secret societies, although with rather changed emphasis. The amorphous quality of Australian political organization is paralleled in the relatively poor Melanesian development of chieftainship and formal political institutions. Lastly, the art of several Melanesian areas is strongly reminiscent, in its colorfulness, motion, and fantastic quality, of the uninhibited vigor of Australian painting.

PART FIVE

Southeast Asiatic Complex

Chapter XIII

Southeast Asiatic Neolithic

As WE SAW in Chapter XI, evidence of many sorts suggests that food-raising was invented independently in Southeast Asia and that a distinctive Neolithic complex was developed there. However, any attempt to reconstruct this complex is fraught with great difficulty. Very little archeological work has been done in Southeast Asia and the adjoining islands and what is available has been directed mainly to the rich and picturesque Hindu and Buddhist cultures of the early historic period. Moreover, as has been mentioned previously, the development of technology in this region seems to have centered on the use of perishable materials, especially bamboo, so that the actual remains from the Neolithic period, mainly surface finds, are scanty and unilluminating.

In the absence of archeological evidence we must turn to that provided by marginal survivals. It has often been observed that when a culture complex has been diffused over a considerable area, older forms will tend to survive around the margins and in regions of comparative isolation long after they have died out in the original center of diffusion. The fact that Elizabethan English ballads are still sung by some of our Southern mountaineers would be a case in point.

The Malayo-Polynesian languages have their center in Southeastern Asia and Indonesia and wherever they are found it is safe to assume that they were introduced by migrants from this general region. Even the ancient Indonesians were excellent sailors and carried their languages and culture eastward to the farthest Pacific Islands and westward to Madagascar. When the same distinctive culture elements are found at the opposite ends of this tremendous area and also among isolated, culturally conservative groups living in remote Indonesian islands and in the mountains of Southeastern Asia, it is safe to conclude that such elements are referable to an old stratum of Southeastern Asiatic culture. It is impossible to say with certainty whether such elements are as old as the

Neolithic, but they certainly belong to the relatively primitive pattern of life which existed in this region prior to the introduction of Hindu and Chinese culture elements.

One may very tentatively reconstruct the Southeastern Asiatic Neolithic as having the following characteristics: the economy was based upon root and fruit crops, supplemented in inland hill regions by unirrigated rice raised by the cutting and burning method. Domestic animals were the pig, chicken, and the ubiquitous dog. The presence of pottery seems questionable since it is lacking not only in Polynesia but even in the more archaic cultures of modern Madagascar. It was replaced by a combination of boiling in large bamboos and baking in earth ovens. Clothing was made from bark-cloth or matting. The loom was unknown. The inventory of stone implements was small and consisted primarily of adzes and chisels which were characterized by angularity and complete polish. Chipped stone implements were rare and crudely made. Knives, scrapers, projectile points were ordinarily made from bamboo. Basketry, matting, and woodworking were probably highly developed.

The most important weapons were the spear and club, both present in considerable variety. The principal missile weapon was the sling. Shields were probably lacking and the bow was unimportant. The failure of the migrant Malayo-Polynesian groups and of even the historic hill tribes of Southeastern Asia to use this implement as a weapon is difficult to explain. It seems to have been used by the food-gathering Negrito peoples whose cultures are certainly very ancient in Southeast Asia, so the Neolithic Malayo-Polynesians must have been familiar with it. It has been suggested that its neglect was connected with a head-hunting complex which made close fighting obligatory if the warrior was to obtain the necessary trophy.

Housing no doubt varied considerably with altitude and temperature, but the fundamental house form was rectangular with gabled roof and floor elevated by building the house either on posts or on an earth platform, usually stone faced. Even in the Neolithic period there must have been excellent canoes capable of extended ocean voyages, and it seems probable that the outrigger and sail were already known.

Political organization was decidedly weak, with no governmental units larger than single villages. Within the village, rule was by family heads under a sort of oligarchic arrangement with, perhaps, nominal chiefs whose powers were mainly advisory. Each village was normally endogamous and had few friendly relations with other settlements, even those which were similar in language and culture. Within the settlement, individual status and social interactions were based on a combination of kinship and wealth with considerable emphasis on the latter.

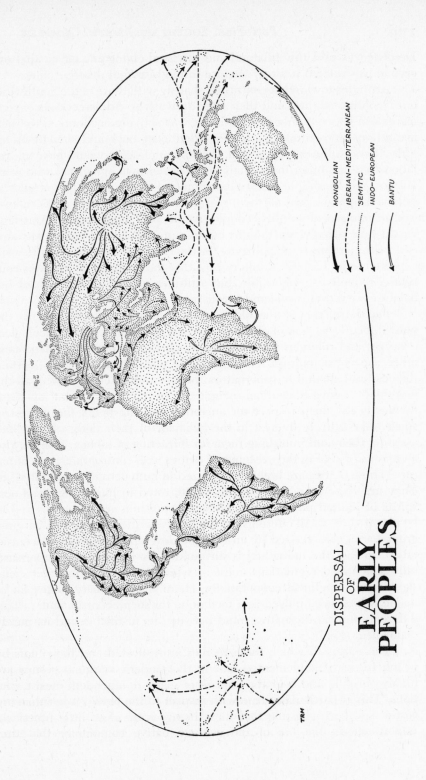

DISPERSAL
OF
**EARLY
PEOPLES**

MONGOLIAN
IBERIAN-MEDITERRANEAN
SEMITIC
INDO-EUROPEAN
BANTU

TRM

Descent was probably bilateral and the local endogamy meant that everyone was related to everyone else through several different lines.

Attitudes toward sex contrasted sharply with those of the Southwestern Neolithic cultures and their later derivatives. Adolescent sex experimentation was not only tolerated, but was actively encouraged by such institutions as separate houses for adolescent boys and sometimes for girls. It was anticipated, as well, that the adolescent would have sex relations with all other individuals in his or her own age group who were not covered by simple incest taboos much like our own. This would be followed by a gradual narrowing of interest until, by the end of the period of adolescent sterility, couples would be "going steady." Marriage would take place when the girl became pregnant. Monogamy was normal, with perhaps some polygyny for the rich, and married couples were expected to be faithful. Adultery by either the husband or wife was considered equally reprehensible, but attitudes toward all sorts of sex behavior were rather casual and permissive.

Reconstruction of the old Southeast Asiatic religion presents the most difficult problem of all since, contrary to general belief, theological concepts and religious practices are much less conservative than many other aspects of culture. However, it is possible to recognize certain themes fundamental to supernatural beliefs and practices among all the marginal Malayo-Polynesian peoples. The most important of these themes is the deep respect for ancestors and the belief that ancestral spirits take a lively interest in the behavior of their descendants, both assisting them and punishing them for infraction of taboos. There is also a universal belief in the existence of deities who control the forces of nature. These deities are highly specialized in both activities and interests. They are remote and, in general, uninterested in human affairs. Local spirits of limited power and uncertain disposition are numerous and to be placated by small offerings. At the behavioristic level all the marginal groups are characterized by an extreme development of the concept of taboo, so that the individual is surrounded by innumerable supernaturally sanctioned regulations, most of which have no recognized social significance or ethical connotations. There is everywhere some fear of magic, which is employed as a technique for social control, and a sharp differentiation in the native mind between its justifiable and its purely malevolent use.

The myths in which these themes are reflected and the rituals by which they are implemented among the modern marginal groups are highly variable and bear the imprint of many independent local evolutions. This is particularly true with respect to the beings other than ancestral spirits, suggesting that these beings were of so little functional importance in the life of the average native community that they provided a free field for elaboration through speculation and fantasy.

The migrations of the Malayo-Polynesian speaking peoples from their homeland in Southeastern Asia and the adjoining islands present one of the most amazing phenomena in history. In spite of their atomistic political patterns, which made it impossible for them to organize large communal projects, and their late acquisition of metal, they were able to encircle a full third of the globe in their voyages of exploration and to establish permanent settlements at points as remote as the island of Madagascar, only 250 miles off the East African coast, and Easter Island, only 2200 miles from the coast of South America and nearly due south of Denver, U.S.A.

Migrations from Indonesia certainly began while the Malayo-Polynesians were in the Neolithic stage of culture and continued until recent times. Thus, Malayan trepang fishermen still visit the coast of Northern Australia, where they have left mixed blood offspring and have exerted considerable influence on the aboriginal culture. However, the great period of migration seems to have begun around 2000 B.C. and to have ended by 500 A.D., about the time when Southeast Asia and Indonesia came under the dominance of Indian culture.

It is generally believed that the originators of the Malayo-Polynesian family of languages and of the Southeast Asiatic version of Neolithic culture were of the physical type known as proto-Malay. Tribes predominantly of this type still survive in the interiors of the larger Indonesian islands and around the margins of the Malayo-Polynesian area. The proto-Malays are brown skinned, long headed, wavy haired, and straight eyed, with features much like Europeans. They are generally classed as belonging to the Caucasic stock. In view of the ancient occupation of Southeast Asia by Negrito and Australoid peoples, it seems improbable that they evolved in this region, but we cannot trace them to any outside source. Following the proto-Malays there was a steady infiltration of Mongoloid tribes coming from the north. This infiltration seems to have been slow enough for the newcomers to adopt most of the language and culture of the proto-Malay population while gradually replacing its physical type with their own. The modern inhabitants of Southeast Asia and Indonesia are predominantly deutero-Malays: brown skinned but round headed and straight haired, with slant eyes and Mongoloid features.

This gradual change in physical type is reflected in differences in the appearance of the population in different parts of the Malayo-Polynesian area. The people of the outer Polynesian islands and the older stratum in the population of Madagascar are both predominantly proto-Malay. Western Polynesia and Micronesia show a much greater proportion of deutero-Malay, while this element is also dominant in the Imerina tribe who are, traditionally, the descendants of the last group of Asiatic migrants to reach Madagascar.

Between Southeastern Asia and Indonesia and the open reaches of the Pacific there lies an almost continuous chain of islands extending from the Japanese archipelago through the Philippines to New Guinea and the various Melanesian groups. All these islands were in easy reach for sailors as expert as the ancient Indonesians. Malayo-Polynesian migrants reached the Philippines very early in their wanderings and successive migrations continued until the late 14th century, when the ancestors of the Moros, Malays converted to Islam, established themselves in Mindanao. There can be little doubt that early migrants also reached Japan and made significant contributions to the later Japanese population and culture. This will be discussed elsewhere.

The Melanesian islands are remnants of what was once a northern extension of the Australian continent. Many of them must have been occupied at one time by people much like the Australian aborigines but, by the time of the first European contact, most of the Melanesian population was more nearly Negroid than anything else. Negrito (black Pygmy) groups are found in refuge areas, from New Guinea to the Andaman Islands in the Bay of Bengal. Several hypotheses have been advanced to account for the presence of Negroid peoples so far from Africa and with no other Negroid populations to bridge the gap, but none of them seem satisfactory. Although the Melanesian Negroids have the required dark skin and kinky hair, they are highly variable in their other physical characteristics, and there are very few of them who might be mistaken for members of any African tribe. It seems most probable that the features which they share with the Africans are a result of convergent evolution. The climatic conditions in the large Melanesian islands are, after all, not too different from those in the West African lowlands, the center from which the true Negroes seem to have spread to the rest of the continent.

Whatever the origins of Melanesian Negroids, it seems safe to assume that at the time the Malayo-Polynesian migrations began, the region was occupied by dark-skinned people of Negroid or Australoid stock who were culturally backward. Lying as it does on the margin of the Malayo-Polynesian home territory, Melanesia was subjected to a constant flow of invaders. By the beginning of the historic period, Malayo-Polynesian languages had been established everywhere except in the interiors of a few of the largest islands. However, in spite of a great many local variations in physical type, the result of social isolation and close in-breeding, even today the population is still predominantly Negroid or Australoid. Proto- or deutero-Malay groups are to be found only on a few small off-shore islands, and even these groups appear to be descendants of Polynesians who drifted back into the region from the east in fairly recent times.

The best explanation for this curious inconsistency in the distribution of language and physical type seems to be that the Malayo-Polynesian migrants found the Melanesian environment much more hostile than the Melanesian natives. Even modern Europeans with modern medicine have found it hard to survive in Melanesia. There are a great many endemic diseases, among which numerous strains of malignant malaria occupy a prominent place. The early Malayo-Polynesian migrants probably made numerous settlements on the Melanesian islands, intermarrying with the local aborigines. Their descendants were hybrids from every point of view. They spoke a variety of languages, in all of which the Malayo-Polynesian elements predominated, and practiced a great variety of local cultures based on various combinations of aboriginal and Malayo-Polynesian traits. However, the aboriginal physical type, with its superior environmental adaptation, gradually replaced that of the invaders. A similar situation can be recognized in some of the older tropical colonies established by Europeans. European languages and much of European culture survive, but present populations show few traces of European blood.

The Malayo-Polynesian occupation of the Philippines and their penetration of Melanesia were only the first steps in their eastward movement. When these were passed, the whole Pacific lay open to them with a multitude of uninhabited islands waiting to be colonized. One migration route seems to have been through Melanesia and along the relatively close-lying Polynesian Islands from Tonga and Samoa eastward to the Society group, the Marquesas, and ultimately Easter Island. Another migration route ran far to the north, taking the migrants into the small and widely scattered Micronesian Islands, from which they eventually reached Hawaii.

The settlers who came by each of these routes bore the marks of their journey. The descendants of the first migrants to enter Polynesia by the southern route survived into historic times in the Marquesas Islands, Mangareva, and Easter Island. They also formed an important element in the great 12th century migration to New Zealand. Although they showed little or no Melanesian blood, they shared various culture traits with that region. The most important of these were a vigorous head cult, with headhunting and the preservation of the heads of both enemies and ancestors, cannibalism of a gastronomic rather than ceremonial type, extreme political fragmentation and constant intertribal warfare, and a vigorous, predominantly curvilinear representative art in which human figures were the usual subjects.

The migrants who came by the northern route occupied Micronesia and seem to have been the first settlers in Hawaii. A radio carbon date from Saipan in the Carolines gives approximately 1500 B.C. for a settlement there, but sporadic migrations have continued into modern times and the bulk of the Micronesians are of deutero- rather than proto-Malay physical type.

After a sojourn in Micronesia and cultural adjustments to atoll conditions encountered there, descendants of these migrants moved southward into Polynesia. Their heaviest impact seems to have come in the west, on Samoa and Tonga, where they modified the older culture so completely that if it were not for physical and linguistic factors, these island groups would certainly be classed as Micronesian rather than Polynesian. From Samoa and Tonga they spread eastward across the intervening groups to the Society islands. The invaders were technologically inferior to the tribes whom they found in possession. During their Micronesian sojourn they had lost much of their skill as farmers, makers of stone implements and bark cloth, and as wood carvers. To compensate for this, they had developed a superior type of canoe and sail, and patterns for the political organization and exploitation of conquered tribes. They found the Polynesians of the older stratum divided into innumerable little local tribes quite unable to cooperate against the invaders. They were thus able to establish themselves as a ruling aristocracy and to set up states involving a sort of feudal organization. A high chief stood at the head, with lower chiefs drawn partly from the invaders, partly from the hereditary chiefs of subjugated tribes.

However, it seems that by no means all the tribes were willing to submit. In later times the Polynesians recognized a type of surrender with honors of war in which a defeated group was given time to make and provision canoes and then allowed to depart in search of a new home. We do not know whether such a pattern existed at this time, but the arrival of the Micronesians certainly set in train a new period of voyaging and exploration which lasted from the 10th to the 14th century A.D.

New Zealand had been discovered and lightly colonized long before, but now there were the great migrations from which most of the modern Maori claim descent. During this period also, migrants of mixed blood and culture sailed northward from the Society group to Hawaii, where they established themselves as rulers of the older population and also, if the traditions are to be believed, introduced various food plants and other elements of higher culture.

The westward migrations of the Malayo-Polynesians are more difficult to reconstruct, but that these migrations were on no inconsiderable scale is proved by the presence in Madagascar of a population not only Malayo-Polynesian in language and culture but also both proto-Malay and deutero-Malay in physical type. The Indian Ocean is the most benevolent of the earth's oceans. Its monsoons make it possible to sail with a steady following wind either east or west, according to the season. It is highly probable that while the Greeks were still harbor-hopping along the barren coasts between the mouth of the Red Sea and India, the seawise Malayo-Polynesians had found their way from Java and Sumatra to East Africa.

The Imerina tribe of Madagascar have preserved a tradition of their own migration. On linguistic evidence they seem to have come from Sumatra in about the 5th century A.D., certainly long after the first settlement of the island. According to this tradition their ancestors left a homeland in the East in search of a "land where there was no death." After a long voyage they made a landfall among the amiable black people and, since they saw no tombs, concluded that their search had been successful. They were disillusioned when they discovered that these people ate their own dead. They sailed southward following along the coast and made another settlement among people who were also friendly but who had tails. This finally offended their aesthetic sense to the point where they once more took to their boats and sailed southward again, making their last landfall at Tulear on the far southwestern corner of Madagascar. From there they traveled northeastward over land to the central plateau where at last they rested.

If one substitutes for the romantic phrase "land where there was no death," the more prosaic one, "region where there was no malaria," such repeated onward movements become more reasonable, since the east coast of Africa is malarial and the Madagascan plateau has been fever free until very recent times (see pp. 26, 395). There is also much realistic support for the conjecture that the Malayo-Polynesian's migration route took them well to the north of Madagascar and then down the African coast. The Mozambique current sets southward so strongly that sailing canoes would have found it difficult to beat up against it. Even today outrigger canoes, with sails of very nearly marginal-Polynesian type, are used on the west coast of Madagascar but are unknown on the east coast. Lastly, had the migrants sailed directly across the Indian Ocean they could hardly have missed the Mascarens (Mauretius and Reunion) or Seychelle Islands. These groups were not only uninhabited at the time of their discovery by Europeans but also sheltered giant tortoises and succulent wingless birds which disappeared within a few years of the first human settlement.

Much of the east coast of Africa is bleak and inhospitable, offering little encouragement to settlement by migrants accustomed to the lush tropics of Indonesia. Nevertheless, there are small scattered areas in which settlements could be established with an economy based on southeast Asiatic crops. Prior to the introduction of American food plants, the most important crops in tropical Africa were the yam, banana, and taro, all of Southeastern Asiatic origin and probably introduced by proto-Malay migrants. Rice may well have been introduced into tropical Africa from the same source, since a primitive type of rice culture exists in Madagascar.

The earliest date for the Malayo-Polynesian movement to Africa and Madagascar can only be conjectured, but stone implements of the characteristic Southeast Asiatic Neolithic types have not been reported from either locality. This does not mean that they may not come to light when intensive archeological work is undertaken in these areas, but on the basis of present knowledge it seems improbable that the main Malayo-Polynesian migrations took place before the migrants had become acquainted with iron working. Conversely, the techniques of African iron working, the shapes of many African tools and weapons, and particularly the use throughout Africa of various modified forms of the piston bellows, an East Asiatic appliance, suggest that the iron working of Negro Africa was borrowed from Malayo-Polynesian sources. (See p. 110.)

Chapter XIV

Oceania and Madagascar

THE MARGINAL Malayo-Polynesian cultures which have survived in Oceania and Madagascar have contributed little to the main streams of cultural evolution. However, they have provided students of society and culture with some of their most interesting comparative material. The relative isolation of many of the islands and the general tendency of the Malayo-Polynesians to live in small endogamous tribes, or even villages which avoid outside contacts, has provided an excellent opportunity for the study of the results of independent cultural growth. One finds every conceivable change rung on a small series of cultural themes which are present almost everywhere. Needless to say, this cultural variety makes generalization difficult. Parallel independent developments seem to have taken place in some regions, while the freedom of movement of the Malayo-Polynesian sea rovers has resulted in a series of broken distributions which defy the neat culture area classification possible in continental regions. Thus, in a general description of Polynesia, a number of the statements true for most Polynesian localities simply do not apply to Samoa. This group was a sort of aristocratic republic whose members paid little attention to genealogy and even less to religion. The regular Polynesian gods appeared as figures in a pleasant and interesting mythology, but there was not a single temple or professional priest in the entire group and the ubiquitous ancestral spirits received scant attention.

The most famous of the "primitive" Malayo-Polynesian areas is Polynesia. Unfortunately it is also one of the areas whose aboriginal cultures are least known, since it received the full impact of late 18th and early 19th century missionary ardor, epidemic diseases, and commercial exploitation. By the time modern ethnological methods for collecting and analyzing cultural material had been developed, most of the Polynesian cultures were moribund. Early visitors have left valuable records of what they saw but usually misunderstood. They interpreted the Polynesians as a happy combination of the Natural Man, then being idealized by Rousseau and his romantic followers, and the aristocratic, class organized society so dear to all "right thinking" gentlemen of the period. The casualness of Polynesian sex mores and the beauty of the Polynesian women, especially as viewed by sailors many months at sea, also contributed to the picture of an earthly paradise. Unfortunately, the combination of misunderstanding and romanticism led to the development of certain stereotypes regarding Polynesian culture; stereotypes which were followed unquestioningly by later authors of travel books on the area and also by many serious students. Even today there is a tendency to view Polynesian political organization in terms of European monarchy and Polynesian religion in terms of classical mythology and an established church.

It is unfortunate that the early visitors who wrote about Polynesian culture did not include at least one "braw Highlander," who might have recognized how much Polynesian tribes and Scottish clans were alike. In both, the clansmen occupied a particular territory, claimed descent from a remote common ancestor, and normally intermarried among themselves. In both the chief was simply the man who traced his descent from the common ancestor in the most direct line. He could never lack for a successor since, if the tribesmen were taken away one by one beginning with the individual of highest descent, the last survivor could legitimately assume the chiefly title and insignia. The respect and obedience accorded the chief by the clansmen were owed to him less as an individual than as a symbol of the clan. Chief and followers were united by reciprocal obligations springing from their ties as kindred.

To this extent Polynesians and Scots were alike. In New Zealand, the Marquesas Islands, and a few other localities, every tribe stood alone

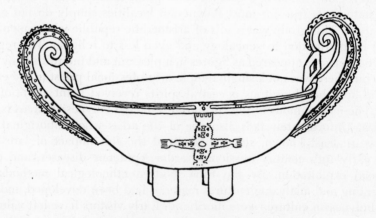

FOOD BOWL, ADMIRALTY ISLANDS

except for temporary alliances, much as in the Highlands. In those Polynesian areas where the later migrants had set up states, notably Hawaii and the Society Islands, the chief of the dominant tribe became a king and received tribute from the other tribes, usually interpreted as an offering in repayment for the use of his supernatural powers in their behalf. The other members of this tribe enjoyed added prestige but they

FLY WHISK HANDLE, TAHITI

were not transformed into feudal nobles. Unless they reinforced their position by marriage with high ranking families from the subject tribes, they had to work like anyone else.

Polynesian kings surrounded themselves with courts which were supported by forced donations from their subjects. The court was made up partly of royal kindred but mostly of individuals chosen for special abilities without regard to their origin. Visitors from other islands gravitated to the court, where, if they possessed the necessary personal qualifications, they would be made royal body servants. Since they were not descended from the local ancestors, they were non-conductors of the local variety of *mana* (see p. 189) and could touch the royal person and belongings without danger to themselves or others. Famous warriors also came to court, where they not only formed a royal guard but also stood ready to enforce royal decrees. Councilors were chosen for their wisdom irrespective of their origin. Lastly, every court included a large number of male and female entertainers. In southeastern Polynesia these entertainers were organized into a society whose members were vowed to celibacy though by no means to chastity. They traveled from court to court in troupes, putting on dances and dramatic performances of an erotic character. It is interesting to note that the natives themselves regarded the royal courts as centers of idleness and profligacy.

There were two points at which the Polynesian social system was unique. Instead of looking back to a great age, the Polynesians looked forward. They conceived of the tribe as an "upward growing, outward pushing tree." Each generation was superior in *mana* to the generation before and the eldest child in a family ranked its own parents. This was carried so far that in many Polynesian localities a chief automatically

OUTRIGGER SAILING VESSEL

lost his status as tribal head on the birth of an heir and ruled as regent only, until such time as his son became old enough to take over.

The second distinctive feature of Polynesian social organization, and one which has caused endless confusion to students, was their peculiar system for reckoning descent and establishing rank. The first born child, whether boy or girl, had highest rank within the family. The second born came next, and so down the line. In recounting genealogies, the line was traced through the ancestor of highest rank in each generation, whether man or woman. Polynesian descent was thus neither matrilineal nor patrilineal but primogenitural, an arrangement found nowhere else in the world. In theory, the social position of the individual was established by both his own birth order and that of his ancestors. Since all a tribe's members were descended from the tribe's founder, the relative ranks of any two individuals within the tribe could be established simply by tracing their genealogies. The more eldest children in such a genealogy, the higher the rank. Since genealogies were also used to establish the individual's rights to land and to other privileges, such as a seat in the tribal sacred place, they were kept with great care. Authentic genealogies running to twenty and thirty generations were not uncommon, while some, probably mythical in the early parts, ran for as much as eighty generations.

The primogenitural method of reckoning descent and rank had important repercussions on Polynesian social and political organization. It meant that many sisters were socially superior to their brothers, wives superior to their husbands, and so forth. This resulted in an unusual degree of equality between the sexes. Although women were subjected to a few taboos which did not affect men, and each sex had its own prescribed interests and activities, there is probably no other "primitive" group in which men and women stood so nearly on a par socially.

The primogenitural pattern also had important effects on the political organization. If the eldest child of a chief was a daughter, she would enjoy the highest social rank in the tribe and transmit this to her eldest child. At the same time it was impossible for her to perform the complete functions of a chief, which included acting as war leader. In such cases the chieftainship would temporarily pass to the oldest of her brothers, but if her eldest child was a son, the chieftainship would revert to him. If the senior line had first-born daughters for several generations while the junior lines had first-born sons, the chieftainship would tend to become fixed in the junior line. At the same time, the senior line would maintain its higher rank and even broaden the social gap between itself and the ruling line generation by generation. Thus in 18th century Tonga, the individual of highest rank was the first-born daughter of the king's elder sister, also first born. Whenever the king met the lady he had to acknowledge her superior rank by stooping and removing his upper garment. It is said that the king resented this so intensely that whenever he knew the lady was in the neighborhood he kept a screen of scouts out so that he would be warned in time to avoid meeting her.

When a first-born son appeared in the senior line a serious problem would arise, since the junior line, understandably, would not want to surrender its powers. The usual system was to make the representative of the senior line a sacred chief immobilized by his sanctity. In extreme cases such a chief rendered everything he touched, even the ground he walked on or a tree his shadow fell on, *taboo,* so that he could only go out at night and had to be carried even then. None except the designated servants could touch his person or handle his clothes, and any vessel from which he ate or drank had to be promptly destroyed to preserve others from injury. One is reminded of the plight of the equally sacred and impotent Japanese Emperors under the Shogunate. (See pp. 582–583.)

Several of the Polynesian groups had found brother and sister marriage a simple answer to the problems raised by the primogenitural descent system. If the eldest child was a girl, she was married to her younger brother. In this way all conflicting claims to the chieftainship were eliminated while the offspring received a double dose of the hereditary *mana.* In most parts of Polynesia, brother and sister marriage of

WOOD PILLOW, NEW GUINEA

any other type was as rigidly reprehended as among ourselves. However, in Hawaii, the desire to build up *mana* seems to have led to the marriage even of elder brothers to younger sisters, an arrangement which was regarded as scandalous by the other Polynesians.

BIRD MAN, EASTER ISLAND

It is impossible to understand Polynesian political organization and government without reference to the concepts of *mana* and *taboo*. Unfortunately, neither of these terms can be directly translated into English. The nearest equivalent for *mana* would be "power for accomplishment." Thus any object or person who was capable of more than ordinary performance, whether the subject was a hook that caught more than the usual number of fish or a chief who was more than usually good in diplomatic maneuvering, showed in this way that it had mana. A similar idea is found among many uncivilized people, but no other group had systematized it as thoroughly as the Polynesians. They developed it into a logical philosophic concept by which all manifestations of superior ability were reduced to a common denominator.

Mana was completely inanimate and non-sentient, like our own concepts of force or energy. It was thought of as universally present and available for use, given the correct techniques. One might compare it to radio waves, and the people or things which manifested it to receiving sets. Gods and spirits as well as human beings owed their power to their ability to receive and concentrate mana. The ability varied greatly in degree, so that a living chief might actually possess much more mana than a ghost or even one of the less important gods. Mana was highly

infectious and anything which had come in contact with an individual
or object of high mana was thus rendered dangerous for individuals of
lower mana.

While the mana belief was superficially similar to such American
Indian concepts as *maniton* power and *orenda,* there was one very fundamental difference which reflected the different attitudes of Polynesians
and Indians toward what we call the supernatural. The American Indian
recognized the presence of power by a subjective test. He knew it was
there because he felt awe, wonder, or what Goldenweiser would call
the "religious thrill." The Polynesian had no such subjective test for
mana. He could no more recognize its presence before he saw it act than
one would recognize that a wire was charged with electricity before he
experimented with it. For this reason objects or places which mana
rendered dangerous had to be marked. Everywhere in Polynesia *taboo*
signs were used to indicate that a place was sacred or that property was
under magical protection.

Taboo also has no exact equivalent in English. The word first became familiar to Europeans through the publication of Captain Cook's
writings in the late 18th century, but it supplied a previous lack in the
English language so neatly that it was immediately adopted. To the
Polynesians *tapu* meant something forbidden, something involving supernatural danger either to oneself or to others. Tapu did not imply that
the thing was immoral or even illegal. The tapu object or act was always
associated with mana. Violation of the tapu by one with less mana than
the one in whose name it was imposed was automatically followed by
calamity.

It was only in the conquest states where the rulers and subjects were
not linked by ties of kinship that the taboo institution was used for exploitation. This reached its maximum in Hawaii where, following the
eighteenth century conquest of the entire group by Kamehameha I,
successive rulers and a well-organized priesthood imposed more and
more taboos until the commoners were reduced to poverty and despera-
tion. Deliverance came as a result of a struggle between church and
state. The king himself broke the taboo by eating publicly from the same
dish with his queen. When it was seen that nothing happened to either
one of them, word spread like wildfire. The entire institution collapsed.
The commoners rose, overthrew the priests and destroyed the temples,
so that Hawaii was without an official religion when the first missionaries arrived.

Polynesian religion, like Polynesian social organization, has been
extensively misinterpreted. The only supernatural beings worshipped
everywhere (except Samoa) were the spirits of the tribal ancestors.
Each tribe had its own sacred place used for this worship and also in

connection with funeral rites. The souls of dead chiefs were especially powerful because of their identification with the tribe as a whole. At a greater emotional distance than the ancestors, but not necessarily more powerful, there were a host of highly specialized deities which took care of every conceivable activity. Thus there were not only gods of canoe makers and fishermen, but also gods of thieves and even of various sexual practices which the natives themselves regarded as perversions. Many of these divine specialists seem to have been the ghosts of especially skillful practitioners of the craft involved, preferably tribe members. Deities whose aid was in demand might have shrines where small sacrifices were made by individuals needing their help.

Lastly, there were a series of great deities who were associated with creation or who supervised whole departments of the cosmos. Thus

STONE TIKI, MARQUESAS

Tangaloa was God of the Sea and, quite understandably, the special patron of the Polynesian aristocracies which traced their origin to the later invaders from Micronesia. Rongo was God of Vegetation and, by extension, patron of both forests and agriculture. These great deities were sometimes made the subjects of formal state cults in the regions where states existed, but in most of Polynesia they had been "gently relegated to the abyss of first causes." They were literary deities, a fact which most writers on Polynesian religion failed to realize.

Where groups of tribes had been organized into states, as in Hawaii and the Society Islands, there were elaborate temple establishments in which rites were performed on behalf of the state and its rulers. The attendance of the subjects was insisted upon as an expression of political loyalty although they might not be allowed to take part in the actual ceremonies. Thus in Hawaii only members of the chiefly group could enter the temple enclosure. The commoners stood outside and went through the required genuflections and responses when signaled by a priest who stood on the wall. Sacrifices were elaborate, with human sacrifice a feature of most state cults, and rituals were long and complicated. As in ancient Rome, any slip in the performance of a ritual made it necessary to begin again at the beginning, and, in Polynesia, carelessness was usually discouraged by executing the one who made the mistake.

Professional priests were required even for the tribal ancestor cults. They were of two classes, ritual priests and inspirational priests. The ritual priests knew the procedures required in various ceremonies and also were repositories of tribal lore of all sorts. The inspirational priests were hysterics who had the happy ability of becoming possessed by gods or ancestral spirits. While in a trance state they acted as divine mouthpieces, giving oracles, demanding sacrifices, and so forth. Both inspirational priests and images were regarded as media through which the gods and their worshippers could be brought into closer contact. The god was called into his image to receive the sacrifice or hear the prayer, just as he came into the inspirational priest to make known his wants. It is significant of Polynesian attitudes in general that ceremonial priests everywhere ranked inspirational priests so greatly that the two did not conflict.

The intricate designs used for the decoration of utensils and clubs and in tattooing seem to have had no magical significance. However, the quality of Polynesian art as a whole is highly suggestive to anyone familiar with the rules for interpreting modern psychological projective tests such as the Rorschach. Polynesian art, outside the area already noted as showing Melanesian influences, was characterized by extraordinary feeling for form and finish combined with a curiously static quality.

WARRIOR, NEW BRITAIN

Surfaces were divided into many small sections filled with innumerable repetitions of small design details, suggesting the work of compulsive neurotics. The absence of color was striking. Wood was polished to bring out the natural grain or, at most, blackened. Except in Hawaii, bark cloth was painted in muted browns and blacks when it was decorated at all. These features certainly suggest a low level of emotional response in the artists, something quite in line with the actual conditions.

The Polynesian approach to life was kinetic rather than emotional. One apprehended reality by working with it, and found the universe orderly and comprehensible. If one seeks for a single term to characterize their culture the best one would be *manipulative.* The highest prestige was accorded to the most skilled technicians, no matter what the activity might be. Even in the field of interpersonal relations technique reigned supreme. The rules governing social behavior were elaborate and formal and could never be ignored. Social interaction took on the aspects of a chess game in which the player who made the correct moves in the correct order could compel compliance with his demands. Sex was regarded as an enjoyable physical function on a par with eating. Romantic love was considered an adolescent aberration, and admiration went to the skillful amorist of either sex rather than the faithful one.

Even in its ruins Polynesian culture has maintained these fundamental attitudes. European visitors are usually charmed by the Polynesians, who take as much pride in their skill as hosts as a good Swiss hotel keeper would, but there is as little emotional involvement in one case as in the other.

Melanesia shows a greater variety of cultures and languages than any other world area of the same size. This makes generalizations exceedingly difficult, and the statements which follow must be understood to refer to a substantial majority of Melanesian cultures rather than to the area as a whole. Although Polynesians and Melanesians spoke languages of the same stock and were both Stone Age agriculturists, the two regions differed fundamentally in their approach to most of the problems of existence. The Melanesian world view was infinitely more primitive than the Polynesian one. Their universe, in so far as they conceived of one, was unorganized and subject to the caprice of innumerable beings, none of whom had more than feeble and local powers. It was a universe without natural laws and thus particularly susceptible to magical manipulation. There were no temples, priests, or actively worshipped beings of divine stature anywhere in Melanesia outside Fiji, where Polynesian influence was strong. On the other hand, magicians were everywhere. Every man knew some magic and would have felt lost without it, since he needed it both to advance his own interests and to guard them against others. The Melanesians were, by and large, a jealous and fearful people who believed that a man's good fortune must be at the expense of someone else. Thus, in the Trobriand Islands, the natives had a saying, "yam feller walk around along night" and believed that a man's success in yam growing depended upon the magic by which he could keep yams from leaving his own field and could lure other men's yams into it.

This did not mean that the Melanesians were not careful and laborious farmers. Many of them were and took great pride in the good appearance of their gardens and even in producing a surplus of food

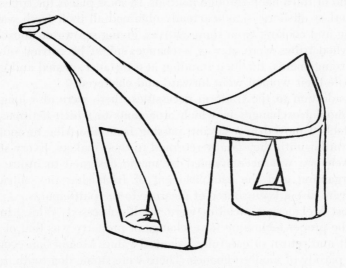

COCONUT GRATER, MARIANAS

which they knew would never be used. They were also competent craftsmen, although their attitude toward technology was different from that of the Polynesians. Many of their appliances were ingenious and effective, even better than the Polynesian equivalents, but the Melanesians in general lacked the Polynesian feeling for form and finish. Surfaces were left rough and elaborate carving might be lavished on an accidentally asymmetrical object. Skilled professionals of the Polynesian sort were to be found only in those parts of Melanesia which had come under Polynesian influence.

Instead, the Melanesians had developed complex patterns of local specialization in which a particular tribe produced one or two things in quantity and traded their products over a wide area. This was the more surprising since every Melanesian tribe was constantly at war with at least some of its neighbors. The result was a curious pattern of economic interdependence and social avoidance.

The tribal specialization often involved the commonest and most necessary tools and utensils. Thus in the Admiralty Islands one tribe made all the matting mosquito bags used in the group, another produced most of the pottery. An interior tribe in one island made all the nets used by the coast tribes for fishing. Still another tribe produced all the weapons used in the group. This specialization probably developed because it was the only tribe which had in its territory obsidian for making dagger blades and spearheads. Even tribes which were at war with the weapon makers relied on them for armament, obtaining their munitions at second or third hand through neutrals. In some places the tribes living on waterless offshore islands actually obtained all their fresh water for drinking and cooking from shore natives, giving sea water in exchange. Even when tribes were at war, exchanges might be carried on under truce arrangements, the men standing at a distance, armed and glowering, while their women went forward and chaffered.

In addition to the trade in necessities, there were also long series of ceremonial exchanges in which ornaments to which fictitious value was attached moved in a circuit, passing from one tribe to another in regular order until they finally returned to their makers. Every stage of such exchange was accompanied by magic designed to insure profit; the bargaining and the establishment of friendship ties outside the tribes were also a keen source of pleasure to the participants.

Most Melanesian societies were wealth-obsessed. While, in Polynesia, the proper technique for exchange of property was that of voluntary gift and return of carefully balanced value, Melanesian economics seem a parody of modern finance. There were stone, dog tooth, feather, mat, and a numerous variety of shell currencies in different parts of the area. Sometimes half a dozen currencies would be in use in a single locality, with fluctuating exchange rates. Moreover, only certain currencies could be used for particular transactions, such as dowry or land purchase. Loans were made with interest rates, shares in pigs were purchased on spec, and the Melanesian financier spent most of his time in trying to collect from his debtors and avoid his own creditors.

All this was really a sort of economic play conducted with surplus. Even the bankrupt Melanesian was still assured of food and shelter. His kin group would make sure that he received these, although their charity would not be tempered by any undue regard for his feelings.

The basic pattern of social and political organization for the area was one of small tribes, each of which embraced several communities. There was no central control within the tribe and the only units larger than tribes were occasional temporary alliances. Within the tribe there were a series of clans, either matrilineal or patrilineal, which often but not always coincided with the communities. As a rule, the tribe was strictly endogamous, the clan exogamous. In some regions there were other and more complicated marriage regulations reminiscent of the Australian system. Adolescents enjoyed a period of premarital experimentation much as in Polynesia, but marriages were usually arranged by the families involved with an eye to financial advantage rather than congeniality of the partners. Even in the matrilineal societies the position of women was relatively low. Polygyny was common and wives were valued mainly for their economic contributions. Women were dominated within the family by either their husbands or their brothers.

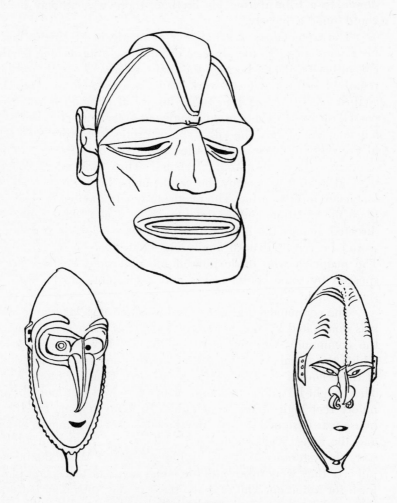

NEW GUINEA MASKS

They were completely excluded from the ceremonial life of the tribe except for providing the necessary mystified audience at public performances, and even the magic which they knew was of a minor sort.

In contrast with the theoretically rigid Polynesian system, Melanesian society was exceedingly fluid. Wealth gave prestige; the loss of it, loss of social position. Genealogies were not reckoned beyond the short distance required by marriage regulations, and every man could find his place in the social hierarchy by his own efforts. There were no hereditary chiefs anywhere in Melanesia outside Fiji where, again, Polynesian influence is obvious. Tribal rule was vested in an oligarchy of wealthy and important men. Although an individual of outstanding ability might dominate a tribe during his lifetime, there was no way in which he could found a dynasty.

The tremendous development of magic in Melanesia has already been mentioned. In the absence of anything approaching law or political authority, magic became the main agency of social control. It was regarded as legitimate to work magic against a recalcitrant debtor or against one who failed to fulfill his social obligations. However, this passed over readily into use of magic out of jealousy or for spite. Malevolent magicians were the only type of professionals present everywhere in the regions. They derived their profit not only from working magic on demand but also from blackmail. Thus, if a man wanted magic worked against an enemy, he would make his arrangements with the magician and pay a fee. The magician would then go to the enemy, explain the situation, and ask how much he would bid to have the magic directed against the first man. This process of playing back and forth would be repeated until finally one contestant had reached his limit. The magician who made himself too obnoxious would eventually be speared by some conscientious and respectable citizen with a strong sense of civic duty.

The ceremonial and aesthetic life of most Melanesian communities was dominated by the men's secret societies. Even the scenic center of the community was the men's house, a relatively huge structure on which the members lavished their engineering and artistic skills. Some of these houses were extraordinary constructions for Stone Age people. They might be as much as four or five hundred feet long and eighty to ninety feet high at the front gable. In many regions the front of the house was designed to look like the head and open mouth of an animal and the house itself symbolized a supernatural being inside whom all sorts of mysterious and magical things occurred. When the boys reached puberty they were taken into the men's house or to a secret place in the bush for initiation. This is reminiscent of the Australian pattern in that the candidate was symbolically killed and revived, actually subjected to various painful mutilations which would later mark him as an initiate, and given instruction in various magical matters.

The first initiation was only a beginning, like the Blue Lodge in Masonry. It had to be paid for, but even the poorest family could usually finance this step for its sons. From time to time, as a man acquired the necessary wealth, he was initiated into higher degrees one after another. Each degree carried with it an increased knowledge of magic, the right to handle certain objects which possessed power and from contact with which the individual drew power, the right to wear special ornaments on dress occasions, and the right to occupy a certain place in the men's house. Membership in the higher degrees of the secret society was not only a symbol of economic success but also contributed to it. When a man took a higher degree he had to distribute a substantial amount of property among those who had already taken the degree. More important, with each degree he learned property-protecting magic and the antidotes for it. It was thus possible for him to exploit the members of all those degrees through which he had passed while he could

BACHELOR RAIMENT, NEW GUINEA

only be exploited by members of his own and higher degrees. A man took as many degrees as he could afford, and at the apex of a society there stood a very small group of old and rich men who constituted the real rulers of the community.

Melanesian art in general was characterized by vigor, not to say violence. Human, bird, and fish forms were combined and distorted with Gothic freedom, color was liberally used, and even the non-representational art was curvilinear, with a fluid, dynamic quality quite at variance with Polynesian norms. The most complicated figures and masks came from New Ireland. These were carved in elaborate open work and painted with numerous small designs. The Sepik River region of New Guinea had a distinctive style in which the nose, here used as a symbol of virility, was always exaggerated. The Sulka of New Britain had masks that looked like surrealist nightmares, with shocking pink as a favorite color.

Melanesian tribal character was too varied to permit a neat characterization of the sort possible for Polynesia. Europeans have disliked the

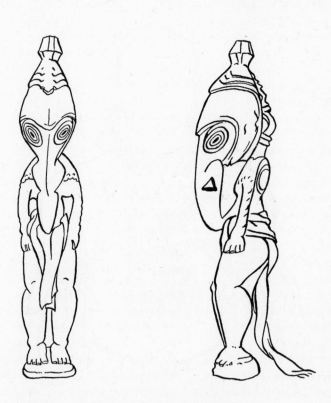

WOODEN FIGURE, NEW GUINEA

Melanesians almost as consistently as they have liked the Polynesians—this in spite of their industriousness and their understanding of our kind of economic values and motivations. Most of the tribes seem to have been the victims of deep-seated psychological insecurity and intense hostilities, which were normally repressed through fear. These attitudes found expression in fear of the supernatural, a fear dramatized in the terrifying masks and costumes of the secret societies, extreme development of malevolent magic, and orgiastic victory rites with prisoner torture and cannibalism.

Micronesia, after long scientific neglect, is now being made the subject of intensive investigations along all lines. When these investigations are finished, more information will be available on this region than on any other part of Oceania, but it is not available at this writing. Micronesia maintained closer touch with Indonesia, and, indirectly, with the Southeast Asiatic mainland than did any other of the marginal Malayo-Polynesian localities. It even received such relatively late Southeast Asiatic culture elements as loom weaving, pottery, and rice. However, most of the Micronesian Islands were atolls, and geography thus imposed strict limitations on cultural development. Agriculture was exceedingly difficult. Taro could only be raised in beds which were dug down to bed rock and floored with soil manufactured by composting. In the Gilbert group, breadfruit trees were planted in pits cut in the coral rock and filled with pumice, which was gathered whenever it washed ashore and pounded to powder. The atolls provided no good stone for implements and very little good wood. In spite of this, the technology was excellent. Emphasis was on utility rather than decoration, and the best work was expended on sailing canoes and men's club houses. The latter served as dormitories for the unmarried men and visitors from other islands and as club rooms, but they lacked any of the Melanesian magical and religious connotations. The sailing canoes were the best in the Pacific. The Micronesians had also developed a real science of navigation, and the combination made possible a network of inter-island trade and political ties. Certain tribes or islands had others as vassals, receiving tribute and extending protection. At the same time patterns of hereditary chieftainship and of extended genealogical records seem to have been lacking. Power rested in the hands of men who had enough knowledge of magic and tribal lore and sufficient strength of character to dominate their tribesmen. Social organization followed the familiar Oceanic pattern of endogamous tribes and exogamous lineages, in this region more frequently matrilineal than patrilineal. Supernaturalism was poorly developed. There was a lively fear of ghosts and sea spirits, but there seem to have been no sacred structures, cult objects, or professional priests.

WAR GOD, HAWAII

Most of the Micronesians were courageous and determined fighters. Inter-tribal wars were common. The Gilbert Islanders fought pitched battles in which the line of battle consisted of champions protected by complete coconut fiber armor and armed with shark-tooth edged swords and daggers. Each armored man was attended by one or more unarmored squires who stood behind him and passed him new weapons as needed.

The Malayo-Polynesian outpost in Madagascar has already been mentioned (see p. 177). Apparently at least two groups of Southeast Asiatic migrants reached the island. Even the first settlers seem to have worked iron, so could scarcely have left Indonesia before 1000 B.C. Although there are traditions of their having found Negrito hunters and food-gatherers in possession, the newcomers seem to have encountered no serious resistance. They spread over the island rapidly and adjusted to the great variety of environments which it provided.

Madagascar is nearly twice the size of Great Britain and Ireland combined. The east coast and eastern slopes of the central plateau are hot all year round, with frequent rain even in the so-called dry season and almost continuous downpours in the wet season. Jungle growth is dense, and fields which have been cleared grow up again in two or three years. The central plateau has a temperate climate, with frost in winter, because of its altitude, and a moderate rainfall concentrated in a rainy season. At the time of the first settlement it seems to have been covered with deciduous forests, but cutting and burning agriculture combined wih cattle grazing had resulted in complete deforestation by the time Europeans arrived. The southern end of the island and the broad western coastal plain are either swampy or arid and unsuited to any economy except cattle raising. Irrigated rice culture is possible in the valleys of most of the westward flowing rivers, but it was unknown there in pre-European times and modern attempts to introduce it have met with considerable resistance from the local tribes.

It has already been noted that the route of migration from Indonesia seems to have passed to the north of Madagascar and down the African coast with first settlements on the western side of the island. The historic distribution of culture elements would seem to bear this out. The most archaic cultures are found in the eastern mountains and along the southeast coast, although the latter region includes tribes who claim Arab descent and show some Arab influence. The central plateau was dominated by the Imerina, descendants of the last Malayo-Polynesian migrants who, on linguistic evidence, probably came from Sumatra in the 5th century A.D. The arid regions of the south and west were occupied by tribes who were strongly Negroid in physical type and who depended largely on cattle. However, all Madagascar tribes spoke mutually intelligible dialects of a single Malayo-Polynesian language and followed the same basic patterns in both social organization and religion.

In spite of these uniformities, differences in technology make possible a partial reconstruction of the cultures of the two groups of Malayo-Polynesian migrants. The earlier group seems to have brought the regular Southeast Asiatic crops, with the possible exception of breadfruit, but placed their main reliance on rice raised by the cutting and burning method. They probably had the pig and chicken, although the former never became economically important. Although they knew how to smelt and forge iron and mined gold, which they regarded as sacred, they were ignorant of pottery making or weaving. Matting and bark cloth were used for clothing. Megalithic monuments were erected as part of the ancestor cult.

The later migrants brought with them irrigated rice culture, pottery making, and highly developed weaving, including the technique of making cloth by the *ikat* technique. They did not introduce either the plow or the wheel, neither of which were known in Madagascar until brought in by Europeans.

Madagascar cattle are of the Asiatic *zebu* type, as are most African breeds. They were probably introduced from Africa at some time between the first and second Malayo-Polynesian migrations and were never very successfully integrated into the utility economy of the tribes living outside the arid regions. Milk was of very minor importance in the diet of any agricultural tribes, hide found so little technological use that animals were usually cut up with the skin on, and even beef was eaten only when animals had to be killed for sacrifice. The irrigated rice farmers found the greatest practical value of their cattle to be manure and kept them in semi-subterranean pens so that none of this would be lost. At the same time, cattle carried tremendous emotional value as symbols of prestige and as the only form of interest-bearing investment possible under native conditions.

The social organization followed the familiar Malayo-Polynesian pattern. The basic unit was the village, an endogamous patrilineal descent group. Several villages which had a common ancestry and occupied contiguous territories might form a clan, but such a group had no internal organization, and any village which became spatially separated from the rest promptly forgot its kin ties. Every village was divided into a number of lineages, each of which traced descent from a particular founder less distant in time than the founder of the village or clan. Each lineage owned a separate ward within the village and had the right to exploit a certain part of the village land. The ranking individual in the village was the hereditary head of the senior lineage. He acted as priest at the ancestor sacrifices and was held in deep respect. At the same time he could scarcely be called a chief, since he had no delegated powers outside his own lineage. All matters involving community interest were settled by an informal council of lineage heads and other important men.

There was a well developed legal system with orally transmitted law codes and a considerable body of regulations dealing with property and contracts. Formal trials were held with the taking of evidence, and decisions were handed down by the village elders. Punishment was by fines or, in extreme cases, by expulsion from the village. Evidence was taken under a system of oaths which passed over into trial by ordeal. Ordeals were used only in cases where the evidence was inconclusive, and physically dangerous ordeals such as swimming a river full of crocodiles were administered only to suspected sorcerers.

In those regions in which there were no political units larger than villages the legal system and its administration were reminiscent of Indonesian *adat* law. Where kingdoms had come into existence, the system was reminiscent of Africa. The king acted as court of last appeal. In particular he had to confirm all capital sentences passed by village courts, since all subjects were considered his personal property, not to be destroyed without his permission. The king also could promulgate new laws and received a substantial share of his income from fines imposed. The ease with which an Indonesian *adat* type legal system could be converted into an African type legal system suggests that this may constitute another unsuspected cultural link beween the two areas.

The development of political units larger than the clan seems to have been due to foreign influence. The ruling clans in these units usually claimed Arab ancestry, and the Imerina empire, which controlled two-thirds of the island during the 19th century, was a later creation whose organization was aided by English missionaries. Traditionally the development of a state proceeded as follows: a strong and pugnacious clan would reduce neighboring clans to vassalage by force of arms. Other clans would then submit voluntarily in order to terminate long-standing feuds. The latter is not improbable since at first submission involved no exploitation. The ruling clan contented itself with superior prestige, symbolized by the exclusive right to wear gold, and with the increased war power provided by contingents from the subject clans. Its members occupied their own territory, depended on their own crops, and carried on all the usual occupations. The head of the senior lineage in the ruling clan was addressed as king and had insignia of office used on state occasions, but even he did not hesitate to work in his own fields.

A state of this sort included three social classes: royal, common, and slave. In cases where a once royal clan had been defeated and ousted from leadership, its members constituted a fourth class, intermediate between royal and common. They retained certain ceremonial rites, usually that of killing the cattle at sacrifices, for which they received a fee, but they were rigidly debarred from any part in government. Each class was normally endogamous.

The slave class included both actual slaves and the descendants of freed slaves. Slaves were mainly unransomed prisoners of war and their descendants. They were attached to particular lineages and their condition differed little from that of poor clan members. Slavery never became imporant in Madagascar economy, and slave markets were a late development under European or Arab influence. In most tribes the sale of a slave was regarded as discreditable to both slave and master.

The final step in the evolution of kingdoms came with attempts of the ruling clan to increase its control of the subject clans, and to exploit them economically. One method for doing this was to place families from the royal clan in each subject village, where they were supported by the villagers and at the same time could watch for signs of revolt. Within a few generations this arrangement degenerated into a sort of decentralized feudal system. The ruling families still formed an endogamous group, but they identified themselves with particular villages or commoner clans which they ruled and led these in war against each other, with a resulting collapse of the central authority. In spite of political disintegration, the blood tie between members of the former royal clan was still emphasized. Commoners would fight against commoners and members of the royal clan against each other. A commoner who killed a royal enemy would be likely to be eliminated by his own ruler. When a village was stormed, if the first attacker to reach the village chief was a commoner, it was his duty to carry the chief out of the village on his shoulders and help him to get away. His own chief would reward him later for saving a kinsman. If the first man to reach the village chief was also a member of the royal clan, the two fought to the death.

A second and more successful system was placing in each village an official appointed by the king. These officials were always commoners selected from clans other than those to which they were sent. Their task was to collect taxes and fines to be forwarded to the king and supervise the administration of justice.

In spite of these attempts at organization, Madagascan kingdoms were always transitory. The culture provided no technique by which the individual's loyalty to his kindred of the clan and village could be extended to a political unit. Religion did much to reinforce this extreme parochialism, since the ancestor cult had absorbed into itself nearly all religious beliefs and practices.

Chapter XV

Southeast Asiatic Post-Neolithic

As WE HAVE OBSERVED, Southeast Asia and the adjoining islands, including the Philippines, constitute a single culture area. Although the peoples involved differ widely in cultural complexity, they all have a common background in the old Southeast Asiatic Neolithic complex and have been exposed to the same influences from the great Indian and Chinese civilizations which are their neighbors. Especially at the village level, their cultural similarities far outweigh their differences. It seems legitimate, therefore, to treat this whole region as a unit, referring to it as the Southeast Asia area and distinguishing between Indonesia and the mainland or between various Indonesian or mainland political units only when these present significant differences.

While the Malayo-Polynesians were establishing their language and culture in the far reaches of the Pacific and off the coast of Africa, conditions in the Southeast Asiatic area were by no means static. In fact many of the differences between various Malayo-Polynesian outposts are most readily explained by assuming that their founders left the Southeast Asiatic area at different times and with correspondingly different cultural equipment. Trade relations between Southeast Asia, India and China must have been established long before the first records of such contacts were written down. By 160 A.D. the Greek geographer, Ptolemy of Alexandria, had heard that the area was rich in mineral resources and mentions it as producing gold and silver. The tin deposits in the Malay Peninsula were certainly known and worked at a much earlier period. Many well-made Neolithic implements have been found in the ancient workings but no metal objects and it seems certain that the local population was mining the tin for export. Since it came in almost pure metallic form it would have found a ready market wherever bronze was made, while its high value relative to its bulk adapted it well to primitive transport.

We do not know where the ancient Malayan tin went but China seems the most probable market. Chinese bronze casting had reached perfection by the Shang dynasty (1765–1122 B.C.), and bronze was the most important metal in China for the next thousand years. Eastern and Southern India, on the other hand, seem to have made little use of bronze and to have gotten iron at nearly the same not very remote date. The South Chinese have been good sailors with large and seaworthy vessels since before the dawn of history, and could easily have visited the Malay peninsula, while the Southeast Asiatics were equally capable of reaching South Chinese ports. Lastly, the possibility of overland trade routes between China and Southeast Asia cannot be ignored. The various questions raised here will no doubt be settled when we have enough analyses of Chinese bronzes to establish the sources of the metal and some information on the archeology of South China, which is now almost unknown for the whole period prior to the Han dynasty (202 B.C. to 9 A.D.).

Stone implements certainly continued in use in the Southeast Asiatic area until very late times. Both bronze and iron seem to have been introduced almost simultaneously. The bronzes of the Dong-son type, tentatively dated at between 600 and 300 B.C., are the oldest metal objects from the region. They are decorated in a style which is emphatically neither Chinese nor Indian. The designs find their closest parallels in the textile designs of some of the more primitive Indonesian groups and in the carvings and paintings of Borneo and some parts of Melanesia. The casting technique, on the other hand, appears to be Chinese. All the Dong-son objects are ceremonial rather than utilitarian, and iron has been found in some Dong-son sites. It seems probable that in this period bronze was employed for ceremonial objects and iron for utilitarian ones, much as it was in contemporary China.

In spite of the indications of frequent contacts between China and the Southeast Asia area, the first Chinese reference to the region dates only from the reign of Wang-mang, 1–23 A.D. At that time a Chinese embassy was sent to "Huang-tche," probably the island of Sumatra, to get a rhinoceros for the Imperial zoo. In 132 A.D., the Indonesian king of "Ye-tiao" sent tribute to the Han emperor. Such a statement means little, since in all official records, gifts sent to the Chinese emperor by other rulers were interpreted as tribute. During the latter part of the Han dynasty, Chinese political control was extended over a large part of Indochina. There are numerous mentions of the region in the contemporary sources and archeological finds there suggest an influx of Chinese officials and even of actual Chinese colonists. However, the best proof of extensive early trading contacts between China and the Southeast Asiatic area are provided by the widespread occurrence in

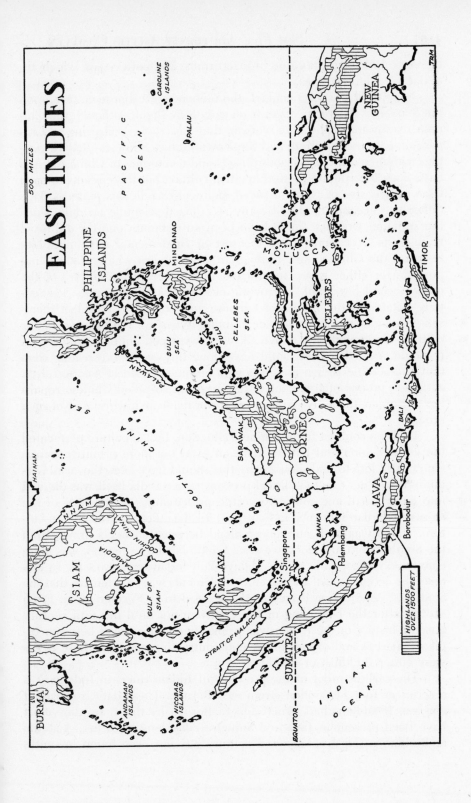

the region of gongs, antique bronze drums, and pottery jars which are of datable Chinese types.

In spite of this long contact, the influence of Chinese culture upon the Southeast Asiatic area has been singularly slight. Although the Chinese readily married native women, they raised their offspring as Chinese and jealously maintained their own culture while the native peoples maintained theirs. Various objects and techniques of Chinese origin have been incorporated into the native culture, but there seems to have been no transfer of Chinese social, political or religious patterns. It is difficult to account for this by any recognized scientific formula, since the situation would seem to have been an optimum one for diffusion. It suggests that there was some sort of fundamental incompatibility between the Chinese and Indonesian world views which made it impossible for either group to understand and accept the culture of the other beyond the simple borrowing of objects and appliances. Particularly notable is the failure of Chinese adventurers to establish themselves as independent princes or to found dynasties. With their superior cultural equipment and, above all, well developed political philosophy, it would seem that they could have done this even more readily than the innumerable Indian migrants who became Southeast Asiatic rulers. Although groups of free-booters did establish so-called Chinese republics in Borneo, the native tribes were never made an integral part of such groups.

In sharp contrast to the Chinese situation, Indian culture permeated the entire region and left its mark on even the more primitive tribes. One is at a loss to understand why this should have been the case. Certainly it was not due to political pressure, since India itself was divided into many small and mutually hostile principalities at the time of the strongest Indian influence in Southeastern Asia. Perhaps the Indian culture, which was itself an ancient blend between elements drawn from the Southeastern and Southwestern Asiatic Neolithic centers, was more emotionally acceptable to the Malayo-Polynesian temperament. In any case, the acceptance of Indian culture elements was so extensive that the Southeast Asiatic area is frequently referred to as Further India. From shortly after the beginning of the Christian era until the 14th century A.D. the history of the region was primarily one of conflict between Indian dynasties and of expanding and contracting empires whose rulers were either Buddhist or Hindu.

The earliest proof of the presence of Indian rulers in Indonesia is a series of four inscriptions from east Borneo. These date from about 400 A.D. If Indians had penetrated to Borneo by this time, they must have been present in Java and Sumatra considerably earlier. A statue of Buddha dating from the 2nd century A.D. has been found in southern Sumatra, but this might have been imported long after its manufacture. The first migrants seem to have followed Brahministic, i.e., Hindu, religious rites.

From the time of the first settlement, Java and Sumatra were the points of maximum Indian influence. In Sumatra, the state of Shrivijaya was in existence by the beginning of the 7th century. Its rulers followed the doctrine of Hinayana Buddhism, but were converted about the beginning of the 8th century to the Mahayana doctrine (see p. 504). Although the Shrivajaya inscriptions are written in the old Pali script of south India, the language is an archaic form of Malay, indicating that the fusion between the migrants and the original population had already gone far. In Java, on the other hand, the language of the early inscriptions is Sanskrit. The first princes of this island were Hindu and seem to have been regarded as incarnations of the god Siva. They instituted a policy of extensive temple building which was carried on by subsequent rulers. In the middle of the 8th century, contemporaneous with the Shrivijaya dynasty in Sumatra, the strong Shailendra dynasty was established in Sumatra. The rulers of this dynasty were Mahayana Buddhists and seem to have come from Bengal. They created an extensive empire which became a sea power, controlling the South China sea and even making war on Cambodia.

At home, they were responsible for the construction of the Borobudur, one of the world's greatest monuments. This structure is a natural hill which has been turned into a gigantic *stupa,* or Buddhist monument. There are seven terraces, the four lower ones rectangular, the three upper ones circular, while the top of the hill has been flattened to represent the roof of a building. The lowermost terrace represents the horrors of Hell and the suffering of those living without salvation. The other rectangular terraces show in great detail first the career of Gautama Buddha as a miraculous teacher and saviour, and then selected episodes from his previous incarnations. When the pilgrim reached the round terraces with his mind prepared for the higher reality, he found a serene simplicity with no ornaments and no sculptures. On the flat top of the hill a central *stupa* of solid stone work contained a statue of Gautama Buddha. This is surrounded by a series of small *stupas* of stone fretwork, each of which encloses a statue of a Dhyani Buddha in meditation.

From the 11th century on there seem to have been no important Hindu or Buddhist increments from India. The process of fusion between the native and imported culture elements went forward steadily, as did the fusion of Hindu and Buddhist religious practices. By the latter part of the 13th century it was possible for a king of Singhasari in Java to build a temple in which the lower floor was dedicated to Siva and the upper floor to Buddha, and it was quite customary for kings to have their ashes divided between a Shivitic and a Buddhist mausoleum. This synthesis was assisted by the fact that these religions were most important to the upper classes. The villagers accepted the rites as superior magic but did not try to understand the doctrines.

The next significant event for Southeast Asiatic culture was the arrival of Islam. The beginning of this can be dated quite accurately. When Marco Polo visited the island of Sumatra in 1292 as an ambassador of the emperor of China, he found that the little town of Perlak, on the northern tip of Sumatra, had been converted to Islam. Most of the Muslim who came to Sumatra were not Arabs but Indians, and the doctrines which they taught had already undergone most of the changes needed to adapt a faith created for desert nomads to the needs of peasants living in the monsoon area. Islam spread rapidly.

BURMESE WATER TEMPLE

The last Hindu Indonesian state of importance was the kingdom of Madjapahit in Java. Under the direction of a prime minister of extraordinary ability, Gaja Mada, it expanded into an empire which took in most of Indonesia. However, new forces were at work and the fall of the Madjapahit empire was even more rapid than its rise. The entire period of its growth and decline extended only from 1293 A.D. to 1389 A.D. After 1400 the Ming dynasty in China embarked on a short-lived program of political expansion in Indonesia. While its control did not extend beyond the collection of tribute, the protection which it offered to princes who would become vassals of China helped in the breakdown of the larger states. As always, the Chinese were interested in trade and political control, not religion, and they accepted Hindu and Moslem princes with equal facility.

The spread of Islam proceeded with great speed. It offered converts release from a Hindu-derived caste system which must have been uncongenial to Southeast Asiatics, and its prescription for forcible conversion of the heathen was highly acceptable to ambitious adventurers and to the Malay pirates who infested the Eastern seas. Any leader who was able to muster a small force and convert a hitherto pagan or Hindu district could be sure of reward. The loot provided an immediate incentive, and the heaven promised believers who fell fighting against the infidel was further recompense.

Before the Muslim could consolidate their holdings, European powers took a hand, beginning with the arrival of the Portuguese, who were able to dominate the seaways of the region by 1515. They were followed rapidly by Spaniards, Dutch, and English, who initiated a period of foreign control which is only now coming to an end.

To study Southeast Asiatic cultures today is like mounting a time machine and going back through successive periods of European, Muslim, and Indian domination to the end of the Neolithic. As one goes eastward from Java to the Philippines or from the coasts to the interiors of the larger islands, one encounters cultures which show less and less foreign influence. However, there are certain features which are common to all or nearly all cultures of the region and others whose distribution points clearly to their origin.

The economic basis everywhere in Southeast Asia is the cultivation of rice. The cutting and burning technique is used in the more backward areas and in places where irrigation is impossible. There are few of the latter, since even in mountain regions irrigated rice is raised in great terrace systems. The plow with either oxen or water buffalo is used by groups who have come under stronger Indian influence, but the favorite instrument for cultivation is a long-handled, narrow-bladed spade, a direct derivative of the Neolithic digging stick. Domestic animals are relatively unimportant as a source of food or transport, and milk is little used even in regions where Indian influence is strong. Fishing is carried on extensively everywhere on the coast and along rivers.

Houses are rectangular with gabled thatched roofs and are always raised above ground, resting on posts in the hot lowlands and on stone-faced platforms in the cooler highlands.

Cloth is woven from a variety of materials, with cotton and silk predominating. It is usually decorated by one of two techniques: *ikat*, designs dyed into the warp before the cloth is woven; or *batik*, designs produced by covering part of the finished cloth with a resist before it is dyed. Very fine metallic brocades are made in a few localities. The whole textile complex seems to have been introduced from India and women of the highest social class pride themselves on their skill as weavers. Bark cloth is still used by many of the more backward groups, but the extent to which it is manufactured is in inverse ratio to the extent of Indian influence in the region.

People in all regions and of all social classes chew *betel.* Slices of the *arecca* palm nut are sprinkled with lime and folded in a pepper leaf. This, when chewed, produces a mild narcotic effect. In more Europeanized territories American chewing gum may now be added to increase the durability of the quid. Tobacco was accepted eagerly when introduced by Europeans after the discovery of America and is now smoked everywhere. Palm wine is widely made and used in spite of the Prophet's prohibition on alcohol.

Primitive methods of fire-making have now been largely replaced by European matches, but prior to this a bamboo fire saw was used by the more backward groups, while the more advanced used the fire piston. This was a horn cylinder with a tightly-fitting piston, to the lower surface of which a wisp of oil-soaked cotton was attached. Driving the piston into the cylinder with a sudden blow compressed the air in the cylinder and generated enough heat to ignite the cotton.

Native metal working has deteriorated in competition with European factory products but was surprisingly well developed even among the more backward groups. Brass, not bronze, was cast by the "lost wax" method (see Chap. IX, p. 106) and decorative work in gold and silver with precious stones was as fine as that done anywhere. The piston bellows was in universal use. Iron was smelted from local ores and steel was made. Tools and weapons were finely tempered and highly finished. The spear and shield were used everywhere. The less advanced tribes employed a flat-bladed axe like a cleaver, while the more advanced groups used a variety of swords which were local modifications of original Indian types. *Krises,* cutting and stabbing swords with wavy blades, were characteristic of the region. In Java these were frequently made from alternate strips of low carbon and high carbon steel which gave the blade a combination of toughness and hardness. The strips were welded together, beaten out, folded, and rewelded, repeatedly. When the blade was finished, it was etched in a bath of arsenic and lime juice which ate away the low carbon steel, producing a highly decorative grain effect like that of weathered wood. The blow gun and bow are known everywhere in the area but neither is important as a weapon.

The less advanced tribes had a veritable cult of antiques to which quite fictitious values were attached. The most generally favored objects were the ancient Chinese jars and bronze drums of various types, some Chinese of the Han dynasty, others of uncertain provenance. Gongs were valued everywhere and figured in many semi-ceremonial transactions. In Borneo, as in Madagascar and West Africa, exaggerated values are attached to ancient beads.

Clothing is usually scanty, the extent of body coverage being roughly correlated with the extent of Indian influence. Men wear a loin cloth or, in more civilized groups, a wrap-around skirt; women a wrap-around skirt. Both sexes usually wear short jackets. Fine fabrics and exceedingly elaborate headdresses and jewelry are worn on ceremonial occasions by the more advanced groups. Tattooing is practiced by both sexes and is understandably more extensive in the groups which wear the least clothing. Teeth are both filed and blackened, the usual explanation for the practice being that human beings should not have teeth which look like those of dogs and pigs.

Premarital sex experimentation was so thoroughly integrated in all the Southeast Asiatic cultures that neither Hinduism nor Islam has been able to eliminate it. In most of the more backward tribes adolescent girls sleep away from the family in a special house where they are freely visited by the unmarried men, and even where this institution no longer exists, the attitudes toward premarital sex are highly permissive. On the other hand, post-marital unfaithfulness in either sex is severely punished. Marriage is usually monogamous, only princes and a few of the rich being able to avail themselves of the four wives and unlimited concubines permitted by Islam. Even in Muslim communities women normally go about freely unveiled, and their social position is little inferior to that of men. Each sex has its distinctive crafts, but it is quite legitimate for men to assist in cooking, baby tending, and other domestic activities. Villages are normally endogamous; kin groups within the village exogamous. The main exceptions to the endogamous rule are in those cases where the establishment of a rigid class system, always traceable to Indian influence, limits the number of families of a particular class in any village to the point where their members have to go outside to find mates.

Legal codes are highly developed and cover every possible phase of social interaction. The attitude toward these codes is much like our own. They rest on social acceptance and are not supported by supernatural sanctions. They are sharply differentiated from the extensive systems of taboos which are also characteristic of the area. An unusual feature of the taboo system is the imposition upon villages of periods of complete isolation and inactivity lasting for several days at a time. During these periods no stranger may enter the village and even the more necessary activities such as cooking and eating are reduced to a minimum.

In spite of the superposition of Hindu, Buddhist, and Muslim rituals, religion still centers around attempts to placate hostile spirits and to get help from the ancestors. The will of the spirits is ascertained through mediums who go into trances and allow the spirits to speak through them. Divination is widely practiced. There is considerable malevolent magic, and poisoning is fairly common.

Except where series of villages had been consolidated into states under a centralized government, intervillage warfare was endemic until terminated by European intervention. It was maintained by the institution of head hunting. This, in turn, stemmed from a concept of power somewhat like the Polynesian idea of *mana.* Each individual and community was supposed to have a certain amount of spirit power. The power of persons whose heads were taken was added to the store already possessed by the successful warrior or his village. Thus, in many tribes, it was believed that a man could not become rich until he had taken a number of heads and added their power to his own. Skulls were preserved, and the successful head hunter's exploits entitled him to wear a costume of a particular sort or to have certain designs tattooed on his body.

Several other culture patterns are, or were, common to those Southeast Asian regions where Indian immigrants had established centralized states. One of these was an incipient caste structure. The extreme avoidance characteristic of the Indian caste system was too incompatible with Southeast Asian values of local solidarity to gain acceptance, but the marriage of a man of lower caste to a woman of higher caste was everywhere prohibited. Differences in social rank were emphasized by elaborate rules of etiquette. Different forms of greeting had to be used for equals, for superiors, and for inferiors of different degrees of social distance, and there were distinct vocabularies to be used in conversations with each.

The head of the kingdom, called by the Indian term *Rajah,* lived in an extensive palace with a large harem, a palace guard, and numerous household and governmental officials. The most important among the latter was a prime minister, to whom all but a few unusually energetic

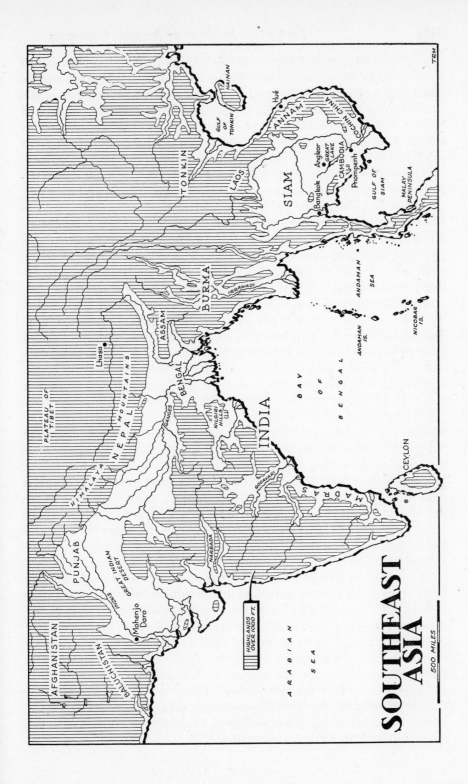

SOUTHEAST ASIA

500 MILES

Rajahs were willing to delegate the business of actual ruling. The *Rajah* as a symbol of the state and semi-divine had performed his most important function when he kept up the religious rites which maintained the state's spiritual power. Virility was one manifestation of this power, and he was expected to add the most beautiful girls in the kingdom to his harem. However, there was only one queen, who was herself of royal stock, and only her son could inherit the kingship.

Numerous temples were built under royal patronage and supported by grants of the revenues from particular villages. Hindu and Buddhist priests, who imitated the behavior of Indian Brahmins, performed the official rites in these and exercised their magical powers on behalf of individuals rich enough to employ their services. Temples and palaces were the centers of artistic activity. The old Southeast Asiatic art forms were infused with Indian motifs. Indian epics were translated into native languages and imitated with fair success. Men of the highest class took pride in their skill as mimes, and painting and literary composition were regarded as proper occupations for the nobility. They had more than enough time for such activities, since the business of ruling reduced itself to making war and collecting taxes from an apathetic peasantry. Although a royal representative, usually some relative of the royal house, was established in each village, the villagers were allowed to govern themselves according to their immemorial *adat* law.

The coming of Islam altered this picture surprisingly little. The Muslim sultan comports himself very much as the *Rajah* did. Even the old pictorial art still flourishes in spite of the Muslim regulation against the making of images. Today, Islam has been established throughout practically the whole of Indonesia and in the southern Philippines. The only places in which the old Hindu-Buddhist patterns still flourish are the islands of Bali and Lombok. "Pagan" tribes still hold out in marginal areas such as the interior of Borneo, and even in Sumatra the Menangkabau, although nominally Muslim, still retain their matrilineal, matriarchal institutions, to the scandal of true believers.

The Southeast Asiatic mainland, lying as it does between China and India, came into contact with both great cultures very early, with the exception of the land that lay to the east of the mountains of Laos, Indian influence has been much stronger than Chinese throughout the mainland. This seems to be due to the fact that the Indians came as colonizers and missionaries, while the Chinese were conquerors or traders. Even after conquest they made few permanent settlements in the territory and kept themselves distinct from native people when they did establish colonies. The Chinese have never been a proselytizing group, but the Indians, whether Hindu, Buddhist, or Muslim, included missionary activity in their colonization.

The oldest kingdom of Southeast Asia was Funan. This country has disappeared so completely that early European historians believed it to have been a legendary kingdom, probably located on one of the islands, until a French sinologist discovered and translated references to Funan in early Chinese annals.

Funan was apparently developed from settlements which spread over the fertile plains along the lower reaches of the Mekong River. In the 3rd century it conquered and subjugated neighboring states until it occupied all of what is now Cochin China and Cambodia, and the northern part of the Malay Peninsula. The Funanese were people of the Mon Khmer family, related to those in Siam and Cambodia. The Malay Peninsula, when Funan made it a vassal state, was already under strong Indian influence. Being on the direct trade route between India and China, it was settled early in the first Christian century by Indian colonists, who brought Indian patterns into Funan.

In the 7th century Funan was conquered by the Khmer people of Cambodia and was completely absorbed. The Cambodian empire extended over most of Indo-China and for a time also embraced northeastern Siam, which accounts for the similarity between Siamese and Cambodian customs, drama, music, and dancing, although the two people speak different languages.

At the head of the Great Lake the Cambodians erected their capitol, Angkor Tom, and adjacent to it the magnificent temple of Angkor Vat. This great complex covered an area of over 10,000 acres and was built between the 10th and 15th centuries under the reign of twenty kings. During the reign of Suriyaravarman II (1113 to 1150) the great temple of Angkor Vat was brought to its full glory. It was erected in honor of the god Vishnu, although the monarch, by some Cambodian twist, identified himself with the god and the temple also became a mausoleum for his majesty. A few Buddhist images have also been found in the temple, indicating that it was at one time also used in Buddhist rites.

The style was predominantly Indian, although the classic Khmer sculptors sought new sources of inspiration in various foreign arts, and developed forms which were distinct and original. The buildings were largely of sandstone, with some brick used for construction work. Pediments, lintels, and columns were covered with delicate and vital designs. The exterior was decorated with 1,750 life-sized figures of *apsaras* (heavenly dancers), each with an individual and intricate headdress. There was at least half a mile of beautifully executed bas reliefs along the walls.

The Cambodian empire collapsed about 1440, after a long and disastrous war with Siam. The Chams were also harrying the empire from the east, and there were clashes, too, with the Annamese. Angkor was sacked by Siamese troops, and the king and the nobles fled the city and reestablished themselves at Pnompenh, the present capital. The people emigrated from the region, too, leaving to the jungle wilderness one of the most magnificent city and temple establishments ever built. That this great city, which had successfully withstood its enemies for two centuries of constant warfare, should have been abandoned so completely, not only by its rulers but by its population, seems strange. It may be that its overwhelming magnificence contributed to its downfall. These glorious buildings must have been constructed and maintained both by slave labor and the conscripted labor of the villagers. To the masses this grandeur may well have represented exploitation and toil from which they were content to flee.

In the early 20th century, when these buildings were freed from the jungle growth by the French government, practically no construction work was needed in the restoration. The masons who designed them had so well understood the stresses of stone and the distribution of mass that the buildings had withstood the encroaching jungle and the passing of centuries. Some of the beautiful carvings and rich decorations were crumbling but nonetheless retained their striking beauty and vitality.

Northeast of the Khmer peoples lived the Cham. They spoke a Malayan language and, in the early part of the Christian era, were a primitive hunting and fishing group. As they were halfway between China and Java, they were influenced very early by both of these superior cultures, although Javanese patterns were most prevalent. The Chams first accepted Hinduism but later were converted to Islam. Their written language was Sanskrit. Both Champa and Annam were invaded by the Chinese on numerous occasions, though Champa, being farther to the south, was never completely subjugated by China. In a war against China which continued from 431 to 446, the Chinese ravaged the Hindu temples of the Cham and were said to have melted down the golden idols and carried back to China 1,000 pounds of gold, which report, even though exaggerated, indicates the wealth and power of the Champa empire at that time. The Champa capital was at Indrapura, some distance south of the present Annamese capital of Hue. The ruins of the Champa temples were second only to Angkor Vat in magnificence.

The Chams built of brick, using stone only for ornamentation and facing. The principal shrine consisted of eight temples raised on platforms and decorated with beautiful sculptures and friezes. Champa still shows predominantly Indian elements, but with considerable Chinese modifications. The Chams warred with the Cambodians, and for a time during the 13th century were subjected to the Cambodian empire. Champa and Annam, occupying adjacent portions of the eastern coast of Indo-China, were continually at war, and in the 15th century Champa was conquered and annexed by Annam. The Chams were largely exterminated, and the remnants of the once powerful kingdom were driven away from the coast and back in the mountain regions, where they still live as a minority group. They are rice farmers, but, unlike other Annamese farmers, they never keep pigs, for the present-day Cham are, for the most part, Muslim who cannot touch the flesh of swine.

In the early part of the 19th century, when the Western powers were beginning to realize the possibilities of exploitation in the Orient, Annam was the dominant culture east of the mountains in Indo-China. This was the one country of Southeast Asia in which Chinese culture was predominant over Indian. For hundreds of years Annam had been alternately subjugated by China and had then regained independence. Although the Chinese and Annamese remained distinct, with little interbreeding or social contact, the religion, government, and family organization of the Annamese were based directly on Chinese patterns. Annamese scholars studied the Chinese classics. The Confucian ethic, with its insistence on respect toward elders and its rules of polite behavior, was the ideal. As in China the family was the basic social institution, and the worship of ancestors and keeping of ancestral tablets were the chief duties of every Annamese household. The religion was a mixture of a sort of easy-going Buddhism, a form of Taoism which was concerned more with the appeasement of local spirits than with the teachings of Lao Tzu, and a half-hearted acceptance of the Catholicism brought by the French missionaries. As in China, the emperor was believed to be a direct descendant of the sun god, and the mandarinate was open to men of all classes who succeeded in passing the competitive examinations, which, as in China, were based on the Confucian classics.

When the French took over Indo-China, the old system was abolished and the mandarinate was replaced by direct control by French officials. The French attempted to administer a policy of assimilation, breaking up the power of the mandarinate and the strength of the communes, or villages, which had been self-governing institutions providing for the welfare and education of their members. Although the French have developed the country, brought more land under cultivation, exploited the mineral resources, and built railroads and motor roads, their rule has not served to unify the people. Under French authority great diversity has persisted in language and culture in Indo-China, and the chief unifying element has been opposition to French exploitation.

Siam, or Thailand as it now prefers to be called, is the only country of Southeast Asia which was able to maintain its independence during the European pressures of the 19th century, which brought her neighbors into political subjugation to Western powers. This was not due to the strength of the country nor to any political astuteness, but rather to

the fact that Siam lay between the English sphere of influence in Burma
and India and the French domain in Indo-China. Either empire would
have been glad to annex Siam, but each knew that such a move would
be bitterly resented by the other; so that Siam, although it lost some
border territory to the French and English, was able to preserve its political freedom.

Siam was settled first by Hindu colonists, but in the 6th century became a Buddhist state. In the 11th century the country was annexed to
the Cambodian empire, which was mainly Hindu. The Thai people,
from whom the country takes its present name, came in during the 12th
and 13th centuries, migrating south from what is now Yunan, apparently
driven down by the conquests of the Mongols. The Thai spread into
Burma, where they are now called Shan, and into Siam, where they settled around the Menam River. In the middle of the 14th century some of
the Thai formed a kingdom which subjugated and consolidated the
other Thai states. In 1767 the Burmese invaded Siam and destroyed the
old capital at Ayuthia. After this defeat a general of Siamese and Chinese ancestry seized control of the country and set up a new capital at
Bangkok. This general was succeeded by another general, Chakki, who
was the first of the dynasty which still rules Siam. The decay of the Burmese royal line and the defeat of Burma by the British in the 1820's disposed of Siam's principal enemy and rival, and the country has flourished under this dynasty.

Although the Thai are of Chinese origin, the culture of Siam has
been more Indian than Chinese. In religion they were chiefly Hinnayana
Buddhist and more orthodox in their belief than most of the other countries of Southeast Asia. Siamese temple architecture, with its tiers of
curving roofs, is reminiscent of Chinese pagodas, although its decoration is strongly Indian in feeling. Like all of Southeast Asia, Siam has
come under Western influence, but Siam, as well as having kept its independence, in the 19th century was more prosperous and had a higher
standard of living than any other Southeast Asiatic country.

PART SIX

Southwest Asia and Europe

Chapter XVI

Southwest Asiatic Neolithic

THE MOST IMPORTANT Old World center of plant and animal domestication lay in Southwestern Asia, in the region roughly bounded on the west by the Mediterranean, on the north by the Black and Caspian Seas and the Eurasiatic steppes, on the east by the central Asian massif, and on the south by the belt of deserts extending from the Sinai peninsula to India. This region was for the most part one of continental climate, hot summers alternating with cold winters. There was very little rainfall in summer, so that the great problem of the later farmers was that of retaining moisture which had soaked into the ground from winter snows and spring rains.

The type of economy developed in this region during the Neolithic was basic to all the civilizations of the Old World with the exception of Southeast Asia, Japan, and Africa south of the Sahara. Most of the culture elements which were integrated in various ways to form these civilizations also originated here. No other cultural co-tradition has been studied as long or as intensively as this one. Two well-known formulations, that of the use of polished stone tools, the bow, and pottery as the criteria for the Neolithic period, and that of a constant sequence of Neolithic, Bronze and Iron Ages in the evolution of culture are based on these studies and only hold for the areas influenced from this Southwest Asiatic center.

At the present time it seems idle to speculate as to the exact origin point within the area of the various grains and animals which were domesticated (see Chap. VIII). We know that by 5000 B.C. village life had been established throughout most of this region and that the various tribes participated in a single co-tradition. Various tribes might make use of different forms and decorations on their pottery, build their houses in slightly different ways, and so forth, but their similarities far overshadowed their differences, and a plant or animal domesticated at

one point must have been diffused within a very short time to all parts
of the area where it would be economically advantageous.

The difficulty of ascribing exact origin points in the area for various
plants and animals is matched by the difficulty of ascribing exact points
in time for the origin of many of the features which together formed the
Southwest Asiatic culture complex and which were diffused to other regions as a part of it. The development of food raising in this region
seems to have been followed by a cultural advance so rapid that the content of various time levels is not clearly ascertainable. We cannot say
with certainty when the first wheel, plow, or loom was made, or when
the first metal was smelted or the first inscription written. We only know
that, in the Old World, all these epoch-making advances can be traced
back to this region and that they occurred between 5000 and 3500 B.C.

Since this Neolithic homeland was also the site of the earliest civilizations, most archeological work has been devoted to uncovering the
temples and palaces. It is only within the present century that significant work has been done on the Neolithic sites, and even today our
knowledge of these is not too extensive. However, this seems to be one
of the regions to which the term "immemorial East" is really applicable.
In many places the peasants still live very much as their Neolithic ancestors did, and the workmen used on excavations can give a clearer
picture of the uses of the various tools and objects found than most
archeologists. This makes it possible to reconstruct the economic life and
technology of the Neolithic period with considerable accuracy. Unfortunately, we can be less certain of the social organization and religion.

Even in the earliest period the people lived in villages. There seem
to have been no isolated dwellings, which suggests the existence of intervillage warfare. Neighboring settlements no doubt quarreled over
grazing land, and domestic animals were a constant temptation to theft.
At the same time the absence of defensive works around villages suggests that the wars were not particularly deadly. It may be noted that
head hunting of the Southeast Asiatic sort seems to have been completely lacking in this culture.

Houses were rectangular, made of adobe or of mats fastened over a
wooden frame and plastered with mud. They were either flat roofed or
gable roofed with straw thatch, depending on the local rainfall. The construction suggests that there was already a shortage of timber in many
localities or that the villagers were reluctant to expend the labor necessary to fell and dress it. Small fields were cultivated where the soil was
good, preferably close to the village. Poor and distant land was used for
grazing and presumably was not individually owned. Farm land remained the property of the families which had brought it under cultivation as long as it was kept in use. Land which was allowed to lie fallow

for several seasons was probably reallocated. In the early period fields were broken with stone hoes and digging sticks. Later, wooden plows drawn by men or oxen came into use. The *ard* type of plow (see Chap. IX, p. 115), which was developed in this region was poorly adapted for breaking sod, but by cross-plowing with it it was possible to pulverize the dry soil of early summer and create a dust mulch which would prevent the evaporation of moisture.

The principal crops were wheat and barley, with lentils, peas, onions, cucumbers, and gourds to vary the diet. After the early period of high fertility fields were cultivated in alternate years. Somewhat later a three-year cycle was followed in which fields were planted to grain the first year and to legumes the second, and were allowed to lie fallow the third. Ripe grain was reaped with sickles made from wood or antler, with flint flakes inset along the cutting edge. Each village had its threshing floor, a level space smoothly floored with clay and usually surrounded by a low stone wall. Such threshing floors served a double purpose, since they provided a most convenient place for village assemblies. The grain was either beaten out of the heads or trodden out by animals who were driven round and round over it. It was then winnowed by tossing it into the air on a windy day. The chaff would be blown down wind, while the grain, being heavier, fell at the feet of the winnower. No part of the crop was wasted, the chaff being used for fuel and the straw for thatch or fodder. The threshed grain was stored in pits dug in hard clay soil or in beehive-shaped mud granaries, usually with thatched roofs. To have mice or rats get into the granary was a major catastrophe, and some of the earliest Egyptian papyri give recipes for the fumigation of the granaries and for keeping rodents out by semi-magical means. The grain was crushed to a coarse meal on a *saddle quern,* a flat slab of stone with slightly roughened surface on which a small flat stone was rubbed back and forth with a motion very much like that used with an old-fashioned washboard. The resulting meal was well seasoned with grit, and old people's teeth were often worn down almost to the gums. The meal was either toasted or, more commonly, boiled as mush. Flat cakes were also made by mixing more finely ground meal with water and spreading it on a hot stone slab or on the outside of a pot filled with hot coals. Leavened bread was still many centuries in the future, but malting and the making of beer had been discovered by at least 4000 B.C. (see p. 94).

Domestic animals were kept in corrals in or near the village. They were cattle, sheep, goats and, less commonly, pigs. Donkeys were used for transport but there were few if any horses. Throughout most of Near Eastern history horses have been luxury animals used only in war and for display. It may be remembered that one king of Israel was criticized for pride because he rode a horse instead of a donkey. All the village animals of each sort were pastured together and herded by children, with a few armed men as guards when such were needed. The stubble of the reaped grain fields provided a valuable source of animal food while at the same time the dung of the animals helped to refertilize the ground. The animals were milked morning and night, and curds and butter seem to have been made from very early times. The latter was more important as a cosmetic than as food, but the dried curds made it possible to store a milk surplus for use in times of shortage. The domestic animals were too valuable to kill except at ceremonies, so meat was little used. The normal diet of the region seems to have been mush and milk, eked out with vegetables, wild plants, game, fish, and in fact anything edible which the region provided.

Women did the cooking and also made the earthen pots in which food was boiled. Before the invention of the wheel these pots were built up by hand from successive coils of clay, apparently in imitation of an older technique for making coiled basketry. They were smoothed inside and out with pebbles, dried and then fired in the open under piles of chaff or dried dung. Pottery was made in a number of different forms, including bowls and jars as well as cooking pots. Vessels which were not meant to be placed on the fire were frequently painted red, black and white with mineral colors. Glazing was still many centuries in the future.

In addition to cooking and making pottery, women wove coarse cloth on simple handlooms. Thread was made from flax or wool rolled on the thigh and then twisted hard with a spindle. Dyeing was discovered at a very early period and fabrics striped in different colors must have been made almost from the beginning, but there were as yet no complicated designs. Clothing was simple, consisting of a kilt for women and a loin cloth for men. A large piece of cloth was wrapped around the shoulders. This was taken off when at work and used as a blanket at night. Cloaks of sheep or goat skin with the hair on were worn by both sexes in cold weather. All garments were made from rectangular pieces of cloth as they came from the loom. It is interesting to note that the tailored clothing, which is now the mark of civilized man, was, even in late classical times, the mark of the barbarian. It derives not from the old Southwestern Asiatic culture but from the hunting peoples of the northern forests, who had to have warm garments which at the same time permitted freedom of movement. Its acceptance by groups whose cultures were derived from Southwest Asia was quite late. Even in the Bronze Age the settled people in Scandinavia were still dressing in uncut squares of cloth draped about the body.

Normal human vanity expressed itself in many ways. To judge from occasional figurines, hairdress was fairly elaborate. The little inhabitants of the human head, which have been associated with man since his first appearance, were discouraged by the use of butter pomade, and by long pins carried in the hair knot and used for scratching. The same figurines which show hairdress have body markings which suggest rather extensive tattooing or body painting or both. It is also probable that people in this region removed their body hair, since this practice has been followed by their descendants since the earliest times of which we have record. In the Bronze and Iron Age city cultures of the region, the only women who did not depilate were the sacred prostitutes attached to temples. The custom of shaving the beard is also referable to this region and goes back to at least the early part of the Bronze Age. Numerous ornaments were worn, particularly necklaces, which were made from beads of shell or semi-precious stone: lapis, carnelian, agate, and amethyst. Analysis of specimens found archeologically has shown that these precious materials were often traded over great distances.

Knives, scrapers and projectile points were made from flint blades retouched by the pressure technique. Polished axes were made from tough stones, such as diorite. These were used for felling trees and dressing timber, but their comparative scarcity in archeological sites and the lack of specialized forms suggests that woodworking was not an important aspect of the culture.

The most significant advance in stone working in this period was the invention of the tubular drill (see Chap. VII, p. 75). Such drills cut a cylindrical hole, leaving a solid core which could be broken out when the drilling was finished. With them, it was possible to perforate heavy stone objects such as axes and mace heads, permitting the type of hafting which we still use. The tubular drill was also used for the manufacturing of stone bowls. After the outside of the utensil had been shaped it was hollowed by drilling a series of closely spaced holes, breaking out the cores and the thin separating walls, and rubbing the interior smooth. From the earliest times a little copper and gold were used for ornaments. These metals were found native and worked cold by hammering and grinding. They were too precious to be used for tools, and, in any case, would have been no better for most purposes than the stone already in use.

Women wove mats and coiled baskets. It seems probable that there were also a considerable amount of skin dressing and use of the resultant leather for sandals, water skins, and containers of various sorts. Weapons were the bow, spear, and shield. The axe seems to have been strictly a tool. The earliest carvings from the region, which are, however, of the Bronze Age, show commanders carrying a peculiar curved weapon, probably a boomerang, and later Neolithic and early Bronze Age sites have yielded pear-shaped mace heads drilled through longitudinally and presumably mounted on a short, straight handle. These are usually made of decorative stone and were probably carried by chiefs. It is highly improbable that armor was worn. Crude four-wheeled carts appear in this region in quite early times but the exact period is not known. The earliest wheels seem to be made in one piece with the axle.

In attempting to reconstruct social conditions we must rely heavily on patterns common to cultures derived from the region, checking by archeological finds where possible. Differences in grave goods indicate that there were already differences in wealth and social position. The attitudes toward wealth which formed a part of the Southwest Asiatic co-tradition differed sharply from those incorporated in the Melanesian cultures or in the more primitive cultures of Southeast Asia. In the latter regions the importance of wealth was consistently played up and social prestige was based directly on financial resources. Even the prowess of the head hunter or the skill of the magician was valued primarily as a means to wealth accumulation. In cultures belonging to the Southwest Asiatic co-tradition, although the actual power which comes from wealth accumulation was tacitly recognized, highest prestige was attached, in theory at least, to other qualities such as valor, strength, or ritual knowledge. Thus, even in our own society, it would be said in praise of a ruler that he was brave, just, or wise, but rarely that he was wealthy.

The main wealth was probably in herds, the only type of interest-bearing investment possible under the conditions, but the finding of occasional hoards indicates that there was also accumulation of capital goods. There unquestionably was trade between neighboring villages and even long-distance trade in highly valued objects. We can be fairly sure that such trade was frankly for profit without the social fictions and magical accompaniments of exchanges of goods in such regions as Melanesia or Australia. It is also safe to assume that there was little institutionalized wealth competition or of the ostentatious waste involved in such institutions as the potlatch of the Northwest Coast of America.

The plan of the villages, the presence of dwellings which must have been occupied by several nuclear families, and the appearance at a slightly later period of tombs with multiple burials obviously made at different times indicates that there was some sort of extended kin group and that more than one of these groups might occupy a single village. It is impossible to say whether the early societies were matrilineal or patrilineal, and descent line quite possibly differed at various places within the region. Thus we know that the middle Bronze Age peoples of the Mediterranean borders of the area were matrilineal while those of the northern margin were patrilineal at the same period. It seems to be a fairly valid generalization that in the long run the descent line in any group will be traced through the sex whose activities are of greatest economic importance. This in turn is linked with an understandable tendency to pass on property from generation to generation within the sex possessing the skills needed for its exploitation. We know that the early Mediterranean peoples were heavily dependent on agriculture, and since there is no indication that the plow came into use in this region before the late Bronze Age, it is highly probable that agriculture was women's work carried on with hoe and digging stick. The patrilineal northern tribes, on the other hand, were in regions where agriculture had become of diminishing importance but where the care of domestic animals, always men's work, was paramount.

Whatever the line of descent, we may feel sure that the region lacked the elaboration of marriage regulations characteristic of Australia or Melanesia and that kinship figured less in the control of personal relations than it did in Southeast Asia. There were certainly nuclear families and we can be fairly sure that most of these were monogamous, although polygyny was probably permitted to those wealthy enough to afford more than one wife. Marriages within the extended unilinearly-defined kin group were almost certainly prohibited, but, in contrast with Southeast Asia, intervillage marriages were probably common. We may also be fairly sure that marriage was regarded as a legal contract rather than as a sacrament and that it was always validated by some exchange of property between the families involved, either bride price or dowry, or more frequently both.

To judge from their descendants, the people of the Southwest Asiatic co-tradition differed markedly from Southeast Asiatics in their attitudes toward sex. In the Southwestern region premarital sex experimentation was discouraged. Many of the societies which shared this co-tradition placed a high value on virginity at marriage, and all of them enjoyed a double standard of sex behavior, permissive for men and restrictive for women. Combined with this was a tendency toward periods of ritual promiscuity, usually associated with the worship of fertility deities. Our own formal attitudes on double standards can be traced back to Southwest Asia as directly as can the oatmeal we have for breakfast.

It is improbable that there were any political units larger than the village, yet villages which shared a common language and culture probably recognized certain ties and were able to combine against outsiders. The village chief led in war, directed communal activities and also, no doubt, exercised his authority to settle disputes and to maintain peace within the community. Chieftainship was probably hereditary within particular families but with the office actually passing to the ablest candidate. Since villages were small face-to-face groups, real power within the community was exercised by family heads and other important men.

The operation of this sort of control can be observed in many peasant communities even today and is as informal as it is effective. The men of the village merely converge on some favorite meeting place, often a threshing floor, in the cool of the evening, and there discuss any matters which may be of interest. Any member of the village is privileged to speak his mind on any matter, but the young or socially insignificant are snubbed, while men of importance are listened to respectfully. The decisions finally arrived at are always unanimous, since long practice enables members of the group to sense the direction in which sentiments are moving, and no one is anxious to find himself the sole representative of a dissenting opinion. As in all small communities, every Neolithic village no doubt had a mass of custom which controlled behavior of all sorts. That which had to do with interpersonal relations was ready to crystallize into law but probably had not done so at that period. A tendency to regard law as something imposed from above and not to be invoked in intra-village disputes is as characteristic of the Southwest Asiatic co-tradition as the constant appeal to *adat* law is of the Southeast Asiatic one.

The Southwest Asiatic attitude toward the spirit of the dead was much like our own uneasy feeling toward ghosts. Property was placed with the dead in order to provide for their needs in the next world but also with a view to giving them the objects to which they had been most attached while alive in order to lessen any incentive for their return. No sacrifices seem to have been made to them after the funeral, and there certainly were no ideas of their constant presence and participation in the affairs of the living. Ideas concerning the afterworld were rather vague, but it seems to have been represented as a place where the ghosts led ineffective existences of absolute boredom, in sharp contrast to the afterworld of Southeast Asia, with its obligations of guardianship for descendants and lively participation in everything going on among the living.

Each village or group of related villages had its own god. These deities might be either male or female. In either case they were provided with divine consorts of secondary importance. While each deity was equated with some natural phenomenon, such as the sun, moon, sky, underworld, and so forth, or linked with a particular activity, such as war or agriculture, his powers were extensive wherever the well-being of his own people was concerned. The god was looked upon as a sort of landlord to whom offerings were made as a rent payment, but who was in turn responsible for the well-being of his tenants. His control was limited to a definite territory and, as in the Near East at a later period, there was probably a strong feeling that he paid no attention to prayers made outside it. This attitude continued well into Biblical times. Readers may remember the episode of Nahman the leper, who, after the prophet Elijah had healed him of leprosy by the power of Jehovah, begged that he might be allowed to take back to Damascus enough of the soil of Palestine to cover the floor of an inner room in his house where he could pray and give thanks to the Divine proprietor of Palestine.

Each village had its local shrine, which was usually a high place outside the village, and there probably were also tribal shrines to which members of several villages might repair. Worship was carried on through priestly intermediaries who knew the proper rituals and received a share of the sacrifices as pay. To judge from the earliest written records from this region, many of the rituals were in fact magical formulae designed to compel the god's assistance quite as much as to implore his help. Since the god was regarded as thoroughly anthropomorphic with physical needs for food and shelter, the relations between him and his worshippers was a reciprocal one. If he did not come across, they did not come across.

It is impossible to say how far these local divinities had been organized into a universal pantheon by Neolithic times. We can be fairly sure that in spite of differences in names, whole series of local gods possessed so nearly the same attributes that they could easily be equated with each other and were in fact fused to form single deities when empires arose in the territory. Divination was important, and, in later times, many local gods had famous oracles available to all comers for a suitable fee.

Outstanding among the gods were a male and female deity, the male usually identified with the sky or the sun, the female with the abundant earth. These also might be worshiped in the form of local manifestations but were the basis of more than local cults. Some tribes emphasized one of these deities, some the other, the distinction presumably following closely upon whether their social institutions were matriarchal or patriarchal. The worship of the mother goddess in particular involved large elements of fertility magic and served as the excuse for periods of license in which the normally repressed sex drives of the worshippers found expression. The cult of the mother goddess goes back at least to the Upper Paleolithic, as shown by the curious little Venus figures, with sexual characteristics exaggerated, which came from various parts of Europe. It survived well into Classical times, although with some of its more spectacular rites eliminated, and traces of it can be found even today in the Maryiolatry of some Christian sects.

The pattern of local divinities equated with one or another of the members of a universal pantheon also has shown great persistence. It was carried to Europe as part of the diffusion of Southwest Asiatic culture and became ancestral there to a cult of local guardians. Thus in Greece half a dozen cities beside Athens had their own Athenas. In Medieval Europe the Virgin of X or the Saint Thomas of Y was recognized by theologians as an aspect or emanation of the Virgin or Saint Thomas, yet at the same time was regarded by townsmen as a special being more deeply interested in their welfare than in that of outsiders. When Christianity became the official religion of the Western world, these local aspects of heathen gods were not infrequently converted together with their worshippers. Particularly in the Mediterranean area, one often finds that the shrine of a local manifestation of an Olympian deity has been used as a foundation for the shrine of a Christian saint, whose characteristics are reminiscent of those of its heathen predecessors.

Chapter XVII

Diffusion of the Southwest Asiatic Complex

THE ESTABLISHMENT of village life based on a combination of grain agriculture and dairying was the starting point in the development of a new co-tradition. The description of this Southwest Asiatic culture must have seemed familiar to most readers, since our own rural culture is, or at least was until the mechanization of agriculture, its direct descendant. Village life in most of the Old World outside the humid tropics still follows the patterns laid down in Southwestern Asia between 7000 and 4500 B.C. The only significant break in this continuity prior to the very recent emergence of the Age of Science has been in those regions in which city living developed or became established. The city was a social invention of such far-reaching consequences that it has served to set the city dweller apart not only from his ancestors but also from his rural contemporaries.

Because of this cultural continuity the familiar divisions of Eurasiatic prehistory into Neolithic, Bronze and Iron Ages has little real meaning for anyone but the archeologist. The grain agriculture and dairying on which village life was based were carried on at first by very simple methods. The invention of the plow, wheel, and loom increased the industrial potential without necessitating any fundamental changes in the earlier way of life. The same may be said for ancient metal working. The war potential of groups who had bronze was greater than that of groups who had only stone, but bronze was so scarce at first that the actual advantage enjoyed by those who had it was slight. Throughout most of the Bronze Age no large military force could be completely equipped with bronze arms and armor. One wonders whether the familiar "heroic" pattern of leaders engaging in combats between the lines, while their followers waited to fly or pursue according to which leader won, may not have been established at a time when only chiefs could be adequately armed with metal weapons. The use of bronze for tools came even later than its use for weapons and merely made it possible for the craftsman to do more and better work in a given length of time.

The introduction of iron was more revolutionary in its consequences, since it led to what V. Gordon Childe has called the proletarianization of metal. Iron ores are abundant and widely distributed, making the new metal cheap and plentiful. It was thus available for tools and even agricultural implements, as well as weapons, and certainly raised the general standard of living. However it had little effect on the already ancient and established patterns of village life. Iron-armed conquerors swept over most of temperate Eurasia, but the villager went on plowing with his oxen, sowing and reaping his grain, wearing the cloth his wife wove, obeying immemorial custom, and placating the supernatural guardian of his fields.

At certain places and times the transition from Neolithic to Bronze Age or from Bronze Age to Iron Age was marked by significant population movements and abrupt changes in culture. In such cases the terms will be used, but it must always be kept in mind that these phases of the Eurasiatic culture continuum differed in length in different parts of Eurasia and that the transition from one to another came at very different times in different regions. Thus the use of metal had become common in the Near East by 4500 B.C. but did not reach the British Isles until 2500 B.C. at the earliest. The Iron Age had begun in Anatolia by 18–1600 B.C. but did not become established in Western Europe until nearly a thousand years later. The most recent phase of the Eurasiatic culture continuum, marked by the production of power and the application of the scientific method, originated in Western Europe about the middle of the 18th century and has not yet reached some outlying parts of the world.

The city was a social invention whose consequences were more far-reaching than those of any technological invention (see Chapter X). For this reason its emergence may be set as a terminal point for the period under discussion. The exact point at which a culture became city-centered and took on urban characteristics is sometimes difficult to establish, yet the city as an institution is unmistakable. It appeared first in Southwestern Asia and was fully developed in Mesopotamia by 4500 to 4000 B.C. It appeared in Egypt about the same time, although in slightly different form. The peculiar settlement pattern imposed by the Nile Valley made the first Egyptian cities little more than religious and administrative centers within a continuous area of dense population. The Indus Valley cities were of a more familiar type, resembling those in Mesopotamia. Although dating for this region is still uncertain, they probably go back to at least 3500 B.C. In China cities did not appear until about 2000 B.C. at the earliest. Turning to Europe, there were few real cities even in Greece before 900 to 800 B.C., while the pattern was not established in Scandinavia until after 1000 A.D.

The spread of Neolithic village life from Southwest Asia involved both migration and diffusion. The increased food supply resulting from combined agriculture and dairying must have produced an exceedingly rapid growth of population. It is estimated that under optimum conditions a human group can double its numbers every twenty-five years. The methods of primitive grain agriculture, without fertilization or crop rotation, lead to rapid soil exhaustion and provide a strong stimulus to migration. Actually, migrants seem to have poured out of the Southwest Asiatic region in all directions.

All the regions which were suited to agricultural occupation offered a supply of wild food and were already occupied by hunting, food gathering tribes. However, these tribes were rarely numerous enough to offer serious resistance, and the progressive conversion of their range into grain fields and pasture must have diminished their food supply and reduced their numbers still further. The situation must have been not unlike that of the Indians and white settlers on our own frontier.

It seems unlikely that many aboriginal groups were converted directly from hunting and food-gathering to settled agricultural life. A change of this sort would have involved not only a reorganization of economic life but also profound changes in attitudes and values. It seems more probable that the first agricultural villagers to enter a region traded with the local food-gatherers and took local women into their settlements. Since the assured food supply of the villagers made it possible for them to increase rapidly, their hybrid descendants would progressively replace the older population. When population pressure caused a new outward movement, many of the migrants would be of mixed blood. These would once more interbreed with the aborigines in newly occupied territory. In this way the original Southwest Asiatic stock became increasingly diluted as the migrants pushed farther and farther out, until we find the Southwest Asiatic patterns being carried into new territory by groups who show no traces of the original racial type or types. Thus we know that the founders of the Shang dynasty in north China were immigrants who arrived from the west at about 1700 B.C., bringing with them such typically Southwestern Asiatic traits as wheat, cattle, the wheel, and the plow. At the same time, these immigrants were thoroughly Mongoloid in their physical type.

Migration was most important in the initial establishment of the Southwest Asiatic patterns outside the area of their origin. The first group to accept the new thing and to integrate it into its culture would modify it enough in the process to make its acceptance by other groups easy. Thus it is unnecessary to invoke migration to account for the dissemination of such devices as the wheel or plow, or even for particular items of social organization or religion. There were numerous movements within the agriculture-dairying area after the initial settlement but these were culturally significant only when they brought into contact groups whose cultures had become divergent.

The most important divergence among the cultures which developed out of the Southwest Asiatic complex was that between the groups who concentrated on the agricultural aspect of the original economy and those who concentrated on the domestic animal aspect. In regions where the local conditions made agriculture precarious the settlers came to rely more and more upon their flocks and herds. Dairying cultures based on Southwest Asiatic patterns emerged in the Eurasiatic steppes and in the more or less arid parts of Southwestern Asia and North Africa, each of these regions developing its own distinctive features. While it is difficult to convert aboriginal hunters and food-gatherers to the dull routine of agriculture, they seem able to take up animal domestication with ease. The reaction of both North and South American Indians to the introduction of the horse would be a case in point. In northern Eurasia various aboriginal hunting groups seem to have been converted to a domestic animal economy, and the northernmost of these groups went their teachers one better by domesticating a new animal, the reindeer. That this was a case of stimulus diffusion, not an independent invention, is indicated by the methods of using the reindeer. These followed those for cattle in western Eurasia, those for horses in eastern Eurasia. In Africa a domestic animal economy based on cattle was transmitted to various Bushmen and Negro groups and became the basis for highly characteristic local cultures.

Still other divergences among the heirs of the Southwest Asiatic village culture can be traced to contacts with various aboriginal groups. These contacts were most significant in regions where the environment was markedly different from that in which the original village complex had developed or where the aboriginal population was numerous and culturally advanced. Thus the villagers who moved into moist, heavily wooded northern Europe found a numerous and well-adapted hunting population already in possession and borrowed from them extensively. Those who moved into the Mediterranean region, on the other hand, found an environment much like that of their Asiatic homeland and a sparse aboriginal population which could teach them little and which was absorbed without leaving any recognizable mark on their culture.

The attempt to reconstruct the population movements and cultural developments, which took place between the rise of the Neolithic culture in the Near East and the beginning of the historic period, is fraught with great difficulty. On the one hand, there are complete lacunae in the record, important regions in which little significant archeological work has been done. Thus the earliest village cultures of the territory extending from the Mediterranean to the borders of India and from the southern shores of the Black and Caspian Seas to the Persian Gulf and the Indian Ocean are still largely unknown, although this was the heartland of the Neolithic development. Research in the early sites of this region has been discouraged by the rich overlay of later civilizations which have left both objects of striking artistic merit and the inscriptions so dear to the hearts of an earlier generation of archeologists. It is only within the last few years that attention has been turned to the older remains. Anatolia, simply on the basis of its position, must have played a highly significant role as the starting point for migrations into Europe, yet Anatolian cultures of the Neolithic and early metal periods are still relatively unknown. The Balkan region of Europe, which, because of its position, must have been reached first by Southwest Asiatic migrants, is somewhat better known than Anatolia but requires a great deal of additional study. In spite of the highly significant work done at Anau, toward the eastern end of the Neolithic heartland, we know even less of early cultural conditions in this part of the area, while our knowledge of the Neolithic cultures of Arabia and the adjoining horn of Africa is still based almost entirely on accidental surface finds.

In contrast with this there are regions in which one suffers from an embarrassment of riches. The archeology of western and northern Europe from the Mesolithic on has been studied intensively and the literature is voluminous. There appears to have been a great variety of local cultures distinguished largely by differences in pottery. The bearers of these cultures were loosely attached to the soil and moved about freely, trading and exchanging ideas with the various groups with which they came in contact. In addition, most European archeologists have been patriots with a tendency to see the center for all important cultural developments or population movements within their own national territories. Readers may gain some idea of the complexity of the data by consulting V. Gordon Childe's recent book, *Migrations in Europe*,[1] which is itself a summarization of an enormous amount of specialized literature. The complexity of the theoretical structures built upon the data and the wide differences in the conclusions of various presumably competent experts is even more striking. Fortunately, the scope and purpose of this book do not necessitate a detailed description of these cultures, and I have

[1] Childe, V. Gordon: *Prehistoric Migration in Europe*. Oslo: H. Aschehough and Co.; 1950. The author wishes to acknowledge his heavy debt to this work which he considers by far the best general work on this epoch in European history.

followed the system of presenting the facts and conclusions on which there seems to be fairly general agreement and suggesting in certain cases still other conclusions on the basis of a comparison of the European material with that from other areas in which the dynamic processes of culture change have been observed directly.

Chapter XVIII

European Neolithic

THE FIRST Neolithic migrants to reach Europe apparently came from Anatolia and established a foothold in the region that is now the Balkans. From this point on there were two main lines of migration. One of these followed the Mediterranean coasts with gradual infiltration of the Italian and Iberian Peninsulas and settlement of the various Mediterranean islands as soon as seafaring had been sufficiently developed. Somewhat later this movement was reinforced by direct sea migrations from the lands at the eastern end of the Mediterranean.

The other migration line was into Central Europe by way of the Danube and its tributaries. The descendants of settlers who had come by this route, reinforced by later migrants from the steppe region further to the east, finally reached eastern France, Germany, and Scandinavia. The two routes brought the migrants into markedly different environments and resulted in distinctive cultural developments in each case.

When the movement of agricultural peoples into Europe began, the Mediterranean region was covered with pine forests. Because of the light rainfall this forest could not reconstitute itself. Wherever it had been destroyed it was replaced by dense scrub, the *maquis,* or dry, aromatic heath, the *garrigué.* However, climatic conditions were much like those in the original Southwestern Asiatic center. The rainfall was concentrated in winter so that the ard plow and the dust mulch which it produced were as functional here as in the Near East. All the original crops could be grown without the need for developing new varieties. The main handicap was the lack of level land, as most of the Mediterranean area is mountainous.

The local conditions were set by certain changes in the original economy. The shortage of level land was partially compensated for by terracing, but irrigated terrace agriculture was not employed because, perhaps, of the poor and seasonally fluctuating water supply. Instead

241

there was a development of tree crops. The fig and olive, both natives of the Mediterranean basin, were domesticated and improved, and various nut trees were planted and tended. The vine was added to this inventory during the later Bronze Age. Although it seems to have been introduced from Asia, it found itself completely at home on the stony slopes of the Mediterranean littoral. Olive oil became indispensable to the Mediterranean economy. It served to cook food, to make bread and salads more palatable, to give light, and to protect the skin against cold and salt water. The wine from the Mediterranean vineyards not only cheered the vine growers but also provided them with a valuable export. Well before the end of the Aegean Bronze Age, olive oil and wine were being shipped to less favored areas. The earliest example of fancy packaging was when, by 1500 B.C., the Cretans were putting up their export oil in gaily painted jars. The Classical Greeks carried this trend still farther, and by the time of the Persian wars Athens was getting most of its grain from the settled Scythians north of the Black Sea.

The Mediterranean settlers brought with them the full Southwest Asiatic series of domestic animals, but here again the environment necessitated changes. The ox remained the only draft animal, but goats replaced both cattle and sheep as the animals of greatest economic importance. Goats could graze on the dry scrub which took over the steep hillsides when the original pine forests had been destroyed. Incidentally, their close cropping and sharp hoofs increased the ravages of soil erosion and were an added factor in preventing reforestation.

To compensate for the relative scarcity of animal products, the sea

HUT, EUROPEAN NEOLITHIC

was always close at hand. The Mediterranean peoples were almost as dependent on fish as the Indonesians. Every coastal village had its fishing fleet, and dried fish was an important article of trade with the interior. Long before the dawn of history the coastal and island tribes had become excellent sailors, and the earliest sea power on record had its center on the island of Crete.

The development of culture in the Mediterranean area was influenced by two opposing patterns. On the one hand, the isolation provided by the islands and by numerous inaccessible valleys on the mountainous mainland made for a high degree of local variation. On the other, the sea made possible contact between even distant regions and the rapid diffusion of some culture patterns over wide areas. To further complicate matters, this diffusion did not proceed systematically but depended upon the degree and nature of contact which various islands or tribes had with the more advanced peoples of the eastern Aegean. Thus it has been suggested, on the basis of recent excavations, that the island of Capri was the legendary Isle of the Sirens. Its Neolithic inhabitants were cannibals and may well have used their women to lure passing sailors ashore. Such a group would have had few opportunities for cultural borrowing. On the other hand, the tribes from the Iberian Peninsula, who were friendly to traders, received strong influences from the eastern Mediterranean in spite of the distance involved.

Certain culture patterns may be noted as of Mediterranean origin and common to the entire area. The changes in food economy imposed by the local conditions have already been mentioned. The dependence on fishing, which was a part of this economy, led to the development of the world's first seaworthy ships. These seem to have been evolved first in the eastern Mediterranean, where the numerous islands provided a good training school for deep-sea sailors. The Mediterranean is a sea of long calms and treacherous currents. A vessel which is dependent on sails alone is likely to drift into dangerous waters or lie for days helpless and rolling. The pictures of boats on Neolithic pottery show them with many oars but no masts or sails. Although the latter had been introduced by 2000 B.C., craft, such as war vessels, which required speed and maneuverability, were oar powered until well into the 18th century A.D. Incidentally, the technique of rowing instead of paddling, without which the later galleys would have been impossible, also seems to have been a Mediterranean invention.

The Mediterraneans of Classical times did not use the rather obvious technique of double or triple manning their oars except in emergencies. The result was a multiplication of oars and benches necessitating an elaborate arrangement of overhanging galleries for rowers. Since hulls were built long to provide space for the many oars required and made narrow for speed, even the galleys of Classical times were top heavy and likely to roll over or break in two in bad weather. Added disadvantages were lack of cargo space and the size of the crew required. Galleys could not keep the sea for any length of time, since they could not feed or adequately sleep their personnel. Even in the Classical period there were no Mediterranean craft capable of crossing the Atlantic. However, the Mediterranean is a relatively small sea with many harbors and islands, and the galleys served their purpose well enough as long as human labor was cheap and abundant.

When the Mediterranean sailors ventured into the Atlantic they had difficulty with the irregular winds and tempestuous seas. Most of their voyaging had to be done in the summer. However, they managed to penetrate as far north as Scandinavia, where the Norse long ships of the Viking period seem to have been simplified and improved copies of early Mediterranean craft. At the same time there was an independent development of shipbuilding along the Atlantic coast. Very large dugouts suitable for short sea voyages and certainly not derived from Mediterranean prototypes have been found in Neolithic and Bronze Age sites. Caesar records in his commentaries that the ships of the Veneti, built to withstand the rough seas of the Bay of Biscay, were massively constructed of oak, with leather sails. He adds that they were so massive that the Roman galleys were unable to ram them successfully but finally overcame them by cutting their rigging and leaving them helpless, an excellent indication that they were sailed, not rowed. We cannot say when this school of shipbuilding came into existence, but we know that it was present in Scandinavia all through the Viking period and that the Norse did most of their traveling and trading in bluff-bowed, slow sailing craft which bore much the same relation to their long ships that a modern freighter bears to a destroyer.

In social organization and religion the Mediterranean patterns also seem to have departed somewhat from those of the Southwest Asiatic homeland. There is no question that many of the Neolithic and even Bronze Age tribes of the Mediterranean coasts and islands were matrilineal and matriarchal. This pattern can be inferred from some of the older Greek legends and survived even into Classical times in various out-of-the-way areas. With it went a heightened social position for women. They seemed to have dominated the ritual life of this region during the prehistoric period, for representations of priestesses are common, while those of priests are exceedingly rare.

The practice of building large tombs which were used for generations indicates that many of the Mediterranean peoples had some sort of clan organization with kin groups which were of long duration. The care expended in the building of these tombs and the presence of consider-

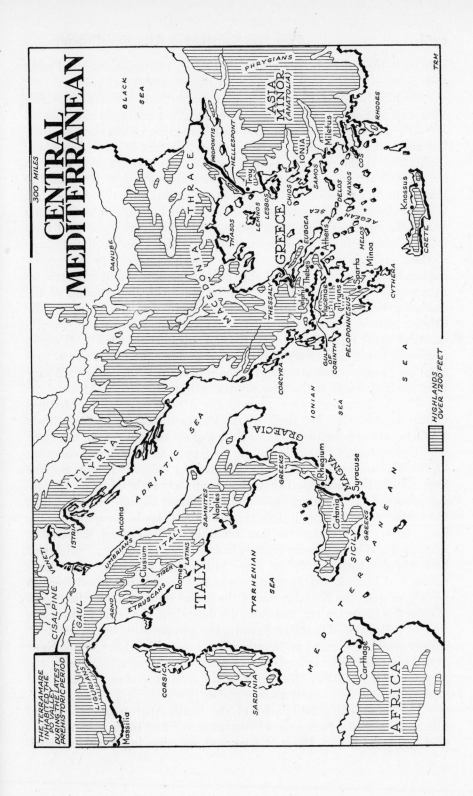

CENTRAL MEDITERRANEAN

300 MILES

THE TERRAMARE
INHABITED THE
PO VALLEY
DURING THE LATEST
PREHISTORIC PERIOD

HIGHLANDS
OVER 1200 FEET

TRM

BLACK SEA

PHRYGIANS

ASIA MINOR
(ANATOLIA)

DANUBE

THRACE

PROPONTIS

HELLESPONT

IONIA

RHODES

Troy

MACEDONIA

THASOS

LEMNOS

LESBOS

CHIOS

SAMOS

Miletus

COS

GREECE

AEGEAN SEA

DELOS

NAXOS

Knossus

CRETE

Thessaly

Delphi

Thebes

Athens

EUBOEA

Mycenae

Tiryns

Sparta

MELOS

Minoa

PELOPONNESUS

CYTHERA

GULF OF CORINTH

CORCYRA

IONIAN SEA

SEA

ADRIATIC SEA

ILLYRIA

ISTRIA

VENETI

Ancona

PO

GAUL

CISALPINE

LIGURIANS

ARNO

UMBRIANS

ITALY

Clusium

TIBER

Rome

LATINS

ETRUSCANS

TYRRHENIAN SEA

SAMNITES

Naples

MAGNA

GRAECIA

GREEKS

Rhegium

Syracuse

Catania

SICILY

GREEKS

MEDITERRANEAN SEA

CORSICA

SARDINIA

Massilia

AFRICA

Carthage

able tomb furniture also suggests that there was an ancestor cult of some sort, an idea foreign to the original Southwest Asiatic culture.

Some other Mediterranean supernaturalistic beliefs and practices were also distinctive. The old Southwestern Asiatic religion had allowed orgiastic practices in connection with the worship of the earth mother, but one feels that in general the emotional content of the religion was slight. The Mediterranean peoples, on the other hand, valued emotion for its own sake and sought ecstatic states in which the individual felt himself to be possessed and in some sense united with the deity. They were profoundly impressed by those crises of human existence which arouse the emotions most (conception, birth, and death) and built their religion about these. Their most important deity was still the earth mother, embodying the reproductive principle. Her rites were conducted by priestesses who probably became possessed and gave oracles as a regular part of the ritual. Side by side with the worship of the mother goddess and her orgiastic rites, there was a worship of the Cthonic deities, powers of night and darkness, who were the embodiments of man's fear of death and the unknown. These rites involved an ecstasy of terror as the rites of the mother goddess did an ecstasy of procreation. Conducted at night and perhaps in secrecy, they may well have been the precursors of the later mystery religions.

The environmental conditions on the African coast of the Mediterranean were enough like those on the European coast, and the cultural contacts between the two were so close and continuous that both can be regarded as forming a single culture area up until the Islamic conquest in the 8th century A.D. The only exception to this was Egypt, but the high civilization developed there had singularly little effect on the development of the Mediterranean cultures. The main difference between the northern and southern Mediterranean coasts lay in the nature of the back country. By the time the first Neolithic settlers arrived, the modern African climatic zones were already in existence. The Sahara, which had been grassland with abundant game at the close of the last glacial advance, had become desert. Great areas were uninhabited and were to remain so until the introduction of the camel shortly before the beginning of the Christian era. Between the desert and the coast there was a zone of light rainfall in which pastoral life was possible, but where agriculture could be carried on in only a few favored localities. Along most of the coast there was enough rain to permit dry farming and the raising of tree crops. The Atlas Mountains, at the western end of the area, had heavier rainfall, with cooler climate and extensive forests.

The most inhospitable part of the North African littoral was in Libya, the region which would be encountered first by Asiatic migrants who had crossed into Africa at Suez and were moving westward overland. There was little incentive for Neolithic farmers to attempt to establish themselves in this region, and this must have slowed down the westward movement until it could be carried on by sea. Beyond Libya conditions gradually improved, and there was a substantial Neolithic population in Algiers and Morocco. This region seems to have shared many of its culture traits with the Spanish peninsula, and in later Neolithic and Bronze Age times the two formed a culture unit, a new center of migration from which settlers voyaged north along the Atlantic coast. There were also voyages to the south. The Canary Islands were colonized by Neolithic settlers from this region.

Although most of the African coast from Morocco to Rio D'Oro was too inhospitable to encourage Neolithic settlement, trade with Negro Africa across the Sahara seems to have been initiated during the Neolithic period. In the absence of camels only a few routes were possible, and it is unlikely that there was any large-scale southward migration of Neolithic peoples. However, there was a diffusion of Neolithic culture elements into the western Sudan and even further south. Polished stone axes of generalized Mediterranean Neolithic pattern are fairly numerous in West Africa from Liberia to the Cameroons, and there have been finds of what is apparently Neolithic pottery; but the nature and extent of Southwest Asiatic Neolithic influence on Negro culture remains to be determined.

Following the initial settlement of the Mediterranean area two cultural centers emerged, one in the Iberian Peninsula, the other in the Aegean Islands. The Aegean center was marginal to the developing civilizations of Mesopotamia and Egypt and was strongly influenced by them. It reached its flowering in the Cretan and derivative Mycenean cultures which, because of their close relations with the later Classical civilizations, require separate treatment.

Neolithic migrants from the Iberian Peninsula settled in the British Isles, where their physical type survives in much of the present population. They also followed the Atlantic coast to Scandinavia, settling most of France and the low countries and eventually pushing inland to Switzerland, where they met and mixed with other agricultural villagers who had arrived by way of central Europe.

The contact between the Iberian Peninsula and the British Isles was particularly close and was maintained all through the Bronze Age. The peninsula seems to have been the starting point for the so-called Megalithic complex of western Europe. This consisted in the building of tombs and the erection of monuments composed of enormous blocks of rough stone. There is no indication that the diffusion of this pattern was accompanied by any large-scale migration. It seems rather to have represented the spread of a religious cult combined, perhaps, with a new form of tribal exhibitionism. In Eastern Polynesia each tribe built its ceremonial structures of the hugest stones possible, since the structure would then stand as an indication of the extent of tribal manpower; one may suspect that the great Megalithic structures of Western Europe, which involved the transportation and erection of stones many tons in weight, may have been inspired in part by similar motives.

There is an extensive literature on the Megalithic culture of Europe, and it may be well to point out that there were two patterns of Megalithic construction in the Mediterranean and adjoining areas which were almost mutually exclusive in their distribution. Around the eastern end of the Mediterranean huge stones were used in the building of fortifications. This was thoroughly functional, since the early stone walls were laid without mortar and could be readily picked to pieces in siege operations unless the stones were too heavy to handle. Big stone was also sometimes used in tomb construction, but this use was not consistent and does not seem to have been an integral part of the eastern Mediterranean mortuary complex. Along the Atlantic coast enormous rough stones were used for *menhirs* and *dolmens* and to form enlignments and circles presumably employed for communal religious rites. *Menhirs* were simple standing stones, usually uncut. Some of the largest weigh thirty to forty tons, and their transport and erection must have required engineering skill of no mean order. *Dolmens* were stone tables, an enormous cap stone being balanced upon several smaller stones in such a way as to form a roofed chamber. Many of the *dolmens* were originally covered with mounds and were used for burial.

However, in Madagascar, where both *menhirs* and *dolmens* were still being erected as late as 1928 A.D., the local *dolmens* were not tombs but memorials to women, while the *menhirs*, with their obvious phallic

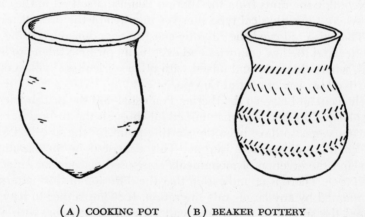

(A) COOKING POT   (B) BEAKER POTTERY

connotations, commemorated men. The Madagascar *dolmens* were also used as tables on which the offerings were arranged for sacrifices to the ancestors as a group. Since graves are very rarely associated with European *menhirs*, they were probably cenotaphs, erected in some prominent place so that they would keep the person they commemorated in mind. The Megalithic ceremonial structures, the best example of which is Stonehenge in England, are usually carefully oriented and were apparently associated with some form of sun worship. Although the Megalithic complex appeared in Western Europe toward the close of the Neolithic, the erection of great stone structures continued during the entire Bronze Age and the ceremonial structures were still in use during the Celtic period, 300 to 400 B.C.

The introduction of metal working into the Mediterranean areas increased the economic importance of the Iberian peninsula, which was rich in copper and other metallic ores. Although the earliest patterns of mining and metal working were probably imported from the east, the peninsula seems to have been the origin point for a curious group known as the Beaker Folk. The remains of this culture are scattered over the whole of Western Europe, with their maximum concentration in regions where there are evidences of primitive mining. They seem to have established real colonies only in the British Isles, Brittany, and Holland, thus following the Iberian migration routes which had been established in Neolithic times. They have left no extensive remains of settlement elsewhere, but many small cemeteries whose graves contain objects indicative of very wide contacts. They may well have been a group of traders and prospectors who pushed into "barbarous" northern Europe following rumors of mineral deposits, and exploited them with the aid of native labor which they trained. It is interesting to conjecture how they obtained the help of the local aborigines in their mining. They do not seem to have been numerous enough to conquer or enslave local populations. Their grave goods are not very plentiful and no extensive caches of trade objects which might be referred to them have been found. The beakers from which they take their name, actually small tumbler-like clay jars, were probably beer mugs, and one is tempted to guess that, as with the early European traders among many different sorts of aborigines, their main stock may have been alcoholic potables.

One last point should be made with regard to the Mediterranean cultures. None of the Neolithic populations who occupied this region or migrated from this region spoke Indo-European languages. The only clues to what their languages may have been are provided by certain late Bronze Age and Iron Age inscriptions from the eastern Mediterranean and by such historic survivals as the Basque language spoken in the Pyrenees and the Berber languages of north Africa. On the basis of

this very scanty information it seems probable that the languages were
of several different stocks.

The second line of diffusion of Southwest Asiatic culture into Europe ran overland from Anatolia to the Balkans and then along the Danube and its tributaries until the northern watersheds were crossed. The
Atlantic river systems were then followed toward the sea. This brought
the central European migrants into contact with the slightly earlier settlements of the Mediterranean migrants and the two traditions blended
to produce a variety of local cultures.

North of the mountains which shut off the Mediterranean Basin
from the rest of Europe, the climate and vegetation changed abruptly.
Except along the Atlantic coast the climate was continental, with hot
summers and cool winters much like those of the central United States.
Rainfall was much more abundant than in the Mediterranean Basin and
was not seasonal. At the time of the first Neolithic migrations most of
Europe was covered with deciduous forest much like that of the eastern
United States at the time of the first European settlement. Along the Atlantic margin there were a few treeless tracts resulting from a combination of light soil and sea winds, while toward the east the forests gave
place to park land. Still farther east this in turn was transformed into
grassland which extended to the Tien Shan Mountains and, becoming
increasingly arid, into Mongolia. North of the deciduous forest there was
a wide belt of coniferous forest which extended clear across the Eurasiatic continent, but most of this lay too far north for pre-scientific agriculture and has remained a haunt of hunters and reindeer keepers until
within the last few years.

The conditions which the Southwest Asiatic migrants encountered
in their movements into Central Europe called for a complete reorganization of their farming methods. Agriculture was carried on by the slash
and burn technique. If one may judge by the agricultural methods of the
Iroquois, a Neolithic people living in New York State and Southern Canada under very similar environmental conditions and with similar technological equipment, the method was probably much more burn than
slash. It was difficult to fell large trees with stone implements and was
really unnecessary if the only intention was to clear land for planting.
Trees could be girdled and allowed to die and tracts burned over without previous felling of timber. The newly burned land gave excellent
crops for the first two or three years, but fields were soon exhausted and
had to be allowed to lie fallow until new forest growth had sprung up.
People who practiced this method had to move their villages frequently.
Among the Iroquois this took place at approximately twenty-year intervals. Such movements tended to push the Neolithic frontier rapidly
northward until it reached the limits set by climate. It also meant that,

as long as there were new lands to be exploited, there was little reason for warfare between Neolithic groups. If they made war at all, it was probably against the comparatively sparse Mesolithic population, who could harass the Neolithic settlers but could make little head against their rapid population increase.

The initial Neolithic settlement had a spotty distribution because of the Neolithic farmers' preference for the loess soils which were best for grain. Until these had been exploited, the Mesolithic population was left in control of regions where the soil was sandy or of heavy clay. This gave opportunity for prolonged contact between the two cultures, and there seems to have been considerable borrowing back and forth. This was no doubt stimulated by the sharp change in environment, which made it necessary for the Neolithic settlers to alter much of their preexisting technology. The mud houses of Southwest Asia were unsuited to the comparatively wet climate of Europe and gave place to wattle and daub structures with high-pitched thatched roofs. When the settlers obtained bronze, wood working became much easier, and even those structures were replaced in many regions by solidly built log houses which were the prototypes of our own frontier log cabins. The forest environment made wood and bark available for all sorts of tools and utensils, and we know that the Mesolithic population were already making extensive use of these materials. The sudden increase in the importance of wood in the economy of the first Neolithic forest dwellers in Europe is attested by the frequency of adzes in their sites. Axes are superior tools for tree felling, but the adze is the wood-working tool *par excellence*. These adzes were frequently hafted in antler sockets pierced for the insertion of a handle, an unquestionable borrowing from the Mesolithic cultures.

The first Neolithic settlers in Central Europe raised wheat of several sorts, barley, and various legumes, and kept a few cattle, although the last were of little economic importance. Crops were cultivated with stone hoes. There seems to have been very little hunting or fishing. Villages were small and had to be moved frequently because of soil exhaustion. The villagers lived in large oblong houses, each of which must have sheltered several families, a good indication that they had some sort of extended family organization. Material culture was simple. The most striking feature was the rarity of weapons. This and the lack of implements of Mesolithic type in the Neolithic settlements suggest that settlers and aborigines practiced some sort of mutual avoidance. Slings were used, but the bow seems to have been lacking. The favorite and almost exclusive wood working tool was the adze. Pottery was molded by hand and decorated with spirals and other curvilinear designs pressed into the clay. There was some trade from the earliest times. Shells from the Mediterranean were carried as far as Czechoslovakia, and stone adzes and even pottery were transported for considerable distances. The archeological record as a whole suggests a hard-working, peaceful peasant society with few differences in wealth or status.

This first phase gradually gave way to a second, in which the emphasis shifted increasingly from farming to stock raising. There was more reliance on hunting and fishing and various tools and weapons show Mesolithic influence. The villagers seem to have borrowed from the aborigines the bow and arrow, with transverse arrowhead, and the hammer axe, based on an antler prototype. Villages were larger than in the earlier period and were occupied for longer times. Some of them were fortified. Houses, on the other hand, became much smaller, suggesting a breakdown of the earlier kin groups. Pottery became increasingly elaborate. It was made in many shapes and the old curvilinear designs were now more frequently painted than impressed. There were numerous small clay figurines, most of which represented women, doves, or bulls. All these were associated with the cult of the old Southwest Asiatic Mother Goddess and indicate that she was worshipped here. Although the standard of living was higher than in the first phase, there seem to have been no clearly defined social classes. There almost certainly were chiefs and either priests or priestesses, but the relation between these and their fellow tribesmen was not an exploitive one.

All through the Central European Neolithic there was a fairly consistent trend toward increased special mobility. There are no indications that any of the Central European people became true nomads, but they moved about with increasing freedom, thanks to their progressive shift from a farming to a herding economy. This was a reaction to the eastward spread of parkland conditions resulting partly from deforestation by human agency and partly from a climatic shift which for some centuries brought warmer, drier weather. With the mobility came a progressive broadening of trade contacts and a great increase in warfare. The latter was no doubt also stimulated by the new herding economy, since domestic animals are easy to steal and have to be protected from both human and animal enemies.

There were a number of resemblances between the Central European cultures and those of the Aegean Islands. Such resemblances can best be explained as a result of contact between each of these areas and some intervening region, probably Anatolia. All through the prehistoric period there was a steady diffusion into Central Europe of culture patterns originating in the Near East. One of the most interesting examples of this was the appearance, at the close of the Neolithic, of a new weapon, a double-bladed stone battle-axe perforated for hafting. The perforation weakened the weapon and made it likely to break in two under a heavy blow, but the whole was a slavish imitation of bronze battle-axes in use in Mesopotamia and Anatolia at the same period. Even the ridges left on the bronze axes by the piece molds in which they had been cast were often copied in the stone reproduction.

Stone axes of this type were in use over much of Northern and Central Europe. In due course various local forms appeared, some of which show the influence of the ancient Mesolithic antler hammer-axe. Various European scholars have taken the original double-bladed form as indication of a distinct "Battle-Axe Culture" brought into Europe from the east by the first of a long series of invasions from the Eurasiatic steppes. Whether there was such a culture and such an invasion cannot be determined at present. The battle-axes are found in many cultures which differ in other respects and if there really was a Battle-Axe people we must think of them as a small, highly mobile and exceedingly warlike group of very simple culture who spread rapidly over Central Europe, establishing themselves as rulers in a variety of different tribes.

The development of metal working in Central Europe also seems to have been due to diffusion. A few small objects hammered from native copper were in use even in the later Neolithic, but the arts of smelting and casting were certainly introduced from the Near East. The mineral wealth of the Carpathians no doubt stimulated this diffusion. Bronze was such a valuable material that, aside from the objects placed in tombs, little of it was lost or destroyed. It was hoarded much as gold has been hoarded through the ages. It is said that the American gold reserve at Fort Knox probably includes gold that was part of the treasure of Egyptian kings in 3000–4000 B.C., although it has been cast in many different forms in the intervening years. Similarly, the supply of bronze accumulated all through the Bronze Age, making it increasingly available and leading eventually to its use for all sorts of specialized tools and even agricultural implements.

Different types of bronze tools and weapons were preferred in different areas, and there can be little doubt that there were not only local bronze workers but journeymen smiths who traveled from tribe to tribe and stayed for a time wherever their services were needed. A similar situation has existed until very recent times in Africa, where clans of iron workers might serve several tribes without being considered really a part of any of them. There also were itinerant merchants who covered long distances in their journeys and carried with them scrap bronze as a part of their merchandise. By 1500 B.C. regular trade routes had been opened up from the Baltic to the Aegean, Mediterranean bronze and other luxury objects being carried northward and furs and Baltic amber traveling southward in return. The itinerant smiths and merchants, with their knowledge of local languages, must have played an important role in the diffusion of ideas as well as appliances.

Two important additions to the Central and Northern European equipment were made during the Bronze Age: the plow and the horse. The Neolithic Europeans had done their cultivating with stone hoes, which were well adapted to grubbing in root-filled soil left after forests had been burned. The use of the plow indicated not only that cleared land had been brought under genuine cultivation, but also that some method permitting continued land use had been substituted for the old slash and burn agricultural technique. It is highly probable that the Bronze Age witnessed the introduction of the three field system, which was kept up throughout most of Europe until after the discovery of

HEAVY PLOW

America. In this system, as we have seen, a field was planted with grain one year, with legumes the second and allowed to lie fallow the third; throughout the entire time animals were pastured over it whenever crops were not growing. The ancient ard plow of the Near East was unsuited for breaking sod or for turning over water-logged heavy clay soil, and during the later Bronze or early Iron Age a different and much heavier type of plow, equipped with a mold board, was invented in Northern Europe. But this plow was also unable to deal with the tough sod of long-established prairies. Even in America, settlers using the North European agricultural equipment were unable to conquer the prairies until the invention of the steel plow in the 19th century. The Eurasiatic grasslands presented a more serious challenge to agriculture than any other part of the continent except the sub-Arctic zone and have remained a preserve for pastoral peoples until recent times.

The introduction of horses into Europe was an event of prime cultural importance. A wild forest horse was native to Western Europe, a shaggy, heavy-boned animal which was hunted like other game. It does not seem to have been domesticated during Neolithic times, although it may have been crossed in later time with the imported type. Some of its blood may survive in the heavy draft horses of Northwestern Europe.

The first domestic horses appeared in Central Europe early in the Bronze Age, and were of a fast, light boned Central Asiatic breed. Horses were not particularly profitable animals to raise for either milk or meat, and it was a long time before horse harnesses suitable for heavy traction were developed. There can be little doubt that the horse was brought to Europe as a fighting animal and that it came as a fundamental part of the equipment of invaders from the east. However, these Bronze Age horse drivers must not be confused with the later and much more efficient mounted invaders who came from the same region. The first evidence which we have for the riding of horses in Europe comes from the Hallstatt culture of the early Iron Age.

The first use of the horse was as a draft animal, in imitation of the slow and docile ox, and the earliest harness was modeled on the ox yoke. The war chariot as we know it from Homeric times or as it was used by the Iron Age Gauls was a highly specialized appliance which could be made only by skilled craftsmen with excellent tools. It certainly was not in use as a developed appliance at the time the Bronze Age horse drivers brought the first horses into Central Europe. Since ox carts were in use in the Near East by 4000 B.C., the first fighting vehicles were probably copied from them. A crude war wagon with four solid wooden wheels and planked or wicker-work sides is shown on the Sumerian standard from Ur. Some of the so-called "hearses," whose remains have been found in the burials of Bronze Age chiefs, may well be the remains of such fighting vehicles. It is highly improbable that there were any drilled troops in Europe at the time the horse was introduced. Bronze Age armies, like the Homeric ones, were unruly mobs of competitive heroes. A war wagon driven at full speed into such a mob would break any line of battle which might have been formed, and when its charge bogged down, it would still provide a platform from which its crew could throw spears and wield axes as if from behind breastwork.

The light, two-wheeled, two-man war chariot appeared in Central Europe by the last half of the Bronze Age, but riding came still later. Bronze Age tombs show no traces of saddlery. Horses were ridden all through the Iron Age, but efficient cavalry did not appear in Europe until very late. Even in the time of Caesar's wars, the cavalry of the Gauls and Germans was essentially mounted infantry. Horses were used as a means of rapid transportation but riders usually dismounted to fight. Lacking adequate saddles and stirrups, their seat was too precarious for hand-to-hand battle.

During the late Bronze Age important social changes took place throughout most of Europe. Kingdoms and even empires appeared in the eastern Mediterranean, while throughout most of the continent new aristocratic patterns emerged. Scandinavia supported a population of well-to-do, free-holding farmers but elsewhere the peasantry was ruled by chiefs or petty kings. Such rulers concentrated the society's economic surplus in their own hands and used it to employ foreign craftsmen, buy foreign goods and provide themselves with pretentious equipment for the next world. These changes may have been due to the diffusion of political techniques and governmental patterns, for they seem to have been marked by no sudden or extensive changes in the technology of the various cultures in which they appeared. However, it seems probable that they were due to the penetration of Europe by some people with military and administrative skill but poor technology, who established themselves as rulers of the earlier population. The problem is actually very similar to that posed by the hypothetical Battle-Axe people previously discussed. Europe has witnessed so many "barbarian" invasions that one is tempted to refer their beginnings to the prehistoric period and to explain prehistoric culture changes in the familiar terms.

In summary, one is forced to conclude that the overland route was more important for the development of European culture than the Mediterranean. Most of the technological and social inventions which reached Europe from Southwest Asia appeared first in Eastern and Central Europe, and the successive waves of migration which laid the foundation for later European civilization all came either from Central Europe or even further east. The priority which has been given to the Mediterranean and coastal route is largely a result of historic accident. The earliest studies of European history were made along the Atlantic coast and the richness of the Central European remains has only become evident within the last fifty years. The Classical civilizations have cast a spell over European scholars, yet one must admit that the modern mechanized civilization of Europe owes more to the North European cultures and their barbarian background than it does to either Greece or Rome.

Chapter XIX

Aryans and Turko-Tatars

THE SPREAD of village culture from Southwestern Asia carried its economic and social patterns not only westward into Europe but also northward into the Eurasiatic steppes. Here settlers encountered conditions not unlike those which confronted our own pioneers when they reached the Great Plains. The western steppes provided excellent pasture, but the soil was difficult to bring under cultivation. There were no forests to serve as a basis for slash and burn cultivation, and the age-old prairie sod could not be broken with primitive plows. To complicate matters still further, the steppes had long climate cycles like those of our own Plains: a run of wet years alternating with a run of drought years. Under these circumstances the immigrants turned more and more from agriculture to stock farming. Since the pasture was good enough to make cattle more profitable than sheep, the emotional and economic focus of this culture was on cattle and cattle products, with horses, apparently first domesticated farther to the east, as a second but less important interest.

At a pre-scientific level of culture the very fact of cattle raising has certain unavoidable consequences. A cattle people cannot choose but be warlike. Cattle are easy to steal and their owners must guard them constantly while under equally constant temptation to add to their herds at the expense of their neighbors. A cattle people cannot be genuinely nomadic. As any dairyman can testify, cows that are kept constantly on the move will give very little milk. Herds may be shifted to different pastures with the changing seasons, but when the pasture is reached they must be allowed to graze undisturbed.

Lastly, a cattle economy lends itself readily to the development of aristocratic social patterns. For the cattle owner, wealth produces wealth automatically. All that is needed is adequate protection of the herd against thieves and wild animals. A family without cattle is condemned to hopeless poverty; one with cattle can at least hope for wealth. At the same time considerable social mobility is inevitable. A rich family may be reduced to poverty overnight by an enemy raid or, nearly as rapidly, by an epidemic. Conversely, for the ambitious young man, cattle-lifting has all the excitement and financial possibilities of stock market speculation among ourselves. The successful cattle thief is the most admired member of the community. Failing this, it is a regular pattern for poor young men to attach themselves to rich cattle owners, preferably kinsmen. They help to guard and care for the patron's herds, receiving in return his protection and a share of the herd increase. Since manpower is usually at a premium, distant kinsmen or even outsiders are sure of a welcome.

Except for graves, cattle people leave few clues for the archeologist. Their economy is best carried on from small, widely scattered settlements like the *kraals* of the South African Bantu. However, it seems safe to conclude that cattle cultures of one general type were in existence over most of the western Eurasiatic steppes by the middle of the Bronze Age.

We have already seen how grassland replaced forest in much of Central Europe during the late Neolithic and Bronze Ages, and the cattle culture spread eastward to occupy the new territory. Part of this spread was a result of diffusion, part of actual migration. The latter carried it still farther west, beyond the limits of the grasslands, for the cattle people found in the agricultural peasantry of Western Europe a new and highly profitable breed of domestic animal. When a peasant community had been captured, no very difficult task, it became a steady source of income. The only danger involved was that some other family of peasant-keepers might try to steal it. The situation for the first few centuries after the arrival of the cattle people was probably much like that which Herodotus describes among the Scythians. The Noble Scythians retained their cattle culture but supplemented it by exploiting the Common Scythians, who raised grain and docilely turned over their economic surplus to their rulers.

Between 1800 and 1500 B.C. cattle-keeping tribes pressed southward from the steppes along a front extending all the way from India to the Balkans. Records left by the civilized groups whom they attacked indicate that these invaders all spoke languages of the Indo-European stock. The tribes who invaded India called themselves *Arya,* hence the much abused term *Aryan.* One may use *Aryan* to designate those tribes who were of cattle culture and Indo-European speech, but the term should not be applied to groups who lacked either of these characteristics. It seems highly probable that all the tribes who shared the cattle culture of the steppes were not Indo-European speaking. The culture area probably took in certain Turko-Tatar tribes on its northeastern borders. Conversely, there are indications that Indo-European languages were spoken outside the cattle area even in very early times. In regions such as the Eurasiatic plains, where there are no natural barriers to movement, single linguistic stocks tend to extend over wide areas, and it must be remembered that in spite of the gradual change from grassland to forest as one moves westward, the plains themselves extend from the Tien Shan to the Baltic. Both archeological finds and historic records indicate that there were Indo-European speaking peoples in Turkestan and the Tarim basin until shortly before the beginning of the Christian era, and it seems quite possible that the linguistic stock had a parallel extension to the west. One exceedingly primitive Indo-European language, Lettish, has existed in the forests bordering the Baltic since time immemorial, and the existence in Anatolia of another group of primitive Indo-European languages has been revealed by the Hittite archives.

The spread of Indo-European languages over Europe has often been noted as an inexplicable phenomenon. According to the standard theory, the continent was occupied in Neolithic times by tribes speaking many languages of many different stocks and scholars have always been puzzled by the apparent ease with which they surrendered their original tongues and accepted that of their presumably Aryan conquerors. It seems well within the range of possibility that this ancient linguistic diversity was characteristic of the Mediterranean and Atlantic borders of the continent rather than the interior. Central and Eastern Europe may well have been Indo-European speaking even in Neolithic times. Certainly there is no indication here of the sort of linguistic competition which studded Western Europe with non-Indo-European place names and left the Basques in linguistic isolation.

All the Aryan tribes were illiterate at the time of their first appearance in history. However, they have left records which make it possible to reconstruct their life with considerable accuracy. Various writers have pointed out that there seems to be some intimate connection between a cattle economy and epic poetry. The Aryans were no exception to this rule. Bards had an important place in their society, acting as a combination of historical library and publicity agent. The bards composed, or more often, memorized, metrical compositions dealing with historic happenings and the deeds of heroes. In spite of their blood and thunder subject matter, modern readers find these epics insufferably dull. New epics were composed whenever a great event or wealthy patron provided the necessary stimulus. It was the great ambition of every Aryan chief to be commemorated in this way, and there can be no question that the models of heroic behavior enshrined in the epics and the desire to be remembered as a hero had a very real influence on behavior. Certainly it was behind the widespread Aryan belief that how a man won or lost was almost as important as whether he won.

The bard who inserted the name of his host's ancestor or a locally popular episode into a well-known epic was certain of an extra fee, so the historical value of these compositions is not too high. At the same time, the picture which they give of the culture is reliable, since it is quite unconscious. From the common denominator of Aryan epics that have been preserved in regions as diverse as India, Persia, Greece, Ireland, and Scandinavia, it is possible to reconstruct the life of the Aryans at the time when they were adjusting to their new role as rulers of conquered peasant populations. For the earlier period, before they had left the steppes, some evidence is provided by the root words common to all, or a large majority, of the later Indo-European languages. However, this linguistic evidence is so fragmentary that it seems best to limit this description to the conquest period.

When the Aryans emerged from the steppes they seem to have been casual agriculturalists as well as dairymen, but they cheerfully relinquished plowing and planting to their subjects. Trade was regarded as a slightly dishonorable substitute for robbery with violence and was employed only as a last resort. Loans with interest were considered on a par with petty larceny. The dominant interests of the society were war and the breeding or theft of cattle and horses. It is suggestive that sheep and goats figure very little in the epics, although they were certainly kept by many of the conquered peasant communities. Horses were important and were both driven and ridden, although there are few mentions even in late epics of fighting on horseback. The favorite conveyance of early chiefs and heroes was the war chariot.

Technology followed the general Southwest Asiatic pattern, with little or no adaption to nomadic life. The Aryans had no portable shelters comparable to the *yurts* of the Turko-Tatar peoples. Wherever they settled for a few days they built wattle and daub huts, easily made and easily abandoned. Clothing was of loom-woven woolen cloth, draped, not tailored, although trousers soon came into use among the tribes in Northern Europe. The wheel and plow were known and pottery was made. All metals except iron were worked at the time of first emergence from the steppes, and the use of iron was soon learned. The weapon inventory was extensive, including spears, swords and axes of various sorts, the bow and arrow, helmet, and shield. The use of body armor during the early period is uncertain. Wealthy men and women wore many gold ornaments, and the most honorable gift was one of these stripped off and given to the recipient directly. During the early period there were Aryan craftsmen, especially smiths, who occupied a good social position. Later, most manufacturing was relegated to the conquered.

The Aryans were not nomadic, merely loosely attached to the soil. On any excuse they would pile their goods in ponderous ox carts, burn their huts, and set out on long treks into unknown territory. Their invasions completely lacked the lightning speed and mobility of the much later Hunnish and Mongol attacks. The whole tribe moved as a ponderous unit, complete with its cattle. Victory meant new pasture lands to be occupied, defeat annihilation. As the Aryans became better adjusted to the role of a conquering nobility these mass tribal movements became less frequent, but they continued into the Classical period and were the terror of the civilized Mediterranean peoples. Note the Roman reaction to the invasion of the Cimbri and Teutones, and the migration of the Helvetii which set in motion the Roman conquest of Gaul.

All the epics picture a three-class society, consisting of nobles and commoners, who together formed the Aryans proper, and serfs, who represented the conquered local population. There were no kings, in the ordinarily accepted meaning of the term, although able chiefs might become the leaders of alliances of tribes. Families which had produced leaders over several generations formed the highest aristocracy, and their members would be considered first when a high chief was needed. Chattel slaves seem to have been very rare in the early period. Few if any male prisoners were taken in war between Aryan groups, while women became the concubines of the victors, and were eventually assimilated into their tribe. Commoners and nobles were frequently related, the difference being mainly one of wealth and prestige. Serfs, when they appear at all in the epics, figure as socially inferior to the nobles' horses and dogs. The Aryans felt strong affection for these animals, and their names and individual qualities often appear in the epics beside those of their masters.

Aryan society was essentially patrilineal, but such great value was placed upon individual independence and initiative that it could scarcely be called patriarchal. Sons could escape from paternal authority as soon as they were grown. Kin ties were reckoned on both sides of the house and for as long as they could be remembered. This gave poor men and younger sons a wide range of choice among family groups to which they might attach themselves. The most generous family head naturally drew the most followers, and stinginess was the most contemptible vice with which an Aryan noble could be charged. Hospitality was indiscriminate and unlimited, and the host-guest relationship established a tie which might be transmitted to the descendants of both parties.

An Aryan tribe consisted of a series of households, each composed of a household head, his wife or wives and children, younger brothers

and their families, unless they had had the energy to strike out for
themselves, and various more or less distant relatives who had chosen
to attach themselves to the group. Household heads constituted the
nobility, their poor relations the commoners. Each household owned a
particular territory with the serfs living upon it. Thus, in order to be
rated as noble in early Ireland, a man had to own twenty cattle or five
families of serfs. The chief of an Aryan tribe was simply the head of
its wealthiest and most important family. His establishment was like
that of any other family head except for its larger scale and the greater
number of voluntary followers. Many of these could claim remote kinship with the chief, but manpower was so valuable that even unrelated
men would be accepted. Such voluntary followers were supported by
the chief's generosity and gave complete loyalty in return. They formed
the chief's bodyguard in battle and, if he were killed, they were supposed to die with him. In them one sees the prototype of King Arthur's
Round Table and the less well-known Red Branch Fellowship of ancient Ireland.

The post of chief carried more responsibility than economic reward.
No taxes were paid to the chief, and he was expected to meet the costs
of his establishment out of the income from his own estate. Even medieval European kings adhered to this pattern, and it has echoes even today in North European countries and in the United States, where government posts are regarded as a combination of honor and duty rather
than as a source of income. These are the only places in the world where
an honest man's acceptance of a government post normally entails severe financial loss.

Although the living arrangements of Aryan households differed
somewhat from one locality to another, the basic patterns were much
the same everywhere. There was a central building, the Hall, with
smaller buildings grouped about to serve as stables, work shops, storehouses, and living quarters for serfs attached to the household. The
household head and his relatives lived in the Hall, where all ate and
slept together. The family head, his close relatives, and honored guests
occupied a raised platform at one end of the Hall. At mealtimes trestle
tables were set up and the company was seated at these in order of importance, the most important closest to the dais. At night the tables were
cleared away and the company slept on the floor, although the family
head and a few other important persons might have built-in bunks. Light
and heat were provided by fires built along the center of the floor, the
smoke going out through a slot along the center of the roof. The whole
arrangement was much like that of a British Columbian Indian house of
the early 19th century. Where the conquered population were numerous and accustomed to town living, as in Mycenean Greece, the

ruling household's establishment was heavily fortified and might form the center of an extensive settlement. In northern Europe, on the other hand, each household lived in isolation, with no defense except the valor of its members.

Life in these households was not too dull. There were always feuds to keep the members on the *qui vive* and cattle raids against neighboring tribes provided both pleasure and profit. Wandering bards came and stayed as long as the host's generosity warranted. Gambling was usual and heavy drinking was the rule.

The early Aryan attitude toward sex and marriage, as revealed in the epics, can best be described as casual. Although there was no recognized period of premarital experimentation, as in Southeast Asia, little value was attached to virginity. An exchange of gifts usually accompanied marriage, but there seems to have been no formal bride price or dowry during the early period. Lacking such economic stabilizers, marriages were brittle. A woman's ties to her own family were always regarded as stronger than her ties to her husband, and in case of a feud she was expected to side with them. Marriage was normally monogamous, as it actually is everywhere, but a rich or attractive man might have two or three wives. Women often took the initiative in cases of this sort, preferring a share in a superior man to complete possession of an inferior one. Concubines, taken from the serf population, were usual. Concubines and wives all lived in the Hall and their children were reared together. A common North European folklore motif of the hero's foster brother who resembles him so much that he can impersonate him is a memory of the days when the foster brother was really a half brother, son of a concubine.

A woman derived her social position from her own kin group, with the result that wives not infrequently ranked their husbands. Such women not only dominated the household but had as much freedom as men in the distribution of their favors. Although polyandry was very rarely institutionalized, a series of lovers do not seem to have been considered to a noblewoman's discredit.

Aryan attitudes toward the supernatural were also rather casual. In the earliest period family heads acted as priests, a practice which continued in Scandinavia until the introduction of Christianity. Elsewhere, specialists in dealing with the supernatural emerged, but their social status was low. They were kept in noble households to insure the proper performance of rituals but were treated like family chaplains.

Worship centered around a collection of supernatural Beings known collectively as "The Bright Ones." During the early period many of these do not seem to have been clearly individualized, but all of them were anthropomorphic in their needs and motivations. A male Being,

resident in the sky, was preeminent, and it is significant that there was
no Earth Mother whose importance corresponded to that of the Sky
Father. Male and female Beings were usually paired as husband and
wife, but each had his or her own activities and the pair did not act as
a unit, an obvious reflection of the normal Aryan marriage situation.
The qualities of Beings other than the Sky Father were so vaguely defined that they could easily be adjusted to the preexisting religious concepts of the various regions into which the Aryans came as conquerors.
The same holds for the organization of the pantheon. Thus, while the
Norse deities and the Olympian Beings of classic mythology were organized along the lines of an Aryan household, the Celtic, Iranian, and
Indian deities do not seem to have shared this pattern.

Certain additional features of Aryan religion may be noted. There
were no animal deities or even zoomorphic demons. Even such a Being
as the early Persian "Ox Spirit" seems to have been conceived without
animal form. The favorite Aryan method of disposing of the dead seems
to have been cremation. This is a technique which is ordinarily believed
to break the ties of the deceased with earth completely and to protect
against the return of the ghost. As might be expected under such circumstances, ancestor worship was conspicuously lacking. Lastly, all the
Aryans seem to have believed in the existence of Fate, an impersonal
mechanism which was superior to both gods and men and which could
not be influenced by prayer, sacrifice, or even magic. This belief made
the Aryan hero resigned to ill fortune, but it also justified him in his
belief that he might win through, even against the hostility of the
gods.

The Aryan culture was so simple that its bearers were able to make
few direct contributions. On the technological side, these contributions
were almost entirely connected with weapons and techniques of warfare. On the social side, their influence was much more far-reaching.
The institution of the noble household's protecting and exploiting the
peasantry living upon its estates became the normal one for Celtic and
Germanic Europe. While it is ordinarily supposed to have disappeared
in Gaul and Britain during the period of Roman domination, it is impossible to say how far it persisted in rural regions even during this
time. The ease with which it was re-established after the Roman collapse suggests that it must have been well remembered. In any case, the
pattern had been retained by the Germanic tribes who invaded western
Europe and was embodied in the feudal system. The French *menes* of
the Dark Ages, from which the more familiar term *desmenes* was derived, was essentially the old Aryan household. The only important
point at which the feudal organization differed from its ancient predecessor was in the superposition of an all-over organization by which

weaker families assured themselves of the support of stronger ones by their promise of aid in war. Aside from military service, feudal dues were normally so light as to have little more than symbolic value.

Perhaps the most important contribution of the Aryans to later civilization was the establishment of the aristocratic pattern which survived in Europe until recent times. Any culture of national scope is inevitably composed of numerous sub-cultures. While the peasant and bourgeois sub-cultures of various European countries have been distinctive, their aristocratic sub-cultures have been so similar that an aristocrat from one nation could understand the attitudes and values of an aristocrat from another nation better than he could understand those of his own lower classes. The outdoor hunting life has been an aristocratic prerogative since the dawn of European history. When it was no longer required to supplement the food supply, it continued as a sport and as a symbol of membership in the aristocratic group. The nobleman had to be a good horseman, and in fact, such terms as *ritter* and *chevalier* reduce to this. It has been said that even in 19th century England any young man of the aristocratic class would much rather have his morals aspersed than his horsemanship.

The European nobleman was strictly limited in his occupations. He could not work on the land himself without losing caste, nor could he engage in trade. The one gainful pursuit which was open to him was horse and cattle breeding. It is interesting to note that now that the horse has lost its economic importance, young Englishmen of the upper class can, by a transfer of the sort familiar to anthropologists, become automobile salesmen without violating the taboo on trade. Intellectual and artistic pursuits were regarded with some contempt, once more following the original Aryan pattern. The aristocrat might act as a patron of the arts and science, but he was not supposed to engage in either himself. Until very recent times most European aristocrats have been poorly educated, and the schools designed for them have been more interested in "character building" than in providing the student with useful knowledge or practical skills. It has been said that the battle of Waterloo was won on the playing fields of Eton, and one might add that Singapore was lost in its classrooms.

The aristocrat might go into the church, especially if he was a younger son, but religiosity was frowned upon and Christian taboos more honored in the breach than in the observance. Sex mores retained the old Aryan casualness. Aristocrats were expected to marry within their own caste to insure the legitimacy of their descendants, but no high degree of chastity was required either before or after marriage and the use of lower-class women in casual liaisons was taken for granted. In this connection it should be noted that in spite of the formal monogamy demanded of Christians, European royalty has been polygynous until quite recent times. It was expected that a king or great noble would have a number of concubines, usually drawn from various aristocratic families who hoped in this way to obtain additional political influence. The offspring of such concubines, although excluded from the succession, nevertheless had a recognized social position within the aristocratic hierarchy. Since they were debarred from the succession and their fortunes depended upon the good will of the royal parent, they were in general more trustworthy than legitimate heirs and could be placed in positions where a legitimate heir might foment revolt. Thus the "Grand Bastard of Burgundy," a title as specific as that of "Prince of Wales," was by custom commander-in-chief of the Burgundian armies.

Gambling and heavy drinking could also be indulged in by the aristocrat without loss of caste. The only requirement was that he gamble honestly and give his gambling debts precedence over all others, perhaps because these were debts normally owed to equals. To cheat at cards was an unforgivable sin, only one degree less deadly than physical cowardice. From the time of the first Aryan invasions, chiefs had been expected to lead their followers in battle and to risk their own persons recklessly as an example to the rest. Since the supremacy of the aristocratic group rested upon the tradition of their superior courage and pugnacity, anyone who showed himself lacking in these was regarded as a traitor to his class.

The Eurasiatic steppes are bounded on the east by the Tien Shan and Altai Mountains, between which the narrow Dzungarian plain leads into the Mongolian plateau. These mountains form a natural barrier between two different environments and what were once two markedly different cultures. The western steppes are fairly well watered, with abundant pasture making possible the mixed dairying and incidental-grain-farming economy which has just been described as the cattle culture. The Mongolian plains, on the other hand, are much drier and stand at a higher elevation. They include such inhospitable stretches as the Gobi Desert and are in general too poor to make cattle raising profitable. At the same time the pasturage is sufficient for sheep, camels, and horses. Since the horse was in many respects the most important animal in the local economy, we will call the particular pattern of culture which developed in this region the horse culture, in contrast to the cattle culture of the west.

The cultures and populations of these two regions originally presented marked differences. In the western plains the early population was, for the most part, Caucasic in physical type and Indo-European in language. We do not know how far east this condition once prevailed, but the presence of an Indo-European language, Tokarian, in the Tarim basin directly south of the Tien Shan mountains suggests that a population of western type ran to the Dzungarian gateway. The cattle culture typical of this population was unquestionably an outgrowth of the Southwestern village pattern, and comparatively few elements in it can be traced to any other source. The people of the Mongolian plateau have been Mongoloid in physical type since the most remote period for which we have evidence and have spoken languages of the Turko-Tatar stock. Although most of their domestic species seem to have come from the west, their culture owed little to that of the Southwestern Asiatic villagers. It shows so many similarities to the Circumpolar culture that it can best be interpreted as consisting of a northern Mesolithic culture base upon which pastoral patterns have been superimposed.

It is rarely realized how late the appearance of the fully developed horse culture was. Tribes, who sometimes rode their horses instead of driving them, did not necessarily share the rest of the horse culture complex. The Achaemenid Persians, who are ordinarily thought of as a horse people, were actually a cattle people. The ox spirit was constantly invoked in the hymns of Zoroaster. Although they were better horsemen than the Greeks, they were culturally much closer to the primitive

MONGOL MERCHANTS IN LHASA

Aryans than to the nomads of the eastern Asiatic plains. During the initial period of Persian conquest the great king marched on foot at the head of his troops. In later times he rode in a chariot, but the 10,000 immortals, his bodyguard, were always infantry. The Scythians had acquired more elements of the horse culture, but they were still primarily a cattle people, depending heavily on dairying, practicing considerable agriculture, and lacking the horse culture's elaborate adjustments to nomadic life. Turning to the eastern end of the Eurasiatic plains, we know that the horse was introduced into northern China by the founders of the Shang dynasty, roughly 1700 B.C., but it was used with chariots, not ridden. In the Shang inscriptions their western neighbors are referred to as sheep-herds and seem to have been able to offer little resistance to incursions into their territory. Shang inscriptions record sacrifices of so many oxen and so many shepherds as though the two were considered very much on a par. Chinese records state that the Huns did not have horses before 500 B.C. This seems highly improbable, but 500 B.C. may very well represent the first appearance of the particular combination of cultural features which transformed the people of the Mongolian plateau from relatively harmless sheep-herders into effective cavalry.

The principal reason for treating the horse culture of the Mongolian plateau at this point is that the history of the steppes has been one of the steady westward pressure exerted by the horse people on the cattle people. The beginnings of this pressure date back to the second or third century B.C., and it was continued with only occasional interruptions until about 1250 A.D., when the movement was completed with the Mongol conquest of Russia. In the course of these invasions most of the bearers of the original cattle culture were driven out of the western steppes and replaced by tribes predominantly of horse culture. There seems to have been plenty of mixture during this period, since conquered tribes were regularly incorporated and used in further conquests. Thus Attila's heavy cavalry were Goths, and the composer of the Nibelungenlied notes with astonishment the variety of peoples at Attila's court.

Such groups as the Huns, Avars and, later, Magyars and Mongols even penetrated beyond the plains into Western Europe, but were unable to maintain their distinctive culture in what was still largely a forest environment, and either withdrew to the steppes or were absorbed into the local populations. Only the Magyars were able to maintain their cultural integrity and national coherence; this was probably due to the shallowness of their European penetration, which had not carried them beyond the limits of the grasslands. The Turks, although they came from Central Asia, can scarcely be classed as one of the waves of nomadic invaders. They became so thoroughly acculturated in the course of their infiltration into Southwest Asia that their empire must be considered a cultural as well as political inheritor of Persia and Byzantium.

The horse culture of the steppes was the most perfect example of a nomadic domestic animal economy which the world has ever seen. The tribes who followed it were thoroughly averse to agriculture. Sometimes they sowed millet, which would grow untended, but they did this mainly as a reserve against famine. Under normal conditions they made no use of agriculturally produced foods or materials. Their domestic animals were sheep, horses, Bactrian camels, and cattle, in order of their

BAGHIRMI WARRIOR IN QUILTED ARMOR (SUDAN)

economic importance. Sheep were raised in enormous numbers. The historic Kazaks of the region counted their flocks, not by individual animals, but by the number of dogs required to herd them. Sheep were sometimes milked, but their main importance lay in meat and wool. Mutton was the staple everyday diet and was eaten in tremendous quantities. One sheep per man per day was regarded as a standard ration. Wool was used for felt.

The great importance of the horse lay in its use as a fighting animal. It was ridden or used as a pack animal, never for draft. Horse meat was regularly eaten, and the flesh of a young mare was regarded as a special delicacy, usually reserved for feasts. When food ran short, soldiers drank blood drawn from their mounts. Mares were milked and their milk fermented to make *kumiss.* Mare's milk was much richer in sugar than cow's milk, and by proper fermentation it was possible to produce an alcoholic beverage with considerable authority. The horse people in general were heavy drinkers, and the end of a successful banquet saw all the guests unconscious. Genghis Khan is reported to have said: "A

MONGOL PRINCE

man who is drunk is like one struck on the head; his wisdom and skill avail him not at all. Get drunk only three times a month. It would be better not to get drunk at all. But who can abstain altogether?"

Camels were used both as pack animals and to draw baggage carts. They were rarely milked or eaten. Cattle were of minor importance in the Mongolian plateau but became more significant as the horse culture expanded westward. Cattle were both milked and eaten, and oxen were used for draft.

The origins of Mongolian domestic animal economy present certain interesting problems. Of the four species involved, sheep and cattle were certainly of Southwest Asiatic origin. It seems probable that they were diffused into the Mongolian plateau from the west and that the first domestic animal economy to develop there was built about them. Horses are generally believed to have been domesticated somewhere in Central Asia rather than in Mongolia, since the wild ancestor of all the present domestic breeds seems to have been the Tarpan, a Central Asiatic rather than Mongolian species. The central position of the horse in Mongolian culture would not preclude such a foreign origin, since we know from the history of the American Plains Indians that within the space of 150 years a new domestic animal can be incorporated into a pre-existing culture with revolutionary results. There can be no doubt that the Bactrian camel was domesticated in the Mongolian plateau, although the date is uncertain. It seems probable that this took place after the introduction of at least sheep and cattle.

It is interesting to note that the attitudes of the horse people toward their domestic animals seems to have been a highly utilitarian one. There are no famous individual horses or dogs described in their epics. Animals were mass produced and mass consumed. The Mongol warrior took with him a string of anonymous mounts to be abandoned or slaughtered for food when they gave out. Perhaps life in the plateau was too hard to allow for sentimental attachments to pets. The horse people seem to have carried over into the pastoral stage the attitude of hunters who looked upon animals simply as potential meat. Even in the days of the Mongol conquests, hunting remained more of a business than a sport in this region. Great surrounds were organized from time to time, and all animals caught in the circle were shot down and eaten.

Hunting and herding produced not only food but also clothing. The normal costume consisted of trousers, boots with upturned toes, a sleeved, shirt-like upper garment, short skirted for men and long skirted for women, and a cap or hood. Over this a cloak was worn in bitter weather. All clothing was made of skins or felt, the only exception being occasional festive garments of cloth obtained through trade or loot. The favorite material was sheepskin worn with the wool inside. Felt seems to have been an invention of this area. Anyone who has seen a camel in the process of spring shed can understand where the original felt makers may have gotten the idea. In making felt, wool was boiled, then spread out evenly on a mat or hide and the whole rolled up. The roll was then beaten or kicked back and forth between two lines of seated workers until the wool was thoroughly felted. From time to time the bundle would be unrolled, more wool added in places where it was thin, and the whole sprinkled with boiling water. Felt lacks tensile strength, but it is wind proof and more water resistant than cloth. It makes a perfect material for winter garments and is excellent as a tent cover, the only drawback in this usage being its weight.

The adaptation of the horse people to nomadic life was as perfect as any that has so far been devised. It must be understood that such an adaptation is in no sense primitive. It represents long experience and the exercise of great ingenuity. Developed nomad equipment bears much the same relation to that required for settled living that a modern trailer bears to a city apartment. All objects used by the horse nomads were light and relatively indestructible. Housing consisted of *yurts,* perhaps the most effective form of portable shelter so far devised. The side walls of the *yurt* were made from slats which crossed each other diagonally and were tied together at their intersections, an arrangement very much like the folding gates we use to keep small children from falling downstairs. A few sections of this lattice work were set on edge to form a circle with a single opening left for the door. Rafters radially attached to a central

YURT HOUSES

ring, much like the ribs of an umbrella, were placed on top of these walls. The frame was then covered with large pieces of felt and the whole lashed down with ropes passed back and forth over the outside.

The internal furniture consisted of felt rugs on the floor, used for both sitting and sleeping, a few wooden chests for valuables, cooking pots, originally of pottery, later of metal obtained by trade or loot, leather bags for milk and *kumiss,* and utensils of wood or horn. The house was the care and property of the woman, who was able to dismantle and pack the entire establishment in an hour or two and to erect the house again with equal speed.

In the early period all goods were probably packed on animals when the camp moved. Later, camel carts came into use but it is significant that vehicles were rarely, if ever, drawn by horses. Where the ground was level enough, as in the Khirges steppes in central Asia, houses on wheels might be used. These steppes were far enough west for cattle to be common, and oxen were used as draft animals. The wheeled houses, *kibitka,* were simply *yurts* permanently erected on platforms sometimes as much as twenty feet across and drawn by many yoke of oxen. It is said to have been the eldest daughter's duty to stand outside with a bull whip and keep the house on the move when camp was being shifted.

Horses were probably used as pack animals in the Mongolian plateau even before the introduction of the wheel, and it may be conjectured that the first saddles were pack-saddles and the first riders small children settled among the bundles when camp moved. From the wooden pack-saddle to the tree-saddle, the most important invention made in this area, was a short step. The tree-saddle consisted of a rigid frame of wood with raised pommel and cantle, the whole suitably padded to make it more comfortable for man and beast. Stirrups also seem to have been invented in this region, although we do not know the exact date. In any case they appeared later than the tree-saddle, and we have no record of their use much before the beginning of the Christian era. A tree-saddle, especially when combined with stirrups, gives the rider a freedom and a control over his mount otherwise impossible.

Even when the successors of the cattle people unhitched their horses from their chariots and began to ride them, they employed only pad saddles, and their cavalry was correspondingly inefficient. Since, in physics, every action has its corresponding reaction, the classical cavalryman could not charge with lance in rest without going over the tail of his mount when he struck his target. Neither could he handle a bow efficiently, since too much attention had to be devoted to controlling his mount and keeping his seat. The combination of the tree saddle, the composite bow (which was brought to its highest perfection by the horse people), and the lance made possible the development of a new cavalry tactic which eventually gave the horse people control of the whole Eurasiatic plains. In this tactic, the cavalrymen softened enemy resistance with showers of arrows so strongly driven that they could penetrate plate mail. Then, when the enemy ranks had been thrown into disorder, they changed to their lances and charged home. To this was added, in the eastern steppes, the development of drilled cavalry charging in line and with spaced ranks. This combination, plus rigid discipline and the high mobility given by the use of strings of horses, produced invincible armies.

We do not know when this combination first emerged or when its potentialities were first realized, but it evidently came into existence rather late. The sudden expansion of the horse culture during the centuries immediately before and after the beginning of the Christian era suggests that it developed at about this time. We find the Chinese on the western frontier suddenly changing from charioteers and infantry to cavalry shortly before the beginning of the Han dynasty (late 3rd century B.C.). There was also an exodus of Chinese peasantry into the steppes at this time, probably to take advantage of the potentialities for conquest and loot provided by the new arm. It has even been suggested that the building of the Great Wall was designed to keep the Chinese peasant in as well as to keep the horse culture invaders out.

The social organization of the horse people differed from that of the early Aryans in certain respects. Marriage was regularly polygynous and was accompanied by the payment of a bride price. At the same time the position of women was relatively high, although not as high as among the cattle people. Both sexes herded and milked the domestic animals. Women rode like men and also fought in emergencies. Wives could acquire property, including animals, by gift or inheritance, and the husband had no control over this. Each wife had her own *yurt* where she lived with her children. The first wife was generally regarded as head of the family group and took charge of the entire establishment, including the husband's flocks and herds when the husband was away. The husband's control was more autocratic than in the Aryan family. There was no regulation as to how much time he should spend with each wife. Sons were subject to their fathers and younger brothers to their elder brothers. The tie between mother and son seems to have been particularly close and to have persisted throughout life.

Class distinctions were based mainly on wealth, although the clans in a tribe were arranged in a hierarchy of importance. There were no serfs and few if any chattel slaves, since the economic patterns made them useless. The Mongol custom of massacring all but a few selected captives at the end of a campaign, when the army was to return to the steppes, was carried out simply because they did not know what else to do with captives.

The local economy made it necessary for the horse people to live in small, scattered family units throughout most of the year. In summer a man and his wives and children usually camped alone. Summer pasture was abundant enough so that the land which provided it had little value and was not regarded as property. Winter pastures, and particularly

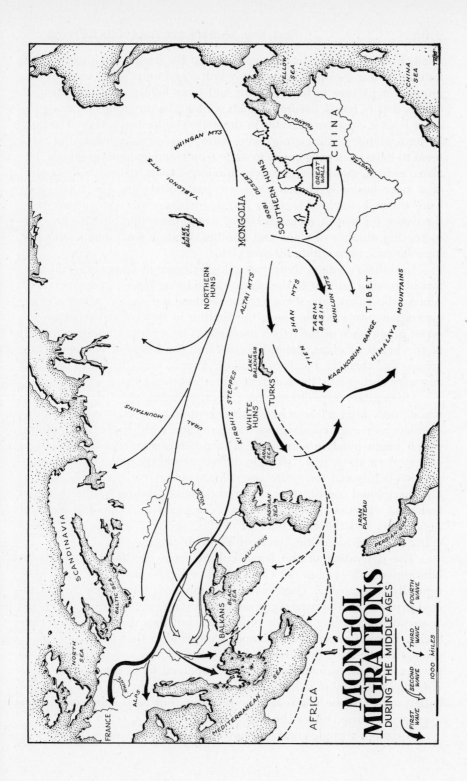

MONGOL
MIGRATIONS
DURING THE MIDDLE AGES

springs which did not freeze, were owned by groups of closely related families. These groups were strongly knit social units. They fought other groups for pasture in hard seasons and were held responsible for each other's acts in feuds. Several of such winter pasture groups claiming descent from a common ancestor in the male line formed a clan. The family and winter pasture group were always exogamous, while the clans seem to have been exogamous in some tribes, endogamous in others. The clans, in turn, grouped themselves into larger units, tribes, under control of a ruler normally chosen from one particular clan. The tribal units were vague, being held together mainly by fear of an enemy attack or by the desire for loot. A successful chief would draw into his tribe an ever-increasing number of clans and families, while a weak one would lose his followers, even within his own clan.

In ordinary affairs there was a high degree of democracy, all matters of general interest to the clan or tribe being settled in open council. Among the Yakut, who seem to have retained the ancient patterns of organization into modern times, the seating in this council reflected the social importance of the tribe's members. The innermost circle consisted of the heads of clans. Behind these came the heads of winter pasture groups and then the heads of families. Anyone was entitled to speak on any subject, but only the words of important men carried weight.

On military expeditions, on the other hand, strict discipline was maintained. After a leader had been accepted, his word was law and disobedience or even carelessness was punished with death. This pattern, which made possible coordinated long-distance maneuvers like those of a modern army, was strikingly different from the undisciplined, competitive heroism of the cattle people. It may have originated in the rigidly disciplined coordination required to make hunting by the surround technique effective, and parallels to it can perhaps be found in the hunt regulations and the hunt policies of the otherwise anarchically democratic and individualistic American Plains Indians.

The derivation of the horse culture from the older Circumpolar hunting complex comes out clearly in its religious patterns, which were typically shamanistic. There were no temples or images and no organized priesthood. Shamans cooperated at certain ceremonies and differed in prestige according to their reputation, but they did not form a hierarchy. Regular seasonal ceremonies were held in the spring and fall to dramatize the struggle between light and darkness and to reinforce the powers of light. Animal sacrifices accompanied these ceremonies, horse offerings being most valued. Public sacrifices on behalf of the clan or tribe might also be made in time of stress, but most religious observances were carried on for the benefit of individuals.

Although a single great and powerful deity, resident in the sky, was

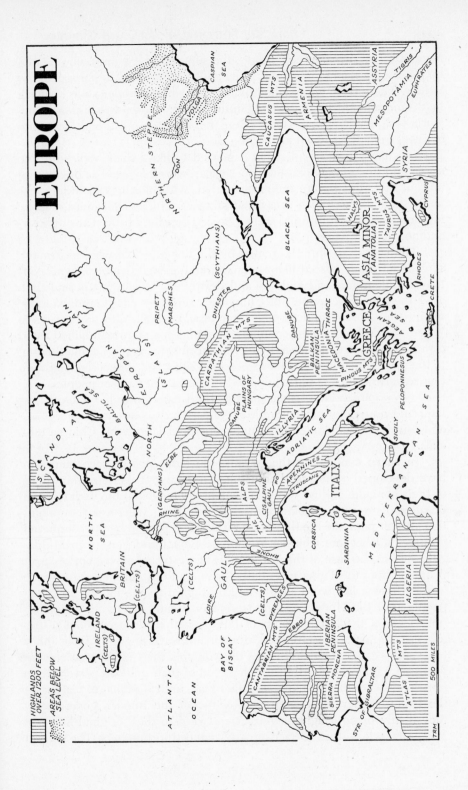

recognized as the source of power, the supernatural beings who had to be placated were mainly local spirits and those related to particular activities. These were approached by the shaman in a trance state induced by drumming and singing. While in the trance his soul left his body and journeyed to the spirit land, where he interviewed the Beings and learned from them what had to be done to achieve the desired ends. Even ordinary men's souls were supposed to leave their bodies during sleep, and dreams, as real soul experiences, were regarded as highly significant. The dead were regularly buried, with offerings including domestic animals and even occasional human sacrifices, but ideas regarding details of the future life were vague. There was little fear of ghosts and no ancestor worship.

The conquest-empires created by the horse people were in general short-lived. They passed like a scourge, taking for themselves whatever they could understand and use and destroying the rest. It is said that after the Mongol conquest of China they seriously considered exterminating the Chinese and turning their territory back into pasture land. Where they settled among conquered populations, they maintained their clan and tribal organization, living in concentrated groups and adhering to their old nomadic life as far as possible. They had in their own culture few patterns which could be applied to the rule of subject peoples, and the high organization of such units as the Liau empire in China or the later and much more extensive Mongol empire was due to the adoption of Chinese models and was actually operated largely by Chinese officials.

In sharp contrast to the Aryans, the horse people seem never to have developed a successful adjustment to conquest. Perhaps the values of their nomadic culture were fundamentally incompatible with the role of rulers over settled communities. In any case, wherever they abandoned their nomadic life they were rapidly assimilated by the conquered groups, and became Chinese in China, Muslim and Persian in Middle Asia, and in the case of the last significant westward movement of horse people, that of the Turks, essentially Muslim and Byzantine.

Perhaps a last word should be said regarding the fate of the horse people after the Mongol conquests. As has already been said, these conquests swept the last remnants of the original cattle people out of the western steppes and established Mongol and Turkish groups throughout their entire extent. One division of the Mongols, the Golden Horde, were drafted by Ivan the Terrible and deprived of their political power. They remained in southern Russia, on sufferance, until the time of Catherine the Great. Under the increasing pressure of the Russian government, they finally made a fighting retreat eastward to their original home in Mongolia, where they arrived greatly reduced in numbers. The central steppes, which were occupied by nomadic tribes of Turkish stock both before and after the Mongol sweep, remained for centuries a breeding ground for tough fighters and, even more, for able generals. Individually or in small groups, these Turks infiltrated the higher cultures to the south and finally seized control of the Near East, but after the Mongol conquests the steppe peoples launched no more major offensives.

Some writers have seen the cause for this in the conversion of the Mongols to Buddhism, but most of the steppe peoples to the west of Mongol territory were converted to Islam, hardly a pacifist religion. The real answer probably lies in the increasing mechanization of warfare that came with the introduction of gunpowder and with the development of disciplined troops and skilled tacticians outside the steppe area. The steppe people, with their atomistic settlement patterns and their relatively crude hand industries, were incapable of producing the weapons which the new situation required. The influences which brought about their downfall were beginning to exert themselves even in the time of Genghis Khan, whose armies were accompanied in their later campaigns by contingents of Chinese engineers whose appliances included flame throwers and probably gunpowder bombs. As long as the steppe peoples had superior discipline they could compensate somewhat for their technological deficiencies, but when other armies became as well disciplined as their own, their fate was sealed. The last European appearance of the mounted bowmen who were once the "Scourge of God" came during the Napoleonic wars, when a Khirgiz contingent was included in the Russian forces. The French soldiers were vastly amused and dubbed them "cupids." *Sic transit gloria mundi.*

Chapter XX

Semites

THE NEAR EAST and Northern Africa have been progressively drying up ever since the end of the last glacial advance, perhaps 10,000 years ago. All through these regions Paleolithic and Neolithic sites are found in places where no one can live today. The desiccation seems to be part of a general climatic trend which will presumably continue until the present inter-glacial reaches its maximum. However, in the Near East the process has unquestionably been speeded up by human agency. Forests which had once been cut or burned over were unable to reconstitute themselves in the face of dwindling rainfall, while the breaking of soil for fields and the grazing of goats and sheep destroyed the ground cover and speeded up run-off.

The first Neolithic farmers were able to raise crops throughout most of the Near East and established their villages everywhere in the area. By 2000 B.C. much of southern and eastern Palestine and most of Arabia, Iraq, southern Iran, Sinai, and Baluchistan had become arid or semi-arid, and the villagers were retreating to mountain slopes and upland valleys where the rainfall was heavier, or to river valleys and oases. In the face of the new conditions the sort of shifting agriculture which had been practiced by the first Neolithic farmers was progressively abandoned. Permanent villages were set up wherever rainfall was sufficient to grow grain or where there was enough water for irrigation. Such settlements were made easier by the fact that soils in arid regions preserve much more of their mineral content than do soils in wet areas. The same once-arid fields will grow crops for many years when they are supplied with water.

In most of Southwestern Asia the rains come in winter and spring. The first summer warmth brings an outburst of vegetation which provides rich but short-lived pasture. The Neolithic settlers took advantage of this by moving their flocks and herds to distant pastures at this season, bringing them back in the fall to graze on the stubble of the fields surrounding the village. Some of the younger and more active members of the community with, perhaps, a few of the poorer families who owned no land, would go with the animals, while the rest of the village stayed behind to attend to the fields. The villagers thus developed a dual pattern of life, with adjustments both to nomadic herding and settled farming. As the aridity increased, the amount of land available for cultivation shrank steadily and the good pasture areas became fewer and more widely distributed. Eventually certain groups abandoned settled village life altogether and became year-round nomads.

The people of the Southwestern Asiatic arid lands once more illustrate the thesis that, within a region having few natural barriers and a uniform ecology, languages and cultures will also tend toward uniformity. Practically all the occupants of the Southwestern Asiatic arid lands spoke Semitic languages and adhered to the same patterns of symbiotic interdependence between villagers and nomads. The Southwestern Asiatic ecology continued across most of Northern Africa and so did the linguistic and cultural similarities. Although the historic importance of two of its languages, Hebrew and Arabic, has led Western scholars to treat Semitic as a distinct linguistic stock, modern research has shown that it is actually only one division of a larger family of languages which are spoken throughout Africa north of the Sahara as well as in Southwestern Asia. There is probably no other example of such a close linkage between a particular linguistic family and a particular environment. The wide distribution of specifically Semitic languages in Africa seems to be a relatively recent phenomenon linked in part to the rise of Islam, but the other divisions of the African-Asian linguistic family have certainly been established in the African arid lands since very ancient times. We know that one of them, Kushiti, used by the ancient Egyptians, was already present as far back as 4000 B.C. There were numerous cultural similarities between the now arid portions of Southwestern Asia and Northern Africa even in Upper Paleolithic times, when both were grasslands, and it seems probable that both regions were occupied by Asiatic migrants who shared a common hunting-culture and spoke related languages ancestral to the later Asian-African stock.

The shift of certain Semitic tribes to complete nomadism was no doubt accelerated by the domestication of the Dromedary camel, an animal which is adapted to hot desert conditions very much as its two-humped Bactrian relative is adapted to cold desert conditions. Camels can live in territory which cannot support even goats and, particularly in Arabia and later in Africa, their domestication opened wide stretches of real desert to human occupation. The camel's mouth and alimentary tract seem to be copper lined. He can chew up and digest camel thorn, which is about as tender and succulent as barbed wire, and can grow fat where a mule would starve to death. His hump provides him with a mechanism for fat storage, so that he can go for weeks on very scanty rations, while his multiple stomachs provide a parallel arrangement for water storage. The camel is thus invaluable to desert dwellers, but anyone who has made the acquaintance of the animal must marvel at its ever having been domesticated. Even the finest modern breeds seem to a European to be phenomenally bad-tempered, stubborn and malodorous. It must be admitted that the Arab does not agree with the European on this point. He regards the camel as a paragon of virtue and an epitome of loveliness. Pre-Islamic Arabian literature is full of poems extolling the beauties of the beast.

The shrinkage of the agricultural area and the development of camel nomadism produced a distinctive pattern of life which was almost ideally suited to the local conditions. In it one can find the best example of the much-advertised but rarely encountered "unchanging East." Although the rise of Islam introduced certain modifications, the life of the modern nomads is little different from that of the Hebrews before their settlement in Palestine, as described in the Old Testament. The continuity has extended even to continuous occupation of the same territory by the same tribes. Thus, some of the Arabian tribes mentioned by Herodotus are still living in the regions to which he assigned them.

Wherever agriculture was possible, people lived in settled villages or even cities. The development of irrigation techniques was one of the first accomplishments of the Near Eastern civilizations. It was in use by 3500 B.C. in both Egypt and Mesopotamia and must have been diffused into the arid regions at a very early date. Arroyas were dammed to form reservoirs, and, where the run-off could not be trapped, the settlers resorted to wells. The word *oasis* usually brings to the American mind a picture of three palm trees and a well standing among sand dunes. Most of the arid territory in the Near East is actually hard baked earth and rock, not sand, and an oasis usually covers several square miles surrounding springs or a brackish lake. Great ingenuity is shown in the conservation and distribution of water. It is carried to the outermost fields by tunnels to reduce the loss by evaporation and is then carefully distributed over the crops. Many of the irrigation systems still in use go back to prehistoric times, and the technique is certainly very old.

The towns, with their associated agricultural areas, were the centers of population and also of manufacturing and trade. Many of them specialized in particular products for export. The regions between the towns were occupied by nomadic tribes who represented the pastoral half of the original dual culture. While the patterns of town life were typically Southwest Asiatic, the patterns of pastoral life were distinctively Semitic. The main animals raised by the nomads were sheep, goats, and camels, all adapted to poor pasture. Very few cattle were kept outside the agricultural areas, and even then their main value was as draft animals. The only important baggage animals were camels. These were infrequently milked and still less frequently eaten.

The famous Arabian horses were reserved entirely for fighting and parade. They were never used for draft and were not even ridden when the tribe was on the march. Since the pasture was usually inadequate, horses were fed on grain purchased from the agricultural areas. They were frequently stabled in the owner's tent. An unusual feature of Arab usage was the preference for mares as fighting animals. The pure Arab horse had only two gaits, a walk and a gallop. Although the nomads became excellent horsemen, they never learned to use drilled cavalry or developed any great skill as mounted archers. Their horses were used as transport on fast long-distance raids rather than for line of battle combat.

The complete dependence of the nomads upon the townsmen becomes obvious when one examines their culture. Although their women weave the coarse, black, goat-hair cloth which is used for tents and the men know how to repair their saddlery and other gear, the nomad tribes have practically no manufactures. The entire equipment of the modern nomad dwelling is obtained by either trade or loot, and this seems to have been the case since time immemorial. Even the standard food is an unleavened bread made from wheat grown in the agricultural settlements. This bread is simply a thin batter of flour and water spread on hot stones or sand. A sanitary version of it is familiar to many Americans as the Passover *matzoh*.

The relations between nomads and town dwellers clearly reflect their close original kinship. Both groups speak the same languages, and not infrequently a single tribe will contain both townsmen and nomads. Tribesmen are usually willing to settle when the opportunity presents itself, but at the same time there is little of the unshakable attachment to the land which characterizes the agricultural peasant elsewhere. Pastoral life is idealized and the nomad considers himself superior to the villagers. Whenever taxes become too oppressive or crops fail for a few years, the village population will abandon its fields and follow its flocks into the wasteland. Readers who know their Bible may remember that in the troublous days following the death of King Solomon the new exactions of the central authority were several times met with the cry, "To your tents, O Israel!" Confronted with the prospect of the loss of so many taxpayers, the king was always brought to terms.

The condition of widely spaced settlements with nomadic pastoralists between was highly favorable for the development of trade. The

nomads, moving from pasture to pasture, came back to the same places
year after year. It was comparatively simple for them to pick up the special products of a town at one end of their circuit, transport them in lei-
surely fashion to a town at the other end, and bring back to the first
town other products given in exchange. It was only a step from this informal carrier service to the organization of caravans. Camel nomads in
particular were ideally suited for this, since they knew the desert trails
and water holes, had the necessary pack animals, and knew how to handle them. Professional caravaneers and long-distance caravan routes
were well established by 1000 B.C.

The Semitic people around the Persian Gulf and on the Red Sea
and Indian Ocean coasts of Arabia took to the sea at a very early date.
Mesopotamian inscriptions from about 2500 B.C. on refer to a "Kingdom
of the Sea" situated toward the mouth of the Persian Gulf, and it is
highly probable that this date does not mark the beginnings of Semitic
voyaging but simply the time at which the Mesopotamians established
contact with the Semitic seamen. Both the Red Sea and Persian Gulf are
relatively placid oceans. The scarcity of food on these barren coasts must
have tempted the local population to fishing, while the difficulties of
travel overland were an added stimulus to seafaring. When, at a much
later time, the Phoenicians reached the Mediterranean coast and
wrested the control of that sea from the Cretans and other "People of
the Isles," they were following a Semitic tradition which was already
old.

On land the caravan trade provided profit not only for the caravaneers but also for the various nomad tribes through whose territories the
caravan routes passed. These tribes operated a system which is, unfortunately, quite familiar to modern Americans. For a fee they would provide the caravan with a "guard" of hungry and thievish tribesmen who
accompanied it across their territory and turned it over to another group
of racketeers at the border. This sort of "protection" was based on the
certainty that a caravan which did not pay would be attacked. Costs
varied with the strength and proximity of the trading centers dependent
on the caravans. When the trading centers were strong and well organized, there were slim pickings for the nomads.

The relations of nomads with the civilized states on the borders of
their territories also followed a consistent pattern. The nomads were
quite willing to enlist in wars between these states and were regularly
used as scouts and light cavalry. However, they were loyal only to their
own interests. They came for loot, and when the tide of battle turned
would turn with it against the losers. When the civilized states were
strong, the nomads kept the peace. When they were weak or disorganized, the nomads would raid them and carry off what they could. It

must be remembered that their military tactics were those of undrilled guerilla fighters and their military equipment generally inferior to that of the settled groups from which it was obtained. Until Islam united the Arabian tribes and endowed them with a common and enduring purpose, they were more of a nuisance than a threat to their civilized neighbors.

As regards the cultural equipment of the nomads, it has already been said that practically all of it was obtained from the settled people. Their distinctive habitation was the tent, a low structure of coarse black goat-hair cloth supported by numerous short posts. Its main function was to provide shade, and it was actually more like a spread awning than anything else. Other equipment included the usual metal cooking pots, wooden bowls and utensils, rugs, and so forth. Men's costume consisted of a long robe over which was worn, on dress occasions, an almost equally long coat of richer material, which was left open in front. A sash about the waist supported at least a dagger. Sandals were worn on the feet, and the head and back of the neck was covered with a cloth held in place by rings made of heavy bundles of cords. The women's dress consisted of two oblongs of cloth, front and back, caught together at the shoulders and again at the waist and partly sewn up at the sides. Women also wore a head cloth, one end of which could be drawn over the mouth, but women of the nomad tribes generally did not veil. Clothing was usually made of coarse woolen cloth, which gave protection against both the chill of the desert nights and the heat of the desert sun. Much jewelry was worn, and a girl would frequently wear her entire dowry on her person in the form of head band, necklace, and the like, of gold coins.

The social and political organization of the nomads was based upon tribes, patrilineal endogamous groups occupying particular territories. Larger political groupings were ephemeral, breaking down when the dominant tribe lost control. All tribe members were related, and it was unthinkable that a family should try to change its tribal affiliations. Control of the tribe was vested in a sheik, whose post was normally hereditary in a particular family line. Preference was given to the eldest son by the first wife, but there was no absolute rule, since under nomad conditions the post was far from a sinecure and had to be filled by the best man available. The relation of the sheik to his tribesmen was modeled on that of a Semitic father to his family. He directed tribal activities and administered justice. It is impossible to say how far formal law codes were recognized by the nomads in pre-Islamic times, but in the administration of the law the sheik was expected to show wisdom in determining who was the real offender and to make the punishment fit the crime. The judgments of Solomon as recorded in Near Eastern folklore are in

the best pattern of both nomads and settled people. Although in practice the sheik was influenced by the opinion of tribal members and did
his best to function by persuasion rather than force, his powers were autocratic and, in theory, absolute. Needless to say, these patterns had
their effect on the development of Islamic patterns of government.

The nomad tribes were constantly at war among themselves, but
since the main motives for these wars were loot or revenge for the murder of a tribal member, the losses ordinarily were not large. Even in the
bitterest war the side that had won the victory contented itself with killing all adult males in the losing tribe and carrying off the tribe's domestic animals. The women and children were left, and, if they were able to
survive, the children could be relied upon to renew the feud as soon as
they grew up. Defeated tribes who wished to avoid this fate often fled
to foreign parts.

In spite of the feuds, all the Arabian nomads recognized their ultimate kinship and, long before the rise of Islam, had established a month
of truce during which pilgrimages to the shrines of various deities could
be undertaken and, still more important, fairs and literary contests held.
These get-togethers helped to maintain a common culture and the unified values out of which Islam was to emerge.

Slaves were fairly numerous among the nomads but occupied what
was, from a European point of view, a peculiar position. The exigencies
of nomadic life and of herding provided slaves with so many opportunities for escape that it was necessary for their masters to win genuine
allegiance from them. They were regarded more as retainers than as
chattels. During the historic period the slaves were mainly Somali and
Abyssinian, so that there was a racial difference between slave and master. Nomads took slave concubines, but marriage with a slave was regarded much as it would have been in our own Old South. The city
dwellers kept white slaves, and attitudes there differed, especially after
the rise of Islam. Masters took pride in the appearance of their slaves,
and they were frequently dressed, armed and mounted better than poor
free men. They fought beside their masters, and Antar, the hero of the
greatest pre-Islamic Arabian epic, was the son of a slave woman. Today
slaves of Arab rulers are regarded as, in a very real sense, extensions of
the ruler's own person. Thus, at a feast, it is a special honor to a guest to
have one of the host's slaves dismember the food which he is served and
feed it to him. It is socially equivalent to having the host do so himself.
Also, when a ruler sends his orders to a subordinate, if the message is
sent by a free man, even a close relative of the ruler, the recipient knows
that he has a certain amount of leeway. If it is sent by one of the ruler's
slaves it is as though the ruler had come himself, and prompt obedience
is demanded. The various institutions which have made Islam the out-

standing slave culture of all history have their roots at least in part in these attitudes.

Among free men within the tribe there were families of greater or less importance and genealogies were kept with Polynesian thoroughness. Readers may remember the famous chapter of *begats* in the Old Testament. However, the very fact of tribal membership conferred upon individuals dignity and prestige. In dealing with both fellow tribesmen and visitors, courtesy and consideration were the rule, and any departure from these was likely to be rewarded by a knife thrust.

The Arabian nomads not only practiced tribal endogamy but also approved of the marriage of certain close relatives. They were one of the few groups in the world in which marriage with a father's brother's daughter was not only permitted but preferred. This pattern was incorporated into Islam and still survives in many Islamic countries. Marriage among the nomads seems to have been normally monogamous, but with polygyny permitted for those who could afford it. Certainly this was the rule of the early Hebrews. The situation in pre-Islamic Arabia is difficult to assess. It must be remembered that Mohammed was a townsman, not a Bedouin, and that the forms of multiple marriage against which he inveighed were those which might well arise in a town population given over to trading and containing a fair proportion of transients. Thus it is questionable whether the pre-Islamic nomads practiced fraternal polyandry or the still more interesting system by which a lady acquired different husbands for the different days of the week. Both of these are mentioned in Arab tradition and were condemned by the Prophet.

A striking aspect of all the Semitic cultures seems to have been extreme insistence on virginity at marriage. The exhibition of tokens of virginity is still a part of the regular wedding ceremony in most Islamic countries, and the values which this reflects certainly go back to pre-Islamic times. This insistence was only one aspect of a cultural preoccupation with sex and the sexual organs which found one expression in the practice of circumcision. This was shared by practically all Semitic peoples. Corresponding mutilation of the female organs was also widespread, reaching its greatest development in parts of the Sudan, where all the external female sexual parts were cut away and the vaginal opening so nearly closed with scar tissue as to make intercourse impossible. The bridegroom was thus insured of a virgin bride, but had to win her consent to a further operation before the marriage could be consummated.

The exigencies of nomadic life made the seclusion of women impossible for all but a few of the richest families, but death was inflicted upon both the unchaste girl or the unfaithful wife and her lover. Since unchastity in men was not disapproved, they made the most of their vis-

its to the town, where the sexual vigor of the Bedouin was as famous as
that of sailors among ourselves. In pagan times these masculine needs
were taken care of in part by a regular institution of temple prostitutes.
A further corollary of the situation was a high development of male
homosexuality, which even today is widespread in Islamic countries. It
is mainly carried on by unmarried men and boys and gives place to normal heterosexual relations when these become possible.

The family control was rigidly patriarchal. The father had complete
control over his wives and sons throughout his life and even beyond. A
father's blessing was an important asset, while a father's curse could ruin
his son's future. Note the story of Jacob and Esau. Daughters were
under the father's control until marriage but thereafter passed to the
control of their husbands. The average Semitic father seems to have
taken more pride in his sternness than in his justice. The son's attitude toward him was one of fear and respect. Especially in polygynous families
the strongest emotional tie was between mother and son. There was real
affection in this relationship and very commonly the two formed an amiable conspiracy to circumvent the father.

The whole situation was such as might be expected to develop a
strong and censorious superego in the individual. The Hebrew picture
of an all-powerful deity who could only be placated by complete submission and protestations of devotion, no matter how unjust his acts
might appear, was a direct outgrowth of this general Semitic family situation. Another product of the exaggerated superego to which it gave
rise was the elaborate system of taboos relating to every aspect of behavior. One system of this sort has been recorded and codified in the
Laws of Moses, but these laws were by no means an isolated phenomenon. All Semitic tribes had similar series of regulations differing only in
content. Such codes provided those who kept them with a sense of security, comparable to that of the good child who is able to remember everything that his father ever told him not to do and carefully abstains
from doing it. The Hebrew Iaveh was a portrait of the Semitic father
with his patriarchal authoritarian qualities abstracted and exaggerated.
The combination of patriarchal suppression and sexual deprivation has
left its mark on the Semitic basic personality. From Moses to Freud,
Semites have been preoccupied with sin and sex.

The Semitic religion was a direct outgrowth of the patterns of supernaturalism developed in the Southwestern Asiatic center. Where settled life was possible the worship centered about local deities who were,
at the same time, manifestations of natural forces. Among the tribes who
followed nomadic patterns these local deities were replaced by tribal
deities and their attachment to the land was replaced by their attachment to the social unit. The principal difference between the two con-

cepts was that the power of the nomad deities was no longer limited in space. They could help or punish their people no matter where their people happened to be. The settled people had sacred places, preferably on hilltops, where offerings were made, and increasingly represented their deities by images. The nomadic groups, on the other hand, represented their deities by portable symbols of various sorts, including images. Such objects were carried with the tribe in its movements and were frequently taken into battle so that the full force of their *mana* could be directed against the enemy. The Ark of the Covenant was such a symbol, and the disastrous results of the Hebrews having taken it into battle against the Philistines is recorded in I Samuel, Chap. 4.

The tribesmen did not deny the existence of deities other than their own any more than they denied the existence of other tribes. They merely were not interested in Beings who presumably were not interested in them. The Ten Commandments did not state that Iaveh was the only God, simply that he should be the only God worshipped by the Hebrews. This attitude is clearly reflected in the earlier books of the Old Testament, where the backsliding of the Hebrews after their arrival in the Promised Land was a constant worry of the Prophets. The Hebrews were, in effect, becoming settled and civilized through their contacts with the more advanced but also Semitic Canaanites, and, since they were now in the territory of the Canaanitish localized deities, it seemed logical to them that they should pay them their long-established dues. Because of these attitudes, the earliest Semitic records show a great number of gods but only vague organization of a pantheon. It was only in the city civilizations of Mesopotamia that the multiple cosmic deities were brought into something like logical order and their relations to each other defined. Even there each city exalted its own deity at the expense of the rest and attached to its god or goddess many of the same myths which were attached to other gods elsewhere.

This focusing of interest on the tribal or local god resulted in an emotional attitude unknown in most other ancient religions. The Semites did not develop elaborate theologies. Their relation with the deity was felt rather than reasoned. In the long run this feeling was to produce the intense monotheism of Judaism and of Islam with their ecstatic devotion to the one all-powerful God. Christianity, stemming from the Judaic monotheism, fell among the non-Semitic Greek philosophers and *mystoi* and emerged with a complicated theology which seems inconsistent at certain points with its avowed monotheism.

Primitive Semitic ideas regarding a future life were vague. In spite of the interest in genealogy, there was no suggestion of ancestor worship. Like practically all peoples, the Semites believed in some sort of survival after death, but the underworld to which ghosts were relegated was gray and uninteresting. They seem to have had no concept of post-mortem rewards and punishments. These were administered either to the individual while alive or to his descendants, the latter no doubt reflecting the strong identification of the Semite with his kin group. The lively and imaginative heavens and hells of the Muslims and Christians stemmed from non-Semitic sources, partly from the Egyptian concepts of the judgment of the dead and the destruction of wicked souls, but even more from the Zoroastrian Persians.

The Red Sea is a narrow sea and seems to have united quite as much as it separated the peoples of Arabia and the adjoining African coast. The environment is so similar on its two shores that migrants could pass from one to the other with no significant changes in their way of life, and any new pattern which had been integrated into Arabian culture could easily be accepted on the African side. The linguistic similarities have already been mentioned, but the cultural similarities are equally strong. The Abyssinian plateau, rising out of the northeast African desert, matches in many ways that section of far southeastern Arabia known to the ancients as Arabia Felix. In both, altitude brings increased rainfall and temperate climate. Abyssinian archeology is still almost unknown, but if the Russian botanists are to be believed, there was an independent center of plant domestication here comparable to the original Southwestern Asiatic center in the number of species brought under cultivation. Most of these species paralleled Southwestern Asiatic ones and the complex which emerged was fundamentally of Southwestern Asiatic type. It produced village life of the familiar Semitic pattern and in due course of time gave rise to an Abyssinian state which was Asiatic rather than African in its patterns of rule and organization.

The interaction between Abyssinia and Arabia was close through the whole period of recorded history and was by no means one-sided. Abyssinia has played an important role in Arabian politics since ancient times and at one period came very close to conquering the peninsula. The Abyssinian conversion to Christianity in the 2nd century A.D. did little to change their Semitic culture patterns, while the added importance given to Arabia by the rise of Islam made the Abyssinians eager to emphasize their Semitic heritage. The claim of the Abyssinian kings that their line stems from Solomon and the Queen of Sheba incorporates a cultural and racial truth no matter how far it may depart from historic accuracy. The modern Abyssinian reveals his Semitic origin in his fine features and light brown skin as well as in his culture and language.

The Somali, the prinicipal Semitic-speaking people of the northeast African deserts, are less advanced in culture and darker in skin color than either Abyssinians or Arabs, but both these deviations are understandable in terms of their environment. There has been some diffusion of both blood and culture from Negro Africa, although the influence of both is surprisingly slight in view of the long contact involved. Physically the Somali combine features of Semitic regularity with very dark pigmentation and a peculiar hair texture unlike that of either Negroes or Mediterranean whites. The hair is coarse and closely crimped, result-

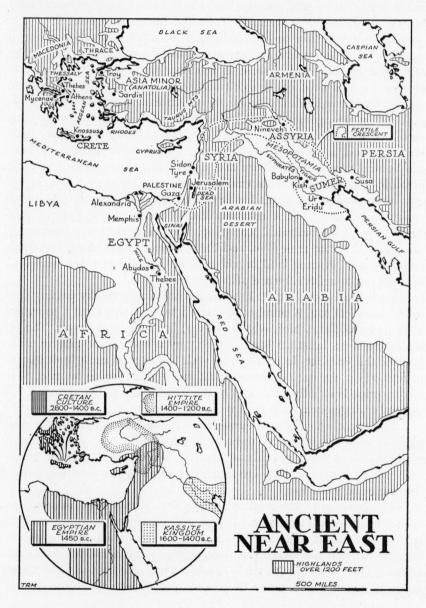

ANCIENT
NEAR EAST

CRETAN CULTURE
2800–1400 B.C.

HITTITE EMPIRE
1400–1200 B.C.

EGYPTIAN EMPIRE
1450 B.C.

KASSITE KINGDOM
1600–1400 B.C.

HIGHLANDS OVER 1200 FEET

500 MILES

ing in a stiff bush which may stand out fom the head for a foot or more.
The heavy skin color is easily understandable in view of the local conditions. The desert on the African side of the Red Sea is one of the driest
and hottest in the world, and heavy pigmentation has unquestionably
had a survival value.

The culture of the Somali seems to represent a desperate attempt to
retain primitive Semitic patterns in the face of an unconquerably hostile
environment. It differs strikingly from the cattle cultures of the Negro
peoples living farther to the south and west. The Somali economy is
based upon sheep, goats, and camels with a limited use of cattle. Actually most of the local pasture is too poor to make cattle profitable.
Horses are also kept but are culturally unimportant. The attitudes toward domestic animals are decidedly un-African. Women do most of the
milking, an arrangement unthinkable in the Negro cattle cultures. In accordance with the ancient Semitic blood taboo, living animals are never
bled for food, a common Negro practice. Like other nomadic Semites,
the Somali turn to agriculture and settled life wherever this becomes
possible. There are numerous trading towns in their territory, and, wherever there is enough water for irrigation, groups settle down, usually
under the direction of a religious leader whose sancitity gives them
some protection from raids. The people live in local groups made up of
men related in the male line, and their wives and children. The group
members hold grazing land in common, but any fields which have been
brought under cultivation are private property.

Each local group has its head man, the office normally passing from
father to eldest son. A number of related local groups form a tribe, also
with its hereditary chief, who, however, has little real power. The Somali have been fanatical Muslim for many centuries and adhere to the
laws of the Prophet. In accordance with this, a man must limit himself
to four wives, for each of whom a stiff bride price has to be paid. Most
of this price is usually passed on to the wife by her father. Tribes are in
general endogamous, local groups exogamous.

The Somali have a well-earned reputation as fighters, and in some
tribes a man cannot marry until he has killed an enemy and brought
home the dead man's genitals as a trophy. Barbarous as some of the Somali practices appear, they are much like those of the Asiatic Semites a
few thousand years ago.

The position of the Asiatic Semites was particularly favorable for
cultural advance. They were in close and continuous contact with the
world's two oldest centers of civilization, Mesopotamia and Egypt, and
by 2300 B.C. had conquered the Mesopotamian center and assimilated its
culture. Their addiction to trade brought them into contact with a wide
range of peoples and made them keenly conscious of cultural differ-

ences. They were always ready to borrow new appliances or art styles when this was advantageous. At the same time the Semitic cultures have shown a fundamental continuity perhaps unequaled by those of any other group. Whatever they borrowed was reinterpreted in terms of their own values and interests, which survived with little change.

The most important Semitic contributions to civilization have been in the fields of mathematics and astronomy on the one hand, and religion on the other. It is a curious fact that we owe to them both the concept of a mechanistic universe and that of one completely subject to the will of a single all-powerful deity. The first was evolved from the Mesopotamian priests' age-long observation of the wheeling heavens. The second grew out of an ecstatic devotion to the tribal deity, a devotion so intense that all other Beings and forces ceased to exist for the worshipper. The Semitic quest was always for absolutes, and it has been the bad fortune of their cultural heirs that they should have found two of them and that the two were polar. All monotheistic faiths of which we have records can be traced to Semitic sources, and all of them are confronted by the same enigma of an all-powerful deity in a universe governed by law.

Chapter XXI

Mesopotamia

EVERYTHING INDICATES that the pattern of village life developed in Southwest Asia spread over the rest of Eurasia and into Northern Africa with considerable rapidity. The modifications which it underwent as adjustments to various environmental conditions have been discussed in previous chapters. The rise of the earliest civilizations can hardly be interpreted in similar terms. They were not necessary for existence in the regions in which they arose, but conditions in these regions made them possible. The results of the spread of Southwestern Asiatic village culture over the temperate Old World were comparable in certain ways to the results one gets when one draws a loop which has been dipped in a bacterial solution across a gelatin plate. In due course of time, isolated dense colonies of bacteria will appear at various spots. In the same way, spots of dense population appeared at various points in the territory the village culture had reached. The civilizations sprang up at those points where a combination of dense population and certain cultural and environmental factors made city life possible.

The significance of the city as a new and distinctive type of social grouping has been discussed in Chapter X, along with the conditions under which cities can exist. They require not only a dense settled population but also the technological equipment needed to transport food and other bulky raw materials to the city site and to distribute the goods produced by the city's skilled craftsmen. City living seems to have arisen spontaneously in several localities in the Old and New Worlds where these conditions were met. In others the diffusion of patterns for city life which had been developed elsewhere created the necessary local conditions.

In the Old World the earliest centers of civilization, which may be taken as synonymous with city life, were all in the valleys of great rivers. Here the rich soil could support a numerous peasantry, while water

transport made the supplying of cities easy. After urban organization
had been established in these centers it was diffused outward from each
center over wider and wider areas. Its spread was encouraged by the
need for raw materials and by application of irrigation techniques developed in the great river valleys to smaller local areas. It cannot be emphasized too strongly that the first centers seem to have arisen independently. Their resemblances were due to their common derivation
from the Southwest Asiatic village culture and to the similar problems
which the new type of social grouping presented to all of them.

The first cities were built beside the Nile, the Tigris-Euphrates, the
Indus, and the Hwang Ho. City life came to Europe exceedingly late.
The early Greek and Italian cities were really small towns, economically
self-sufficient. The first European culture complicated enough to be
classed as a civilization, that of Crete, also was not a city culture. The
island population, although relatively dense, was distributed in many
small towns, thus minimizing the need for transport of goods in bulk.
The skilled craftsman who produced the goods which the Cretans exported were concentrated at a few places on the coast, where ships
could bring the raw materials and carry away the finished product. True
cities did not appear in Greece until after the first Olympiad (776 B.C.)
or in Italy until the Greek (6th–7th century B.C.) or possibly the Etruscan (8th century B.C.) settlements. They were even later in the rest of
Europe and did not appear in Scandinavia until almost the end of the
Middle Ages.

Egypt and Mesopotamia were probably the first centers of city life.
Its beginnings in these two regions seem to have been independent and
practically simultaneous (about 4000 B.C.). Although there were occasional contacts between Egypt and Mesopotamia as early as 3500 B.C.,
real interaction between the two civilizations did not begin until Egypt
became a military power with Asiatic commitments (1500 B.C.). The beginnings of the Indus Valley civilization are more difficult to determine,
since we have no way of establishing a local chronology. However, this
center lay so close to the origin point of the Southwest Asiatic village
culture that settled life must have been established there at a very early
time. Trade objects prove contact with Mesopotamia by 3000 B.C., and
the beginnings of the civilization are undoubtedly older. The Hwang Ho
Valley civilization in northern China was established much later than
the others. Even if one accords the status of a civilization to the Black
Pottery culture which preceded the Shang Dynasty in this region, the
earliest date for its development cannot be much before 2000 B.C.

Mesopotamia has influenced our own civilization more than have
any of the other earliest centers. We are only beginning to recognize
how heavy a debt Classical Greek culture owed to this region. The debt

of the Hellenistic cultures was still heavier, since the economic and political patterns which they incorporated came directly from this region
with the Assyrian and Persian civilizations as intermediaries. Through
the Hellenistic cultures, these patterns were transmitted to Imperial
Rome and became a part of the Western European tradition.

The Egyptian contributions to our civilization have been next in
importance but are much less numerous. They have been mainly in the
fields of technology and theology and were filtered through the Hellenistic civilization before they reached the West. Egyptian culture followed a divergent line of development based on values and interests
which we find hard to appreciate. Its preoccupation with the future
life, and its enthusiastic acceptance of the Pharaoh as a God upon whose
well being that of the nation depended, are incomprehensible to Europeans.

The Indus civilization, in interaction with the Southeast Asiatic
Neolithic culture which seems to have been contemporaneous with it in
eastern and southern India, produced a distinctive culture configuration.
Additional elements were introduced by the Aryan invasion of northern
India, but it is becoming increasingly evident that the Aryan contribution was much less than has been supposed. In India as in Europe the
Aryans gave a language and borrowed a culture. In spite of long contact
with the West, Indian civilization has contributed little to our own. The
so-called Arabic numerals are really Indian. Certain Indian philosophical concepts may also have been transmitted through Hellenistic intermediaries, but Indian civilization, like the ancient Egyptian one, is profoundly different from our own in its values and interests.

The Hwang Ho center became ancestral to the great Chinese civilization which infused and revolutionized the earlier cultures of Korea
and Japan and left its mark in Indo-China and Tibet. That this civilization has contributed so little to that of Europe seems to be mainly an
accident of time and space. Certainly Chinese values and interests are
quite comprehensible to the modern European. Ingenious Chinese technicians have contributed, through Near Eastern intermediaries, such
items as paper, printing, gunpowder, silk and porcelain.

In attempting to describe the ancient cultures which have contributed to the development of modern civilizations, one of the greatest difficulties is that of deciding which time-level to take. Our information on
these cultures becomes increasingly vague and fragmentary as we go
back in time. When each culture emerges into the full light of knowledge there are indications that most of its fundamental patterns have
already been in existence for a long while. Although at least two of the
civilizations had their beginnings in periods of exceedingly rapid change
which must be considered genuine cultural mutations, all of them seem

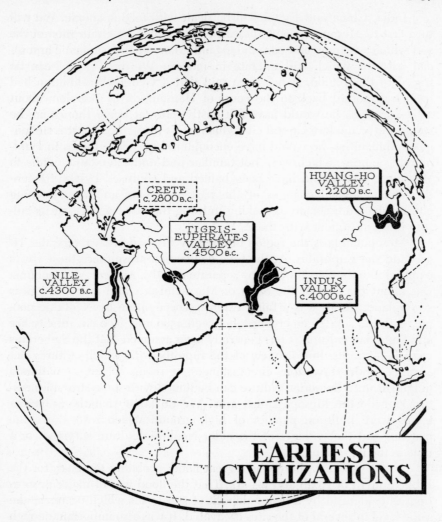

CRETE
c. 2800 B.C.

HUANG-HO
VALLEY
c. 2200 B.C.

TIGRIS-
EUPHRATES
VALLEY
c. 4500 B.C.

NILE
VALLEY
c. 4300 B.C.

INDUS
VALLEY
c. 4000 B.C.

EARLIEST
CIVILIZATIONS

to have become well integrated at an early period and to have carried on
with only slight modifications, until their courses were altered by conquest and the resulting close contact with other cultures. Under the
circumstances it seems best to take as our base level for descriptive
purposes the point in their history at which the culture configuration
becomes clear, referring to earlier periods only incidentally. For Mesopotamia this base level would be roughly 2000 B.C., for Egypt approximately the same time, for China the period of the later Chou dynasty,
about 500–400 B.C., while for India the cultural record remains confused and confusing until after the Islamic invasions of the 9th century, A.D.

India, China and Egypt will be dealt with in due course. We will turn first to Mesopotamia as the earliest example of a civilization of the sort which we know and can understand. Many of the economic and social patterns which still operate in modern Western society can be traced to this region. It has been said that if George Washington had been transported back to the court of Hammurabi of Babylon, about 2067–2025 B.C., he would have felt vastly more at home there than he would in the modern capital city which bears his name. Apart from language difficulties, he would have encountered very few things in Hammurabi's empire which were not familiar and understandable, while in Washington he would have been baffled and confused by the tremendous technological changes of the past 200 years and the fumbling efforts which our society is making to bring the other aspects of its culture into adjustment with these.

Mesopotamia is the region drained by the two great rivers, the Tigris and the Euphrates. At the time civilization arose there these rivers emptied into the Persian Gulf by separate mouths. Ancient Mesopotamia was about the size of the State of Massachusetts and much of it was swampland. There was a fairly extensive occupation by Neolithic people, with the sudden emergence, between 4500 and 3500 B.C., of city life and Sumerian culture. It has generally been assumed that the Sumerians were immigrants, but, in view of the rapidity with which cultures can advance under favorable circumstances, it seems wisest to withhold judgment until Sumerian culture can be linked with some still older culture outside the Mesopotamian area. We do know that the Sumerian towns were built on patches of high ground which rose above the marshes and that villages of the older Neolithic culture survived for a time in the marshland.

About 3500 B.C. there was a great flood, probably the basis for the Biblical myth of Noah and his ark. That the flood was of major proportions is evidenced by a heavy deposit of sterile silt which occurs at the same level in several of the sites excavated. It was also important enough to serve as a datum point in the Sumerian time system, and their later king-lists are divided into an antediluvian and a postdiluvian period. The flood overthrew some of the Sumerian cities and was even more catastrophic for the less advanced swamp dwellers, most of whose villages must have been wiped out. After the flood the Sumerians not only rebuilt their towns but spread out and took over the whole of the lower valley. They very early developed techniques for building combined irrigation and drainage canals. These transformed much of the swampland into deep, rich soil which would provide two heavy crops a year without fertilization. The population increased rapidly, and, from 3000 B.C. until the Mongol conquerors of the 13th century destroyed the canals and let the land revert to swamp, Mesopotamia remained one of the most densely populated and culturally advanced areas in the world.

The Mesopotamians seem to have been racially mixed even in the earliest times. The main types represented were long-headed Mediterraneans and the big-nosed, short-headed type known as Armenoids. The latter seems to have been the admired, aristocratic type, since it was the one regularly represented in the oldest idealized statues and reliefs. It did not appear with any high degree of frequency among the figures which were intended as portraits. If either of these types was the result of a major invasion it was pretty certainly the Armenoid type, which might be thus equated with the hypothetical Sumerian migration.

The early Mesopotamian language situation is better known to us than the physical type, thanks to the development of the cuneiform script and the custom of writing on clay tablets which, when baked, were practically indestructible. Although Mesopotamia is in the middle of a Semitic area, Sumerian itself is emphatically not a Semitic language. We can read the Sumerian inscriptions without difficulty, since the later Mesopotamian scholars were already studying it as a dead language by 2000 B.C. and have left us numerous dictionaries and phrase books in which it is equated with their own Semitic tongue. Sumerian does not seem to be closely related to any living language. Its grammatical structure shows some resemblance to Turkish but its vocabulary was entirely different. A few Sumerian words occur as root words in the Indo-European linguistic family, suggesting early contact between the Sumerians and the people of the steppes. Further evidence of this contact is provided by the shape of certain metal and even stone battle axes of the steppe people which are clearly derived from Sumerian originals.

The Sumerian technology was essentially that of the Southwestern Asiatic Neolithic center with a few additions and a marked increase in technological skills. The Sumerians knew and worked practically all the metals except iron, which was found only in meteorologic form and was therefore too rare for ordinary use. They cast by the lost wax method (see Chap. IX, p. 106), drew wire, and were able to solder pieces together. Their jewelry shows filigree and grain work. During the early Sumerian period the difference in value between metals was slight. Copper and bronze were so scarce that they were almost as valuable as gold and silver. Spears, daggers, and battle axes, actual weapons, not ceremonial objects, were made from alloys of gold and copper or gold and silver. These alloys were practical working metals, hard and resistant to corrosion. Pottery was made on the wheel and was turned out in great quantities by potters who were obviously professionals. Their product was standardized and strictly utilitarian. Luxury utensils were made from metal, stone, or shell.

The most important advance was the emergence of many sorts of skilled craftsmen who depended on their skills for a living. Among the earliest documents are contracts for teaching particular crafts. It seems highly probable that by 2000 B.C. craft guilds were already in existence in the cities.

The Sumerians were always threatened by the Semitic-speaking villagers and nomads on their borders and finally succumbed to a Semitic conquest in roughly 2000 B.C. The invading Semites rapidly took over much of the Sumerian culture, and the relations of the two groups are perhaps best illustrated by the numerous carvings in which a Semitic king with embroidered robe and tiara and long, formally curled hair and beard is attended by a Sumerian scribe with shaven head, cloak, and kilt. After a few generations the two groups fused. The Semitic language triumphed but the Sumerian culture, already well stabilized at the time of the conquest, was continued with little change. Not a single item of the later technology was introduced by the invading Semites.

The Sumerian city was surrounded by a tremendous wall built of mud brick, faced with a few layers of burned brick. Since cities were often occupied for many centuries and the wall was reinforced from time to time, some of them grew to enormous size. At the time of Herodotus the walls of Babylon were 80 miles in circumference, 90 feet high, and so wide that two chariots could pass each other driving along the top. Such walls served not only as defense against enemies but also as levees, protecting the city against floods. Within the city there was usually one broad avenue running from the main gate to a central temple enclosure. Otherwise, the streets were only narrow, twisting alleys laid out on no regular plan.

Houses were built of mud bricks reinforced with timber. They frequently collapsed, particularly in the rainy season. The timbers would then be salvaged, the mud leveled off, and a new house built on top. Since there were no sewers and all garbage was dumped into the streets, the street level rose progressively until the water drained back into the house in time of rain. At this point the house would usually be reconstructed on a higher level. Within a few generations each city stood on a mound of its own creation. Mesopotamia today is dotted with artificial hills called *tels* which have been produced in this way. The archeologist who digs in one of them discovers layer after layer of occupation and a continuous series of buried towns going right down to the water level.

The houses of the middle class, and there was a considerable middle class in Sumerian cities, were much like the modern Near Eastern or Spanish American city houses. Outside there was a blank wall with a single large door. The rooms were built around a central patio with kitchens and storerooms on the ground level and the living rooms on the second floor connected by a gallery overlooking the patio. The second floor probably had windows on the street. There was usually a bathroom with a drain to carry off the bath water, but no toilet. The people probably used the street for their excretory functions, as in much of the Orient today. The roofs sloped inwards so that rain water ran down into the patio, where it was drained off by a deeply buried vertical pipe. The furnishings of the house were quite modern. There were chairs and beds, the latter with woven strips of rawhide in lieu of springs, quite as comfortable as a modern camp cot. There were rugs on the floor and hangings on the walls.

Wealthy Sumerian families apparently owned two or three homes and, like the Elizabethan English, moved from one to another, leaving the vacated house "to sweeten." This was made more desirable by their practice of burying dead relatives just under the floor of the dwelling. When the departed commenced to smell too high for comfort, the living moved out, leaving the ghosts in possession until their earthly miasmas had passed off.

Each walled city was dominated by a temple enclosure, also walled, which covered several acres and included living quarters for the entire temple entourage, as well as storerooms and workrooms. In the center of the enclosure would be an artificial hill known as the *ziggurat,* on top of which stood the shrine of the city god. The shrines of several minor gods would also be built inside the enclosure but at ground level.

The shrines themselves were small, windowless rooms lighted only from the doorway. At the rear of the room in mysterious shadow stood the image of the god, usually carved in stone but small enough so that it could be taken from the shrine and paraded through the streets on festivals. It cannot be told from the inscriptions whether the image was regarded as the actual God, as a body into which the God could enter temporarily to establish closer contact with his worshippers, or merely as a representation of the deity. Probably the early Mesopotamians did not worry their heads about such fine distinctions. In any case, the image of the god of an enemy city was an exceedingly important prize. It was treated as an honored captive and it was believed on both sides that as long as the conquerors had it in their possession the conquered had little chance for revolt.

The principal god of the city was usually provided with living quarters furnished like those of a ruler but even more richly. He was also provided with priestly servitors of various ranks and with a harem modeled upon royal lines. At the head of the harem stood the *entu,* who was the god's head wife. This woman was supposed to be faithful to her divine husband and was well chaperoned. She also was, as a rule, the sister or daughter of the ruler of the city. In some cases she regularly slept

in the living quarters of the god. She always slept there on the night before some important political decision with the idea that her divine husband would visit her and give her the answer. The ruler might also sleep
in the shrine when he was confronted by a difficult problem. The god
would come to him in a dream and tell him what to do. Since the
god's head wife was always a close relative of the ruler of the city, the
god's orders and the ruler's will were rarely in conflict.

Below the head wife in the social scale were the god's other wives,
known as *Sal-me.* These women seem to have been regularly married to
the deity and to have brought with them a dowry. They usually lived in
the temple grounds but could come and go freely and even keep a house
outside the precincts. They could own property and engage in trade.
The only business which was out of bounds for them was that of tavern
keeper. The conflict between religion and alcohol, still familiar to us,
apparently goes back to at least 2000 B.C., for the code of Hammurabi
specifies that a *Sal-me* who keeps a wine shop shall be burned. These
secondary wives were under no pledge of chastity. Any children they
bore were considered the children of the god, which accounted for the
frequency with which the heroes of ancient legends were able to claim
divine paternity. A rather curious provision was that which allowed
Sal-me to marry but not to have children by their human husbands.
This was regarded as an infringement of the rights of the god, and if a
married *Sal-me* had a child she was executed. Apparently *Sal-me* wives
usually bought their husband a concubine to take over the child-bearing
function. One suspects that such marriages were usually contracted by
older women who entered them for business purposes or to gain congenial companionship.

Below the *Sal-me* came the *zikru* and *kadishtu,* who were the concubines and serving women of the god. The existence of two terms indicates that there was some difference in their status and functions, but
the inscriptions do not explain what it was. These women were prostitutes who had rooms in the temple precinct and whose earnings went to
the temple. They were a regular part of the divine establishment even
when the deity worshipped was a goddess. Children born to them were
usually adopted by families outside the temple organization. Their social position was not unlike that of better class prostitutes among ourselves, and young men were frequently warned against them and their
wiles. When they became too old for this service, they were put to work
at menial tasks in the temple and were also employed as weavers. Tablets have been found with lists of the women employed in this way, the
amount of food issued to each, and the amount of cloth they had produced.

Several gods were worshipped in each city, but main devotion was always given to one God, or less frequently, Goddess, who was the city's special guardian and, indeed, owner. His priests formed the highest order in the priesthood, while other gods were worshipped in lesser establishments and by lesser priestly orders. With the rise to empire of first one city and then another, the power of the various city gods also rose and fell. The god of an imperial city would dominate the entire pantheon. When a city was defeated and destroyed, its god would drop to the bottom of the divine hierarchy. There is a passage in a play by Lord Dunsany in which a prophet, speaking to a king and foretelling the doom of the city, says, "Already the gods in heaven shun thy god, for they know his doom. He seeth oblivion about him as a mist." This was exactly the Sumerian attitude. The gods had no love for each other or for men. They were completely unethical in their dealings with both and were interested in humans only for exploitative purposes.

The temple dominated the intellectual and economic life of the city as the *ziggurat* dominated its buildings. It was a huge corporation which, as time went on, drew more and more of the wealth of the community into its hands. The city god was owner of all the land and ten per cent of the produce was paid to him as ground rent. Peasants and artisans paid their tithes in kind. The raw materials obtained in this way were worked up in the temple factories and the finished goods were exported and sold through agents in other communities. This temple trade required a great corps of clerks and accountants, all of whom were officially classed as priests of lower grades. The higher level priests formed a self-perpetuating board of directors for the temple corporation, which continued in operation for as long as a dynasty lasted. Money and goods which once found their way into the temple coffers were never redistributed, while the temple's custom of lending money at rates which we would consider exorbitant hastened the concentration of wealth. This tendency for wealth to accumulate in the hands of religious organizations can be observed in many cultures. At the time of the Protestant Reformation, the Church owned about a third of the total area of Europe and was rapidly creeping up on the rest.

The temples were the only educational centers and maintained schools which were theoretically co-educational, although few girls attended. These schools trained students for the professions of scribe, doctor, and lawyer, as well as for the priesthood. All professional men were rated as priests, although most of them were in independent practice with only a formal connection with the establishment of one or another god. There were two orders of priests: the ceremonial priests, who saw that the rituals, including sacrifices, were performed properly, and the diviners, who answered questions and made prophecies based on various methods of divination.

The diviners were considered of lower rank than the ceremonial priests but are of particular interest to us, since they were the earliest scientists. Even the method of divination from the entrails of animals was carried on according to strict rules. Clay models of livers with the meanings of various anomalies written on them were used to instruct young diviners, and there is even reason to believe that the results of various predictions were noted down with a view to improving the method. The most important contribution of these Mesopotamian diviners to later civilization came from their study of the stars. Although the Egyptians also studied the heavens, learned the true length of the year, and discovered the cycle of more than a thousand years intervening between the time that the star Sirius rose at a certain point on the horizon and returned to the same point, the Mesopotamians elaborated the science much further. It is to them that we owe the concept of the zodiac and the recognition of the difference between planets and fixed stars. It is interesting to note that they included the earth and the moon among the planets. The Mesopotamian star watchers kept records over the centuries of planetary movements and of the eclipses of the sun and moon. In due course of time they learned to predict at least lunar eclipses with great accuracy and were able to put this knowledge to good use in their prophecies. Although their astronomical knowledge has come down to us through the Greeks and the Arabs, they were unquestionably the originators of the still flourishing pseudo-science of astrology. Even more important than their astronomical discoveries was the concept of a mechanistic universe resulting from these. A world in which planetary movements and eclipses can be accurately predicted centuries ahead is no longer a world ruled by the casual whims of deities. Upon this recognition is based the search for regularities and natural laws which is the fundamental activity of the scientist.

The Sumerian city was a theocracy in the most complete meaning of the term. The city was thought of as so completely under the divine control that the earliest treaties between cities were always phrased as agreements between their gods. The names of the human rulers often were not mentioned. Below the deity stood a governor who was thought of as a sort of steward of the divine estate who took his orders from the deity. During the later Sumerian period a division between church and state began to appear, and, after the Semitic conquest, kings emerged as distinct functionaries respectful to the city god but not his direct representative. The throne was hereditary in a royal family, with the succession normally going to the ablest, not necessarily the oldest, son of the head wife. If none of her sons survived, the heir was chosen from among those of the secondary wives or even concubines. The duties of the king were no sinecure. He was expected to administer justice, direct public works, and lead the armies in wartime. If these duties were not performed successfully, the dynasty fell, with the destruction and misery for the common people inevitably associated with any revolution.

Especially after the small city states began to coalesce into empires, the duties of the king were more than any one man could perform, and the well known Near Eastern pattern of the *wazir* emerged. The *wazir* was an administrator appointed by the king and exercising absolute power, subject only to the king's veto. Since the veto was very likely to be accompanied by an order for the *wazir's* execution, the post was one of both honor and peril. At no stage in Mesopotamian history was there development of anything like a representative legislative body. The nearest approach to it seems to have been during the late Babylonian or Assyrian period, when cities within empires had their councils.

The Sumerians seem to have been the first people to make slavery a formal institution, and the patterns which they originated have persisted in the Near East until very recent times. Slaves were chiefly prisoners of war, with a few criminals and debt slaves. Earlier peoples had killed off war prisoners, but the Sumerians, living in a settled community where there was much rough work to be done, realized that even an enemy was worth more alive than dead. Slavery for crime and debt are often misinterpreted. Enslavement of criminals was designed less as a punishment than as a means of insuring good behavior of troublesome individuals. It was used mainly in the case of persistent petty offenders. The master who bought such a slave was responsible for any offense which he committed and could be counted on to watch him and to give him a thrashing when he misbehaved.

Debt slavery was merely the end-product of a system under which a man could borrow beyond the amount of his assets. He put himself up for security, and, if he was unable to repay his borrowings within an agreed length of time, became a slave of his creditor and by his labor reimbursed the creditor for the loss of the loan.

Sumerian slavery was not particularly onerous. Since the slaves were captured from nearby cities or had been members of the community, there was no difference in physical type between slave and free. The slave could own property, could borrow money if he could offer security, and could buy his freedom. The slave could also protest his own sale in court, that is, he could show that the man who wished to buy him had a grudge against him and was likely to mistreat him. Runaway slaves were severely punished, as were those who aided them in their flight. Slave women were automatically concubines to their owners. However, at the master's death the concubine and her children were

free. The owner of a slave was recompensed if the slave was injured, just
as in cases of other property damage. Any damage done by a slave had
to be made good by the slave's owner.

Next in rank above the slave was a social group which we would call
the free commoners. These were known as *mushkinu.* They were farmers, laborers, artisans, toolmakers, shopkeepers, and merchants. Many of
the *mushkinu* were educated and often seem to have been wealthier
than some members of the upper class. The *mushkinu* carried on most
of the peacetime activities of the community and in war provided light-
armed skirmishers.

The highest class, known as *amelu,* included government officials,
priests, and soldiers. In Sumerian-Akkadian times the names of the
members of this group show them to have been an almost equal mixture
of Semites and Sumerians. It seems likely that the Semitic invaders
found the class system already in existence and allied themselves with
its highest division. The law code of Hammurabi distinguishes between
amelu and *mushkinu* at various points, but not always to the advantage
of the former. The legal status of the two classes was the same with regard to all situations which did not involve physical injury. However,
damage to the person of an *amelu* was punished much more severely
than a similar injury to a *mushkinu;* conversely an *amelu* was fined more
heavily than a *mushkinu* for several offenses. The heavier fines may have
been based on an assumption of greater capacity to pay, but actually
many of the *amelu* seem to have been small farmers who held their land
in return for personal military service. The regulation which forbade
foreclosure on an *amelu's* property while he was away on a campaign
has a familiar ring.

The best explanation for the legal distinctions seems to be that put
forward by Wooley that it was a reflection of the military system which
the Sumerian-Akkadian empire had inherited from its Sumerian predecessors. The majority of the *amelu* group were trained soldiers. Bodily
injury to them was therefore punished more heavily because it meant
loss to the state of the investment which their training represented. Conversely, since *amelu* were subject to military discipline, their punishments were naturally heavier than those of civilians. A similar distinction between ordinary and martial law has been retained even in our
own society.

The Sumerians were the first people in history to organize and drill
their armed forces. The early wars were local affairs, quarrels between
city states over fields or water rights. Later, as the city states expanded,
long-range campaigns of conquest were inaugurated. By 3000 B.C. we
find Sumerian cities fighting for the control of trade routes. The earliest
monuments show four-wheeled battle wagons drawn by teams of don-

keys. However, it must have been extremely difficult to maneuver with these or even to drive them into the thick of an attacking force. Donkeys, unlike horses, are inclined to use their own best judgment on these occasions. By Akkadian times horses were present in Mesopotamia and the superior two-wheeled chariot was known, but there are no indications of the use of effective chariot tactics.

The strength of the Sumerian army lay in its drilled infantry. The Sumerians were the first people to develop the phalanx, ascribed by most historians to Epaminondos of Thebes some two thousand years later. In this formation the front rank carried large square shields which protected them from the neck to below the knees, and carried short swords or battle axes for hand-to-hand fighting. They marched shoulder to shoulder holding up their shields, while behind them came three ranks of soldiers whose spears projected out between the shields, forming a bristling front. Such phalanxes were formidable war machines, especially on level ground, but their effectiveness depended upon drill of almost Prussian thoroughness. The men of the phalanx must have been trained to march in step and to whirl as a unit at the word of command. Individual phalanxes seem to have been kept up for generations, like our own regiments. They had names and special insignia, and there was a tendency for membership to be hereditary. Members of a phalanx who failed to report for duty or who tried to send a substitute were punished by death. In return for their long training and frequent absences from home they were protected from foreclosure on their property, held their lands tax free, and were rated as members of the highest social class. A poor *amelu* farmer ranked a much wealthier *mushkinu* merchant socially.

Monuments of 2500 to 3000 B.C. show these phalanxes marching to battle with the king gallantly striding in front wearing a gold helmet and carrying a scimitar or mace. He must have skipped to the flank before the phalanxes met. The opposing phalanxes operated somewhat like the flying wedge formation familiar to night club waiters. The two phalanxes would advance at the double, gathering speed until they crashed front to front. There would follow a pushing contest, aided by hand-to-hand fighting between the shield bearers, until one side gave way. The members of the broken phalanx usually fled in panic and most of the slaughter took place during the pursuit. Heads of vanquished enemies were brought back and piled in the temple grounds as an exhibit, but there was no genuine head hunting and these trophies were not kept.

The Semitic conquerors of Sumer found themselves confronted with the problems that have plagued conquerors ever since. They were themselves villagers and nomad tribesmen, and as soon as they had taken over the civilized Sumerians they discovered that running an empire was no sinecure. It is easy for nomads to loot a country, but when they try to move in to collect taxes and to keep up production and really profit by their conquest, they are forced to turn to those who already know something about government administration. Within a few years after the Akkadian conquest, the conquerors were using the old Sumerian bureaucracy to keep the system going. Within a few generations the shaven headed Sumerian scribes, who are shown humbly following the gorgeous Akkadian kings, had gotten most of the real power back into their own hands. In the long run the pen is a deadlier weapon than the sword.

Mesopotamia was the first civilization to have business as one of its major interests. Trade was necessary to any sort of civilized life, since the only raw materials which the valley provided in adequate quantity were clay, reeds, and grain. Even the beams needed in house construction and the stone from which the images of the gods were made had to be imported. As the Sumerians made increasing use of metal their trade routes extended farther and farther. Trading posts staffed by Sumerian merchants were established as far afield as Asia Minor and Palestine. They also seem to have carried on a fairly extensive sea trade by way of the Persian Gulf, since we have one record of a trading expedition which was gone for over three years and came back loaded, no doubt, with "ivory, apes, and peacocks." Goods from the upper river districts, which were the principal sources of lumber and animal products, were brought to the Sumerian cities by a method still in use. A bull boat, which was simply a large circular basket woven of osiers and covered with hides, was loaded with produce and floated downstream. The bull boats were large enough to carry two or three men and one or two donkeys in addition to their payload. When the boat reached the city it was broken up and sold together with the cargo. The crew stowed their personal possessions and purchases on the donkeys and walked home.

All the appliances for effective business were established by 3000 B.C. Standard weights and measures were developed. Those of the various cities probably differed at first as they did in Medieval Europe, but the spread of empire resulted in increasing standardization. The earliest medium of exchange was a fixed measure of barley, the measure being, in many cases, carved in stone and set up in the market place so that if a farmer thought he was being short-changed he could measure out the grain. By 3000 B.C. metal currency was beginning to replace barley currency, and the government was beginning to worry about the shortage of money. The code of Hammurabi attempted to stabilize the relative value of barley and metal, with serious penalties for abuse of the standard. A merchant, who refused to take barley in payment for his wares forfeited his life, as did anyone who refused to exchange metal money for barley at the current rate.

Metal was cut and weighed at each exchange. The Sumerians did not have coins. The difficulty was, of course, in assessing the purity of the metal, and in later times private banking houses stamped metal ingots with their seals as a guarantee against adulteration. These "stamped shekels" were the ancestors of our own coins. In the Sumerian-Akkadian period the ratio of silver to gold was 12 to 1.

We have cuneiform records of elaborate financial transactions, loans with fixed rates of interest running up as high as two or three hundred per cent in cases in which the individual had no security. The lowest rate was 25 per cent per annum. There were principals and agents and also joint projects, corresponding to our stock companies and corporations. It is interesting that, in the laws governing principals and agents, an agent who defrauded his employer was punished only half as severely as the employer who defrauded his agents. Apparently the financial forces were already operating to squeeze the little fellow, and the law was attempting to protect him from the big operators, particularly the temple corporations.

Because of the Sumerian habit of making contracts for all important transactions we have an amazingly complete picture of the life of these people. Not only documents and contracts but a good deal of private correspondence have been preserved. One tablet from before 2000 B.C. contains the familiar lament of an old man about the degeneracy of the younger generation. Another personal document which shows a high continuity of pattern is a letter written to his parents by a boy at school complaining about the food.

From the legal documents and private correspondence we gain an excellent picture of Sumerian home life. The Sumerian family was much like our own. There were no clans or extended kin groups. This was probably a reflection of city living, since it is very difficult to maintain extended family patterns in a city population which is constantly shifting and being recruited from the outside. Any city population tends to be made up of isolated individuals, and consequently the small family with only the parent-child tie is the strongest social unit.

Marriage was monogamous, except that a rich and important man might have several concubines. Marriages were arranged by parents on a strictly contractual basis. There were no religious ceremonies or sanctions. The marriage was a written contract in which the rights and duties of both parties were outlined precisely. Causes for divorce and even the amount of alimony to be paid were also specified. At the betrothal the bridegroom made a gift of money to his prospective father-in-law, which was forfeited if he broke the engagement. If the girl withdrew, the father had not only to return this sum but to pay an equal amount to the jilted suitor as a fine. If the marriage was consummated, the payment from the bridegroom and the contribution made by the bride's father became the girl's dowry, to which she held inalienable rights. It went to her children and her husband couldn't touch it.

Family capital was held and used jointly. Women could run businesses, lend money, make legal contracts in the absence of their husbands, and, in short, held positions of economic equality. As a matter of fact their legal position was much better than that of the English woman prior to the Married Women's Property Act of 1926. A wife was not responsible for debts that her husband had contracted before marriage, and vice-versa; but, after marriage, debts contracted by either party were family debts and either party could be held for them. A husband could sell his wife under certain circumstances but only with her consent. If she preferred being a concubine in a rich man's house to being a hard-working wife in a poor family, she could ask her husband to sell her. A husband could put his wife up as security for a loan up to three years. As in the case with all other securities, the lender had the right to use the pledge until it could be redeemed. Although the rights of women were carefully guarded, the laws also provided some protection for husbands. One passage in the Code of Hammurabi reads, "If a woman gads about, speaks disrespectfully of her husband, and neglects his house, she shall be drowned."

The Sumerians had a great desire for children, but infant mortality rates must have been very high. A family of more than three or four children was exceedingly rare, at least among the class who left written wills and testaments. If a wife were barren she could be divorced. The husband had to have the wife's consent to the divorce, however, and she kept her dowry and received a money compensation as well. If she refused her consent, the husband could legally take a second wife, but it was specified in the contract that the first wife retained her status, and the second wife had to wash the feet of the first one and carry her stool when they went to the temple. The more common arrangement was for the barren wife to buy a concubine for her husband, a slave woman who took over the wife's reproductive function. Any children born to such a concubine were rated as the wife's legal offspring. A barren woman who was willing to buy a concubine for her spouse could not be divorced.

Sumer was the first place in history to have a fully developed concept of law and written and published law codes. The Indonesian development of *adat* law cannot be dated, but must be ascribed to a later time. The first complete Mesopotamian law code which has been preserved is the Code of Hammurabi, which was drawn up in 1940 B.C.

However, fragments of a number of older codes have survived, and their compilation must be regarded as a sort of Code Napoleon, intended to simplify and unify the preexisting legal system of a whole series of cities. This was made necessary by the spread of the Sumerian-Akkadian empire of which Hammurabi was ruler.

Hammurabi was a Semite and, to judge from the fragments of earlier codes, the Semitic conquest led to a considerable stiffening of penalties and a worsening of the status of women. Incidentally, according to his own statement, the infant Hammurabi was found floating in a reed basket in a drainage ditch and adopted by a gardener, thus antedating Moses by some 500 years.

Hammurabi had his code inscribed on pillars which were set up in the market places of the various cities in his empire. The laws were stated with a brevity and conciseness which is rarely found in our own. The king had important judicial powers and represented the court of last appeal. This pattern has been continued by some Near Eastern rulers down to the present day and seems to be a characteristic Semitic pattern. It provided a method by which the king could make himself accessible to his subjects and gain their favor. A king who made wise judgments, was able to evaluate conflicting evidence, and detect false witnesses gained tremendously in prestige. Solomon, who held court in good Sumerian fashion, was such a king, and his judgments are still famous.

The higher officials whom the king had appointed to outlying districts performed his judicial functions there. There were both ecclesiastical and civil lower courts, but the jurisdiction of each type was not too clearly defined. Presumably the system had originally been weighted on the ecclesiastical side like the rest of Sumerian culture, but the civil courts had arrogated additional power to themselves. By the time of Hammurabi the ecclesiastical courts could pronounce judgments in affairs pertaining to the temple, but even these decisions were subject to royal review. Ordinary civil suits were heard in civil courts by judges appointed by the king.

In the legal procedure the plaintiff first made application to a functionary called the *mashkin,* who acted as arbitrator and tried to settle the case out of court. If he failed in this, the case went to a court which was presided over by two to four professional judges. The *mashkin,* who was already familiar with the facts of the case, was associated with the judges on the bench. The principals and witnesses gave testimony under oath, documents were produced and examined by the court, and the decision was handed down on the basis of precedents. In important cases the accused would be represented by counsel. A judge who reversed his decision could be fined and disbarred, as it was assumed that he had been bribed to do so. However, a case could be appealed to a higher court if the judgment was unsatisfactory, or new evidence could be brought in. Court stenographers recorded all cases on cuneiform tablets, which were put down in sand in large jars. There were heavy penalties for perjury and contempt of court. In fact, the whole courtroom procedure would be entirely familiar to a modern lawyer.

Some of the most interesting sections of the code are those dealing with economic matters. Prices were rising steadily, and the poor land owner was being progressively squeezed out. There was legislation directed at the redistribution of agricultural land which was not kept in use. In these codes we can observe the first attempts to control wages, rents, working hours, etc. In fact, there is a recently translated tablet from the Sumerian period in which there is a dispute over portal to portal pay. This controversy was brought to court and decided in favor of labor, a not infrequent result in Sumerian courts. However, in spite of the effort to fix prices and wages throughout Mesopotamian history we can trace a steady rise in the cost of things, comparable to that which has been going on ever since.

Sumer even had its New Deal and social reform instituted from the top down, which was undertaken by Urukagina of Lagash in 2630 B.C. In his inscriptions Urukagina is exceedingly vague as to his ancestry, which suggests that he was a commoner who had risen to power. One of his first acts was to reduce taxes and to cut the excessive charges which the priests were making for necessary services such as funerals and divination. In fact he tried to introduce socialized divination, putting the diviners on a straight government salary and forbidding them to receive extra fees. He also tried to institute agrarian reforms, breaking down the large estates and redistributing the land to the peasants. This naturally earned him the enmity of all the better people, who called upon the ruler of a neighboring city for help. In the resulting rightist revolution Urukagina was killed and everything returned to normalcy. One of the most personal of ancient documents which has come down to us deals with this event. An unbaked clay tablet was found buried in a rubbish heap outside the city wall of Lagash. Upon this tablet a minor priest, who must have been a friend and partisan of Urukagina, had listed the shrines destroyed and looted by the foreign allies of the conservative faction and had eased his mind by calling down a comprehensive curse upon the traitors.

Chapter XXII

Near East and Mediterranean

THE PROGRESSIVE DESICCATION of the Near East which led to the development of the Semitic culture patterns also served to concentrate population in the river valleys and on the flanks of the mountain ranges. The most important of these ranges were the Zagros mountains which bordered Mesopotamia on the east, the Elbruz immediately to the south of the Caspian Sea, and the Taurus mountains in southeastern Asia Minor. In addition, the whole of Khurdistan and much of Armenia and Asia Minor were broken plateaus where small ranges alternated with fertile valleys. Unfortunately, the archeology of most of these mountain regions is still largely unknown, but the presence of Neolithic and Bronze Age settlements is attested by the numerous *tels,* tall mounds of accumulated debris. The few excavations which have been conducted outside Mesopotamia indicate a steady development of culture throughout the prehistoric period with numerous diffusions both westward to the Aegean Islands and Europe and eastward through Turkestan. The finding in Kansu, China, of Neolithic painted pottery similar to that from early levels from Susa in Persia shows how far the diffusion extended.

As our knowledge increases, Anatolia, at the western end of the Southwest Asiatic massif, is beginning to emerge as an important center of culture growth. Most of the new elements which appear in central Europe from the Neolithic on can be traced to this region, and it seems increasingly probable that it was a genuine origin point for new ideas and techniques rather than a mere transmitter from the more advanced cultures of the south. Although Syria and Anatolia could not support the dense population or develop the thoroughly urbanized culture of Mesopotamia, its valleys and plateaus were fertile enough to support numerous villages and to provide considerable economic surplus. Fairly large towns grew up in many places and the technology, especially in pottery and metal working, was little, if at all inferior to that of Mesopotamia.

In Anatolia at least, the ethnic and linguistic situation seems to have been exceedingly complex. As in all mountainous country, the local conditions made for isolation, with corresponding cultural and linguistic diversity. Although few, if any inscriptions are available for this region before the rise of the Hittite empire, about 1800 B.C., the first written records reveal a situation not unlike that in the modern Caucasus. There were certainly a great variety of languages and cultures functioning within a comparatively small area. Tablets from the Hittite archives in Boghaz Keui are written in at least 17 different languages, several of which cannot be related to any known linguistic stocks. Data on physical types is lacking, but since the tribal groups were small and normally endogamous, each of them probably had its own distinctive physical characteristics based on "family resemblances." The earliest sculptures from Anatolia and Syria show the big-nosed, short-headed Armenoid type which is still strong in these regions. The fact that this type also seems to have been the artistic ideal of the Sumerians, although it is very poorly represented in Sumerian skeletal material, raises some interesting questions. Since the early Sumerian representations are at least 1000 years older than the Hittite ones, whatever copying of ideal types may have occurred was from south to north. Perhaps a small group of Armenoids invaded Mesopotamia from the north and became an aristocracy which survived long enough to leave their imprint on the art style.

In spite of local variations, the later Neolithic and Bronze Age cultures of Syria and Anatolia show certain basic similarities. Pottery was elaborate, with numerous shapes and fine polychrome decorations. It was superior to anything made in Mesopotamia during the Sumerian or Akkadian periods. Mesopotamian traders had penetrated Syria by 3000 B.C. and were using the region to the north as a source of metal. There was a considerable exchange of metal objects, and it is highly probable that there were also journeymen metal workers like those already mentioned in central Europe. A variety of metallic ores were available in Anatolia, giving an opportunity for experiment and improvements in technology. The local smiths passed from copper to bronze by way of the smelting of mixed ores, and perfected a number of new implement forms in the latter. They then became the first craftsmen, as far as we know, to smelt and forge iron. The first evidence for the use of smelted as distinct from meteoric iron comes from the Hittite territory in northern Syria between 1500 and 1800 B.C. At this time all the great civilizations were still using bronze, and iron must be considered a geographically marginal invention. Apparently the Hittites tried to keep a monopoly of the new metal. A suggestion of the Egyptian king that he and the Hittite king should exchange gold and iron was met by evasion and a royal gift of two daggers with gold hilts and tempered iron, not steel, blades. One of these, apparently preserved as an heirloom, was found in the tomb of Tutankhamen.

Unfortunately, our information on Asia Minor is woefully inadequate. The inscriptions from this region are not numerous, and even now many of them cannot be read. Thus, although the Hittite language is known to us from numerous cuneiform inscriptions, the Hittites' own system of writing still has not been deciphered. However, it seems that the Hittite empire, which came into being about 1800 B.C., was a confederacy which brought together numerous tribes of divergent language and culture. The best record of its membership has been left by its Egyptian enemies. The frontiers of the two empires met in northern Palestine and they fought back and forth for centuries. In one of the Egyptian temples there is a series of reliefs showing the various contingents of the Hittite army, each contingent with its proper arms and equipment. Among them one finds the "Men of Troy," who are shown driving chariots, wearing crested helmets much like those of the Classical Greeks, and carrying the typical figure-eight shields used by both sides in the Trojan wars. The physical types and equipment of the other contingents are exceedingly varied and bear out the impression of heterogeneity conveyed by the many languages present in the royal archives.

The Hittite language was certainly Indo-European, as are some of the other languages preserved in the archives, while the names of most of the tribal chiefs also seem to be Indo-European. The first invasion of Greece by Indo-European speaking tribes seems to have taken place

SWORD SCABBARD FROM HALLSTATT

shortly after the founding of the Hittite empire, and it seems probable that both were part of a single movement originating in Asia Minor. The early Hittite empire was probably not so much an organized confederacy as it was a group of tribes held together by aristocracies of common origin. The Greek principalities which combined to make war on Troy were united on a similar basis. That numerous tribal languages were still in use within the Hittite enclave would not be surprising if the Indo-European expansion had been a comparatively recent event.

We know little of the early organization of the Hittites. The later Hittite empire was obviously modeled on the Mesopotamian ones, and the inscriptions show a well-developed bureaucracy and, still more interesting, a formal code of laws reminiscent in some ways of the Code of Hammurabi and probably modeled upon it. It is interesting to note that the penalties in this code were in general milder than those in the Code of Hammurabi, and that sex offenses of various sorts were treated with much greater leniency.

The Hittite state, whether as confederacy or empire, was certainly effective for both offense and defense. It survived 500 years with only one brief interval of eclipse, established its rule over Syria and much of Asia Minor, and pressed southward until its frontiers finally met those of the Egyptians in Palestine. For a short time it seemed that the Hittites might even dominate Egypt as had their predecessors, the Syrian Hyksos.

The name of Tutankhamen is probably better known to Americans than any other pharaoh, but few have heard of his young queen, who seems to have been the better man. When the pharaoh died there were forty days of mourning, during which no political action could be taken. The queen knew that the dynasty was crumbling and the last of Akhenaton's reforms would be swept away with it. She wrote to the Hittite king begging him to send his son to marry her so that the Hittite armies might help her hold the throne. There are two accounts of what followed. According to one, the Hittite king replied cautiously, "Let us see first what the queen's captains say." According to another, a Hittite prince was actually sent to Egypt but was ambushed and murdered by Egyptians *en route*. In any case, at the end of the forty days of mourning, one of the queen's captains seized the throne and the little queen disappeared from history.

In the early 12th and late 13th centuries B.C. the Hittite power came to an end. Hittites and Egyptians had fought each other to a standstill and, after its defeat in a battle at Kadesh in the Orantes in 1288 B.C., the Hittite empire fell to pieces. The disintegration was hastened by the attacks of new barbarian tribes from the north. The Greeks placed the Dorian invasion at only a slightly later period, and apparently another wave of Indo-European speaking peoples, perhaps the true cattle-keeping Aryans, were now pressing southward and westward. In order to escape them, various non-Indo-European speaking tribes began to evacuate Asia Minor and the Aegean Islands. Although the Egyptian records refer to these tribes collectively as "The People of the Isles," the evidence seems to point to the mainland, specially the south coast of Asia Minor, as their most probable point of origin. Some of them no doubt came from the Aegean Islands, but it is hard to believe that these small and relatively barren islets could send forth such a swarm of varied tribes. Also, it seems that some of the tribes came southward overland with ox carts, something most unlikely for an island people.

These invading tribes had already been known for some centuries to the Egyptians and Hittites, who had employed them as mercenary soldiers. They ran over the Syrian and Palestinian coasts and staged a great but unsuccessful attack on Egypt. When they were beaten off, two of the tribes seem to have migrated westward, establishing themselves in what were still barbarian lands. The peoples, whose name the Egyptians wrote S'rd'n, were pretty certainly the same as the later Sardinians. Egyptian representations of this tribe agree in details of their rather unusual costume and equipment with figurines found in the island of Sardinia. However, this could scarcely have been their point of origin. Egyptian and Hittites of the 16th century B.C. were not likely to have been recruiting mercenaries from an island between Italy and Spain when even the Cretan sea rovers had barely penetrated that far west. It seems much more likely that the S'rd'ns, after the failure of the attack on Egypt, sailed westward, overpowered the older Sardinian population and settled there, giving the island their own name. These "People of the Isles" were already using iron as well as bronze tools, and the extensive deposits of iron ore in Sardinia may have provided a stimulus to the settlement.

At least part of the Tyrrheni, another tribe of the "People of the Isles" migrated to Italy and became the Etruscans. However, this movement seems to have been delayed for at least two centuries and was a matter of gradual infiltration rather than mass invasion. The Etruscans contributed heavily to the development of the Roman culture and will be discussed later.

A third group have a peculiar interest for us, although they played a very minor role in history. These were the people known as the Philistines, who settled along the coast of what is now Palestine and gave the region their name. The Philistines established themselves there between approximately 1300 and 1000 B.C. The Children of Israel, who arrived at nearly the same time but from the opposite direction, found the Philistines already in possession of the coastal lands. The older Canaanitic population, who were settled Semites, were caught between the two.

The Hebrews, at the time of their arrival, were still in the Bronze Age, while the Philistines were using iron. Bible readers may remember that the charges which the Philistine smiths made for sharpening the Hebrew's iron tools were regarded as exorbitant. The "sharpening" was probably the reforging or welding of worn-out tools, processes requiring the skill of trained smiths. After a long-drawn struggle recorded in the Book of Judges, the Hebrews conquered and eventually absorbed both Canaanites and Philistines. According to the Hebrew records, the Philistines came from Caphtor, usually equated with the island of Crete. However, none of the Minoan (early Cretan) carvings show the characteristic Philistine headdress, a feather war bonnet almost identical with that worn by the Blackfoot Indians of our own Plains. Neither do the Philistine archeological remains nor the few Biblical references to their ethnology fit with what we know of the Minoans. It seems much more probable that the Philistines followed the example of the Sardinians and the Tyrrheni and established colonies on Crete after the failure of the Egyptian attack. By 1200 B.C. the brilliant Minoan civilization had collapsed, and a group of foreign invaders might well have gained a foothold. It may be noted in this connection that one of the symbols on the Phaestos disc, a unique inscribed tablet found in Crete, is the head of a man wearing what looks very much like a Philistine war bonnet. The Egyptians were already familiar with the Minoan Cretans, with whom they had traded for centuries, and distinguished clearly between them and the Philistines, whom they regarded as part of the general southward migration of the "People of the Isles."

In later times the native peoples and cultures of Asia Minor were caught between the great Asiatic powers to the east, first Assyria, and then Persia and the expanding Greek civilization. They have left little mark on recorded history. Nevertheless, on the cultural side their contributions were by no means inconsiderable. As has already been said, the region seems to have been one of the earliest centers of metal working and may well be responsible for both the invention of bronze and smelting of iron. The Etruscans played an important role in the shaping of the Roman civilization and through this left their mark on later cultures of the west.

Lastly, events in Asia Minor left an enduring monument in the Homeric epics. As we have seen, Troy was part of the Hittite confederacy. So long as the Hittite power continued the mainland Greeks did not dare to attack the city, although they probably had causes for irritation considerably more important and less romantic than the elopement of Helen. The city of Troy was a small affair. In the Homeric period the total space within its walls was roughly equivalent to that covered by Grand Central Station in New York. However, it was strategically situated at one of the few spots along the Aegean coast where ships voyaging northward to the Hellespont and Black Sea could obtain water and could be beached for the night. The Trojans would have been less than human if they had not taken advantage of their position to try to dominate the Black Sea trade. After the battle of Kadesh and the Hittite collapse, the Greeks saw their opportunity to dispose of a long-standing rival and did so.

PART SEVEN

Mediterranean Complex

Chapter XXIII

Crete

THE DISCOVERY of the early eastern Mediterranean cultures is one of the most romantic stories in archeology. The *Iliad* and the *Odyssey* contain frequent references to objects quite unlike anything known to the Classical Greeks and implying a level of technological skill which even they lacked. To give a single example, the shield of Diomede, on which a picture of men picking grapes in a vineyard was worked out in metals of many different colors, would have been beyond the skill not only of the Classical Greeks but, until a century ago, of any people except the Japanese. Although the Greeks themselves had taken the Homeric epics as serious history with only the embroidery allowed by poetic license, the European scholars of the 19th century relegated them to the realm of fantasy and reduced the heroes and episodes to cosmic deities and solar myths.

One man refused to be convinced. Heinrich Schliemann, born the son of a poor pastor in 1822, was a familiar German type, a romanticist with an *idée fixe*. He has written a very interesting autobiography in which he tells how his passion for the Greek classics began when he was a small boy. In his native village there was a poverty-stricken alcoholic who, in his better days, had received a classical education. When this man was drunk he would recite Homer in the original Greek. Young Schliemann would save his pennies until he had enough money to provide the necessary stimulus, then listen to the rolling lines of Homer, no word of which he understood, with tears of emotion rolling down his cheeks. He determined that when he grew up he would find and excavate the city of Troy and promised to take a little girl who was his first love with him. Although the girl dropped out of the picture, he retained this ambition during years of poverty and even when he was an itinerant laborer. Eventually, he made a fortune by smuggling tea into Russia, an occupation which at that time compared in both its respectability and returns with bootlegging in the United States of the late 1920's. In 1870, when he was forty-eight years old, he was finally able to implement his ambition.

In preparation for the resurrection of Troy, Schliemann had taught himself Greek and had studied Homer intensively. He refused to accept the place which was then supposed to be the site of Troy because it lacked certain springs mentioned in the *Iliad*. Other reasons for rejecting it were that it was too far from the coast and that it would have been impossible for Achilles to pursue Hector around the city walls unless they both had indulged in some fairly stiff rock-climbing. Finally he decided upon a mound on which the village of Hissarlik had stood as the most probable site and began excavations with vast enthusiasm but little professional competence. In the course of his work he unearthed, and hopelessly scrambled, the remains of a whole series of superimposed

MINOAN JAR

towns which showed that the site had been occupied almost continuously from Neolithic to Roman times. In one of the occupation levels, which was later proved to be some centuries older than Homeric Troy, he found a collection of gold objects which had evidentally been hidden in haste and which he gleefully dubbed "The Treasure of Priam."

The rumors of treasure brought down upon Schliemann a horde of hungry Turkish officials and he was forced to abandon work at Hissarlik before he had completed the destruction of the site. He moved to the Greek mainland and began work at Mycene, which was the reputed site of the Atridae, the royal house to which King Agamemnon had belonged. The Roman writer Pausanius, who had written a sort of Baedeker of the Greece of his time, reported that a certain place at Mycene was pointed out to tourists as the tomb of Agamemnon. Digging in the area indicated by Pausanius' account, Schliemann uncovered a series of royal tombs with unbelievably rich furniture. In one he found the skeleton of a tall man with his face covered with a bearded gold mask and with a magnificent bronze rapier by his side. Other tombs yielded a wealth of metal objects, the most extraordinary of which were daggers inlaid with scenes of men hunting lions, of a wildcat pursuing birds among the reeds, and with rows of lilies, all worked out in many colored metals. One of the most intriguing finds was a silver cup with bird figures on the handles. With a very slight stretch of the imagination, this could be regarded as the veritable cup of Nestor, described in the *Iliad*. Schliemann wired to the German emperor: "I have found the tomb of Agamemnon," and shortly thereafter died happily.

We know today that this could not have been the tomb of Agamemnon but came from a period at least three or four centuries earlier, but Schliemann's labors had brought to light a chapter in Greek history which had been completely lost. If he had lived only a few years longer he would have completed his work by discovering the center of this great Aegean culture, for at his death he had already made plans to dig in Crete. As it was, the Cretan work was carried on by other archeologists, especially Sir Arthur Evans, who devoted his life to the gradual uncovering of the great site at Knossos where the Cretan civilization seems to have reached its climax. Unfortunately Cretan culture has to be reconstructed from artifacts, buildings and frescoes, plus some Greek legends. To judge the authenticity of the latter, one must remember that the period separating the climax of the Cretan civilization from the climax of the Athenean culture was roughly the same as that separating the Norman conquest of England to the present day and that these legends had been handed down by word of mouth. The Cretans had developed a system of writing, apparently a mixture of syllabary and ideographic signs, but even if it could be deciphered it would give us little help, since they have left no long inscriptions. This in itself may be significant, for it indicates that the Cretans did not accord their rulers the adulation given to Mesopotamian kings or Egyptian pharaohs. Most of the examples of Cretan writing which have come to light so far are on tags which apparently were for marking bales of merchandise.

The Cretan civilization was derived from the same Southwestern Asiatic Neolithic center which was ancestral to the other ancient cultures just discussed. However, it seems to have been more strongly influenced by Egyptian civilization than by Asia. Crete lies about halfway between Egypt and the Greek mainland, a position which proved highly advantageous, since it made it possible for the Cretans to dominate the carrying trade between these two centers in later times. The first Cretan settlement seems to have been made about 5000 B.C., probably by migrants from the Greek mainland. Their culture was a simple Neolithic one, but they could reach Crete by island-hopping without having to cross more than 50 or 60 miles of open sea at any point. This would be quite possible in dugout canoes in calm weather. Racially, the settlers were long-headed, dark-haired, slender Mediterraneans. Even in Classical times the back country Cretans did not speak Greek, and from this and the Minoan (early Cretan) inscriptions, we feel sure that the original language of the island was not Indo-European.

Contact with Egypt seems to have been established before the end of the pre-Dynastic period there, roughly 4000 B.C. So many Egyptian elements appear in Crete during the next thousand years that some authorities believe there was an actual migration from Egypt. In the classical period the Cretans were famous for two things: their archery and their mendacity. They seem to have used the composite bow, even in Minoan times, having presumably acquired it through trade contacts with Asia Minor. The mendacity was presumably a local development. There was a Classical Greek phrase, "to lie like a Cretan," which acknowledged their supremacy in an art at which the Greeks themselves were no novices.

Even in Neolithic times Crete must have been a relatively poor region for agriculture. However, the island was well forested, providing timber for ships, and the olive tree was well adapted to the stony slopes which were left when the forests had been cut off. The Cretans seem to have been one of the first peoples to domesticate this tree. Olive groves are profitable only for a thoroughly settled population, since it takes them about 30 years to come into full bearing, after which they will keep on bearing for about 100 years. Throughout Cretan history olive oil was one of the island's main exports. Their use of the fine pottery which was produced locally for the fancy packaging of this product has already been mentioned.

The main Cretan domestic animal seems to have been the goat
Horses reached the island before the Minoan culture was overthrown,
but they were of little importance. Cattle were also kept and bulls had
very definite ceremonial and religious connotations. However, the Cretans must have got most of their protein food from fish. The poverty
of the Cretan soil and the proximity of the sea led them to seafaring
and commerce. They were the first people in history to develop a civilization of the modern commercial type. Throughout the period when
Crete was a great power, the Cretans lived much as the English have
lived in recent centuries, by their control of the ocean-carrying trade
and by the sale of manufactured products. Much of their food must
have been imported. Crete was densely populated even in Homeric
times, when the civilization was in a state of relative collapse. The
Homeric poems constantly speak of the "many-peopled Crete," and the
Greeks of this period were greatly impressed by the number of towns
and the crowded streets of the island.

By 3000 B.C. copper was being obtained in trade from the island of
Cyprus. Our own word for copper, passed down through many languages, really means "metal of Cyprus." Bronze, silver, and gold were
in use by 2400 B.C., and since there were no rich ore deposits on the
island, all of these must have been obtained through trade. Iron did not
reach Crete until after the collapse of the Minoan civilization. It may
well have been brought in by those Philistines whom we have already
discussed. The Cretan artists of the late Minoan period, 1600–1200 B.C.,
developed a skill in alloying which has rarely been equaled. They tried
out all sorts of metallic mixtures and finishes, until they were able to
literally paint in different colored metals. Relatively few examples of
this work have been found in Crete itself, and one wonders whether its
products were intended primarily for the non-Cretan mainland princes
for whom the Cretan artists produced luxury objects. Perhaps the metal
painting was too flamboyant for the highly refined Cretan taste.

Pottery was known from the first Cretan settlements. Although they
had frequent contacts with Egypt, where the technique of making
faience was well developed, most of their vessels were unglazed. Nevertheless, the forms are excellent and the decoration not only beautiful but
painted with a freedom and skill which marks the professional. Not until the great age of the Greek vase painters do we find pottery of equal
artistic quality.

The Minoans also must have been excellent woodworkers, although
no examples of their craft have survived. We know that they built
chariots and seagoing ships, both of which require careful preliminary
design and expert joinery. It is interesting in this connection that the
few Minoan tools which have survived include a fragment of what seems

to be a large bronze crosscut saw, probably used in sawing out planks for shipwrights. Other Minoan tools are much more like modern European hand tools than are those of the Mesopotamians or Egyptians. A modern craftsman could use them with little change in his muscular habits.

The ingenuity and technical skill of the Cretans was recognized by the later Greeks in their legend of Daedalus, the master craftsman who contrived numerous machines for the use of his royal master. At least one of the devices with which he is credited, the ball and socket joint permitting universal motion, may well be a Cretan invention. According to the legend, when he fell from favor he escaped with his son Icarus by means of artificial wings. The fate of Icarus, who ventured too near the sun, is still familiar as an example of disastrous pride.

Minoan art represented an early flowering of that keen observation of nature and attempt to reproduce it, while maintaining balance and harmony of design, which was so characteristic of the later Greeks. Like

MINOAN JAR

the Greek art of the later Classical period, Minoan art was instinct with life. Its artists did not represent remote and awful deities or divine kings, but proud and happy humans. Minoan pottery was decorated with floral and marine forms of surprising naturalism, and similar forms, particularly dolphins, were used as repeat designs in the frescoes with which the Minoan palaces were decorated.

A striking feature of Minoan art, as it has survived, is the small size of most of the objects. We have figurines obviously intended for ceremonial purposes, but no life-size statues. This is in sharp contrast to the fresco art in the palace at Knossos, where life-size figures are common. There is even one frieze of more than life-size male figures modeled in stucco in relief. We have the tradition of the bronze man which Daedalus made to serve as a guardian for Minos, and there are a few skillfully cast bronze figurines. One wonders whether there may not have been larger, perhaps life-size, metal statues which have disappeared in the course of the numerous lootings to which the island was exposed from 1400 B.C. on. Whether there were larger statues or not, the miniature products of the Minoan art show extraordinary skill and naturalism. The tiny face of one ivory figurine representing a priestess is so live and so charming in its irregularity of feature that it may well be a portrait. Another object which unfortunately has survived only in part is a group showing the favorite theme of the bull sport. In this a delicately carved ivory athlete, caught in mid-leap, seems to have been supported on gold wires above the figure of the bull.

Thanks to frescoes and figurines it is possible for us to reconstruct various details of Cretan equipment. The usual costume of young men was a scanty loin cloth and a broad belt designed to produce a wasp waist. Older men wore a long gown, and apparently cloaks were worn for warmth or on solemn occasions. The women's costume gives a curious feeling of modernity. The upper garment was a short-sleeved bolero jacket worn with or without a blouse of thin white material. With this was worn a flounced bell-bottomed skirt or wide-bottomed lounging pajamas gaily decorated with ruffles. Color was extensively used. The footgear for both men and women was completely modern. Men are sometimes shown wearing sandals but more commonly wearing a solid shoe much like the army field shoe. Women wore high-heeled, open-strap slippers almost identical with those shown in the summer displays of Fifth Avenue shops. Women also wore large, gaily decorated hats which might well have come from the workroom of Lily Daché. Both sexes were addicted to elaborate ornaments of gold and gems, and the variety of costume details shown in paintings and figurines suggest that the Minoan ladies, like our own, followed the dictates of frequently changing fashions.

The Minoan warriors are shown wearing crested bronze helmets but no body armor. The basic defensive weapon was a large shield shaped like a figure-eight. The indentations in the center were no doubt designed to give the bearer room for work with spear or rapier, but they formed a weak spot in his defense. It may be remembered that in the Homeric poems most of the heroes were wounded in the side toward the waist, the place where the Minoan shield gave the least protection. The main weapons were the spear and sword. The double-bitted axe, which must originally have been a real battle axe, seems to have been relegated to ceremonial use by Minoan times. The swords were long, straight, bronze rapiers, tapering very gradually from a slender tip to a widest point just in front of the grip. Hilts were made of gold, ivory, or crystal, elaborately worked. These rapiers had been developed from earlier daggers and were used exclusively for thrusting.

Unfortunately, we have little information on the Cretan shipbuilding, which must have been one of the high points in their technology. They seem to have been the first people to develop large seaworthy vessels. To judge from engravings on gems and occasional representations on pottery, these ships were galleys with single banks of oars. They seem to have been decked over for their entire length and to have had one to three masts with square sails. The bow and stern were high and sharply upcurved and, at the bow, the keel projected for some distance beyond the cutwater. This arrangement must have been designed for ramming, and we know that by the end of the Minoan period fighting ships had rams which were shod with bronze. They were thus the originators of what was to be the main naval tactic throughout the Classical period. It may also be noted that the Minoans were the first people to develop the type of anchor still in use, complete with flukes and rig.

If they were able to ram successfully, the Minoan galleys must have been fast and maneuverable. They enabled the Minoans to establish the first sea empire in history. In order to maintain this, they set up naval bases around the eastern Mediterranean. Their bases in the Nile delta were leased from Egypt. Those in less civilized areas were probably established by force. Such bases were the earliest examples of the deliberate colonization brought to such a high point by the later Greek cities. While these bases were mainly useful for trade, the Minoans also no doubt indulged in piracy. It may be remembered that in the *Odyssey* King Nestor politely asks Odysseus' son Telemachus whether he is a trader or a pirate. Both occupations were regarded as perfectly respectable at this period and were obviously merely alternate ways of getting what the voyager wanted.

The Cretan communities seem to have been more prosperous than any of the early city civilizations. Certainly the economic surplus was more evenly distributed. The Egyptian cities consisted of a few great temples and palaces surrounded by extensive slums. There was a larger middle class in Mesopotamia than in Egypt, but even there the proportion of middle-class families seems to have been much smaller than in Crete. The Minoan towns suggest a predominantly bourgeois population. The settlement pattern was that of open villages, each with its outdoor shrine as a center for community life. Houses seem to have been built of timber and stucco and, except for flat roofs, looked very much like Elizabethan English cottages. There were plenty of windows which, to judge from the pictures, were covered with some brown translucent substance, probably oiled parchment. Nobles and kings had larger houses, but only one really huge establishment has been discovered to date.

No buildings which seem to be slave quarters have been found so far. The rowers on the Cretan galleys, like those of the Greek galleys as late as the battle of Salamis, may well have been free men and members of the crew. There probably were some domestic slaves, the only satisfactory answer to the servant problem prior to the machine age, but they do not seem to have been numerous or economically important. Although the island of Crete apparently was not politically unified until about a century before the final collapse of the Minoan culture, the Cretan villages were all open towns. The Minoan control of the sea made defense against foreign invasion unnecessary. There seem to have been no fortifications on the island, which suggests that the various districts must have had some sort of confederate organization. Apparently the Cretans lived at peace with each other, aside from the usual family feuds. This was in sharp contrast to the mainland settlements.

The largest establishment on Crete was the great building at Knossos, usually referred to as the palace of the Minos. Minos was the title of the Cretan priest-kings, as Pharaoh was of the Egyptian divine kings. The palace was a vast complex which had apparently grown over several hundred years until it had come to include over 1000 rooms. None of the rooms was very large and the construction was of a sort easily accomplished without the use of mass labor. The building contained a throne room and living quarters for what must have been a ruling family, but most of the complex was taken up with storehouses and workshops. It seems to have been more a community center and factory than a palace. In the throne room there was a gypsum throne with guardian griffins painted on the walls on either side. In the royal living quarters were bathrooms and toilets much more modern than anything in most of the villages on the island of Crete today. There was a good sewage system, with drains arranged in such a way that when it rained the water from the roof would flush the sewers and keep them clean. The sewers also had manholes so that workmen could go down into them for cleaning and repairs. The Cretans were the first sanitary engineers in history.

A combination of palace and factory such as the great building at Knossos was quite in line with the importance of trade and manufacturies in the Cretan economy. Trade between Crete and Egypt began as early as 4000 B.C., and by 2000 B.C. the contact was close and continuous. Cretan art objects were thought worthy of inclusion in the tombs of the Egyptian pharaohs, and Egyptian frescoes show the arrival of Cretan merchants with characteristic costumes and wares. Even the Minos of Crete traded with the Egyptian pharaoh, although their business transactions were phrased in the lofty terms of a gift exchange. Thus, we have a copy of a letter from a pharaoh complaining to the Minos that the last shipment of olive oil had not been up to specifications. There must have been many other traders, and the finding of what can only be described as country villas suggests a class of wealthy merchant princes.

Cretan trade and manufacturing seems to have left the local population with plenty of time for spectator sports. As part of the Knossos complex there was an open-air theater which, to judge from the frescoes, was used mainly for bull baiting. The bulls were the wild aurochs of Europe. These looked much like the modern Spanish fighting bulls but were considerably larger and more ferocious. From a slightly later period we have some marvelous gold cups showing how wild bulls were caught with nets. The frescoes show young men and women dressed only in loin cloths and shoes baiting these dangerous animals. Apparently the trick was to meet the charge of the bull between his spreading horns, catch them, swing up and vault over the bull's back when he tossed his head. The trick must have demanded perfect timing and acrobatic skill. Since the bull baiters were unarmed, the bulls were unhurt, but the actors must have suffered numerous casualties. Apparently bulls were in some way associated with the Cthonic deities of the old Mediterranean religion, and the sport, if one can call it such, probably had religious connotations.

Unfortunately, we have little information on Minoan religion. To judge by the representations, the most important deity was female, the old Earth Mother. She is shown in almost constant association with the snake, an obvious phallic symbol. Other animals associated with her in Minoan art are lions and doves, while mountains and forests also seem to have been connected in some way with her worship. Perhaps she was similar in her attributes to the Syrian Great Mother, who also had these as her symbols. She was certainly served by priestesses rather than priests. There are no indications of human or even extensive animal sacrifices. Her favorite offerings seem to have been the fruits of the field. No male deities can be identified in the art, but very early Greek legends have it that Zeus was born in a cave on the island of Crete, and one may suspect that, as in the case of the Syrian Great Mother, there was a male deity of secondary importance who was at the same time the son and lover of the goddess. There seem to have been no real temples, but there were village shrines and the Knossos complex contained a small room which must have been a sort of chapel.

We also have little information on the social or political organization of the Cretans. The finding of communal tombs in which burials had been made over several generations indicates the existence of some sort of extended kin groups. At the same time, the size of the dwellings in the villages is proof that the family was a simple unit much like our own. Probably there was some sort of clan organization with villages consisting of unilinear kin groups.

Women occupied a high position. There is no suggestion of veiling or seclusion for them. The frescoes show them crowding the bleachers at the bull sport and also taking part in the bull baiting, although women bull baiters may well have been captives. Apparently the noble-women even took part in war. As late as the Greek and Persian wars a half-Cretan queen of Halicarnasus, Artemisia, led her own contingent of

BULL BAITING

ships at the battle of Salamis and was one of the valued military advisors of the Persian king. The Greeks were infuriated at having a woman take the field against them and made a desperate effort to recapture her galley, but she escaped from them after a fierce fight.

All this makes it highly probable that the Minoan society was matrilineal and matriarchal. Certainly this condition was widespread among the pre-Aryan tribes of the eastern Mediterranean.

Our only guides to the reconstruction of the Cretan governmental system are a few doubtful Greek legends. According to these the ruler was a priest-king who bore the title of Minos. He was selected by the will of Zeus, which probably meant that he was chosen by some sort of lot. He held the office for nine years. At the end of this time he had to enter the Diktaian cave, where the god Zeus was reputed to have been born, and give an account of his stewardship. If Zeus approved of his administration, he returned and served for another nine years. If Zeus did not approve, he did not emerge from the cave. Apparently the Minos was not a war leader but an administrator and judge. We know nothing of Cretan law, but it seems probable that there was a well-developed legal system. A trading culture of the Cretan sort could scarcely have functioned without one. This must have impressed the barbarous Greeks of the mainland, for in later time they made Minos the all-wise and incorruptible judge in Hades.

Not only do the Greek legends throw light on ancient Crete but the discoveries in Crete throw light on ancient Greek legends. One of the most famous of these legends is that of Theseus and the Minotaur. According to this story, when Theseus, son of the king of Athens, returned to claim his birthright, he found that Crete was exacting from Athens a tribute of seven youths and seven maidens who had to be sent to Crete every ninth year to feed the Minotaur. This was a bull-headed, human-bodied monster sprung from the unnatural union of a Cretan princess and a bull. The cunning craftsman Daedalus constructed the labyrinth, a vast and complicated building in which it was penned. The passages were so complicated that once the victims had been driven into the building they could never find their way out. Theseus insisted on joining the tribute group and when he reached Crete, won the heart of Ariadne, the daughter of Minos. On the night before the youths and maidens were to be offered to the Minotaur, she gave him a sword and a ball of thread. By tying the thread to the door post of the labyrinth and unwinding it behind him, he was able to find his way back and lead his comrades out of the labyrinth, after he had met and slain the Minotaur. They then seized a ship in the harbor and set sail for Athens, bearing Ariadne with them. At the island of Naxos Theseus abandoned her asleep on the shore and continued on his way to other adventures.

There can be little doubt that the labyrinth was none other than the palace of Minos, a building complex enough to completely bewilder a mainland Greek of that period, who had probably never seen any structure with more than two rooms, while the bloodthirsty Minotaur can scarcely be other than the bulls of the Cretan sport.

There is another and less-known Greek story which may have a similar basis in fact. According to Clidemus, as quoted by Plutarch in his *Life of Theseus,* the mainland Greeks had agreed not to build any boats carrying more than five men. After his return, Theseus secretly raised a fleet, descended on Crete, burned the Knossos, slew the Minos, and brought the Cretan thalassocracy to an end. We know that the end of the Minoan period came with startling suddenness. There are no indications that any preparation for defense had been made before the blow fell. A new section of the palace at Knossos was under construction, and the workmen's tools and materials were found where they left them, ready for the next day's work. The attack seems to have coincided with an earthquake which shook down sections of the palace, but this did not prevent the attackers from doing a singularly complete job of looting. They even stripped off the gold leaf with which various stone objects had been covered. The neat combination of earthquake and attack suggests an internal enemy, possibly a slave revolt. However, it can scarcely be doubted that it was the work of foreign invaders. The collapse of the Minoan culture was complete, and after this attack there was a recognizable change in Cretan physical type, such as might have resulted from invaders having killed the Cretan men and taken the Cretan women for themselves.

After the fall of Knossos, Crete rapidly sank into a cultural and political insignificance. However, by this time its culture had taken root on the mainland. At some time before the fall of Knossos, perhaps between 1700 and 1500 B.C., Indo-European-speaking invaders reached the Greek peninsula and established themselves as an aristocracy among the tribes already settled there. These tribes were of diverse culture and at various levels of advancement but the later Greeks designated them all by the term *Pelasgi.* Apparently they followed the familiar pattern of conquest, each noble family among the invaders setting up a separate principality. They concentrated in their hands the economic surplus of the conquered communities and employed it first in the building of great fortified holds from which they dominated the surrounding countryside, much as the Normans dominated the Irish from their castles. These holds were built of enormous uncut stones fitted together in mosaic pattern, the so-called Cyclopian masonry (see Chap. XLI, p. 653). They were usually built on abrupt, rocky hills and were the origins of the later Greek city *Acropoli.* Inside the fortification was the palace, a comparatively small building on the lines of the later Greek *megaron* house. There seem to have been no temples at this period. Such buildings were not a part of either the Minoan or Mycenean tradition.

The Greek peasantry at the time of this first Indo-European-speaking invasion were very much on a par culturally with their conquerors. Both were in full Bronze Age. The two groups intermarried and, here and there, rulers of the older stock remained in control. The resulting society was further modified by contact with Crete and the result was the Mycenean cultures, the last phase of which was recorded in the Homeric poems. By this time the fair-haired Achaeans, descendants of the conquerors, were fighting side by side with and listening to the advice of the dark and crafty Odysseus, personification of the older Pelasgian element.

Some of the finest examples of Minoan metal work have come from mainland tombs, and Minoan pottery and other luxury objects were also imported. Mainland palaces were frescoed by Cretan artists, who, however, represented scenes from the life of the Mycenean employers rather than from Crete. Thus the women in the frescoes are shown wearing robes much like those of the Classical Greeks, while men wear the tunic. Women are shown hunting, driving chariots, and otherwise engaged in what are commonly considered masculine activities. Both these representations and the Homeric poems suggest a much greater degree of freedom than was enjoyed by Greek women in later times. Although this may be explained in part by the old Indo-European heritage, there is also good reason to believe that many of the Pelasgian tribes were matrilineal and matrilocal. Perhaps the attitudes engendered by this carried on into the Mycenean culture. In any case, the repression of women in Greece seems to have come fairly late.

It has even been suggested that matrilineal succession provides a clue to the importance attached by the Greeks to the theft of Helen and the way in which all the Achaean kings rallied to her husband's aid. The Achaeans were Indo-European-speaking invaders who had conquered various tribes on the Greek peninsula and ruled over them in much the way that the Normans ruled over the Saxons in England. In cases where these tribes were matriarchal and matrilineal, the invaders may well have re-enforced their claims to the territory they had seized my marrying women of the native royal line. They would then rule in the name of their wives, but their children would be unquestionably heirs to the kingdom. It has been suggested that Helen carried the hereditary rights to the kingdom and that Menelaus ruled through her. Since her escape held possibilities of a general revolt with Trojan assistance, all the Achaean kings felt that their own interests were involved and combined to recapture her. This is, of course, surmise, but it seems more in line with what we know of Achaean values than the romanticized version of Helen's elopement told in Greek myth.

The Myceneans have left no inscriptions. The best picture of their society and religion is probably to be derived from Homer. One finds an arrangement of nobles, commoners, and serfs, with few chattel slaves. There was no over-all control of the various principalities but a strong feeling of unity among the Achaean nobles and a capacity for combining forces under a chosen leader when they became conscious of a general threat. Women of the noble group took charge of the family and even the principality when their husbands were absent. There was normally only one wife in the noble family, but captive women, and no doubt others selected from the prince's subjects, were regularly kept as concubines. Warfare was a matter of struggles between champions, while the common soldiers remained in the background ready to rush forward or flee according to which champion won. No male prisoners were taken, but women were carried off as part of the spoils of war. To judge from Homer's accounts, the heroes were not particularly heroic by our standards and discipline was nonexistent.

In religion the Achaeans seem to have recognized the Olympian deities, but they performed their sacrifices to them at altars set up in the open air. A few images were in use, but the Greeks seem to have brought none with them. The Trojan Palladium and its theft both sound much more Asiatic than Greek. Human sacrifice as well as that of animals was practiced. There were no temple establishments, but the pattern of oracles which reached such a high development in later Greece was already in existence. It may be significant that the givers of oracles were almost all priestesses rather than priests, and it seems probable that the pattern was carried over from the Pelasgian level.

There is only one significant point at which the archeological findings do not bear out Homer. This is in the matter of mortuary practices. No cremated burials of the type described in such detail by Homer have so far been found in the Mycenean area. Nobles seem to have been buried either individually in shaft graves with abundant offerings, or placed in large beehive shaped tombs which were used by the same families for centuries. However, the rites described by Homer are much like those performed in Central Europe during the early Iron Age (Hallstatt period).

We do not know whether the Myceneans were responsible for the sack of Knossos and the overthrow of Cretan sea control. However, it may be significant that Egyptian objects of a sort which might have been sent as royal gifts appear in Mycenean sites dated shortly before the Cretan catastrophe. It seems quite possible that the Egyptians were egging on the Myceneans and that the legend of Theseus previously mentioned is a folk memory of the Mycenean attack. If so, they were given little time to enjoy the fruits of their victory. About 1100 B.C. a new group of invaders, ancestors to the later Dorian Greeks, swept down into the peninsula. They were more completely pastoral than their Achaean predecessors; in fact, legends suggest that they may have had no agriculture at the time of their arrival. However, they had abundant iron weapons, which gave them a considerable advantage. They seem to have been exceedingly destructive and to have wiped out what was left of the Mycenean culture on the mainland.

Their invasion ushered in a Dark Age which ended with the first Olympiad, 732 B.C. During this Dark Age, traces of the Mycenean culture survived among the Ionian Greeks on the Asiatic coast. Strong influence of the Mycenean art forms can be traced in the Ionian pottery. In due course of time this art was reintroduced into the mainland and seems to have played a significant role in the development of Classical Greek art, especially as this was represented by vase paintings.

One last contribution of Cretan culture may be suggested. It seems highly probable that Crete gave us one of our own most fascinating myths, that of the lost Atlantis. This myth, as related by Plato, may well have been elaborated for his own symbolic purposes, but it seems improbable that he invented it out of whole cloth. According to the legend, the Egyptians told Solon of Athens (6th century B.C.) that there had once been an island, Atlantis, whose fleets controlled the Mediterranean, held Athens to tribute, and traded on equal terms with Egypt. A great earthquake had destroyed the island almost overnight. By the time that the Greeks emerged from the Dark Ages, the Minoan civilization had been completely forgotten. When confronted by the necessity for finding a site for Atlantis they were in much the situation that we would be if we had no written records, but were told by the Abyssinians that a few centuries before there had been a great power which held the whole of the East African coast to tribute, captured cities in India, conquered the spice islands, and fought England on equal terms. It would scarcely occur to the modern American to equate such a power with present-day Portugal, and similarly, it did not occur to the Greeks that Atlantis might be Crete. Since they knew the Mediterranean geography quite well by this time and nothing seemed to fit the story, they placed the island beyond the pillars of Hercules in the wastes of the unexplored Atlantic. Actually the few bits of information which the legend gives us about the habits of the Atlantians are not inconsistent with the Cretan ascription, while even the last catastrophe might be a folk memory of the earthquake which seems to have overthrown the palace at Knossos.

Chapter XXIV

Greece

WITH THE EMERGENCE of Greek civilization Europe passes from the pre-historic to the historic period. It is salutary for us, as Europeans, to re-member that Mesopotamia and Egypt had made this transition almost two thousand years before. After the 7th century B.C. we have in-creasingly complete written records covering wider and wider areas within Europe until the whole continent is included. Where these rec-ords are available it becomes possible to apply the historian's techniques for determining their authenticity and for fixing the dates of particular events. I have no intention of trespassing upon this well-cultivated field. I also feel considerable hesitation in approaching the Classical cultures from an anthropological viewpoint. The study of these cultures has oc-cupied many of the best minds of Europe for centuries. There are in-numerable works dealing with the philosophies and value systems of the Greeks and Romans and, more recently, with their economics and social and political patterns. The most that I will attempt is to give a brief de-scription of certain features of Classical culture which, it seems to me, have not been sufficiently emphasized in the literature but which exerted considerable influence on later cultural developments in Europe.

The first fact of which the average reader needs to be reminded is that the great periods of Greek and Roman civilization were by no means contemporaneous. The Age of Pericles was separated from the Age of Augustus by an interval nearly as long as that from the discovery of America to the present. At the time of the Athenian ascendency, Rome was little more than a village, and the Romans were vastly inferior culturally to those Asiatics whom the Greeks were accustomed to call barbarians. By the time the Romans had completed the subjugation of their Etruscan and Italic neighbors and were making war on the Greek cities in Sicily, Alexander had made his conquest of Persia, and the hy-brid Greco-Asiatic culture which we call Hellenistic was rapidly taking form. When Rome suddenly and quite unpredictably became a world power, this culture was well established throughout most of the civilized world, and it was this culture which the Romans assumed in their own transformation from barbarism to civilization. Classical Greek culture bore about as much and as little similarity to Hellenistic culture as the culture of our 18th century ancestors bears to our own. It was in the Hellenistic culture that Greeks and Romans were able to unite with Asiatics and Egyptians in an *oikouméné,* which had become for the first time something more than a geographic division.

The influence of the Hellenistic culture was so far-reaching that it must be dealt with separately. Similarly, the Greeks and Romans of the pre-Hellenistic period differed in so many respects that any attempt to deal with them simultaneously can only result in confusion. Grecian culture is the obvious starting point for any study of the development of European civilization within the historic period. However, the influence of Classical Greece runs through that civilization as a bright colored thread rather than a broad skein. Its heavy strands were drawn from Rome and, even more, from the northern barbarians whose culture stemmed, in turn, from Central Europe.

GREEK SHIP WITH FURLED SAIL

As always, Greek culture cannot be understood without reference to its background. We have already discussed the Aegean peoples, the Cretans, and the Indo-European-speaking invaders whose blood and cultures blended to produce the Greeks. Still another element contributed to this mixture, although its importance is difficult to evaluate. After the destruction of the Minoan sea power a Semitic people, the Phoenicians we have previously discussed, dominated the Mediterranean. Their earliest cities were on the Syrian coast but, like their Minoan predecessors, they soon felt the need of naval bases and founded colonies at various points in the west. One of these colonies, Carthage, was destined to play a significant part in later history. In the eastern Mediterranean they were always in competition with Greeks and Egyptians, but they made the seas beyond Sicily their own and profited greatly from their exploitation of the mineral wealth in Spain. They also explored north and south along the Atlantic coast and reached the British Isles.

The Phoenicians were mainly interested in trade and profit, and cared little about political affiliations as long as commerce was not interfered with. They were quite willing to become a part of the great empires which emerged successively in Western Asia. They have left few records, and the accounts of Carthaginian culture given by the Romans can be largely discounted as war propaganda. Their main role in the development of the Greek and other Mediterranean cultures was as intermediaries between Asia and Europe. Their most significant contribution to Greek culture was the alphabet, a Semitic invention. As good businessmen they had been quick to appreciate the advantages of a system of writing so simple that professional scribes became unnecessary. The Minoan system of writing had completely died out in Greece during the Dark Ages following the fall of Crete and, according to Greek tradition, it was Cadmus, a Phoenician, who reintroduced the art. This much is certain: the Greek alphabet was taken from the Phoenician one.

In Greece alphabetic writing encountered a particularly favorable milieu. As traders the Greeks could appreciate the immediate advantages of the system, but they combined with their business interests a range and variety of other interests and lively curiosity which the Phoenicians lacked. The Greeks liked to find out new things and to tell as many people as possible about them. Moreover, their religion was simple and relatively unorganized, with no strong priestly class which might have pre-empted the new skill. In Greece, writing escaped at last from both the counting house and the temple and became a medium for the exchange and preservation of ideas.

Greek culture not only was of mixed origin but also demonstrated what the biologists would call hybrid vigor. It gave to and borrowed from every culture with which the Greeks came in contact. All cultures

owe much of their content to borrowing, and it is no disgrace to the
Greeks that they took advantage of the unusual opportunities offered by
the time and place. The rise of the Asiatic empires had broken down
the old patterns of tribal isolation over wide areas and created an insatiable demand for mercenary soldiers. During their Dark Ages Greeks
wandered all over the Near East and served in the armies of Egypt, Assyria, and lesser states. By the Classical period they were traveling simply to satisfy their curiosity, like modern tourists, while their philosophers, who were also their scientists, were eagerly contacting people
with similar interests in all the places they visited. One can recognize in
these early Greek travelers an attitude much like that of the 19th
and early 20th century Japanese. While their belief in their own
fundamental superiority was never lost, they were keenly conscious of
their inferiority in certain directions and had an overwhelming eagerness to learn. They borrowed shamelessly, and there were few items in
Classical Greek culture which could not be traced to outside origins. The
distinctive element in the Greek situation was the catalytic quality of
the Greek mind. Ideas brought together in its presence combined to produce new and unexpected results.

Each of the older civilizations contributed its quota. The Egyptians
impressed the Greeks by the magnitude of their structures and, above
all, by their claims for the immemorial antiquity of their civilization.
They regarded the Greeks as amusing parvenus and the Greeks, who
had forgotten their Minoan ancestry, shamefacedly concurred in this
opinion. At the same time the animal gods and essential confusion and
illogic of Egyptian religion had little appeal for the highly logical

CHIMERA OF AREZZO

Greeks. They were not greatly impressed by the Egyptian priests' claims that these things only concealed deep mysteries. The Egyptian political system, with its god-king, was equally incompatible with Greek values. Although they learned what they could from Egyptian astronomers and mathematicians, time showed that these were inferior to the Mesopotamians, while the technological knowledge, in which the Egyptians excelled, was ignored as beneath the notice of gentlemen. On the other hand, Egyptian art, with its vigorous if conventionalized use of men and animals and its success in depicting motion, struck a responsive chord and strong Egyptian influence can be traced in the development of Greek art, especially sculpture.

In Mesopotamia the Greeks found a science which they could appreciate and a mechanistic view of the universe which was quite in line with their own skepticism regarding the extent and nature of divine interference in human affairs. They brought back from their Mesopotamian contacts a much improved knowledge of astronomy and a better mathematics, both freed from the shackles of priestly control. These led to a great expansion of the Greek mental horizon. When wedded with the keen Greek interest in natural phenomena and vital behavior, they produced Greek philosophy, with its essentially agnostic approach to the universe, and also the much-overrated Greek contribution to later science.

The ascription of high scientific ability to the Greeks rests mainly upon the fact that a study of the Greek philosophers reveals in one place or another conjectures which foreshadow most of the discoveries of modern science. However, it must be remembered that these were conjectures. They were developed as parts of logical systems and were completely unsupported by what we would regard as scientific evidence. If one takes the collection of "scientific" theories which the various philosophers found it necessary to include in what each of them attempted to make a comprehensive interpretation of the universe, one finds that the Greek score was relatively low. For every suggestion which later science has shown to be correct, there were at least a dozen which were later proved to be wrong.

A disconcerting by-product of these Greek philosophies was the need felt by the early Christian fathers for a cosmology as well as a theology and an ethic. Without some explanation of the universe, the Christians found themselves at a disadvantage in their competition with the philosophies which were their most dangerous rivals in their struggle to win over the educated minority. Modern fundamentalism thus owes its existence to a pattern based on pagan pseudo-science.

In Alexandria at the close of the Classical period the Greeks seem to have made some feeble gestures in the direction of real science based on experiments and observation. However the entire Greek system of thought suffered from one incurable defect. The average Greek always preferred talking to working, and the Greek philosopher believed that ultimate truth in any situation could be arrived at through verbal manipulation. The Greeks never seem to have been able to appreciate the distinction, difficult enough for ourselves, between the external reality and its verbal symbol. The Greeks were the originators of the analytic method, by which configurations of phenomena were broken down so that particular items or sequences within the configuration could be conceptually isolated for independent study. They never were able to realize the importance of configurations *per se* or to understand that, in the presence of multiple factors, the logical extrapolation of assumptions based on a few of these may, in the long run, lead the logician further and further from reality. The modern scientist accumulates as much data as possible, develops his theories logically on the basis of this data, and then checks them by the experimental method or whatever technique it may be necessary for him to substitute for it. The Greek philosopher began with little data, developed his theories by the application of logic, and then stopped. *didn't check by experiment*

No doubt this arrangement was satisfactory to the Greek philosopher, since he conceived reality as existing on a different level from that which we recognize. The concept expressed in Plato's *Universals* makes the ultimate reality and the verbal symbol practically identical. Unfortunately, this concept of reality does not lend itself to the successful manipulation of the material world, but the Greeks were little troubled by this. The attitude of the Greek intellectual toward technological advance is beautifully illustrated by the following passage from Plutarch: [1]

> *These machines he [Archimedes] had designed and contrived, not as matters of any importance, but as mere amusements in geometry; in compliance with King Hiero's desire and request, some little time before, that he should reduce to practice some part of his admirable speculation in science, and by accommodating the theoretic truth to sensation and ordinary use, bring it more within the appreciation of the people in general. Eudoxus and Archytas had been the first originators of this far-famed and highly-prized art of mechanics, which they employed as an elegant illustration of geometrical truths, and as means of sustaining experimentally, to the satisfaction of the senses, conclusions too intricate for proof by words and diagrams. . . . But what with Plato's indignation at it, and his invectives against it as the mere corruption and anni-*

[1] Plutarch: "The Life of Marcellus." In *The Lives of the Noble Grecians and Romans.* Translated by John Dryden and revised by Arthur Hugh Clough. New York: The Modern Library; 1932, p. 376.

hilation of the one good of geometry, which was thus shamefully turn-
ing its back upon the unembodied objects of pure intelligence to recur
to sensation, and to ask help (not to be obtained without base supervi-
sions and depravation) from matter; so it was that mechanics came to be
separated from geometry, and repudiated and neglected by philoso-
phers, took its place as a military art.

The influence of this attitude was reflected in Greek technology.
Until well into the Hellenistic period it was characterized by an increasing perfection of manual dexterity and an almost complete lack of new
basic inventions, or even of borrowings which might have fundamentally
altered the existing technical patterns. Thus the arch and dome, which
had been known for millennia in the Near East, were not adopted by the
Greeks in spite of their obvious practical advantages for many purposes.
The most revolutionary change which took place in their architecture,
from the late Mycenean on, was the substitution of stone for wood in
their public buildings, and even here the forms developed in the older
material were almost slavishly preserved. At the same time their skill
in manipulating the existing techniques reached an amazingly high
point. The essentially primitive architectural forms were refined until
they showed perfectly balanced proportions and such subtleties as those
of the Parthenon columns, in which the sides are slightly bowed outward

MUSIC LESSON

in order to give the visual illusion of a continuous straight line from top to bottom.

This lack of basic technological changes has been ascribed to the predominance of slave labor in the Classical Greek state, but the perfection achieved by the technology within its limits is not congruous with such an assumption. The architects who designed the Greek buildings certainly were not slaves, and at least as late as the time of Pericles most of the artisans were free men. If the master craftsmen who designed the perfect proportions of Attic pottery and applied its spirited decoration were slaves, at least they were slaves with a real pride of craft and with an appreciative audience. The truth was that the Greek interest lay in other directions. For gentlemen, the predominant interests seem to have been war and philosophy, while for all Greeks, irrespective of class, politics amounted to an obsession.

The Greek political systems should be of particular interest to us, since the Greek city-states were confronted with certain problems not unlike those of our own municipal governments today. In both cases a culture, which had been developed under essentially rural and village conditions, and which had inherited patterns of attaching extreme value to personal independence and individual initiative, found itself confronted with the problems of city living and of far-reaching changes in the economic structure. True cities did not appear in Greece much before the Classical period. It has already been mentioned that the Classical Greeks lived largely by exporting both manufactures and their specialized agricultural products of olive oil and wine. The replacement of subsistence farming by staple crops raised for export is always hard on the small landowner, who finds himself at the mercy of the middleman. Although the Classical Greeks did not develop great plantations worked by slave labor, as the later Romans did, many peasants lost their holdings. There was an increasing concentration of population in the cities, with the breakdown of the older extended groups, and a developing potentiality for individual anonymity such as we have today.

The Greeks met this situation in part by their rigid rules of citizenship, which limited the electorate to individuals either born of citizen parents or, more rarely, those upon whom citizenship had been conferred. Every city contained a large number of aliens who might be respected and affluent members of the community but who were not allowed to participate in government. While the number of individuals was too large for the citizens to function as a face-to-face unit, even in cities the size of Athens or Corinth, any candidate for office would be personally known to a great many of the electorate, while the candidate's record would be well-known to all. The limitation of the electorate made the problem of representative government simpler, but this was counterbalanced by the low level of education in much of the electorate and by the Greek basic personality, which combined individualism with high emotionalism and intense jealousy.

The culture pattern established political participation as not only a privilege but a duty of citizenship. The Greek citizen seems to have spent a large part of his time and energy in discussing politics and in the intrigues which were inseparable from it. Coupled with this there was a survival into urban life of the loyalty and strong in-group sentiment characteristic of the primitive tribe. It would have been quite unthinkable for a Greek dramatist to open a new play in any city other than his own. Even artists and authors felt obligated to give their own cities the first fruits of their genius, and only moved on to greener fields when their own cities had rejected them or when their genius had been generally recognized and added to their city's fame.

The development of most Greek city governments began with the old Indo-European pattern of a king and a tribal council dominated by the heads of noble families, but with free discussion and any tribesman allowed to speak his mind. The king was primarily a war leader and executive instrumenting the council decisions. He had no hint of personal divinity and even his priestly functions were unimportant. With the rise

GREEK WARRIOR

of the new commercial urban culture the power of the king and the nobles evaporated, giving place to an oligarchy dominated by the *nouveau riche*. The oligarchies were followed in turn by democracies, which soon came to be dominated by demagogues. Finally a strong man would seize power and rule like a king, but usually with careful avoidance of royal symbols. The position of such a man would correspond roughly to that of the boss of a well-entrenched political machine in one of our own cities. Although the outward symbols of democracy would usually be preserved, all power would be gathered into his hands. The Greeks applied to such city bosses the term *tyrannos* (master), which was the origin of our own word *tyrant*, although in its original uses it lacked most of the connotations of cruelty and oppression which that word carries for us. The first "tyrant" in any city was often an able and benevolent ruler, but in due course of time one of his successors would become cruel and oppressive. The "better element" would then oust him and establish an oligarchy. This in due course of time would give place to a democracy and the democracy to another tyranny. The Greeks recognized this cycle and regarded it as a sort of natural phenomenon which could be postponed but not averted.

With this as a starting point the Greeks developed various constitutions, none of which seem to have worked successfully for very long. The drawing up of a constitution was part of the advanced planning which went into the founding of a new city, and these constitutions represent the highest points reached by Greek political theory. Unfortunately, they very rarely remained in force for any length of time. None of them provided for a successful civil service which might have had a stabilizing effect, and, in politics as elsewhere, the Greeks were poor losers. Defeated candidates for office were likely to stir up revolt, and this was the basis for the institution of ostracism, by which the losing candidate was exiled from the city for a period of years.

In one respect at least the Greek cities were more fortunate than the later Roman cities. They did not have an idle, pauperized proletariat which would be at the beck and call of any politician who wanted to create a disturbance. During the Classical period the exclusion of non-citizens from political life and the relatively small size of the citizen body prevented this. There must have been a fair number of impoverished citizens, but there were not enough to require a regular and continuous dole of the Roman sort. During the late pre-Classical and much of the Classical period, the poor and the surplus population drawn cityward from the surrounding countryside were taken care of by the founding of new cities. Most of them were in the western Mediterranean, especially in southern Italy, which later came to be known as *Magna Graecea*, "Greater Greece."

Result a Greek urbanization

The ability to establish planned colonies at favorable locations was no mean cultural accomplishment in itself. Apparently the Delphic oracle operated as a clearing house for news of available sites. A city aiming to found a new colony consulted the oracle, and the priests, drawing upon the pooled knowledge which they had acquired from other clients, suggested the best place. The colonists were selected from among those citizens who volunteered to go. They were provided with necessary equipment and food to tide them over until they could plant and harvest their own crops, and the mother city helped them until they could take care of themselves. Although there was no continuing tie between the daughter city and the mother city, there was a strong emotional attachment and, as a symbol of the continuity, sacred fire was usually carried from the mother city and used to kindle the first fires in the new settlement. Many of these new cities came to have greater wealth and larger populations than their parents on the Greek mainland, but in artistic and intellectual matters they were regarded, and regarded themselves, as provincials. Any famous Greek who took a colonial tour was as sure of profit as an English literary light visiting the United States.

The development of the Greek pattern of colonization is difficult to trace. No doubt it was greatly stimulated by the presence of uncivilized but not unfriendly tribes to the west who offered high profits to the Greek traders. However, the resettlement of several hundred people involved in the founding of a new city is a very different matter from the mere establishment of trading posts and requires careful planning, as the failure of many of the American colonizing attempts shows. The Phoenicians also were establishing colonial outposts in the period from 1000 to 700 B.C., although they seem to have been less systematic about it than were the Greeks, and the Greeks may have used them as models. More probably, both Greeks and Phoenicians learned the necessary techniques from their contact with the Minoans, whose widespread naval bases have already been mentioned. The Assyrians also had been carrying on extensive resettlement programs for a long period as part of their imperial policy, and the Greeks may have borrowed some techniques from them.

One other result of Greek urbanization should be mentioned, since it has exerted an important influence on certain aspects of our own culture. Although each Greek city of the period had its temples to the Olympian gods and had selected some one of them as its guardian and the recipient of its special devotions, the worship of these deities became more and more an excuse for pageantry and ritual from which the participants and observers derived aesthetic satisfaction rather than spiritual refreshment. It has been said, probably truthfully, that after Salamis the Olympian deities were dead.

The pre-Indo-European religious practices, on the other hand, now reasserted themselves and acquired new meaning in the urban context. What had been before local rites carried on with the orgiastic accompaniments characteristic of many of the old Mediterranean cults were now reorganized and extended beyond their original local contexts to become the mystery religions. The urban populations, especially the many individuals who were living in cities of which they were not citizens, felt a strong need for some system by which they could establish ties with others in the same position. Human beings seem to have a deep seated need for social contacts and for membership in in-groups. Viewed from this angle, the rise of the mystery religions can be seen as a result of the same frustrations which have led to the tremendous multiplication of organizations of all sorts in our own society. Wherever patterns of spatial and social mobility break down kin and local groups, substitutes will develop.

The rise of the mystery religions cannot be explained entirely on these grounds. The lack of opportunity for unconscious identification with a larger social group increased the tendency toward individualism, already strong among the Greeks. The unattached, anonymous individual could no longer satisfy his desire for posthumous survival by contemplating the continuity of his kin group or tribe. He began to yearn

OFFERINGS TO THE DEAD WITH SPIRITS HOVERING

for assurances of his own immortality, and with this came the natural desire for a pleasant and satisfying future life. The Greek Hades must have appeared even duller to an urban slum dweller than it did to a villager. Lastly, the informal social controls which enforced ethical behavior upon the villager were no longer operative in the city, and to those who had been born and reared in smaller communities, always the majority of an adult urban population, this must have been felt as a tremendous loss. In the absence of personally applicable public opinion there was a need for some effective substitute. The old gods had been essential amoral in their outlook. The new ones became a source of supernatural sanctions, rewarding good behavior and punishing evil, even when these remained unnoticed by the individual's contemporaries.

Out of this combination of factors there developed a series of sects which had certain features in common. Entry into all of them involved some preliminary instruction and a ceremony of initiation, in which the individual was prepared for his later psychological identification with both the deity and the cult by repeating, in company with others, certain experiences of the deity. All the cults promised their initiates survival and a happy after-life, and all involved certain obligations of ethical behavior, at least toward other members of the cult. A mystery religion was thus not only a religion but also a secret society with obligations of mutual help among the members, and with ethical precepts which made it possible for these members to feel secure in dealing with each other.

As the Classical period in Greece passed into the Hellenistic period, with its much greater urban concentrations and increased spatial mobility, these mystery religions increased in number and took on added significance. Local chapters included not only citizens and resident aliens but also slaves. In view of the common Greek pattern of selling whole city populations as part of the spoils of war, there were inevitably many slaves who had been initiated into the mysteries before they were enslaved and who therefore had to be accepted as brothers if the secrecy was to be maintained. The various cults emphasized their autonomous existence by having their own status-systems based on different degrees of initiation, and a man who was a slave outside the lodge might occupy the highest position inside it.

The trend toward mystery religions which began in Classical Greece increased rapidly during the Hellenistic period, since all the conditions to which these religions were a response were then intensified. Not only were pre-Indo-European deities and rites revived, but foreign gods were accepted and their worship internationalized and reorganized on the mystery pattern. Thus, in later Hellenistic times, we have the mysteries of the Egyptian Isis and the Persian Mithras, and only slightly later the emergence of Christianity which, beginning as a minor Jewish sect, was opened to Gentile converts through the ministry of Saint Paul, and was then reorganized by these converts upon the familiar mystery pattern.

The total Greek contribution to our own culture has been so extensive and is so well known that this brief summary of some of the less-emphasized aspects of the contribution must suffice. The most important thing to remember is that the Classical Greek culture, like all other cultures for which we have records, borrowed widely. At the same time it reintegrated and reinterpreted its borrowings to an unusual degree and gave the resulting culture complex a distinctive quality. One who digs into the background of Greek culture finds its roots extending far into the past and branching and rebranching to draw upon many different sources, but the keen curiosity and the analytical attitude which characterized the Greeks were their own contribution.

Chapter XXV

Barbarians

AT THE FOUNDATION of all European history has lain the *drang nach Westen,* the steady pressure of peoples forcing their way into the continent from the east. The steppes have been an inexhaustible breeding ground for warriors, and barbarian tribes have flowed out of them in successive waves. We do not know what has been responsible for these movements. Some of them may have been due, as Elsworth Huntington has suggested in *The Pulse of Asia,* to an alteration of long periods of abundant rainfall and good pasture, causing population increase, with drought periods which squeezed out the surplus. We also know that shortly before the beginning of the Christian era the development of superior military equipment and techniques among the peoples of Mongolia resulted in the displacement westward of a whole series of tribes who were less effective fighters. However, we need not seek for any single cause. For a nomadic or seminomadic tribe, migration is the simplest answer to pressure of any sort, including cupidity. When the steppe people discovered how much loot was to be obtained in the more civilized areas beyond their borders, no local calamity was required to set them moving.

    Throughout most of the prehistoric period the movements from the east seem to have been carried out by small groups. They were in the nature of a gradual infiltration rather than a massive conquest. The newcomers spread themselves over the pre-existing populations and became assimilated in them. From the Bronze Age until the arrival of the Mongolian Huns and Avars after the Roman collapse, the cultures of all the barbarian invaders seem to have been of the general type already described for the early Aryans. The patterns by which a hunting, cattle-keeping aristocracy dominated a much larger peasant population were transmitted from one conquering group to another with little change. The differences which existed among the conquerors were mainly a mat-

353

ter of sophistication, based on the amount of their contact with the more civilized peoples of the south, plus, in the case of the Germans, a few borrowings from their Circumpolar neighbors.

The introduction of bronze into Europe has already been discussed. The far more revolutionary introduction of iron does not seem to be traceable to any one group of invaders. As we have seen (p. 109), iron working was certainly of Southwestern Asiatic origin. The necessary techniques were known to the Hittites as early as 1600–1800 B.C. The diffusion of these techniques into Europe following the collapse of the Hittite empire may well have been due to journeymen smiths comparable to those of the late Bronze Age. The so-called Hallstatt culture (see p. 255), which was the earliest Iron Age culture of Europe, was actually made up of a great number of local cultures which, aside from iron working, had only a few elements in common. The best explanation would seem to be that the Eastern European tribes who were the first to obtain iron exploited the military advantage which it gave them and progressively established control over their neighbors, but that the change did not involve any fundamental alteration in the European patterns; in other words, that the tribal movements which ushered in the Iron Age were on no greater scale and originated no farther afield than those of the Celts and Germans in the early historic period.

Certain new features do appear in Western Europe at the beginning of the Iron Age, roughly 1000 B.C. The most important of these was the use of a new weapon, a long, straight, double-edged sword with a broad point, obviously intended for slashing rather than thrusting. This might well have been used by men on horseback, and in the grave-finds of this period single sets of horse's equipment become increasingly common, suggesting the use of single mounts rather than chariots. Another new feature which appears at this time is cremation and the burial of ashes in urns. It is usually assumed that radical changes in burial practices indicate the arrival of new populations, but we have plenty of evidence that this is not the case. Such practices seem to be highly dependent upon fashion and can be changed with considerable speed.

The first Classical accounts of the barbarians reveal the presence of two groups in Western Europe north of the Mediterranean basin, the Celts and the Germans. The Gauls, who figure so largely in Roman literature, were a division of the Celtic group who had their center in what is now France. The Germans were mainly east and north of the Rhine at that time and were the more barbarous, since they were the more distant from the southern centers of civilization. The description of the Germans given by Tacitus, a Roman contemporary, shows that they were a cattle people, and he notes that, like the modern cattle tribes of

Africa, they rated their wealth by the number of their animals, paying little attention to their quality. They raised only grain and cultivated new fields each year, facts which, since most of their country was heavily forested, probably mean that they followed the cutting and burning technique. There were no large towns in their territory, and even in their villages the families lived some distance apart. Their houses were of wood, crudely built but painted with colored clays. The men's costume consisted of a long cloak worn over skin-tight trousers, apparently an early version of the long hose worn by most North European groups in the Middle Ages. The body was bare, and the arrangement suggests a

VISIGOTHS AFTER THE BATTLE

compromise between some ancient pattern of male nudity except for a cloak and the exigencies of the German winter climate. The women wore the familiar straight dress made from two strips of cloth fastened together at the shoulders and again at the waist. They wore cloaks in cold weather, and crude, massive jewelry, which was sometimes made of iron.

The Germans attached little value to the utensils of gold and silver sent to them as gifts by the Romans. They were indifferent metal workers and even iron was in poor supply. Their weapons were long swords of the type already described, light spears with small heads, and shields. A few men wore helmets, usually of leather, but body armor was infrequent. A young man was given the right to carry arms at a solemn ceremony which no doubt marked his assumption of full adult status. Such an investiture is reminiscent of the Medieval ceremonies by which a squire was raised to knighthood and given for the first time the right to carry a sword.

The family was monogamous, and Tacitus insisted on the high moral standards of the Germans, whom he held up as a model for the Romans of his time. The husband paid a bride price, which was then returned to the new family as the bride's dowry, the wealth exchanged at this time being in weapons. A mother's brother was considered as close a relative as a father, an arrangement which may indicate earlier matrilineal patterns but is more likely to have been a reflection of the bilateral reckoning of kinship characteristic of most of the Circumpolar people.

Hospitality was universal and unstinted. During the winter season groups would go from house to house, staying at each until the owner's supplies were exhausted. This custom is reminiscent of the Medieval pattern by which a king or noble was entitled to so many days of entertainment a year for himself and his *entourage* as part of his feudal dues. In a time and place where transportation was difficult, this arrangement had the great advantage of bringing the mouths to the food instead of vice-versa. Chiefs kept considerable state, and were surrounded by young tribesmen, not necessarily relatives, who received food and shelter but no pay. The main duty of the chief was as a war leader, and he was expected to distinguish himself by his courage in the field. His companions were expected to equal him in bravery, and it was a deep disgrace for them to survive him if he fell. Even common soldiers had to bring back their shields, the first encumbrance which a fleeing man would discard, and if they failed to do this they were permanently disgraced. Although there seems to have been no drill, the warriors used a flying wedge formation in attack and probably formed a shield wall in defense. The women and children accompanied the men on campaigns, acting as an informal service of supply and medical corps, and in case of defeat took an active hand in the fighting, regarding death as preferable to capture and enslavement.

The Germans were characteristically great eaters, heavy drinkers, and confirmed gamblers. Tacitus says that a gambler who had lost all his property would frequently wager his own person and, if he lost, become a slave to the winner. Such a prize was embarrassing, and the winner would usually sell him or otherwise dispose of him as soon as possible. When a campaign was to be planned, the chief feasted his warriors and encouraged all of them, when they had drunk well, to state their opinions and air their resentments. This cleared the air, and all plans were reviewed the next morning in the cold light of the inevitable hangover.

The German society was divided into chiefs, commoners, and serfs. The Roman commentators seem to have been puzzled by the German institution of serfdom and remarked on the fact that although such "slaves" could not be sold, their owners could and frequently did kill them without incurring any penalties.

The one road to advancement was war, just as, in the absence of trade and manufacture, looting was the one road to wealth. A commoner who was a successful warrior was honored almost as highly as a man of chiefly family. At the same time great importance was attached to high descent, and anyone who aspired to chieftainship without it would be regarded as a usurper. Tacitus says that the Germans chose their chiefs by inheritance and their generals by ability.

The men of the tribe met in council once a month at the time of either the new or full moon, the tribal priest presiding. Such councils combined the functions of a legislature and a court of justice. The chief was an executive carrying out the mandates of the council and was bound by its decisions. There were law codes which distinguished between offenses against the community and against individuals. The former were treated as crimes, and the offender was punished in his person, usually by death. The latter could be compensated by payment of damages. Murder was regarded as an offense of the second class and could be atoned for by payment to the murdered man's kin group.

There is very little information on early German religion, and it is dangerous to try to reconstruct it from the later Norse beliefs, since these show considerable foreign and even Christian influence. The Germans worshipped a pantheon of deities who were individually enough like the Roman gods to be equated with them. Thus Tacitus says that the main German deities were Mercury, to whom human sacrifices were made, Hercules, and Mars. There were numerous sacred groves, and there were also images which were kept in the groves and carried by the tribe when it went to war. Temples, when they existed, were small buildings used as storage places for the images and other religious paraphernalia. All ceremonies were performed in the open air. Tribal ceremonies were held on fixed dates throughout the year. Each grove had its priest or priestess who officiated at the rites performed there, but it is improbable that these formed an organized priesthood. In sacrifices on behalf of kin groups, the head of the group officiated.

There was heavy reliance on divination, which was performed by throwing a bundle of short sticks on a white mantle and observing the way they fell. The behavior of birds and animals was watched for omens. Women also acted as oracles, giving answers to questions while in a trance state. Death practices followed the old Iron Age tradition. Bodies were cremated with a minimum of offerings, and the ashes were buried in an urn under a small mound.

The Gauls occupied the territory south and west of the Germans, and closely related Celtic groups were in possession of Britain and Ireland. The Gauls had been in contact with the Mediterranean civilizations for centuries, alternately trading with and raiding them, and had absorbed much of Mediterranean culture. Remains from the region immediately west of the Alps show that, by the 5th century B.C., the Gauls had achieved extraordinary skill in working iron, bronze, silver, and gold. The metal objects were decorated with elaborate and beautiful scroll designs embellished with colored enamels, coral, and gems. Many of the objects produced by this so-called La Tene culture were technically equal to any made in the Mediterranean basin at this time. It is significant that even after the Roman conquest of Gaul native craftsmen continued working in their own style for the Roman trade.

The main southern influence on the culture of the Gauls came from the Greeks. By 400 B.C. there was a Greek settlement at what is now Marseilles, and Greek traders were penetrating the hinterland. In the 3rd century B.C. a Greek geographer and explorer, Pythias, even sailed northward along the Atlantic coast until he reached Scandinavia and heard rumors of an island to the northwest, which may have been Iceland. Among other things the Greeks introduced the use of money, and coins struck in Gaul by local chiefs show a fascinating series of simplifications of original Greek patterns.

The Gauls also came in contact with the Etruscans, who had established themselves at the head of the Adriatic by 800 B.C. The light chariot, extensively used by the early Gauls, may well have been developed from Etruscan prototypes. Its use had died out on the European mainland by Caesar's time, but he found the Celtic Britains still using scythe-armed chariots. In Ireland chariots survived even later.

The accounts of the Gauls which have been left by Classical writers have to do mainly with their fighting ability and the ravages which they inflicted on their southern neighbors. They invaded Italy repeatedly, and when Caesar finally "pacified" Gaul, the Romans rejoiced less at the

GAULS

addition to their territory than at the removal of what they had come to regard as an ever-present threat. The Gauls also raided into Greece and Asia Minor, and the famous statue from Pergamum which we know as the dying gladiator actually represented a dying Gaul, a monument to the defeat of one of these expeditions.

The Roman conquest of Gaul resulted in the collapse of the local culture and the Latinization of the survivors. The conquest of Britain was later and less thorough, but here also the Roman overlay obscures the features of the earlier culture. The best picture of early Celtic life is provided by Ireland. Here the Celts succeeded in maintaining their independence through the Roman period and did not succumb completely to foreign control until the time of Cromwell. Even Christianity, which the Irish accepted with enthusiasm, was revised in Celtic terms.

The Irish economy was based primarily on domestic animals: cattle, horses, and pigs. Cattle were not only milked but also bled periodically and the blood boiled and eaten. Horses were neither milked nor eaten. They were driven in chariots or, later, ridden. Cavalry played little part in the Irish forces, perhaps because they never acquired the tree saddle. In the 14th century A.D. the English authorities passed a law fining any Irish-born Englishman who rode without a saddle "in the Irish fashion." Pigs, then as later, were the mainstay of the small householder. Ham and bacon seem to have been Celtic inventions, and even the Romans spoke with admiration of the hams prepared by the Gauls.

Although there were seasonal movements of whole families and their cattle in search of new pasture, there was little adjustment to nomadic life. On these expeditions, the Irish built brush shelters reminiscent of those of our own Apache Indians. Great quantities of meat were consumed, but the main diet of the poorer classes consisted of mush and milk eked out by game. The great emotional value attached to domestic animals is shown by a curious arrangement under which cattle and possibly horses, but not pigs, were considered the property of kings or higher nobility and were leased to their followers in return for an annual payment. No such payment was assessed for land use. Plowland was farmed cooperatively by small groups of families, normally related.

Stone construction was unknown in Ireland until comparatively late times, and, when it did appear, was due to Roman influence. The mainland Gauls fortified their cities with dry stone walls, but both cities and walls were a very late development. The poorest Irish people lived in round or square wattled huts, the more affluent ones in oblong wooden houses. The size of a man's house and the number and size of outbuildings which he was permitted to build were strictly fixed by his rank. Every householder controlled the land for a fixed distance on all sides of his dwelling and could punish trespass and extend protection to any stranger or guest who was in this territory.

Men's clothing normally consisted of a tunic much like that of the Classical Greeks and Romans, with a heavy cloak which was taken off indoors. In general the Irish did not wear trousers, although the mainland Gauls certainly did. Women wore a straight two-piece dress and belt much like that already described for the Germans. The garments were made of cloth, and those of the better classes were dyed in bright colors and elaborately embroidered. Embroidering-women are listed among the indispensable craftsmen in early law codes. The commonest clothing materials were linen and wool, but silk was mentioned even in pre-Christian epics and was evidently highly prized. Elaborate jewelry of gold, silver, and enamel was worn by both sexes, and the skill of the Irish goldsmiths rarely has been exceeded. The Irish designs can be traced directly to the continental Celtic art of the La Tene culture, but the forms were refined and elaborated. After the Irish became Christian, the same designs were used for illumination, resulting in books that are still among the wonders of the world.

Irish armament differed from that of both the Gauls and Germans. The favorite weapons were the spear and light axe. The long slashing sword of the continent was replaced by a medium length stabbing weapon, and the entire armament is suggestive of Bronze Age forms reproduced in iron. Defensive armor was limited to a round shield and, occasionally, a helmet.

The Irish social organization throws much light upon that of the mainland Celts. The basic unit was an extended kin group made up of several related families who shared in the ownership of farmland but leased cattle from their noble patrons independently. Most families were monogamous, but a man was permitted to have concubines. In pagan Ireland the concubine relationship was often entered into for a year at a time, usually from May to May, and terminated at the end of the year unless renewed. A bride price was paid by the husband, but, especially in the upper classes, marriages seem to have been dissolved easily and frequently great ladies enjoyed as much freedom in the distribution of their favors as did their lords. In spite of this freedom, it may be noted that the bride price to be paid for a woman diminished with each of her successive marriages.

There were no villages, but a group of related families usually lived in the same neighborhood and shared in the cultivation of plowland held in common. The political unit was the *tuath,* sometimes mistermed a clan. Although many of a tuath's members might be related by blood, the unit also included serfs and craftsmen who might be of foreign origin, and refugees who had been allowed to settle within the tuath's limits. At the head of the tuath was a king, the post being filled in each generation from a particular family line, all of whose members ranked as royal. This, coupled with the fact that many of the Irish "kingdoms" were little larger than a New England township, explains the frequency with which the "king of Ireland's son" occurs not only in Irish but in continental romances. Below the king came the nobles; then the "worthies," freemen with the right to keep cattle and share in plowland; and lastly, the serfs. At the bottom of the scale were chattel slaves who were bought and sold freely, slave women being ranked with cattle as units of value. Nobles and "worthies" were further divided into numerous subgroups based on wealth and descent.

Side by side with the secular organization just described there was a hierarchy of learned men: bards, priests and those skilled in the law, who gave Ireland cultural unity. In spite of the apparent fragmentation and the almost constant raiding between kingdoms, every individual and social unit had its place in a single, all-embracing system and every person held the same rank everywhere. For legal purposes this rank was indicated by his *dīre* or honor price, which determined the amount of damages which he could collect in case of injury to his property or person and, conversely, the size of the fines which could be assessed against him. It is interesting to note that Irish law, like Medieval European law, was phrased in terms of the privileges allowed to persons of different rank rather than in those of things prohibited to them. Thus a "worthy" of the lowest grade was one who: [1]

. . . held enough land to support the seven cows and the bull which he was entitled to lease from the king for a rent of one of the cows at the end of each year along with the seven sheep and a riding horse. He was competent to be a partner in a ploughland, owning his ox and ploughshare and goad and halter, and his share in a kiln, a mill, a barn, a cooking pot. He was allowed *a house of nineteen feet long made of wicker work in the lintel with two doorways, a door in one, a hurdle in the other; a bare fence of boards around it; an oaken plank between every two beds. Three "chattels" of kine were his honor price, because the establishment of his house was not complete,* and he could not *guarantee for the full honour price owing to the smallness of his means.*

Under the honor price system, rank and wealth were inseparably linked, and a family rose or fell according to the establishment which it could maintain. Thus a "worthy" family which acquired wealth equivalent to that of a noble and retained it for three generations was accounted noble. Conversely, a family which could not maintain "noble"

---

[1] Green, Alice Stopford: *History of the Irish State to 1014.* London: Macmillan and Co., Ltd.; 1925, p. 194.

economic status after three generations dropped to the "worthy" class. The three generation rule, when applied to kingship, became one of the most perfect systems ever developed for maintaining constant turmoil. A family line whose head had not actually ruled within three generations was demoted to noble level and lost the right to rule in the future. Since all of a king's sons and grandsons were accounted royal, but only one of them could be king at any given time and transmit royal rank to his descendents, there were always numerous pretenders to every throne and fratricide was the commonest road to succession. After the Irish became Christian the situation was mitigated somewhat, the king being allowed to nominate his successor and share rule with him, but assassination and invasion by claimants who had been ignored were still rife.

In spite of the constant turmoil, the organization of the whole of Ireland under the High King was more than a legal fiction. The High King made tours from time to time and, in fact, was required to do so in order to validate his claim to office. On these tours he held assemblies and heard cases appealed to him from the lower courts. Regular assemblies for the hearing of law cases were held in various places at fixed times, and matters of policy were also debated on these occasions.

The gatherings for these councils provided an opportunity for fairs at which goods of all sorts were exchanged. There was an extensive system of roads, and a special rank was accorded to those who had houses of hospitality. These were wealthy men, the equipment necessary for setting up such a house being elaborately specified in the law code. They received travelers as guests but expected to be reimbursed by gifts, and the post carried both prestige and economic rewards.

The basic uniformity of culture was maintained by the fairs and councils and, above all, by the professional bards, priests, and law-men. All the Celts accorded these great respect. In Ireland the bard was entitled to the seat on the king's left, while the law-man sat across from him on the queen's right. Under the sumptuary law bards could wear five colors and the king only seven. Famous bards wandered from court to court and through their control of publicity were able to operate rackets not unlike those of the modern columnist. Failure to entertain them properly would be punished by a satire, which seems to have been feared as a form of malevolent magic over and above the resulting ridicule. Lesser bards were attached to the courts of various kings. Both verse and versifiers were robust. The royal bard was expected to take his place beside the king in the line of battle so that he could contribute the magical efficacy of his satires, as well as be able to observe the royal deeds and celebrate them properly in his verse.

Accounts of the religion of pagan Ireland and, indeed, of that of the Celts in general, are fragmentary. Students have had a tendency to assume the existence of a much more organized theology than there is any real evidence for. There seems to have been the usual Indo-European assortment of male and female deities, enough like the Olympian gods for Classical writers to equate the two. On both Ireland and the continent certain deities, for example a god with stag horns shown in numerous carvings from Gaul, may belong to a still older cultural stratum. Ceremonies were held in the open, and where there were Megalithic circles and alignments these continued in use until almost the beginning of the Christian era. The rites were presided over by priests, the much-advertised *druids* who, in addition to directing sacrifices and other rites, performed divination and worked magic. These priests seem to have been graded in some sort of hierarchy which was recognized across tribal lines, but it is impossible to say in how far they formed an organized group. After the Roman conquest of Gaul many of the native priests and learned men fled to Britain, and from there continued to stir up revolt until the Romans conquered that island also.

The Irish records all come from a time considerably after the period when the mainland Celts were making themselves a terror to their Mediterranean neighbors, and it is probable that the Irish social system had become considerably more elaborate than that of the Gauls of Caesar's day. However, partly hereditary, partly local groupings of the *tuath* type; the organization of local chiefs under a paramount chief; the grading of individuals even within the threefold division of chiefs, nobles, and commoners; a system of vassalage by which men received cattle from the chief and paid him rental for these rather than for the use of land; a well-developed legal system with law-men; an extensive literature transmitted verbally; and an exaggerated respect for learned men: all these seem to have been present among the Gauls.

One is forced to conclude that, aside from the lack of writing and the rarity of cities, the Gauls were little inferior culturally to the Romans of the Republican period. How much of this culture was able to survive the Roman conquest is a problem deserving further study. In the new society which emerged in Western Europe after the fall of the Roman empire, German and Latin elements were predominant, but the Celtic social institutions must have survived in rural districts long after the Roman conquest and prepared the population for the feudal system.

Chapter XXVI

The Roman Peninsula

ROMAN CULTURE has been even more thoroughly studied and described by scholars than Greek culture. The extent of the Roman contribution to later European civilization is evident to anyone who is familiar with the languages spoken over nearly half of the European continent; the letters of the alphabet, the solemn and massive architecture of our governmental buildings, our devotion to the letter of the law and to legal procedure, and our crippling system of checks and balances in government are only a few of the things which we have inherited from them. In addition there is the legend of Rome as the world state, the bringer of universal peace. All this has served to overshadow the fact that until well after Rome had become a world power, the Romans were themselves barbarians. Even Pyrrhus, the Epirote, who encountered them almost a hundred years after the time of Alexander the Great, regarded them as such and noted with surprise that there was nothing barbarous in the way they handled their troops. Their conquest of the Greek cities of southern Italy, and the amazingly rapid expansion which established their power over the eastern Mediterranean in the short space of fifty years, must have been regarded by the civilized populations of the regions as very much on a par with a Gaulish invasion.

Culturally, Italy lagged behind the Aegean countries throughout most of its history. This was merely a reflection of the well-known fact that it takes time for any culture pattern to spread from the point of its origin and that, other things being equal, the greater the distance from the origin point to a particular region, the longer the culture lag. The first Neolithic settlers of Italy came from the east, either by sea or following the coast, and were a part of the Mediterranean wing of the Neolithic colonization of Europe. The culture of these first settlers was relatively simple and there were no significant new developments after they reached Italy. The Neolithic period in Italy was also shorter than it was in Northern Europe, since Italy in particular contained considerable mineral wealth which lured in foreign miners and merchants. Both traders from the Aegean and Beaker Folk from Spain had reached Italy by 1200 B.C., but seem to have had no great influence on the local cultures.

About 1500 B.C. bronze-using invaders established themselves in the Po Valley. These people seem to have come from Central Europe, possibly Hungary, and almost certainly spoke an Indo-European language. They established fortified villages from which they dominated and finally absorbed the older Neolithic population. Their villages were occupied for longer periods, and their sites are marked by mounds of gray, greasy earth called *terramare,* which the Italian peasants were accustomed to dig out and spread on their fields as fertilizer. In the course of these diggings many objects came to light, and in the 1880's systematic excavations were undertaken. Unfortunately, the science of archeology was still in its infancy when this work was done, and none of the sites were dug with the care or techniques which would have been employed today. The bronze objects found are of Middle European type. The pottery, on the other hand, is suggestive of the earlier Italian cultures. The plan of the Terramare villages was almost identical with that of the Roman legionary camp. The village was defended by an earth embankment, with a moat into which a running stream was diverted. The entrance to the village was by way of a single bridge over the moat and a narrow passage through the embankment. From the entrance a single broad road led across the village. At the further end there was a mound containing three sacrificial pits, obviously marking the site of a sacred area. The main road was intersected at right angles by another broad way, and the houses were arranged in regular rows between. The houses seem to have been built on piles, and the whole arrangement was suggestive of a lake-dwellers' village reproduced on dry land.

Such carefully planned, laboriously constructed villages would seem congruous with the interests and attitudes of Roman culture in the Republican period. Certain features of the plan would also explain puzzling elements in the later Roman culture, particularly their preoccupation with bridges. Since the safety of the Terramare village depended upon the bridge, it would not be unnatural for the villagers to call their priests *pontifs,* literally *bridge makers,* a feature otherwise hard to explain. Moreover, the bridge and entrance were narrow enough to be held by a single champion against an army, and the stirring tale of Horatius at the bridge may well have been a folk memory of Terramare days.

From the Terramare period on there were repeated incursions into northern Italy, first by representatives of the Hallstatt culture and later by Celtic tribes. The Celtic invasions were of little significance, since, after each inroad, most of the raiders retired behind the Alps with their loot. The Romans themselves first emerge in history as a group of traders and farmers who settled on a group of low hills on the left bank of the Tiber River about fifteen miles from its mouth. The settlement became a thriving trading center, and by 753 B.C. it was a small city-state governed by a king. The Roman feeling for republican rule was apparently inculcated early, for in 509 B.C. they deposed the king, who was an Etrurian from across the Tiber, and wiped out the dynasty. They spent the next hundred and fifty years warring with their neighbors, subduing them, and bringing them into the Roman orbit. In 390 B.C. Rome was invaded by the Gauls, who plundered and sacked the city before they were driven off. However, by 338 B.C. Rome had made herself mistress of all Latium. Roman power grew rapidly after this. A series of successful campaigns subdued the Samnites, the sturdy highland tribes of central Italy. Etruria was brought under Roman domination, which gave Rome access to Adriatic ports and increased trade. By 270 B.C. Rome had succeeded in doing what no Greek city-state had ever done: she had welded the whole southern peninsula into a single confederacy completely under her domination. The Gauls continued to harass Rome from the north, however, until Caesar reversed the usual direction of movement by invading Gaul and pacifying the Gauls.

There was one group of invaders who came to stay and left a deep and enduring stamp on Roman culture. The Etruscans were the first really civilized people to reach Italy. They left few inscriptions, and even these were mainly brief epitaphs which throw little light upon their culture or origins. The most that can be learned from these inscriptions is that they wrote with an alphabet obviously derived from a Semitic rather than a Greek prototype, and that the Etruscan language was neither Indo-European nor Semitic. Scholars have surrounded their origin with mystery, but the Romans, who both conquered them and incorporated much of Etruscan culture into their own, had no doubt as to where they came from. They believed that the Tyrrheni, as the Etruscans called themselves, came from Asia Minor, and until quite late in Roman history the anniversary of one of the earliest Roman victories over the

ETRUSCAN DAILY LIFE

Etruscans was celebrated by leading mummers dressed in Asiatic fashion through the streets, while criers shouted, "Sardinians for sale!"

The Etruscans seem to have arrived in Italy between 800 and 900 B.C. Their movement may have been a last act in the diffusion of the "People of the Isles" from Asia Minor. Their settlements were made in northwestern Italy, suggesting that they may have followed in the footsteps of the Shardana (see Chap. XXII, p. 317). Although by 800 B.C. the use of iron was well established in the Near East, bronze still remained a precious metal much in demand for all sorts of ornamental objects and eagerly desired by the tribes beyond the Alps. The presence of rich deposits of copper and tin in northern Italy may well have been the original reason for the Etruscan settlement.

Apparently the Etruscan movement was neither a mass migration nor a planned colonization. They seem to have come a few shiploads at a time, settling first along the coast and establishing themselves as an aristocratic class ruling over the native population. Each Etruscan city seems to have been founded by a different kin group, and the remains show significant cultural differences. The relations between conquerors and conquered followed much the same pattern as the Aryan conquests elsewhere, although the organization of the noble group itself was quite different.

The noble rulers of various cities carried on intricate feuds, but all of them would combine to come to the rescue of an Etruscan overlord in case of a revolt of his subjects. This throws light on some episodes in Roman history. The expulsion of the Tarquins, who were the early kings of Rome, has been romantically ascribed to the crime of Sextus, one of the king's sons, who raped a Roman matron and drove her to suicide. The Tarquins were in fact an Etruscan dynasty, ruling over what was at that time one of the minor Etruscan principalities. Their family tomb has been found near the ancient city of Caere. We do not know what the real cause of the popular revolt may have been, but when the Tarquins were thrown out they appealed to their Etruscan kinsmen, who sent a mixed force under the command of Lars Porsena of Clusium, the leading

ETRUSCAN DAILY LIFE

city of the loose Etruscan league. Anyone who has read the *Lays of Ancient Rome* has got a good Roman version of what followed.

The social organization of the Etruscans was an aristocratic one. At the top were the *lucumones,* the nobles of Etruscan blood; below them, the bourgeois middle class who were attached to them as clients, in the Roman usage of the term, and who were probably of mixed origin. These included skilled craftsmen and merchants. At the bottom of the scale were the peasants and ordinary artisans, who were largely of aboriginal stock. Class membership seems to have been strictly hereditary. There was no way in which a bourgeois or peasant could become a noble. The nobles were tremendously proud of pure blood and kept extensive genealogies. After the fall of the Etruscan power, many of the noble families were incorporated into the Roman state, and many of the Roman patrician families boasted of their Etruscan origin.

All wealth seems to have been concentrated in the hands of the patrician families, and their great rock-cut tombs and the wealth of objects placed in them contrast sharply with the simple cremations of the lower classes and indicate how complete the economic control of the nobles must have been. These tombs were veritable houses of the dead, furnished with all sorts of objects of both utility and luxury. They were used generation after generation and indicate both a strong kin organization and the presence of an ancestor cult.

In early times each Etruscan city was ruled by a *lars,* a priest-king whose functions were as much religious as political. It was his task not only to administer justice but also to act as high priest and to interpret omens. Later the Etruscan cities seem to have become aristocratic republics ruled by hereditary oligarchies much like that of Venice. The organization of republican Rome after the expulsion of the Tarquins, with its rigid division of the population into patricians and plebeians and its restriction of all offices to the patricians, probably was in accord with the Etruscan patterns. Throughout Etruscan history the nobles always retained control of religion, and the priesthood was recruited exclusively from their ranks. Their presumed magical powers no doubt helped to maintain their control over the commoners. The Roman pattern, by which the priests of the higher orders were civil officials elected for secular rather than religious reasons, probably derived from the Etruscans.

The Romans had two sets of deities. One consisted of the family gods, *lares* and *penates,* who were ancestral spirits and guardians of the household. These were probably of Etruscan origin. They were small, intimate beings who could be loved and dominated by their worshippers and, in so far as emotion entered into Roman religion at all, it found its outlet in the familial cult. The second group of gods were merely personifications of virtues or qualities. Thus there was Terminus, the god of boundaries represented by the boundary stone; Vesta, the goddess of the hearth, represented by a sacred fire; and a whole series of similar impersonal deities. The worship of these was a function of the state, and the priests who presided over their rites were government officials who were letter-perfect in the rituals. The relation between the deities and the state was regarded as a contractual one in which, if the state performed its part, the deities would perform theirs. If divine help was not forthcoming, it was assumed that there had been some slip in the ritual, and it is on record that, in at least one case, the same ceremony was repeated seven times because a minor slip had been detected in each of the first six performances. Such deities and such attitudes toward them might be expected from the Terramare people, but certainly were alien to the Etruscan temperament.

Since the Etruscans have left no literature we can only judge what their temperament was from their art. Their tombs are filled with pictures of banquets and decorous revelries in which both men and women participated. The Romans, who were an exceedingly puritanical people, especially in their earlier period, had a great deal to say about the general profligacy and degeneracy of the Etruscans, but there is little real evidence for this. Roman men were not supposed to strip in each other's presence, while the Etruscans followed the Greek tradition and used nude figures in their art. They evidently knew how to enjoy themselves and how to live luxuriously. Thus, Etruscan gold work was the best in the ancient world, and the frescoes show them wearing mantles bordered with the purple which later became the mark of Roman senatorial rank.

The tomb materials show extensive contacts, and it seems highly probable that the Etruscan nobles, like the later Italian ones, themselves engaged in trade. They certainly lacked the Greek contempt for technology. They were good farmers who introduced the grape and olive into Italy, and they probably were responsible for the use of the plow and crop rotation. The later Roman interest in agriculture and its practice by patricians probably stems from Etruscan origins. The Etruscans were also the best bronze workers of their times, their superiority being acknowledged even by the Greeks.

In the 7th century B.C. bronze cauldrons of Etruscan workmanship were dedicated at Olympia by Greek cities, not as curiosities or spoils but because they represented the finest craftsmanship available.

Etruscan art reveals a curious situation. In spite of their technological excellence, they seem to have been uninventive as regards style and subject matter. They copied the artistic forms of the various peoples with whom they traded, Syrians, Egyptians and Greeks, and produced curious hybrid products which often appear clumsy in concept if not in execution. The only art in which they excelled was that of portraiture. At a time when even the Greek atttempts at it were stylized, they were working from models and producing faces which were strongly individual. Most of their portraits were cast in bronze, but the Etruscans were also famous for their colossal pottery figures. These were sometimes fifteen to eighteen feet high, decorated in polychrome. To construct and fire such immense earthenware objects required a mastery of technique which has never been surpassed. The first Italian artist whose name has been preserved is one Volca, an Etruscan sculptor whom the Romans employed to make earthenware statues for the temples on the Capitoline Hill, when these were rebuilt after the city had been burned by the Gauls.

The Romans finally succeeded in breaking the power of the Etruscans and incorporating their fragments and those of various conquered Italic tribes into a single state. It may be noted that in this incorporation they did not show their reputed genius for statecraft. The conquered groups were given no share in government, and, although they were expected to furnish levees for the Roman armies, they were so thoroughly exploited both militarily and economically that most of them were ready to side with any enemy of Rome. Having consolidated the north, the Romans gradually extended their power southward through their progressive conquest of the Greek cities in southern Italy and Sicily. These Italian Greeks were vastly more civilized than the Romans, who regarded them with envious contempt. The city fathers at this time made numerous attempts to prevent the younger generation in Rome from accepting Greek culture, but its attraction proved too strong for censorship and repressive legislation.

The subjugation of the Greek cities brought the Romans face to face with the Carthaginians, a Phoenician group who at that time dominated the western Mediterranean from their bases in North Africa, Sicily, and Spain. The final destruction of Carthage after the Punic wars created a vacancy in the Mediterranean power alignment, and the Romans were swept into this. In reading the records, one feels that the Roman overseas empire originally came into being more by chance than by intention. Roman isolationists, not unlike our own, protested every step in the early growth of the empire, and, when Rome finally found herself a world power deeply involved in world affairs, she had no constructive plan for meeting the situation. Within fifty years she had passed from an insignificant barbarian state on the outer edge of civilization to control of the whole Mediterranean basin, including its Asiatic coasts. The only previous parallel for such an expansion had been the conquests of Alexander the Great, and, in these, power was already centralized in the person of the conqueror.

The Roman republican system, with its paralyzing elaboration of checks and balances, proved quite inadequate to the new conditions. The Roman virtues were the parochial virtues of poor, hard-working peasants. Republican Rome had had no educated or leisure class, and its poor patricians, laboring as cultivators on their own lands, could not afford most of the vices they condemned. When wealth began to flow into the city from the East, their virtues proved to have no solid basis. The last days of the Republic were marked by a wild scramble for money, the sort of ostentatious waste to be expected from *parvenues,* and a callous indifference to all human values. The commanders of the conquering armies and the governors whom the Senate sent out in their wake devoted themselves to looting on an unprecedented scale. Determined revolts in the East, where the population had been abused beyond the endurance of even Asiatic peasants, and the struggles for power between various generals, completed the collapse of most of the old Roman republican institutions.

The one institution which was able to survive and perform its original functions effectively under these circumstances was the Roman military establishment. The old army tradition of loyalty to the state was increasingly replaced by loyalty to the commander, but discipline remained firm and the Roman military techniques were superior to those of any of their antagonists except the Parthians, whose mailed and mounted archers were more than a match for the legions. Except on the Parthian front, the limits to Roman conquest were set only by the increasing poverty and cultural backwardness of the tribes whom they encountered. Good businessmen as always, the Romans established their frontiers at the point where the anticipated income from new territories would not pay the cost of conquest and administration.

The evils of the period of conquest reached a climax in the wars of Marius and Sylla, which paved the way for the creation of the Roman empire under Augustus. In this the Roman Senate and the old forms of the Roman Republic were maintained for their psychological effect but were carefully shorn of real power. The state which emerged was a Hellenistic monarchy of the type which had already been developed in the Near East through centuries of trial and error. The worship of the emperor, which was an integral part of the Hellenistic system, was accepted reluctantly by the early emperors, who found it rather ridiculous. Augustus himself carefully avoided any of the old titles which bore connotations offensive to Republican ears; nevertheless, he was in complete control. The empire was treated as the personal estate of the emperor, and no distinction was made between the national treasury and his private fortune. Since he was also commander-in-chief of the army, he was able to attach to his person both such loyalty to the state as had survived and the devotion of the soldier to his commander.

The Roman imperial organization called for the creation of an honest and devoted professional civil service. The peculations of Roman officials in the provinces, which under the Republic had been taken as much for granted as the grafting of American politicians, now became embezzlement of the imperial property. It is interesting to note that the secretaries of Augustus, who would correspond to our own presidential cabinet, were, with few exceptions, Greeks, and several of them were Greek freedmen who had been reared in the Near East and were thus familiar with the Hellenistic patterns both for government and for the management of great estates. With their aid Augustus organized the empire on such a sound basis that it was able to carry on for centuries in spite of vicious and incompetent emperors and even the wars of rival aspirants to the purple. After the initial period of conquest had come to an end and during the long periods, when contests for the purple did not reach the dimension of civil wars, the Roman empire conferred genuine benefits upon its members. It maintained peace among its subjects and protected them from barbarian inroads. It established new trade routes and improved old ones. It gave the most civilized part of the ancient western world a common system of laws and a common language, the latter increasingly Greek rather than Latin.

Lastly, the Romans were the first to make constant use of the device of awarding citizenship with all its accompanying rights and privileges to a selected group of individuals among the subjects. This arrangement not only gave the subjects the hope of final social equality, but performed the more immediate function of detaching many of their ablest potential leaders and affiliating them with the dominant group.

In spite of these advantages, the Romans never developed an adequate fiscal policy, and from the time of the establishment of the empire on there was a gradual decline in the extent of Roman resources. Even under good emperors it became increasingly difficult to finance the defensive wars against barbarians. It should be pointed out that the Hellenistic patterns of government which the Romans had made their own had been developed in the Near East, in a territory in which a dense rural and urban population had been supported from time immemorial by irrigation, the practice of crop rotation, and a high development of trade and manufactures. Europe, even Italy, was by contrast a backward region with a sparse and dwindling rural population whose lands were becoming increasingly impoverished, and with few and insignificant cities. In the long view of history, one must think of the Roman empire as a westward extension of the Hellenistic civilization which had its origin and continuing center in the Near East. As with many other advances of culture into regions to which they were ecologically unadapted, the Hellenistic civilization never really took roots in the West. In due course of time the Celtic and Germanic cultures reasserted themselves, and the Hellenistic civilization retreated eastward, where it survived in Byzantium, the so-called eastern Roman empire, until the 15th century A.D. Its retreat left the control of Europe to the barbarian tribes whose culture had been enriched but certainly not transformed by contact with Hellenistic Rome. These tribes had found many elements of the Hellenistic culture incompatible with their own long established institutions, and, while the great legend of Rome predisposed them to accept the outward forms of the Roman state, they reinterpreted these in terms of their own values.

In Western Europe the chaos, following the Roman collapse, crystallized into the feudal system, which, as H. G. Wells remarked, was not a system but "confusion roughly organized." With the breakdown of authority the prevailing need of early medieval society was for protection. Governmental control, which normally guards the rights of citizens, was lacking. The peasants and small landowners were easy prey for any roving band of invaders who descended upon them. They were therefore obliged to seek protection where they could find it and pay whatever was demanded. Thus the powerful landowner with a retinue of fighting men could force his weaker neighbors to become his dependents in return for his protection. This resulted in a system of nobles holding the manors, with the peasants working for him as serfs and fighting for him when necessary.

The foundation of feudalism was the *fief*, which was usually land but might be other privileges, such as the right to operate a mill, collect revenues, or hold some other lucrative post. Each noble tried to collect as many fiefs as possible, and in exchange for a fief gave an oath of fealty to the lord from whom he had obtained it. This meant sending the required number of fighting men to the lord if he was at war and being loyal to his interests at all times. The nobles were a military aristocracy trained in the arts of war, the most important of which was the ability to fight in heavy armor—a skill which takes considerable practice, as a suit of plate armor might weigh as much as 150 pounds. The nobles lived on their manors, which were practically self-sustaining, providing food and processed goods and services for the lord and his retinue and also for the peasants on the estate.

Feudalism was essentially a rural society, with the nobles established on the manors. In the towns was a small group of burghers who produced the few specialized things which could not be made by the peasants. With the rise of the cities, feudalism collapsed. In fact, in the region around the Mediterranean, where city patterns survived the fall of Rome, feudalism never became strong as it did in the north.

Feudalism presented a rigidly stratified society in which, theoretically at least, no man could rise above the position into which he was born. However, as in most integrated social systems, a safety valve was provided to draw off the energies of able and aggressive members of the lower class who might otherwise have revolted. The one outlet for social advancement was through the Church. The villeins were chained to the soil and could be sold along with a plot of land, but the son of a serf, if he were able and ambitious, could go into the Church. In this organization it was theoretically possible for him to rise to the position of Pope and to stand on a par with the emperor, who was the secular head of the heirarchy. In this way the Church succeeded generation after generation in drawing off the best brains of the society and also in providing an outlet for the restless and aggressive ones who were potential troublemakers in this rigid system.

The Church shrewdly prevented the priesthood from becoming an hereditary aristocracy by passing two basic regulations: first, the clergy were forbidden to marry, and second, no illegitimate son could take orders in the Church. Consequently the road to advancement in the Church was always open, and new blood was constantly being drawn from all levels in society.

The Church, which had modeled its organization on that of the Empire and even taken over many of the Empire's secular functions at the time of the Roman collapse, had remained the last Hellenistic stronghold in Western Europe. Its incompatibility with the barbarian cultures led to innumerable clashes between Church and State which finally culminated in the Protestant Reformation.

Chapter XXVII

Islam

WHEN THE ROMAN EMPIRE went into a decline in the West, the eastern Empire carried on. Two great powers emerged from the Near East. One was called the Byzantine Empire, which is a much better term for it than the eastern Roman Empire, since its official language was Greek and its cultural background was predominantly Greek and Syrian. The other power, lying farther to the east, was the Persian Empire. The Romans were never able to conquer the Parthians, the people living in what is now Persia, but who at one period extended their boundaries as far as the Tigris and Euphrates. Here, in the early centuries of the Christian era, a strong and highly civilized power emerged.

The Sassanian kingdom was the direct descendant of the Persian Empire with which the Greeks had fought. In the course of time, the dynasties had changed, yet the general patterns had carried over. It was highly organized and civilized. Zoroastrianism, the state religion, was for a time the great opponent of Christianity. The Persian religion was a fundamental dualism. It was based on the idea that the universe was controlled by two contesting forces, darkness and light, or evil and good. Ormuz was the God of Light; Orimon, the God of Darkness. The struggle between them was an equal one, so that the outcome was constantly in doubt. Neither of them was all-powerful, as the Christian God is supposed to be. It was the duty of the good man to align himself with Ormuz, and to take an active part in the struggle. Christianity borrowed one very important thing from it: the idea of the Devil, and of the evenly balanced struggle between God and the Devil, which left the outcome in doubt.

To the west of the Persians the Byzantine Empire was developing, becoming more and more rigid and formalized, but accomplishing one thing which was exceedingly important. It managed to incorporate people of many different cultures into itself and to do it successfully.

375

Its lists of officials, emperors, and generals name men of the most diverse origins. For instance, Belesarius, the great Byzantine general, was the son of a Slavic peasant from the Balkans. Several emperors were Arabs; some of the others were Slavs, Greeks, and Syrians. Probably none of them was of pure Roman ancestry. Apparently Byzantium had no particular consciousness of racial or national differences. Anyone could come into the system, and if a man possessed the necessary qualities, for the most part qualities of which we do not approve, such as ability for intrigue, knowledge about the suitable administration of poison, and so on, he was able to rise to a high position.

In this connection it is a very interesting fact that after the rise of Nazi domination, before the war and Germany's collapse, some of the more serious German scholars were making quite extensive studies of the Byzantine system. They knew that if Germany should conquer Europe it would have to incorporate the vanquished peoples; they were interested to see how this had been accomplished by the Byzantine Empire. These investigations were not carried far enough to disclose exactly how the Byzantines did this so successfully.

Incidentally, during this period, there was a surprisingly close connection between Byzantium and Scandinavia. The Scandinavians came down across the Russian flats, choosing places where they could get their long-ships down with only short portages. Some were traders; others were assembled by the emperors of Constantinople to form an imperial guard, the Varangian Guards, patterned after the old Praetorian Guard. It was the proper thing for Scandinavian princes, especially for high-spirited young men who had killed an opponent in a duel and wanted to get out of the country until the affair was forgotten, to go to Constantinople, join the Varangian Guard for a few years, and then to return home with their earnings. More Byzantine coins have been found in Scandinavia than anywhere else in the world. Apparently, the Scandinavians buried the loot they took north instead of spending it. The earliest account that we have of the pagan Norsemen is written in Arabic by an Arab who visited their encampments in Russia. He has left us a very good and circumstantial account of the Viking funeral, with its human sacrifices, which checks almost exactly with the descriptions given in the sagas.

Byzantium was constantly being exhausted, on the one hand by its wars with the Sassanian Persians; on the other, by successive raids from the north by Bulgars, Slavs, and the like. In the 7th century A.D. Byzantium and Persia had just about fought each other to a standstill, and had reduced the peasantry in the fought-over territory to a condition of complete despair and indifference. The rulers' technique for getting taxes was to make the richest man of each district the tax collector. If, given a free hand as to methods, he could not raise the required taxes, he had to supply the difference out of his own pocket. This hardly engendered enthusiasm toward the central government.

It was upon this scene that the conquering Arabs of Mohammed's immediate successors appeared. This background has been described because the usual and far more dramatic picture suggests that small Arab armies came from the desert and overthrew the forces of the two mightiest empires in the world. But great empires are not easily conquered unless they have rotted from within. Here we find a situation which slightly parallels the invasions of the barbaric tribes. But the significant difference, which facilitated the Arab conquest, was the fact that while the earlier barbarian invaders of the Roman Empire had a tribal organization, which meant a certain amount of resistance to outsiders becoming part of the tribe, the Arabs were united by a common faith which was a vigorous, proselytizing religion, and were eager for converts. In the early days of their conquests, anyone who accepted their religion became a brother in Islam. Many of these early Arab invasions undoubtedly bore many of the earmarks of a social revolution, which gave the proletarians a better chance than they had had under the existing systems of the old empires.

Mohammedanism, or more properly, Islam, began with the teachings of Mohammed. He was an historical figure whose life is amply documented. He was born in Mecca in 570 A.D. of a good family, but his father died before his birth and his mother when he was six. His childhood was insecure and difficult, for the orphan was handed around to various foster-mothers and relatives. During his early adolescence he served as a shepherd, which gave him much time for contemplation. At seventeen he went to Syria with an uncle and fought in a local religious war. When he was twenty-four he became commercial representative for a caravan owned by a wealthy widow. A year later, in 595, he married the widow, who was then forty, had been married twice before, and had borne her former husbands two sons and a daughter. She bore Mohammed two sons, who died in childhood, and four daughters. From 595 to 610 Mohammed was a respected businessman in the city of Mecca. He was given the surname Al Amin, The Just, because of the wisdom of his decisions. At the age of forty, however, he began to feel dissatisfaction with his tranquil and prosperous existence and retired for meditation to a cave outside the city. Revelations in the form of dreams came to him, and he was convinced that he had been chosen by Allah as a vehicle of enlightenment.

As well as being an important town in the caravan trade, Mecca was a center for religious pilgrimages, for it was the shrine of an important deity of the old Arabic religion. Because of this, the Meccans were highly attuned to religion; also their contact with traders had exposed them to the Jewish and Christian ideas. Mohammed's revelations attracted a number of followers and he began to preach and make further converts. Like all Arab towns, Mecca was split into various factions. A powerful group who disliked Mohammed's clan, and saw in his new teaching a threat to the old pilgrim trade, made an unsuccessful attempt to assassinate him. Mohammed and his small group of loyal disciples fled to Medina on July 16th, 622. This is a very important date, for it is the year of the Hejira, or flight, from which all Mohammedans reckon, just as Christians date their calendar from the time which is assumed to be the birth of Christ.

The people of Medina, a town lying north of Mecca, welcomed Mohammed, chiefly because they were old rivals of the Meccans. Towns frequently followed the policy of taking in an exile and helping him to become a distinguished citizen in order to make trouble for the town from which he had fled.

There were numerous small battles between Mecca and Medina. Finally, the Meccans mustered a large army to try to take Medina. The level of Arab culture at that time can be deduced from the fact that this siege is known in Mohammedan sacred history as the "Battle of the Ditch." Under the direction of a Persian in Medina, who had been converted to Mohammedanism, Medina was fortified by a moat. At this time the desert Arabs had so little experience in coping with any kind of fortification that this "ditch" completely baffled them. They camped outside the town, without the slightest idea of how to gain an entry. After a certain amount of skirmishing the siege began to look like a stalemate. The attacking force was of heterogeneous origin, made up of clans, most of which were feuding with each other. Since there was no actual battle to consolidate them, they began quarreling among themselves and finally dispersed. After this bloodless victory, Mohammed's influence in southern Arabia was never questioned. In 630 he drove a bargain with the Meccans: in return for his safe conduct to Mecca he would agree to make this city the center of the new religion, thus retaining and augmenting its pilgrim trade.

Mohammed returned to Mecca in 630. He destroyed the idols of the old religion and forbade any pilgrims except the Faithful of Islam to enter the city. He ruled that the idol-worshippers must be either converted or slain, but the "People of the Book," meaning Christians, Zoroastrians, and Jews, were allowed to worship in their own way, although they were assessed a special tax.

Two years after his return to Mecca, Mohammed died at the age of 62, a ripe age for a prophet. Most of the great religious leaders died long before the religious ideologies which they inspired were formu-

lated. The doctrine of the Trinity, the nature of the Holy Ghost, and
other theological concepts which arose subsequent to the original doctrine of Christianity, and which have been the concern of divines for
centuries, would probably also have puzzled Jesus of Nazareth. But
Mohammed, as a religious leader in Medina and then in Mecca, coped
with immediate questions of doctrine. Following the tradition of Arab
sheiks, he administered justice and handed down decisions.

Mohammed died a successful and prosperous citizen, which is also
outside the pattern for prophets. He was a man of experience, having
been a herdsman, a warrior, and a trader. He had a thorough understanding of Arab culture and his teachings were adapted to the needs
of the people and made no demands which would disrupt their patterns of life. He worked for unity and a funneling of the old tribal loyalties into a new religious allegiance. Certainly Mohammed's teachings
were more direct and comprehensible than those of Zoroastrianism or
Christianity, the religions with which Islam had to compete at the time
of its origin.

The Arabs, who were familiar with Jewish and Christian ideas, had
felt themselves at a disadvantage because they had no scriptures nor any
written tradition. The desert Arabs were just beginning to learn to write
at this time and had the awe and respect, characteristic of all illiterate
people, for written records and their apparently magical effects. Out of
the pronouncements of Mohammed came the Koran, which filled a long-
felt need in Arab life. Much of the Koran was dictated by Mohammed
while in a state of possession and is phrased in Arabic poetry, a mixture
of mystic prayers and exhortations to the faithful. Other sections are
pronouncements of all kinds. Although this book abounds in obscure il-
lusions which are dull and confusing to the modern reader, these referred at the time when it was written to contemporaneous events with
which the community was thoroughly familiar. Mohammed's pronouncements were occasionally inspired by momentary irritations. For instance,
after a difficult session with a strong-willed, old lady litigant, he made
the statement that no old woman would be accepted in Heaven, since
Heaven was designed as a peaceful place. He later relented on this
dictum, but the question as to whether or not women have souls is still
a point of doctrinal disagreement among various sects of Islam.

Although Mohammed did not live long enough to answer all the
questions that arose, he laid the foundation of a creed and a legal system which were later supplemented by his followers. The *Koran* contains innumerable laws governing all phases of behavior. Supplementing
the *Koran* proper, which contains the actual words of Mohammed, is
the *Hadith,* which contains the traditional sayings and decisions of Mohammed as these were recalled by his followers after his death. Some

Koran

Hadith

were reported by those who had known Mohammed, others were based on hearsay evidence. After Mohammed's death all the scribes of Islam began a frantic collection of all the sayings and episodes which could be recalled at first or second hand. This went on as long as there was anyone alive who had been alive in Mohammed's time. From these sacred works developed the peculiar pattern of Islamic sacred history which is still the background of Islam.

The legal content of the Koran was derived, for the most part, from the pre-Islamic customary law, with only minor variations by Mohammed himself. These in every case were ameliorations of earlier laws, for Mohammed was a social reformer. Thus, there is a statement in the Koran to the effect that a master must be kind to his slaves. Another specification on which Islamic peoples laid great stress was that all true believers were brothers and social equals. Coupled with this was an extraordinary degree of vertical mobility. A man born into any position in society, even that of slave, could rise to any heights. This was logically consistent for, since Allah controlled the universe, he could make a man a beggar one day and a sultan the next if that were his will. Islam has represented throughout its history an unusually flexible social system.

Within about fifty years after Mohammed's death, Islam split into three main sects, which were later still further divided. Although Mohammedanism began with fairly simple teachings, elaborations of doctrine served to carry various groups off in different directions. Because of the collapse of the neighboring tribes, the Arabs at this time were in possession of rich territory, the control of which was a plum worth fighting for. Therefore the question of the legitimate succession to the Caliphate became very important. Mohammed's sons had died in infancy, and his two nephews were killed in an interclan fight for the Caliphate. He had designated as his successor Abu Beker, his father-in-law and one of his first converts, but he was already an old man and died two years after Mohammed. It was on this point of succession that Islam first split into three camps: the *Sunni,* the *Khawarij,* and the *Shiites.*

The Sunni believed that any member of Mohammed's clan could be elected to the Caliphate, which made the choice exceedingly wide. They regarded the Caliph as the direct successor of Mohammed and as such, commander-in-chief of the army and head of the religion. The Khawarij held that the Caliphate was open to any true believer, since all were brothers in Islam. This group is now extinct except for a few small sects in North Africa. The third group, the Shiites, believed in absolute succession from Ali, who was Mohammed's nephew and adopted son, and husband of his favorite daughter, Fatima. Ali was regarded by the Shiites as an incarnation of Mohammed's power. Philo-

DRAWING FROM AN IRANIAN MANUSCRIPT, XV CENTURY

sophically this meant that the Caliph was an individual to whom the power and authority of Mohammed had been transmitted by Allah. He was not a reincarnation of Mohammed himself, but was semi-divine because of the divine power vested in him.

Since the Khawarij have faded from the scene, the main divisions in the Mohammedan world is between the Sunnis and the Shiites, each group considering the other heretic. The Sunnis, who held Arabia and Egypt, have remained closer to primitive Islam. Although they are a conservative group, their doctrines have been modified by the introduction of the concept of the *Ij'ma*. This is the belief that since the will of Allah controls everything, any custom which is workable and approved by the people must be in existence because Allah wills it so, even though it may be in opposition to the code of the Koran and Hadith. This concept has been extremely useful to the Sunnis in their missionary work, particularly in Africa. They have been able to adapt the doctrines of Islam to the local customs of the African Negro in a way in which the Christian missionaries have failed to do, with the result, that unless something unexpected happens, Negro Africa is likely to become Mohammedan rather than Christian.

The Shiites, who were essentially Persian, combined the pre-Islamic philosophy and customs of the old empire with the teaching of Mohammed and developed various mystic sects. Both Shiites and Sunnis were actually cultural extensions of the pre-Islamic civilization of the Near East.

The desert Arabs were not a large group. Their armies, although they were augmented by converts to Islam, were still small. However, Islam has never been a peaceable religion, and its followers have always been good fighters. Amru, the Arabian general, invaded Egypt in 639 with an army of only 3000 men, although the Egyptian population was between three and four million at this time, and held the country for three years until reinforcements arrived to complete the conquest. The Arabs were a desert people of simple culture who were able to take over the territory of more highly civilized groups through superior fighting ability. As is usual in such cases, they took over the patterns of the conquered groups. However, conquerors of lower culture than the conquered always find themselves confronted by a multiplicity of administrative problems. In the case of an old empire, such as Egypt was in the 7th century, the techniques for handling problems of government had already been worked out and it was easier for the conquerors to make use of the old bureaucracy than to attempt to train a new group, for the handling of men in large masses requires very specific techniques. So within a few generations the Arabs had absorbed the patterns of the divergent civilization of the areas which they had conquered.

They were eager to accept civilization, which they recognized as much more comfortable than their old desert existence. The Persian Empire and that part of Byzantium which they overran were exhausted empires, rotten from within, but with much that was new and stimulating to offer to the invaders. A tremendous upsurge of intellectual vigor resulted, which made the Islamic world for a time a center of intellectual activity. Although the Arabs shed their old patterns, they imposed the faith of Islam on the conquered peoples.

There is not space in this volume to give the history of the Islamic conquests, which absorbed the rotting empires on both sides of Arabia with amazing speed. Except for the excursion into the monsoon territory of Southeastern Asia, the spread of Islam has been closely connected with a particular environment and has never taken strong roots in any other kind of country. The typical environment is semi-arid country with

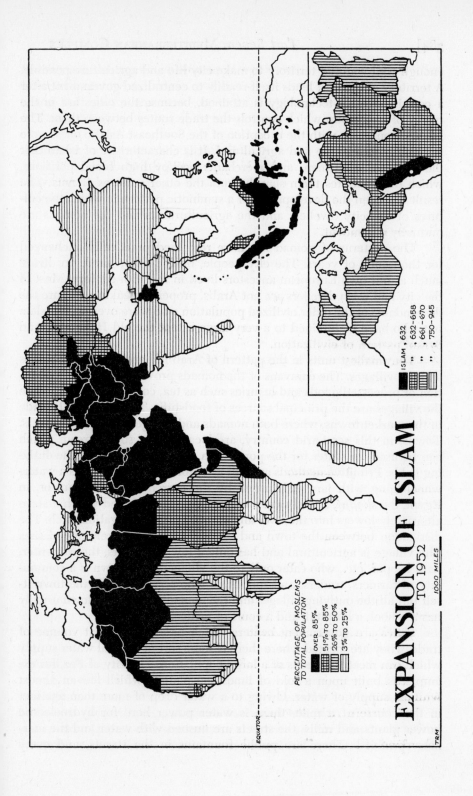

EXPANSION OF ISLAM
TO 1952

1000 MILES

PERCENTAGE OF MOSLEMS
TO TOTAL POPULATION

OVER 85%
51% TO 85%
26% TO 50%
3% TO 25%

ISLAM, 632
" , 632-658
" : 661-670
" . 750-945

EQUATOR

T.R.M.

enough well-watered territory to make city life and agriculture possible. A territory of this sort lends itself readily to centralized government after a certain level of technology is attained, because the cities are at the mercy of any group which controls the trade routes between them. The Islamic countries, with the exception of the Southeast Asiatic ones, were essentially mercantile and agricultural. It is characteristic of Islam that the artisans, craftsmen, and merchants occupy high social positions, which differentiates them sharply from the other cultures of Asia. The result has been the development of a symbiotic pattern in which the cultures of the city dwellers and the agriculturalists and the nomads are mutually dependent.

The patterns of nomad life have remained practically unchanged for thousands of years. The city people, on the other hand, are living much as our own European ancestors lived in the 16th century. Most of the city and town dwellers are not Arabs, properly speaking, but are the descendants of the older civilized population who were overrun by Islam but who have maintained to a very large extent the old Hellenistic and Syrian pattern of civilization.

The smallest units in the pattern of Arab life are the nomad camps and the villages. The caravans of the nomads provide for the transportation of processed goods and luxuries such as tea, coffee, and sugar, while the villages are the principal sources of foodstuffs. The exchange is made in the market towns, where both nomads and villagers bring their goods. Towns, in this semi-arid country, are located near some stream which can be used for water for the population and for irrigation of the outlying fields. Primitive methods are still used for irrigation, such as a water-wheel hung with jars and turned by the current of the stream or, in Egypt, the *shaduf,* a well-sweep with a large jar attached which a slave alternately lowers into the river and empties into an irrigation ditch. The distinction between the town and the village is not merely one of size. The village is agricultural and has only a few specialists, the carpenter, bath keeper, etc., who cater only to the villagers. The town is a community of farmers, traders, and specialists who serve not only the town itself but all the outlying villages and the nomad camps. The town usually has a school, a hospital, and a court of justice.

Cities are government centers which handle the great volume of trade. They are located where there is some sort of natural water supply which can meet the needs of a large population. The city of Fez, for example, is built upon a fold of limestone plateau which has an almost limitless supply of water. Owing to a water drop of more than 250 feet in the course of a mile, there is water power here for hydroelectric power plants and mills; the streets are flushed with water and the markets sprinkled. There are public fountains in the streets, and every wealthy householder has a gushing fountain in his garden. Muslims delight in running water, and a courtyard fountain or a country house with a pool and stream is the ambition of every family in the Middle East.

Cities are a maze of narrow streets, cut through by a few wide thoroughfares. House walls are at street level and unbroken on the ground floor except for big doorways wide enough to drive a car through. The ground floor is usually used for cooking and storage; living quarters are on the second floor. In wealthier families the women stay on the upper floors and occupy themselves by watching the world go by from grilled windows overlooking the street.

Mohammedan family life is rigidly secluded. On the rare occasions when visitors are invited to the home, none of the womenfolk appear. Social life for the men centers in the mosques, the markets, the coffee shops, and baths. The only place where the women can gather for gossip are the cemeteries, since a husband cannot refuse to allow his wife to go to mourn her dead relatives. Young women are kept in strict seclusion, but, after middle age, women go about fairly freely, although still veiled. Even in this supposedly male-dominated society the household is frequently run by strong-willed old ladies, as it is in most places.

Islamic markets differ from those in European cities, where the intention is to have a center where goods of all sorts can be found within easy reach. To Muslims, bargaining is more important than saving time or shoe leather. In Islamic cities one finds the street of the leather workers, the street of the brass workers, and so on. The purchaser can go down the line comparing qualities and prices. Bargaining is raised to a fine art here and enjoyed by all concerned. Handicrafts are still dominant throughout these countries, in spite of the fact that more and more machine-made goods are available. In the markets, the local wares are made by people who, like the guildsmen of the Middle Ages, are both manufacturers and sellers. In the little shops the work of the goldsmith and leathermaker is carried on in plain sight. Craftsmen are held in high esteem, and the people have a great respect for and appreciation of technical skill. Each city has a special craft determined by the raw materials available in the region. Many craftsmen occupied in one specialty stimulate one another to greater achievment until this particular craft is raised to a high point of accomplishment, and the city achieves a world-wide reputation as the center for some *de luxe* type of object. Handicrafts flourish both in town and city, but what distinguishes the city is that there are so many workers in each craft that some sort of organization beyond the control of the provost of the market is enecssary. The workers and traders are formed into guilds much like those in Medieval Europe, with a head man in each guild who is responsible to the market provost.

One important effect which the guilds had on the development of economics in these countries is that their organization succeeded in keeping slaves out of the manufacturing industries. In Classical cultures slave labor was employed for cheap mass production, duplicating, to some extent, the effect of the modern machine. But in Islamic countries, slaves were almost never allowed to practice the crafts, even if they had

LUSTRED TILE, 1263, KASHAN

been expert craftsmen before their enslavement. They were used for rough mass labor or for house servants.

Slavery is still practiced in Islam, though it has declined decidedly. However, in the old days an upper-class Islamic family employed many slaves. It was taken for granted that attractive female slaves of suitable age would become the concubines of the owner. In this way they became casually incorporated into the household. If a slave bore a child to her master, both she and the child automatically became free. This custom led to some curious situations in high places. During the Turkish dynasty the succession in the House of Ottoman always went to a sultan's son by a slave concubine. Since the handsomest and brightest young women were selected to serve in the palace, this proved an excellent device for introducing new blood into the royal line. It also meant that there was very little of the blood of Ottoman in the later sultans.

Female slaves in a royal establishment thus could become the mother of a sultan, but male slaves were also in a position to take over more and more power. This was due to the fact that the Islamic peoples had never developed patterns of elective or representative government of any sort. The sultans had absolute control, which could be tempered only by riots and palace revolutions. The sultan who made a decision which was too unpopular with his subjects was apt to be attacked by a city mob, as this was the only way that disapprobation could be expressed. Under this absolute control, the most dangerous threat to the throne was the potential heir. If the prince were given authority, he would probably try to dispose of his father as soon as he had established himself firmly enough in the good graces of the people so that he could look forward to being accepted as successor. Therefore the only men whom the sultan could trust as administrators were newcomers of such low background that they would have no claims on the throne, or, preferably, slaves. A slave in high position who had done away with his master would never be accepted as successor by the populace. Consequently kings surrounded themselves and filled all high administrative offices with slaves, for slaves who had been given positions of responsibility and power had the strongest possible motives for keeping their rulers alive. This system of slave administrators finally passed into a situation in which the slaves became the actual rulers.

In what later became Persia and India, a series of dynasties was founded by slave kings. The Islamic conqueror of northern India, Mohammed of Gazni, was originally a slave. Several of the most successful kings were captives taken from the Turkish tribes in the steppes. These men proved themselves good fighters and able administrators. A slave who showed such qualities would be purchased by another ruler, trained in the duties of his new position, and then passed along. It is recorded that one of these Turks who became a Mohammedan slave-king was purchased by his predecessor for a quarter of a million dollars with the deliberate intention of training him as heir to the throne, in this way insuring an able and well instructed successor.

In other Islamic countries slave corporations were established, of which the Mamelukes of Egypt were the outstanding example. The early Islamic rulers of Egypt brought in Mamelukes, which literally means "white slaves," as mercenaries, since the Egyptians were good craftsmen but poor soldiers. The Mamelukes were, for the most part, Slavs, Circassians, and Greeks. They were organized first as a bodyguard to the Sultan, then as a standing army. They finally had complete military control of Egypt and decided they could dispense with the sultan, which they did. They ruled Egypt for several hundred years as a corporation, purchasing more slaves to keep up their military forces. They were organized in a military hierarchy with what would correspond to captains, colonels, and generals up to a commander-in-chief, who was actually the ruler of Egypt.

The Janissaries, the slave soldiers of the Turkish Empire, provide another example of this type of slave organization. They were recruited by the Turks through a regular levy on their Christian subjects. Promising boys between eight and ten years of age were sold into slavery by their parents. This was done without too much reluctance, for these boys were trained not only as soldiers but as administrators, and in time came to hold the real power in Turkey, making and unmaking sultans as they wished. The Turks owed much of their success in conquest during the 15th and 16th centuries to the Janissaries, who were the best infantry regiments in the world at this time.

The Mohammedan house of worship is the *mosque.* At certain intervals, seven times during a twenty-four-hour period, the *muezzin* climbs to one of the towers, called minarets, and chants a call to prayer. Bells and music are forbidden in the mosques for in Mohammed's time these were part of the Christian religion. Images of any sort are not permitted, for these recall the old pagan religion which Mohammed drove out of Mecca. The only furniture in the mosque is the pulpit. Sometimes the floors are carpeted, but usually the worshipers bring their own prayer rugs with them. The aesthetic interests of Islam find expression in the wall decorations of the mosque, which are usually complicated arrangements of colored tiles. A whole series of decorative scripts have been perfected, which serve artistic as well as semantic purposes.

There is usually a courtyard in the mosque with a colonnade where men can talk and rest after prayers, and a tree or two for shade. A fountain for ritual cleanliness is prescribed. No business is conducted in the mosque, but it is a pleasant gathering place.

In addition to attending the services in the mosque, every loyal Muslim must make the pilgrimage to Mecca at least once during his lifetime. When this regulation was passed by Mohammed, the area of Islam was small and the edict was presumably made to encourage the Meccan pilgrim trade which had proved so profitable in the past. Since Islam has expanded to all parts of the world, many sects have established shrines for local Islamic saints. In North Africa, for example, seven pilgrimages to a local shrine may be equated with one pilgrimage to Mecca. The rituals performed by the pilgrims at Mecca are too complicated to be described fully here. However, the most important ritual is that of running around the Kaaba, the small building in which 360 idols destroyed by Mohammed were once stored, and in kissing the Black Stone of the Kaaba, a meteorite which was an ancient sacred object of the Arabs and has now been set in the wall of the Kaaba at a suitable height from the ground.

Although the intellectual life of Islam is at present perhaps old-fashioned, Mohammedanism is still a strong and alive religion which is a force in the lives of its followers. In Islamic countries the mosque services and the reading of the Koran are always in Arabic. This means that all educated people in the widespread Islamic countries have a common language, much as all educated people in the Middle Ages in Europe understood Latin, which was the language of the Church. Thus, behind all the political divisions of Islam there is a solid core of common learning and common understanding. Islam rises superior to international political lines, an important point to consider when attempting to predict the reactions of the Islamic world in any world crisis.

Common language, learning, + understanding

PART EIGHT

Africa

Chapter XXVIII

Prehistory

STUDENTS of cultural history find the Dark Continent well named. Although it was certainly one of the first, if not the first, continent to be occupied by man, its past is shrouded in obscurity. Outside the narrow limits of Egypt, Abyssinia, and the northern littoral, there are no written records earlier than those of the medieval Arab travelers. The great Negro kingdoms which are ranged across the continent south of the Sahara have oral traditions which carry the record two or three centuries farther back, and their king-lists and tales of migration and conquest certainly contain much truth. However, as history, they are subject to the limitations imposed upon all records which are handed down by word of mouth. For the regions still further south even these aids are lacking, and tradition becomes folklore.

Remains of human occupation are to be found everywhere in Africa, yet vast areas are still, for all practical purposes, archeological *terra incognita*. Surface finds of Old Paleolithic implements have been made in all parts of the continent where some missionary or government official has troubled to look for them. In many areas they are so numerous as to suggest either a relatively dense population or a very long occupation. The latter seems more probable.

The dating of the early African remains presents serious problems. The tremendous climatic cycles which produced the European glacials and interglacials produced little more than fluctuations in rainfall in Africa. Changes in animal life were so gradual that fossils are of little aid in dating finds, and the evolution of culture, and very probably of man himself, followed a slow and placid course all through the Pleistocene. This was in marked contrast with conditions in Europe, where, during the successive ice advances, man could retain only a precarious foothold along the southernmost margins of the continent. During these catastrophic periods, Africa, like the Church in Toynbee's formulations, became a refuge for the cultural gains which had been made before, and it was from Africa that man re-emerged to occupy western Eurasia whenever the weather there warmed up sufficiently. Since the African climatic conditions were fairly constant and the occupation continuous, the African Lower Paleolithic record lacks the abrupt changes which distinguish the various Lower Paleolithic periods in the European sequence. The earliest African cultural remains so far found come from Northeast Africa and show a crude flake and chopper culture vaguely reminiscent of Southeast Asia. Following this, for many millennia, Africa, from the Mediterranean to the Cape, was occupied by hand-axe cultures. In these the tool forms gradually evolved through the types shown in the successive European hand-axe cultures.

We have lamentably little information on Africa's Lower Paleolithic population. Recent South African finds suggest that man may actually have originated on the continent. Certainly the erect terrestrial anthropoids of the Australopithicine group came closer to being "missing links" than any other fossils which have been found to date. The curious Rhodesian skull and a recently reported find of what may be a Neanderthal from the Belgian Congo indicate the presence of later, but still pre-Sapiens, populations, but the evidence is still far too fragmentary for definite conclusions.

After the Lower-Paleolithic period it becomes even more difficult to apply the conventional European archeological sequences to Africa. Although there are implements from several parts of Africa which resemble the European Flake cultures once called Mousterian, their antecedents and position in the African series are too uncertain for us to say whether or not there is any real relationship. On the evidence now available it seems more probable that these industries were developed in Africa as a result of contact between surviving hand-axe users and invaders who brought an Upper Paleolithic blade-industry with them.

The earliest African blade-industries resemble those of Europe and the Near East in so many respects that there can be little doubt that they were introduced into Africa in developed form. However, they underwent numerous local modifications there and passed, by a gradual metamorphosis, stimulated perhaps by later Asiatic increments, into industries of Mesolithic type. Such industries have been reported from all parts of the continent for which we have adequate archeological data, and they were certainly very widespread. They were also of relatively long duration throughout most of the continent. The Bushmen of far South Africa were still producing Mesolithic implements at the time Europeans arrived. Whether the Pygmies of the western jungles ever did so is an open question. Archeological evidence is lacking, and their modern technology provides no clues. Due to their long dependence upon their larger neighbors and the iron implements thus made available, they have completely lost any stone-working skills they ever possessed.

The skeletal material coming from Upper Paleolithic and Mesolithic sites is of special interest because of the light it throws on African racial history. Although the remains are not numerous, they indicate two things: that a number of different human breeds and types were present on the continent at this time, and that Negroid physical characteristics were less pronounced and less widely distributed at this period than they became later. The North African population associated with Upper Paleolithic industries was predominantly Caucasic and showed many of the characteristics of the modern inhabitants of the same region. Scattered finds made in the African plateau from the eastern Sudan to South Africa indicate that the Bushman-Hottentot type once extended much farther north than it has in the historic period, while Caucasic elements extended farther south. Lacking any clues as to pigmentation, hair form, and so forth, some of the East African remains would probably be classed as Caucasic if found anywhere else.

Conditions in humid West Africa are most unfavorable for the preservation of skeletal material, and we have almost no data from this region, but by a process of elimination one must conclude that the center for the development of the aggregate of physical characteristics which we ascribe to the Negroid stock lay here. One must also conclude that these characteristics have been progressively spreading from West Africa. One may even hazard a guess that this spread has been related to the relatively high tolerance for malignant malaria characteristic of West African Negroes. Even today most members of this group are malaria carriers, and, whenever they have come into a region where there was a vector (anopheles), they have introduced the disease, with catastrophic results for the local populations. The resulting vacuum has been filled by an increase of the Negroes and less susceptible mixed bloods.

The African Neolithic cultures present a series of problems which can only be solved by much more excavation and particularly by systematic research in two key regions: Abyssinia and the Sudan. Both of these are still almost unknown archeologically. That the African Neolithic cultures stem from the Southwestern Asiatic center previously described (see Chap. XVI) can hardly be doubted. Their technologies are basically similar, and everywhere north of the Sahara the African Neolithic economy seems to have been based on Southwestern Asiatic plants and animals. Although there may have been some mixture between these imports and closly related native species, there is no good evidence that any economically important animal was domesticated on the African continent. It has been suggested as an origin point for the donkey and for one sort of sheep, but this has not been proven. The Egyptians did domesticate the cat, but this animal has contributed more to man's psychological than to his physical satisfactions.

We have no direct evidence as to the crops grown by Neolithic societies south of the Sahara, but we do know that very few of the Southwest Asiatic grains could have been raised there. Most of the crops grown in West Africa and the Sudan today are of either American or Southeast Asiatic origin. The remainder seem to have been domesticated for the most part in Abyssinia. If the Russian botanical reports are to be believed, a surprising number of species were brought under cultivation there. Those, which seem most likely to have been grown south of the Sahara in Neolithic times, are various sorts of millet (sorghum, eleusine, and pennisetum) and ground nuts (voandzeia). If these really were domesticated in Abyssinia, one more problem is added to the already complicated question of African Neolithic origins and movements.

The main migration route of Neolithic settlers coming into Africa seems to have been by way of the Sinai Peninsula and across the Red Sea. It is a curious fact that, in spite of the close contact between Abyssinia and Arabia all through historic times and the frequent and fairly large-scale movements of population back and forth which have occurred during the past two thousand years, Neolithic culture is poorly represented, if present at all, in the Horn region of Africa. Although very little archeological work has been done in this region, one would expect Neolithic tools to turn up in the hands of modern natives if such tools were present. The ubiquitous stone celt (hand-axe) is regarded everywhere in the Old World as a magical object, associated with lightning, and is treasured accordingly. Since none have been reported from this region, they must be exceedingly rare if present.

The best explanation for the absence of Neolithic remains in East Africa would seem to be that, at the time of the Neolithic migrations from Asia, much of the African coast of the Red Sea was already too dry to support the mixed agricultural and domestic animal economy of the ancient Southwest Asiatic villagers, while the pastoral adaptation which later made possible the occupation of this region had not yet been developed. Some of the early Egyptian Neolithic cultures are believed to have come into Upper Egypt from the Red Sea coast, but if so they have left no known settlements to mark their migration route. Climatic conditions may also explain the rarity of Neolithic sites in much of the Sahara, which had been progressively drying up since the close of the glacial period. When the techniques necessary for a pastoral economy had been developed, there were numerous migrations from Arabia into the Horn of Africa. These apparently went on all through the later prehistoric period, which in this region extended until after the beginning of the Christian era. Still later, the development of Islam was responsible for an extensive movement which carried Arabian pastoral tribes over much of semi-arid North Africa.

In this connection it should be noted that the horse and camel were both comparatively late arrivals in Africa. The first appearance of horses anywhere on the continent seems to have been with the Hyksos invasion of Egypt in about 1500 B.C. The Egyptians took over the animal from their temporary conquerors, but used it only for fighting. Horses were driven in light one-man chariots. The driver's main weapon was the bow, and in action he freed his hands by fastening the reins around his waist. Egyptian ingenuity and interest in fine craftsmanship made the Egyptian chariots the lightest and strongest in the ancient world. At the same time, Egyptian conservatism was such that, once the technical problems had been solved, chariots of the same type continued in use for many centuries. The Egyptians never developed native cavalry, and used their chariots for skirmishing and in pursuit of routed foes, rather than against battle lines for shock effect.

We have very little information on the diffusion of the horse from Egypt westward. We know that by Roman-Carthaginian times it was in common use throughout North Africa as a fighting animal. Numidian cavalry was one of the most effective parts of Hannibal's army, and for centuries thereafter it served with the Roman forces. There are suggestions of the existence, in the drier parts of North Africa in Classical times, of a pastoral economy centered on horses as the later Sahara cultures were on camels. A careful study of Greek and Roman sources would probably reveal many details of this culture which cannot be gleaned from the scanty archeological record. Horses were eventually diffused over the whole of the Sahara, and their importance in the Sudan in historic times was much greater than is usually realized. The great kingdoms which developed in the eastern and central Sudan were dominated by a mounted aristocracy, and mailed cavalry formed the nucleus of their armies.

The camel was not used in Egypt until the Ptolemaic period, although its existence seems to have been known long before that. There is at least one unmistakable carving of a camel which goes back to early dynastic times. It was probably first imported from Arabia into the Horn of Africa and adopted by the Hamito-Semitic tribes of that region. From there it seems to have spread rapidly throughout much of the Sahara. It opened up additional areas to occupation, since after the brief rainy season camels can live upon the fresh herbage without water. It also made possible the maintenance and extension of trans-Saharan caravan routes whose existence the progressive desiccation of the area at this time was rendering precarious.

In the light of our present very scanty information, it seems that stone industries of Neolithic type survived throughout East Africa and the entire plateau from the Sudan to the Cape until they were replaced by metal, and that this replacement occurred in comparatively recent times. There was no Bronze Age in Africa, a fact often attributed to an early and independent discovery of iron. It now seems more probable that stone tools continued in use in Africa until after iron had replaced bronze in the adjoining parts of Eurasia. Techniques and tool and weapon forms strongly suggest that Negro Africa derived its iron-working from India or Indonesia rather than Europe or the Near East.

Remains of Neolithic cultures of regular Southwestern Asiatic pattern are found in Egypt and along the Mediterranean littoral. They reached their climax in Egypt and in far western North Africa, which formed part of a distinct Hispano-Mauritanian Neolithic center with a heavy population and advanced culture (see p. 243). There are no indications that the Egyptian Neolithic cultures penetrated to the Eastern Sudan. Throughout the entire stretch between Egypt and Morocco, Neolithic sites become less frequent as one goes southward from the Mediterranean Coast, and it seems certain that much of the Sahara was not occupied during this cultural stage. However, Neolithic sites increase in numbers when one reaches the western Sudan. In this region, fine chipped-stone implements, celts, and hand-molded pottery are fairly plentiful, but because of an almost complete lack of systematic archeological work it is impossible to say what connection there is between these cultures, the Hispano-Mauretanian center to the north, and the later Negro civilizations of West Africa.

Scanty as the records of African Stone Age culture are, those of the next period are even scantier. Between the end of the Neolithic and the records left by Medieval Arab visitors, the cultural history of West Africa is a complete blank. We may be sure that there were occasional contacts with the Mediterranean littoral by way of the Sahara caravan routes. Phoenician traders also may have reached the West African coast, but the only evidence for this consists of a few possible Phoenician elements in the art of the region, and certain ancient beads treasured by the present natives.

In the East African Horn region the Abyssinian civilization had come into existence by the beginning of the Christian era. It seems to have been strongly influenced by the marginal Greco-Roman civilization which developed in Nubia during Ptolemaic and Roman times, and may also have received some increments from India. The *Periplus of the Erythraean Sea* mentions a settlement of Indian merchants in Somaliland in the first century A.D. The Abyssinians were converted to Christianity in the 3rd century A.D. and thus came under Byzantine influence, still manifest in their art and church rituals. While there is an extensive

Abyssinian literature, very little of this has been made available to Western scholars, and one may doubt how much light it will throw on the development of Abyssinian civilization even when it has been translated.

Somaliland was visited by at least one Egyptian expedition, that sent out by Queen Hatshepsut in about 1500 B.C., but we do not know how long the contact was continued. The Ptolemaic Greeks have left us a brief account of the East African ports in the just-mentioned Periplus. However, the earliest materials of value for cultural study are the narratives left us by Arab and Portuguese travelers from the 13th century on. These indicate conditions much like those which existed in the same region up until roughly 1900 A.D.

Lastly, as one of the earliest and most distinctive of the world's civilizations, Egypt stands apart from the general course of African culture and deserves separate treatment.

Chapter XXIX

Egypt

EGYPTIAN HISTORY and culture have been subjected to highly specialized research for over a century. A number of excellent books dealing with them are available in most libraries, and this discussion will be largely limited to those aspects of Egyptian civilization which have had significance for cultural developments in the world outside Egypt.

Egypt's Asiatic neighbors and even the Greeks borrowed from her unashamedly, but they took mainly what they could see without having to understand. Although Egyptian culture had its foundations in the same Southwestern Asiatic Neolithic which fathered the civilizations of Eurasia, it developed into something profoundly alien. A modern student feels this, and the classical writers, who were able to observe Egyptians in their daily life, had the same reaction. Herodotus wrote that the Egyptians were the strangest of human beings and did everything by opposites. They even retired indoors to perform their excretory functions instead of using the street like civilized people, i.e., the Greeks.

Why there should have been such divergence is an interesting problem in itself. The developing Egyptian population and civilization undoubtedly absorbed many elements from the pre-Neolithic inhabitants of the region, but this in itself can hardly account for most of the peculiarities. Some of these were certainly a result of the local geographic conditions. The land of Egypt was nothing more nor less than the valley of the Nile, an elongated oasis extending for 675 miles from the First Cataract to the sea, and as far east and west as the Nile's water spread in flood. Outside this everything was desolation, the realm of Set, the enemy of the life-giving god Osiris. For the first 500 miles the valley was a canyon, never more than twelve miles wide; for the last 175 miles, a spreading fan of swamps through which the river wandered sluggishly in many branches. The Nile, unlike nearly all other rivers of historic significance, flows from south to north, and Upper Egypt lies south of Lower Egypt.

The flood water evaporated rapidly, and although early Egyptian records mention occasional rains in regions where no rains fall today, agriculture could not be carried on without irrigation. Governments capable of organizing the mass labor necessary for the digging of canals and building dams, and with power to settle the inevitable disputes over water rights, came into existence long before the dawn of history. It seems probable that these took shape first in the delta region, where drainage as well as irrigation was required, but the interdependence of the various provinces, all of which drew their water from the same river, must have provided a strong incentive for unification into larger and larger states.

Egypt is the ideal territory for the historic archeologist. There are endless inscriptions and even numerous manuscripts. The dry climate has preserved delicate and perishable materials intact, and the Egyptian's unquestioning belief in a future life much like the present, and his attempts to equip the dead for it, have resulted in the preservation of an almost complete inventory of objects of daily use. Unfortunately, the situation for the prehistoric archeologist is much less satisfactory. The annual deposition of Nile mud has resulted in the gradual building up of the valley so that Upper Paleolithic and even Neolithic settlements on the valley floor are now buried under many feet of accumulated silt. Most of our information on the prehistoric periods comes from sites around the edges of the valley, and especially from the cemeteries, where the dead were buried beyond the borders of the arable land and out of reach of the Nile floods.

Although the earliest record is gradually coming to light, there are still many points that remain unsettled. In the previous chapter African prehistory was discussed in terms of the entire continent. In Egypt the hand-axe culture was followed by a flake culture, the *Aterian*, reminiscent in certain ways of the Middle Paleolithic of Europe. This in turn gave place to the *Sebilian*, a Microlithic culture much like those which survived until comparatively recent times throughout the African plateau.

In about 6000 B.C. Asiatic migrants brought in domestic plants and animals and Neolithic technology. In the delta, the *Merimdeans* cultivated wheat and barley and kept cattle, sheep, and goats. They reaped their grain with wooden sickles edged with inset flakes of flint and stored it in mat silos. They were a sedentary people, living in stockaded villages of oval wooden-framed huts. They had pottery of two types, simple undecorated cooking pots and a fine red and black ware. They were excellent stone workers. Their products included slate palettes, upon which paint for body decoration was ground and mixed, polished stone axes, and extraordinarily well-made knives and projectile points of chipped flint. They also made fishhooks and piercers of bone. About 4500 B.C. they began to use some copper.

In Upper Egypt a different and less advanced type of Neolithic culture (*Tasian*) appeared slightly later. These Tasians seem to have been semi-nomadic, or at least they lived in open camps and had shelters so flimsy that they have left few traces. Aside from this, their technology was much like that of the Merimdeans. The most important difference was in their pottery, which consisted of black tulip vases encrusted with white patterns. While the ancestors of both these groups unquestionably came from Southwest Asia, those of the Merimdeans probably crossed at the Isthmus of Sinai, while the Tasians' ancestors seem to have reached Upper Egypt from the direction of the Red Sea, coming overland rather than up the Nile.

Lower Egypt was united under a single ruler by 4500 B.C. and conquered Upper Egypt about 250 years later. The date can be set with considerable accuracy on the basis of the Egyptian calendar, which had as one of its units the Sothic cycle of 1460 years. The first of these cycles, based on observations made at Memphis and Heliopolis on the borders of Upper Egypt, began at this time. The northern conquest was short-lived, and by 4000 B.C. the two regions were once more independent. From this time until the beginning of the Dynastic period, 3300 B.C., little is known of Lower Egyptian culture. However, a rich culture, the *Badarian,* was flourishing in Upper Egypt. This is the best known of all the predynastic cultures. It was vigorous and dynamic and seems to have been stimulated by repeated Asiatic contacts. One of its phases, the *Gerzean,* apparently coincided with an actual invasion of Asiatics which introduced a round-headed element into the previously long-headed population. The invaders seem to have come overland from the Red Sea rather than up the Nile.

It was during this 700 years of independence that the foundations of the later Egyptian civilization were laid. The people still lived in oval huts like the Merimdean ones and had not discovered how to build in permanent materials, but they had learned how to weave linen, how to smelt and cast copper, and how to make blue-green faience and enamels of pounded rock crystal. These techniques were the precursors of glass-making, a later Egyptian invention. They made a red pottery with black edges, the two colors being produced by differential firing. Work in bone and ivory was highly developed, and graves frequently contained small figurines of nude women carved from these materials. The slate palettes of the earlier period became increasingly elaborate and showed

PRIEST. CARVED WOODEN PANEL, THIRD DYNASTY

in their decoration the unmistakable beginnings of the later Egyptian artistic conventions. The dead were carried beyond the area reached by the Nile floods and buried in oval pits with elaborate grave furniture. The bodies were laid on their sides in a flexed position and covered with mats. The warm and completely dry sand, which soon packed itself about the body, mummified it more successfully than any of the later and more elaborate processes, and there can be little doubt that it was from this that the later Egyptians got their ideas of body preservation.

By 3300 B.C. each of the two Egypts had its king and court, its royal symbols, and its national gods. Upper Egypt had the white crown, was under the guardianship of the vulture goddess, *Nekhebet,* and had as its emblem the sedge. Lower Egypt had the red crown, was under the protection of the cobra goddess, *Buto,* and had as its emblem the bee. The differences between north and south survived throughout the whole period of Egyptian history and went deeper than mere political organization. One can see certain parallels in the case of the Scots and the English. The up-river Egyptians were hardy, quarrelsome, suspicious of refinements, forthright and, from the Egyptian point of view, puritanical. The delta Egyptians were gay, clever, pleasure-loving, and eager for novelties, but preferred battles of wits to those of arms. They regarded the Upper Egyptians as barbarians and poked fun at their harsh dialect and crude ways.

Even when the two kingdoms were united under Menes, the Upper Egyptian conqueror, he found it politic not to try to consolidate their governments completely. Instead he ruled as king of Lower Egypt and again as king of Upper Egypt, much as in Europe the same individual was emperor of Austria and king of Hungary. Pharaoh had a palace and an independent bureaucracy in Lower and in Upper Egypt, and functioned sometimes as king of one and sometimes as king of the other, his status at the moment being shown by his wearing of either the red or the white crown.

The period immediately following the unification of the two Egypts was one of tremendously rapid cultural advance. From 3300 to 2563 B.C. Egypt was the scene of one of those culture mutations whose causes are one of the main problems still to be solved by the investigators of culture dynamics. During the first 500 years of this period Egyptian technology achieved its final form in everything but architecture. Specialized craftsmen supported by the ruling group were producing vases carved from the hardest decorative stone, a wealth of beautifully wrought copper vessels, and ornaments of gold, lapis lazuli, and turquoise. More practically, the beginning of the dynastic era saw the introduction of the plow. We do not know whether this was a local invention or an Asiatic borrowing, but in any case it lightened the labor of agriculture consider-

ably and released for use on national projects manpower which had
hitherto been tied to the fields. Hieroglyphic writing was perfected (see
Chap. IX, p. 112) and so firmly integrated into religious and governmental practice that it underwent no significant changes after this time.
There seems to have been an outburst of all sorts of intellectual activity.
The first scientifically conceived treatises on the diagnosis and treatment
of disease and injuries date from this time. Religion was organized and
the elaborate rituals of temple and court were crystallized. Lastly, the
ruling group developed one of the most thoroughly organized and politically centralized systems of government the world has seen.

Toward the close of this period the great pyramids of Giza were
built. How extraordinary these structures were can be appreciated if one
realizes that the first, largest, and best constructed was erected less than
two hundred years after the Egyptians first essayed to use stone in any
sort of construction. The pyramids were built with the simplest appliances: ramps, rollers, and levers. Even the pulley was unknown. They
represent a triumph of sheer manpower and persistence. To organize
and supply the tremendous labor force which worked on them year after
year was an administrative accomplishment of the first magnitude. It has
been said that the common Egyptians were enthusiastic about the work,
since they believed that they were building the dwelling of a god on
whom the future well-being of the nation would depend. Nevertheless,
they had little choice in the matter. The Egyptian peasants of this period
were serfs attached to the land and organized in army-like units under
overseers whose positions were like those of non-commissioned officers.
They were subject to draft for public work, quarry labor, and military
campaigns, and apparently regarded all three of these occupations as
very much on a par.

The last two dynasties of the Old Kingdom period became obsessed
with the desire to conquer Nubia and waged constant war with the Negroes there. This, and the unproductive labor expended in pyramid and
temple building, finally overtaxed the patience of the peasants and exhausted the land's resources. The Old Kingdom period ended, about
2300 B.C., in political breakdown and confusion. When effective central
government once more emerged in 2065 B.C., the common people had
won their freedom from serfdom, and, although they were still subject
to royal tax collectors, and more often than not tenants upon the royal or
temple lands, they possessed and thereafter retained much greater freedom. Above all, it was possible for individuals to rise in the world. Many
a high official boasted in his funeral inscriptions that he was a self-made
man, son of a middle-class or even peasant family. Advancement depended upon a combination of abilities. The ambitious official had to be
able not only to perform his office successfully but also to ingratiate him-

self with superiors. All wealth and honors were distributed downward and were the outpourings of Pharaoh's splendor.

Egypt's most significant contributions to the growth of world civilization were in the two fields of technology and religion. Its governmental forms were too rigid and too permeated with theocratic patterns to be acceptable outside the Nile Valley. A peasantry which is accustomed to defending itself against outside attacks cannot be expected to grovel before innumerable priests and officials. The relative safety of Egypt, fortified by its deserts, made possible a degree of absolutism which could not be enforced elsewhere.

The Egyptians were by far the cleverest craftsmen of the pre-classical world. By 1500 B.C. they had learned to mix their copper with tin to produce bronze. The introduction of bellows at about the same time facilitated the work of smelting. They were familiar with most of the ordinary metals used today. Iron was rare before about 1000 B.C., and even then was mainly obtained in trade. The Egyptian hieroglyph for it, meaning star metal, shows that they realized the meteoric origin for their early supplies. Gold was more plentiful in Egypt than in any other ancient civilization. It was pounded out of veins of gold-bearing quartz which threaded the local granite and was also sent from Nubia as tribute. A natural alloy of gold and silver, electrum, was much prized, while silver itself was exceedingly rare, so much so that its value exceeded that of gold. The work of the Egyptian jewelers can hardly be bettered today. They were familiar with all the modern techniques of gold working with the exception of electroplating. Their enamel work was superb. They had discovered how to make colored glass in many different shades, but used it mainly for beads and inlays. The techniques of glass blowing seem to have been developed outside Egypt, probably in Syria.

Wood had been rare in the Nile Valley since ancient times, and even in the Old Kingdom it was being imported from Syria and the Lebanon. The scarcity of the material and the need for utilizing even scraps led to a surprising development of joinery and cabinetwork. All the various joints used by modern cabinetmakers were known, and the Egyptians also were experts at marquetry work and veneer. They were the first to realize the aesthetic possibilities of ebony and to utilize this hard and brittle wood; they also developed the art of ivory and pearl inlay to a high point. They were the first people to bark-tan leather, inventing the techniques still in use throughout most of the world. They also seem to have been the first to tool their leather with designs, and the modern saddlers' knife is still made on an Egyptian model. In textiles they wove linen cloth as fine as any which can be produced by modern looms. Wool was known and used sparingly, but its non-Egyptian

PHARAOH MYCERINUS WITH GODDESS HATHOR AND GODDESS OF THE
JACKAL NOME

origin was attested by the prohibition against bringing it into temples. Cotton and silk were unknown.

One other aspect of Egyptian technology deserves mention. The Egyptians were as much devoted to artificial beauty aids as modern Americans, and physicians regarded the provision of these as a legitimate part of their activities. Medical papyri include recipes for removing wrinkles and darkening gray hair. Kohl was used for lengthening the eyebrows and lining the outer corners of the eyes. Eye shadow was of two sorts: green, made from malachite, and gray, made from lead ore (galena). Red ocher was used for rouge, but heavy rouging was not fashionable. The nails, the palms of the hands, and the soles of the feet were dyed with henna. Wigs made of human hair over which melted beeswax had been poured were worn by both sexes, and members of the upper classes kept a number of wigs suitable for different occasions. Women wore the wig over their natural hair, but men shaved both hair and beard. Both sexes removed all body hair. Ladies who wished to be in the height of fashion gilded their breasts and painted their nipples blue. The Egyptians were apparently the originators of the process of making oil perfumes, still practiced in the Middle East, and both sexes kept their skins soft by oil rubs. At banquets it was customary for the host to place upon each guest's head a cone of scented unguent which, in the heat of the banquet hall, gradually melted and ran down over the guest's face and body. Both sexes wore many ornaments, the most important being heavy collars made from rows of beads of different colors, and huge earrings.

The Egyptian artificers expended their best skill on luxury objects, and the great demand for these, created by the custom of burying them with the dead, had a curious by-product. The tombs of the Pharaohs and their nobles were filled with treasures of gold and precious stones, and, although tomb robbers returned much of this to circulation, the supply could not keep up with the demand. The dead are not hard to deceive, and the Egyptian craftsmen soon began to produce imitation gold work in which the metal was simulated either by gilding or by surface finishes which made base metal look like gold. It was in these efforts to imitate precious materials and to find substitutes for them that the science of alchemy, ancestor of our own chemistry, originated. The earliest alchemic texts, which come from Ptolemaic Egypt but probably embody much older material, are, with few exceptions, recipes for making alloys or giving surface finishes which will look like gold. It is significant that the same texts include recipes for making a dye which would imitate the costly Tyrian purple. Alchemy thus began in a search for cheap substitutes, and became confused and transformed into a mystic search for the philosopher's stone only after the Neo-Platonic philosophers had captured it from the craftsmen.

To the modern Westerner, reared in the tradition of Greek logic and of constant sequences of cause and effect, Egyptian religion appears quite incomprehensible. According to his personal predilections, he will interpret its recorded content either as childish nonsense or as hints of an esoteric knowledge revealed only to initiates. As a matter of fact, it was neither. A wise Eskimo medicine man once summed up his people's relation to the supernatural by saying, "We do not believe, we fear." The Egyptian might have summed up his with, "We do not believe, we manipulate." The names of at least 2000 Egyptian gods are known to us, yet there were none of these whom their worshippers regarded with real affection or before whom they felt genuinely powerless. Every deity could be circumvented and controlled if one could only learn the words of power. The Egyptian deities could not be categorized as good or bad. Even Set, slayer of his brother Osiris and lord of the desert, was by no means the equivalent of a Christian devil. He was the ancient patron of *nomes* (provinces) in both Upper and Lower Egypt, and as such was assured of worship by their inhabitants. He also held an honored place among the warriors of Ra, the Sun God, and was himself worshipped as a war god. The aid of deities could be invoked quite as well for unethical as ethical purposes, and the elaborate rituals which were performed in the temples were as much incantations as acts of worship. The Egyptian was interested in the methods by which his deities could be controlled and their powers used for his own benefit or for that of the community. He was essentially uninterested in problems of deities' origins or their exact nature. For this reason he never developed a coherent theology, and even the Egyptian mythology was totally illogical and inconsistent. It would seem that the Egyptians actually preferred a half-dozen myths explaining the same phenomenon to a single myth.

While this lack of logical consistency reflected a pattern of thinking, historic factors also contributed. In the whole of Egypt there were 42 nomes which had originally been politically independent groups and which always retained minor cultural differences. In the beginning, each nome had had its own pantheon of deities, one or more of whom served as the nome's special guardian and received the bulk of its worship. Even after the political consolidation of Egypt, these nome gods retained the special devotion of nome members. The various pantheons were all modeled upon much the same lines, with series of deities who performed similar functions. This made easy the process of *theocrasia*, i.e., fusion of several deities into one. However, in this process the Egyptians were unwilling to surrender any of the stories which had adhered to the various local gods. As a result, a dozen different and frequently conflicting stories might be told about the same Being. In the same way, items of local ritual would continue to be practiced locally. All this led to endless contradictions and inconsistencies.

The importance of deities rose and fell with that of their cities or districts. However, there were certain centers whose gods retained their influence throughout Egyptian history. Thus the oldest of the great principal gods was *Ra, Atum,* or *Ra-Atum,* god of Heliopolis. He was a sun god, a world creator always depicted in human form. Below him in the doctrine of Heliopolis were a series of eight other gods, including *Osiris* and *Isis.* Their son, *Horus,* headed another ninefold group of deities, but in good Egyptian fashion he was specifically identified with Ra-Atum under the name of *Harakhte* and was known as the son of Ra. More concretely, Horus was personified as the rising sun, Ra as the midday sun, and Atum as the setting sun, represented as a tired old man.

At Hermopolis the principal deity was *Thoth,* pictured as a man with the head of an ibis. He controlled the seasons, the moon and the stars, and had invented hieroglyphic writing, mathematics, the keeping of accounts, languages, magic, law, and even the game of chess. He was also prime minister and scribe of the gods. Like Ra-Atum, he had created the world, but by a different method. He and his associated deities were central to the doctrine of Hermopolis.

During the early period both these doctrines found themselves in competition with a third, the doctrine of Memphis, which had as its principal figure *Ptah,* the god of that city. According to this doctrine, Ptah was more ancient than Atum himself, and had created Ra-Atum by means of a profound effort of the mind. All gods and men were projections of his intellect. The falcon god, Horus, was his heart, and Thoth, the god of wisdom, his tongue. He was the special patron of artists, artificers, and men of letters, but the doctrine in which his worship was embodied was too abstract to win general support from the concrete-minded Egyptians.

In the contest between these doctrines that of Heliopolis was finally victorious, largely because it could be adapted most readily to the doctrine of Pharaonic divinity, in which the dead Pharaohs were equated with Osiris and the living one with Horus. The last of the great national gods was Amon-Ra, the god of Thebes. Originally an insignificant god of the Scepter nome and not even its principal guardian, he rose to power under the Theban Pharaohs, and, after these had gained control of Egypt, his cult grew steadily until his high priests became the real rulers of the nation. It was against his priesthood that Akhenaton, the Heretic King, waged and lost his battle for religious reform.

The doctrine of Osiris differed in several respects from the other

great doctrines. His legend falls into two parts which seem only incidentally related. In the first, he ruled in Egypt together with his queen-sister
Isis. His brother Set desired her and, by a trick, murdered Osiris and set
the body afloat in a chest which drifted to Byblus in Syria. Isis followed
and brought it back to Egypt, where the god *Anubis* mummified it under her direction. The soul of Osiris then descended to the underworld,
where he became ruler of the dead. Isis took the mummy to a hiding
place in the marshes of Lower Egypt, where she contrived to get herself
impregnated by it. (The inconsistency might be resolved by the *Ka* belief [see p. 413], but the Egyptians themselves probably were not troubled by it.) In due course of time she gave birth to a son, Horus. Set also
had been searching for his brother's body. He discovered it in Isis' absence, carried it off, dismembered it, and scattered the pieces throughout the length of Egypt. Isis sought them out and reassembled them.
When Horus grew to manhood he set out to avenge his father's murder
on Set. An epic but inconclusive battle ensued. In the end the quarrel
was submitted to the arbitration of the earth god, *Geb,* who first
awarded Lower Egypt to Horus and Upper Egypt to Set but later
placed both kingdoms beneath the sway of Horus.

In the first half of this legend Osiris appears as a typical Near Eastern vegetation god. Many of the incidents resemble those told of *Adonis*
of Byblus and *Tammuz* of Mesopotamia. Like them, Osiris was killed,
dismembered, buried and resurrected, a cycle annually reenacted in the
reaping and threshing of the grain, and the planting and growth of the
new crop.

The second part of the legend is an allegory of Egyptian history
providing divine sanction for the rule of Pharaoh. Isis was the ideal
queen-sister and loyal wife, and Horus the perfect son who defended his
father and avenged his death upon his murderers. The initial division of
Egypt between Horus and Set is a folk memory of the actual division
of Egypt in prehistoric times, while the final assignment of the whole of
Egypt to Horus commemorated the first unification of Egypt, which took
place under Lower Egyptian rule.

Osiris, as benevolent Pharaoh and a ruler in the land of the dead
who was willing to share his immortality with all his subjects, became
the most popular deity in Egypt. Where the gods of the other doctrines
were worshipped mainly by the upper classes, the Osirian trinity was
worshipped by all classes, from Pharaoh to the peasants. At his great
shrine at Abydos, the incidents of his life, death, and resurrection were
reenacted in a sort of passion play which continued for many days. The
important roles were assigned by the king to high officers of state, the
part of Horus, the ideal son, being regarded as a special honor. The local
population and the thousands of pilgrims who came to the celebration

joined in the proceedings as extras. The ceremony culminated in an epic battle between forces representing the armies of Horus and those of Set, Osiris' murderer, during which no one was killed but many eyes were blacked and heads were broken.

Last but by no means least among the Egyptian deities was Pharaoh himself. At his coronation Pharaoh *became* the god Horus and at his death was transformed into Osiris. His spiritual potency, on which the well-being of the land depended, was increased by the purity of his royal blood, and for this reason the Pharaoh was married in childhood to the most suitable of his small sisters or half-sisters. When he became a man he was permitted to take as many additional wives and mistresses as he desired, but it was desirable for his heir to possess the strongest possible strain of royal blood. To insure this, Pharaohs not infrequently married their own daughters.

Pharaoh's palace was constructed in the form of a temple and was actually regarded as such. He himself was both a high priest and an embodiment of the god. The daily liturgy which he performed rendered efficacious the liturgies celebrated everywhere else in Egypt. As Horus, his acts and costumes were regulated throughout the day by long-established rules. He maintained two complete establishments, one in Upper and one in Lower Egypt, and was supposed to divide his time equally between them so that both lands might participate in the supernatural benefits of his presence. Even after his death the king's influence continued. He became a national guardian, and his pyramid city or mortuary chapel was staffed by hereditary priests who remained in his service for many generations.

There were hundreds of other gods of which we know little more than the names and the shapes in which they were represented. The Egyptians had a penchant for showing their gods in part animal, part human form and, in later days, worshipped animals as divine incarnations. Many of the nomes also had as their symbols particular animals which they were forbidden to kill or use. The whole arrangement is very suggestive of totemism. There are two curious aspects of these animal gods and symbols. Although the predynastic Egyptians' culture was largely Asiatic in its origins, the wild animals represented are all African; at the same time, two most impressive African animals, the elephant and the rhinoceros, are conspicuous by their absence.

The most important ritual associated with the worship of all gods was that known as the "Rite of the House of the Morning." Pharaoh or the high priest of any temple, acting as his substitute, was first bathed with water brought from a sacred pool, part of the ritual equipment of every temple and palace. He was then anointed and invested with the insignia of his office by two priests wearing the masks of Thoth and

Horus. The importance of masks in Egyptian ritual is very rarely mentioned in popular accounts of Egyptian religion, but they were used in numerous rites, an interesting link between Egyptian and later African cultures. Following this investiture the two priests took the officiant by the hand and led him into the sanctuary, where there was an image of the god in a closed shrine. The officiant broke the clay seal which held the doors of the shrine together, threw them back, prostrated himself before the deity, and woke the god by reciting the hymn of morning worship. The priest then took out the image, purified it, went through the motions of feeding it, robed it in colored cloths, rouged its face, and adorned it with its appropriate emblems. He then replaced the image in the shrine and sealed the doors. He walked backwards as he left the sanctuary and swept out his footprints with a palm branch. Any special requests addressed to the Egyptian gods were accompanied by offerings, but they very rarely required human sacrifices, and even the slaughter of any large number of animals seems to have been discouraged. In line with the semi-magical attitudes of the Egyptians toward their deities, the exact performance of elaborate rituals was more important than the making of offerings.

The Egyptian concepts of the spiritual element in man and its fate after death were as disorganized and non-logical as the rest of their religious beliefs. Description is made even more difficult by the transformations which some of these concepts underwent in the course of Egyptian history. The predynastic Egyptians certainly believed in individual survival for all classes, for they provided all their dead with tomb furniture, varying in amount and quality with the resources of the family. The Old Kingdom centralization of power deprived the common people not only of freedom but even of the hope of immortality. For a time at least the only individuals to enjoy life after death were the Pharaoh and the nobles to whom he communicated certain magical formulae, and whom he allowed to be buried near him, thus sharing a portion of his divine life-force. We do not know whether the commoners concurred in this opinion or not, but that they never lost their desire for immortality is proved by the rapid development of the cult of Osiris, Isis, and Horus after the Old Kingdom collapsed.

The Egyptians believed in the existence of at least two and possibly more spiritual entities connected with the individual. The most clearly defined of these was the *Ka,* the individual's double. There is some reason to believe that in the earliest times this was equated with the placenta. The Ka was born with the individual, maintained a separate existence during his lifetime, and was reunited with his body at the instant of death. If the body was seriously damaged or destroyed, the Ka would perish, hence the practice of mummification and the custom of placing in the tomb an image of the deceased which the Ka could occupy if the body was destroyed. The Ka lived in the tomb, feeding upon the offerings, and the elaborate tomb furnishings and wall carvings were for its benefit. Every Egyptian attempted to assure his Ka not only of shelter but of a steadily renewed food supply. The worship of the dead by their descendants was obligatory, since the dead were able to control the destinies of the living. The sacrifices in connection with the ancestor cult were much more numerous than those given to the gods and included animals and libations of blood, milk, and wine. Certain passages in the pyramid texts may indicate that human sacrifices were made before the individual's death to assure him proper service in the next world.

The relation between ancestor and descendant was a reciprocal one. While the ancestor could bring his descendant good or bad fortune, the descendant, by withholding his sacrifices, could make the ancestor exceedingly uncomfortable. There are frequent records of a disappointed worshipper threatening a dead relative with suspension of his sacrifices if a particular request was not granted. The presence of ancestor worship of even a truncated sort in a society without clans or lineages is unique. Like certain other aspects of the culture, it strongly suggests that the earliest Egyptian pattern of social organization included localized enduring kin groups like those still common in Negro Africa. The elaborate provision which individuals made for their own comfort in the next world suggests that they realized the probability of their line becoming extinct or its members indifferent, features which do not have to be anticipated where there is a functional clan organization.

Beliefs regarding other aspects of the personality were much less precise. The individual was believed to have a *Ba,* which left the body at the moment of death. In the hieroglyphics this is represented as a stork or as a bird with a bearded human head and a lamp, the latter referring to a very ancient belief that the Ba became a star. However, it could also return to earth as a ghost in the form of the dead man, or assume the body of a bird, an animal, or a fish. Whether it was the Ba which underwent the judgment of the dead and found happiness in the underworld under the rule of Osiris, or whether it was still another entity, is not clear. The soul as it wandered through the Elysian fields was often referred to as the *Akh,* the effective spirit, and was supposed to be a radiant counterpart of the body as it was when alive. Lastly, the vital essence (life force?) of the individual was sometimes referred to as the *Sekhem.*

After the rise of the Osirian cult, Pharaoh still went to his heaven in the sky, but the souls of all others inhabited an Underworld which ran parallel to the Nile Valley and partly beneath it. This Underworld was separated from Egypt by a mountain range, with a narrow gorge through which the sun and the spirits of the dead could enter. The spirit passed first through a dark and fearful region haunted by fiends and monsters. It also had to pass through a series of gates which opened to it only when it gave the proper password. At the end of this journey the soul arrived at the realm of Osiris but still had to undergo a last hazard: the Judgment of the Dead. The trial was presided over by a company of forty-two gods or demons, each of whom was associated with a particular offense, and the deceased had to be able either to declare his innocence of each delict or to repeat the magical formula which would restrain the particular being from speaking against him. As a form of accident insurance, those who could afford it were provided with a scroll, the Book of the Dead, which contained directions for proper behavior at each stage of the journey, and also the words of power to be used whenever the soul was guilty. It is an interesting commentary on Egyptian business morality that these scrolls not infrequently were incomplete. Only the first few feet of the scroll were inscribed, the seller acting on the assumption that the buyer would not trouble to unroll it all.

At the end of his negative confession, the dead man's heart was weighed against a feather while he stood near it and begged it not to inform against him. A fierce monster with the head of a crocodile, the forepart of a lion, and the hindpart of a hippopotamus waited to devour the soul if the judgment went against it. If it was declared worthy of immortality, the judgment was written down by Thoth, and Horus took the soul by the hand and conducted it into the presence of Osiris. It should be noted that, although this Egyptian judgment of the dead has often been considered the origin of the Christian belief in the last judgment, the resemblances are rather superficial. In the Egyptian myth Osiris did not act as judge and neither Osiris nor Horus acted as Savior. Moreover, the forty-two "sins" had to do for the most part with infractions of taboos or offenses against property. Very few of them involved what we would consider ethical issues.

The Osirian realm was also much more like Egypt than it was like the Christian heaven. It consisted of two fields comparable to Upper and Lower Egypt. These were located in the western corner of the Underworld. In them the soul was reunited with its dead relatives and enjoyed all the pleasures of the flesh. It was also subject to various human disabilities, one of the more onerous being forced labor. A number of little figures were placed in the tomb to substitute for the dead man. When he was ordered to do something one of the figures would promptly call out, "I'm doing this," and hasten to obey the command.

Before leaving the subject of Egyptian religion, it is only just to make some mention of the Heretic King, Akhenaton, whose defection from the official religion has been so frequently applauded by modern writers. He has often been referred to as the first *individual* in history, and has been praised as a sort of John the Baptist of monotheism. Actually, contemporary evidence would seem to place him in a less exalted role. Akhenaton's father, Amenophis III, was one of the most powerful and autocratic rulers of the 18th Dynasty, the royal house whose kings made Egypt a world military power for the first time in its history. He fell in love with a woman who was "impossible" from the point of view of the Egyptian nobility, since she was both a Semite and a member of a middle-class family, and he had the arrogance to make her his chief wife and queen. The reaction of the priests of Amon was not unlike that of the British clergy under somewhat similar circumstances, and even the usually obsequious courtiers seem to have snubbed her. The king countered by compelling them to wear huge scarabs inscribed with the queen's name and titles as reminders of her position.

The son of this union, originally named Amenophis after his father, was not a legitimate heir by priestly reckoning and had every reason to hate the established religion. Aton, the sun disc, was a Semitic deity who had been known in Egypt for some time, but who was worshipped mainly by commoners of Semitic origin. It is highly probable that the young Pharaoh's mother was one of his devotees. The Pharaoh changed his own name to Akhenaton, thus honoring Aton, and set up Aton's worship as the state religion. In this he followed a pattern already familiar in Egypt, in which the founder of a new dynasty would usually make the god of his home district the center of the national worship. While Akhenaton insisted on the preeminence of Aton, it is highly improbable that he was a monotheist in the sense of denying the existence or even the power of other deities. At least he continued to go through the rituals which, as Pharaoh, he was obligated to perform for the good of the land.

In his attempt to break the power of the priests of Amon, Akhenaton built a new capitol and tried to usher in a new era in art and ritual. Egyptian art had become highly conventionalized, and the statues and pictures, in spite of high aesthetic quality, had come to represent offices rather than real persons. However, side by side with this conventional art there had emerged a livelier style of carving and painting which bore much the same relation to it that our own comic strips bear to our fine arts. Artists, decorating tombs with the endless friezes of food, furniture, and servants at work depicted there for the benefit of the Ka, amused themselves by making humorously realistic details which they tucked away in odd corners. The same sort of free, unconventional drawing appears in various papyri made with humorous or pornographic intent. Akhenaton turned to this free style and attempted to develop it in opposition to the priestly style. He himself was physically deformed, and he insisted that his deformity be shown in his portraits. He also had life masks made of himself, his wife, and his courtiers, so that his artists could have exact models from which to work. Fortunately, his sister-wife, Nefertiti, was a worthy subject, and her head, carved by some emancipated sculptor of the period, is one of the world's great pieces of portrait art.

Aton was a god of "peace on earth and good will to men." Akhenaton took these doctrine seriously, and, in an attempt to implement them, he sent out letters to the kings of neighboring states indicating his eagerness to make peace with all of them. Unfortunately, he did not wait for proof of their good intentions before reducing his military forces. As a result, the Egyptian empire, which had extended to the Euphrates and far into Asia Minor in the days of his father, was completely wiped out.

The last king of the tottering dynasty was Tutankhamen, whose very unimportance may have helped to save his tomb for the modern world. He was forgotten so quickly that a slightly later Pharaoh built living quarters for his workmen over the entrance passage, thus effectively concealing Tutankhamen's resting place from robbers. Although most of the splendid furniture of Tutankhamen's tomb was of the sort placed with any Pharaoh, there were some unusual features. Tutankhamen died of tuberculosis when he was only sixteen. Even during his brief reign the priests of Amon had recovered their power and were vigorously trying to re-establish the old order. They even forced him to change his name from the original Tutankhaton to Tutankhamen. Apparently the royal family realized that the dynasty was coming to an end, and placed in the tomb foreign gifts which had been made to Pharaohs of the dynasty in the time of its greatness, along with numerous articles which were family heirlooms or were closely associated with the Aton cult. Since the tombs of Pharaoh's were sacred, this was the best method for keeping such objects from falling into the hands of the priests of Amon.

The social and political organization of Egypt is less well known than one might anticipate. Personal documents and court records which might illustrate social relations are comparatively rare, and the Egyptians took their own institutions too much for granted to think of describing them in inscriptions. The basic social unit seems to have been a simple nuclear family much like our own. No lineages or clans were present during historic times. No bride price was paid, and it appears that the first marriages, at least, were usually love matches. There seems to have been a considerable number of women who elected not to marry, and these were allowed to administer their own property and to distribute their favors as they wished. The position of women was high, married women controlling their own fortunes and taking charge of their husband's businesses in their absence. However, polygyny was the preferred form of marriage. There was always a head wife, the other women being secondary wives or concubines. The more women in a man's establishment the higher his social prestige.

The royal marriages of brother and sister have already been mentioned, and, after the fall of the Old Kingdom, this practice, like other royal privileges, was extended to the nobles. We do not know whether it was taken up by the artisans and peasantry. In funeral inscriptions men of all ranks, if rich enough to afford such memorials, frequently referred to their head wife as "sister." However, we know that this was a term of endearment as well as a relationship term, so the question of how widely the practice spread must remain unanswered for the present.

Various classical writers state that the Egyptians traced descent through the mother, but there are few indications of this in their inscriptions. It seems more probable that descent was actually bilateral, as among ourselves, property and office being inherited through either parent. Such a system would have appeared extraordinary to the highly patrilineal Greeks and Romans. It may be added that the Classical explanation for Egyptian matrilineal descent was that the Egyptian women were so much addicted to adultery that the paternity of their children was always doubtful.

The next organized social unit above the family was the nome or province. In historic times the nomes functioned mainly as administrative units. Nevertheless, the inhabitants of a nome united in the worship of a nome deity, had their cases tried in the courts of a hereditary nomarch who also supervised local public works, and felt considerable local pride and hostility toward persons from other nomes. It seems probable that during the oldest period, when the forty-two nomes were politically independent, they were endogamous localized kin groups of the sort still widespread in Negro agricultural Africa.

In historic times Egyptian society was class-organized, but with considerable opportunity for vertical nobility. In the Old Kingdom there were actually only two classes, royalty and commoners, all important offices in both the governmental bureaucracy and the priesthood being filled by royal relatives. The large harems maintained by men of the royal group insured an extensive supply of these. As time went on, the society was differentiated into a peasantry, a middle-class of craftsmen and professional soldiers, and an aristocratic group of nobles, administrators, and priests. Above them all towered the Pharaoh, whose divinity set him beyond classification as a mere human.

It may be noted that slaves are not mentioned in the list just given, since they were never important in the Egyptian economy. Criminals and prisoners of war were either drafted into the army or sent to the quarries, where their life expectation was short. A few slaves, particularly slave women, were employed in domestic service, but these were regarded more as family retainers than as property. As always, in countries where a huge supply of free labor existed on the level of bare subsistence, it was uneconomical to employ slaves for ordinary work. It was cheaper to hire men when they were needed than to incur the lasting obligations that went with ownership.

The virtual enslavement of the peasants in the Old Kingdom times has already been mentioned, as has the collapse of the system at the end of the 6th dynasty. In later times the Egyptian peasant was no longer a serf. He was assigned land, sometimes in freehold, sometimes on one of the royal or temple estates. In either case the holding was inalienable and descended to his children. He was under obligation to pay taxes on his produce, as well as rent to the owner, and long custom decreed what crops should be raised in particular districts. Although the peasant was no longer tied to his holding by law, he was tied to it by economic necessity, since all land had long since been allocated, and if he left his holding his only recourse would be to become an unskilled laborer.

Craftsmen were concentrated in the cities, where all the workers in one craft commonly lived together in a particular quarter. Each establishment was a combined workshop and store, and the craftsmen were organized into guilds much like those of medieval Europe. We have no way of estimating the income of the skilled craftsmen, but their lot was certainly better than that of the peasants.

There were few professional soldiers in the Old Kingdom days, but as time passed the military establishment became more and more important and permanent. The men of Upper Egypt were much better soldiers than those of Lower Egypt, but even they had no great love for war, and the Egyptians very early began to use foreigners in their forces. These were drawn at first from Nubia and Syria, while the Shardana, the "Men of the Isles," had a high reputation for courage and were frequently used for Pharaoh's personal bodyguard. Although some of the foreigners were volunteers, many of them were actually slaves. We know that, during the 18th dynasty, campaigns in Nubia were often preceded by raids into Syria to get soldiers, and vice-versa. Needless to say, such forces could not be used successfully against their own tribesmen, but in distant campaigns slave soldiers had definite advantages. They were, so to speak, on life enlistment and had no civil rights which had to be regarded. They could be subjected to the strictest discipline, and, since their civilian ties had been broken at the time of their capture, homesickness would never lead to mutiny. From the slave's point of view, war, with its excitement and opportunities to loot, was vastly preferable to labor in a quarry or on public works. The pattern of slave soldiers thus established survived in Islamic countries until exceedingly late times. Outstanding examples are the previously mentioned Janisseries in Turkey and the Mamelukes of later Egypt.

Greek mercenaries

Beginning in the 8th century B.C. the Egyptians employed more and more Greeks, who proved themselves superior mercenaries. From the 19th dynasty on soldiers played an increasingly important role in politics. The peasantry were powerless and politically indifferent, and rival claimants to the throne or founders of new dynasties relied upon the Libyan, Nubian, or Greek mercenaries for support, while rulers in power had to placate them with gifts. By the time of Herodotus there were nearly one and a half million professional soldiers in the delta alone, all either holding grants of land or receiving generous rations of grain, beef, and wine. One of the curious incidents of the later period was the mutiny of 4,000 Gauls in the army of Ptolemy Philadelphos. They planned to seize the government and did succeed in looting the treasury. When their coup failed, they retreated to an island in the Sebennytic arm of the Nile, where they all committed ritual suicide, a Gaulish pattern comparable to Japanese hara-kiri.

It may have been noticed that in the enumerations of middle-class groups no merchants were mentioned. Egyptian internal trade was nearly all carried on locally in the city markets and by a system of barter. Although standard weights and measures were in early use, there was no fixed standard of value until the 12th century, B.C. Prior to that time there were elaborate tables in which the value of one commodity was established in terms of half a dozen other commodities. After the 12th century, ring-money of gold, silver, and copper came into use but had to be weighed at each transaction. Coins were introduced at the time of the Persian conquest. Since taxes, rents, and tithes were collected in kind, both the temples and government were deeply involved in business. Such foreign trades as existed seems to have been largely in their hands. In the case of the Pharaoh, trading was phrased in terms of tribute or royal gift exchanges. As a result of this there was no opportunity for the development of wealthy merchants or bankers comparable to those of Mesopotamia.

Scribes

On the borderline between the middle and upper classes stood the scribes. The old saying that knowledge is power was nowhere truer than in Egypt. It required years of assiduous study to master the intricacies of the hieroglyphic writing, but the scribe's training by no means ended there. He was expected to know the ancient literature and also to have mastered enough mathematics and engineering to be able to cast accounts, design buildings, and supervise public works. His royal master might even call upon him to lead a military expedition. The biographies which some successful scribes have left in their funeral inscriptions suggest a versatility like that of Leonardo da Vinci.

Since an aspirant's family had to be able to support him during several years of study, there were economic prerequisites which debarred the sons of most peasants and craftsmen. However, once the skills had been acquired, any scribe might hope to attain any post in the government, even that of vizier. It may be noted in this connection that the stronger the central power, the greater the tendency for Pharaoh to make administrative positions appointive rather than hereditary and to fill them with commoners whose loyalty could be counted on because of their dependence on his favor. Since appointments were given by favor, advancement depended as much upon absolute obedience to the royal will and ingenious flattery as upon ability. Not only royal gifts, but also donations from individuals seeking various sorts of favors, made it possible for the holders of administrative positions to acquire wealth, intermarry with the hereditary nobility, and have their descendants acquire full noble status.

The Egyptian upper class consisted of government officials, hereditary nobility, and the priesthood. As just noted, officials might be of either common or noble origin, but the higher positions in the priesthood were normally held by nobles. The situation was not unlike that of the medieval church in Europe. The officials were divided into the administrators and the court group, who were particularly concerned with the care of the Pharaoh's person and establishment.

At the head of the administrative hierarchy stood the Vizier, who took over all the routine secular duties pertaining to Pharaoh's office. These duties were heavy. The Vizier acted as a supreme court and had to hear all cases referred to him from lower courts. Great stress was laid on his expeditious handling of cases. He superintended public works and, three times a year, received reports on conditions in the various nomes. Tax authorities sent their accounts to him and he issued receipts from the royal storehouses. He also recruited the Pharaoh's bodyguard and took care of all the arrangements when he traveled. Every morning the Vizier went to the palace, met the Pharaoh, inquired after his health, and then reported to him on the state of the nation.

Closely associated with the Vizier was a second great minister known as the Director of the Seal. He was in charge of the financial affairs of the kingdom. It was he who assessed taxes and saw to their collection. Since the taxes were paid in kind, not cash, he was further responsible for the distribution of the goods turned in and, in later times, for their conversion into money. He also managed the incredibly complicated affairs of the funerary foundation and temple estates. Lastly, he had to fix wage scales for labor on the royal and temple estates, which thus set a general standard for the kingdom. During most of Egyptian history, there were a single Vizier and a single Director of the Seal, but, by the New Kingdom, administration had become too complex to be handled in this way, and there were separate Viziers and Keepers of the Seal for Upper and Lower Egypt.

The office of Vice-roy of Nubia was created in the 18th dynasty. Because of the distance of his province and the necessity for quick action in case of attack, the Vice-roy had practically royal powers and headed his own separate court and administration closely modeled on those of the Pharaoh. All these officials were surrounded by a numerous corps of scribes. Below this level administration was handled independently in the various nomes, the nomarch being held responsible for the behavior of his subjects, with duties which repeated on a smaller scale those of the Vizier.

The palace officials were exceedingly numerous. Closest to the king's person were a group of intimate advisors known as the Honored Ones. This group automatically included members of the royal family but was primarily made up of men who had proved their worth by many years of administrative service. The Honored Ones were maintained at court at the king's expense, but their most prized privileges were the provision which the king made for their splendid burials and his permission to be laid out to rest near his own person. Individual Honored Ones were also assigned posts connected with the operation of the court and the care of Pharaoh's person. These posts carried honorary titles such as "Lordship of the Secret of the Royal House," i.e., custodian of the crown jewels. Court protocol was exceedingly elaborate. The king's person was attended by a Director of the King's Dress, under whom were a Valet of the Hands, a Director of the Oils and Unguents, a Keeper of the King's Wigs, and many others. The queen and ladies of the royal harem had even more elaborate personal staffs. Even the staff of the royal kitchen was organized in a rising order of precedence. The three royal meat carvers preceded the cake maker, who in turn preceded the soufflé maker, who in turn preceded the jam maker.

The most important group in the hereditary nobility was composed of the nomarchs and their relatives. These were the descendants of the kings who had ruled over the various nomes before the unification of Egypt. Although every strong dynasty tried to limit their power and minimize their importance, they retained the devotion of the nome members and, whenever the central power weakened, functioned as petty kings. The nomarch was really a sort of Vice-roy in his province, combining administrative duties with religious functions as high priest of the nome god. The hereditary nobility were in general supported by

estates which had been granted to the family in the past by Pharaoh.
Although many of the noble families boasted long descent, able commoners might be promoted through Pharaoh's favor and become the
founders of noble houses. It is interesting to note that the Egyptian nobility was not primarily a warrior caste. Although a few of the great
families produced able generals through several generations, many others concerned themselves mainly with religious or administrative activities or were simply courtiers.

The priesthood was one of the most important elements in Egyptian
society. In addition to the observance of the daily rites and the annual
festival of the god, which often lasted for weeks, the priests gave oracles
and presented individual requests to the god in return for suitable fees.
Unfortunately, our knowledge of the staffing of the temples is limited to
the names of the various officials. The priests as a whole were divided
into two classes, consisting of prophets and ordinary Priests. No matter
what the duties of these two groups may have been in historic times, this
division is highly suggestive of the well-nigh universal one between the
inspirational priest, who goes into a trance state and permits the deity
to speak through his mouth, and the ritual priest, who takes charge of
the proper performance of the formal rites. Every temple was staffed
with a Chief Prophet, Deputy Prophet, Priest, Deputy Priest, and so
forth. Priestesses were ranged in a hierarchy of their own, but were
much less significant in religious exercises than the priests. Their principal duties consisted in providing music and dancing on religions occasions. Sacred concubines and sacred prostitutes were attached to the
temples of most gods. A separate group of priests supervised the worship and offerings in the royal mortuary temples.

Lastly, most of the schools in which advanced education was given
were associated with temples, and it was customary for Egyptian professional men, doctors, and lawyers to take orders and to be nominally
connected with some temple establishment. A similar arrangement was
common in Europe during the Middle Ages.

The study of Egyptian culture leaves one with the feeling that the
Egyptians were a clever and ingenious people whose progress was stulti-
fied by the development of one of the most rigid and highly centralized
governmental systems which the world has seen. There was a complete
union of church and state, with a correspondingly complete control of
the subjects' bodies and minds. Such systems can function successfully
only through a rigid maintenance of the status quo. The Egyptian inventions which eventually became incorporated into the general stream
of developing Eurasiatic civilization were almost all made during the
first 500 years of Egyptian history. It is even doubtful whether the Egyp-

tian contributions outside the field of technology were not a result of the classical misinterpretation of Egyptian beliefs and rituals rather than an authentic diffusion of Egyptian elements.

With respect to the African cultures, particularly the African civilizations, the situation is quite different. While it is exceedingly difficult to find exact parallels between Egyptian civilization and those of the great Central and West African kingdoms, nevertheless one feels a basic similarity. This will become evident in subsequent chapters.

Chapter XXX

Historic African Peoples

THROUGHOUT the entire historic period Africa has been divided racially and culturally by the Sahara desert. North of this tremendous waste the African population has been predominantly Caucasic, and the African cultures essentially Eurasiatic. North Africa has been a part, first of the classic Ecumene and, from the 8th century to the present, of the far-flung Islamic civilization. South of the Sahara the population has been predominantly Negroid and its cultures, in spite of occasional accretions from outside sources, have remained distinctive. It will not be necessary to record the cultures of the North African peasants and city dwellers. Apparently the local populations have conformed readily enough to the patterns set by their successive rulers, Phoenicians, Greeks, Romans, Byzantines, and Arabs. In the Atlas and at those points in the Sahara where a scanty rainfall permitted pastoral occupation, elements of the older culture survived through all these vicissitudes, but the information which we have on these from either archeological or classical sources is negligible.

With the Islamic conquest most of the distinctive North African culture survivals were eliminated. The North African environment was so similar to that of the Arabian regions in which Islam had its source that the Islamic culture patterns could be introduced almost *in toto*. In addition, whole tribes of pastoral Arabs moved into the North African interior and, backed by the prestige of Islam, were able to establish a cultural ascendancy over the local population.

In historic times only one group in the Sahara had kept a distinctive culture derived from the pre-Islamic period. These were the Tuareg, a Berber people who occupied the Western Sahara. Although nominally Muslim, they had many practices which were highly unorthodox. The position of women was extraordinarily high. Descent was traced in the female line and women were the guardians of the intellectual and artistic

activities of the tribe. They were usually literate, while the men rarely
were, and there were women poets and musicians who were nationally
famous. Women were never secluded. Girls and young men were allowed to indulge in petting parties reminiscent of American college
undergraduates, while friendships between married women and men
were taken as a matter of course. The men spent their time in camel
breeding and raiding. During the time between engagement and marriage a prospective bridegroom was expected to steal from enemy groups
the camels needed for the bride price, and, since the larger the bride
price, the greater the honor to both parties, marriages were often delayed until middle age. Women did not veil but all men wore veils of
heavy cloth which were never removed, even when eating or sleeping.
Women frequently embroidered their fiancés' or men friends' veils with
appropriate mottoes. The Tuareg themselves explained male veiling as
simply a defense against flies and sun. Since the nobles were of almost
pure Caucasoid stock and were frequently light-skinned and grey-eyed,
this was probably correct.

Political organization was a loose confederacy in which a few aristocratic clans dominated a more numerous servile population. While the
noble clans were Caucasoid, the servile ones had a heavy admixture of
Negro blood. They were the descendants of slaves and small aboriginal
Negro groups who had assumed Tuareg culture and had finally been
admitted to Tuareg tribal membership. Since it was customary for men
of noble clans to take mistresses from the servile clans during the long
period before marriage, there was a constant infiltration of Caucasoid
genes into the servile clans, with little penetration of Negro genes into
the upper classes.

The Tuareg were primarily camel breeders, although they also
kept sheep and goats and the servile clans also practiced agriculture
where possible. Much of their regular income was derived from policing
the caravan routes and robbing caravans which had not paid "protection." They were ferocious warriors who extended their conquests as far
as Timbuctu on the Niger River.

Northeast Africa east and south of Egypt forms a distinct province
both racially and culturally. The local population, generally referred to
as the People of the Horn, have physical characteristics which place
them in an intermediate position between the Negroid and Caucasoid
stocks. They combine exceedingly dark pigmentation with Caucasic features. Their hair is quite different from that of typical Negroes, being
coarse and closely crimped, so that when allowed to grow long it stands
out from the head in a bush. The origins of this type are uncertain. Although it is generally regarded as the result of an ancient mixture between Negroes and Caucasics, the mixture has become so thoroughly

stabilized, if this is the case, that it must be regarded as a sub-race. Since the region is one of intense heat and violent sun, heavy pigmentation is advantageous and might have become fixed as a result of natural selection.

Three distinct cultures were represented in the region, two in the lowlands and one in the Abyssinian highlands. Both of the lowland cultures were based on animal economies. One, that of the Somali, followed in most respects the familiar Semitic pastoral pattern. Its economic emphasis was on camels, sheep, and goats, with cattle few and incidental. The other domestic animal culture, characteristic of the Galla, was a dairying culture of distinctively African type with cattle as the most important animals. The Abyssinian culture was based on a mixed agricultural and domestic animal economy but with agriculture paramount. Since the Abyssinians had been Christianized in the 3rd century and had maintained contact with other Christian and later Muslim societies all through the historic period, this civilization was less African than Near Eastern. It showed strong Byzantine and Arab influence, and the governmental institutions were essentially of Semitic type.

Negro Africa extended from the southern borders of the Sahara and Eastern Sudan to far South Africa, where one encountered the some-

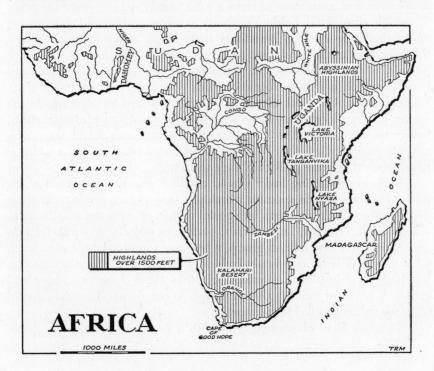

AFRICA

1000 MILES

HIGHLANDS OVER 1500 FEET

what divergent Khoisan, i.e., Bushman-Hottentot physical type and cultures. In spite of numerous local variations, certain features were present throughout this entire region, making it appear probable that the various cultures shared a remote common origin. The diversity was most marked in the fields of technology and economic organization, aspects of culture which are most readily affected by differences in natural environment and by foreign contacts. There were also marked differences in the size and patterns of organization of political groups.

Certain social patterns were present everywhere in Negro Africa. Polygyny was universal and was correlated with an equally universal surplus of women, due partly to the more dangerous activities of men and partly to a strong tendency for females to exceed males in both birth and survival ratios. Payment of a bride price was practically universal. This payment was construed primarily as reimbursement to the woman's family for the loss of her services and those of her potential children. It did not make the woman one of her husband's chattels, and it did not prevent her from dissolving the union under sufficient provocation.

Although both matrilineal and patrilineal descent were present, marriages were nearly everywhere patrilocal. The normal family establishment was a compound in which each of the multiple wives and her children had a separate dwelling. There was a strong tendency for a man's sons and grandsons to form a joint family, i.e., to continue living in a single compound, holding property as a corporation and cooperating under the direction of a hereditary male head. Men who could afford the necessary outlay preferred to break away, establish their own compounds, and thus become the founders of new joint families. Several families which had been formed in this way and still recognized their kinship constituted a sub-clan, and several sub-clans a clan. Outside the region of large kingdoms, clans were usually localized territorial units. Sub-clans were, almost without exception, exogamous. Clans were usually exogamous when they formed part of larger political units, endogamous when they were politically independent.

Each kin grouping had its head or chief who derived much of his power from his role in ancestor worship. Clans and even sub-clans often distinguished their members by special details of costume, scarification, and so forth. Totems, i.e., animals, plants, or objects which stood in a special relation to a human group, were very common at the clan level. Clan members were commonly forbidden to kill or use their own totem but had no objection to members of other clans doing so. There was usually a myth explaining the relationship, but belief in actual descent from the totem was lacking in most cases.

Societies were class-organized, with a threefold division of chiefs, free commoners, and slaves. The relations of inferiors to superiors were strongly autocratic. This began in the family, where children were expected to show exaggerated respect to their parents and young people to their elders. Similar attitudes were reflected in the behavior of subclan and clan members toward the heads of these units and of all lower orders toward kings and officials. Patterns of popular election and representative government were completely lacking. All political offices were either hereditary or appointive. Democracy existed only at the village level where, as in villages everywhere in the world, policies were decided through informal discussion among the natural leaders of the community. Chiefs had counselors, but they selected them themselves and allowed them only advisory activities.

In spite of these autocratic institutions, concepts of law strikingly similar to the European one were present in all the agricultural and most of the dairying societies. The chief was allowed to exercise his autocratic powers only within clearly understood limits. Law codes were no less valid because they were transmitted verbally. One of the main functions of chiefs was to act as magistrate. Cases were pleaded before him, evidence taken, frequently on oath, and precedents were cited. The chief was expected to show his wisdom and fitness for office by the skill with which he disentangled conflicting evidence and made the punishment fit the crime. When there was a hierarchy of officials, cases could be appealed from lower to higher courts until they reached a prime minister or even the king himself. Trial by ordeal was universally allowed, but was resorted to only when the evidence was so inconclusive that no decision could be reached.

Puberty rites were universal. Groups of boys and girls were initiated separately, frequently in camps established at some distance from the regular settlement. Here they were kept under the watchful care of adults, never their own parents, who hazed them in various ways and finally gave them sex instruction and, frequently, esoteric religious knowledge. Mutilations of various sorts were often inflicted at this time. Boys were circumcised, girls had the clitoris removed and, in regions where scarification was practiced, both sexes received their clan or tribal marks.

The basic, universal religion of Negro Africa was ancestor worship. This was directed primarily toward founders of kin groups and heroes whose exploits were remembered. It was firmly believed that the dead took a lively interest in the doings of their descendants, that they were able to help or harm them, and that they could be influenced by prayers and, especially, sacrifices. Upon these basic assumptions numerous local beliefs and practices had been developed. In addition to the ancestral spirits there were non-human deities, but their number and importance varied greatly in different parts of the area. Outside a few of the great kingdoms, god cults were less important than the ancestor cults.

There was a lively belief in magic of all sorts, and the medicine men, its practitioners, held an honored position. Professional priests were in charge of the shrines of various gods and directed their worship. Supervision of ancestor worship was normally a function of the head of the kin group. There were also professional diviners who practiced no other type of magic; medicine men's activities were directed mainly toward the healing of disease.

The medicine man was usually an individual with hysteric tendencies, and, since the post was socially important and financially rewarding, such tendencies were watched for in children and encouraged, their expressions being shaped to the culturally approved forms. Contrary to popular belief, the medicine man was rarely if ever a genuine psychotic. To be a successful practitioner required a firm grasp of reality and superior intelligence. At the same time, the average medicine man was not a charlatan. He believed in his own powers and frequently possessed abilities in what is now called extra-sensory perception. He was also, in most cases, an excellent psychotherapist, and possessed a knowledge of genuine and quite non-magical remedies for common ailments. There can be no doubt that a study of African *materia medica* and healing practices would contribute significantly to our own medical knowledge.

The medicine man knew magic of all sorts and could kill as well as heal. He was ready to provide evil charms and directions for their use quite as a modern pharmacist carries poisons. However, this was a very minor feature of his activities. The medicine man must not be confused with the malevolent sorcerers, also found everywhere in Negro Africa. The sorcerer was a constant practitioner of malevolent magic, an all-round virulent enemy of the community devoted to evil for its own sake. Sorcerer's attacks were directed not only against individuals but against humanity in general, and they were killed without mercy whenever discovered. It was believed that the condition of being a sorcerer was frequently involuntary and, indeed, unconscious. It was thought to be due to the presence in the body of a "witch substance," described as a white gelatinous material somewhat like phlegm. This substance might be acquired in various ways or might even be inherited. It was quite possible for an individual to be a malevolent sorcerer without knowing it. Since all members of the community shared in these beliefs, persons who were detected and accused of sorcery by the medicine men would usually confess and submit to execution without protest. While medicine men operated individually, except for observance of professional etiquette, sorcerers were often believed to be organized in groups which met secretly and planned campaigns.

One of the most important activities of the medicine man was the making of fetishes. It is difficult to convey to Europeans the exact nature of these objects. They were not inhabited by spirits and were known to have been manufactured, yet they were regarded as sentient Beings. They were strengthened by offerings, could hear and respond to prayers, and were able to bring good or evil fortune. They owed their power to having been compounded in certain ways of certain materials. Most of these materials were taken from plants or animals, but many of the more powerful fetishes included human blood, bones, or organs. The concept was, after all, not unlike our own attitude toward such a material as gunpowder. Sulfur, charcoal, and saltpeter, each of which is innocuous in itself, have astonishing potentialities when combined in certain proportions and in a certain way.

The cattle brought to Africa by Neolithic settlers could flourish in regions where the crops which they had brought could be grown with difficulty, if at all. The result was the development of an African dairying culture similar in some respects to the Eurasian one already described in Chapter XIX. In historic times, at least, the bearers of the African dairying cultures were almost exclusively Negroes, although frequently Negroes who showed a considerable Caucasic admixture. The center for the development of the dairying complex seems to have been in the Eastern Sudan, and it was here that in later times it showed its most distinctive characteristics. Although it was presumably developed out of the domestic animal half of the original Neolithic economy, there can be little question that it was sometimes taken over directly by groups of hunters and food-gatherers who had never known agriculture. It seems impossible to explain the Hottentot situation on any other basis, and we know that similar shifts from a hunting to a domestic animal economy were made rapidly and easily by tribes in other parts of the world.

All the African dairying cultures centered their economy around cattle. Other animals, especially sheep, were usually kept in small numbers, but their cultural significance was slight. In historic times most of the dairying societies other than the Hottentots practiced a little agriculture where climatic conditions made this possible. Their original crops were probably the African ones previously mentioned, but from the 17th century on these were supplemented and then largely replaced by food crops of American origin, particularly maize, peanuts, manioc, and pumpkins. The introduction of these plants, which were well suited to the African plateau environment, may have resulted in a heavier reliance by the dairying peoples upon agriculture.

Cattle were the emotional and cultural center of native life. All work with them was pre-empted by the men, and all cultures having this economy were strongly patriarchal and patrilineal. The bride price was always paid in cattle, and in some tribes sex relations between two persons whose mothers had been bought by cattle from the same herd were considered incestuous. In others, a wife who had been purchased with cattle which a man had acquired for himself, instead of having received from his kindred, became a "hill" and the founder of a new genealogical line. Wealth was reckoned in terms of the size of a man's herd, exclusive of quality, an attitude which in modern times has resulted in both inferior stock and bad overgrazing of native reserves. A man's love for his animals was proverbial. Even owners of several hundred head knew every animal belonging to them. Cattle were penned at night and grazed during the day with boys as herders. They were milked morning and night and also bled, the bleeding being done with a miniature bow and arrow which was driven suddenly into one of the neck veins. A quart or two of blood was drawn off and the wound closed. To judge from the animal's behavior, the operation caused little pain. This technique does not seem to have been practiced by the Egyptians, and, in view of the negative attitudes of all Semitic peoples toward the use of blood in any form, it is a strong argument for the Negro origin of the African cattle complex. It also suggests the presence of a hunting component among the originators of the complex, since all people who

NILOTS AND FRIEND

live by hunting regard blood as an important article of diet, and the arrow is primarily a hunter's weapon.

Although most of the historic dairying societies conducted mass hunts to destroy lions and other predators, they rarely hunted for meat. Since game was abundant everywhere in the plateau, this neglect of a significant natural resource seems curious. In several cases the dairying tribes shared their territory with hunting tribes of inferior social status, from whom they obtained the skins of antelopes and other wild animals which they used for clothing. Technology was rather poorly developed in all the dairying cultures. Iron was in universal use for tools, weapons, and even ornaments. The metal seems to have been most plentiful and most skillfully worked in the northern part of the plateau. Smiths everywhere formed a distinct caste of low social status. This may indicate that the iron-working technique was introduced by foreign craftsmen. Mats were woven but the true loom was unknown.

Costume was fragmentary, many of the northern dairying people going completely nude except for ornaments. Farther south both sexes wore small aprons. Blankets, made from skins of antelope or other wild animals, were a constant item of clothing throughout the entire area. Most utensils were of wood or gourd shell, although simple clay cooking pots were made by many tribes. Art was rudimentary, being limited to simple geometric designs frequently burned on utensils. In sharp contrast with West Africa, there was an almost complete absence of sculptured figures, masks, and other ceremonial equipment. This was no doubt related to the simple and relatively unorganized character of religion in the area.

Economic organization was simple. Aside from smiths, there were no specialized craftsmen. Markets, important elsewhere in Negro Africa, were not characteristic of the dairying cultures, and, where they occurred, could usually be traced to foreign influence.

In the dairying tribes religious beliefs and practices were exceedingly simple. There were no doctrines regarding the nature of the soul, and beliefs concerning conditions in the next world were vague. Attitudes toward individual survival were rather neutral even in the most warlike groups, where the individual's life expectation was low. Some of the northern dairying tribes agreed with Goethe that a soul was not a gift but an accomplishment, and limited survival to chiefs, medicine men, and heroes. Most of the dairying tribes recognized a supreme Being and a few other deities, but the elaborate and highly organized pantheons found among some of the agricultural people were notably lacking. In general, neither gods nor ancestors received worship except in times of emergency, and rituals were simple. Animal sacrifices were offered on occasion, but human sacrifice was very rare.

Cattle rustling
small scattered
settlements
peas and communities
were captured
Exploited agriculture
warlike

Shelter

Dairying itself imposes certain patterns of settlement (see Chap. XIX, p. 258). The African groups who shared this economy normally lived in small, widely distributed *kraals*, each occupied by a joint family. The houses of the various wives, sons and their wives, and so forth, were usually arranged around a central cattle pen. Since the cattle were a constant temptation to raids, most of the African dairying groups were exceedingly warlike, a characteristic which stood them in good stead in their contacts with their less aggressive agricultural neighbors and led eventually to the establishment, along the margins of the cattle area, of numerous states in which a cattle-keeping aristocracy ruled over predominantly agricultural commoners. A curious feature of these states was that many of those along the southern edge of the Sudan were of quite recent origin, having been set up as a result of an eastward movement of the Fullah. This group, who are difficult to place ethnically, since they show a stabilized mixture of Negroid and Caucasic traits, seem to have originated in Senegal, and, after their conversion to Islam, began a rapid eastward expansion. Wherever they went they successfully dominated the Negroes and even today, and in regions where they do not hold formal rule, they succeed in controlling the agricultural Negro populations.

political
organ

Outside the areas where they ruled as conquerors, the political organization of the Sudanese and East African cattle people was rudimentary. The usual pattern was a federation of clans and sub-clans organized in a prestige hierarchy. Slavery was economically unimportant and frequently lacking. Such political control as existed was usually vested in clan chiefs or hereditary medicine men whose main function was that of making rain. Legal patterns were less developed than in agricultural Africa. The most distinctive social feature was the great emphasis upon male age-groupings. All the males of a particular age group were initiated into manhood at the same time and circumcised with the same knife, thus establishing a bond of blood brotherhood. Such a group served as a unit in the army, and its members had strong reciprocal rights and duties, extending in some cases to wife-lending.

Most of the plateau from Kenya south was occupied by Bantu-speaking tribes who were comparatively recent arrivals in the region. Although cattle dominated their economy at the time they were first encountered by Europeans, they depended much more heavily on agriculture than did the Sudanic and East African dairying tribes. This tendency may have been increased by the fact that they were already in possession of American crops at the time when Europeans first visited this region. There can be little doubt that before their entrance into the plateau the culture of these Bantu invaders was much like that of the West African agricultural villagers. They seem to have brought with them more advanced patterns for political organization, and during the 18th and early 19th centuries a number of ephemeral empires were developed in this region, each one centering about some great leader and military organizer. None of these empires developed the professional administrators who gave the agricultural kingdoms their continuity. The most famous of these empires was that of the Zulu, created by Tschaka.

In far South Africa a highly aberrant version of the dairying culture was carried on by the Hottentots, closely related to the Bushmen in both physical type and language. There can be little doubt that they originally had a culture of Bushman type (see Chap. XII, p. 157) which was modified by contact with some dairying group. Before the invasion of the plateau by Bantu-speaking people, the Hottentot range extended much farther north, perhaps even to the borders of Kenya. Their principle domestic animals were cattle and fat-tailed sheep, both of which were milked. Milking was done by women, and cattle were used as pack animals, practices which the other African dairying peoples regarded as little short of sacrilegious. Instead of occupying more or less permanent kraals, the Hottentots lived in temporary camps and moved frequently. There was a heavy dependence on hunting, carried on by men. The basis of social organization was the localized, exogamous, patrilineal group, but there were numerous traces of a matrilineal, or at least bilateral, reckoning of descent. Characteristic social features were the extreme respect, amounting to avoidance, which brothers were expected to pay to sisters, and the strong ties between a man and his maternal uncle. Political organization was negligible. Although each band had a head man, such leaders exercised no real authority. Religion was an unformalized ancestor worship. The moon figured prominently in the mythology, but only three other supernatural beings were regarded as more important than the ordinary ghosts of the dead, and even they were believed to be of human origin. The most important religious ceremony was an annual rain-making ritual held in November or December, when the summer rains were due.

In Africa the line between farming cultures and dairying cultures was closely related to rainfall. From the borders of the Sahara rainfall gradually increased southward through the Western and Central Sudan until one reached the humid tropics of the coastal lowlands and the Congo basin. The transition was gradual enough so that farming and dairying cultures were able to co-exist over a fairly wide strip of territory running east and west. Although some tribes practiced both herding and agriculture, the dominant pattern was a symbiotic relationship, dairymen and farmers operating side by side and exchanging their products. However, political dominance of the dairying people over the farmers was the usual pattern. Along the western edge of the great African plateau, on the other hand, the climatic transition was abrupt, and the frontier between the dairying and farming economies closely followed the line of forty-inch rainfall. Where the precipitation was more than this, the presence of the tsetse fly, which carried a disease deadly to cattle, made dairying unprofitable.

The farming economy provided a basis for the development of great and relatively permanent kingdoms which, by all tests except that of literacy, fully merit the title of civilizations. These kingdoms, which will be discussed in the next chapter, were most numerous and most highly developed in regions immediately south of the Sudan. Although the imperial patterns also penetrated into the Congo, most of the states set up there lacked the elaborate organization of the more northerly ones and certainly represented a less advanced stage of development. Still further south, political centralization disappeared, leaving autonomous communities or small groups of villages recognizing only local chiefs. The patterns of peasant life were so similar throughout the whole area in which the main economic dependence was on agriculture that one is forced to conclude that there was an older cultural sub-stratum, upon which centralizing political institutions had been superimposed in various regions without greatly altering the daily life of the common people.

In the regions of heaviest rainfall the only domestic animals were goats, chickens, and dogs, with rare and sporadic pig culture. Toward the margins of the farming area a few cattle were kept, but there was a strong tendency toward specialization in this as in other economic activities. Cattle-keeping tribes interlocked with farming tribes, and the two exchanged their products. The principal crops of the heavy rainfall area were banana, yam, and taro, the last usually referred to in the literature as *bull yam*. Banana and taro were of Southeast Asiatic origin and must have been introduced into Africa from across the Indian Ocean. At least one of the yam species grown was also Southeast Asiatic. The main agents in the introduction of these crops were presumably the same Malayo-Polynesian voyagers who settled Madagascar. Since, except for yams, none of the economically significant crops raised in the humid African tropics were of African origin, it is probable that these regions were left to primitive hunting and collecting tribes until a comparatively late date. In the regions of less heavy rainfall, maize, manioc, various millets, sorghum, peanuts, and ground nuts were raised, but it should be noted that here also most of the historic staple crops were not of African origin. It seems safe to assume that anything like intensive agriculture, making possible dense and non-migratory populations, was a relatively late development in Negro Africa. Since strong centralized states cannot exist without such populations, the Negro civilizations must also be of relatively recent origin.

Most of the territory now occupied by the farming cultures was originally forested, while such areas as the lower Congo basin and coastal lowlands of West Africa were covered with heavy jungle. There was thus an abundance of hardwood and other forest products, making possible the development of an elaborate and well-balanced technology, although one whose content was largely perishable. It follows that the archeologist working in this region finds himself confronted with a situation somewhat like that in Southeast Asia. After the introduction of metal, stone-working of any sort seems to have been abandoned, while wooden objects, which must have been numerous at all periods, have succumbed to the ravages of termites and tropical climate. In recent years the value attached to antiquity *per se* has led Europeans to ascribe considerable age to many West African art objects. However, none of the wooden sculpture now extant can be more than two, or at the most, three hundred years old, while it is rarely safe to ascribe even a hundred years to any object which is not known to have been taken out of Africa before 1900.

Basketry and mat weaving were well developed throughout the entire agricultural region. The weaving of cloth, on the other hand, was most highly developed in the northwestern part of the area, suggesting that it may have been introduced as part of the Neolithic complex which seems to have reached this region from the Mediterranean. In the eastern and southern parts of the farming area, woven cloth was largely replaced by bark cloth. This, like the Southeast Asiatic bark cloth, was made from trees of the *ficus* family, but certain details of manufacture suggest an independent origin. Pottery was made throughout the entire area, but the rarity of ornamental pottery or painted wares suggests that it was primarily a cooking appliance. Eating utensils were uniformly made of wood or gourd shells. Houses were made of wood and thatch, appropriate to the climate, but the construction was usually excellent, and town houses were often large and elaborate structures.

Iron-working, including the smelting of local ores, was present throughout the region. In addition, casting brass and gold by the lost wax (see p. 106) process was a highly developed art. These metals were employed for ornaments and ceremonial objects. Bronze was unknown. The Negro metalworkers did not know how to produce alloys. Gold was worked as it came from alluvial mines and brass was obtained by trade. The use of the wheel in any form was unknown, a curious lack in view of the long trans-Saharan contact.

In contrast to the dairying cultures, most of the farming cultures produced wood carvings of considerable aesthetic merit. Practically all the objects to be seen in modern exhibits of African art were made by tribes having this economy. Artistic production reached its high point in the great kingdoms of West Africa and in the Cameroons, Gabun, and the Congo Basin. In the great kingdoms the concentrated economic surplus of subject populations made it possible for the ruling class to support professional artists, while the demand for luxuries provided a steady market. It must be emphasized that, even in the regions where there was no such concentration of wealth, the artists were, with very few exceptions, professionals. The term "primitive" is emphatically a misnomer when applied to African sculpture and any attempt to compare it to the work of children or the insane is nothing short of ridiculous. The different emphases embodied in African abstraction, and the peculiarities of presentation to be seen in African art, are the direct result of long-established traditions. Although some of the African work may appear naïve in terms of a European value system, it was no more primitive than any other highly stylized art such as the Byzantine.

One of the most outstanding features of African art was the high development of masks. These were intended, not only to disguise the wearer, but also to temporarily confer upon him the qualities of the Being which the mask represented. In many cases masks were in themselves fetishes, and as such had to receive periodic sacrifices in order to maintain their power and retain their good will.

Ivory was used mainly for ornaments and charms, and was carved with great skill, the small masks and grotesque figures of the Warega tribe and the huge carved tusks which formed part of the Benin altar arrangements representing the high points in this craft. Ornamental metal work was also highly developed in West Africa. Although some tribes did elaborate iron forging, the principal medium was brass, an imported material which was cast by the *lost wax* method (see Chap. IX, p. 106). The finest examples of the craft are the portrait heads of 11th century kings of Ife, which, in both conception and technical perfection, compare favorably with the finest Egyptian portraiture. The Ashanti are still famous for their small brass figures, sometimes arranged in intricate groups illustrating proverbs, and for their cast gold work. The artistic excellence of the life-size, conventionalized bronze heads and intricately cast plaques from Benin have received universal recognition.

In the division of labor men habitually worked in wood and metal. They also made bark cloth, a sharp departure from the Southeast Asiatic practice, and worked as potters and weavers in most areas where these crafts were highly developed. In agriculture they cleared the land but

WEST AFRICAN FEMALE FIGURE

usually left the planting and cultivation of crops to women. There were some exceptions to this in the West African civilizations, but farm work for men was generally considered degrading and was left to slaves when possible. Wherever there was a mixed agricultural-domestic animal economy, men cared for the animals. Whatever time women had left over from farm work, housekeeping, and baby tending was devoted to making utility pottery and baskets or, in the more advanced cultures, was spent in trade. The small business of the markets was almost entirely in their hands. Every woman tried to produce some food surplus, and the profit from this became her property.

There was a strong tendency toward professionalism in all the agricultural tribes. This reached its highest development in the civilizations, where most crafts were carried on by hereditary groups. Local specialization based on availability of particular materials or knowledge of particular skills was also common. Long-distance trading expeditions were carried on in many regions, while markets were almost universally present. These reached their highest development in the civilizations, where sales taxes and duties formed an important part of the royal revenue.

Trade was facilitated by the use of numerous local currencies in which blocks of salt, copper ingots, standardized iron tools and weapons, and so forth, served as media of exchange. Over most of agricultural Africa the standard unit of value was a cowrie shell which came originally from the Maldive Islands, off the coast of India. Millions of these shells were in circulation even in West Africa when the first Europeans arrived. They must have been traded clear across the continent, and their presence indicates the extent of African trade connections even under aboriginal conditions.

Farming methods were relatively primitive. Plows were unknown, the favorite agricultural implement being a short-handled hoe whose user had to bend almost double. Fertilizers and crop rotation were rarely used. The staple crops of various regions had a strong influence on settlement patterns. Land clearing was most laborious in the rain forest areas, but the crops habitually raised, yam, taro, and banana, depleted the soil slowly and made possible long-continued occupation of the same sites. In drier territory land could only be used for two or three years after clearing, and then had to be allowed to lie fallow for ten to twenty years. This cycle seems to have been due less to soil exhaustion than to the growth of weeds on the cleared land. Native farmers could not cope with this, and found it easier to abandon the field until the return of larger growth had smothered out the weeds. Under this system villages had to move every twenty or thirty years, and land ownership, except on a broad territorial basis, became correspondingly less important. The larger the local unit, the sooner it would have to move, and there was a

Cooperative labor

tendency for villages to break up into scattered compounds wherever the existence of a strong central authority made this safe. Since the clearing of new land could be done most efficiently by the combined labor of many men, cooperative labor organizations were a frequent feature of the agricultural societies.

In spite of the limitations imposed by the pattern of shifting agriculture, many regions in West Africa contained cities of considerable size. These cities served as royal residences, religious centers, and trading centers, much like the early cities of the Near East. They were made possible by the high development of trade which insured their supply of food and raw materials.

Polygyny was thoroughly approved by both sexes. Women preferred it because it reduced their labor, while men had other reasons. In many tribes sex relations with a wife were prohibited during the time that she was nursing an infant, and, since nursing was normally continued until the second or even third year, the husband of only one wife was seriously deprived.

Because of their economic importance, the status of women was exceedingly high. The rights of plural wives were guarded by elaborate regulations. The first wife, or the one of the highest social rank, functioned as head of the women's half of the family, directing the women's joint activities. The husband was expected to divide his time equally among his wives, usually a specified number of days with each in fixed succession. During this period the wife had exclusive rights to the husband and frequently was entitled to a share of any profits he might make. The arrangement was actually not unlike monogamy in installments. In general, the selection of a new wife was subject to review by all the previous wives, and it was not uncommon for a man's wives to urge him to marry a particular woman whom they found congenial and would like as a working partner.

In a well-organized family, each wife would devote her period with the husband to intensive domesticity, cooking and child-tending for the group and thus releasing the other wives for work in the field or for other economic activities, such as selling in the markets. Strange as such a system seems to European values, one must admit that it provided one of the best solutions so far discovered for the feminine problem of how to combine domesticity with a career. The husband was theoretically in control of the family, but only an exceedingly courageous man would defy his wives when they presented a united front. The tie between mother and son was exceedingly close throughout life. The relation between father and son was distant, and little love was lost between brothers, especially those by different wives.

Matrilineal and patrilineal descent were both present among the agricultural peoples. Even in many of the strongly patrilineal societies, there were various institutions which suggested an earlier matrilineal condition. The inconsistency between matrilineal descent and patrilineal residence was resolved in matrilineal tribes by sending sons back to their mother's sub-clan shortly after they were weaned. There they would be reared by one of her real or classificatory brothers, and in due course of time would marry and function as members of his joint family. Another interesting development frequently found in these cultures was the presence of simultaneous matrilineal and patrilineal descent groups, each of which had its own prescribed social or religious functions. Every individual belonged to two such groups, and his marriage with members of either was usually prohibited. The descent regulations of the farming societies, taken as a whole, strongly suggest that the original descent pattern in the region was matrilineal. An alternative explanation might be an early pattern of localized endogamous kin groups like those of Oceania. Within such groups the tracing of descent tends to be bilateral, and, with a shift to exogamy, either patrilineal or matrilineal institutions may develop.

Society was class-organized, with three levels: chiefs, who were normally hereditary; commoners; and slaves. Although the institution of slavery was greatly stimulated by European contact from the 17th to the early 19th centuries, there can be no doubt that it was old. In general, two types of slaves were recognized: recently captured enemies, who were considered on a par with any other domestic animals; and slaves who were members of long-established slave families or were fellow tribesmen enslaved for debt or minor offenses. Slave families were often associated with the same free family for generations, and the sale of such a hereditary slave was regarded as equally disgraceful to the slave and to his owner, since it indicated that both had failed in a legitimate social relationship. Debt slaves and petty criminals could be sold within the tribe, but their sale outside was forbidden or at least strongly disapproved. The relations of slave and master were covered by long-established patterns which guaranteed all but the enemy captives a considerable degree of justice and freedom of action. Owners were responsible for their slaves, and the hereditary slave of a chiefly family actually enjoyed a better position in many respects than a poor freeman.

Within the stratified society, the clan and sub-clan chiefs occupied an important position. The office was normally hereditary in a particular family, the one which was regarded as standing closest to the direct line of descent from the common ancestor of the kin group. The chief was chosen from among the sons in this family, usually on the basis of ability rather than birth order. He was regarded as an embodiment of the spiritual force or genius of the kin group, and as such played an important role in all rituals intended to promote its well being. At the secular level he acted as director of the group's activities and functioned as a judge.

All the societies who shared the farming economy had well-developed law codes and formal systems of legal procedure. Laws were precisely stated and legal precedence carried heavy weight. Witnesses were called to testify under oath, professional pleaders were employed by both sides, and the whole procedure was strikingly like the European one. Also, as in medieval Europe, trial by ordeal was resorted to in those cases where the evidence was so conflicting that the judge could not arrive at a decision, or in trials for malevolent magic where the actual practice was usually impossible to prove. Poison ordeals were common and far from uniformly fatal to the accused.

Religion in general was much more important among the farming than among the dairying societies. The ancestors were regarded as ever-present, and not only aided their descendants but also disciplined them for any moral slips. The male ancestors in particular were regarded with much more fear than affection, and it may be noted that in many cases conversion to Christianity, with the consequent relegation to limbo of

MUD HOUSE, NIGERIA

these invisible guardians of the status quo, has resulted in a distinct breakdown in native mores. In addition to the ancestors, there were often regular pantheons of deities, usually organized on the model of the human kin groups. These deities were, for the most part, associated with forces of nature, but the greater ones were often provided with supernatural messengers and servants who operated as intermediaries in the deity's dealings with humans. The good will of these was often sought more earnestly than that of their divine superiors. As might be anticipated, the god cults reached their highest development in the great kingdoms. For the average villager the gods were little more than literary deities, Beings who were the subject of fascinating myths, but with whom one had little dealing.

Aside from the ever-present ancestral spirits, interest centered in the village fetish. This was prepared by a medicine man at the time the village was founded, and was carried to the new site whenever the village moved. It was usually kept in a house either in or just outside the village, and it assured the health and good fortune of the community. It had to be propitiated with sacrifices and was treated like a deity. In addition to the village fetish, there were usually other community fetishes designed to give aid in specialized activities such as hunting, fishing, and agriculture. Each of these had to be strengthened by periodic ceremonies and sacrifices. Lastly, each individual possessed personal fetishes, some of which were worn, others kept in his house. Some of these were for general good fortune, others for aid in specific activities such as hunting or money-getting.

Lastly, mention should be made of the men's secret societies, which were widespread among the farming tribes. Curiously enough, they seem never to have been adopted by the dairying peoples. The origin of these societies is obscure. It has been suggested that they were developed in imitation of the Marabout orders of the North African Muslim. They may also have been developed out of the puberty initiations universally present. In any case, they were one of the most striking features of the African agricultural cultures. The societies were in part cult groups, but were also organizations for mutual aid, for social control, and not infrequently, for blackmail. Each society had its masks and characteristic costumes and gave occasional public performances at which these were displayed. Women, children, and any men who were not members were supposed to believe that the masked dancers were supernatural Beings, and anyone who discovered their real identity was killed. The societies had regular recognition signs and passwords, and members were pledged to mutual aid much as in Freemasonry.

The societies thus provided a unifying factor in regions where large political units were lacking, and enabled their members to travel out-

side their home territory with reasonable safety. Where political control
was strong, they were often quite understandably regarded with dis-
favor by authorities, and in Dahomey they were forbidden on pain of
death. Their activities varied with the region, but one of their main functions seems to have been the enforcement of local mores. "Uppity" wives
and other non-conformists were likely to be severely beaten or even
killed by masked members. The resemblance between the Ku Klux Klan
and these West African societies is striking, and may well be more than
coincidental. In addition to these socially approved secret organizations,
there were others whose activities were unqualifiedly anti-social. The
witch-societies, previously mentioned, may not have existed in fact, but
there was a Leopard Society, whose members regularly practiced murder and cannibalism, apparently as accompaniments to black magic.

Chapter XXXI

African Civilizations

FEW AMERICANS realize how rich and complex the cultures of many African societies were at the time of the first European contact. In the regions from which most of the American Negroes' ancestors were drawn, there were a series of strong and enduring kingdoms which deserved the name of civilizations on every count except that of literacy. In their arts and crafts these societies were little, if at all, inferior to medieval Europeans, while, in the thoroughness of their political organization and the skill with which social institutions were utilized to lend stability to the political structure, they far exceeded anything in Europe prior to the 16th century. It is not too much to say that in their home territory the African Negroes have shown a genius for state-building unsurpassed by any other people, except possibly the Incas of Peru.

Every civilization has drawn into itself elements from many sources, and those of Negro Africa are no exception. Contacts between them and the civilizations of Egypt and the Mediterranean littoral have existed since ancient times. Egypt is known to have traded and fought with the Negro tribes of the Upper Nile since at least 3000 B.C. During the 18th dynasty (1580–1320 B.C.) Nubia was conquered and occupied by the Egyptians and a vice-roy established there. The Nubians seem to have been overawed by Egyptian civilization and accepted it enthusiastically. They became devout worshippers of the Egyptian Amon-Ra, and close ties grew up between his holy city of Thebes and the Nubian capital at Napata. When Shashank and his Libyans conquered Egypt, many of the Theban priests fled to Napata and continued the work of acculturation. In 730 B.C. the Nubians conquered Egypt itself, but by this time they had become more Egyptian than the Egyptians. During the brief period of their power they attempted to restore rites which had already become moribund even in this unchanging land, and during the later

445

years of Assyrian and Persian domination they welcomed Egyptian refugees.

Nubia retained its independence under the Ptolemies and Romans, and during the first six centuries after Christ developed an independent civilization in which Egyptian, Greek, and Roman elements were combined with considerable originality. In the 6th century the Nubians were converted to Christianity and were able to beat off successive Muslim attacks until the middle of the 14th century, when the Christian kingdom of Dongala fell to the Funj, Arabized Negroes from the Blue Nile. From that time on Nubia participated in Islamic civilization.

It can be seen that there was abundant opportunity for Egyptian, Near Eastern, Greek, and Roman influences to reach Negro Africa by way of the Eastern Sudan. How much these contributed to the foundation of the Negro civilizations lying to the south and west it is difficult to say. One might expect to find the oldest borrowed elements, i.e., those of Egyptian origin, surviving around the margins of the area to which they had been diffused, and there actually are a number of items in some of the more advanced Negro cultures which are strongly reminiscent of Egypt. The widespread idea of a sacred king upon whose vigor the national welfare depends would be a case in point. Still more suggestive is the institution of the queen-sister, found in many central African kingdoms. In this the queen, with duties, privileges, and an establishment closely paralleling those of the king is always his sister. It may be remembered that in Egypt she was both sister and wife, and even this practice was followed by the Bahima, a Uganda tribe. Yoruba and Ashanti religions, with their elaborate priesthoods, numerous gods as objects of individual cults, and sacred animals, are also suggestive of Egypt. Lastly, the Ashanti believed in a spiritual double which visited the tomb after death, and it was for this that offerings were provided, quite as the Egyptians furnished their tombs for the comfort of the *ka.* To complete the picture, the Ashanti double was called a *kra.*

These and other features suggestive of Egypt show such an irregular distribution that it is hard to explain them on the basis of Egyptian diffusion. It seems more probable that their presence in both Egypt and Negro Africa was a result of independent development from a common basis in an ancient Hamitic culture. We know that Hamitic tribes not only settled the Nile Valley, but also extended their occupation over most of the Sahara at a time when the climate there was more benevolent than it is at present. Everything indicates that the Caucasic Hamites began infiltrating the Negro peoples to the south in Neolithic times if not before. The Berbers, who were the historic descendants of the Saharan Hamites, continued this process. Their conversion to Islam, which gave this southward penetration the sanctions of a crusade, merely accelerated what was already a long-established pattern. By the 9th century A.D., Berbers, with some slight Arab admixture, were already establishing a chain of kingdoms throughout the Western Sudan. The most important of these were Songhai and Ghana, in the region of the Niger. In the 14th century the Mandingo kingdom of Melle conquered the entire Western Sudan.

Berbers and Negroes mingled their blood freely, and even the ruling dynasties of these Sudanese kingdoms were predominantly Negro. However, they were self-consciously Islamic in culture, and their political organization followed regular Islamic lines. It has generally been assumed that the pagan Negro kingdoms which arose still farther south derived from those of the Sudan. However, the structure of the pagan kingdoms differed so much from the Islamic patterns that only some sort of stimulus diffusion seems possible. The pagans far exceeded the Islamic peoples in the complexity of their political organization and in the skill with which they utilized existing institutions to strengthen royal power.

As examples of these pagan kingdoms we may take Uganda (the civilization of the Baganda peoples) and Dahomey. The former lay at the eastern end of the whole line of pagan kingdoms and had received minimal Islamic influence. Dahomey, toward the western end of the line, was a much more recent creation. There had been numerous earlier kingdoms in the same region and these, in turn, had had extensive contacts with the Islamic kingdoms about the Niger. The West African coastal region had had still other civilized contacts. Although the expedition of Hano, the Carthaginian, is the only one of which a record has survived, there can be little doubt that other and less official voyages occurred both before and after his attempt at planned colonization. The gold and ivory of the West coast, which have given their names to two of the regions' modern political divisions, must have been a strong lure, and the Carthaginians were noted for their skill and courage in pursuit of profit. Dahomey also was in the region which received the first impact of modern European penetration. Although it is impossible to say how far this contact modified the native institutions, it unquestionably changed the native economy, shifting the emphasis from ordinary agricultural production to the slave trade and to wars for profit.

The kingdom of Uganda lies northwest of Lake Victoria. It includes a considerable stretch of shore line protected by outlying islands, so that coastwise traffic was easy. Although the Baganda never developed sails or any craft more elaborate than large plank canoes, the high level of their technological development was reflected in the excellence of these. Canoes were used in war expeditions against neighboring tribes, and the admiral of the canoe fleet was an important officer. More prosaically, fishing was a main source of protein food. Fish were dried and distributed throughout the whole kingdom in trade.

According to the native tradition, the organization of the Baganda kingdom was begun by Hamitic dairying people who invaded the region about 500 years ago and founded the dynasty which still rules. By the time of European contact these invaders had been completely absorbed both physically and culturally. Due to constant intermarriage, royalty and commoners were of the same Negroid type. The main economic dependence of all classes of the population was on agriculture. Some cattle were kept but they had become essentially luxury objects. The commonest domestic animal was the goat, and a commoner who was so fortunate as to own cattle normally kept them with the herd of his chief. Herding was done by a hereditary group, the Hima, who did not occupy a particularly high social position.

While a variety of crops were raised, the main sources of food were bananas and plantains. These were rarely eaten raw, being by preference steamed and mashed to a pulp. Banana mash was the bulk staple of the native diet, comparable to rice in the Orient, and although other foods were eaten with it, they were regarded as incidental and desirable mainly because of the flavor and variety they gave the meal. It may be noted that milk of either cattle or goats was very little used. In addition to various food crops, a species of fig was planted to provide bark for the bark cloth of which the native costume was originally made.

Baganda agriculture had significant effects on their patterns of production, settlement, and social organization. The banana plants, once established, would continue to send up new shoots and produce fruit for twenty-five or thirty years. This made possible relatively permanent settlements. Moreover, the yield was so heavy that a dense population could be maintained, even though women did all the agriculture. It is said that one woman could care for enough banana trees to feed four men. At the same time losses in males through war and through the huge human sacrifices required on various occasions were so heavy that the population contained three women for every man. The result was a society in which there was a very considerable surplus of time and energy, with possibilities for the development of correspondingly excellent manufacturies and complicated rituals.

The technology was essentially the same as that already described in the generalized account of agricultural tribes. However, the Baganda differed from most African peoples in their insistence on complete clothing. Although before puberty boys went naked and girls wore only a girdle with a fringe of shredded banana leaf, after puberty women dressed in a wraparound garment reaching from the armpits to the feet.

Men were even more heavily dressed, with a loin cloth, a kilt, and a toga. All garments were originally made of bark cloth, and the manufacture of this cloth was one of the men's main industries.

The peasantry lived in widely spaced compounds rather than in villages. The compound was surrounded by its banana plantations, and both compound and plantation were fenced. Houses were circular conical structures completely covered with thatch. The doorway was protected by a small inset porch or vestibule. The establishments of chiefs and even of the king himself followed essentially the same pattern, except for their much greater size and the larger number of their occupants. Thus the royal compound, which stood on a hill near Lake Victoria, was a mile and a half long and half a mile wide. Between the king's house and the main entrance lay the establishments of hundreds of officials and guards as well as slaves, while on the roads outside the enclosure were clustered the compounds of the great chiefs.

An unusual feature of the Baganda kingdom, and one which no doubt contributed to the successful functioning of its centralized government, was an extraordinarily good network of roads. These were frequently as much as twelve feet wide, hard surfaced, and with causeways running across swampy ground. The chief of each district had as one of his duties the maintenance of a road between the king's establishment and his compound, while each of the nobles in a district had to maintain a road between his compound and that of the paramount chief. The road system made possible rapid troop movements and an extensive exchange of manufactured goods. There were numerous markets to which both professional craftsmen and local peasantry brought their products. Markets within easy walking distance of each other were usually held on different days, forming a cycle, so that itinerant merchants, at the close of one market, could pack up their wares and move on to the next. Each market was in charge of an official who was responsible for maintaining order and punishing unfair dealing. The government imposed a ten per cent sales tax.

The social and political organization of the Baganda bore out their traditions of the origins of the state. There were only three hereditary classes: slaves, commoners, and members of the royal family. Since polygyny was the rule and the kings were expected to exceed their subjects in the number of wives, as in all other symbols of prestige, the royal group was fairly numerous. However, as a preventative of civil war, it was customary to kill most of a reigning king's brothers when he came to the throne, and to kill any of his daughters who married or bore a child. As a result the royal group was largely reconstituted in each generation.

Below the members of the royal family, who were debarred from

holding administrative offices, there were numerous officials who functioned as administrators. This group bore a superficial resemblance to
the European feudal nobility. However, all of them were appointed by
the king and owed allegiance directly to him. Since every appointment
automatically terminated at the king's death and any free man was
eligible for office, these administrators never developed into a distinct
hereditary class.

Slaves were, for the most part, prisoners of war or their descendants, although there were also Baganda slaves, children who had been
pledged as security for debt and whose labor provided the creditor with
interest on his loan. Slaves were in general well treated. Women became
concubines and were freed as soon as they bore a child to their masters.
The main disadvantage of slavery for men was their immediate eligibil-
ity for the numerous human sacrifices required by Baganda ritual.

Commoners were originally grouped in thirty-six patrilineal exogamous clans, but by the time of the first European contact six of these had
almost lost their identity through fusion with other clans. Each clan had
its chief, selected by a council of the clan elders. Upon his accession, the
clan chief took the name of the clan founder and was regarded as in
some degree his reincarnation. Each clan had two totems, usually animals, and took its name from the more important of these. Clan members were forbidden to kill or utilize their totems, but had no objection
to members of other clans doing so. A clan divided into a series of sub-
clans. The central feature of a sub-clan's territory was a graveyard for
its members. After it had been in use for three generations this graveyard, with the plantations about it, became the inalienable property of
the sub-clan, not subject to royal seizure. Each sub-clan had its chief
and usually a temple in which its founder or some clan deity was worshipped.

The organization of clans and localized sub-clans was certainly
older than the Baganda state. The Hamitic invaders superimposed the
administrative framework of the state upon it and were careful to keep
the two severely separated. Clan and sub-clan chiefs were in general
debarred from participation in the national government, and officials
were rarely appointed to rule over their own clansmen. At the same
time, through the ascription to the various clans of numerous more or
less honorary offices, the clan loyalty was used to bind the subjects to
the central government. To cite only a few examples of these, the post
of custodian of the royal tombs was hereditary in the Monkey Clan, the
king's guard was drawn from the Rat Clan, the men who carried the
king on their shoulders whenever he went outside the royal compound
were recruited from the Buffalo Clan, the royal gatekeepers came from
the Mushroom Clan, and the royal drummers from the Hippopotamous

Clan. A wife from the Otter Clan made the royal bed. Every clan sent wives, and from time to time levies of boys and girls were drawn from the various clans for service in the royal compounds and the households of the highest officers.

The whole structure of the state centered on the king, whose functions were as much religious as political. Immediately below him were two officials, the *Katikiro,* or prime minister, and the *Kimbugwe,* keeper of the king's umbilical cord. The former took charge of the administration of the kingdom, while the other had charge of the national shrines. Their offices thus corresponded to the two major aspects of the royal office. The entire kingdom was divided into ten districts, over each of which ruled a great official *Basaza,* or earl. Within his district the principal duties of the *Basaza* were to administer justice, maintain order, and supervise public works. He also had to provide a contingent of troops in time of war, keep certain buildings in the royal compound in repair and provision the king's household for one month in every ten. The earl of each district had special duties. The *Basaza* of Kayadondo, the district in which the royal establishment was situated, substituted for the king on the various occasions when the monarch was in seclusion. Because of the sacred nature of the royal office, these were fairly frequent. The *Basaza* of Busugu occupied a position of great importance, since he had charge of all the royal offspring, who were forced to reside in his district, and played a major role in the selection of a new king. The *Basaza* of the district of Busiro was custodian of the royal tombs, and his post was the only one which was hereditary in a particular clan. All other *Basaza* appointments were terminated with the death of the king, although a *Basaza* might be reappointed and, in any case, would usually be succeeded by another member of the same clan. Every *Basaza* kept one establishment in the capital and another in the district which he ruled. Each establishment was supervised by a steward who acted for the earl in his absence.

Below the *Basaza* there were six grades of minor nobles ruling over sub-districts. These nobles were appointed by the king with the advice of the earl but were responsible to the king alone. Like the *Basaza,* they maintained establishments in the capital, and all officials were expected to spend much of their time there. The whole order of nobility together formed the great council of the kingdom, which was in almost constant session.

One of the main duties of all officials other than palace functionaries was the administration of justice. Personal revenge was rigidly forbidden except during the lawlessness of an interregnum. There was an elaborate law code which was amended from time to time by royal decree. Nobles of each grade acted as magistrates in their own districts, but appeal was possible from lower to higher courts until the case reached the king himself. In litigation both the plaintiff and the defendant were required to post a bond in the same amount, and this was forfeited by the loser, a useful mechanism to discourage unnecessary litigation. Ordeals were resorted to when the evidence was inconclusive, and torture was used to extort confessions. Suspects might be kept in the stocks while waiting trial, but there were no facilities for prison sentences and the commonest punishment for minor crimes was mutilation, ranging from ear or nose clipping to castration or amputation of limbs. Those guilty of capital crimes were often reserved for human sacrifices.

Taxes were collected irregularly and levied whenever the royal treasury became depleted, but the methods of collection were well organized. Six tax collectors were appointed for each district, one each by the king, the queen-sister, queen-mother, the prime minister, the keeper of the national fetishes, and the earl of the district. The collectors visited each noble and fixed the tax to be paid by his territory on the basis of the number of compounds it contained. Taxes were paid in kind, and two months were allowed between the levying of the tax and its collection to give the peasants time to get together the necessary goods. The king received half of the total. The rest was divided beween the queen-mother, the queen-sister, and the two great ministers, while each *Basaza* and baron received a share of the tax collected from his district. Peasants were drafted as soldiers and also for labor on public works. There was a curious arrangement by which a man who had been drafted for labor had to pay a substantial sum to the overseer before he began work, although he received no compensation for his work.

Royalty was sharply differentiated from commoners and administrators. The central figures were the king, the queen-mother, and queen-sister. All of these, but the king in particular, partook of a personal divinity reminiscent of ancient Egypt. He was hedged about by elaborate ritual, and everyone who approached had to prostrate himself. Although the king never submitted to marriage, he had innumerable wives who had been presented to him as gifts or bribes, whom he had inherited from his father's harem, or who had simply caught his eye. Among these, the wife who had been acquired for him by his royal father was preeminent. All wives lived in the royal compound and were subject to strict chaperonage to insure the legitimacy of any children born to them. All kept their mothers' totems in recognition of their kinship with her clan. In addition they respected the lion and leopard totems.

Each prince, as soon as he was weaned, was turned over to the earl of Busugu, who appointed a guardian for him and assigned him a small estate. The eldest son, who was debarred from inheriting the kingship, shared with the earl the supervision of his royal brothers, while the eldest daughter of the king was similarly responsible for her sisters. Few of the royal sons survived the death of the father for any great length of time. When the heir had been selected, he and his mother gathered up all brothers who might have any claim to popular support and sent them to a particular place where they were put in a stockade under strict guard and allowed to perish of thirst and hunger. The royal daughters were treated with great respect. They were forbidden to marry or to have offspring but were not required to be chaste. Some of them became priestesses, while others, as free women supported by small estates, lived in promiscuity.

At the death of the king there was a hurried conference of the great ministers, the earl-guardians, and the king's eldest son. When they had decided who the next king was to be, the royal death was announced by extinguishing the sacred fire which burned before the entrance of the king's house, strangling its keeper, and sounding a special drum used at no other time. The drum telegraph carried the news to all parts of the kingdom, and the country immediately fell into anarchy. Earls and barons fought with each other, and the strong looted their weaker neighbors. All the princes were summoned to the capitol, and the earl-guardians announced who would be the next king. After this, the prime minister challenged any disappointed candidates and their supporters to a test of arms. The mother of the new king assumed the office of queen-mother, and one of his sisters or half-sisters was selected to be the queen-sister. Some of the most important officials were also appointed at this time. The king went through a complicated ceremony known as "eating up the country" in order to legalize his claim to the throne, but the coronation was postponed for six months, during which time the new king was in mourning for his father.

The earl-guardian of the royal tombs took the dead king to his district, where the body was mummified. When mummification was completed, the body was carried to the building which served as its tomb. Subjects brought offerings of bark cloth, which were piled inside until the house was filled to the roof, after which the door was sealed. Four of the king's personal attendants, four of his wives, and hundreds of slaves and captives were clubbed to death and their bodies left lying around the building. Six months later the house was opened and the head of the mummy removed and cleaned. One man drank beer and milk from the skull and thereafter became the medium through whom the ghost of the dead king spoke to the people. The skull was replaced in the tomb, but the jawbone, together with the umbilical cord, was deposited in a temple in the dead king's compound. Each king's establishment was kept up in perpetuity. The dead monarch's ministers, palace officials, and numerous wives continued to serve his spirit, and, as each

official died, a new man was appointed as substitute. The reigning king
was expected to visit his father's temple once during his reign. At the
conclusion of this visit he gave a signal, and hundreds of the onlookers
who attended every royal progress were seized and sacrificed to his
father's ghost.

The coronation came at the end of the king's mourning period. He
and the queen-sister took the oath of office and were invested with the
royal robes. Two men captured on the highway were blindfolded and
brought before the king. One of these he wounded with an arrow, and
this unfortunate was taken by a raiding party to the borders of a neighboring kingdom with which the Baganda were habitually at war,
maimed, and left to die. The second man was taken to a place of sacrifice, where eight other men were slaughtered one after the other and
their intestines draped around his neck. Thereafter he received a special
title and was placed in charge of the king's wives. Lastly, the earls built
new compounds for the king and for the queen-mother and queen-sister.
Each of these ladies had her own court, ministers, and court officials
paralleling those of the king in title and function.

Baganda supernaturalism was strongly tinged with magic. Here, as
everywhere in Africa, there were medicine men whose activities included the making of fetishes, working of magic, and healing of disease.
Medicine men were sharply differentiated from priests, who were attached to the service of particular deities, but there was some duplica-
tion of function between the two groups. Thus divination, which was
one of the medicine men's important activities, was also carried on by
the priests. While the medicine men divined by observing the fall of
cowrie shells, studying the entrails of fowl, and other objective techniques, the temples maintained oracles.

Baganda religion centered about the worship of the dead. Ordinary
souls were believed to become reincarnated a few years after death in
children of the same clan. The child was given the dead person's name,
and worship of the soul ceased. During the interval between death and
reincarnation, sacrifices had to be made to the ghost. Although generally
friendly to relatives, ghosts were quick to revenge neglect and to punish improper behavior, and their anger was frequently considered a
cause of disease.

Even the greatest gods of the Baganda were really ghosts, since all
of them were believed to have once lived on earth as men. Each clan
worshipped as its principal deity the spirit of its first ancestor. This ancestor was also incarnated in the clan chief, who assumed the ancestor's
name when he took office. As a spirit, the ancestor was provided with a
temple, priests, and all the appurtenances of divinity. The logical inconsistency involved in such multiple beliefs troubled the Baganda no

more than it did the ancient Egyptians. All dead kings were regarded as national deities and were frequently consulted by the reigning monarch.

Gods, as distinct from ancestral spirits, were equated with various natural phenomena. The most important of the Baganda gods was Mukasa, a deity associated with Lake Victoria. He provided fish, controlled storms, and was also a god of fertility. Every god had one or more temples, each with its corps of priests, its estates, and slaves to work them. The more important deities usually had one main temple for the use of the king and high officials and several small ones, scattered throughout the country, for the use of the common people. In each temple there was a medium who acted as intermediary between the worshipper and the god. He transmitted the worshipper's question or requests to the god and then, in a state of possession, gave an incoherent answer which was interpreted by the priest. All prayers were accompanied by offerings, which differed with the importance of the request and the standing of the worshipper. The darkest aspect of Baganda religion was the prevalence of human sacrifices. These were required as part of the worship of all the more important deities, and when a general calamity was feared several hundred persons might be sacrificed at one time. There were thirteen places in the kingdom where such mass sacrifices might be held. The method of sacrifice differed with the place. At one site the victims were clubbed to death and their bodies left to be eaten by hyenas and vultures. At another the victims' arms and legs were broken and they were left on the beach for the crocodiles to devour alive.

The fate of Uganda has been happier than that of most other Negro states. Difficulties of transportation and the absence of oil or other natural resources of outstanding value have protected it from foreign exploitation, while the climate has discouraged European settlement. The founding of a British Protestant mission in 1877 and a French Catholic mission in 1879 soon put an end to the more sanguinary aspects of the native religion. After the death of King Mutesa in 1884, the country was laid waste by wars between Protestant, Catholic, and Muslim candidates for the throne, and in 1894 Uganda became a British protectorate. The Baganda have shown themselves eager for education and there can be little doubt that they will play an important part in the development of a modernized African civilization.

Dahomey, on the slave coast of West Africa, had longer and closer contact with Europeans than any other Negro kingdom. Visited first by the Portuguese in the middle of the 15th century, it became of great importance in the slave trade. In the first half of the 19th century it was better known to and more frequently visited by Europeans than any other Negro state, even Ashanti. The West Africans were already accus-

tomed to trade and commercial production when the first Europeans
arrived. Most crafts were carried on by hereditary specialists, whose kin
ties made it easy for them to form guilds, and the traders in various commodities frequently organized to maintain prices and insure fair competition. Thus the mercantile activities resulting from European contact
were novel mainly in their scale. The integration of foreign merchandise
into the culture, the necessity for distributing the imported goods
throughout the kingdom, and, above all, the volume of value involved in
the slave trade made it possible for commoners, including women, to
amass considerable fortunes. Even the king himself was a trader and derived much revenue from this in addition to his income from taxes and
custom duties.

The European contact may have played a similar stimulating role in
the development of Dahomean technology. All the peoples of this part
of Africa were expert metal workers. The discovery of a series of magnificent portrait heads of the 11th century kings of Ife proves that this
skill was well developed before Europeans arrived. Nevertheless, there
was a tradition in the neighboring kingdom of Benin that the art was introduced in the 15th century by a Portuguese craftsman from whom a
clan of hereditary brass-casters traced their descent. While Europeans
certainly did not introduce this technique into Africa, they may well
have contributed to its perfection in Benin. After the 15th century the
art of the region also shows European influence in its subject matter, although not in its conventions. Muskets are represented as frequently as
any aboriginal weapons, and individual Europeans are depicted with
more cleverness than sympathy.

Dahomean society was strongly class-organized. At the bottom of the
social scale stood the slaves, who in this case were foreign captives or
criminals. There were no hereditary slaves in Dahomey because of a
long-established law that any person born on Dahomean soil was free.
However, this did not prevent the enslavement of Dahomean subjects
for numerous offenses, a tendency which was stimulated by the ready
market provided by the European slave traders. Not only criminals, but
even members of the royal family whom the king suspected of political
ambitions, might be enslaved and shipped overseas. The African ancestry of the Negro slaves sent to America was as socially diverse as that of
the occupants of Nazi concentration camps.

Between slaves and freemen there was a class of serfs, children of
royal slaves, who worked on the royal estates. These could not be sold
but could not leave the land. Commoners, who formed the bulk of the
population, were organized into forty non-localized clans. Each of these
had its hereditary chief who, in addition to settling disputes between

clan members, supervised their marriages. Since all bride prices passed through his hands, the post was a lucrative one. He also had the usufruct of all clan corporate property and the right to call on clan members for labor. His importance derived from his role as high priest in the worship of the clan ancestors, and he owed his power to his intimacy with the ancestral spirits. The oldest women of the clan also exercised great power, since they were soon to become ancestral spirits.

The clan members were scattered throughout the kingdom, and solidarity was maintained by yearly assemblies at which all deceased clan members, including those who had been enslaved and deported, were worshipped. Within the clan the principal social unit was the joint family. The joint family head administered its property and was treated with the utmost respect while alive and deified after death. It was every man's ambition to found a joint family of his own and have it grow into a sub-clan. A curious by-product of this system was that, since women could engage in business and accumulate wealth like men, techniques had been developed by which they could become founders of joint families. A woman who had accumulated sufficient wealth would buy land, build a compound, and purchase wives whom she would loan to selected young men for breeding purposes. The "wives" would address her as "husband," while their children, who formed the new lineage, would address her as "father" and show her the formal patterns of respect due a real father. In the next generation the sons in such a lineage purchased wives and brought them into the lineage establishment in normal fashion. The daughters, on the other hand, did not leave the establishment but brought their husbands into it. Matrilocal marriages were also resorted to by lineages which lacked sons, but this was a temporary arrangement. Only woman-founded lineages continued generation after generation. As a result, these lineages grew rapidly and were usually more than ordinarily numerous and prosperous.

For meritorious service the king conferred estates upon commoners. The estates were inherited by primogeniture and resulted in the creation of a semi-nobility known to Europeans as the *Caboceers*. These were subject to military service, like all free Dahomeans, and formed the nucleus of the national cavalry. All the descendants of Dahomean kings enjoyed princely rank. By the 19th century these princes had become so numerous that they constituted about ten per cent of the total population. The women of this group were not prohibited from marriage, but, since their marriages were usually contracted with commoners, they were dominant in the household and were famous for the casualness of their sex behavior. The king was allowed to marry princesses when the actual blood tie was distant, but his sons by princesses were debarred from the succession, since it was thought that their legitimacy would always be in question. The princes and princesses were not supposed to occupy themselves with trade or with any sort of manual labor. They were also, in general, prevented from holding any sort of administrative office. Their support came from hereditary estates and royal gifts.

Kin ties were exceedingly strong in Dahomey and the individual's obligation to innumerable relatives hampered his movements at every turn. It may have been in response to this situation that the distinctive Dahomean institution of Best Friend was developed. Every Dahomean man or woman had an individual of the same sex, never a relative, in whom complete trust could be reposed. The relationship was recognized in Dahomean custom and law, and even the king had his own Best Friend, a commoner. The Best Friend acted as confidante during the individual's life and was expected to assist him in all of his activities, legitimate or otherwise. If a man committed a crime and escaped, his Best Friend would be seized and tortured, since the real criminal, on hearing of this, would be sure to give himself up out of loyalty. A Best Friend might also assist a man by providing funds for the purchase of a wife. In such cases it was understood that when the first daughter of the union came of age the Best Friend would get her as wife without paying bride price. This arrangement was supported by some of the most vigorous sanctions in Dahomean law. If the girl eloped or was seduced, all women of the Best Friend's clan who were married to men of the seducer's clan were immediately and automatically divorced. The offended gentleman was then given his choice of all marriageable girls in the clan of the defaulting fiancée without payment and without reference to any marriage commitments which might have been previously made for them. When a man died, his Best Friend was expected to conduct his funeral and also to execute his will, which was usually confided to him rather than to any member of the family. The relationship was so important that most Dahomeans had second and third Best Friends who could be advanced to take the place of the first Best Friend if the latter died.

The royal establishment in Abomey included about 8,000 persons, nearly all of whom were women. The king had 40 "leopard wives," who attended his person, and several thousand other wives, the majority of whom never had any contact with their royal husband. Thus, the 2,500 Amazons who constituted the *corps d'élite* of the Dahomean standing army were classed as royal wives, although most of them were virgins and sex relations were forbidden to all of them under pain of death. Other "wives" were utilized as living archives, in whose memories the complicated affairs of the kingdom were preserved. Every official, from prime minister to local magistrate, had ascribed to him one of the royal wives as "mother." This woman was supposed to be present on all occasions when he acted in an official capacity, in order to remember what took place and to be able to report to the king.

The king had two great ministers, both of whom were selected from among the commoners. One of these, the *Mingan*, was originally the royal executioner. Later his duties were amplified until he became actually a prime minister handling the administration of the kingdom. He always married the king's eldest daughter and stood at the right side of the throne at formal functions. The other great minister, the *Mehu*, was charged with the administration of the royal palace and with the supervision of all members of the princely group. He married the king's second daughter and stood on the left side of the throne. There were numerous other officials involved in the administration of the kingdom. Although these were all commoners, there was a tendency for their offices to become hereditary. Each of the more important officials had a prince assigned to him as lieutenant. These lieutenants enjoyed some of the benefits of the office but had no power. The king's heir was chosen by him during his lifetime. He was normally the eldest son of the first wife given to the king by his father, but fitness was also considered. The heir apparent was given estates and numerous wives and was associated with his father in rule even before the king's death.

The kingdom was divided for administrative purposes into twelve districts, each under a hereditary district chief. Within each district there were several villages, also with hereditary chiefs. Each chief had his insignia of office: a carved staff and stool, which varied in design according to the particular office and had a height proportional to its importance, a pipe, and an umbrella carried over him on state occasions. The main duties of the chiefs were judicial. State finances were on a sound and regular basis, with sales taxes the most important source of income. Inheritance taxes were also levied, and the king received the confiscated estates of criminals. A commoner who made undue display of his wealth was very likely to be condemned on some trumped-up charge. There were numerous minor officials, and the whole bureaucracy was watched by an extensive, well-organized secret service.

Census taking was a distinctive feature of the Dahomean state activities. Every year there was a careful enumeration of the Dahomean population, including reports on births and deaths. Each individual was represented by a pebble. Special officials were charged with enumerating slaves, war captives, and deaths in battle. The pebble record was divided into fifteen units, one each for adult males, adult females, and children of each age group up to thirteen. The bags of pebbles were stored in a special house at the capital and constituted a lasting archive from which it was possible to see whether the population was increasing or diminishing and to govern policy accordingly.

Another distinctive feature of the Dahomean state was the existence of a standing army. All able-bodied free men were expected to respond to the annual levy, which took place at the beginning of the dry season, when there was a break in the farm routine. The general levy, being untrained and poorly armed, was of little military value. The strength of the state lay in its regular army. This was made up of palace guards, court attendants, sons of chiefs, certain classes of criminals, and the Amazon corps. The whole force was organized into regiments, each with its officers and distinctive uniform. Men formed the wings of the force, the Amazons the center. There were about 2500 Amazons divided into five groups: the musketeers, who were most numerous and formed the main body; the blunderbuss corps, older women who were veterans; the elephant huntresses, the most daring of all, who also accompanied the king on his hunts; and the razor women, a small group armed with straight razors with eighteen-inch blades which were especially designed for decapitating enemy chiefs. Lastly, there was a group of young girl archers who participated in parades but did little fighting. The Amazons went constantly armed and were kept in top training through frequent maneuvers. They proved their mettle during the French wars of conquest, and were probably the best native troops in Africa.

The king of Dahomey regularly made war every year against one or another of his neighbors. The motives were almost exclusively economic, the loot and especially slaves resulting from such expeditions forming an important addition to the royal income. Many features of the war pattern were reminiscent of the techniques used by European totalitarian states. The territory to be attacked was investigated by spies disguised as traders, and foreign officials were suborned whenever possible. A careful campaign was carried on to arouse the war spirit at home. Government agents were sent to the markets to spread rumors about atrocities committed by the state selected for attack, and everything was done to make it appear that the enemy was the aggressor and that Dahomey had gone to war against its will.

Dahomean religion was thoroughly organized about two groups of supernatural beings, the ancestral spirits and the national gods. The Dahomean concept of man's spiritual nature was much more complex than the European one. Every Dahomean had associated with him a supernatural being, the spirit of an ancestor. This being provided the material from which the individual's body was fashioned and afterward served as his guardian and helper. Each individual also had his private destiny, revealed to him by a diviner. Although this was not clearly personified, it had to be propitiated by sacrifices at least three times a year. In addition to these external entities there were three internal ones. The individual's personal soul was believed to have fashioned the body from the material given by the guardian spirit. It resided in the head and governed the thinking processes. It left the body temporarily in sleep, and dreams were its experiences. A personal "serpent," equated with the umbilical cord, was the individual's vital principle. If this were well treated and propitiated, it would bring its owner wealth taken from other men who had neglected their "serpents." Lastly, every individual had a divine spark, a bit of the goddess Mawu, which gave him his intuitive powers.

On death the various entities dispersed. The guardian spirit found other protégés until it had returned to earth sixteen times. The life principle, if it had been properly worshipped while the individual was alive, would join and strengthen that of the clan. Otherwise it drifted away to the mountains and might cause trouble. The divine spark returned to the goddess Mawu. The personal soul became a ghost, tarrying on earth until it had received a proper funeral. This had to be held within three years. If there was no funeral, it became a permanent ghost, very hostile to its neglectful relatives. After the funeral the soul went to the goddess Mawu to render an account of its life, being accompanied by the divine spark, which bore witness if it testified honestly. It finally reached the land of the dead, where it lived much as on earth. However, it retained a lively interest in the doings of its living relatives. It usually became the guardian of one of them, as already described. It was to this part of the individual's spiritual nature that the ancestral rites were primarily directed.

Each clan worshipped its own ancestors at a great annual ceremony, and once a year the king worshipped the royal ancestors on behalf of the entire nation. At this national ceremony, known as the "customs," several days of feasting and wealth display culminated in a spectacular ceremony held in the great plaza before the royal palace. The royal executioner, and representatives of all his predecessors in office, stood beneath a high platform from which animals were thrown down to be beheaded by them. As the culmination of this rite twenty or thirty men were thrown down and similarly beheaded, after which their bodies were exhibited hung from scaffolds about the square. At the great "customs" following the death of a king and the inauguration of his successor, many of the dead king's guards, wives, and palace officials, several hundred victims in all, were killed to provide him with a suitable entourage in the next world. Human sacrifices would also be made whenever it was desired to communicate important matters to the ancestral spirits. The victim would be given a message to be delivered to them and then executed. In spite of these practices, human sacrifice was much less important and extensive in Dahomey than it was in Uganda. One suspects that the value of human beings of any sort for the slave trade may have been partly responsible for this.

Side by side with the ancestor cult there flourished the worship of gods who had never been human. These formed three pantheons: the Sky, the Earth, and the Thunder deities. At the head of the Sky pantheon stood the Moon goddess Mawu; she was reputedly the mother of all other gods, although she was not regarded as a supreme Being or even a creator. Her consort was Lisa, the Sun god. The gods of the Earth pantheon were, with one exception, males. At their head stood a pair of twins, the first born of Mawu and Lisa. The other gods of this pantheon were their offspring. The Thunder pantheon was headed by the second son of Mawu, who had been given control of thunder, rain, fire, and the sea. Each of the three pantheons had its own cult, whose followers formed a sect. These sects corresponded in many respects to the secret societies present in other parts of West Africa but rigidly prohibited in Dahomey.

Every god had one or more temples, circular thatched houses containing his image set on a clay platform. The temple establishment consisted of a chief priest, a number of assistants drawn from the older cult members, a body of fully initiated lay members, and a number of novices undergoing initiation. The last lived in a special building on the temple grounds. Each sect had slightly different rituals, but they all conformed to the same general pattern, one of the most important aspects of which was possession of the priest by the god. Ritual dancing by the worshippers, also leading to possession, was a common feature of the ceremonies. Sacrifices were required as accompaniments to all requests. Individuals might join the cult either by inheritance or in fulfillment of vows. When a cult member died, his place was filled by another individual from his clan. Children were frequently vowed to a cult and were put through a long course of ceremonial initiation. In the course of this the novice was supposed to be killed by the god and resuscitated, subjected to various ordeals, possessed by the god, and finally ransomed by his family with a large sum of money. Members of the various cults had their hair cut in characteristic ways or wore distinctive ornaments. These Dahomean cults are of considerable interest to Americans, since they formed the basis of the much misunderstood American Negro voodoo practices. Both they and their voodoo derivatives were essentially benevolent in purpose and should not be confused with the practice of malevolent magic, to which the cult members were strongly opposed.

After the suppression of the slave trade the importance of Dahomey waned, and in the late 19th century European scramble for colonies it fell to the share of the French, who captured the capitol of Abomey and sent the last king into exile in 1892. Although the Dahomeans succumbed to the force of French arms, they had never given up hope of regaining their independence and restoring the monarchy. It is said that there is still a designated incumbent for every office in the kingdom and that, if the Europeans withdrew, the old patterns of government could be reinstated overnight.

In summary, the social and political organization of all the Negro kingdoms had numerous features in common. It would seem that their basic institutions all represented various elaborations of much the same themes. In all of them the peasantry was organized into more or less extended kin groups, with chiefs who functioned both in adjusting disputes between members and as priests of an ancestor cult. This kin organization was kept rigidly separate from the bureaucratic organization upon which the functioning of the state depended. Even when posts in this bureaucracy were hereditary, the kin group leaders were debarred from them. All the Negro kingdoms were highly autocratic, with power of life or death vested in the king. He also represented the court of last appeal in legal cases, and one of his important functions was dispensing justice. While benevolence in a king was appreciated, he was likely to be regarded as a weakling if he never utilized his powers arbitrarily. The person of the king was always sacred, and his physical condition was thought to affect the well-being of the state. In conjunction with this there were often formal previsions for the killing of infirm or senile rulers.

The royal ancestors were everywhere the subject of a national cult and functioned as guardians of the kingdom. The royal establishment was always elaborate and absorbed much of the national revenue. It included guards, an elaborate cadre of court officials, and hundreds of wives. Although rarely rigidly secluded, the king's wives were usually guarded to prevent adultery. None of the Negro kingdoms had legislative bodies or any other device for popular representation in government. Although the king usually had a council, the members were appointed by him and their duties were purely advisory. Like the kin group leaders, the king's own kindred were normally excluded from office. Women of the royal group everywhere enjoyed a high degree of freedom in sexual behavior, yet they were either prohibited from bearing children or their children were excluded from the succession.

It seems unlikely that, in the resurgence of African culture which may be expected to take place within the next century, these long-established patterns will be ignored. In particular, it is highly improbable that any attempt to impose the reality, as well as the outward forms of democratic government, upon the African civilization will be successful.

PART NINE

The Orient

Chapter XXXII

Prehistoric India

EUROPE OWES its continental status to Greek parochialism; India has been deprived of such status by the same sort of limited perspective. The great peninsula is as large as the continent of Europe exclusive of Russia, and its inhabitants comprise one-fifth of the world's population. Its climates present every gradation from glacial peaks to lush tropical jungles, and to deserts as forbidding as the Sahara. Throughout the historic period there has been no other region of equal size occupied by as great a variety of races, languages, and cultures, and this situation continues even today. Tribes of genuinely primitive hunters and food-gatherers are to be found within two or three hundred miles of great modern cities, and the largest steel mills in the world match their assembly lines against village artisans carrying on hereditary occupations by techniques which were old when Alexander of Macedon made his raid into the Punjab. No adequate description of such a country can be given in a single volume, let alone within the scope of a few chapters. The present discussion will, of necessity, be confined to those aspects of Indian life which serve to indicate the place of Indian civilization in the world picture and the role which it has played as both a receiver and donor of culture elements.

India is geographically more isolated than any other part of Eurasia. On the north it is cut off from the rest of the continent by the enormous barrier of the Himalayas, a sort of Maginot line against invasion. The western end of this rampart rests upon the deserts and mountains of Baluchistan, while its eastern end is buttressed by the equally formidable jungles and swamps of Assam. Like every static defense, this Himalayan bulwark was breached repeatedly, but behind it India presented a more formidable defense in depth. A Mongol general who had raided into the Indus Valley wrote back, "This is an evil land. The water is bad and the sun kills men." The successive waves of

hard to conquer due to barriers & mts, swamps, disease, heat

northern invaders found themselves in a crowded and a long-lived-in land where, no matter what their skill in arms or the rapidity of their initial conquest, they were confronted thereafter with an unending war against climate and disease. In the slow, continuous struggle for survival which followed every new conquest and occupation, the older population always came off best. The invaders could survive only by mingling their blood with that of the conquered and accepting much of the Indian way of life. Their descendants became an integral part of India, finding places in the elaborate yet flexible structure of Indian society and religion. In India the mosaic pattern, already mentioned in connection with the Near East, reached its climax. There the problem of integration was solved by creating a sort of jig-saw puzzle in which innumerable sub-societies of diverse origin were fitted together to form a coherent picture, a working whole in which each unit has its place, protected by specialized activities and religious sanctions. Thanks to this system, Indian civilization has been able to maintain itself for at least three thousand years as a distinct, easily recognizable cultural entity. It has borrowed extensively, like all civilizations, but it has borrowed selectively and shaped its borrowings to its own patterns.

The diversities of India stem in part from natural environmental factors. The peninsula falls into four geographic zones. Along its northernmost edge the heavily forested slopes of the Himalayas support a sparse population. Between the Himalayas and the Vindhya Mountains to the south lies a region of fertile river valleys and plains which the Indians themselves regard as the heart of their homeland. This was the region in which Indian civilization assumed its historic form. Even this "Land of the Five Rivers" has a far from uniform climate. At the western end lies the Indus Valley, once a forested region and seat of a great civilization, now deforested, and with a precarious rainfall which makes agriculture impossible in many places and dependent on irrigation in the rest. To the east lies the Ganges Valley, with its superabundant rain and hothouse climate, while between is a region of little rainfall, with seasonal alternations of tropical heat and cool temperate weather. South of the Vindhya Mountains the central part of the peninsula is occupied by a moderately high plateau, the Deccan, bordered on the east and the west by abrupt hills, the Ghats, which run parallel to the coasts and converge in the extreme south to form the Nilgiri Hills. The elevation of this plateau brings a temperate climate into what otherwise would be a tropical region, while the Ghats cut off the full effects of the monsoon, resulting in a moderate rainfall. Most of this region seems to have been covered originally with deciduous, not very dense forest. Between the Ghats and the sea, on both sides of the peninsula, lies a rather narrow plain with many lagoons. This is a region of intense heat and heavy rainfall, ecologically related to the Malay Peninsula and Indonesia. The seaward slope of the Ghats are covered with dense tropical jungle, and some of the most culturally backward peoples in India and, indeed, in the world, have succeeded in holding out here. On the coastal plains and in the Deccan live civilized groups whose physical type and language attest their aboriginal ancestry.

The most important feature of Indian climate, and the one which affects the entire continent, is the monsoons. There are only three seasons in India: a cool, dry period from October to February; an intensely hot, dry period from March to June; and a rainy season extending from June to September. Practically all the rain on which agriculture depends everywhere in India falls in these four months. Moisture-laden winds originating far out over the ocean between India and Africa reach the Malabar coast in Southwest India about the end of May. From there they move diagonally across the peninsula until they reach the Bay of Bengal, where they gather up more moisture and deposit the heaviest rain over Burma and the Northeastern Indian provinces of Bengal and Assam.

The Himalayas deflect the winds back in a northwesterly direction and they pass slowly across the whole of Northern India, depositing less and less rain as they go westward. The southwest monsoon usually reaches this region three weeks after it has appeared in the south. About the beginning of September it dies out, and the northeast monsoon begins to blow. Coming from the interior of Eurasia and passing over lands which are already arid, this wind brings cold air but little or no rain. It ushers in the pleasant climate of the Indian winter. Only far Southern India receives any appreciable amount of winter rain. Because of the long dry season, irrigation has been in use in much of India since prehistoric times. However, crops and people are heavily dependent upon the monsoon. Experience has shown that the rainfall in most parts of India is insufficient approximately one year in five, while one year in ten the failure is complete enough to threaten famine. These recurrent famines have provided a cruel but effective solution to the Indian problem of overpopulation, a problem to which no gentler answer has been found to date.

From the point of view of the social anthropologist India has no race problems. Physical type is only incidentally an indication of social status. Although *Varna*, meaning color, is the Sanskrit term for the four great divisions in the system by which castes are classified, and the classical explanation for caste is that it came into existence to protect the dominant Aryan group from miscegenation, today the black South Indian Brahman is no less aristocratic for that reason, nor is the white-skinned, grey-eyed untouchable of some northern Indian regions any more elevated because of his pale complexion. Fairness, however, is a criterion of beauty much as it is among American Negroes.

For the study of race as a physical phenomenon India presents a fascinating series of problems. Recent developments in the study of race, which are substituting dynamic for the long-established static concepts, have increased rather than diminished the complexities. It was difficult enough to account for the Indian racial diversity in the days when races were regarded as fixed entities. Modern recognition that the phenotype can be altered by a whole series of very little understood environmental influences, and that new human breeds may come into existence through the fixation of hybrid characteristics, opens an endless field for study. Indian social conditions were ideally suited to the production of a tremendous variety of human breeds. A nearly constant feature of the Indian caste system was its insistence upon endogamy. At the same time, any new social group which came into existence in India was presently transformed into a caste.

Invaders who entered India in complete ignorance of the caste system and took to themselves concubines from the local population were, within a few generations, converted to caste practices and began carrying on a quite unconscious experiment in the fixation of hybrid characteristics. Gangs of bandit adventurers who gained control of territories in times of confusion soon claimed caste status for themselves, in bland indifference to their heterogeneous origin. Lastly, practically every religious reformer who has arisen in India has begun by denying caste and welcoming converts from all regions and levels of society, only to have his sect transformed into a caste within a few generations. Furthermore, since each caste has its own dietary rules and its own costume and social conventions, including rules of marriage, the possible permutations and combinations of genetic and environmental influences are almost astronomically numerous. What one actually finds at present, if one studies Indian castes as the functional local groups on which the system is based, is that the members of any caste, even one only a few centuries old, tend to show a sort of family resemblance.

India would thus offer the world's best field for studying the dynamics of human evolution if we only knew exactly what racial elements had gone into the making of the present population. Unfortunately, any attempts to reconstruct Indian racial history must be largely conjectural and are likely to remain so. The practice of cremation is certainly ancient throughout most of India, and, while it has both aesthetic and sanitary advantages, it writes "finis" to the anthropologists' attempts to trace racial history on the spot. We can only reconstruct India's racial past on the basis of cultural hints and resemblances between current Indian physical types and those found in other areas.

Paleontological work as intensive as that which has been carried on in Europe may well bring to light the most ancient Indian. There can be no doubt that the peninsula has been inhabited continuously since a time when its population had not yet acquired the practice of cremation or, indeed, of any ritual type of disposal of the dead. As far back as the Miocene, India was the home of a surprising variety of anthropoids, including the large and presumably ground-living Dryopithicine group who, until the recent African discoveries, appeared the best candidates for the honor of a position in the direct line of sub-human ancestry. Certain geological episodes, such as the elevation of the Himalaya Mountains, must have disturbed the peaceful existence of these ancient anthropoids and quite possibly affected their evolution, but there is no indication that any environmental changes within the peninsula were extensive enough to destroy its primate population.

If India was not within the area in which our own species evolved, it was certainly one of the first regions to be occupied by our peripatetic ancestors. Even today there are groups in the south of India whose physical type differs in only minor respects from that of the Wadjak man of Java, the oldest recognized representative of our species. Various breeds of proto-Australoids, as this archaic generalized type is usually termed, still occupy most of Southern India. It is interesting to note that their physical "primitivity" is in no way related to cultural backwardness. In fact, they produced and perpetuated civilizations which compare favorably with anything developed by the much advertised Caucasic Aryan of the north of India.

Since ancient skeletal material is almost completely lacking in India, one must turn to current distributions as a basis for reconstructing racial history. In the south of India the population is predominantly of the proto-Australoid type just mentioned. The main racial component in Northwestern India seems to be a Mediterranean-type Caucasian, differing from the Western representative of the type mainly in somewhat taller stature and markedly darker pigmentation. These differences can readily be accounted for as results of long residence in a tropical or semi-tropical environment with strong sun. In the same region and extending for some distance down the west coast of India, there is a factor of round-headedness which does not seem to be consistently linked with other racial criteria. Its presence may be due to an invasion from beyond the northwest frontier, a region where round heads are still common.

In the Himalayan foothills there is a fairly strong Mongoloid element, easily explainable as the result of infiltration from across the mountain barrier and eastward from Assam. In Northeastern India one finds a rather distinctive physical type characterized by a combination of round headedness, dark pigmentation, and a somewhat Mongoloid cast of countenance. This type can most readily be explained as a result of mixture between proto-Australoids and Mongoloids.

These various types have mixed to produce an infinite variety of local breeds. In general, the proto-Australoid elements are strongest in the south of India and from there northward along the east coast. The Mongoloid elements are strongest in the Northeast and do not penetrate Southern India in strength. The Mediterranean-Caucasic element is strongest in the Indus Valley and seems to have diffused from there eastward and southward. There can be little doubt that the proto-Australoids formed the aboriginal population of the entire peninsula. The first invaders were probably the Mediterranean Caucasians. From finds of skeletal remains we know that this type was associated with the Indus Valley civilization, which in turn showed many resemblances to the civilizations of Mesopotamia and other regions to the west.

The Mongoloid element was probably the last one to enter India in force, but it established itself by a process of gradual infiltration rather than by large-scale invasion. In addition to these main elements, there have been innumerable minor accretions of foreign blood. Greeks, Scythians, Mongols, Zoroastrian Persians, Muslim Persians, Arabs, Syrians, Malays and Chinese have all entered India and contributed their genes to the present rich and diverse mixture. Curiously enough, the racial element introduced by the invading Aryans cannot be identified. It has usually been assumed that they were blond Nordics, but one looks in vain for any surviving enclaves of this type. Indian heat and sun provide an environment unfavorable to blonds; if this racial group ever invaded India in force, it has disappeared without a trace.

The linguistic situation in India is almost as complicated as the racial one, but as in the latter the infinite local variety can be reduced to a few main stocks. The smallest but in some ways the most interesting of these is the Austric stock. Languages of this stock are found throughout Southeast Asia and the Pacific. In India their speakers are, almost without exception, groups of simple culture living in refuge areas, suggesting that this stock is very old in the peninsula. Languages of the Dravidian family are spoken throughout the whole of India south of the Godavari River, with an isolated example, Brahui, in the far northwest. The presence of various Dravidian words and phonemes in the Indo-European languages of Northern India suggests that Dravidian languages were once spoken throughout most of the peninsula. Lastly, the Indo-European, i.e., Aryan, languages are spoken throughout the whole of Northern India.

The Dravidian distribution in particular raises some exceedingly interesting problems, and emphasizes once more that physical type and language are by no means necessarily linked. If Dravidian languages were originally linked with the proto-Australoid type, as current distributions would suggest, it seems highly probable that the Mediterranean Caucasic population of Northwestern India had been converted to their use during the interval between its own arrival in India and that of the Aryan conquerors of approximately 1500 B.C. If, on the other hand, the Dravidian languages were brought into India by these same Mediter-

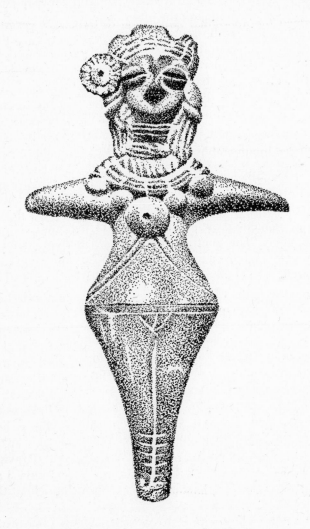

GODDESS, INDUS VALLEY, 2000 B.C.

ranean invaders, one is confronted with the more difficult problem of how the whole south of India, where the Mediterranean racial element is certainly insignificant, could have been converted to their use.

Our knowledge of Indian prehistory is still extremely sketchy and based largely on surface finds rather than systematic excavations. However, these indicate that India, since the most ancient times, has been the meeting ground for two fundamentally distinct culture complexes. In the Old Paleolithic, Northwestern India was the seat of a hand-axe culture belonging to the general African-Western Eurasian co-tradition. Eastern and Southern India, on the other hand, had chopper- and flake-using cultures of the Southeast Asiatic co-tradition. The border between these two cannot be accurately traced at present. It is highly probable that it fluctuated with climatic changes during the many thousand years that the two co-traditions shared the peninsula. One may anticipate that the distribution of each will be found linked to particular ecological conditions, the hand-axe cultures occupying regions where the natural environment was like that of Southwestern Asia, the chopper- and flake-using cultures regions where the ecology was of Southeast Asiatic or Indonesian type.

Upper Paleolithic and Mesolithic remains have been found in several places in India, but too little work has been done to make it possible to give distributions or suggest outside connections.

Neolithic remains show a continuation of the Southeast-Southwest Asiatic dichotomy. The Southern and Eastern Indian Neolithic inventory is characterized by a multiplicity of adze and axe forms and a relative scarcity of chipped stone implements. Most of the adze forms, some of which are highly specialized, can be duplicated in Southeast Asia. The Northwestern Indian Neolithic, with its stone celts and emphasis on numerous pottery types, has unquestionable Western affiliation. A recent find of a Neolithic tool factory in the province of Madras in Southern India suggests an extension of the western Neolithic complex toward the Southeast. In addition to adzes, axes, and chisels, the Madras inventory includes a considerable variety of small chipped implements, knives, scrapers, arrowheads, and so forth. These are out of place in the Southeast Asiatic co-tradition, with its heavy dependence upon bamboo for projectile points and cutting tools.

The outstanding feature of South Indian technology during the whole period from the Neolithic to the dawn of history was the high development of Megalithic construction. Megalithic sites are exceedingly numerous in this region. It is said that there are about a million of them in the Deccan alone. They include circles, menhirs, dolmens, and rock-cut tombs and were constructed from both uncut and dressed stones.

The tombs contain skeletons, an indication that the practice of cremation had not yet begun. The physical type was proto-Australoid, like that of the present inhabitants of the region. With the burials were placed coarse pottery vessels, apparently as containers for food offerings, and a variety of stone ornaments and weapons. In the later part of the Megalithic period metal objects were placed in the tombs in considerable numbers, but copper, bronze, iron, and gold are intermingled in the same deposits from the beginning. In this respect the South Indian Megalithic culture resembled the Dong Son complex of Southeast Asia, which was also associated with Megalithic construction. Unfortunately, neither can be dated with any accuracy. It seems probable that metal-working was introduced into Southern India and Southeast Asia in fully developed form, but, if so, the South Indians seem to have improved upon their instructors at least in iron-working. As far as we know, South India was the first place in the world where steel was made deliberately, and the simple but effective methods used in producing this alloy of iron and carbon are still used here.

The number of Megalithic sites and the size of the stones transported and erected suggest a dense ancient population in Southern India. Agriculture seems to have been practiced from very ancient times. Rice has been identified in the food offerings placed in Megalithic tombs and was presumably a staple crop. In view of the Southeast Asiatic affiliations of their culture, it seems highly probable that the Megalithic builders also grew the root and fruit crops, hard to identify archeologically, of the Southeast Asiatic center and practiced irrigation. We have no evidence as to whether they knew the plow or had as yet domesticated the water buffalo, without which the plow would have been of only moderate value for work in irrigated fields.

The only clue to social or political organization is the presence of group burials, with indications that the same tombs were sometimes used over a considerable period. Both this and Megolithic construction, with its requirements of organized manpower, suggest the presence of extended kin groups. Since nothing resembling royal tombs has been discovered, it seems probable that there were no centralized states with autocratic governments at this period.

In contrast to the confused archeological situation in Southern India, the northwestern part of the peninsula provides a coherent picture whose outlines are becoming increasingly clear. Since the existence of the Indus Valley civilization has only been recognized for about thirty years, there are still numerous gaps in the record, but excavations under way or projected should fill most of these. By 3300 B.C. at the latest, the Indus Valley was occupied by a great civilization which had been developed out of the Southwestern Asiatic Neolithic base. There is little direct evidence for the origin of the Indus civilizations in the Indus Valley itself, since the lowest levels in most of the sites excavated are under water, but numerous finds in adjoining Baluchistan and Seistan indicate that there were Neolithic cultures there very similar to those in Mesopotamia in pre-urban times.

Even if its exact origin and line of development are never discovered, the Indus Valley civilization itself provides abundant evidence of Southwest Asiatic affiliations. It followed the Southwest Asiatic tradition in passing through successive stages of copper and bronze utilization. It had come to an end before the introduction of iron. The staple foods were wheat and barley. No rice has been found so far. Numerous representations of cattle, including some showing their use as draft animals, suggest that the economic base of the culture was a mixture of farming and dairying. The wheel and loom seem to have been known from the first. It is impossible to say whether the plow was used, since no examples or representations of it have come to light. This is in sharp contrast with the numerous miniature carts, modeled in clay or cast in bronze, which seem to have been favorite toys of the Indus Valley children. Grain was apparently hulled in mortars, and one of the sites shows brick-floored circles polished by generations of bare feet, in the center of which the wooden mortars were set.

Cotton probably was cultivated, since cotton cloth has been found. Flint, copper, and then bronze were cast in a variety of forms. Tools included adzes, axes, and saws with offset teeth. One of the most interesting finds is a piece of a bronze ruler with divisions accurately marked, showing that the Indus Valley people were already conscious of small exact measurements. There were also bronze weights arranged in a complicated scale. Pottery was abundant, and even that from the lowest level so far excavated was wheel-made and well-fired. Much of the pottery was coarse cooking-ware, but the better jars were painted black on a red ground and burnished to a lacquer-like finish. The designs were mainly floral and showed little vigor or originality. There were innumerable little clay figures which are presumed to have been toys. So many of these have come from one site that it must have been a center in which they were manufactured for export.

Crude female figures, nude except for elaborate ornaments, are exceedingly numerous and probably represent a mother goddess connected with domestic fertility cults. A curious feature of the culture is the almost complete lack of sculpture. This is the more striking since the examples which have been found show extraordinary skill and a developed style. A red sandstone male torso is better executed and more naturalistic than even Egyptian work of the same period. The head was separate, and the neck socket suggests that the piece may have had multiple heads reminiscent of the many-headed, many-armed deities of later India. It seems probable that most large sculpture of this period was done in wood and consequently has not survived.

The most interesting artistic products which have survived are flat rectangular seals usually cut from soft, white limestone. They are carved with figures of animals and supernatural beings executed with great skill and vitality. All the animals represented are Indian, but not all of them are now found in the Indus Valley. A figure of an elephant wearing a blanket is of special interest since, aside from a mention of a blanket-wearing elephant in the Gilgamesh epic, it is the earliest indication that this animal was tamed. Numerous figures of trees with animal figures below indicate tree worship, while a three-faced human figure seated in one of the Indian ascetic attitudes of meditation may be a prototype of the historic deity Siva. Many of the seals bear brief inscriptions in a character unlike anything known elsewhere. The precision with which the characters are drawn and their number, too great for an alphabet but too few for ideographs, indicate that the Indus civilization used a syllabary. No other inscriptions have been found, and it is safe to conclude that records were kept on perishable materials. The recent findings at Mohenjo Daro of a jar with an inscription in early Sumerian characters raises hopes that a bilingual inscription may sometime be found. Failing this, we have no clues to the spoken language.

The cities of the Indus civilization reflect an even higher level of culture than the arts. They were carefully laid out on a gridiron plan, with a main thoroughfare or thoroughfares connected by narrow ways. There can be no question that they were deliberately planned and then constructed, a practice which has continued all through Indian history. A striking feature of all the sites so far excavated is the absence of anything which could be construed as a temple or palace. At Mohenjo Daro there are the remains of an extensive roofed area with numerous pillars but no interior walls, probably a bazaar, a large building with numerous rooms which may have been an administrative center, and a large and extraordinarily well-built swimming pool surrounded by cubicles which look like dressing rooms. It seems likely that the last was used for some sort of ceremonial purification comparable to that practiced by modern Hindus.

It is hard to believe that such a rich culture lacked temples. Perhaps the later Indian reverence for hermits and forest retreats was already present, and worship was carried on at shrines outside the urban area. Only one burial ground has been discovered to date. This contains urn burials of ashes and bone fragments, indicating that cremation was already in use. The lack of palaces in the sites is also surprising. It seems best explained on the theory that only provincial cities have been excavated to date and that the capital of what had been a veritable empire still awaits discovery.

Dwellings were two stories high and were built of hard-fired brick. Walls were plastered or lime washed but show a complete lack of decoration. Probably the inside walls were covered with hangings. Furniture consisted of chairs and probably tables and bedsteads.

The first city of this culture to be excavated, Mohenjo Daro, was unfortified and there was a striking lack of weapons among the finds. This led early writers to picture an idyllically peaceful society. Subsequent excavations have shown that some of the cities were walled, while at least one had a heavily fortified acropolis. Even at Mohenjo Daro there were signs that the city had been attacked and its inhabitants slaughtered.

The Indus civilization was by no means limited to the Indus Valley. Sites have been found in Baluchistan, Seistan, and as far south as Kathiawar. Objects of Indus Valley origin have also come to light in the Ganges Valley but no occupation sites of the Indus culture have so far been found there, suggesting that even at this time the immemorial dichotomy between the Southeastern and Southwestern Asiatic co-traditions was still being maintained.

The lowest levels in most of the Indus Valley cities are now below water level and cannot be investigated. However, the civilization certainly goes back to 3300 B.C., as established by cross-dating with Mesopotamian sites. The culture showed great stability and seems to have already reached its highest development by the earliest period now accessible. After this there was a gradual deterioration in culture and diminution in population, with the occupation of most of the cities coming to an end about 2500 B.C. There is good reason to believe that there were significant climatic changes between the initial development of the civilization and its fall. The hard-fired brick from which even ordinary dwellings were made required abundant fuel, while the construction of the houses and the large street drains suggest that carrying off heavy rain was a problem. The ancient climate was probably wetter than it is at present, and the forests were certainly much more extensive. Deforestation, soil exhaustion, the souring of the soil under irrigation without underdraining, and the climatic change may all have contributed to make the region inhospitable. The signs of loot and murder at Mohenjo Daro may indicate that the *coup de grâce* was administered by barbarian invaders, but if so there is a significant difference in time between this hypothetical invasion and the 1500 B.C. usually given as the approximate date of the Aryan invasion.

The Aryans have been the most advertised of all the groups which have invaded India, and numerous beliefs regarding them have become practically religious dogmas. According to the classical formulation, they entered India about 1500 B.C., killed or reduced to slavery the aboriginal population, established the institution of caste in order to maintain the purity of their blood, and then turned from warfare to mysticism and developed the pantheistic and spiritual evolutionary concepts upon which all later systems of Indian philosophy were based. They became the ancestors of the three highest groups in the caste classification and gave their language to most of India.

These beliefs were developed on the basis of a devout and far from critical study of the Sanskrit literature. The Aryans did give their language to the whole of Northern and Central India, but beyond this the dogmas need to be subjected to a sort of higher criticism. The literature itself contains numerous inconsistencies, and it is possible at the present time to check the picture which it gives against a greatly increased knowledge of both pre-Aryan India and the probable culture of the Aryans at the time of their arrival.

The Aryan invasion of India was, after all, only one of a series of movements which carried Indo-European speaking people from the eastern steppes into the more civilized regions. The invaders everywhere created and preserved a considerable literature, verbally transmitted, and the accounts which all these literatures give of their life have so many features in common that their original culture can be reconstructed with considerable accuracy. The picture it gives is of semi-nomadic tribes of cattle-lifting, chariot-racing raiders, equally addicted to gambling and hard liquor, and interested in the supernatural only in time of need. Even then they seem to have felt considerable doubts as to the efficacy of their worship and to have tended toward the semi-mechanistic fatalism embodied in Beowulf's often repeated comment, "Weird goeth ever as she must." It is conceivable that such a people might settle down and become contented cultivators, as the Aryan literature pictures them doing in India, but it is much more difficult to imagine them turning to deep philosophical discussions or developing patterns of asceticism and reverencing sages who retired to forest hermitages for meditation.

The material on which reconstruction of Aryan life must be based is the direct antithesis of that available for that of the Indus Valley civilization. The latter has left a wealth of remains and no written records. The Aryans in India have left practically no remains, but a wealth of literature. It is a case of circumstantial evidence versus testimony. A few stone posts which may have been used in the sacrificial rites described in the *Vedas* have been found, but no Aryan occupation site or graveyard has ever been identified. The literature on which reconstructions of early Aryan life are based is included in four collections known as the *Vedas.* The *Rig Veda* which, on the evidence of its language, must be the oldest, consists of hymns partly sung, partly recited at sacrifices. The *Atharva Veda* is the most primitive of all in content if not in its language. It is a book of magic consisting mainly of spells, incantations, and medical prescriptions. The *Sama Veda* is a collection of the songs used at sacrifices. It includes verses from many of the *Rig Veda* compositions, together with others of later origin. The *Yajug Veda* consists of *Mantras,* i.e., prayers and mystic formulae.

Whether the system of writing used by the Indus Valley culture was completely lost or whether it contributed to the development of later Indian alphabets is still an unsettled question, but in any case there seems to have been a long period of illiteracy in northern India. During this time the Vedic literature was handed down by word of mouth. In later times there was strong insistence on the exact rendition of this literature, and it was believed that mistakes or interpolations would result in the death of the offender from supernatural causes. However, we cannot be sure that such regulations existed during the early period, while the minimal time of one thousand years intervening between the composition of the earlier hymns in the *Rig Veda* and their commitment to writing would have given abundant opportunity for changes. Even the hymns of the *Rig Veda* must have been composed over a considerable stretch of time, since they indicate two distinct economies. One set of hymns reflects a semi-nomadic dairying culture closely similar to that of the people of the eastern steppes, while the other assumes a predominantly agricultural and settled village culture functioning in a forest environment in which the economic importance of cattle was secondary. The best explanation would seem to be that during the period that the hymns of the *Rig Veda* were being composed the Aryan invaders were adjusting themselves to Indian life and that different hymns reflect the needs and attitudes related to various stages in this adjustment.

As the Aryan invaders settled down they could scarcely have failed to take on many elements of blood and culture from the older population. They seem to have been unusually reluctant to admit this. One of the most puzzling features of the Vedas is the references to the aboriginal population, the Dasyus, as black-skinned and flat-nosed. While these adjectives might be applied to some of the proto-Australoid people of Southern India, they certainly were not applicable to the predominantly Mediterranean population of Northwestern India, the people with whom the Aryans must have had their first and presumably hostile contact. The Dasyus are also described as savages in some hymns, while in others the gods are appealed to for aid in overthrowing their cities and stone-walled forts.

There can be no doubt that the Indus culture contributed very heavily to the development of later Indian civilization. In fact, one can recognize many more resemblances between it and the historic civilizations of India than between the latter and the semi-nomadic cattle-keeping culture of the steppe region from which the invading Aryans came. One is tempted to believe that during the interval between the arrival of the Aryans and the completion of the Vedas a fusion took place between the invaders and the survivors of the Indus civilization. In the growth of a hybrid folklore it would be quite possible for memories of the struggle which the ancestors of the Indus Valley people had had with proto-Australoid aborigines in Northwestern India to become confused with the battles between the Aryans and the weakened and culturally decadent survivors of the older civilization. Even the terms "black," "flat-nosed," and so forth may have become more or less conventional epithets applied to enemies, like our own use of "Huns" for the Germans in World War I.

This suggestion may seem far-fetched, but a close parallel can be found in the British Isles, where the Picts became the subject of an extensive folklore. We know from contemporary sources that the Picts were actually Goidels, Celts who originally shared the Hallstatt culture, who came into Scotland from Ireland in the period of confusion at the close of the Roman domination of Britain and who survived as a politically and culturally independent group until the 5th or 6th century A.D. In physical type they appear to have been much like the tall, red-haired, freckled Scottish lowlanders. Nevertheless, they figure in folklore as a small, dark, uncanny people living underground, practicing obscene rites and brewing a mysterious but tremendously potent beverage, heather ale. There can be little doubt that these details represent a folk memory of the Neolithic aborigines of Scotland, conquered many centuries before by metal-armed Celts.

The life of the early Aryans has already been described (see Chap. XIX). That of the Aryans in India at the close of the Vedic period seems to have been essentially like that of the rural North Indian villages of historic times. Northwestern India had regressed until it supported only a sparse and backward population. Even the Indus Valley was regarded as a provincial area, the center of population and cultural activity being in the upper Ganges Valley. Wheat and barley were the staple crops. Cattle were kept and milked but seem to have owed much of their importance to their use as draft animals. The plow and the wheel were in long-established use, and all the more familiar metals were known and worked. Horses had become luxury animals used only in fighting. They were driven in two-horse, two-man chariots but do not seem to have been ridden. Warfare was carried on briskly between the various

Aryan groups, but was beginning to be a specialized occupation and was regulated by various chivalrous practices.

The later Vedas give an idealized picture of what a village should be. It should be built in a forest clearing and should be rectangular, with a stockade and a gate and watchtower in the center of each side. The gates should be connected by two broad straightways which intersect in the middle of the town. At the intersection a platform shaded by a thatched roof or a large tree served as the meeting place of the village governing body, a council of five elders known as the *panchayat.* Inside the stockade there was a broad pathway running around the entire village. This served for processions. Houses were built of wattle and daub or bamboo, with thatched roofs. Cultivated fields radiated from the village in narrow strips, each of which was assigned to a different family. Grazing ground was held and used in common. This rectangular town plan was preserved with religious care by later Hindus and may still be seen in some of the great Indian temple cities.

The main difference between the later Vedic and the historic periods was in connection with social structure and religion. The institution of caste had not yet come into existence. There was a division of the population into warriors, farmers and craftsmen, and priests. An arrangement similar even to cognate terms for the various groups was also present among the earliest Persians, to whom the early Indian Aryans were closely related. It is significant that in neither system was there a category comparable to the later Untouchables. Even priests were not yet a clearly differentiated group. Every head of a family functioned as a priest in the frequent sacrifices which the Vedic religion required. The Brahmans of the period were a small group of experts who served as chaplains to aristocratic warrior families, and whose services were sought on occasions when difficult rites had to be performed correctly. They were still dependent on the warrior aristocracy and clearly subservient to them.

Ascetics were already present by the end of the Vedic period. They were individuals who had withdrawn from ordinary social contacts and activities and had retired to a hermitage in the forest. There they gave instruction to those who sought to penetrate into the nature of the universe and of man. Even at this date the emphasis was on man. The later Hindu concept of the material world as illusion was already present at least in embryo form. Ascetics were supported by voluntary contributions from the local villagers, who were glad to provide the food and minimal comforts required in the Indian climate in return for the magical benefits conferred upon the community by the ascetic's presence. Even the touch of his hand when receiving a gift conferred a part of his spiritual power on the donor.

The Indian village of this period consisted of a number of families related in the male line. Although the extended family pattern was beginning to emerge, such units seem to have been of small size and relatively short duration. The typical Vedic family was monogamous, although polygyny was permitted and was practiced by those who could afford it. Child marriage was unknown and the remarriage of widows was permitted. There was no bride price, and the wife brought a substantial dowry into the new family. Villages were normally exogamous, as in modern India.

Several villages were united in a clan while several clans formed a tribe. According to Vedic tradition there were five original Aryan tribes, but after their arrival in India the number increased rapidly. The various clans forming a tribe were organized in a prestige series, with one or more noble clans enjoying the highest status. Village government was thoroughly democratic, both legislative and administrative functions being vested in a council of family heads. If the original *panchayat* of five, mentioned in the *Rig Veda,* ever existed, it soon gave place to a larger group, and, since meetings were public and informal, there was abundant opportunities for villagers to express their opinions on all matters of interest. This democratic tradition was strong even at the tribal level.

At the head of the tribe stood the king, whose duties were those of a war leader and an executive. The post was usually hereditary in a particular clan, but the incumbent was elected by the tribesmen from among its members. Democratic tendencies were still strong. In a few tribes the king was elected at regular intervals, while confederacies of tribes with governing assemblies survived until the 4th or 5th century B.C. In return for his services the king was allowed to collect a tax, never more than one-sixth of the harvest, but he very definitely held his office on sufferance and could be deposed for misconduct. Although later times witnessed a progressive increase in royal power, the old democratic patterns survived in a number of localities, and it is interesting to note that the kingdoms from which came both Gautama Buddha and Vardhamana, the founder of the Jains, were still following the democratic pattern.

Since the Vedas deal mainly with religious matters, our knowledge of this aspect of early Aryan culture is particularly extensive. The pantheon of deities followed the general Indo-European pattern. The most important gods were Agni, the god of fire, who acted as messenger between men and gods, and Indra, god of the middle Heavens and storm clouds, who was also a war god, leading the Aryans in their struggles with the Dasyus. Indra seems to have been the ideal Aryan warrior of the earliest Vedic period. He dashed into battle joyously, wore golden armor, and was able to consume the flesh of three hundred buffaloes and drink three lakes of *soma* at one time. The sun was worshipped in many aspects and under at least five names. Vishnu, who became one of the chief gods of later Hinduism, was a sun god but occupied a very minor place in the Vedic pantheon. The wide sky was worshipped under the name of Dayous-pitar (cf. Jupiter), and was a benevolent deity. The storm god Rudra was more feared than loved. Later he became identified with Siva of the Hindu trinity.

Lastly, Varuna, another sky god personifying all embracing space, was the most powerful of the Vedic gods. He was unique among them in his interest in human behavior, and prayers to him implored him to forgive the supplicant's sins. The heavenly bodies were his eyes, through which he watched the doings of men on earth, and nothing that happened there escaped his notice. The gods demanded burnt offerings of animals and libations of *soma*. Although *soma* figures largely in the Vedic rituals and was appreciated as much by men as by gods, all that we know concerning it is that it was an intoxicating drink brewed from the juice of some still-unidentified plant. The worshippers believed that the gods consumed the sacrifices and were nourished by them in quite material fashion. Agni, as the messenger of the gods, bore the essence of the offerings upward to them in the smoke of the sacrificial fire.

Up to this point there was nothing in Vedic religious concepts or practices which was in any way inconsistent with the culture of any of the Indo-European speaking peoples who emerged from the eastern steppes into the light of history. However, a new element appears even in the *Rig Veda*. In the Tenth Book there are numerous abstract and philosophical hymns which are in a different vein. Here one finds the concept of *Purusha,* a universal being: "enveloping the universe on every side, He exists, transcending it. All this is He—what has been and what shall be. The whole series of universes expresses his glory and power. All beings of the universe form, as it were, a fraction of his being." These pantheistic concepts lay at the foundation of all later Indian religion and philosophy, but it is hard to believe that they sprang from the minds of the same naïve, unreflective tribesmen who, in another hymn of the *Rig Veda,* declared that: "Indra lows like a bull for his *soma.*"

How much later Hindu religion owed to the Aryans is still an open question, but their contribution was certainly less than that ascribed to them by Brahmanic writers. Of all the Vedic gods, only Vishnu survived to become an active deity of developed Hinduism, and even his attributes had been changed beyond recognition. The doctrine of reincarnation, basic in later Hinduism, seems not to have been held by the early Aryans. The patterns of asceticism, and of a hereditary priestly group

dominating society by its learning and skill in dealing with the supernatural, were both highly incongruous with ancient Aryan values as
these appear in related cultures outside India. If one turns directly to
the original evidence, ignoring the wealth of rationalizations and interpretations developed by later writers, one is forced to conclude that the
Aryan invasion of India followed very much the course of most subsequent invasions. In these the early political and military dominance of
the invaders was followed by their absorption, and a resurgence of the
older culture. In the long run the Aryan invasion may prove to have
been little more than an episode in the long evolution of a distinctive
Indian civilization.

The main argument which can be advanced against this view is the
acceptance of Aryan languages throughout most of India. However, this
problem is not exclusively an Indian one. In nearly all the regions invaded by Indo-European-speaking peoples they succeeded in establishing their languages, even though their culture and even physical type
soon disappeared. In fact the only region in which this did not occur
seems to have been in the general Mesopotamian area, where the Indo-
European languages came into competition with equally vigorous and
equally foreign Semitic tongues. Why certain languages survive in acculturation situations and others do not is one of the most interesting
problems of culture dynamics, and one for which we have as yet no
solution.

Chapter XXXIII

Early Historic India

ANY DISCUSSION of Indian history is complicated by the singular lack of interest in history which the Indians themselves have displayed. A *Weltanschauung* which regarded the universe as an illusion and events as occurring in repetitive cycles was understandably uninterested in exact details of time and place. The Brahmans, who enjoyed a monopoly on education, fixed their attention on philosophy and religion rather than on the passing show. Moreover, since they always claimed to find ancient sanction for their current practices, they were less than interested in tracing cultural developments. As a result, Indian cultural history must be reconstructed mainly from the incidental background materials in romantic and religious literature, from archeological monuments, and from the accounts of foreign visitors.

Even Indian political history is vague at many points. It does not begin to meet Western standards of precision until after the first Muslim invasion. To one who is not a specialist in the field, the names of the innumerable Indian dynasties and kings who have functioned during the last 2500 years are largely meaningless, and their rise and fall matters of indifference. For that reason the only political events mentioned will be those which seem to have had lasting cultural significance.

On the basis of the source materials available for the earliest historic period, it is possible to divide the whole of India into three regions. Northwestern India was brought into contact with Western civilization by the 6th century B.C., when Darius the First annexed the Punjab and Sind to the Achaemenian Persian Empire. This was followed by the conquest, actually little more than a raid, of Alexander the Great and the establishment of successive dynasties of invaders from the Northwestern mountains and steppes, all of whom rapidly assumed the more obvious elements of Hellenistic culture. European descriptions of the region began with an account by Skylax, a Greek, whom Darius sent to explore the Indus in approximately 500 B.C. (This is known only from extracts from later writers.) They continued until the final extinction of the Hellenistic kingdoms in the 3rd and 4th centuries A.D. By far the most valuable of these records is that left by Megasthenes, an ambassador of the Near Eastern Seleucid Empire, who arrived in India in 302 B.C. and spent many years at the court of the Mauryan emperor, Chandragupta.

For Northeastern India we have no early foreign sources and almost no local historic writings. However, there are abundant references to the contemporaneous culture in early Buddhist literature and legend. This material goes back to the 5th century B.C., the time of the Persian domination in Northwestern India. By the 2nd century A.D., Buddhist art depicts the Enlightened One as carrying on his mission against a background of scenes from everyday life, thus providing additional information.

In Southern India the record begins somewhat later. The oldest writings do not go back much before the beginning of the Christian era. However, this region was in frequent contact with other ancient civilizations, and there are numerous references to it in Greek literature from the first century on. There are also various Chinese references, less readily available to the Western scholar. Protected by sea, Southern India was not invaded in force until after the Muslim conquest of North India in the 9th century A.D. However, from at least the 7th or 8th century B.C. traders had come to the Southern Indian ports from the west. By the 2nd or 3rd century B.C. the trade with both East and West was flourishing, and Southern Indian ships were sailing to Arabia, the East African coast, Indonesia, and Southern China. Western contacts reached a peak around the beginning of the Christian era. The Romans had an insatiable appetite for Indian gems and spices, particularly pepper, and, since they had few products which the Indians would take in exchange, these imports were paid for in gold. Roman gold coins were regularly used as currency in much of Southern India; Roman and Greek soldiers served Southern Indian kings as mercenaries; and two Roman colonies were actually established in Southern India, with a temple to Augustus at one of them. Other foreigners to settle in Southern India included Jews and Syrian Christians who arrived in the 1st century A.D., Persian Christians who came in the 4th; and Arabs, whose descendants still form an important element in the population of Malabar. There was also a considerable trade with China, which was still going on briskly in the time of Marco Polo.

By the dawn of their respective histories the three Indian regions had numerous cultural features in common, but there were also well-marked local differences. Northern and Southern India were sharply divided by language. The Indo-European-speaking peoples of the North had inherited more of the Aryan tradition. The Dravidian-speaking peoples of the South had retained numerous practices which were certainly non-Aryan. There were also well-marked differences within Northern India between the East and West. The West was open to raids. It formed the gateway by which new tribes had infiltrated the peninsula since before the dawn of history. Northeastern India, the Ganges Valley region, was much less accessible to invasion, and its climate and natural resources enforced a greater degree of cultural continuity. Invaders who entered its lush tropical environment from the North or West found it necessary to adopt local ways of life in order to survive. Southern India was in a position to receive and transmit cultural elements without outside pressure. It seems to have been much more important as a donor than as a borrower, sending out missionaries and adventurers who carried Indian civilization into Indonesia and the adjoining mainland. What it borrowed from foreign sources it took selectively and shaped to its own patterns.

There is little direct evidence for the cultural effects of the Achaemenid invasion of Northwestern India. Darius organized the Punjab and Sind into the 20th Satrapy of what was then the world's greatest empire. Herodotus records Indian troops in the huge heterogeneous armies which the Persians led against the Greeks. More important, the Indian Satrapy paid an annual tribute of ten tons of gold dust, about one-third of the total revenue of the Persian Empire. It is safe to assume that the Persians, who were master organizers and the first world conquerors to realize that subjects could be better controlled by bureaucracies than by armies, took pains with the administration of such a valuable property. It seems highly probable that they gave to Indian culture new patterns of political organization and even, perhaps, the concept of empire. At least it is significant that by the end of the Persian occupation one finds great conquest states in Central India as opposed to the semi-tribal kingdoms into which the contemporary East and South were divided. The structure of the Mauryan Empire, as revealed in the records of Megasthenes and in the native Arthsastra of Kautilya, shows strong Persian similarities. There was also a Persian influence on Northern Indian art, clearly shown on such monuments as the columns erected by King Asoka, but this soon vanished under the impact of Hellenistic art forms.

The conquest of Alexander the Great was little more than a raid, and the Greek garrisons which he had left in India were wiped out within fifty years of his departure. The Mauryan Empire, which followed and became the first of the extensive Indian empires, was strongly nationalistic. The Classic influences in Indian culture date much less from

Alexander than from the barbarian kings, Scythians and especially Kushans, who established dynasties in Northwestern India around the beginning of the Christian era. These barbarians felt the prestige of Hellenistic culture and hastened to copy its outward forms. Although the contact with the Hellenized West continued for generations, few elements of Greek origin were incorporated into Indian culture. The homeland Greeks were always weak in the fields of government and social organization, and in Hellenistic times usually adopted the patterns of the states they had conquered. Greek technology, in spite of its superb artistic productions, was in most respects only equal, if not inferior, to that of India, while Greek philosophy and learning were alien in their spirit to those of Buddhism and evolving Hinduism. In the single area of representational art the Greek influence had a lasting effect. The conversion of the Kushan kings to Buddhism, and their use of Greek provincial artists in creating the innumerable images which soon became a feature of the religion, left a lasting mark upon the style of Buddhist art throughout the East.

By the 5th century B.C. Northern India had developed many of the cultural characteristics which have survived there to the present time. The life of the ordinary villagers seems to have changed little between that period and the revolution which is now being initiated with the arrival of radios and easy transportation. The modern time-traveler who returned to this horizon would be impressed by the extent of the forests and the universal use of wood for construction. Even such great cities as the Mauryan capital of Pataliputra, with its palace and temples, was built entirely of wood and protected by a stockade and a moat. In much of the same region today the peasants are hard put to it to find sufficient timber for rafters and do their cooking with cakes of dried cow dung. He would also have been impressed by the comparative scantiness of the clothing worn in the eastern part of the region. The ordinary costume of men was limited to a loincloth made from a single narrow strip of cotton, while women wore only a short kilt. The rich compensated for the inexpensive character of such dress by the fineness of the fabrics used and by jewelry so abundant that women must have found it a genuine burden.

The same differences in economic status which impress the modern traveler in India today seem to have been present even in this period. Although the villager's economic status was probably better than it is today, he paid one-sixth of his harvest in direct tax and was further exploited by a state salt monopoly, a sales tax, and various other exactions. However, it seems that even at this date differences in income were reflected more in display than in standards of living. The pillars of Chandragupta's palace were sheathed in gold, but he slept on a mat and ate much the same simple, if highly spiced, food as the average peasant. When, in his old age, he retired to a forest hermitage, he had to surrender few creature comforts.

The same crops, wheat and barley to the west and rice to the east, were being cultivated in the same manner as today. Cattle were driven in to be milked at the "hour of cow dust," but they had not yet acquired the sanctity which they have for the modern Hindu. Animals were still sacrificed to the gods in rituals of increasing expense and complexity. In social organization, the joint family and the village were already long-established units, and it is probable that villages were strictly exogamous as they are today. In each village the bulk of the inhabitants were cultivators, with a few families of craftsmen, perhaps a smith, a carpenter, a potter, and a priest serving their immediate needs. The four great caste divisions, Brahman, Kshatriya, Vaisya, and Sudra, were already in existence in Northern India, but there are no indications of the innumerable subdivisions of these which characterize the modern caste system or of the elaborate ceremonial regulations which govern the interrelations of individuals of different castes today. It is impossible to say whether Untouchables existed at this time. Megasthenes does not mention them, and, if they had been present in Northwestern India in the 3rd century B.C., it seems unlikely that they would have escaped the notice of such a keen and interested observer.

By the time of Buddha, in the 6th century B.C., there were veritable universities to which young men of good families went to receive instruction in the sacred writings as part of the education suitable to their station. One of these universities was in Taxila in Western India, the capital of the ancient Persian Satrapy. All men of the three upper caste divisions received instruction in the sacred lore and rites. This was congruous with the older Aryan patterns, according to which the head of a family sacrificed for his kindred, and the ruler might sacrifice for his subjects. However, there are numerous indications that, by the 6th century B.C., the Brahmans were arrogating to themselves more and more power and control. This movement was less significant in Northwestern India where the frequent incursions of non-Hindu peoples tended to maintain power in the hands of the Kshatriyas, the fighting ruling group, who seem to have been willing to incorporate foreign conquerors. In Northeastern India the struggle for power between Brahmans and Kshatriyas had not yet been resolved at this period. The Brahmans had not resigned themselves to the role of advisors to kings or realized the numerous advantages of power without responsibility, nor had the Kshatriya given over all claims to learning or to direct access to the supernatural. It is interesting to note that the activities of the Kshatriya were much more in keeping with the character of the earlier Aryan invaders than were those of the Brahmans.

There is always a strong tie between the gods of a conquered people and the land they have watched over. They are likely to be hostile to newcomers, and again and again one finds conquerors acknowledging the magical powers of the conquered and calling upon their priests and medicine men to intercede for them with the ancient proprietors of the soil. It has already been mentioned that the gods of later Hinduism were not the gods of the Vedic Aryans, and that, even in the case of those whose names survived, such as Vishnu, the correlation of their earlier Vedic with their later-Brahmanic character represented a philosophical *tour de force*. The increasing importance of the Brahmans at this time may well have been a reversion to pre-Aryan patterns.

By the beginning of the historic period, religious beliefs and practices in Northern India had taken on a number of distinctive characteristics. Outstanding among these was the belief in reincarnation and the concept of *Karma*. Although the Greek Pythagoras had taught reincarnation, and there are references to it in Celtic mythology, the belief does not seem to have been present in the older Vedas, nor did it form a part of the general Indo-European cultural heritage. We know that a belief in reincarnation, with various elaborations, has arisen independently in many parts of the world, and its Indian form may very well have been developed by pre-Aryan philosophers seeking to find a logical solution to the problems created by man's determined denial of the possibility of his own extinction.

Whatever its origin, the Indian version of the soul's destiny was far more logically consistent and intellectually satisfying than that developed within any other cultural tradition. While the doctrines of various Indian sects differed as to the beginning and the end of the soul's journey, they all were in essential agreement on the middle portion, that which had to do with the individual's immediate past and future. The soul began as an unformed, amorphous aggregate of spiritual forces, which infused the body of some low form of life. Upon the death of its host it passed to another body, bringing with it the experience which it had acquired in the previous incarnation. Through life after life this accumulating experience molded and consolidated the soul. In addition to experience, each soul accumulated a running account of what might be termed spiritual credits and debits, the result of good and evil deeds performed in its incarnations. These together constituted the individual's *Karma,* which determined the particular position in society into which he would be reborn and the good or bad fortune which he would experience.

The belief in *Karma* was of great importance to the operation of Indian society, since it provided a rationalization for the caste system. One who was born a Sudra or Untouchable occupied this unenviable position because it was the place in society to which his *Karma* fitted him, the one where he could acquire the type of experience needed for his soul's further development, and receive the rewards or punishments to which his past behavior had entitled him. As a corollary, one who attempted to leave his caste threw the pattern of his soul's development into confusion and would be demoted many steps in his incarnation. It was desirable to acquire good *Karma* through sacrifices and the meticulous performance of rituals, the giving of alms to Brahmans and ascetics, and the practice of general benevolence. However, the most important thing for the soul was the increasing awareness and wisdom which carried it upward in its evolution. One who devoted himself entirely to good deeds might acquire so much credit in his account that he would be delayed through several pleasant but unprofitable incarnations, in order that he might enjoy the benefits which he had previously earned.

The most direct road to spiritual advancement was to become an ascetic. Megasthenes noted the existence of communities of ascetics which reminded him of the contemporary Hellenistic academies. He said that the discussions of these Indian philosophers were concerned entirely with death, a preoccupation which probably struck the life-oriented Greek as extraordinary. Since even by the time of Buddha the doctrine of reincarnation had become thoroughly established in India, it seems probable that the discussions which Megasthenes mentioned had to do with the operation of *Karma* and the successive stages in the soul's evolution.

By the time of Megasthenes the ascetic had already been a familiar object on the Indian landscape for many centuries. One of the seals from Mohenjo-Daro shows a figure seated in an attitude prescribed for ascetics in later times. There can be no doubt that the institution was of Indian origin, and it seems highly probable that it was pre-Aryan; at least, it finds no parallel in the early cultures of Indo-European-speaking peoples outside India.

In its inception, Indian asceticism may have been psychologically related to the vision quest of the North American Indians. In this the suppliant fasted and underwent self-imposed sufferings in order to excite the pity of a supernatural being. If he was successful, the being would appear to him and promise to help him, at the same time specifying various taboos that the human must observe in order to maintain the relationship. The hypnotic state induced by continued fasting and pain made it possible for the suppliant to see visions and hear voices which, in retrospect, could be organized into a coherent supernatural experience of the sort which the suppliant's culture had led him to anticipate. The situation was not unlike that in which the modern psychoanalytic subject finds himself honestly reporting Freudian dreams if he has a Freudian analyst, and Jungian dreams if he has a Jungian one.

Whatever its origins, by the time Indian asceticism emerged into the light of history the practice of austerities had come to involve aggression against the supernatural; the ascetic "fasted against" the deities in order to increase his own spiritual power. Some of the earliest legends imply that an ascetic, who could perform heavy enough penances, could build up his power to the point where he could compel the deities to obey him. As pantheistic concepts developed, this attitude waned and was replaced by another in which ascetic practices were directed toward the subjugation of the body in order to release the mind, and the more fundamental entity which Europeans would term the soul, from the limitations imposed by the flesh. We cannot determine accurately the times at which these various changes took place, but during at least the last 1000 years the principal object of Indian asceticism has been to aid the soul in its attempt to achieve identification with the infinite and to experience states of ecstasy in which it apprehended the universe.

The ascetic progressed to his goal by successive steps. The first of these was the breaking of all worldly ties, including those of family and fortune, and retiring to a forest retreat where he could devote himself to meditation and to various physical exercises designed to give him complete control over his body. In these, breathing and posture were emphasized. While there is an extensive and florid folklore on the subject, many ascetics unquestionably did achieve extraordinary control of the functions normally controlled by the autonomic nervous system. The miracles which this made possible astonished the laity and no doubt helped to keep the begging bowl filled, but such training was not an end in itself. Its purpose was to prevent the body from intruding upon the activities of the mind and soul.

The next step after the conquest of the body was the conquest of the mind, achieved when the individual was able to empty his mind completely of conscious content and to arrest the thought process, thus freeing the soul for deeper experience. The emancipated soul could experience moments of unity with the world soul and return from these with superhuman wisdom and power. If the individual was sufficiently benevolent, he would share this potency and heightened knowledge with those who had not undergone the experience themselves and thus hasten their *Karmaic* development. Even if he gave no instruction, the strength and spiritual benefits were conferred by touching his person, and the worshipper who filled his begging bowl was thereby rewarded.

Whatever the skeptical Westerner's reaction to these concepts, he must recognize the value of Indian asceticism as a social mechanism. Sacred books composed near the beginning of the historic period say that the ascetic life was open to members of all three of the higher castes but prohibited to Sudras and, of course, Untouchables. The institution provided an escape for the maladjusted, and functioned much as did the Western religious orders in the Middle Ages, appealing to both mystics and those unable to face the stresses of secular existence. Not only the seeker after spirituality, but the prince who tired of his role, the husband who found his wife insufferable, or even the merchant relentlessly pursued by his creditors could join the ranks of holy men. He retired to the forest, where he led a simple, chaste life. He usually became a disciple of some holy man of established reputation, acting as his servant and receiving instruction in return. In some localities there were whole colonies of hermits who spent their time in philosophic discussion and in studies of the sacred literature, as well as in meditation. During the early historic period much of this literature was still transmitted by word of mouth and had to be learned by rote.

From the very beginning of the historic period there was a sharp distinction between the Brahmans and the ascetics. Brahmans could become ascetics, but most of them did not. The Brahmans were skilled workers with the supernatural, professional priests who knew the long and complicated rituals prescribed by the Hindu religion. Outside their religious duties they led normal lives, except for the limitations imposed by the regulations of their caste. Many of them were eager for wealth and social control, and it is clear that during the early historic period they were constantly building up their power in Northern India and seeking to convert aboriginal tribes to Hinduism.

The increasing pretensions of the Brahmans, and the development of more and more elaborate and expensive rites which only they could perform, was met in the 6th century B.C. by a religious revolution instituted by two great leaders, Gautama Buddha and Vardhamana Mahavira, founder of the Jains. Both of these men were born as members of the Kshatriya caste, both became ascetics, and both accepted the doctrines of reincarnation and *Karma* without question. However, in both cases their teachings were antithetical to Brahmanic ritualism. The Jains still survive as a minor sect, characterized by a highly developed ritualism and an extreme reluctance to take life in any form. The Jain priest going about his duties swept the path before him with a broom to remove any insects which might be trodden upon, and would not drink water in the dark lest he swallow and destroy some minute form of life. The most important tenet of the faith was its insistence upon *Ahimsa,* "harmlessness," a pattern of consistent non-resistance. The late Mahatma

Gandhi, although not a Jain himself, had been strongly influenced by Jain doctrines. Although Jain missionaries made many converts in Southern India, the religion had never spread outside the peninsula. The doctrines of Buddha, on the other hand, have been a force in world affairs for 2000 years, and for this reason will be treated in a separate chapter.

We have already mentioned that the South Indian record does not go back much before the beginning of the Christian era, and that for even that period the information is far from adequate. Quite as in the North, the material culture and patterns of village life seem to have acquired very much their modern forms by the dawn of history. The economy was predominantly agricultural, but with all branches of technology well developed. All the Southeast Asiatic crops were raised, but the most important crop was irrigated rice. The plow, drawn by water buffalo, was used in preparing the rice paddies. Since this animal was also milked, in sharp contrast to the Southeast Asiatic pattern of animal usage, it seems probable that its utilization was modeled upon that of cattle in regions further north. The technology was equal, if not superior, to that of Northern India in the same period. Important buildings were of wood and were large and firmly constructed Metal working was highly developed and steel was already being manufactured and exported. The aesthetic urge found expression in ivory and wood carving, weaving, and metal work. To judge from the artistic productions in the region in the somewhat later period of Buddhist dominance, the art was naturalistic and characterized by unusual vigor and motion.

The social organization and religion of the South are even more difficult to reconstruct. The best contemporary source is the *Tolkappiyam,* a Tamil work attributed to about the beginning of the Christian era. Although this is primarily a study of grammar, it includes dissertations on many other subjects. For purposes of cultural reconstruction it has the added advantage that Tamil seems to have been the most purely Dravidian of the languages spoken in South India and by far the most widespread at this period. The information which the work contains may therefore apply to much of Southern India.

According to this treatise, the Tamil-speaking people were originally divided into four groupings: the people of the mountain, of the forest, of the plain, and of the seacoast. Each division had its chief, and each carried on specialized activities based on the resources which its natural environment provided. Each division was composed of numerous groups, who had different occupations and no doubt exchanged their products for those of other groups or divisions. Thus the people of the coast were divided into fishermen, pearl fishers, boatmen, makers of boats, salt makers, workers in shell, and merchants engaged in foreign trade. The early sources do not indicate whether these subdivisions were hereditary, but, in view of the situation existing in most cultures which shared the Southeast Asiatic co-tradition, it would seem highly probable that they were.

Modern ethnological studies in Southern India reinforce this conclusion. A similar division of activities still exists among the non-Hinduized tribes of the Nilgiri Hills. One of these tribes, the Toda, has become, largely by accident, the Indian group most frequently mentioned in ethnological literature. A plateau in the Nilgiri Hills is occupied by three tribes, the Toda, Kota, and Badaga. The Toda herd and milk buffalo and prepare the clarified butter which is an indispensable part, not only of the food supply of other tribes, but also of their ritual procedures. They carry on no other economic activities. The Kota are farmers, cultivating grain, while the Badaga are craftsmen, merchants and also musicians. The three tribes are completely interdependent economically and share the same territory amicably. At the same time they live in different villages, and each tribe is strictly endogamous. Each tribe also has its own distinctive patterns of costume, housing, social organization, and religion. There are various taboos governing behavior between members of different tribes, particularly in cases where the exercise of tribal skills is involved. Thus it is forbidden to an outsider to enter a Toda dairy when churning is in process. Although the Toda are recognized by the other two tribes as the original proprietors of the district and are accorded additional respect for this reason, the system lacks the rigid stratification which characterized the Hindu caste system, and the religious rites of each tribe are performed by tribal members.

The social organization within the numerous tribes which existed in Southern India at the beginning of the historic period cannot be reconstructed. However, studies of the modern aboriginal Dravidian peoples suggest that it may have been of almost Melanesian complexity, with clans, moieties, and elaborate marriage regulations. The only fact which is clear is that most, if not all, of the Tamil-speaking groups were originally matrilineal and even in some cases matrilocal. The position of women was and has remained exceedingly high, with older women in particular exercising dominance in family affairs. Although the introduction of Hinduism brought with it Hindu sex mores, with insistence on virginity at marriage and subsequent female chastity, the evidence of the surviving aboriginal tribes and certain traditional practices strongly suggests that patterns of pre-marital sex experimentation usual in cultures of the Southeast Asian co-tradition were present in the earlier period. Polyandry was probably approved in some tribes, as among the Toda, but it is unlikely that it was a general practice, since this institution seems to be uniformly linked with a paucity of natural resources and control of population through female infanticide. That there was a lively interest in sex can be deduced from the fact that, of the eight classical Tamil anthologies which have survived, three contain 400 love poems each.

The early literature gives no descriptions of the functions of division chiefs, nor of the extent to which the divisions were politically organized. Kingdoms cutting across division lines were certainly present from very early times. The main functions of such kingdoms seem to have been to make war and collect taxes. The early history of Southern India is one of almost continuous warfare, and it is amazing that such a high level of culture could have been maintained. Apparently the wars were carried on by professional soldiers, and subjects changed hands with little interruption of their daily lives.

Megasthenes notes the importance of popular assemblies in the government of Southern India. In his time and in later times there was a strong democratic tradition in government. Although this would seem to be inconsistent with the long record of warlike dynasties, even kings hesitated to act without consulting the representatives of the people. At lower levels, social units of every size and sort were governed by elective assemblies operating through committees. Such bodies existed not only for villages and districts but also for trade guilds and religious groups. The pattern of village organization as recorded in the 10th century A.D., when it was already considered ancient, was especially interesting. The land was held by the village as a corporation, and its use, and indeed all aspects of village life, were controlled by an assembly. Members of the assembly were chosen by lot and served for one year. All persons with property rights in the village, including women, were eligible to serve if they were of good character and had some knowledge of Hindu law. Committees appointed from the council were in charge of the care of gardens, land usage, irrigation, land survey, village servants, justice, the collection and payment of taxes, temples, and charities.

It is impossible to reconstruct Southern Indian religion of the pre-Brahmanic period. It seems certain that there were numerous tribal deities, some of which were equated with natural phenomena, while others seem to have been deified ancestors or local heroes. There was certainly serpent worship, and some other animals may have been revered. There can be little doubt that the pre-Brahmanic religion was heavily concerned with phallic worship and fertility rites of various sorts. Magical practices seem to have been more important than in the North.

The northern empires of the pre-Islamic period were in general unable to extend their control over the Dravidian South. Only Asoka in the 3rd century B.C. conquered the Deccan, and his successors soon retreated northward. As a result, the Dravidians were under no compulsion to accept the culture of the Indo-European North, and what they took from it they took selectively. Their acceptance of Buddhism and later Hinduism was no doubt facilitated by the numerous non-Aryan features, presumably drawn from Northern Dravidian cultures, which had been incorporated into these religions. Northern tradition has it that the first Brahmans visited Southern India in about 800 B.C., and by the 2nd and 3rd century B.C. Brahman, Jain, and Buddhist missionaries were operating in the region in considerable numbers. The Dravidians seem to have welcomed all three, no doubt largely because of their interest in the magical powers which the new cults claimed, and the whole South, with the exception of a few backward hill tribes, accepted the Northern religions. The process of Northern cultural penetration was probably much like that which took place in Indonesia at a somewhat later date. We know that there Indian princes or Brahmans, reinforced by the prestige of their higher culture, established themselves among the native tribes and either allied themselves with ruling families by marriage or enjoyed highly lucrative positions as prime ministers or as intermediaries between the new converts and the Hindu gods. It is interesting to note that by the 3rd and 4th centuries A.D. there were Brahman kings in Southern India. The acceptance of the Northern religions seems to have been enthusiastic. Their missionaries were showered with royal gifts, and some of the most striking monuments of the Buddhist period in India are in the South, where monumental stupas of the 2nd and 3rd centuries still survive.

Chapter XXXIV

Buddhism

BUDDHISM has been India's most important contribution to civilization. Although now practically extinct in its homeland, it has become a world religion, with innumerable sects and with followers half again as numerous as all Christians combined. Buddhism is important not only as a religion but as an expression of basic Indian philosophy. Siddhartha, also known as Gautama, as Sakyamuni, and as the Buddha, was a historic personage who was born in 563 B.C. and died in 483 or 486 B.C. Europeans find these multiple names puzzling. Siddhartha was his childhood name, Gautama his clan name, Sakyamuni his title as an ascetic, and "The Buddha" his divine appellation. He lived to instruct numerous disciples and to supervise the organization of the religion which he founded. The records of his sayings and of the various events in his life, although transmitted for at least a century by word of mouth, are probably accurate. However, as with the founders of all great religions, the myth which has sprung up about him has become more important than the facts.

There is an ancient Hindu doctrine that a god will incarnate when some great evil threatens the world and thus save it. Thus Vishnu, as preserver, has had numerous *avatars*. According to orthodox Buddhism, Sakyamuni was only one of a series of Buddhas who have come at various times in the past and who will come in the future. He had already experienced innumerable incarnations, stories of which are preserved in the *Jatakas,* a charming collection of folklore. Having achieved the highest point of spiritual development, that of a Bodhisattva, he rested with the gods in the highest heaven. Moved by compassion for mankind, he took upon himself the burden of a last reincarnation. He called all the gods together and instructed them in Buddhist law. He also presented to them his successor, the Bodhisattva Maitreya, the time for whose appearance on earth the Buddhist world believes is approaching. Gautama

499

then looked about for a suitable mother from whom to be reborn. He chose Maya, the wife of the rulers of the Sakyas in Nepal, on the border of Northeastern India. When he announced his decision, all nature made demonstrations of joy. A cloud of singing birds settled on the palace and all the trees bloomed out of season. Maya retired to the women's quarters, where the Bodhisattva appeared to her in the form of a pearly white elephant with six red tusks, certainly a more picturesque visitant than the Christian Angel of the Annunciation. When her time arrived, Maya went to the park of Lumbini outside the gates of the city, and Buddha was born from her right side as she stood erect. The gods Indra and Brahma received the newborn child in their arms, and the two kings of the Nagas, the serpent deities of aboriginal India, sent streams of hot and cold water for bathing the child. The moment that he was born, Siddhartha took seven steps toward each of the four cardinal points, thus taking possession of the world.

Mother and child were borne to thè palace in a chariot drawn by angels. The mother died of happiness seven days after the birth and was immediately reborn in heaven among the gods. Siddhartha was reared by his mother's sister, Mahaprajapati. The child, according to the legend, was born with various auspicious marks, such as webbed fingers; a bump on his head; large, elongated ears; and the marks of the wheel of the law on the soles of his feet. A great sage who saw him prophesied that he would either become King of the World or the Savior of Mankind. When the child was first taken to the temple, the statues of the gods prostrated themselves before him. He disputed with the wise men, his teachers, and astonished them by his wisdom. When, in his early teens, he sat in meditation for the first time in the shadow of a tree, the shadow of the sun remained stationary so that he would be sheltered and his meditation undisturbed.

When he came of age his royal father chose a wife for him, but his future father-in-law doubted whether the beautiful, dreamy young man had the necessary strength to make an able husband and ruler. He therefore resorted to the competition of suitors, a theme which occurs in legends the world over. He offered his daughter to the one who could draw the strongest bow and shoot an arrow farthest. Siddhartha, of course, far outshot any of his competitors. He then married Yosodhara and a series of secondary wives who were sent with her. However, the delights of the harem failed to satisfy him, and he meditated upon the sorrows and evils of the universe.

His meeting with an old man, a sick man, and a corpse, and his charioteer's assurance that these things were the unavoidable fate of man, focused his discontent. He begged his father to allow him to become an ascetic. His father refused and tried to divert his mind with new pleasures. A son was born to him, and the event was celebrated with a great festival, but Siddhartha himself greeted the news with: "This is one more tie to break." On the very night of the festival he fled the palace, accompanied by his charioteer, Chandhaka. The deities bore up his horses' hooves in their hands so that the guards would not hear his passing. At the edge of the forest Siddhartha said good-bye to horse and charioteer. He cut off his long hair and exchanged clothes with the first peasant he met, who was, needless to say, a god in disguise. He visited various groups of holy men and finally became the disciple of Arada Kalama. After undergoing the usual instruction in meditation and ascetic practices, he became a holy man. He finally settled in southern Bihar, chosen because of its natural beauty, and gathered about him a group of five disciples. He practiced great austerities and his fame spread far and wide.

At length Siddhartha's austerities became so great that the gods feared for his life and sent his mother from heaven to beg him to desist. In less romantic terms, he came to the conclusion that austerity could not give him what he sought. He ate, bathed, and announced his decision to give up fasting and yoga practices. His five disciples promptly left him. He wandered for a time, then, at Bodh-Gaya, seated himself beneath a pipal tree and entered into the sublime meditation which was to reveal to him the path of salvation. Mara, King of the Demons, recognized the threat to his dominion on earth and tried to divert him. He sent monsters to terrify him, but Siddhartha, now become the Buddha, ignored them. Mara then sent his beautiful daughters, offering all the pleasures of the flesh, but Buddha ignored these also. Enlightenment came with the realization that the root of all suffering lay in desire, springing from wrong concepts of the self. If desire was eliminated, grief and suffering would cease.

After he had experienced enlightenment, Buddha stayed on for four weeks under the pipal tree. In the fifth week a great storm arose, but the Naga King, in the form of a giant cobra, spread his hood over the Enlightened One, sheltering him from the rain. Only the final task, that of giving his doctrine to the world, now remained, and when Indra and Brahma came asking him to do this he set forth on his mission.

From this time on, Buddha's career, as recorded in the legends, was a continuous series of miracles. In sober fact, he seems to have lived for forty years after the enlightenment and to have dealt wisely and realistically with the innumerable problems which arose during the founding of the new religion. Although at the beginning of his mission he met with some skepticism and even open hostility on the part of a few individuals, he was never persecuted. He even underwent successfully the acid test for any prophet, returning to his home and convert-

ing the members of his own family. He enjoined poverty, chastity, and
benevolence in his followers, and gave them a distinctive costume, the
yellow robe and tonsure. He organized them into monastic groups,
whose government was modeled upon that of the small republics still
extant in Northern India at the time. During the dry season the monks
and nuns, for women had been admitted to the religious community with
some reluctance, went forth to preach the gospel. In the rainy season

SEATED BUDDHA AT SARNATH

they returned to the monastery and spent the time in meditation and discussion.

In its original form Buddhism, like Christianity, was simple and direct. Many of Buddha's sayings have been remembered:

"There are two extremes which should be avoided. There is the life of pleasure, which is base, ignoble, opposed to the intelligence, unworthy and vain; and there is the life of austerities, which is miserable, unworthy, and vain. The perfect one has remained far from these two extremes and has discovered the way which passes in the middle, which leads to rest, to knowledge, to illumination and to *nirvana,* its final escape. Behold, O monks, the holy truth about pain. Birth, old age, sickness, death, and separation from that which one loves, these are pain. It is the thirst for pleasure, the thirst for existence, the thirst for that which is evanescent. Behold the truth about the abolishment of pain. It is the extinction of this craving by the annihilation of desire."

Again he said: "Alms, knowledge and virtue are the possessions which do not fade away. To do a little good is worth more than to accomplish difficult works. The perfect man is nothing unless he spends himself in benefits to living beings."

"My doctrine is the doctrine of pity. That is why the happy ones of the earth find it hard. The way of salvation is open to all. Annihilate your passions, but know that he who believes he can flee from his passions by establishing himself in the shelter of a hermitage is deceiving himself. The only remedy against evil is sane reality."

During the forty years after his enlightenment Buddha lectured to his followers and gradually clarified his doctrine. He denied the value of caste distinctions, not as difficult at this time and place as it became later. He also denied the efficacy of ritual and sacrifice, a body blow at the Brahman supremacy. He did not deny the existence of the gods, but he claimed that they were unable to aid men in their striving toward the final goal; they too were tied to the wheel of life. Even more significant, he condemned the belief in the transmigration of souls, although this was so deeply rooted in Indian thought that it became one of the basic tenets of the emergent religion. He even questioned the existence of the soul as a distinct entity, holding that it was merely the Karmic accumulation of good and evil deeds held together by desire. When one of his disciples questioned him regarding the beginnings of the world, he answered that the question was unprofitable, thus forever saving Buddhism from the conflict between a primitive cosmology and an evolving knowledge of the nature of the universe which has so plagued Christianity.

All this negativism was intended to strip away superstition and to leave the individual free to follow the eightfold path. This involved, first, right views, which seems to have meant largely the insistence upon truth as this could be arrived at by logic. Second was right aspirations, which were to take the place of the base personal cravings which he condemned. They included such things as an abstract love for the service to others, love of justice, and the like. Third, fourth, and fifth were right speech, right conduct, and right livelihood. Sixth was right effort, which meant the intelligent planning of action toward the ends indicated in the rest of the doctrine. Seventh, right mindfulness, seems to have meant the elimination of individual pride of accomplishment in the face of the realization of individual imperfection. Eighth, and least clear, was right rapture, which seems to have meant the joy to be derived from meditation and contemplation as distinct from ecstasies of the Dionysian type.

Needless to say, these doctrines were so simple and called for so much personal soul-searching that they failed to appeal to the average individual. As time went on, there were increasing accretions of ritual, while doctrinal disputes led to the founding of various sects. The transformation into Mahayana Buddhism (the Greater Vehicle) was clearly annunciated in the 1st or 2nd century A.D. by Nagarjuna. Mahayana doctrine postulated the existence of beings known as Bodhisattvas, who consciously rejected nirvana in order to remain on earth to assist in the ultimate salvation of all life. This was in contradiction to the Hinayana (the Lesser Vehicle) belief in salvation as the reward of one's own efforts. The postulation of a greater number of divinities, however, led to changes in the attitude toward the Buddha himself; instead of being an enlightened individual, he became a god in the Western sense. The new doctrine, with its almost unlimited potentialities for religious and magical accretions, spread the popularity of Buddhism throughout India and into Tibet, and from there to China and Japan. The relatively simple Hinayana doctrines, with their closer adherence to primitive Buddhism, have survived in Ceylon and in parts of Southeast Asia. Even these have become highly ritualized.

Buddhism, in its early rise to the status of a world religion, owed much to royal favor. In the 3rd century B.C. Asoka, the emperor of the Mauryan Dynasty and the first conqueror to extend his rule over much of Southern as well as Northern India, became a convert. Horrified at the sufferings brought on by war, he voluntarily ceased his conquest and devoted his later years to good works and to the propagation of the faith. His royal edicts, carrying the tenets of the new religion, were inscribed on pillars and rocks throughout the empire. Three centuries later the Kushan kings of Northwestern India also became converted. The founders of this dynasty seem to have been Turkish nomads who had raided down into India from the steppes following the immemorial invasion routes, but they were eager to appear civilized. Kanishka, the greatest of their kings, called a synod to clarify Buddhist doctrine, in an attempt to heal the schisms which had developed.

The introduction of Buddhism into Tibet is attributed to a pious queen of Indian birth, while in Japan the first Buddhist missionaries arrived by royal invitation. However, the most powerful weapons in the Buddhist conquest of Asia were the religious doctrines and philosophic concepts of the Buddhists and their patterns of mendicant missionaries. The great university of Nalanda in southern Bihar, which at one time housed nearly 10,000 monks, served not only as a training school for monks but also as a goal for devout pilgrims from other countries. The famous Chinese pilgrims, Hsüan Tsang and I Ching, both studied there in the 7th century, and left vivid descriptions of that seat of learning, the vast ruins of which may still be seen today.

The incoherent animistic beliefs of the farther Asian peoples could oppose no resistance to the closely reasoned, logical systems which the Indian missionaries brought, while the religious paraphernalia of images and pictures, and the beautiful and dignified rites which accompanied them, had an overwhelming appeal. Even in China, where Buddhism was faced with a group of well-defined philosophic systems, the metaphysical doctrines and comprehensive appeal of Buddhism won the support of a large segment of the population during the disordered period from the 2nd through the 6th century A.D. Later, when Buddhism was dying in India, new sects were being created in China under the inspiration of Sanskrit texts brought back from India by zealous pilgrims. The new doctrine then spread from China to Japan, where even today Buddhism is a living philosophy.

India was the first region in which missionary activities developed. and they seem to have come about as a direct result of the emergent Hindu and Buddhist philosophies. The animist, or even the later worshipper of local or tribal deities, did not attempt to convert others to his faith. Conceding as he did the existence of gods who were limited in power and in the scope of their interests and activities, he felt that every new worshipper diminished the power and interest which his god might exert for his benefit. It was only with the emergence of the concept of deities of infinite power, who were capable of aiding all men in all places, that this older belief gave way to the idea of attaining divine favor by bringing the god additional worshippers. With the early Buddhistic denial of the very existence of deities, plus its tremendous insistence on benevolence and good works as the surest road to individual salvation, missionary patterns assumed a new vigor. In Buddha's own lifetime he sent forth hundreds of disciples to carry the good news to all parts of India, thus acquiring merit.

The Indian patterns of asceticism and withdrawal from the world, already well established by Buddha's time, added an important ingredient to this missionary complex. The begging priest could move among hostile peoples and disordered nations with impunity, since he was too poor to be worth robbing and also carried with him the mystery of supernatural dedication. One does not lightly injure a man from whose death or robbery nothing is to be gained, especially when, at the same time, there is an excellent chance of offending the higher powers by such an act. It was not until more than 1000 years after Buddha's death, when his monks found themselves confronted by Muslim fanaticism, that they lost this immunity. Prior to that time they were able to wander east and west over the immemorial caravan routes and seaways, bearing with them everywhere the tidings of the law and welcomed alike by villagers and kings.

By the beginning of the Christian era they had arrived in Alexandria and, although their teachings made little impression, since their philosophy could not compete successfully with the elaborate Greek systems, they seem to have been responsible for many of the forms of asceticism and of monastic organization which characterized the early centuries of Egyptian Christianity.

Chapter XXXV

Pre-Colonial India *Fusion of Aryan culture*

THE DEVELOPMENT of modern Indian culture has involved a synthesis of elements from many sources. The fusion of Aryan culture with what were probably numerous aboriginal cultures went on for millennia, the Aryan elements being diffused progressively eastward and southward. Beginning with the Persian and Greek invasion, Northwestern India was the scene of numerous evanescent conquests, in all of which the cycle of events seems to have been much the same. The early and rapid victories of the invaders were followed by gradual absorption and the final overthrow of alien rule by neighboring native states. The Muslim invaders were to introduce a new pattern.

In 712 the Arabs conquered Sind in the lower Indus Valley, and the province became the first independent Muslim state in India. From the 8th to the 11th century, Western India was in close contact with the Arab world through trade, cultural relations, and missionaries who brought the religion of Islam to a tolerant India. It was not until about 1000, when a Turk from Afghanistan, Mahmud of Ghazni, cruelly pillaged Northern India and annexed the Punjab, that Islam became equated with political power, brutality, and religious fanaticism. After Mahmud's death there were no invasions until the end of the 12th century, when another Afghan conquered Delhi, this time establishing a Sultanate which, during the next 150 years, gradually spread its dominion southward on the heels of refugees from Muslim tyranny. During that time the conquerors, an Indo-Aryan people closely allied to the Indians, underwent some Indianization through cultural synthesis. Towards the close of the 14th century Delhi was mercilessly sacked by Timur, who left all of Northern India greatly weakened. In 1526 Babar, a cultivated Turco-Mongol descendant of the Timurids, took Delhi and founded the Mogul Empire in India.

The Moguls were not barbarous invaders but representatives of the

Hindu Buddah
Islam Mohamed

ancient civilization of the Near East, reinvigorated by Muslim fanaticism. They were not impressed by Indian culture in the north, which was in a state of decay, and they missed the luxuries of their homeland in Central Asia. (It was Babar, for example, who laid out the plan for the city of Agra; his grandson, Shah Jehan, who built the glorious Taj Mahal.) Nor did they value the abstract philosophy in which the Indians were supreme. Continuous relations with the West and prescribed pilgrimages to Mecca kept these invaders in close touch not only with the Muslim center but also with the Safavid Renaissance in Iran.

Between the Weltanschauung of Hinduism and Islam there lay an unbridgeable gulf. It would have been difficult to find two civilizations more antithetical. The Muslim invaders were uncompromising monotheists, with a burning faith in the immanence of a highly personalized anthropomorphic deity; the Hindus were polytheists willing to recognize the existence of innumerable deities, since they regarded all of these, in the last analysis, as merely manifestations of an impersonal world soul (Brahman). The Muslims had a violent aversion to all forms of image worship; the Hindus had been accustomed for millennia to approach their deities through visible material representations. The Muslims insisted upon the brotherhood of all true believers and in practice allowed a high degree of individual social mobility. The familiar *Arabian Nights* motif of the mendicant raised to wealth and high political office overnight was only the romantic expression of a cultural ideal. The entire Hindu social system was based on social inequality and fixity of inherited status. Most of all, Muslim values were dynamic. "Islam" meant "submission to the will of God," but in practice consisted in the dignified acceptance of a *fait accompli* when no alternative appeared possible. The Hindus, on the other hand, glorified passive resignation and other-worldliness. The Hindus' loss of political power after the Muslim invasion no doubt reinforced tendencies toward passivity and denial of the reality of the external world. They cloaked themselves in a protective mantle of exclusiveness. The caste system crystallized and the seclusion of women (*purdah*) developed rapidly, as did untouchability. But exclusiveness, passivity, and other-worldliness were already present when the Muslims arrived. Since, as we have seen, they were foreign to the early Vedic religion, they may well have been of Dravidian origin, becoming more deeply impressed upon the Indian population during the long period when Buddhism was ascendant.

Between such opposites there might be compromise and some synthesis, such as occurred in music and language (*Urdu*), but no real fusion. Following the Muslim conquest, various spiritual leaders and even the Emperor Akbar attempted religious unification. Yet, with the exception of the Sikhs, their followers always found themselves in one or another of the two camps. Although the conquerors adopted many elements of the Indian technology and even, as their contacts with the Hindus continued, took on certain aspects of the caste system, they remained a distinct and, in most regions, politically dominant group. Since the Muslims were highly conscious of their status as conquerors, they were constantly galled by the rules of avoidance insisted upon by caste Hindus, and the feeling of resentment on both sides was no doubt increased by the fact that the numerous Hindu converts to Islam were drawn from the lower castes. In spite of their doctrine, by no means all of the Hindus were pacifists. The Rajputs in Rajputana held out for centuries, partly by their fighting ability, partly by the development of techniques which made their conquest unprofitable. When the fall of a city was imminent the defenders fired it, thus destroying all loot. The women and children committed suicide and the men, dressed in their nuptial garments, rode out to die fighting. At the time of the Mogul Empire they became vassals rather than subjects. Their noble houses gave brides to the Mogul emperors, and much of the military strength of the Moguls was derived from the Rajput battalions incorporated in their army.

Even when the Muslim conquest had been rapid and complete and a *modus vivendi* had been established, riots between the followers of the two religions were frequent. There were even conventionalized forms of incitement to riot. Hindus who wanted to start a disturbance would play music outside a mosque when services were going on, while Muslims who wanted to start one would publicly butcher a cow, with appropriate comments.

The presence of Muslim overlords presumably had much to do with the development and hardening of Hindu culture into its modern form. Various writers on India have noted with surprise that in spite of the extensive Buddhist and Jain remains dating from as far back as the 3rd century B.C. there are comparatively few Hindu remains until the 5th century A.D., that is, during the later Gupta period which is generally known as the Classic Age of Indian culture. This period gave to India the writings of Kalidasa, poet-dramatist and author of *Shakuntala*, and the paintings and sculptures of the cave temples at Ajanta in the northern Deccan. One of the earliest extant, and most beautiful, Hindu shrines (Deogarh) also dates from that epoch. There is evidence that Vaisnava and Saiva shrines existed even before the Christian era. A few coins and some stone images have come down to us from the 2nd and 1st centuries B.C. The prominence given to Siva even on the coins of foreign conquerors (the Kushans) shows how widespread the worship of Siva was at this time. But there was nothing to compare in magnitude or number with the monolithic structures of the Mauryas or the later stone work of the Buddhists and Jains.

This has been attributed to accidents of survival but there are other possible explanations. The Brahmans, from whose activities Hinduism has been inseparable, may have been ultra-conservative and insisted on constructing their temples and images from wood long after stone had come into use by the heretical Jains and Buddhists. It is also possible that, when these latter two sects dominated Indian religion, the Brahmans, since they were in eclipse at the royal courts, may well have continued to carry on their studies and revisions of the sacred literature in their forest retreats and to perform their rites for conservative village communities. A parallel case would be survival of heathen practices among Western Europe villages for centuries after Christianity had become the state religion.

Buddhism had as one of its most important precepts the veneration of sacred relics. The converted Mauryan Emperor, Asoka, remorseful at having laid waste the province of Kalinga (Orissa), which he had recently annexed, and anxious to convert his people, was personally interested in erecting lasting monuments to his new faith. He may even have used the services of craftsmen skilled in the Greco-Persian tradition of stone cutting, for Achaemenid influence is strongly present in the great monolithic pillars produced during his reign. His imperial patronage ushered in a golden age of indigenous religious art which, despite the changing fortunes of Buddhism and Brahmanism from the Gupta period on, continued until the establishment of the Delhi Sultanate and the Muslim introduction of a totally new aesthetic in architecture and design. The great and little domes and minarets of Muslim mosques and tombs changed the landscape of India. Yet the style of Islam underwent modification, largely because of the technological knowledge and skill which the Indian stonemason acquired during centuries of temple building. The artistry that had created the elaborate images on Hindu temples was now employed in the carving of arabesques and Arabic calligraphy, and in the use of dressed stone instead of the more common stucco and brick of the Near East.

By the time of the Arab invasion in the 8th century, Buddhism was already on the decline in all but Bihar and Sind. The destruction of monasteries and libraries and the ruthless massacre of Buddhist monks which accompanied Mahmud of Ghori's conquest completed its extinction; many of the surviving monks fled to Nepal and Tibet. Hindu temples were brutally torn down and, in their haste to erect their own houses of worship, the Muslims hacked away the images and re-used the stone in many of their early mosques. Later, however, even where the

Muslim rulers were religiously inclined, their zeal to wipe out Hinduism was always mitigated by the knowledge that under Koranic law, unbelievers were subject to various taxes from which true believers were exempt. Thus we know that in the early Islamic conquests in the West, Muslim governors were warned to discourage wholesale conversions, which were affecting the revenue of the Caliphate.

It is quite impossible to trace the successive steps by which Indian society and religion arrived at the forms which they manifested at the time of the first European contact. As has been previously noted, the Indians have been singularly uninterested in history and the applied sciences, and the Brahmans have maintained the pattern of claiming both remote antiquity and Vedic origin for any and all forms which they favored. By the Colonial period Indian religion and society had been integrated into an indissoluble whole. Daily life and social intercourse were ritualized to a greater extent than in any of the other world civilizations, and every detail was reinforced by supernatural sanctions. Even the caste system was justified by elaborate theories of spiritual development. As the result of the work of many sages over centuries, Hindu religion and philosophy had been brought into a working whole.

In contrast with the universal gods of the Vedic Aryans, the Dravidians seem to have had innumerable local deities. Thanks to the pantheistic concepts of the Brahmans and their doctrine of reincarnation, it was possible for them to equate the local gods and heroes with beings of their central pantheon, thus converting both the deities and their worshippers. The conflicting attributes of these adopted deities and the contradictions in the legends associated with them could always be explained by the concept that the gods, like men, were reborn repeatedly and that the conflicting tales referred to different *avatars* (reincarnations). Many of the deities which had been locally popular in the Dravidian south had considerable popular appeal, and their worship spread over most of Hindu India. Buddhism and Jainism were both heresies of an orthodox Brahmanism. Buddhism, particularly in its early stages, was, as we have seen, fundamentally philosophic and monastic and probably was continually in conflict with popular belief in local deities, although many of them were incorporated into the Buddhist pantheon. When Buddhism suffered for want of royal patronage these aboriginal deities reappeared in a resurgent Hinduism which, around the 6th century, began to weaken the Buddhist hold on India.

The two main deities of this later Hinduism were Siva and Vishnu. The chief gods of ancient times, Indra and Brahma, fell into virtual obscurity. Vishnu, orginally a form of Surya (the sun) now became the god sustaining the universe. His numerous avatars show how various divinities were consolidated in the person of one god. Even the Buddha

was explained as an avatar of Vishnu. Siva seems to have been a pre-
Vedic divinity; his home, Mount Kailasa, was in the Himalayas, and the
forms of most Hindu temples reflect the outlines of his mountain abode.

Although in common practice Hinduism is polytheistic, it may be
said to be monotheistic in that all divinities are regarded as aspects of
one universal power. Hindu philosophy posits three great beings or
manifestations of the basic world force: Brahma, the creator, Vishnu, the
preserver, and Siva, the destroyer. This is consistent with the Indo-Euro-

SIVA, FOUR ARMED, TANJORE, X CENTURY

pean pattern, in which 3 is the most sacred of all numbers and the male principle is uniformly given precedence over the female. But, according to the Saivas all three are manifested in Siva himself, and according to many, Siva and Vishnu are only aspects of the One. This philosophic attitude led to complete tolerance among the various sects, so that almost entirely different practices and ways of thought were acceptable within the one religion. The worship of vital forces was uppermost in Saivism, while other sects paid devotion to the *Sakti* (female principle). During the 7th and 8th centuries the doctrine of *Bhakti* (devotion to a personal god) came into prominence, and soon thereafter the great philosopher-missionary Shankar organized the first Brahmanic monastic orders and, in his remarkable travels all over India, preached for the unification of beliefs. The thousands of Hindu temples constructed during and after the time of Shankar reflect the fervor of that Hindu Renaissance.

The source of much of Hindu doctrine is the *Bhagavadgita* (*Gita*), an enchanting dramatic poem in dialogue which is primarily ethical in its teachings. It condemns inaction and posits three main paths to salvation (*moksha*): action (*karma*), knowledge (*jnana*), and devotion (*bhakti*). The *Gita,* which was written some time during the first two centuries B.C., is a section of the *Mahabarata.* This work is a repository of Indian mythology, legendary history, and early philosophic speculation. The other epic, the *Ramayana,* has been a source of great inspiration to the Hindus, especially through its vernacular rendering in medieval times. For centuries their tales of gods and goddesses, heroes and heroines, have been woven into the fabric of the people's lives. From them various sects chose their deities, both major and minor.

There are numerous Vaishnava and Saiva sects and sub-sects, each directing its worship toward a particular avatar. In addition there are miscellaneous cults directed toward minor deities, such as the Nagas (snakes) and Yakshas (tree gods), who are not commonly regarded as avatars of the great gods but who are mythologically connected with them in one way or another. Each avatar has its temples, in which it is represented by images or symbols and in these temples there are still carried on rituals handed down from great antiquity. Even today the god is treated in the temple as a resident king or queen, and the ritual is an enactment of the ancient royal daily round. All twice-born Hindus, i.e., members of the upper three castes, are expected to perform daily rituals. This is described by S. Bhattacharya as follows: [1]

While the temples are dedicated to many different deities, the daily practices in the temples follow a common pattern. They begin with

[1] "Religious Practices of the Hindus," in *Religion of the Hindus.* Edited by K. W. Morgan. New York: The Ronald Press Co.; 1953, pp. 156–157.

the auspicious lamp ceremony at the last eight of the night, when the deity is awakened. Then the deity is bathed, and worshipped; at midday, cooked food is offered to the deity, followed by a lamp ceremony, after which the deity rests until late afternoon, when there is the anointing and decorating ceremony. In the evening there is an elaborate lamp ceremony, after which food is again offered to the deity, followed by the final ceremony at which the deity is retired for the night. In addition to these daily ceremonies, there are elaborate rites, often lasting several days, at the time of the important festivals. It should be borne in mind that while the five daily offerings are obligation for the Hindu, there is no obligation to participate in the ceremonies at the temple. Some very devout Hindus go to the temple rarely, if at all.

The Hindu peasant left philosophic speculations to the Brahmans, and followed the prescribed rites in order to get practical benefits. In addition to the particular god of his sect, he worshipped local spirits, legendary heroes who were in some way connected with his caste or region, and even in some cases prayed to his own ancestral spirits. He would attempt at least once in his life to make a pilgrimage to one of the great temples dedicated to his patron deity. The festivals of different gods were held at different times and places. Such gatherings brought together great numbers of worshippers and provided a welcome break in the monotony of village life. A fair was usually combined with the religious celebration. Between pilgrimages he might worship his particular god at a private shrine, but he would not neglect the village shrine dedicated to some local deity. This was presided over by a resident priest, not always a Brahman, who would be called on to assist whenever elaborate rites were needed. In addition, he would address any god who might be of assistance to him in current need. Thus the merchant would pray to Ganesh, the elephant-headed god, for help in business, while at the time of a smallpox epidemic offerings would be made to Durga, the goddess of smallpox, one of the less lovable consorts of Siva. The average Hindu, whether peasant or Brahman, did not question the existence of innumerable deities and was as tolerant of other sects as the followers of one Christian saint are toward those of other saints.

The village temple was the center of Hindu culture. There the people worshipped, were educated, and obtained medical relief and charity. There the fine arts—music, poetry, sculpture, and the dance—received encouragement. The activities of the temple were financed by public and private funds. Under Muslim rule, with its lessening sympathy for Hindu life, heavier exactions were made and the sources of village revenue declined. As a result the general cultural life of the Hindu community was adversely affected.

On the whole the democratic pattern of the Indian village as developed in Aryan times changed little. Under the Muslims the separation between state and religious affairs was maintained, the village council continued to rule civic affairs, and the Brahmans retained their supremacy in all religious and social matters. The economic basis of pre-colonial village life lay in a delicate balance between agriculture and industry. Cities were primarily administrative and religious centers, and were usually small, except for those on the coast or on rivers where water transport simplified problems of supply. A striking feature was the building of fortified cities and the development of city planning as an art common to both Hindu and Muslim. A ruler, wishing to escape from the influences of his predecessor's reign, would pick a new site, construct a planned city, and then move a population into it by a combination of force and persuasion. The duration of such cities depended to some extent on the skill with which the site had been chosen. In most cases the movements were only over a short distance, and in many localities there are clusterings of old and new cities within a small area.

The bulk of the Indian population occupied rural villages with an average of 400 inhabitants. Groups of villages were often united in a county council, which acted as the final tribunal in civil affairs. Many of these communities were isolated, with little outside contact. Land holdings followed the immemorial pattern of the Near East, with cultivated fields immediately above the village and pasture beyond. Joint property ownership and survivorship inheritance, which also followed Near Eastern patterns, prevented excessive fragmentation of holdings. The joint family also provided for the needs of each worker and non-worker among its members. The village grain share system (*Jajmani*) continued to provide a fixed annual share of the harvest to the village carpenter, smith, potter, priest, barber, etc., in return for services performed throughout the year. Economic patterns remained stabilized and there were few mechanical improvements in workmanship. Techniques of craftsmanship were transmitted within hereditary groups (castes) and guarded as trade secrets. The lack of material advance may have resulted from these occupational monopolies, which limited competition and discouraged invention.

Indian culture was characterized by an extreme development of ascribed status and role, which made it the most static and most perfectly integrated culture so far developed. The foundation of the society was threefold: village self-government, the caste system, and the joint family. The caste system was reinforced by a series of supernatural sanctions and rationalizations derived from a highly complex and formal religious and philosophical system. A caste is a closely organized body equipped with a common tradition and a strong esprit de corps. It has a chief and a council. Its members meet on occasion in assembly of more or less plenary authority. They join in the celebrations of certain festivals and they have jurisdiction over their members, with power to impose penalties, the most severe of which is expulsion from the caste.

In addition to the marriage regulations imposed by the caste system, the Indian village was, with few exceptions, an exogamous unit. Groups of villages intermarried and were thus bound together by ties of blood. Child marriage, although by no means universal, became increasingly common during this period, and stems from a combination of factors. It was incumbent upon a father to obtain a husband for his daughter before she reached puberty. Also, residence was strictly patrilocal, and it was easier for a child, transferred to another joint family in another locality, to become integrated into it than it was for an adult. By child marriage the father shifted the responsibility for the behavior of his daughter to the husband's family. In most castes which practiced child marriage both parties were children, and the marriage was not consummated until they were well grown, by which time the wife had lived for some years in the husband's family and was ready to take her place as one of its members.

A caste was normally a hereditary monopoly of a certain activity or occupation. In any district in India the caste activities were organized in such a way that different castes did not come into economic competition. Secondly, in sharp contrast to the economic interdependency, there was the factor of self-containment. In general the caste institution provides a certain sense of security because it delimits the area of social and economic rivalry. Caste distinctions were less rigid prior to the 12th century, when the Hindu began to protect himself from Muslim contact by various devices of seclusion. Since that time intercaste marriages have been exceptionally rare, although they seem to have been quite common earlier. The other great taboo, that of dining between members of different castes, may also have become more restrictive at that time. The Brahmans, in order to preserve their ceremonial purity, developed laws pertaining to what cooked or uncooked food may be accepted by certain classes of non-Brahmans. The rigid stratification of castes and subcastes led to a general ritual of social relations.

No matter how diverse the actual origins were, all castes are, in theory, arranged in a graded series of social prominence, based on their supposed derivation from Brahma's body. Each of the four main castes is divided into hundreds of sub-castes, each of which has one above and one below it in the social order. Since the Indian populations have been relatively static, this arrangement could be maintained. While it is impossible for an individual to rise in the caste hierarchy, it is possible for an entire caste to rise as a whole. This is done by keeping the formal regulations with respect to prayers, ceremonial cleanliness, and so forth, with special strictness. A Sudra cannot become a Kshatriya, and no caste can become Brahman, but it is possible to elevate a sub-caste a notch or two by this method.

The caste system is excellently adapted to keeping a highly complex but static culture functioning successfully. Caste has become a basic pattern of Indian life and most new social elements are interpreted and adjusted in its terms. Even the native Christians and Muslims, although they did not accept the Hindu hierarchy, divided into sub-castes. On the other hand, many Untouchables espoused Islam, and later Christianity, in order to escape from their miserable status.

In the matter of social organization, the differences between North and South are still recognizable. The penetration of the South was almost entirely by Brahmans and even today the only caste categories which are significant there are Brahman and Sudra. Groups such as the Nayars, whose activities as rulers and professional warriors would normally equate them with the Kshatriya, are nevertheless classed as Sudra. At the same time, the innumerable groups of local specialists which constitute the real functional basis of the caste system are multiplied to a much higher degree in the South and East than in the Northwest, and the taboos governing their interrelations are more numerous and onerous. In particular, the South presents unusual elaboration of the group lying below the Sudra in the classificatory system. These are now commonly referred to as the Depressed or Scheduled Castes, since this category is also subdivided and organized along caste lines. Gandhi called them Harijans, or Children of God.

The regulations governing the interaction of members of different castes are much more elaborate in the South and East than in the Northwest, and the whole system much more rigid. In Southern India members of lower castes could pollute a Brahman or a sacred place by approaching within distances which varied with their position in the local caste series. Some castes in the Scheduled groups polluted ground simply by walking over it and therefore were required to use special paths and to abstain from the public highways, where members of higher castes might pass. There were even a few unfortunates at the very bottom of the series whose sight was polluting.

The restrictions imposed on Hindu castes vary in degree rather than in kind but they are numerous at all levels. In general, the higher the caste, the more elaborate the restrictions on its members' behavior. There are various exceptions to this, as to practically all generalizations dealing with caste, but the Brahman is in nearly every case more hedged about and restricted by caste regulations than the members of lower groups. It is quite inconceivable that such a system could have been imposed by force or from above. It is interesting to note that the closest parallel to the Hindu avoidance system is to be found in Polynesia, in connection with the constant, as distinct from imposed taboos. The Polynesian regulations were directed primarily toward the well-being of the group and the safety of individuals of lower rank, and stemmed from the Polynesian concept of *mana*. The chief, as symbol of the tribe, enjoyed the highest mana, while other tribe members possessed the quality in diminished degrees. Contact between an individual of high mana and one of low mana might result in some loss to the higher but was injurious mainly to the lower individual, for whom it frequently had fatal results. We have seen that the surviving non-Hindu Dravidian tribes have various taboos and avoidance practices which are reminiscent of some of the caste regulations, and it has also been pointed out that Southern and Eastern India seem to have participated in the Southeast Asiatic co-tradition of which Polynesian culture was a part. It seems highly probable, therefore, that the caste regulations were originally designed quite as much to safeguard the spiritual potency of individuals and groups, and to prevent injury to those of lower potency, as to impress inferior groups with their social disabilities.

The four-category system was, as we have seen, a feature of early Persian society and was presumably brought into India by the Aryan invaders who were closely related to the early Persians. Hereditary occupation groups tending toward endogamy were a frequent feature of Old World societies. They seem to have been more frequent in advanced than in simple societies, perhaps because economic factors connected with maintaining craft monopolies were involved. There is good reason to believe that such groups were present in the advanced Dravidian cultures of India. Elaborate regulations of behavior, based on the fear either of loss of power or on a belief in the danger of coming into contact with power greater than one's own, were a common feature of the Southeast Asiatic co-tradition. A combination of these three elements would be enough to produce the Hindu caste system, the Aryan social categories or classes being superimposed upon the Dravidian occupational groups and the whole being organized into a single system in which each caste was placed in a particular category, thus establishing its superiority or inferiority with regard to other castes. Lastly, the insistence on endogamy and the establishment of formal rules of behavior governing the interaction of individuals of different castes served to maintain the system.

British colonial rule in India, among other things, dealt a body blow to the autonomy and self-containment of the village and further fractured the caste system. Today in independent India other significant forms of social relationships are in the process of drastic reform. Through the enactment of new laws, changes are now taking place in caste relationships, land ownership, and in the structure of the joint family. These events, the consequences of which are still being worked out, will not be discussed in the present volume.

Chapter XXXVI

Prehistoric China

CHINA HAS HAD a culturally unified population for a longer continuous period than any other civilization of the world, although it is by no means the oldest. China's civilization took shape much later than those of the Indus Valley, the Near East, or Egypt. China's culture, however, became integrated early and, unlike the other great early cultures, has never collapsed, but has continued its development with varying degrees of effectiveness ever since. Contacts with other cultures have been numerous. The Chinese have been conquered and ruled by several foreign dynasties, but have always managed to impose their own culture on their barbarian conquerors and eventually to absorb them and re-establish their own line. They were the first civilization to evolve a really workable and stable government which could handle a large population made up of both city and rural areas, and they have never been truly overthrown.

According to the Chinese historian, Mencius, Chinese history moves in 500-year repetitive cycles. The pattern has always been: domination by a foreign conqueror; absorption of the conqueror; a period of confusion; and finally, when the Chinese are once more reorganized under a Chinese dynasty, a period of aggressive world policy and conquest. If history repeats itself, China should be able to dispose of the Russians and become a world power in its own right within another couple of hundred years. The idea that the Chinese are a simple, friendly, non-warlike people is far from the truth. China has been a world power during several periods of her history and has spread her conquests to an amazing distance.

The earliest Chinese date which can be assigned with any probability is 2250 B.C., based on an astronomical reference in the *Book of History*. However, development was rapid, and, by the beginning of the

520

Shang Dynasty, approximately 1750 B.C., China had drawn abreast of the Western civilizations. Since that time it has maintained an enviably high level of culture, and a continuity of tradition unequaled elsewhere.

Several factors contributed to this. Chinese crops and cultivation methods were probably the best in the world prior to the introduction of modern scientific agriculture. They made possible the support of a population as dense as that of Egypt or Mesopotamia over a vastly larger area. The Chinese, from very early times, concerned themselves with the practice and theory of government, and well before the beginning of the Christian era had developed techniques for recruiting superior minds into the government service. Wicked men, and equally wicked women, have ruled in China, but few fools have held power, and these only briefly. Thanks to techniques of training and selection, the Chinese administrative system during the last 2000 years has been able to combine the advantages of the British government service with a broad utilization of human resources like that created by the American democratic system. Lastly, the development at an exceedingly early time of a system of writing, which was divorced from spoken language, made it possible to incorporate into a single state and cultural tradition groups speaking many different dialects. It also made available to the administrator the experience of past rulers in a way impossible in the West, because of the frequent language changes which have taken place in the history of every European state.

The distinctive qualities of Chinese culture have been due at least in part to geographic conditions. China faces east and is rimmed about on the south and west by almost impassable mountains. Even communication in these directions has always been difficult. On the northwest the mountain barrier breaks down but is replaced by arid plains, while to the north the great Circumpolar forest extends, or did extend, across Manchuria. None of the frontier regions was capable of supporting a numerous settled population, or one at a high level of cultural complexity. The only frontier on which China was threatened was the northwest, where it impinged upon the Asiatic steppes with their population of warlike nomads. As a matter of fact, all the foreign invaders who have succeeded in conquering China, with the single exception of the Manchus, have come from this direction. Chinese diplomacy and Chinese culture have dominated the eastern steppes since ancient times, and the invading Huns, Turks, and Mongols were already conscious of the grandeur of the Chinese tradition. The various nomad dynasties which have ruled in China for longer or shorter periods have always found it necessary to avail themselves of the services of the existing Chinese scholar-bureaucracy, while their followers have been unable to

compete with the Chinese on a peaceful footing. In spite of attempts to
maintain their barbarian way of life, a few generations have seen them
thoroughly acculturated.

Chinese cultural self-sufficiency has been greatly aided by the natural environment. Chinese climates are as variable as those of the United
States. Northern China has a temperature range much like that of our
own Northern Plains, while far Southern China is semi-tropical. There
are very few crops which cannot be grown somewhere in the empire.
Much of China is mountainous, but a coastal plain and three great river
valleys, the Hwang Ho on the north, the Yangtze Kiang in Central China,
and the Chu Kiang on the south, provide large areas of fertile land. The
Hwang Ho and the Yangtze are linked by the 850-mile Grand Canal,
which extends from Hangchow to Tientsin. The construction of the
project was started by Fu Ch'ai, king of the state of Yüeh, in the 5th
century B.C. The oldest portion, connecting the Hwang Ho and the
Yangtze, was completed under the emperor Yang, who reigned from 605
to 617 A.D. The remainder, including an extension to Peiping, which is
now filled in, was constructed during the Yüan Dynasty, 1279–1368 A.D.
Thus, by the beginning of the 7th century A.D., it became possible to
reach most parts of the empire by boat and to exchange the products
of the most distant regions at slight expense. The mineral deposits were
sufficient for the support of a culture still operating on the level of
hand industry. Chinese resources of coal and iron are limited by modern
standards, and it seems doubtful whether they provide a basis for heavy
industry of the European type. However, the Chinese have exploited
the deposits successfully for some 2000 years. They discovered the use
of coal long before the Europeans did.

Most of China seems to have been covered with great forests in
early times. These were especially heavy south of the Yangtze, and this
region is warm enough for the growth of bamboo, one of the most
variously useful products of nature. All in all, China has been a highly
desirable region for human settlement, and one of the few capable of
supporting a dense population at a high level of cultural complexity
without foreign trade. The Chinese were able to produce all necessary
goods within their own borders. Their trade with the West, carried on
by sea and by the immemorial caravan routes crossing central Asia, was
a trade in luxury objects. They sent silk westward and received in return
other luxuries: Syrian glass beads and vessels, finely wrought precious
metals, and, in still later times, dancing girls and fast horses.

In sharp contrast with the Indians, the Chinese have always been
historically minded, and the amount of Chinese literature dealing with
the past is enormous. Unfortunately, their desire to use past events to
point a moral and their fondness for systematic organization have re-

sulted in the frequent rewriting of the earlier records. Thus, the *Bamboo Books,* which give earlier accounts of the same period covered by other classics, present a much less idyllic society. However, much of the cultural information presented incidentally in all of these writings undoubtedly has a sound factual basis. It is fortunate for the student of Chinese origins that this is the case, since there is no area of equal size and cultural significance anywhere in the world whose archeology is as poorly known as that of China. For this reason the few regions and periods which have been studied have received what may prove to be undue emphasis.

The excavation of a single site near the modern city of Peiping has yielded some of the earliest physical and cultural remains of man. These are dated tentatively as early in the last Interglacial period. Following this there is an almost complete blank for at least 200,000 years. Beginning at 3000 to 3500 B.C. at the earliest, a series of moderately diverse Neolithic cultures can be identified in various parts of northern and northwestern China. These lead into the sudden cultural flowering of the Shang dynasty in approximately 1550 B.C., and the beginnings of a civilization immediately recognizable as Chinese. From this time on cultural developments in Northern China can be traced through inscriptions and other literary records, which become more and more plentiful as time advances.

South China, on the other hand, is known to us only as it gradually emerges into the light of history as a result of its penetration by North Chinese culture, and of its progressive conquest by various North Chinese dynasties. The South Chinese archeological record is still, to all intents and purposes, a blank. From occasional surface finds this region seems to have shared the Southeast Asiatic Neolithic co-tradition. Some of the stone implements are strikingly similar to those of Southeast Asia, and there seems to be a corresponding lack of finely chipped stone projectile points and knives. The last named characteristic may be more apparent than real, since implements of this type are less likely to be recognized and preserved than the larger ground stone objects. There is also the interesting and highly suggestive conclusion of Vaviloff that the mountains of Southern China were an important center of plant domestication, and that a surprising number of root and leaf crops originated here. That there have been significant cultural differences between Northern and Southern China since at least Neolithic times cannot be doubted, and such differences exist even today.

Reverting to the archeological record, it is clear that the beginnings of human occupation in China go back to exceedingly ancient times. A protohominoid, *Sinanthropus,* occupied Northern China during the last interglacial. This form was similar in most respects to the Java man,

Pithecanthropus, although somewhat closer to modern man in his evolutionary position. On the basis of physical characteristics, any surviving representatives of this group would probably be consigned to a zoo. Nevertheless, the behavior of Sinanthropus was much more human than anthropoid. The species used fire and made stone tools which show considerable skill in the techniques of blade-striking. Some of these are so well-shaped as to suggest that they were deliberately designed for use as specialized tools: knives, scrapers, or even projectile points. The species also followed the human practice of cannibalism, unmistakable evidences of which have been found in the single site of this period so far excavated. Since no indication of burials or other ceremonial treatment of corpses has been found, it seems highly probable that they ate their own dead. This practice has been current among several historic peoples, where it was instigated not by hunger but by an understandable desire to keep the virtues of the deceased in the family.

To judge from accidental finds, this culture passed over into one with larger and more crudely worked flakes and choppers, resembling in many respects the old Paleolithic of Southeast Asia. At a somewhat later period than that of Sinanthropus, and farther to the Northwest, there seems to have been another Old Paleolithic culture which used large flakes and occasional crudely chipped pointed implements reminiscent of the European and African hand-axes. However, a gap of at least 100,000 years separates even these fragmentary Paleolithic finds from the first Neolithic settlement in Northern China. In spite of a few seemingly Upper Paleolithic objects from the upper cave at the Sinanthropus site, this gap still remains to be bridged. Some indication of what may have been the cultural situation in Northern China during the late Upper Paleolithic or Mesolithic can be gained from discoveries in Mongolia. Here surface sites have yielded great numbers of small cores from which slender blades have been struck. Very few of the blades themselves have survived, but there can be little doubt that they were inset in bone or wooden implements to provide a sharp cutting edge. It seems safe to assume that there was also a considerable bone and antler industry. Although only one or two implements of these materials have been found, they would be very unlikely to have survived in open sites. The whole complex suggests a hunting-gathering economy without permanent settlements, carried on under environmental conditions more favorable than the present. A few fragments of checked stamped pottery, and some bar-shaped ground stone objects which might have been used both as pestles and grinding stones, have been found on some of the Mesolithic sites, but probably belong to a later period.

The earliest Neolithic phase in Northern China was clearly a part of the Circumpolar co-tradition. The sites contain circular pits usually

referred to as pit-houses. These are so small that they are more likely
to have been underground granaries or storage rooms. If lived in at all,
they probably served as cold weather dormitories. Ground stone celts of
simple generalized type were in use, as well as chipped-stone knives
and projectile points, and bone projectile points and awls. Some of the
chipped-stone and bone implements have forms which are already distinctive and ancestral to those used in later Chinese metal objects. Pottery was fairly abundant and was in the Circumpolar tradition, being
beaker-shaped and grit-tempered. It was frequently cord-marked or
roughly modeled. Three-lobed cooking pots, made with three bodies of
ordinary beaker form sloping toward a single mouth at the top, were
not uncommon, and may indicate the origin of the tripod vessels so
popular in later Chinese periods.

The earliest crop seems to have been a large, strong-stalked millet,
kaoliang, like that still grown in the region. Some of the accidental im-
pressions on pottery have been interpreted as made by rice, but, if so,
the presence of this cereal in Northern China by at least 2500 B.C. presents a puzzling problem. With the millet and rice (?) culture the
people also kept dogs and pigs, both used for food. Before the close of
this early Neolithic phase sheep and cattle also appear, but the infrequent horse bones found in sites probably indicate that the animal was
hunted rather than domesticated.

Toward the close of this period a new type of pottery appears in
Kansu province in Northwestern China. This is a red, black, and white
ware decorated with spirals and other curvilinear designs. Large water
jars painted with a broad band of design on the shoulder are the most
characteristic utensils, but there are also bowls and smaller vessels. The
cooking pots are still of the old beaker-shaped, grit-tempered type. This
painted ware is very similar to the Neolithic pottery from Persia and
even the Danube Valley. There can be little doubt that it was introduced into Kansu from the West, but, since no other new and distinctive culture elements appear with it, it must have been brought in by
diffusion rather than a migration of Western tribes. This whole complex, including the painted ware, is called the *Yang Shao* culture. It has
been very tentatively dated at 3000 to 2500 B.C.

In Northeastern China, in Shantung province, there is a considerably
richer Neolithic culture, called the *Lung Shan.* The two cultures meet
in the region about the bend of the Yellow River. In the few sites where
both are present, Lung Shan remains overlie Yang Shao ones, indicating
a later date for the former, perhaps 2300 to 2000 B.C. for its beginnings.
The antecedents of Lung Shan are not clear, but it contains a number
of new elements and represents the highest level of complexity attained
by any Eurasian culture which lacked metal.

The Lung Shan people built large towns fortified with walls of tamped earth, a building material still used in the same region. The old Neolithic pit-houses were still present, but there were also the tamped earth foundations of fairly large rectangular houses built on low platforms. To judge from the arrangement of the posts, these houses were much like those still in use in Northern China. Stone and bone work resembled that of the Yang Shao culture, but there was considerable use of shell for both implements and ornaments. The characteristic pottery was an exceedingly thin, hard-fired black ware made on the wheel, and if this appliance was present one can scarcely doubt that the Lung Shan people also knew the cart and chariot. Millet and possibly rice were raised and the soya bean, although not found in any sites to date, may well have been present. Domestic animals consisted of pigs, dogs, cattle, sheep, and horses.

This Lung Shan culture seems to have provided the foundation on which the civilization of the Shang Dynasty was erected. In spite of the Shang use of bronze and the superb skill with which it was worked, the peasant population remained essentially Neolithic for centuries. It is noteworthy that in the "Tribute of Yü" section of the *Book of History,* presumably dating from near the close of the Shang dynasty (1027 B.C.) "arrowhead stones" are listed in the tribute paid by two provinces of the empire. Although the reference is obscure, the character may well refer to flint or other easily flaked stones, rare in the loess land surrounding the Shang capital.

There are no inscriptions from any period earlier than Shang. The *Book of Changes,* which deals with origins of things Chinese, states that before the invention of written characters records were kept and messages sent by means of knotted cords. The Peruvian use of these appliances (*quipus*) proves how effective they can be. The *Book of Changes* itself was revised and re-edited several times, so the statements contained in it must be taken with all the usual reservations. As a further complication, the scholar-philosophers, through whose hands it passed, thought in terms of a logically organized universe whose order was perceived by the semi-divine rulers of the earliest times. Only when these rulers had established the observances necessary to strengthen and maintain the cosmic order did they turn their gifts to the invention of utilitarian appliances.

One of the first creations of a primordial demigod was the sixty-four hexagrams, figures composed of parallel solid and broken lines arranged in different combinations. Each of the sixty-four figures carried a different meaning, and all had a magical significance. They were and still are used in divination for the purpose of finding out whether conditions are propitious for any activity. According to the *Book of Changes,* the first emperors arrived at the invention of useful objects by meditating upon the hexagrams. The three lords, Huang Ti, Yao, and Shun "tamed oxen (in carts) and yoked horses (to chariots), thus providing for the carriage of what was heavy and for distant journeys, thereby benefiting all under the sky." The idea of this was taken, probably, from the hexagram *sui* ("Following": cheerfulness over movement).

In spite of its revisions and its preoccupations with ritual and the supernatural, the *Book of Changes* offers valuable information on the pre-Shang culture of North China. Thus the deity Shen Nung is both inventor of agriculture and Lord of Fire, a good indication that agriculture was carried on at first by the slash and burn technique. The book contains numerous references to battles between the *Hsia,* as the Chinese called their own ancestors, and the *Miao,* an aboriginal group whom they found in possession of at least part of Northern China. The Miao are associated with the sea in the ancient writings, and their totem animals were sea animals, sea monsters, and winged creatures. The totems of the Hsia, on the other hand, were tigers, leopards, and two sorts of bear.

Archeological work in Northern China has done little to clarify these legends, aside from showing that there were distinct, at least partly contemporaneous Neolithic cultures in the eastern and western parts of Northern China. It seems highly probable that the same participants in the Southeast Asiatic co-tradition whose northward voyages took them to Japan and Korea also settled on the Chinese coast and even followed the Yellow River inland, but proof of this is lacking.

Hsia society was divided into the "Nine Tribes of the Ruler," the "Hundred Clans" and the "myriad Black-Haired People." The last seems a curious appellation for a group in a region where any other hair color is practically unknown today, but red hair and grey or green eyes are by no means unusual among Paleoarctic peoples. Ghengis Khan belonged to a Mongol clan called "The Grey Eyed Folk," and Subatai, his greatest general, was famous for his flaming red hair. In later times the Chinese viewed these physical characteristics without enthusiasm. In fact, they ascribed them to their devils. However, it seems quite possible that the Hsia contained a fair proportion of individuals showing them. The Miao, on the other hand, were always described as darker skinned than the Hsia, and were presumably black-haired. Various aboriginal groups in far Southern China are still called Miao, and Chinese scholars have assumed that these are the descendants of Northern tribes who fled before the Hsia. It seems much more probable that the name Miao

was applied to several non-Hsia tribes living in Northern China, and
that most of these were progressively civilized and absorbed into the
historic Chinese population.

From the material in the *Book of Changes* it seems that the Miao
were matriarchal, and the Hsia patriarchal but by no means as strongly
so as the later Chinese. Many European scholars have been confused in
their interpretations of this material by the now discredited cultural-
evolutionary theory that matriarchal institutions always preceded patriarchal ones. Actually, patrilineal descent and patriarchal institutions are
characteristic of all the Eurasiatic peoples with a hunting or herding
economy. The presence of the radical "woman" in the Chinese character
for "clan" and in most of the oldest recorded clan names is less likely
to be a memorial to an evolutionary stage than to the importance of the
Miao element in the Chinese society of the pre-Shang period.

It is difficult to reconstruct the social and political organization of
Hsia society because of the scantiness of the records and their extensive
revision in Chou times. There were peasants, military aristocracy who
fought from chariots, and a leader of the whole Hsia people, who seems
to have been much more priest than king. The relation of these divisions
to the "Nine Tribes of the Ruler," the "Hundred Clans" and the "Black-
Haired People" is not clear. The most probable assumption seems to be
that there were villages of the "Black-Haired People" exploited and
dominated by families of one of the other groups in a sort of unorganized, uncentralized feudal system. It is interesting to note that the ruling
group does not seem to have followed the extended-family patterns
characteristic of later Chinese aristocracy.

The duties of the priest-king were primarily to act as a mediator
between the nation and the celestial beings. He is occasionally mentioned as leading his people in war against the Miao, or against rebels
whose most serious offense seems to have been trying to introduce a
new calendar in opposition to the one which he maintained. However,
it is clear that he had little political power. There also seems to have
been no fixed capital of the nation, the king going wherever his services
were required.

There were innumerable supernatural beings associated with various places and activities, but ancestor worship seems to have been much
less important than it became later. Beings important enough to be
classed as gods were divided into two groups, the celestial deities and
the chthonic deities. The former were generally beneficent and were in
charge of the seasons, the round of agricultural activities, and the
weather. A deity enthroned at the North Pole was pre-eminent among
them and has almost the importance of a supreme being. Their worship
was closely associated with astronomical studies. Rites in their honor

were performed by the priest-king annually on particular dates, and were intended to insure the regular return of the seasons and the growth of the crops. These rites were performed in the open air, and seem to have been highly formal even in the earliest times. The offerings to be made and the vessels to be used in each rite were rigidly prescribed.

The chthonic deities appear much less frequently in the records, probably because they were so much feared that their names were never mentioned. Their place was underground, and they were associated with darkness, death, and evil. There is little information on their worship, but we know that their rites were held at night or in dark places. At a later time animals offered to them were burned alive in pits, and there can be little doubt that they received human sacrifices as well. Sacrifice was an important feature of all the ancient rites and there is good reason to believe that the most important sacrifice, reserved for calamities, was that of the priest-king himself. As late as the Chou period (1027–221 B.C.) it was customary in time of drought for the emperor to pray that the sins of the people might descend on his head, and then cut off his front hair and fasten it on the forehead of a black bull which was sacrificed in his stead.

This early Chinese dualism is very reminiscent of aboriginal Siberian shamanism, with its summer and winter deities linked with light and darkness and served by different groups of shamans. There are also occasional mentions of mediumistic practices reminiscent of aboriginal Siberia and far North America, and the Chinese magical number at this period was *four*, as among the North American Indians.

The historic period begins with the Shang Dynasty (1766–1122 B.C.). Although frequently mentioned in the classical literature, this dynasty was considered mythical until a few years ago, when bones scratched with very archaic characters came to light in the region about the great bend of the Hwang Ho. Since then royal tombs of the dynasty have been systematically excavated, and most of the Shang emperors listed in the *Book of History* have been identified in contemporary inscriptions. The combination of excavated objects, contemporary inscriptions, and traditional literature makes it possible to get a better picture of the conditions during this dynasty than we have for many later periods. The Chou dynasty, which succeeded the Shang, has left a wealth of literary records, but no Chou site has been excavated by satisfactory modern scientific methods. Chinese antiquarians' interests have provided a market for ancient bronzes and stone carvings, and tomb robbing has been a common if disreputable occupation since at least the beginning of the Christian era. It has brought to light many wonderful works of art, but not much can be told from objects out of context. The excavation of the Shang royal tombs at An-yang still remains an isolated example of scientific work, and no later finds have proved as valuable as the Shang oracle bones for throwing light upon the daily life of the upper classes.

It is clear both from archeological finds and from the "Great Plan" section of the *Book of History* that the rulers of the Shang period were deeply interested in divination and practiced it according to several methods. In one of these a turtle shell was subjected to heat and the answer to the question put to the diviner was deduced from the cracks which appeared. In a second and closely related system a series of oval pits were cut on one side of a piece of bone, usually a sheep's shoulder blade. A red-hot metal point was thrust into the depressions, and the answer was read from the cracks that appeared on the other side of the bone. Scapulimancy (divination employing a shoulder blade) was widespread in far northern Eurasia and America. Turtle shell divination, on the other hand, seems to have been of southern origin, and the Shang rulers imported and kept tortoises of a southern species in order to have shells of the right sort. In their scapulimancy the Shang diviners scratched questions to be answered on the bone before heating it. This may have been due to the belief, present in China at a later date, that the gods were deaf and could only understand requests addressed to them in properly written memorials, a belief which one presumes the scribes did nothing to weaken.

The inquiries dealt mainly with affairs of the royal palace, proper times for performing rituals, probable outcome of raids, and weather and crop prospects. Many of the scapulae were ground flat, and some of them were numbered, suggesting that they may have been filed for future reference. An amusing sidelight on the possible attitude of the diviners comes from one bone on which the inquiry, "If the king goes hunting in the eastern hills on (such and such a date), will it rain?" and the bone's affirmative answer, is supplemented by a brief notation: "It really did rain."

The Shang characters were drawings, many of them quite naturalistic, which had begun to take on ideographic meaning. They were directly ancestral to modern Chinese writing by way of the rectangular, clearly outlined "seal characters" of the Chou and early Han periods. The form of the modern characters has been modified by the method of writing with a brush on paper. The Shang writing was a well-developed, conventionalized system which must have taken generations to reach the state in which it first appears. However, it bears no resemblance to anything known from outside China and probably originated there in Neolithic times.

The Shang population lived in villages, and there was at least one city which served as a capital and regular place of residence of the ruling dynasty. Classical literature, particularly a poetic work, the *Shih Ching* contains numerous references to the life of the common people. Apparently it was much like that of their predecessors of the Neolithic Lung-Shan culture. Both sexes were completely clothed, wearing trousers and a long coat with sleeves. Houses were one room mud structures, with a door on the east and a window on the west. The hearth was in the center of the floor, with an open vent in the room above. The family slept in the sacred southwest corner of the house. Here the seed grain was stored and Ao, the house deity, and Tsao, guardian of the hearth, received their offerings. Women controlled the house and carried on the indoor activities, while men did the agriculture and cared for the domestic animals. Winter was spent in spinning and weaving. Hemp, jute and bast were the fibers used in the most ancient times, but silkworms had been imported from the South by the beginning of the Shang period. Caring for them was one of the women's duties.

All the families in a village were related in the male line. Village government was based on kinship and inter-generation obligations, and the community was controlled by the old men who were family heads. It is interesting to note that each village had a town house, in which the council met and some communal ceremonies were held. Between times it served as a men's clubhouse, in which they gathered for drinking bouts and other amusements. Outside the village there was a sacred grove with a running stream. If possible, the village was so placed that both grove and stream would be to the south, forming a protective barrier against evil influences coming from that direction. The sacred grove was the scene of spring and fall rites. The spring rites were intended to promote fertility. They were celebrated by the young men and women and had an orgiastic character. The fall ceremonies were a farewell to the growing season and a thanksgiving for the harvest. They included dances by men wearing animal masks, and were accompanied by heavy feasting and beer drinking. They were presided over by old men. Instrumental music, to which magical efficacy was ascribed, figured largely in all ceremonies. The beings propitiated in the village rites were largely local nature-spirits and animals, among whom snakes, bears, and the clever shape-changing fox seem to have been the most important. There was also some ancestor worship at the peasant level, but the rites seem to have been directed to the ancestors of the village as a group. The rites directed toward the great beings were performed by the kings and nobles.

The Shang aristocracy seems to have led a luxurious existence. Evidence of this is to be found in the royal tombs of the dynasty, since these tombs were regarded as dwellings for the dead and were fitted up with the furnishings appropriate to a palace. The tomb chamber was solidly constructed of heavy timber and was placed at the bottom of a shaft forty or more feet deep. A ramp gave access to the tomb. When the interment was completed, the whole excavation was filled with rammed earth. Unfortunately, in recent times this feature has served to show the location of tombs, and the huge prices paid for Shang objects has led to wholesale looting. The personal servants and favorite women of the ruler were killed and buried with him, and, while the excavation was being filled, numerous freshly severed human heads were thrown in and stamped down with the earth. Many of the heads found were still wearing bronze helmets, suggesting that they belonged to members of the rulers' guard rather than to slaves or captives.

The inner walls of the tomb were decorated with conventionalized designs. The tomb furniture included bronze vessels clearly intended for ritual use, weapons, and stone carvings, including numerous jade objects. Large marble figures, which, although rigidly stylized, possessed great artistic merit, were of especial interest, since they are not mentioned in early writings. Although chairs and tables were not used at this time, there were undoubtedly many wooden objects and other perishable offerings such as food, garments, and bolts of silk. The stone carvings show great technical skill. Both the jade and marble objects seem to have been sawn out, rather than shaped by the usual Neolithic techniques of battering and grinding. Stone-sawing was also used by some of the early cultures in Southeast Asia, in Japan, and by the Alaskan Eskimo and Indians of British Columbia, in their manufacture of jade implements. It once more suggests the influence of the mysterious sea people previously mentioned.

Weapons were of bronze. The favorite weapon for hand-to-hand fighting seems to have been the "ko," a sort of tomahawk copied directly from a primitive sickle used in North China in Neolithic times for harvesting grain. From literary sources we know that the Shang nobility drove two-horse chariots, that the Shang armies consisted of charioteers and light-armed foot soldiers, and that the favorite weapon was the bow, presumably of composite type. Bronze helmets were worn and probably plate mail as well, which was made by sewing plaques of metal or bone upon a flexible base.

The most interesting of the tomb remains are the bronze ceremonial vessels. These reveal a vigor and sophistication of design and a technical skill in casting which have never been surpassed anywhere at any time. The entire vessel was frequently given bird or animal form, and small animal figures were often used for surface decoration. The choice of animals is suggestive. Although the Shang territory lay far north, and the founders of the Shang dynasty were presumed to have come from the west by way of the steppes, very few northern animals are shown. The high development of bear ceremonialism throughout Northern Eurasia and the fact that two species of bear were Hsia totems makes the omission of this animal the more remarkable. The favorite subjects were tigers, water buffalo, rams, and bulls, depicted as conventionalized split animals known as *T'ao-t'ieh*. This selection makes it appear improbable that Shang art was developed out of animal art of the steppes, and suggests a southern rather than western origin for it. At the same time, the forms of the bronze vessels seem, with few exceptions, to be derived from wooden, pottery, and horn prototypes. The vessels in animal shape, with deeply incised decoration, are suggestive of wood carving. It is impossible to say whether the conventionalized designs with which all surfaces were covered were purely decorative or had symbolic significance, although in view of the high ritualization of Shang life the latter seems more likely. No close parallel for designs can be identified outside of China, but the present writer feels that they show a kinship with the Dong Son designs, and also with the historic arts of certain culturally conservative areas in Indonesia and Melanesia, and even with the arts of the Polynesian Marquesans and Maori. Although the assumption is quite unprovable, I would not be surprised if archeological research eventually reveals the presence of an old Southeast Asiatic art style from which all of these, including Shang, was derived.

The technical perfection of the ritual bronzes is impressive, but it is literally too good to be true. Even the best metal-caster has occasional bad luck. It must be remembered that the objects available for study have been carefully selected. Only the finest of the bronze objects reaching the market from tomb robbers have been ascribed to the Shang period. It is quite possible that, when information on the entire bronze inventory becomes available, cruder pieces will come to light. The perfection of the workmanship may have been due not only to the skill of the craftsmen but also to the use for which the vessels were designed. Imperfect sacrificial vessels might have been as offensive to the gods as carelessness in the ritual. In Shang times bronze was still so scarce that it must have occupied very much the position of gold in our own culture. Flawed or imperfect pieces may well have been melted down and recast repeatedly until a perfect object was obtained. Casting was done both by the lost wax method and in terra cotta piece-molds, fragments of which have been found on the site of the ancient Shang capital. The source of the bronze has not yet been determined. Two of the districts listed in the *Tribute of Yü* (see Chap. XXXVI, p. 526) are mentioned, each as producing three kinds of metal, so that both the copper and tin may be of Chinese origin. However, the rich tin deposits of the Malay Peninsula were worked by the local natives at a time when they themselves were still using Neolithic implements. This suggests an ancient trade in the metal. An analysis of the Shang bronzes should reveal whether any of the tin came from this source.

The structure of the Shang Empire seems to have been intermediate between that of a conquest state and a federation. The various districts which composed it were politically self-contained, and there was no suggestion of anything like an imperial council or general assembly of nobles. Each district was ruled by its own hereditary noble family, who had submitted to the emperor and shared the benefits of the rites which he performed. The strength of the central power depended largely on the personality of the emperor. When the emperor was weak, the nobles made war upon each other. At all times the empire was at war with one or another of its non-Chinese neighbors. There are repeated references in the oracle bones to a tribe designated as "shepherds," who lived to the west of the Shang territory. These were regularly raided for slaves and particularly for sacrificial victims. In the lists of sacrifices one finds "shepherds" noted on a par with other domestic animals offered.

There is little information on the internal organization of the districts, but it is clear that there was a sharp distinction between nobles and commoners. We do not know the financial arrangements, but it is probable that, as in Chou times, the peasants supported their lords by cultivating certain fields set aside for them. The villagers also provided their lord with light-armed infantry when he went to war. It should be noted that even the Shang nobility were light-armed by European feudal standards, while the peasantry were trained in the use of the terrible composite bow which could drive an arrow through any armor known at this time. This situation endured long after the Shang Dynasty, and it has been cynically suggested that the extreme interest in the well-being of the peasantry expressed by the Chinese philosophers, themselves of the upper class, may have been related to this fact.

Shang culture had an unusually strong religious and magical orientation, although at the same time it was quite devoid of mysticism. Each village performed its own ceremonies related to its annual round of activities and also worshipped its own ancestors. The district nobles performed other rites for the benefit of the district. Apparently each district had a somewhat different series of secondary deities, as well as spirits of the local mountains and streams. Lastly, the emperor performed rites in honor of the highest group of deities, especially the celestial beings, thus benefiting the entire state. The rites performed by the nobles and by the emperor were rigidly formalized. There were strict regulations as to the type of sacrificial vessels to be used on each occasion and the appropriate offerings. There can be little doubt that the procedure followed in the rites was equally conventionalized.

Animals were regularly offered, and human sacrifice was commoner in the Shang period than at any other time in Chinese history. Ancestor worship, directed not only to the ancestral spirits as a group but also to the more important individuals in each past generation, was a regular feature of the noble and imperial rites. The rigidity of the rites suggests that they were as much magical as religious in their purposes. The importance of divination has already been mentioned. While diviners may have constituted a distinct group, the rulers were expected to perform the rites themselves and to combine in their persons the functions which in other societies were divided between secular rulers and priests.

In order to perform their duties properly, the nobles had to be educated, and most of them seem to have been literate, thus differing sharply from the Western feudal nobilities. There was already considerable official correspondence, and the skill with which letters and memorials were composed was a matter of pride. The consciousness of an audience which was such an important feature in later Chinese culture was already present, together with an eagerness to be revealed to posterity in the best possible light. Although the nobles claimed authorship of their official correspondence, it is highly probable that there was already a class of professional scribes who acted as advisors to the rulers and played a considerable part in governmental administration.

The origins of the Shang are obscure. Apparently their ancestors came into China from the Northwest by the route which conquerors have followed throughout Chinese history. Moreover, the beginning of the dynasty, approximately 1500 B.C., corresponds rather closely to the invasion of India by the Aryans and of the Near East by various steppe peoples who were also horse breeders and chariot users. The generally accepted theory is that the Shang were responsible for the introduction into China of a whole series of culture elements of Western origin, notably the cultivation of wheat and barley, the use of horses, chariot fighting, bronze casting, and writing. Wheat and barley do appear first at this period and are unquestionably of Western origin, but horses as well as cattle and sheep were already known to the Lung Shan peoples. There is no indication that the establishment of the Shang dynasty led to any great increase in animal husbandry. Moreover, they did not use milk, an incomprehensible feature if the Shang culture was derived from either of the co-traditions of the steppes.

That the wheel was known in pre-Shang times is indicated by the presence of wheel-made pottery in the Lung Shan culture, and the *Book of Changes* assumes that the cart and war chariot were both used by the Hsia. To judge from such peoples as the Polynesians and Mayas, making these with stone tools would be a laborious but by no means impossible task. The use of bronze and the techniques employed in casting it are almost certainly of Western origin, but the forms of most of the Shang weapons and vessels are unlike anything now known from the West and, like the decoration, seem highly distinctive. As regards Shang writing, no close similarities can be traced anywhere outside China, and it may be pointed out that the steppe invaders who make such havoc among civilizations farther west were uniformly illiterate. Lastly, the preoccupation with ritual and divination and the strong sense of dependence upon higher powers which characterizes Shang culture is quite at variance with either of the steppe co-traditions.

The most probable explanation of this situation would seem to be that the founders of the Shang Dynasty were a relatively small group of invaders who practiced the mixed agricultural and domestic animal economy of the pre-nomadic steppe peoples. Through their contacts with the West they had acquired a knowledge of bronze, in common use there by 1500 B.C., and had learned to rely heavily on war chariots, which tools of the new material made it easy to produce. The superiority which this gave them, coupled, perhaps, with a better military organization, made it possible for them to conquer the already advanced Neolithic population of Northern China. However, they followed the same course as the later conquerors of China. They enriched the local culture by the addition of a few Western elements and stimulated further developments within the Chinese tradition, but they brought about no cultural revolution.

Whatever the Shang origins may have been, the beginnings of this dynasty found Northern China a region of independent tribes with varied Neolithic cultures, while its end saw the same region possessing a unified, unmistakably Chinese civilization. In many ways the Shang period foreshadowed the later course of Chinese history. It began with a foreign conquest, followed by the acculturation of the conquerors. It witnessed the elevation of writing to the position which it enjoyed in later Chinese culture and the emergence of respect for learning. It saw the formalization of religious rituals and the triumph of technique over emotions in the relation of man to the supernatural. Above all, it crystallized the pattern of assigning the most important secular and sacred duties to the same individual. The development of a literate aristocracy who were simultaneously priests, warriors, and rulers resulted in a complete and indissoluble fusion of church and state.

Moreover, the result was in no sense a theocracy. Chinese attitudes were eminently practical and made religion a supplement to administration. These patterns survived throughout Chinese history and saved the country from the struggles between priest and ruler which disrupted so many other civilizations. Even the downfall of the Shang dynasty set a pattern for propaganda which was followed by each of its successors. The Chou invaders who overthrew the dynasty depicted the last Shang emperor as a monster of vice and cruelty, and themselves as liberators sent by a benevolent supreme being to punish the Shang Dynasty for its crimes and to restore order to the commonwealth.

Chapter XXXVII

Early Historic China

WITH THE CHOU DYNASTY China emerges into the full light of history, and Chinese culture takes on most of its characteristic patterns. Many of these patterns were already in existence in Shang times, but it was during Chou that they became integrated into a coherent whole. The Chou was less a dynasty than a period. Although in the dynastic lists it is usually given as extending from roughly 1000 B.C. to 221 B.C., the temporal control of the Chou emperors came to an end about 770 B.C., when the capital was moved east to the city of Lo-yang. Even before this, the disruptive forces inevitable in any feudal system had begun to weaken the central power. The accomplishment of the Chou dynasty proper was to set up a system of thoroughly integrated social, political, and religious institutions within which culture patterns already present in China or borrowed from the barbarian cultures to the west could be developed and organized. It is difficult to tell how far the founders of the dynasty were personally responsible for this, but they or their councilors certainly were responsible for reducing the pre-existing patterns to a system. The first Chou emperors were in an unusually good position to do this, since they had already had experience in integrating elements from the Hsia culture with that of the barbarians of the steppes.

Although later Chinese scholars manufactured a descent from ancient Hsia kings for the house of Chou, it seems that the founder of the line was a Hsia noble, Liu, who settled on the northwestern frontier of the Hsia territory in the 18th century B.C. The barbarians whom he encountered there and reduced to vassalage were probably the same stock as the "shepherds" so systematically exploited by the Shang. The conquered population may well have looked upon their Hsia rulers as protectors, since the motto of the Chou reigning house always seems to have been "benevolence is the best policy." In the 14th century B.C. the pressure of tribes still farther west forced the Chou and their vassals to migrate further into China, where they occupied territory in the modern district of Feng Siang and became vassals of the Shang emperors. At the time that they arrived in this region their culture had a strong steppe flavor. They were strictly patriarchal and patrilineal. Horses seem to have been important in their economy and at first were ridden rather than driven. That the Chou turned to the use of war chariots, as soon as they had gained the necessary resources, indicates that they had not yet developed adequate cavalry tactics or equipment.

The history of the Chou rulers, as recorded in the *Bamboo Books,* reveals a combination of an inflexible will toward power, worship of order, and a profound respect for the proprieties. Until the very end of their vassalage to their Shang emperors they treated these with all the outward symbols of respect, while drawing more and more of the petty states which composed the empire under their own control. When King Wen deposed the last of the Shang emperors and founded the Chou dynasty, he did so with all the marks of polite regret, and proceeded at once to put the society and state in order on the basis of what was, on paper, or more properly bamboo, a rigid system. According to the Chinese historians, always devotees of the Great Man theory, the new system involved changes even in family organization, and it apparently did involve a change in the rules of descent among the nobility. However, to change the family structure of any society is a task of the first magnitude, and it seems probable that what actually happened was that the noble families who had survived from the Shang Dynasty were encouraged to alter a few of their practices in order to bring their family system into accord with that already existing among the Chou nobility. Since the main function of the peasantry was paying taxes, it is highly improbable that the new dynasty tried to modify their familial habits.

The Chou nobility were organized into joint families much like those of the Chinese aristocracy in all later periods. The nucleus of these families was a group of males descended from a common ancestor, sharing a common residence and functioning as a corporation under the control of the oldest member. The joint families and the larger name-groups to which such families belonged were strictly exogamous. Control was strongly patriarchal. Women born into the joint family were not regarded as actually belonging to it. They were not introduced to its ancestral spirits, but on marriage were introduced to the ancestral spirits of the husband and became thenceforth members of his family group. Marriage was theoretically monogamous, but when a noble bride went to her husband's house she was usually accompanied by a younger sister and various serving women who automatically became the husband's concubines. The position of women was high. Although noble women were secluded, they were not confined in harem fashion. Even at this period women frequently received a literary education, and there are many indications that husbands frequently consulted their wives even in affairs of state.

In the organization of the Chou empire the basic relations existing between males within the family were taken as a model. The most important of these was that between father and son. This was supposed to be mirrored in the relations of the emperor to the supreme being and to his subjects. This period saw the birth of the imperial title, "Son of Heaven." The emperor stood in the relation of a son to the supreme being, while at the same time he stood in the relation of father to his subjects and was supposed to exercise toward them the twin parental functions of benevolent support and enforcement of good behavior. A second familial relationship strongly insisted upon was that created by the age differences between different generations, and between older and younger brothers. Juniors should always respect and obey their seniors. This was reflected in the attitudes and obligations of different ranks of the nobility toward each other. Lastly, and not of familial origin, was the relationship of mutual assistance and trust implied in friendships which could be used as a basis for loyalty between the feudal lord and his noble followers.

Under the Shang Dynasty there had been a steady growth of cities, and the trend continued in the Chou period. The Chou nobles were city dwellers. Towns were fortified, and served as centers for administration and for the concentration and storage of the taxes paid in kind by the peasantry. They also became centers for trade and for the manufacture of articles required by court life. The feudal courts consisted of the feudal lord's family, his aristocratic followers, and his advisors and

SHRINE AT YAMADA, PROVINCE OF ISE, JAPAN

officials, not all of whom were of noble origin. They became the centers of learning and luxury, and provided a new stimulus for the development of civilization.

The patterns of peasant life under the Chou were probably little changed from those under the Shang, but the theoretical organization of the Chou state was extended even to specifications for the peasant village. It is impossible to say whether the eight-family system described in the records was ever actually imposed, but it certainly was regarded as an ideal. Under this system, eight related families had their dwellings grouped about a central well. The fields surrounding the village were divided into eight holdings of equal size and value. Each of these was assigned to a different family, and the holdings were rotated at intervals to achieve complete equality of opportunity. A ninth field, somewhat smaller than the others, was cultivated by the joint labor of the village, and the produce was given to the feudal lord. The peasantry were also required to labor without pay on roads, fortifications, and other public works, including the building of palaces for the feudal lords. In the valley of the Yellow River, which still constituted the heart of the empire, the public works also included extensive irrigation and flood control projects, and the necessity for planning and coordinating these undoubtedly strengthened the control of the rulers.

The Chou swept away the last relics of matriarchal institutions and established a pattern of direct succession from father to eldest son. During the Shang period, succession had passed from brother to brother before reverting to the son, with the consequent temptations for fratricide and civil war. Chou society was rigidly stratified. The nobles were graded into five classes, according to the importance of the territories which they ruled. Those of all classes held their fiefs directly from the king rather than, as in the European feudal system, from other nobles of higher rank. In the initial organization of the empire, the Chou rulers eased the transition from the older system by confirming most of the ruling families in the control of their hereditary territories, but any noble who proved incompetent or untrustworthy could be deposed and his fief given to another, frequently a relative of the emperor. Below the nobles there was a group of court officials and administrators who were also directly dependent on the king, since they received their incomes as salaries or from estates which he had granted them. Below the officials there was a numerically unimportant bourgeoisie of merchants and skilled craftsmen, while the great mass of the peasantry stood at the bottom of the scale.

Between the nobles and commoners there was a clearly marked division. Only the nobles attended the higher schools and received a full education in the six liberal arts of the period: ceremonies, music, archery, charioteering, mathematics, and writing. Although the Chou emperors boasted of having established schools for the common people, education in these was limited to knowledge essential for their daily life. In spite of this limitation of opportunity, there is abundant evidence that many of the officials and administrators were recruited from among the commoners, and this tendency became increasingly strong as the disadvantages of hereditary transmission of office became evident. The most important privilege enjoyed by the nobility was that of immunity from the penal code. It was a proverb of the time that "ritual does not extend as far down as the people, nor the penal code as far up as the nobility." No noble could be executed for a crime, although if found guilty of a capital offense he might be pressured into taking his own life. The common people, on the other hand, were exposed to the rigors of a fairly strict penal code and could be punished in both their persons and property.

In return for the common people's forced labor and payment of taxes, the nobility took upon themselves the tasks of defending their subjects and of the amicable and orderly relations with the supernatural upon which the well-being of the state depended. Much as in Shang times, the noble of each grade sacrificed to the beings of his district and to certain of his own ancestors, the number being set according to his rank. Thus the emperor sacrificed to seven ancestors, a noble of the highest order to five, and so down the line. The all-important sacrifices to heaven, upon which the well being of the entire empire depended, were performed by the emperor with special ritual paraphernalia, the imperial tripods. During the last centuries of the Chou period, when the secular power of the emperor had diminished to the vanishing point, the possession of these tripods carried with it the right to use the imperial title and to perform the imperial sacrificial functions.

The highly centralized political system established by the founders of the Chou dynasty soon proved unworkable. Several causes contributed to its breakdown. The original system placed too much responsibility on the emperor, while the strict rules of succession left his personality to chance and often brought to the office weak or evil rulers. The empire was under continuous pressure from barbarian tribes on both the northwest and south. The Chou nobility became more and more a military nobility, whose only congenial activity was war. They were as willing to increase their estates at the expense of weaker neighbors as they were to protect the empire against foreign aggression. As late as 700 B.C. the Chou armies still followed the old organization of chariot-driving nobles surrounded by light-armed infantry, but the old feudal levies of untrained peasants were replaced more and more by standing armies of professional soldiers. This increased the charges upon

the peasantry, who now had to support their lord's military establishments as well as paying the costs of his court. Such courts were now
established in many cities, and vied with each other in luxury and ostentatious display. The border lords employed more and more foreign mercenaries, and the depredations of these poorly disciplined barbarian
troops added to the earlier troubles of the common people. There were
repeated peasant revolts, and one of the causes frequently cited is the
destruction of crops and property during the nobles' great hunting
parties. This suggests that the Chou nobles held large-scale surrounds
and game drives like those of the later Mongols.

Under the stress of constant warfare the nobility increasingly delegated both education and civil administration to an emergent group of
professional scholar-bureaucrats. Education, which had previously been
a monopoly of the noble class, thus became proletarianized, and schools
teaching all of the old noble subjects, with the possible exception of
archery and charioteering, were opened in many cities. The office of
political advisor to a feudal lord offered a profitable career, and commoners who had studied history and learned political skills sought the
patronage of rulers and found it quite consistent with their ideas of
honor to leave their native states and take service with whatever noble
would pay them most liberally. The philosophers of the 6th and 5th
centuries B.C., such as Confucius, Mencius, and others, were drawn from
this group of scholar-bureaucrats, and in view of their background it
is easy to understand the preoccupations of their philosophic systems
with social and political problems.

The constant state of warfare and uncertainty, and the incorporation of more and more barbarians into Chinese society, seems to have
weakened belief in the efficacy of the old formal sacrificial rites. Since
the performance of these rites was, in theory at least, the main function
of the emperor, this also served to weaken the central power. By 700 B.C.
the empire had broken down into fourteen contending states, and the
role of the Chou emperor had become somewhat like that of the Holy
Roman emperor in medieval Europe. It carried great prestige but little
actual power or emolument. The emperor's political control was limited
to the single state, a relatively small one, of which he was traditional
ruler, and his revenues to the taxes paid by its peasantry.

We need not concern ourselves with the names of the fourteen early
states or the kaleidoscopic changes in the fortunes of their ruling houses.
By 468 B.C., the beginning of the period generally known as the "Warring States," only three of the original fiefs of the Chou empire were still
in existence. The most important of these was Ch'i in the northern and
central part of China. This state had enjoyed a period of strength and
property under wise rulers, who had established a sort of state capital-

ism based on government ownership of salt and iron mines and control of trade. In the northwest the new and largely barbarian state of Ch'in was the most powerful, while in the south the new state of Ch'u, occupying the middle course of the Yellow River, was extending its power northward and attempting to bring the whole of China under its domination. Like Ch'in, Ch'u contained strong foreign elements, drawn in this case from the southern mountain tribes.

In approximately the 4th century B.C. a new feature appeared. Prior to this time the strength of the Chinese armies had lain in their armored chariots. Cavalry now began to be used by the northwestern states. It seems probable that this period marked the development, presumably in the steppes, of the equipment and tactics necessary for effective mounted warfare. The combination of the tree saddle, stirrups, the composite bow, and drilled horsemen able to charge in line as well as to maneuver, was an innovation in warfare as revolutionary as the development of the tank or airplane in later times. It changed the balance of power along the entire frontier where China met the steppes.

The war chariot was an expensive appliance. It was difficult to build, and the maintenance of chariot teams in regions where the economy was already based on intensive agriculture was a considerable problem. The well-organized Chinese states had enough economic surplus to enable them to build and maintain considerable chariot forces. The nomads, on the other hand, lacked both the skills and the material resources necessary for the development of this weapon. Armored chariots were irresistible against infantry or undrilled mounted men. It was only in the periods of political confusion that the barbarians were able to invade successfully. Cavalry equipment could be produced by a nomadic herding people with few financial resources. The life of the herdsmen provided long intervals of relative leisure, and even the manufacture of composite bows and tree saddles required no equipment which could not be readily transported when moving camp. After the emergence of the cavalry complex, the steppe peoples raided their settled neighbors almost at will. China bore the first brunt of these attacks, but only a few centuries later Europe, as far west as France, went down before the Hunnish cavalry.

With the coming of the barbarian mercenaries Chinese warfare took on a new and more sanguinary aspect. The civilian population of the fortified cities, which formed the strong point of the feudal defense, was discouraged from determined resistance by systematic massacre inflicted on towns which were captured after stubborn defense. Also, captured soliders, who in earlier days had usually been set free at the end of a campaign with nothing more serious than some mark of humiliation such as a clipped ear, were now systematically executed in order to weaken the trained manpower at the disposal of the enemy. Meticulous records were kept of the number of heads taken, and it is said that after the capture of the city of Ch'angping 400,000 persons were beheaded. Even allowing for the exaggeration usual to Oriental scribes, the continuing loss of life must have seriously depleted the population and left room for a strong influx of immigrants from the neighboring barbarians. Since the Chinese economy depended heavily upon the presence of a large taxpaying peasant population, it is quite possible that this immigration was encouraged by the feudal rulers. The invaders readily became acculturated, and the influx seems to have had little effect upon the Chinese civilization.

In spite of, or perhaps because of, the ills from which the nation suffered, the time immediately preceding the period of the Warring States was one of extraordinary intellectual activity. The rise of private schools, which functioned side by side with those supported by the state and eventually took over most of their functions, and the admission of commoners to these, provided what was unquestionably the largest group of educated intellectuals which existed anywhere in the ancient world. These intellectuals were all confronted by the very practical problem of finding some way in which to alleviate the sufferings, obviously due to governmental mismanagement, which were making life unbearable. Various philosophers found various answers. Among the resulting systems those founded by K'ung Tzu (Confucius), Lao Tzu, and Mo Tzu were the most important. The first two were able to exert a profound influence on Chinese culture, and the Confucian school in particular, thanks to official support, was directly responsible for the development of numerous governmental patterns. It is difficult for a European scholar who is unable to read Chinese characters to get a clear picture of these philosophies. The telegraphic brevity of Chinese sentences is not correlated with an equal clarity, and one finds numerous differences in the interpretations which Chinese scholars themselves give to the earlier texts.

Confucius was of Northern Chinese origin, and the seat of the school which he originated was in the state of Lu, still ruled in his time by dukes of the Chou family. Confucius himself was the greatest scholar of his day, with a deep interest in historical precedents and a belief that the tightly organized state set up by the first Chou emperor had been a golden age. He revised and idealized the records from this period, putting them in the form in which they still survive. His teaching was ethical in intent but was wholly without supernaturalism. It is difficult to translate his concepts into Western terms, but he believed that there was a natural sympathy existing between persons. This found its strongest expression within the family circle, but ideally was extended until it enveloped the whole of mankind. In order to put this sympathy into operation it was necessary to have a correct definition of what he called "names." In the Confucian philosophy this term had a significance reminiscent of the Platonic absolutes. The "names" were regarded as realities existing in the world of ideas.

From the point of view of the modern sociologist, these "names" would correspond rather closely to a combination of a status and its associated role. Knowing a "name" consisted of understanding the exact position of a particular category of individuals in the social structure, and of knowing the rights and obligations which went with this position. The latter were phrased as rules of behavior, making it easy to learn them objectively and automatize them. The proper performance of an individual's role validated his status. Only the prime minister who performed the duties of his office properly was entitled to be termed a prime minister. Similarly the emperor, as an individual, was entitled to be considered the Son of Heaven only as long as he performed the imperial role correctly. When he failed to do this, it became not only the right, but the obligation of the subjects to set him aside and to find another occupant for the imperial throne. Since the well-being of the empire depended upon the approval of Heaven, failure of the emperor in his duties was immediately made evident by a series of calamities, while, conversely, the right of his successor to assume office was demonstrated by success in re-establishing order and prosperity. Confucianism is unique among all the philosophies advanced before the 18th century period of enlightenment in reserving to subjects the right to revolt.

In practice, Confucius was a precisionist and expended most of his energy in clarifying the various social roles. Like other scholar-administrators of the time, he was peripatetic, going from one court to another in search of a patron who would be willing to put his theories into practice. Eventually Confucius was appointed to a minor governmental post in the state of Lu. It is told of him that in his later days at the court of Lu he accompanied his ruler on a tour and remarked that the order of progress illustrated the state of worldly affairs: pride and vice (i.e., the ruler and his favorite concubine) leading the procession, and wisdom and virtue (i.e., Confucius) following far behind.

The Confucian school underwent further development at the hands of two disciples, Mencius and Hsün Tzu, who agreed on the initial concept of "names," but differed diametrically on the question of whether morality was in conformity with nature and consequently on the efficacy of "sympathy" as the motivating force in good behavior. Mencius believed in the inherent goodness of human nature. According to him the individual, if not interfered with, would turn toward good as automatically as water runs downhill. His followers therefore objected strongly to all sorts of social compulsion. Hsün Tzu, on the other hand, held that human nature was intrinsically neither good nor bad. He believed that righteousness was a habit to be acquired only through the repetition of good behavior. He might be thus classed as the earliest representative of the Learning Theory school of personality psychology. Consistent with this view, he also questioned the authority of the remote past and thought of the development of society as a progressive process which could be best understood and guided by contemporary sages.

After various vicissitudes the Confucian philosophy was ostensibly accepted in the later Han dynasty as a guide to the organization of the empire. There is a tradition, probably apocryphal, that one of the Han emperors, who found his rule increasingly disturbed by the resurgent power of the old feudal nobility, called in a Confucian scholar and asked him how this group could be rendered harmless. The scholar is said to have replied: "Allow them to distribute their estates equally among their sons." The emperor was so much struck by the wisdom of this advice that he established Confucianism as the official philosophy of the realm.

Even if this story were true, neither a single episode nor even official favor can explain the way in which Confucian philosophy has been able to dominate Chinese thought for nearly 2000 years. The clue probably lies in that characteristic of Chinese character which Francis Hsu has termed "situation oriented." According to this penetrating analysis, the average Chinese is anxious to understand most situations in which he finds himself and to adapt his behavior to them. His desire to adjust successfully is given precedence over any abstract value system. The Confucian philosophy, with its clear definition of statuses and roles, clarifies the social situations which play a predominant part in any individual's life and provides him with ready-made behavior patterns.

The philosophy of Lao Tzu presents a contrast to that of Confucius at practically every point. Where the Confucian school concentrates on human relations and pays tribute to the supernatural only in its insistence on the proper performance of rites, the school of Lao Tzu ignores human relations and concentrates instead on the understanding of the universe, including aspects of it which we would consider supernatural. Where the Confucian school seeks for an ever clearer definition of concepts, and in this search lays heavy emphasis on scholarship and particularly on the study of history, the school of Lao Tzu turns to meditation and introspection and is content to leave its fundamental concepts vague and to seek the answer to problems in inspiration rather than precedent.

It is an interesting fact that this school, commonly called Taoism, originated in Southern China and was obviously an attempt to organize attitudes and beliefs already long established in that region. Taoism obviously developed from the old nature worship and disorganized supernaturalism which preceded the emergence of a politically unified China. Folk elements entered into it so strongly that we do not even know whether or not Lao Tzu was a real individual. There are a large number of Taoist deities, some of them supernatural beings, such as the king of heaven and the goddess of mercy. This goddess, an ancient deity called Hsi Wang Mu, has been equated with one of the Buddhist saints and also, in some localities which have become Christian, with the Virgin Mary. Other Taoist deities are early heroes of legends. The Taoist god of war is a famous general who died in the 3rd century. It is interesting to speculate whether Taoist mysticism and that of India may not go back to some component of the old Southeast Asiatic co-tradition, since this exerted an influence on both religions.

The fundamental concept in the philosophical system of Lao Tzu was that of a universe in a constant state of change and reorganization within the force field created by two opposing principles, the *Yin* (female) and the *Yang* (male). The Chinese sage did not conceive of these principles as in conflict. They were in balance like the opposite poles of a single magnet. Both forces were completely impersonal and amoral.

TEMPLE OF HEAVEN, PEKING

The idea of the universe as a field of battle between Ormuz and Ahriman or between the Christian God and the Devil, with every individual required to pick his side and take active part, was totally alien to the Taoist philosophy. The Yin and Yang were conceived as being normally in a state of balance which might be temporarily disturbed. The wise man followed the middle way, the Tao, which was revealed to the individual as a result of meditation, especially in the presence of nature uninfluenced by human activity. The typical Chinese landscape, with mountains, a waterfall, great trees, and, somewhere in the foreground, a tiny human figure seated in meditation, was the perfect expression of this Taoist concept. In the presence of nature and its sublime forces man was small indeed, and his wise course was to gain an understanding of these forces so as to avoid interfering with them.

As a logical development of its theories, Taoism turned its back on political activities and advised the individual to find his safety and satisfaction in a meditative return to nature and to abstain from action lest he disturb the Yin-Yang balance. The original Taoist doctrine did not concern itself with social relations, but, in a setting where philosophical thought always eventually turned to problems of government, the Taoists were forced to develop their own theories in this field. The Taoist attitudes toward nature provided the basis for a concept of the natural and therefore happy man. He had big bones, strong muscles and an empty head, qualities to be desired in the subjects of an autocratic state. The duty of the ruler was to see that his subjects were well fed, steadily worked, and maintained in a state of contented apathy. Both for his own good and that of the peasants themselves, the ruler should make no attempt to teach or awaken them. Above all, the governed should be denied any part in or understanding of the processes of government. These tenets naturally aroused strong opposition in the Confucian school.

Early Taoism was "this-world" oriented. Like Confucianism, it had no clear doctrine regarding survival after death. A hazy pantheism allowed for the existence of supernatural beings without clearly defining their attributes. However, the vagueness of Taoist teachings left the way open for the incorporation of all sorts of popular superstitions. Forces of nature and *genii loci* worshipped from prehistoric times were easily incorporated into the system. So was a lively belief in ghosts and demons, the latter frequently malicious ghosts, and in an afterworld modeled on the present. In the later development of Taoism the "situation-oriented" factor of Chinese character came into play. If one accepted the Yin-Yang hypothesis it was highly desirable to know the state of the balancing forces at any given time and place in order to adjust one's behavior to it. As a result, the later Taoism became the resort of magicians and fortunetellers of all sorts. Under the influence of Buddhism it also developed the features necessary to an organized religion: images, temples, formal rites, priests, and even monks and nuns.

The school of Mo Tzu dates from the same time as that of Confucius. Its fundamental principle was that of sympathy, but it ignored the gradations of sympathy based on degrees of nearness which Confucianism insisted on so strongly, and declared that the individual's love should be extended equally to all mankind. In contrast with the other two schools, it was definitely theistic and, indeed, almost monotheistic. The world was not governed by fate but by the conscious will of a supreme being. The existence of other supernatural beings was recognized, but they occupied minor positions. Great stress was laid on the reality of individual survival after death. The love for mankind which the school taught was not regarded as either instinctive or learned but as a religious duty. The attitudes of the school's members were strongly ascetic, and its adherents were expected to sacrifice all comforts and joy to their service to humanity. At the same time they combined a practical attitude with their asceticism and judged the value of various acts on the basis of their utility. For this reason they condemned the teaching of the arts, especially music. The philosophers of this school were noted as fearless and devoted advisors to princes. In accordance with their doctrines, they were willing to sacrifice themselves for the good of the community. Pacifism was an outstanding feature of their doctrine, but they were realistic enough to distinguish between wars of aggression and those waged in self-defense.

Certain parallels can be drawn between the teachings of this school and that of the Quakers. Although the followers of Mo Tzu relied on strict logic and lacked the ecstatic quality which characterized early Quakerism, both were in agreement on the direct relations between man and the deity, and on the obligation of the individual to give his whole energies to the betterment of mankind, while retaining a realistic attitude. In the pacifism of both one can see natural reactions to the sufferings of populations which had been subjected to generations of war. It is a curious commentary on the effects of Mo Tzu's teachings that, after their official suppression, they seem to have survived in the doctrines of the far from pacifist, secret sects which came to the fore repeatedly in China in times of disorder. The most recent of these manifestations occurred in the T'aip'ing rebellion and in the Boxer uprising. The similarities between Mo Tzu's doctrines and some elements of Christianity may have been a factor contributing to the imperial Chinese government's suspicion of Christian missionaries.

The three philosophies just described coexisted for centuries and exerted considerable effect, not only on Chinese institutions but also on

each other. A number of minor philosophies were born from their interaction. The only one of these which exercised significant influence on the
development of Chinese culture was the school of the Legalists. This
had as its main aim the development of effective patterns for state administration. Its concepts were worked out most completely in the
organization of the state of Ch'in, which, a few centuries later, stepped
forward to unite a China enfeebled by the endless wars of a decadent
feudalism. The fundamental idea of the Legalists was that of government by law, with human factors eliminated as completely as possible.
They devoted their attention to the development of statute law, and to
defining its meaning so accurately that individual opinion could not in-
trude into its administration. They were probably the first group anywhere in the world to insist on the equality of all members of the state
before the law. In view of the immunity of the nobles from the Chou imperial code, this was a revolutionary development. The cold imperson-
ality of this school succeeded in welding the state of Ch'in into a formidable weapon and in holding it together during the period of conquest,
but understandably, under the new dynasty, it disappeared as a school
although its principles remained alive under a veneer of Confucianism.
It is interesting to note that during the Chinese republic this philosophy,
largely because of its similarity to European concepts of jurisprudence,
enjoyed a brief revival.

All the speculations of the philosophers could not arrest the increasing disorder of the closing centuries of Chou feudalism. The sanguinary wars which followed the introduction of cavalry greatly reduced
the population, and the systematic killing of prisoners of war resulted in
the elimination of a large part of the feudal nobility. The state of Ch'in,
lying north of the center course of the Yellow River, was saved from
these evils. It was protected from most attacks by a mountain range, and
had a series of rulers and councilors who were statesmen of outstanding
ability. Although their ultimate aim was the conquest of China, they
avoided wars of doubtful outcome and followed a consistent policy
aimed at strengthening the state by exploiting its rich natural resources,
including its inhabitants. The rulers' advisors were largely Legalists, and
under their direction Ch'in was changed from a feudal state of the usual
Chinese sort to a totalitarian conquest-oriented nation of surprisingly
modern type.

Much of the population of Ch'in consisted of Hunnish barbarians
who had drifted into the territory from the steppes. This no doubt facilitated the rulers' plans for social reorganization. The great family and
the eight-family village system were both abolished, but one may doubt
whether either had ever become firmly established in this region. The
old feudal distinctions of rank were completely swept away, with all

power centering in the ruler and his administrators. Each family lived on a separate allotment, and the number of fields, houses, servants, and even garments permitted to each family was strictly regulated. Any family with more than two adult males had to break up or pay double taxes. The whole state was divided into districts with officials in charge. The families within the district were organized in groups of either five or ten. If any members of such a group committed an offense, all members were punished for it, hence they could be trusted to watch each other and to report delicts promptly. The army occupied a favored position. Every man was liable to lifelong military service, and all officials were also army officers. The leaders of successful campaigns and soldiers of outstanding courage were highly rewarded, while failure or cowardice were usually punished by death. The Legalists saw to it that these regulations were enforced with the greatest severity. The main weakness of the system proved to be that it provided no rewards, only punishments, for the peasantry. Such a system could enforce obedience, but not loyalty, and it could not arouse devotion. When the state of Ch'in, under its greatest ruler, known to history as Shih Huang Ti, finally conquered the whole of China, its control was short-lived.

Shih Huang Ti combined the administrative and organizing ability of an Augustus Caesar with the megalomania of a Hitler. In the long run, the consolidation of China which he accomplished and the models which he set for later imperial rule were a distinct gain, yet his name is still execrated for his excesses, and above all for his attempts to destroy the whole pattern of classical education and scholar administration. Born to the rule of Ch'in, he continued the expansion begun by his predecessors. Whenever a feudal district had been conquered, its hereditary nobility were eliminated, and it was incorporated into one of the provinces of the growing empire. At the end of his conquests there were thirty-six of these provinces, to which four more were added later. Each province, in turn, was divided into districts for administrative purposes. This general pattern of organization remained in use throughout all later Chinese history.

The organization of the new united China was characterized by a sharp differentiation between civil and military authority. The two were united in the person of the emperor but were kept separate at all lower levels. At the head of the civil administration was a prime minister, who was concerned only with internal affairs and government. The army was directed by a general who had no power outside the military. Each province and district had cadres of both civil and military officials. Lastly, there was a third and quite independent body of censors whose sole duty it was to check on the performance of officials of the other two classes. To insure their faithfulness to the central government, officials were continually transferred from one district to another. No official was allowed to remain in one place long enough to develop ties with the local inhabitants, and the central power was particularly careful to see to it that appointments were made to provinces as far as possible from those in which the administrator's own family was located.

Under the feudal system there had been numerous local differences much like those of medieval Europe. The units of land measurement, weights and measures, and wagon gauges varied from place to place. The last had considerable effect on long distance transport in a region where all goods had to be carried over unsurfaced, deeply rutted roads. Shih Huang Ti proceeded to standardize all these items. Local laws were replaced by a single imperial code. During the feudal period a number of local scripts had been developed and Shih Huang Ti's minister, Li Ssu, selected eight of these, added one more of his own devising, and decreed each of them the proper vehicles for one of the nine types of literature. The dialectic differences of the various parts of China, however, amounting in some cases to mutual unintelligibility, were too much for even Shih Huang Ti's standardizing ability and have survived down to the present time.

Shih Huang Ti's attempts to standardize thought were less successful. The various schools of philosophy were deeply entrenched in both education and government, and the colleges in which they were taught were centers around which resistance could be organized. On the advice of Li Ssu, the emperor finally adopted the drastic step of decreeing a monster book burning. Books on agriculture, astronomy, and medicine were allowed to continue in circulation, but works on what we would now term social science and those dealing with history other than that of the state of Ch'in were condemned. Copies of condemned works were to be kept in the imperial library, where they could be consulted by properly qualified persons who obtained permission from the government, but their ownership by private individuals was strictly prohibited. That the purpose of this was the control of thought rather than abolition of learning is proved by the emperor's creation of a gigantic library in his capital. In this library ancient manuscripts of all sorts were assembled and its destruction, at the time when the capital was sacked and burned, probably did far more to eliminate early records than the emperor's suppressive measures.

It has been observed that one of the surest methods of preserving a literary work for posterity is to have it condemned by the authorities, with a demand that the owners of all copies turn them in to be destroyed. Under such circumstances the condemned work acquires an abnormal value, and copies of it will be hidden away. After the collapse of Shih Huang Ti's superstate most of the condemned books rapidly reappeared. However, the repression had produced a hiatus in the development of scholarship. As a result of this and of the new standardization of the writing, whose obvious advantages led to its retention, the classics had to be transcribed and undoubtedly underwent various modifications in the process.

The massacre of scholars commonly ascribed to Shih Huang Ti seems to be largely legendary. Some scholars who refused to turn over their libraries were executed, but most of the victims belonged to a group of court magicians who had become unpopular. Like certain other totalitarian rulers, Shih Huang Ti seems to have been extremely superstitious and kept about him diviners and magic workers of all sorts. Those who failed to work promised miracles or made unfavorable predictions were eliminated, but there were always others ready to take their place.

PAGODA, PEKING

The emperor's megalomania also found expression in building on a colossal scale. His palace and tomb were the largest structures which had been erected in China up to that time. Before the palace stood a series of gigantic bronze statues cast from sacrificial vessels of the conquered feudal states, while it is said that the floor of the tomb was laid out as a map of China with running streams representing the principal rivers. These buildings have disappeared without a trace. His lasting monument was the Great Wall. Archeological research has shown that the Chinese of the later Chou, like the Romans of the later imperial period, were much given to building walls along their frontiers. Although such walls would not have been a serious deterrent to civilized antagonists equipped with siege machinery, they did provide some protection against barbarian raids and reduced the utility of the barbarian cavalry, their most effective arm. Before Shih Huang Ti came to power the state of Chao had built and fortified a wall on the northwest which formed the nucleus of the later Great Wall, while the state of Yen had built a similar wall on the east. In each case these walls had been pushed beyond the original limits of the state to enclose lands which were then settled by the state's peasantry.

At the time when Shih Huang Ti came to power, the importance of the Hsiung-nu barbarians was steadily increasing, and their attacks on the frontier were becoming more and more serious. These Hsiung-nu seem to have been the same people as the Huns who later terrified Europe, or at least were of kindred stock and possessed the same military patterns and fighting ability. In the year 215 B.C. Shih Huang Ti dispatched against them the Commander in Chief of the military forces, one of the two greatest officials in the empire, with an army of 300,000 men. He succeeded in beating them back and in annexing considerable territory from them but, as in all wars with nomads, the advantage was only temporary. To defend the newly acquired territory he linked up the existing walls and frontier posts, forming the Great Wall.

It has been suggested that the purpose of the Great Wall was quite as much to keep the Chinese peasants in as to keep the barbarians out. The economy of China in this, as in later times, was completely dependent upon a large agrarian population whose economic surpluses, individually small, could be diverted to the support of the state. There is abundant evidence that in the slightly later Han period numerous Chinese peasants did join the barbarians. Many of the Chinese along the border were the descendants of barbarians who had settled there and had become Sinified during the feudal period. The oppression which all the peasants suffered under Shih Huang Ti must have provided a strong incentive to escape from his tax collections and labor press gangs. Whatever the purpose of the Wall, and no matter how many earlier elements were incorporated into it, it still remains one of the greatest works erected by man and a lasting monument to the superhuman energy and organizing ability of the first authentic emperor of China.

Shih Huang Ti was far too great an egoist to found a dynasty. Men of his type can never tolerate sons who are potentially of their own stature. When he died he left a country seething with discontent, and the feeble son who tried to carry on the dynasty was eliminated in a few months. The imperial peace gave way to a struggle between war lords, with mobs of starving peasants wandering from place to place and leaving disaster in their wake. Out of the chaos there finally emerged a strong ruler, whose possession of the Mandate of Heaven was shown by his ability to restore peace and order. This man, Liu Pang, followed the pattern of later war lords, if he did not create it. He was an illiterate peasant who began his career as a brigand, then made himself Duke of P'ei and finally Emperor. His accession marked the beginning of the Han dynasty in which China became, for the first time, a power in world affairs.

Chapter XXXVIII

Late Dynastic China

FOR 2000 YEARS the Chinese have been the largest politically and culturally unified group in the world. The census made in 100 A.D., during the later Han period, reported a population of 60,000,000, and it should be noted that Chinese censuses are always underestimated, because the peasant quite normally concludes that any official who asks questions is getting statistics for tax purposes and consequently tells as little as possible. For the next thousand years the population of China was almost static, indicating that it had developed to the limit set by the combined resources and technology at this period. From 1100 A.D. to the census of 1736 the population slowly increased. In 1736 it was 125,000,-000. Between 1736 and 1881 it advanced suddenly to 380,000,000 and has been climbing steadily ever since.

At this particular time in history there was a sudden increase in population throughout the Old World. The reason is not clearly understood. In Europe the increase has been attributed to the beginning of mechanization and opening of colonial markets, but the same phenomenon took place in China and India, which were untouched by the industrial revolution at this time. In any case, China has had for a very long time a tremendous population which was much more united culturally than any other population in the world. Even in times of collapse of the central power, when there was confusion and civil war, the Chinese have maintained their tradition of unity and looked upon such times as mere interludes.

This huge population has been of great advantage to China, for it has made the country really invulnerable. The conqueror who established himself over this huge, culturally united, civilized population inevitably found himself swamped, acculturated, and ultimately absorbed. However, such a huge population has also set significant social and governmental problems, problems which we in the West have faced for some time but which we are only beginning to solve. Big populations are a fairly new development in world history. Most of the continental nations, up until the 18th century, were under 25 million, and Great Britain never exceeded 10 million. The necessity for handling hundreds of millions of people under a unified central government poses new problems for which adequate techniques have not yet been developed.

To understand the background of Chinese political organization, it is necessary to take a look at the general social patterns of the country. With the exception of the Northeast part of the country, where families live on large isolated farms, much like the American farm pattern, the single independent homestead is rare in China. The real unit is the village, a collection of families living close together, frequently with a mud wall surrounding the settlement as a protection against wandering bandits. Beyond the villages are a series of cities, which function mainly as administrative centers and as dwelling places for the wealthy part of the population (which in Old China was almost entirely the official class) and for the service occupations, such as the manufacture of luxury objects.

The functioning of the economy differed in certain respects from those of India and the West. There is no suggestion of the Indian caste system, with its hereditary occupational groups. Nor, except within narrow limits, was there the Western pattern of concentrating manufacturing in the cities. There was instead local concentration of particular industries; certain villages in one district would manufacture one item and exchange it for the products of other villages. These exchanges were carried on in market towns, which were intermediate in size between the villages and the cities. The peasants came into the market towns and sold and exchanged their goods for raw materials which they needed, or they came for finished products. This organization of local specialties, by which one small district made all the baskets of a particular type that were used all over China, another concentrating on a special kind of iron tool, etc., reflects the pattern of a unified country with strong central control which made safe trade possible. Even in times of confusion, when it did not operate properly, this organization was retained in the minds of the populace as the ideal pattern.

The bulk of the population were free landholders living in villages. There are two great dividing lines in Chinese society: the line between the man who owns land, even if it is only a minute patch, and the man who does not. The landowner is like the captain of a boat: whether it is a battleship or a barge, he is still the captain and distinct from a mere sailor; similarly, the Chinese peasant with his patch of land feels superior to a landless man. The other dividing line falls between the peasant and artisan groups, who work with their hands, and the scholar and official group.

Since the Chinese peasants do not practice primogeniture but divide their estates evenly among their sons, there is a constant fragmentation of holdings. This means that a section of the peasant population is progressively squeezed off the land and forced to become either city proletariat or, in recent times, rickshaw boys. China, whenever the controls of famine or war are not operating, rapidly builds a larger population than can be maintained at the level of hand industries and uses this proletariat for the heaviest and most unskilled labor. It is because of this constant supply of labor, which will work for anything it can get in order to live, that slavery has never taken hold in China. In the large wealthy households there are women servants who have been bought as children and might be regarded as slaves, but they are actually brought up as members of the family, and their master has a definite obligation to find husbands for them when they are of age. There were slaves in the Imperial Palace, but there was nothing like the mass slavery of the sort which flourished in the West. That could not develop because it was cheaper to use the proletariat, just as it was only after the rise of the machine that our consciences began to trouble us about slavery. With the machine it was obviously cheaper to hire a man, treating his labor as a commodity and throwing him out when he became old or disabled, than to own him as a slave and be obliged to take care of him.

The Chinese village is normally composed of individuals of a single name group. There are in China a limited number of family names, most of which trace their origin to definite localities in China. Some of these name groups may include as many as 4000 people, though many families within such a group cannot trace any genealogical connection. There is no institution in Western civilization which corresponds to these name groups. They include individuals at all social levels, ranging from scholars high in the government to peasants and the disappropriated proletariat. However, these groups are strictly exogamous. The peasant must get his wife from another village, a practice that saves a man considerable trouble with his in-laws, who are never near enough to interfere. Marriages are arranged by go-betweens, marriage brokers who in many cases take a keen interest in knowing the market and making sure that the marriages turn out well. Marriages are of great concern to both families. Parents of a son must provide a wife for him so that the family line will be continued. Since there is no permanent place for daughters in the Chinese household, parents of a daughter must marry her into another family where she will have ancestors and offspring and not be a homeless ghost when she dies. There is no bride-price in China, but there is a ceremonial exchange of gifts between the two families.

The Chinese village community is like our own in being a close in-group, in which everyone knows everyone else's business. Morality and rules of avoidance between the sexes are imposed with as much vigor as would be the case in a village of similar size in Vermont and by much the same technique. The upper classes, of course, are permitted to take concubines, but no peasant has the economic resources to take on a concubine, and there would be strong social pressure against his doing so in any case.

The new wife is completely subject to her mother-in-law and has no status in the family at first. However, a wife who has borne sons and is getting into middle age is in a strong position. When her sons marry and she acquires daughters-in-law to dominate in her turn, she frequently becomes the real head of the family. The peasant family is usually split after the marriage of the sons. The brothers may get along well together and prefer to remain in the family under the direction of the eldest, but the wives, who come in from various outside villages, become jealous of one another, particularly after they have children, and stir up so much trouble that the families tend to break up in the second generation.

However, there is a quite different pattern of family life for the scholar and official class. Here the ideal picture is that of the great family. Such a family is a corporation which persists for generations under the leadership of the oldest male in each generation. When a man builds a fortune, by whatever means, it is his ambition to found a family of this sort. The family establishment is a compound, with each son and his wife and children occupying one compartment of it. The group owns the family wealth, whether it is in land or business or whatever, in common, like a corporation, pro-rating the income to the various members of the group as needed. If a son cannot get along with the others or wishes to try his fortune elsewhere, he will be paid off, given his share, and allowed to go. Families can be kept going in this way for centuries, although as a matter of fact, in spite of the ideal pattern of indefinite persistence, few of the great families have managed to keep going together for more than four or five generations. However, by this time the group may well number over 100 persons, including a collection of poor relations and hangers-on who occupy an intermediate position between family members and servants. The head of the family frequently is vague about where such individuals fit into the family, but it is to his credit to have a large number of persons in this extended family group.

There is in China another family unit made up of individuals who recognize a common descent of a fairly close sort, that is, by genealogical record. They know how they are related to one another, which the name group does not. They have a graveyard in common and also a temple. This temple acts as a sort of foundation. Rich members of the *Tsu,* as this group is called, will bequeath money or land to it, the income of which will be used to help indigent members, or to educate a promising boy to become a scholar or eventually a member of the official class. The Tsu is sort of a mutual aid society, more important in the south of China than in the north.

One of the most significant things about Chinese society is that there is a high degree of vertical mobility, not only in theory but in fact, as much as there is in England, for example, where in spite of strong class distinctions it is possible for a commoner to make a fortune and buy his way to knighthood. In China there is a steady turnover in the population, with families of peasant ancestry gradually rising into the scholar and official class and then dropping out again. Until recent times this worked as follows. The entree to Chinese officialdom was through education and the ability to pass a series of competitive examinations. The Chinese system of writing is so complicated that, before one can become a scholar, his family must have enough economic surplus to support him for a minimum of six years. This is the time required to learn to read the classics (Confucian, Four Books and Five Classics), to compose essays and poetry, and to use a computing machine. These were the things one had to be able to do to pass the first examination.

The scholar held a high position in China, the poorest scholar, a village school teacher, for example, taking social precedence over a rich merchant who was illiterate. Therefore, any family who could afford to do so educated its sons in the hope that they might be able to pass the official examinations. These examinations were one of the few things in early China which were kept reasonably free from graft, because they were regarded as the core of the system. It is true that in the later days of the Manchu dynasty and during some other dynasties also, it was possible to buy lower military degrees which were correlated with academic degrees. The Chinese themselves had a term for it: "a degree by the back door." However, an individual with a back-door degree never achieved an official position in the government.

The examinations were first introduced under the Han dynasty, roughly from 200 B.C. to 200 A.D. There was at this time considerable friction between the emperor and the scholar groups, and it is said that the Han emperor who organized the examination declared: "Now I have the scholars fast in my net." However, it proved to be the scholars who had caught the emperor, for the Chinese government was dominated by the scholar class from that time until fairly recently. The examinations assumed their final form under the T'ang dynasty, between

700 and 900 A.D. They usually consisted of two essays and a poem of twelve lines of five characters each, all on a subject assigned at the last minute. This pattern continued with little change in either form or subject matter until 1912, when the so-called Republican Revolution occurred in China.

It was essential that a candidate for any appointive post pass at least the first examination. Usually two degrees were required. There were four examinations in all, but few were able to achieve this highest degree. Those who did so were taken care of, even if they could not be assigned to an immediate post. They were pensioned and held in reserve until a post became vacant. All the administrative officials above the village level were appointed, the appointees being taken from the lists of those who had passed the examinations. The village had a highly democratic type of government run by a village council, comparable to a New England town meeting. It operated with great effectiveness, for the council was a group of men who were family heads and whose opinions carried authority in the village. However, above the level of the village council, government was from above downward.

The first generation scholar whose parents were from the peasant or merchant class would rarely be able to get a government post even after he had passed the rigidly competitive examination. He usually settled back, content with the dignity received in this way, while his family group worked to accumulate enough wealth so that his sons could continue as scholars. If they passed the examinations they would be in line for the coveted government jobs. However, the competition was so keen that there were always more academically qualified men than there were jobs. Since the contestants were not arranged on any list of seniority according to the highest marks on examinations, obtaining a government job required a pull with officials already in office. The candidates tended to gravitate to Peking where they would wait around, pulling all possible strings.

The successful candidates were usually given jobs in a part of China as remote as possible from their homes. This was done because, as soon as it was known that a member of the Tsu had a government post, everyone who had a kin claim would be around looking for help or minor jobs. The only way to avoid this horde of hungry relatives was to move out of reach. In the old days, when traveling was difficult, an official who was shifted to a distant province left his relatives safely behind. However, with the rise of the motor bus and other handy means of transportation, a flock of poor relations would be sitting on his doorstep by the time a new provincial governor arrived at his post, hoping to make use of the pattern of family loyalty and family obligations for all sorts of graft and patronage.

In theory, every post in the government, except the post of the emperor himself, was open to any man with sufficient ability. There were a few groups, policemen, ferrymen, and slaves, for example, who were not eligible to take examinations, but these were small in number as compared to the Chinese population as a whole. The student who had completed a course of higher learning, which was principally a study of moral philosophy, history, and literature, went up for his first examination. These examinations were held in the prefectural cities of each province twice in three years. The examiners were the district rulers and literary chancellors appointed by the government. When the individual came up for examination he had to file a document giving his age and place of birth, and showing that he was not a member of one of the prohibited groups. He was searched to make sure that he had no cribs or ponies on his person and then put into a small room, the door of which was sealed from the outside with a strip of paper with the official stamp on it.

The examinations covered a broad general field and were designed to demonstrate the scholar's intelligence and ability. The assumption was that a man who was intelligent enough to pass the examinations could soon acquire the special skills needed for a particular job. This is in direct opposition to the American belief that, if a man knows the skills needed in his job, nothing else matters, and to our idea of a politician as an individual who is, not only in his general interest but in his general abilities, as near the common man as possible. The Chinese idea was to devote as much ingenuity as possible to finding a really superior man for legislative and administrative jobs; by superior they meant a man who was honest, disinterested, and devoted to the public good. The rewards were high, unlike the American system where a trained man can make much more money on the outside than he can in a government job, unless he goes in for graft on the side.

The Chinese system was very like that of the British Colonial Service which has been, until recent times, one of the most effective administrative groups in the world. Here too the civil service examinations were directed mainly toward discovering cultured men of high intelligence, and questions varied all the way from one on the book-collecting tastes of Boccaccio to the reading of a weather chart. The Chinese official was a similarly carefully selected man and a man of high I.Q. Any European official who had to deal with the Chinese government in the days when the Manchu dynasty was strong was well aware of the high quality and ability of these men. Occasionally the system might miscarry as, for instance, when a Mandarin of the fourth rank who had never been on the water was appointed to command the Chinese fleet in the first Sino-Japanese war. Naturally the Chinese fleet was rapidly eliminated. The Mandarin followed the best scholarly tradition by writing an excellent literary ode on the subject, transmitting it to the emperor, and then committing suicide. But apart from such emergency situations, the method worked effectively.

Six or seven thousand students would compete in the first examination. From these perhaps less than ten per cent would be chosen. These would then take another competitive examination, and so forth, until not more than one per cent, say sixty out of six thousand, would be given the first degree. Those who passed could go to the prefectural cities and enter universities to prepare for the second examination. A man who had passed the first degree had nothing to worry about. His financial security was assured, for if his family could not help him for further study, the community would pay his expenses on the chance of his passing the second degree and getting a government post. The Chinese have always been gamblers, and they were willing to take the chance of getting a friend in the government who could help the community.

Passing the first degree was a great event. The name of the successful candidate was inscribed on the ancestral tablets of his family. Before the arrival of the telegraph in China there used to be a special group of men who made their living by acting as messengers for such news. They would wait outside the examination rooms until the list of the winning candidates was posted, then ride off to announce the good news to the families in remote villages. The families, filled with good feeling at such times, rewarded the messengers liberally.

The second examination was held in the provincial capital, with examiners appointed by the emperor. The procedure was similar to that of the first examination. The successful candidates were decorated with a collar and a gold flower. The winners then went to the capital, Peking in the old days, for examinations in the third degree. The winners remained to take a fourth examination given, and corrected in red ink, by the emperor himself. The winners of the highest degree were divided into four classes. One group was pensioned and kept in reserve to fill important vacancies. A second group became members of the inner council. A third group was appointed to positions in government bureaus, and a fourth group was sent out as provincial rulers.

Needless to say, the last posts were the ones most sought after, because the ruler was in a position to cut in on the highly organized graft which was an integral part of the Chinese governing system. Since there were not enough posts to go around, getting an appointment, even after passing the final examination, required a combination of skill and influence. The Chinese official who had gone through this process was exceedingly intelligent, and as long as government in China was actually left to this honestly recruited bureaucracy of scholars everything went exceedingly well. The weak spot in the system was that there was no equally rigid arrangement for recruiting emperors. The Chinese did not follow the patterns of primogeniture, although there was a tendency to it in the imperial line. In general, the emperor designated his heir from among his sons. Since the emperor was polygynous and his wives were chosen from various important Chinese families, the scheming and intrigue which this system occasioned can be imagined. When the heir was appointed, his mother worked on him to get appointments for all the members of the family. The sign of impending breakdown of a dynasty was always that the administration began to pass out of the hands of the real scholars recruited by the examinations and into the hands of palace favorites.

The palace eunuchs played a deadly part in the breakdown of Chinese dynasties. The eunuchs in China differed decidedly from those in Islamic countries, where they were usually slaves. In China they were volunteers, in many cases middle-aged men who had already fulfilled their obligations to the clan by marrying and producing sons. They would voluntarily undergo this operation and go into the palace service, where it was possible to rise to a high position. But the eunuchs, in spite of their emasculated condition, had families on the outside, and thus promoted the old Chinese administrative conflict of family claims operating against the national claims. Needless to say, the individuals who abandoned their families to enter palace service on these terms were either men who had been maladjusted or unsuccessful in ordinary life, or those who had such an overweening desire for power that they were willing to make any sacrifice to obtain it. The result was that they were a dangerous group. When the eunuchs became powerful enough in palace administration so that they held administrative posts and brought in their relatives, a dynasty was on the way out.

The weakness of this system was at the top, but as long as the rulers were good, it functioned effectively and made it possible for China to build up and constantly recruit a highly intelligent official class, who were united in education and cultural background. It was, as a matter of fact, the best system for maintaining an aristocracy which has so far been developed. The problem of recruiting really efficient administrators is one of the most exigent problems facing modern nations, and it is also one which we have handled very badly.

The further weaknesses in the Chinese government were the universality of graft and the handling of crime. Chinese graft cannot be judged by Western standards. The Chinese governor was paid a small salary and was expected to take graft. How much he received in this

way was rigidly fixed by custom and became a predictable overhead
for those who had to deal with him. It was what the old Tammany Hall
leaders in New York used to call "honest graft." If the governor of a city
squeezed too much, the merchants and craftsmen would send a protest to the central government. A board of examiners then arrived un-
announced, sealed the accounts, arrested the officials, and went into the
case. If it was shown that the official had been grafting out of reason,
action was swift. Instead of letting the case drag on for ten years and
then fining him three per cent of his known take, in American fashion,
the official was executed. This provided a considerable deterrent to
excess.

The Chinese handling of crime, while bad by our standards, was
harder on the criminals than on the public, which cannot always be said
of our practices. Punishment was meted out swiftly, and there were
many ingenious forms of execution. The criminal, however, had little
right of appeal. Witnesses who had no active part in the crime were
tortured on the principle that a more complete account of the circumstances could be obtained in this way. This, of course, made any witness
flee the scene of crime with swiftness, and evidence was very difficult to
obtain. If the person charged with an offense was an official, and his
crime was not flagrant enough for execution, he would be sent to the
capital to await trial. Here he would be kept for months or years, with
everyone around him extracting bribes until he was finally milked dry.
This, by the way, was a conscious technique for concentrating wealth for
the use of the dominating group. The pattern was to let the minor officials graft all they wished and then pick them when they were ripe. It
was a method coming into usage in Nazi Germany, and one which is
likely to appear wherever there are dictatorships.

China is unique among the great civilizations in that at no time in
its long history has it produced a strong priestly group, To be sure, in the
early times of Shang, Chou, and Han, the emperor was also a priest who
made the sacrifices to heaven on behalf of the entire kingdom, but the
religious functions of the rulers have always been secondary to the business of governing, or at least of providing the sanctions for government,
the actual procedure being in the hands of experts, the trained bureaucracy. China has never, at any stage, had anything corresponding to the
great temple establishments which dominated the intellectual and economic life of such civilizations as Egypt, Mesopotamia, and to a lesser
extent, India.

The most significant element in Chinese religion was ancestor worship. Any religion tends to be a projection of those values and interests
which the society considers most important. The two things which were
most important in Chinese daily life were the patterns of family organi-

zation and the continuity of family. Next in importance were the patterns of politeness, the rules for which were provided at great length in the classics. These two dominant interests were reflected very strongly in Chinese religion. The Chinese, no matter to what creed they gave official allegiance, were always fundamentally ancestor worshippers.

This practice comes directly out of the pattern of family life. To the Chinese the family is more important than the individual, something which continues and which may be said to have a living and a dead division. The ancestors are believed to continue to be much concerned with the fortunes and behavior of the descendants. They are notified of all ceremonial occasions in the family, and offerings are made to them. However, this is not worship in the ordinary sense of the term. The offerings are made as a token of respect and a polite recognition on the part of the descendants that they owe their existence and their good fortune to these people of the spirit world.

Ritual is important in most Chinese religion. The earliest Chinese texts which have been preserved are those prescribing the exact rituals to be used for various sacrifices, giving elaborate specification of how the sacrificial vessels were to be made, what proper procedures were, and the like. It is a form of approach to the supernatural which is largely devoid of emotional content, much like the approach of a well-trained major-domo or court official to the emperor. If you follow the exact rules of etiquette in dealing with the supernatural, you will presumably get results. You are not expected to love god or particularly fear god, but you must know how to approach him properly and how to influence him. Much of Chinese literature has been devoted to these matters.

In the early days the Chinese not only made offerings to the ancestors but at the time of burial provided them with all the tools, utensils, and other equipment which they would need in the next world. In the Shang tombs, about 1500 B.C., tremendous offerings were deposited with the dead. The reason that such fine bronzes have been found in Shang tombs is that a dead king was provided with a full equipment of all the sacrificial vessels which he would need to perform the proper sacrifices as king in the next world, which was regarded as a direct projection of the one on earth. They also gave the king an outfit of servants and frequently a favorite concubine or two. These servitors would be strangled and put into the tomb with their master. Sometimes a devoted noble would commit suicide and accompany his friend to the other world, so that the dead monarch could begin his new existence with a familiar group about him.

This practice continued in the imperial sacrifices for over a thousand years. By the end of Chou, however, feeling against human sacrifices had increased, and the use of substitutes was started. There is a

legend that human sacrifices were abolished during the Han Dynasty
when, after the death of an emperor, the major-domo insisted that the
empress should be sacrificed to accompany her consort. The lady, however, countered that, since the major-domo had run the household and
was more familiar with her master's needs than herself, he would be
more capable of satisfying the emperor than she. The matter was
promptly dropped, and there were no further human sacrifices at the imperial funerals. The magnificent Chinese figurines of dancing girls, warriors, horses, etc., called tomb figures, during the late Chou, Han, and
T'ang dynasties were placed in the tombs to take the place of real people
and real objects.

In modern times the orthodox Chinese continue to provide equipment for the use of the deceased in the next world. However, these are
made of cheap and perishable materials, frequently paper, and are
burned at the end of the funeral procession and thus dispatched to the
next world by way of fire. It is quite usual to have a paper automobile
complete with chauffeur carried in the funeral procession. A paper
airplane was included in the funeral procession of a Chinese general
during the Chiang Kai-shek regime, and was sent flaming into the sky at
the end of the proceedings. This custom of putting property into the
grave or destroying it at the funeral for the use of the deceased had such
wide validity that, as late as 1910, loans were occasionally made with the
understanding that they would be repaid in the next world. There was
also a belief in China that the body remained in the condition in which
it was at the time of death. For this reason the Chinese, even today, are
exceedingly reluctant to undergo amputation, even to save life. If an
amputation is performed the limb must be saved and eventually buried
with the individual. Heads of beheaded criminals are normally returned
to the family and joined to the body when the deceased is buried. If the
missing members were not available, terra cotta substitutes were sometimes placed with the body. The palace eunuchs in the old days had
the organs which had been removed pickled in alcohol, so that when
these gentlemen had reached retirement age they could retrieve the
equipment. It was sewed back on the body at death so that in the next
world one could start out as a complete man. Berthold Laufer, who gave
me this information, had as his prize possession a jade substitute, extremely flattering to the deceased, which was discovered in a T'ang
tomb.

Until recently (and it is difficult to say what the Chinese believe
at present), it was believed that all equipment provided for the dead
was translated into the next world. The Chinese picture of this realm, at
least among the non-philosophic common people, is a practical and
material one. It is an underworld which lies directly below visible and

material China and which corresponds in all details. The imperial rule functions in the underworld as it does in the upper one. When, in the days of the empire, a man was rewarded for meritorious services, his ancestors for five generations back were also ennobled, and patents of nobility were duly dispatched to the next world so that the ancestral spirits could immediately profit from the titles thus conferred upon their descendants. There are also a series of elaborate hells for the wicked, which included various sorts of elaborate tortures by a series of demons. One of the worst punishments, however, did not involve physical suffering. The condemned was forced to stand before a magic mirror and watch the results of his evil deed as they worked themselves out on earth. He saw his family destroyed, his children and friends suffering from his misdeed, until his line was finally ruined and extinguished, while he stood by unable to intervene or to look away.

The Chinese attitudes toward religion are a mixture of superstition and practicality. The folklore abounds in tales of demons and ghosts. The typical Chinese devil is an earthbound ghost who has not been able to pass over, as the spiritualists say. Victims of death by violence or drowning and suicides cannot follow the normal course of reincarnation until they have found a substitute, but are condemned to haunt the place where the tragedy occurred. The Chinese are extremely reluctant to rescue anyone who seems to be drowning, for they believe that the drowning man is being pulled down by a spirit who has been drowned at that place at some previous time and who is trying to get a substitute drowning so that he may go free. If such a spirit is thwarted he will remember and make trouble for the rescuer of his victim.

Although there were some mystics during the early periods of developing Chinese philosophy, the general approach of the Chinese is a thoroughly practical one. The Chinese have always been tolerant of various religions and willing to worship anywhere it will do most good. They never persecuted on religious grounds, and there have been few Chinese martyrs. Such persecutions as there were, notably those of the Buddhists, sprang less from religious causes than from the fear of having the Buddhist church continue to siphon off the wealth of the land. The Chinese are quite ready to switch from one deity to another if it seems advantageous to do so. The principal reason that Christianity has never taken hold in China, aside from its being the religion of a foreign power which is felt to be a threat to Chinese integrity, has been that the Christian missionaries objected to ancestor worship. However, the Catholic Church has recently ruled that the Chinese Catholics may burn incense to the ancestral tablets.

A wealthy Chinese will frequently have on one side of his funeral procession a group of Buddhist monks chanting from the Buddhist scripture. On the other side a group of Taoist priests will recite the proper spells to scare away demons and burn paper money to pay off the beggar ghosts. It is believed that these ghosts attend funerals and may cause trouble for the new arrival in the spirit world unless they are placated.

The most significant contribution which China has made to world culture is its importance as a center for the development and diffusion of civilization. It maintained great city populations when the rest of the world was living in small villages. It met most of the problems of government which confront a huge modern state and found working solutions for them, even to the proposition of how to deal with a small ruling minority. China not only affected all the civilizations of the East, providing a center from which the neighboring cultures were constantly reinforced, but it also influenced Europe. The situation of China with regard to neighboring cultures was much as though the Roman Empire, with its imperial institutions, had endured for 3000 years instead of 500, influencing all the barbarians within radius.

China at various times in her history has been one of the richest and most powerful countries in the world. During the 17th and 18th centuries, the period of European flowering, China was incomparably richer, and by most standards, more civilized than Europe. Europeans traded extensively with China, bringing back fine silks and porcelains which gave the name "china" to all English tableware. In the early 1700's things Chinese introduced a new style and enjoyed a great vogue in Europe. Wallpapers, cabinets, furniture and paintings done in this manner were called Chinoiserie. French nobles built Chinese summer houses in their gardens. Many French Jesuits were sent to China with the hope of converting the Emperor Ch'ien Lung to the faith. They were well received at court, but the emperor was more interested in the scientific, mathematical, and military contributions which the Jesuitical scholars were able to furnish than in their religious offerings. The French Jesuits, however, studied Chinese philosophy and classics. There is good reason to believe that many of the ideas of the period of enlightenment that formed the background of the French revolution actually percolated into French thinking from Chinese sources. The belief that, while the ruled owed allegiance to the ruler, the ruler in turn had an obligation to protect the welfare of his subjects, and that the subjects had the right to revolt if he failed in this obligation, is straight Confucianism. It is difficult to prove at which point this idea came into the European thought stream, but we do know that it makes its first appearance at a time when there was a burst of interest in Chinese art and Chinese philosophy. From what we know of the mechanics of diffusion, we can at least speculate that China was its source.

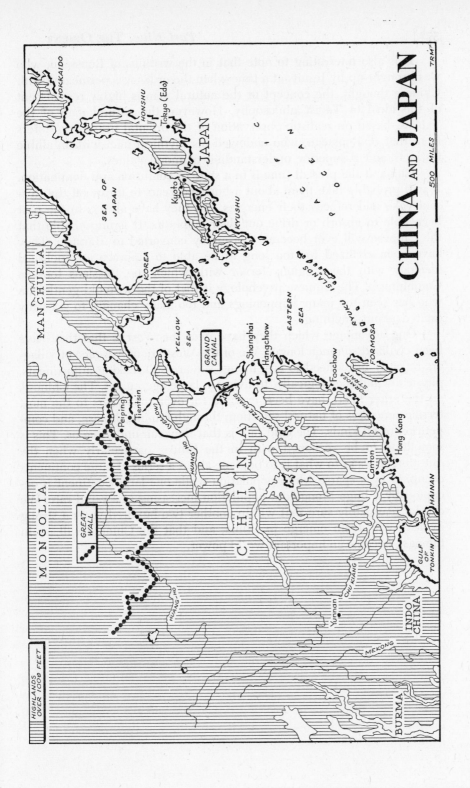

CHINA AND JAPAN

It is also interesting to note that in the writings of Rousseau, who was brought up by Jesuits at a time when the order was permeated with Chinese thought, the concept of the natural man is highly reminiscent of the ideal of Taoist philosophy. However, the natural man of the Taoists, based on realistic observation of the oriental peasantry, differs from that of Rousseau, who endowed his mythical man with infallible instincts and a superior understanding of moral values.

China at the present time is in a state of confusion and domination. It will probably take them about a hundred years to throw off the Russian yoke and refocus their energies, but they have always in the past been able to absorb or drive out their emperors. It is improbable that the Chinese will ever become thoroughly converted to Marxism. They have been civilized for too long to be able to embrace any political ideology with the religious fervor with which the Russians took to Communism. The Chinese psychology is that of the wise old gentleman who has seen too many happenings and too many changes to get truly excited about anything.

One advantage which they have over the West is that they have been civilized so much longer. We of the West are only a race of villagers recently introduced to city living. We are still making adjustments, physically and sociologically, to living in large aggregates. The Chinese, on the other hand, have been exposed for over 3000 years to the most terrific processes of natural selection, through famine, disease, and competition of all kinds. The cold fact is that they can underlive us. This is something to be reckoned with in the future, particularly when the question arises as to what is to be done about a series of large continents occupied by a sparse white population while one large continent is occupied by a huge Mongoloid population increasing at a rapid rate. We can be reasonably sure that within another two hundred years a strong dynasty will again emerge in China, and that the Chinese will, as in the past, become an important world power.

Chapter XXXIX

Japan

JAPAN OCCUPIES a position off the east coast of Eurasia comparable to that of the British Isles off the west coast of Europe. Both are island groups lying considerably north of the zone of comfortable occupation on the mainland and made habitable by warm oceanic currents, the Gulf Stream for Britain, the Black Current or *Kuroshiwo* for Japan.

The Japanese island group is of volcanic origin. This makes for a rugged mountainous terrain. However, all the arable land is very fertile, for volcanic soil, formed from ash and decayed lava, is the richest to be found anywhere. The Japanese have brought under cultivation all the land which is tillable and, by means of terracing, have added much which would not be considered usable in most countries. It is this full use of the soil which has made it possible for Japan to feed its dense population. Since the land is already used to full measure, the introduction of modern farm machinery will do little to increase the food supply. The only agricultural possibility which the Japanese have overlooked is grazing. The higher slopes could be used quite profitably for goat and sheep herds, but pastoral techniques have been foreign to Japanese culture.

The warm current which bathes Japan and gives it a temperate climate brings with it from the south a tremendous amount of marine life. The greatest food source for Japan is the off-shore fishing beds. Except for the period of the Shogunate, from the middle of the 1600's until Perry's visit in 1852, the Japanese have been a seafaring people who built able craft and went on long voyages. Japanese pirates were harassing the Korean coast by the beginning of the Christian era.

Japan has no extensive mineral deposits. There is some coal in the north, but practically no oil or iron and only a little copper and gold. In the old days export of gold from Japan was forbidden on pain of death, because it was so scarce and valuable that the authorities did not want any of it to leave the country. Japan, therefore, has not sufficient mineral resources to keep a modern technology going. Her sudden rise to power in the 20th century was made possible by a political organization which was able to modernize immediately and consciously, employing techniques already developed by the West and making use of every resource possible. This program could not have continued long without expansion of territory to provide raw materials. Unless Japan can have free access to mainland supplies, she is doomed to be a third-rate power.

The origins of the Japanese population are still in dispute. We do not know when the first humans came to the islands. No pre-human remains have been found in Japan, nor even any very early human fossils, in spite of the fact that during the Pleistocene Japan was intermittently linked with the Asiatic mainland. Remains of Indian elephants and other tropical forms have been found. If these animals could have gotten across, humans certainly would have been able to do so.

The curtain does not lift archeologically until the Neolithic. Around 1000 B.C. the northern two-thirds of Japan were occupied by a curious people called the Ainu. These were regarded for a long time as being marginal remnants of a Caucasic race. More recent studies have linked them with the Australian aborigines. They are probably an old, undifferentiated human type from Eastern Asia, which, living in a cloudy northern enviroment, became more bleached out than their southern ancestors. They are light-skinned, with long heads, broad faces, and stubby noses. Their eyes are round rather than almond-shaped. They have liberal whiskers and much body hair. The later Japanese, being a relatively smooth-skinned and beardless people, have always referred to them as the hairy Ainu. The culture of these earliest inhabitants can be reconstructed partly from archeology and partly from the life of the Ainu who still survive in northern Japan.

The Ainu culture was a part of the Circumpolar co-tradition. They were fishermen and food-gatherers. They lived in pit-houses and used Neolithic tools: ground stone celts, ground bone projectile points, etc., and made grit-tempered, cord-marked pottery, almost indistinguishable from that made by the American Indians of the Eastern woodlands, in other words, the typical Circumpolar pattern of early cooking ware.

The social organization of the Ainu was one of small villages with an exogamous totemic group; that is, each group had a sacred animal for which they were named and toward which they held special attitudes. Their religion was a worship of nature spirits, not merely the elements such as the sun and rain, but also waterfalls, rocks, trees, and other elements of nature. Their most important cult centered around the bear, which was the one dangerous animal in this environment and also the largest meat animal. Bears were regarded as people of a different tribe who, when no outsiders were present, took off their fur overcoats and behaved like other human beings. Special rites were performed, whenever a bear was killed, to placate its spirit so that it would pass the word along to other bears that if they let themselves be killed by the Ainu they would be well treated. In fact, even today the Ainu follow the practice of capturing a bear cub which is brought up as a village pet and treated with honor and deference until it is finally sacrificed.

In contrast to the Ainu, the early inhabitants of the southern part of Japan seem to have been agriculturalists from very early times. They brought in taro and probably rice, but they also relied heavily on fishing and built their settlements in coastal areas. The archeological evidence of their culture is scarce, for they used bamboo and wood for building and implements, made no pottery, and used little stone. Apparently this southern group were physically much like what we call proto-Malay, a stockily built, brown-skinned people with little body hair. They had broad faces, small noses, thin lips, and straight eyes.

Between these people and the Ainu, who were at approximately the same cultural level, the frontier fluctuated for some time. Both were good fighters, but the southern people, having agriculture and therefore being able to support larger populations, gradually moved northward, pushing the Ainu back. Still later, somewhere in the 3rd or 4th centuries B.C., there was another invasion of people coming from Korea. These people brought with them bronze weapons, pottery, and well-developed agricultural techniques. In spite of their smaller numbers, they managed with their superior culture to spread out as conquerors over the southern territory occupied by the Neolithic Indonesian group, whom they organized and absorbed. The ancestors of the Ainu were pushed farther north, where they remained, making little cultural contribution aside from forcing their neighbors to the south to maintain military vigilance. Japanese culture has had a military caste from the beginning. Throughout their history the soldier class has been in control, whereas in China the soldier was of minor importance, considered an unfortunate necessity for the defense of scholars, farmers, and merchants.

Descendants of the invaders established a tribal organization which became the background of later Japanese society. Their tribes, or clans, were normally endogamous and were ruled over by a clan chief, who occupied a high position as representative of the clan and carrier of the group *mana*. The clansmen's activities were limited to agriculture, hunting, fishing, and fighting. Manufacturing was carried on by groups of artisans, hereditary craftsmen who were not true clan members, although they were attached to the clan and were allowed to marry local

women. In time the craftsmen's families came to merge with the clan
and to claim its name and a common ancestry. The craftsmen had specialized functions: fine weaving, building, and the making of tools and
weapons. Below the clan and the craftsmen was a small class of slaves,
male and female, usually prisoners of war or their descendants.

Each clan had its own pantheon of deities, including a guardian
god. The powers of these deities were ill defined, and their habitation
and mode of life shadowy. The gods of the various clans were sufficiently similar so that later, when there was political consolidation, the
tribal gods could be equated and merged into a national pantheon. Each
tribe claimed descent from its own deity, and the chief or chiefess of
the tribe was believed to be in direct line of divine descent through the
eldest child of either sex. If the eldest child in a chief's family was a
daughter, she would be the ruler of the tribe. This accounts for the number of empresses who figure in early Japanese history.

The early history of Japan is difficult to reconstruct, for there has
been little good archeological work done there, and the Japanese
learned to write and keep records very late. Legends and traditions were
handed down by word of mouth. Written history does not begin until
after 552 A.D., when there were a number of Korean scribes and Buddhist missionaries coming into Japan. Moreover, Japanese history has
been exposed from its very beginning to propagandistic activities, reinforced by religious and patriotic enthusiasm, and this background is not
conducive to the keeping of accurate records. In the 6th century, when
the Japanese came into contact with the historically minded Chinese,
they felt that they should have a history of their own, and tried to manufacture it from the various legends which had been handed down. Japan
was at this time split into a great number of localized clans. Each scribe
set out with the pious intention of writing a history of Japan which
would show his own clan as having been the ruler of all Japan throughout its history. When the clan which was the founder of the present imperial line became dominant, it was obviously to its advantage to falsify
the records and claim that it had always been on top. In the same way
the ancestor goddess of this clan, Amaterasu, the sun goddess, from
whom the present emperor claims descent, was exalted and put high in
the pantheon of gods, although there can be little doubt that she was
originally a minor deity.

The Japanese empire came into existence when one clan finally
established dominance over the others and its chief arrogated to himself
the title of emperor. The society which emerged was a feudal system,
with numerous clan survivals. The Japanese nobles were originally clan
chiefs but, as the empire was centralized, the clan organization broke
down. It was replaced by an extended family organization, patrilineal

kin groups which included a number of persons but which were smaller than the original clans and which did not cut across class lines. Society was organized into four classes. At the bottom were the *Eta,* or outcastes. The origins of this group are unknown. Its nucleus was probably the war captive slaves of the pre-Imperial period, but it was gradually extended to include outcastes of all sorts: criminals, and even occasional members of the noble class who had not had the courage to commit hara-kiri when good manners required it. Today the Eta do not differ in physical type from other Japanese, although they were consistently Jim-Crowed for centuries. Their touch was considered defiling, and they were limited to "unclean" occupations: scavengers, executioners, tanners, and butchers. These last two occupations are particularly low in a Buddhist country, for Buddhism frowns on all killing of animals, and those who practice these impious trades are at the very bottom of the scale.

Above the Eta were the commoners, who were divided into cultivators, artisans, and merchants. The cultivators, although they were economically unfortunate in that they tended to be taxed by everybody, nevertheless had social prestige. Farming *per se* was an honorable occupation. Even a *Samurai* could become a farmer without losing caste. Artisans ranked below farmers. This was probably because, in the early days of the feudal period, skilled artisans were attached to the ruling families in a sort of client relationship. They were few in number, since they were for the most part foreigners who had been imported from abroad. For instance, a Chinese maker of porcelain would be brought to Japan to ply his trade. He would be provided with a Japanese wife, but his children, following the pattern of patrilineal descent, could not become real members of a clan. They were supported by the noble family but were outsiders.

The merchants originally held a debased position in Japan, but during the "sealed" period in the 17th and 18th centuries, they came into more and more importance. During this period a strong central government had developed, and, in order to control the nobles, the ruling clan insisted that every noble either should be in the capital himself or send some responsible member of his family there. Various members of the noble family might take their turns at court, but the Shogun demanded that there always should be a member of noble family within reach, acting as hostage for his kin. The old feudal economy, which was a production economy, was thus transformed into a luxury and money economy, because the nobles and their families who were settled in the capital had to have cash in order to buy elaborate costumes demanded for court rituals and to keep up the establishments which their prestige required.

At this point the merchants began to move in. Throughout Japanese history there were trade guilds and unions, which operated mainly in the larger centers where the luxury manufactures were located. The Japanese city workers who made up these guilds had never been a docile lower class, and the organized guilds often fought back if they felt the nobles had mistreated them. As there came to be more concentration of population in the cities, the merchants began to acquire wealth, while the nobles kept the prestige. Gradually the merchants began to acquire prestige also. In the last hundred years before the opening of Japan, an impoverished nobleman could recoup his fortunes by marrying the daughter of a wealthy merchant and becoming the adoptive husband in the merchant's family. When there was no son in a Japanese family, it was customary to marry a daughter to a promising young man who would be adopted as a son and given the family name. Some of the greatest of the Japanese merchant houses have been built up in this way in the last 100 years.

The nobles constituted a hereditary military class, the *Samurai.* Since a noble's sons by peasant concubines were rated as noble, this class was constantly increasing. The highest noble was the Shogun. This title, meaning "victorious general," was originally conferred by the emperor on the noble in charge of the northern frontier region, where the Japanese were carrying on their endless war with the Ainu. Later it became the title of the secular ruler who pre-empted the powers of the emperor. Beneath the Shogun were the great military lords, *Daimyo,* and attached to these in turn were minor chiefs and knights. The feudal system differed from the European one in that there was much more concentration of power at the top. In Europe, the knight lived by the direct exploitation of the serfs on his manor. In Japan, taxes were collected by the overlord and then disbursed down to the lower ranks of nobles. This made the nobles highly dependent upon their overlords. The eldest son succeeded his father in receiving this allowance, and, if there was no son, the family lost its right to the allowance. Expropriated Samurai formed a distinct group called *Ronin,* which meant "wave men," and served as mercenary soldiers under various lords. They were readily recruited for attacks on the mainland, and many of them served outside Japan. Thus, for centuries the royal bodyguard of the kings of Siam consisted of Japanese Ronin.

The Samurai evolved their own code of ethics, called *Bushido,* and had their special dress and social ritual. Their armor, made from plates intricately lashed together with silk cords, was effective against the Japanese sword, which was used exclusively for slashing. The swords themselves were among the finest examples of metal-working to be found anywhere in the world. They were made from alternate layers of high and low carbon steel, which were repeatedly pounded out, folded, and welded, until some of the finest blades might have as many as 2000 laminations.

Although equipment and techniques of individual fighting were highly developed, warfare itself was primitive. The feudal Japanese understood little of tactics or military maneuvers. Although they had horses and used mounted men, they never developed cavalry as a distinct arm. War was a matter of brute strength and cunning, and pitched battles usually began with individual champions coming out between the lines and engaging in single combat. It was proper for each champion to introduce himself and recite his genealogy. If the antagonists could point out a flaw in the recital, it was believed to give him a strong advantage in the subsequent combat. In spite of such chivalrous behavior, the battles were sanguinary, and the Samurai code made no provision for either surrender or the treatment of prisoners. Those who could not escape after a defeat were expected to commit hara-kiri. This tradition provided the background both for the Japanese no-surrender patterns of the recent war and for their failure to conform to what we regard as civilized rules of war prisoner treatment.

The patterns of obedience and personal discipline imposed by the feudal system proved a distinct advantage when the Japanese came in contact with the West. They provided the nation with a group of patriotic leaders whom the masses had been trained to follow. The long years of feudalism made it possible for the Japanese to mobilize national energies for the assimilation of those elements of Western culture which appeared valuable to them. Needless to say, the Western military tactics were among the things most eagerly accepted.

At the top of the social scale was the imperial family, who were a social class in themselves. Originally the imperial family had been the chiefs of one of the powerful noble clans, but, as they came to be regarded as of divine origin and became sanctified, they were set apart from the other nobles. Although marriages in the imperial group were permitted only within the imperial clan, an imperial prince could take concubines from among the daughters of the nobles. The children of such unions, according to Japanese rules of patrilineal descent, were regarded as of divine origin and had full imperial powers. The imperial line thus became quite extensive. If the Shogun had trouble with the emperor, there was always a collection of imperial princes, one of whom could be substituted for the refractory ruler. The usual technique was to request the emperor to resign in favor of a young and docile prince.

The patterns of family organization were much the same for all classes. All had the extended family system. All the people in a village were usually related and, in the back country, might even live in one

big communal house. The eldest male served as family head, but was
not accorded the respect nor allowed to wield the authority enjoyed by
a family head in China. The Japanese have always preferred to work
things out in committee, so to speak, whether the problem be social or
political. Therefore the family head in Japan conferred elaborately with
other family members before handing down any important decision.

ENTRANCE TO THEATER, XVIII CENTURY

There has always been considerable prostitution in Japan. The houses of prostitution were staffed largely by girls who had been sold by their families or who had sold themselves in order to pay off family debts. This was considered an honorable and filial thing to do. If a girl could manage to pay off her debt to the house, she could leave it and go back to her village and marry. However, the madames of the houses, like ladies of this persuasion everywhere, usually saw to it that the girls remained in debt. The geisha was quite different from the prostitute. She was a trained entertainer who had to be able to play various musical instruments, to sing and dance, and to make agreeable conversation. The geishas might take care of a patron for the night if they wished to do so, but it was not part of their profession.

The first relatively certain date in Japanese history is approximately 200 A.D., when the Japanese invaded Korea under the Empress Jingo. We have this, not from the Japanese records, for there were no scribes in Japan at this time, but from Korean and Chinese historians. She seems to have been a powerful ruler in central Japan, who succeeded in uniting enough clans to make large-scale continental expeditions possible. It was Jingo who first brought a more or less centralized Japan into contact with the Asiatic mainland, and prepared the way for the flow of Korean and Chinese culture into Japan.

In 284 A.D. the Emperor Ojin called in a Korean sage as his advisor. This man brought writing to Japan for the first time. However, writing did not become established in Japan until two or three centuries later. Japan took on culture and learning from the mainland and became civilized only in the 7th century A.D. The first Buddhist temples in Japan were built just before 600 A.D. under the direction of Shotoku Taishi, the Crown Prince Regent, who is known as the founder of Buddhism in Japan. In 645 the Emperor Kotoku, the great reformer, began his campaign to educate and improve his people. This reforming emperor may appear under other names, as the Japanese custom was to give a child one name at birth, another when he matured and took office, and a third, or divine name, after his death. However, under any name, this emperor recognized the inferiority of his own people as compared with the civilizations of the mainland, and set out deliberately and purposefully to do something about it. This bears the stamp of the sort of Japanese psychology which has persisted up to the present time. The Japanese have always been willing to borrow and benefit by other people's ideas and inventions, though remaining essentially Japanese in their attitudes and loyalties.

Kotoku not only tried to civilize and educate the people but also worked to reorganize the loose tribal government by strengthening the central power, that of his own clan, of course. He also tried to give more recognition and freedom to the common people. The chief contact for this borrowing and organization was Korea. In the next century, when the Japanese were going farther afield from their own islands, they discovered that the real center of civilization was not Korea but China, and that the Korean culture which they had been imitating was a second-hand version of the Chinese. The emperor then sent commissions to China to study and report on Chinese institutions. This was a unique event in human history, the only case on record, except for a Japanese parallel many centuries later, in which a nation deliberately set out to remake its formal structure on a pattern taken from another country. The Japanese commission in China stayed for about twenty years, during which time they selected the most promising craftsmen of all kinds and encouraged them to carry their skills in lacquer work, porcelain, enamel, and so forth, over the sea to Japan. They also sent over many Korean and Chinese scholars, and even persuaded scholars and craftsmen from India and Indo-China to go to Japan.

During the 7th and 8th centuries in Japan, therefore, there was a making-over of Japanese life comparable to that which took place in the late 19th and early 20th centuries. This reorganization was characterized by the same psychological needs: the feeling of intense inferiority and a desire not merely to catch up with the rest of the world but to exceed it.

The attempts to remake Japanese culture along Chinese lines failed at certain points. In China at this time the system of competitive examinations and the establishment of a professional bureaucracy was assuming the form which it was to hold for the next thousand years. Although the Japanese made some attempt to introduce this system into their own country, they were unsuccessful because the bulk of the Japanese aristocracy was still illiterate. There were few Japanese scholars, and no Japanese literature or philosophy upon which an arrangement of the Chinese sort could be established. In China the feudal aristocracy had practically destroyed themselves during the wars preceding the emergence of the Han dynasty. In Japan the feudal aristocracy was never destroyed, and the central government succeeded in bringing them under control only for short periods. The result of this situation was that the Japanese officials were appointed through favor without preliminary selection. Given the Japanese pattern of strong family and clan loyalties, there was a tendency for government offices to be hereditary, with no consideration given to honesty or ability.

The attempt to center rule in the emperor also broke down, following this period of reform. After a series of able emperors, the line began to die out. The Japanese met this in very characteristic fashion. They retained the emperor as a sort of figurehead, making him more and more sacred, while turning over the central control to first one and then another of the great Japanese clans. From the 9th through the 19th centuries the emperor was immobilized by his own sanctity and the taboos which surrounded him. For example, when the emperor sat in state he had to hold himself rigid, for if he turned his head he would cause an earthquake in the direction toward which he looked. His person was so sacred that his hair and nails could be cut only when he was asleep, and his personal belongings or anything he had touched were taboo. The emperor had to be fed out of new dishes at each meal, and the dishes were destroyed after he had finished with them. This was an excuse to use poor and cheap equipment in the imperial palace.

At first the secular rulers showed great respect for the emperor, but later this declined and they regarded him more and more as merely a symbol. The institution of the sacred emperor and the secular rulers was crystallized under Yorimoto, who ruled from 1185 to 1199. At this time there was a terrific war between two of the great clans, with most of the minor clans being drawn in on one side or the other. Yorimoto, whose group emerged victorious, proceeded to reorganize the empire so that he would be able to control it. Up to this time Japan had not been particularly warlike. There were the usual clan feuds, but after this reorganization, which involved also changes in the patterns of inheritances of offices and income, a definite military caste emerged, which remained dominant until the reformation of Japanese politics which took place after Commodore Perry's visit in the middle 1800's.

In 1192 Yorimoto was given the title *Shogun*. This was not a new title, but, after Yorimoto, it took on a new significance and came to mean military dictator. He preserved the emperor and the court at Kyoto. However, without destroying the older civil officialdom, he established a military administration under his control. He made peace with the powerful Buddhist monks and appointed military constables and tax collectors in all the provinces. Yorimoto was a political genius, and his dual form of government lasted until the middle of the 19th century, a period of 650 years.

In the 18th century the Shoguns themselves became puppets. Another ruling house seized power, and another ruling office was established. In the last 200 years before Europeanization and reform, the governmental setup consisted of the sacred emperor in the extreme background and completely immobilized, next to him the sacred Shogun largely immobilized, and then the real rulers, who were successors of Hideyoshi, who had overthrown the Shogunate and had established what was to all intents and purposes a totalitarian state. This government gave the Japanese good training for what was to come later.

The first Europeans to reach Japan were the Portuguese. They arrived in 1542, shortly followed by the Spaniards, Dutch, and British.

Some commerce was established between Japan and Europe, and the Europeans brought with them two things which profoundly influenced the culture of Japan: firearms and Christianity. Firearms gave new strength to the feudal lords, who could now become more independent of the central power. Their old simple wooden houses were replaced by stone castles in more or less European style, for they now needed stronghholds which could withstand gunfire.

The Jesuit, Francis Xavier, was the first missionary to Japan. He arrived in 1549, accompanied by some other members of the Society of Jesus. The missionaries found an immediate response among the Japanese. The doctrine and ceremonial of the Roman Catholic Church was similar to that of the Buddhist religion. The once powerful Buddhist priests were at this time losing their hold on the people, who were ready to turn to new spiritual leadership. The new faith was favored by the central government, for it facilitated trade with the West. Within a generation after Xavier's arrival there were reported to be 200 Christian churches and 150,000 Christians in Japan. The feudal lords sent embassies to Rome, and for a time it seemed that Japan might become a Christian country.

During this period three great leaders arose in Japan: Nobunaga, Hideyoshi, and Iyeyasu. Nobunaga was a feudal war lord who successfully overpowered his neighbors and made himself master of the capitol. He was followed by Hideyoshi, a man of humble rank, not even of the Samurai class, the only instance in Japan's history in which a commoner rose to the highest position open to one not of divine descent. Hideyoshi, having unified Japan under his military dictatorship, undertook foreign conquest also. He overran most of Korea, which he regarded as a gateway to China. It was Hideyoshi who announced that he was going to roll up China as one rolls up a mat. However, the Japanese were no more successful than they were recently in their attempts to conquer China. China does not roll up easily. The Japanese soldiers arrived at a time when the Ming Dynasty was in confusion and there was no strong central power. In spite of this the Chinese rallied under attack.

The Koreans also, although they had never been a particularly warlike or brilliant people, showed unexpected strength and ingenuity in combating the Japanese onslaught. They invented the first "ironclads," and a fleet of these new "turtle boats" sank the Japanese fleet and cut their supply lines. The Koreans also invented at this time the first mortar to throw an explosive shell, an improvement which had not yet come into use in Europe, although it appeared shortly thereafter. Hideyoshi's attack ground to a halt, and after his death the Koreans managed to throw off Japanese control.

This expansion to Korea was actually a diversion which took the military out of Japan and enabled the new government to seat itself more firmly. A war which arouses the patriotism of the population has long been observed to be the best way to unite a nation. This conquest, although unsuccessful in the long run, brought Japanese to the mainland. Also, considerable numbers of Ronin went south and spread through Indonesia and Southeastern Asia, where they served as mercenary soldiers. These migrants were, for the most part, men of the noble class who, through poverty, disgrace, or over-adventurousness, had forfeited their connection with the noble house and were on their own. The recent Japanese expansion into Indonesia actually followed an old pattern, in which the Japanese surplus military population spilled over into the mainland territories.

Hideyoshi was followed by Iyeyasu, who had originally been his opponent, but became his chief lieutenant. Iyeyasu turned his attention to internal affairs rather than foreign conquest, and under his leadership the country was finally consolidated. He had himself appointed Shogun in 1603 and was thus in charge of the feudalized military system which had been inaugurated by Yorimoto four-hundred years earlier. He set up a military capitol at Edo, the present Tokyo, away from the imperial court. Iyeyasu was succeeded by his son and grandson, and under the rule of his family Japan had peace for over two centuries.

During this time the Japanese not only abstained from foreign conquest, but shut themselves away from the outside world entirely. The Japanese rulers did not want their people to know what was going on outside the country, and, in particular, they did not want them to leave. A Japanese who left the island and returned again was put to death. The central powers instituted a complete police state, with innumerable road blocks. Passports were required of people moving from one province to another, and there were local customs charges, as in France. It was a bureaucratic arrangement very reminiscent of the Russian iron curtain.

Before this time the Japanese had always been a sea people. Within a generation after their first contact with Europeans they were building vessels which could cross the Pacific, and were trading on the west coast of America. When Japan was closed, a law was passed making it punishable by death to build ships above a certain burden. There were also regulations limiting construction so that vessels seaworthy for transoceanic shipping could not be built. All foreigners were excluded, except for a few Dutch merchants who were allowed to occupy a small island in one of the harbors. The only outside skill for which the Japanese admitted a need was that of medicine. They permitted medical students to study Dutch so that they could read Dutch medical books.

However, during the time when Japan had been open there had been a surprising amount of borrowing of European technology and

ideas. The Japanese, behind their self-imposed barriers, went on per-
fecting many of the European forms. They developed firearms based on
European models but modified in accordance with Japanese manual
habits. They made elaborate armor, a modification of European plate
armor, made up of lacquered metal and rawhide put together with silk
lashings. Metal work was raised to a high art. Their swords would take
a razor edge but would also stand heavy service. The Samurai lord
would have a variety of sword fittings for his blade, some simple and
refined for religious occasions, and some inlaid with gold for court ceremonials.

The Japanese have always been a beauty-loving people, with a desire for aesthetic perfection. Their art has been basically dependent on
importations from abroad, mainly from China, which were then gradually transformed to satisfy the native sensitivity for harmonious proportions, decorative pattern, and humor. Thus, from the 7th through
the 8th century, and again in the 14th and 15th centuries, when a new
wave of Chinese influence brought with it calligraphic painting, art in
Japan was almost purely Chinese in character. Around 1600, in Hideyoshi's time, this style of painting was once more synthesized, this time
into the brilliant decorative screens that adorned the imperial castles and
temples. With the rise of a bourgeois merchant class a new art was developed through the inexpensive medium of the color woodblock, which
was employed mainly to depict trivia of everyday life. The woodblock
was the first Japanese art form to capture the attention of the West.
More recently we have been influenced by the sophisticated simplicity
of the paraphernalia used in the tea ceremony, which originally derived
from Zen Buddhist ritual. Another profound influence on modern art
has been Japanese domestic architecture.

The Japanese, like the Chinese, have shown tolerance for all sorts
of beliefs. Buddhism was the first world religion to be superimposed on
the aboriginal nature worship. It did not become powerful until the
7th century, when it began to develop various local sects. Christianity
had considerable influence in the 16th and early 17th centuries, but was
banned by the Shogunate and practically wiped out. Side by side with
Buddhism and Christianity was the truly native Japanese religion,
Shinto, which developed from the aboriginal nature worship. During
most of Japanese history Budhhism has been the religion of the intellectuals and aristocrats. Zen Buddhism, with its emphasis on the development of the individual personality, had wide influence, especially
among the Samurai. Attitudes created by this sect permeated the aes-
thetics and ethics of all Japan. Shinto was carried on as an unorganized
back-country cult. After the opening and modernization of Japan, Shinto
was made the state religion.

During the Shogunate the population of Japan was pretty well stabilized. This was accomplished partly by considerable ingenuity in sexual matters and techniques of contraception, and partly by a process, which the Japanese dislike to acknowledge, called "thinning the family." The Japanese did not practice the usual sort of infanticide, in which a superfluous child is done away with shortly after birth. The Japanese family head who had more children than he could properly provide for would wait until the child was two or three years old and his potentials of health and intelligence were becoming obvious. The least promising ones would be eliminated. This "thinning" was done in the same way that one would thin a growing crop, removing the poorer plants so that the surviving ones would have a better chance. However, when the Japanese became mechanized and the developing commercial interest needed cheap labor and the emperor needed soldiers, the people were encouraged to breed rapidly. Being a well-disciplined and patriotic people, they proceeded to do so, and the population took a rapid upswing.

The country was closed in 1636 and remained closed until 1853 when it was opened, so to speak, with a can opener. What happened was that the Americans sent to Japan a fleet of war vessels vastly superior to anything the Japanese had and politely suggested that they would like treaties permitting trade—or else. It was much like the suggestion of an offensive and defensive alliance between Russia and Finland, and the Japanese liked it about as much. They would have preferred to stay comfortably isolated from the world.

A few years after Perry's arrival some of the Japanese shore batteries opened fire on some European armed steamers, which returned the fire with a speed and precision astonishing to the Japanese. It brought home to them very definitely that they were helpless against the modern equipment of European forces, and made them realize that if they were to be drawn into the world once more they would have to modernize themselves as rapidly as possible. The Japanese already had the pattern of deliberately imitating other countries, and China, their previous model, was at this time in a state of confusion and was itself being rapidly brought under European control. The Japanese turned to the West. They sent delegates to various parts of Europe to bring back the skills which had made the Europeans successful. They recognized that different countries excelled in different things. Therefore they organized their army along German lines, the navy along British lines, and finance and manufacturing on French and English models. The United States they ignored at this time as not being far enough advanced to warrant study and imitation.

Perry's visit was in 1853, and by 1867 the internal revolution had been accomplished. Feudal dues had been formally abolished, and the emperor was reinstated as an actual political ruler, not merely a divine symbol. Fortunately, the emperor of this Meiji era was an able man. The Japanese set up a new government which looked democratic and constitutional enough to win the respect of Europeans, although actually it was handled on a sound Japanese basis of family control. It is interesting that in the reorganization, for instance, one of the great clans took over the army, another the navy, while still others went into various businesses.

For a time all the old aspects of Japanese life were devaluated. The population was so dazzled by European pre-eminence that they attached little importance to their own culture. Many of the finest pieces of Japanese art were sold for a song to knowing Europeans, and the Japanese strove to acquire an appreciation of pre-Raphaelite Victorian painting.

A long period of discipline had prepared the Japanese for acting with a united will upon orders. They laid out a careful plan for modernization, for the conquest of world markets, and then, as part of the long-range program, for the conquest of the world so that all races should be brought under the benevolent shadow of the emperor. These plans were carried well forward during World War I, but foundered on Japanese miscalculations in World War II.

PART TEN

The New World

Chapter XL

North American Aborigines

THE CONTINENTS of North and South America were really a New World. Cut off from the Old World centers of development by the two great oceans, they lagged far behind in the timetable of civilization. When the Spanish explorers reached these shores, the peoples of America had arrived at the stage of civilization which Southwest Asia had attained in 3500 B.C. and Western Europe in 1500 B.C. That they had achieved so much in their isolation and had independently made most of the discoveries and inventions on which civilized living is based indicates that they were essentially a gifted people. If they had been allowed to develop their culture and work out their destinies, they might have made significant contributions to the stream of world civilization.

There has been much speculation, and many fancy theories have been spun, about the origin of the American Indian. Even their name springs from a misapprehension on the part of Columbus. At various times, professional guessers have tried to establish that they were descendants of the Ten Lost Tribes of Israel, stragglers from the fleet of Alexander the Great; or emigrants from the mythical continent of Atlantis or a similarly hypothetical Pacific island called Mu. Because the monuments of the Maya in Central America are similar in many respects to those of the ancient Egyptians, attempts were made to prove that the Indians were of Old World origin, ignoring the fact that when the Mayas were building their temples those of Egypt had been abandoned for thousands of years.

The first settlers of America undoubtedly came from Asia by way of Alaska. There was no independent human development on this continent; no fossil remains of any human species except *homo sapiens* have ever been found in America. Man came to this continent as modern man, already equipped with tools and fire and some sort of language. In view of the Arctic regions through which he had to pass, it is safe to assume that he also could provide some sort of clothing and shelter for himself. During the Ice Age, what is now Bering Strait was presumably a land bridge, as the great glaciers stored up enough water to lower the water level. With Arctic waters landlocked on the north, the shores of Alaska and Northeastern Siberia would be washed by the warm Pacific current. This was the hypothetical state of the area at the time of the first migrations. Much of Alaska was ice-free at this time, but the glaciers of the Coast Range would have prevented migrations due south.

It seems likely that the first wave of migrants followed the coastal plain, north and east to the valley of the Mackenzie. There was an ice-free corridor along the eastern side of the Rockies, and also plenty of game. Asiatic animals preceded man to the continent, and both human fossils and early artifacts have been found in association with, or embedded in, the bones of extinct animals: the camel, the giant ground sloth, the Bison *Taylori,* and the original American horse. It was believed for a time that this proved the antiquity of man on the continent, as these animals had been extinct in the Old World since very early times. However, the new Carbon 14 dates indicate that it was the animals who survived to a late date rather than the humans who came early. The earliest dates so far tested go back only about 10,000 years. Several thousand years must be allowed for the migrants to have reached the sites in southern North America where they were found, so that 12,000 to 15,000 years is the limit for the antiquity of man in America.

Two methods of dating which have been developed by American scientists in recent years have done much to clarify the picture. The first was a process discovered by Dr. A. E. Douglass, an astronomer who came upon the method when he was studying sun spots and weather fluctuations. He found, when studying cross-sections of pine trees in the Southwest, that wet and dry seasons were recorded in the width of the annual growth of the trees. By comparison of tree ring patterns of old living trees, beams found in colonial structures, and posts from prehistoric ruins, he was able to establish a calendar of tree ring dating which extended from 11 A.D. to the present. This method has so far proved practical only for Southwestern material.

The second dating technique is a by-product of modern atomic studies. A radioactive isotope, Carbon 14, is constantly being produced on the earth's surface by the collision of cosmic rays with nitrogen atoms. Atmospheric carbon is assimilated by living organisms, both plant and animal, but assimilation stops at death. Since Carbon 14 has a half-life of $5,568 \pm 30$ years, it is possible, by determining the percentage of this isotope in the total carbon of the specimen, to date specimens as far back as 25,000 years. There are a number of other factors which may upset this balance, but this has still proved the most acceptable method of dating ancient materials.

All human fossils discovered fall within the range of the physical variation of the historic Indians. This range is considerable, for, while the first migrants were probably of a generalized Mongolian type, they spread out and settled in small, inbred groups in a variety of climates and soon developed individual physical types. All Indians have dark eyes and hair, medium brown skins, and little or no body hair. However, these characteristics do not show up in fossils. The bones show that some were short, some tall; some long-headed, some round-headed; some had high, narrow noses, some low, broad noses. At the lowest strata heavy flake instruments have been found, crude artifacts reminiscent of early type Paleolithic from East Asia. From a somewhat later stratum a more complete picture can be pieced together, showing primitive man contemporaneous with the mammoth and the sloth.

All the early migrants must have been nomadic hunters and fishermen, since this is the only mode of life possible in the Arctic regions through which they had to travel. As they made their way south down the Mackenzie Valley to the Plains regions, they found a land abounding in game and free from human enemies. Under these conditions they multiplied rapidly. As the ice retreated further north another route was opened between the Rocky Mountains and the Coast Range, leading to the Great Basin. The settlement of America was accomplished not by a single wave of migrants, but by a steady infiltration which continued for thousands of years. All the early migrants traveled south in search of better lands until the last comers, the Eskimo, arrived with full equipment for Arctic life and techniques for hunting the big sea mammals. They settled in the region and cut off further migration.

The population of the continent was very early divided into two recognizable culture complexes, the seed-gatherers and the big game hunters. The seed gatherers were the settlers of the Rocky Mountain Plateau west to California and east across Texas. There was little game in this region but plenty of wild vegetable food, seeds, berries, nuts, roots, and bulbs. Since these people were not hunters, their projectile points were few and crude. They made large flake tools and choppers. They learned how to roast their seeds and grind them in *metates* (concave grinding stones) to make meal, and how to dry their gleanings and store them in tightly woven baskets of twined cord. For this reason their descendants were known as the Basketmakers.

The game hunters centered in the High Plains of the Western United States with some penetration into the Eastern Woodlands and toward the Texas border. Hunting, food-gathering societies are as dependent upon the ecology of the region in which they live as any other mammalian species, and do not penetrate into the territories which will require them to invent or borrow new techniques. To a Plains hunter a thickly forested area presented as effective a barrier as a mountain range. The hunters therefore stayed on the Plains, where game was plentiful, supplementing their diet with wild seeds and roots.

This culture was characterized by an extensive and fine industry of chipped stone projectile points, knives, and scrapers. Two types of projectile points are diagnostic for this culture: the Folsom and the Yuman points, named for the places in New Mexico where they were first discovered. The Folsom is a fluted stone point with lengthwise fluting or grooving on both faces. The Yuman points are long and narrow, with parallel flaking extending across the blade and no fluting. These Folsom-Yuman people were the ancestors of the American hunting tribes. We know that they hunted the mammoth and other extinct animals. The first find of these implements was made at Folsom, New Mexico, where they were found in association with bones of bison of an extinct type. However, the hunting techniques were the same as those used by historic Indians. They had evidently surrounded the animals, herded them together, and finished them off with javelins. Folsom type points were embedded in the bones of the bison. Another interesting feature was that the tail bones of all the bison skeletons were missing. This indicated that the Folsom people skinned the beasts, leaving the tails on the hide. Since the skeletons were otherwise complete, they apparently followed the practice of the historic hunters, who roughed out the skeletons of the buffalo and carried off the meat in large rolls.

Taken as a whole, the earliest remains suggest a movement to America of a people with a crude flake culture and generalized Australoid-Mongolian characteristics. They probably arrived during the period of the last glacial retreat, most likely while the Eastern United States was still under ice, which accounts for the fact that no cultural remains have been found in this region. These migrants spread over most of North America and were the first to reach South America. There were probably no further migrations for a long time because a period of increased cold made passage of the Strait impossible. With milder climatic conditions, migration from Asia started again with a people of Upper Paleolithic culture, who were adjusted to full nomadic hunting life. These people were Paleoasiatic (intermediate Caucasic-Mongoloid characteristics) much like the historic Indians. These carriers of a hunting culture mixed with the older population and adopted seed-gathering in regions where straight hunting was less profitable than food-gathering.

From the time of this second migration there was frequent move-

ESKIMO
ESKIMO
ESKIMO
ARCTIC CIRCLE
BARREN
GROUND
ESKIMO
NORTHWEST COAST
ROCKY
MOUNTAIN
PLATEAU
CALIFORNIA
SOUTHWEST
GREAT PLAINS
NORTHEAST WOODLANDS
SOUTHEAST
WOODLANDS
AZTEC
MAYAN
EQUATOR
ANDEAN HIGHLANDS

NEW WORLD

1500 MILES

TRM

ment across Bering Strait, possibly by boat, though the passage was blocked from time to time by climatic fluctuations. These migrants continued to trickle south and eastward seeking more favorable territory. Then came a group who had developed full Circumpolar culture: ice fishing, bone implements, and the use of bark for canoes and utensils. This group spread from the Bering Straits area southeast across Canada, following the lines of the wooded lakes. These Paleoasiatics were the ancestors of the historic Northeast Indians, the Algonkians. The later migrations were of people of increasingly specialized Mongoloid type. About 1000 B.C. the Eskimo, with a highly specialized version of the old Circumpolar culture, moved into the Bering Strait area. Since they had a full adaptation to Arctic life, they were not impelled to move on in search of a better climate, but settled in the area and cut off the route to further migration.

Archeological finds suggest that agriculture arose independently in several different places in America, with subsequent borrowing of crops. All the important food plants used by the prehistoric peoples of America were of local origin. The most important was maize, a plant which has become so highly domesticated that it cannot resow itself or survive without human care. It was long believed that this originated in the Mexican Highlands, where there are agricultural sites dating back to 1500 B.C. Some later evidence tends to show that the plant or its ancestor was developed in South America, probably Paraguay, though maize of a very primitive type dating from around 1000 B.C. has been found in Bat Cave, New Mexico.

In Middle America it found a favorable environment, and there it was combined with two other locally domesticated crops, beans and squash. Maize, beans, and squash, throughout most of their range from Middle America northward, were planted together. The corn was planted in hills, the cornstalks provided poles for the beans, and the squashes were planted between the cornhills. The Eastern Indians called these three crops the "sacred sisters."

Maize was diffused northward early, but when beans and squash were also introduced, a balanced ration of starch, protein, and vitamins was provided. These crops made possible the settlement of regions where the hunting was too poor to supply protein food. Their introduction was everywhere followed by an increase in population and a rapid upswing in culture.

Animal husbandry was never important in America because there were few animals worth domesticating. Only the dog and the turkey were domesticated north of Mexico. The turkey was domesticated first in the Southwest, apparently quite as much for its feathers as for its meat. The dog was ubiquitous all through America. He probably accompanied the first migrants from Asia and was the companion of men in all their wanderings on this continent. In the Arctic and on the Plains, dogs were used as transport animals. In some places dogs were eaten. The Coast Salish used dog-hair as wool for blankets. The dogs were strung up by the neck and the hair yanked out. Early travelers reported that Salish dogs were extremely ill-tempered beasts, which is not surprising. In the Andean region the llama and alpaca and the guinea pig were domesticated. The first two were used for transport and for wool; the guinea pig was raised for food.

At the time of the arrival of the whites the first reshuffling of the population under the impact of agriculture had already taken place. Settled life in semi-permanent villages, supported by agriculture, had spread as far north as the crops would support it. A series of regional culture patterns had emerged, linked with particular climatic and environmental areas. The prehistoric peoples north of Mexico can be roughly divided into nine main groups: (1) Eskimo; (2) Barren Ground; (3) Northeast Woodlands; (4) Southeast Woodlands; (5) Plains; (6) Rocky Mountain Plateau; (7) Southwest; (8) California; (9) Northwest Coast; Areas 1, 2, 3, 5, and 9 were predominantly hunting or fishing cultures closely related to the Old World Circumpolar culture. In areas 4, 6, 7, and 8 vegetable food was most important, with incidental dependence on hunting or fishing.

It is impossible to give a detailed account of these areas in this vol-

ESKIMOS

ume. The following descriptions attempt to show the focal points in the
organization of the cultures and the characteristics which set each area
apart from its neighbors.

(1) The Eskimos lived along the Arctic coast from the mouth of
the St. Lawrence to Southern Alaska. Their culture was dominated by
unusually severe climatic conditions, in which the need for food and shelter overshadowed everything else. Lack of shelter in this region led not
merely to discomfort but to extinction. The struggle for existence absorbed the attention of the group so completely that their social organization and religion remained at a low level of complexity. They had no
clans, no formal patterns of government, nor even any clearly defined
tribes. The typical Eskimo settlement consisted of a group of families
bossed rather than ruled by the man who was strongest in both physique
and personality. There was a high degree of sexual laxity, again brought
about by the exigencies of Arctic living. Wife-lending was quite common. For instance, one man might be going up-country for caribou while
another stayed on the coast and fished. If the fisherman's wife was skilled
in preparing caribou skins, while the hunter's wife was not, the two men
would swap wives for the season.

The winter dwelling for the Eastern and Central Eskimos was the
snowhouse, or igloo, which was made from snowblocks fitted together
to form a self-supporting dome. The Western Eskimos used semi-subterranean sod houses. Houses were heated with seal oil lamps, which were
also used for cooking. These lamps heated the igloos so thoroughly that
people ordinarily stripped off their clothing inside the house. In the
summer the people lived in tents of deer or sealskin. Sometimes these
tents were set up inside the igloos in winter to make an air chamber between the tent wall and the snow-wall to prevent the interior heat from
melting the snow.

Religion centered around hunting, about which there were innumerable taboos. If the hunting was bad it was assumed that a taboo had
been violated. The medicine men, called *angekoks,* were called in to discover who was guilty and compel the offender to make public confession. Spiritualistic seances in which the *angekoks* called up the spirits
were held during the long winter nights and days. (See discussion of
Old Circumpolar religion, pp. 153–156.)

The main deity was a goddess called Sedna, who lived at the bottom of the sea. She controlled the sea mammals and the game, and, if
displeased, withheld the animals so that hunting was poor. Once a year
she was called up by the *angekok* in a dance ritual, propitiated, and sent
back to the sea in good humor. The Eskimos were fearful of death and
ghosts. They destroyed or removed any property which had been in

contact with the dead or dying, and usually broke camp and moved to a new location after someone had died.

In spite of this relatively low development of many aspects of the formal culture, the Eskimos were an exceedingly intelligent, self-reliant and aggressive people, who exercised most of their ingenuity in the development of material culture. They always loved gadgets. Wherever they came in contact with Europeans they took to mechanical devices with ease and skill. Between 1870 and 1880 Alaskan Eskimos frequently shipped as donkey-engine men on whalers. An agent in Bering Strait told me that he had once turned a broken watch over to an Eskimo friend. The Eskimo had never seen a watch before, but he took it apart, studied it, tinkered with it, and in a few weeks had it running again. Duncan Strong told of an Eskimo in Labrador who assembled and set up a kerosene stove which had been shipped to the camp in sections and which completely baffled the anthropologists. The Eskimo had never seen such a stove, but he studied the diagram and had it together in record time.

The Eskimos showed extraordinary ingenuity in making all sorts of appliances. They invented the sealing lance, snow goggles, and oil lamps. The Eskimo sledges were better than anything Europeans were able to devise. They were made from numerous pieces of wood, lashed together with rawhide but not joined, so that they were flexible enough to go over rough ice and broken ground without jarring themselves to pieces. The runners were shod with strips of ivory. Oddly enough, the Eskimos never made use of snowshoes or skis. Sledges were drawn by dogs. An ingenious harness was devised for the dog teams. The traces were prevented from tangling by toggles carved from solid ivory, while the pin to which the traces were attached ran through a ring fastened in back so that it could turn freely.

For summer hunting the Eskimos used the kayak, a boat made of walrus skin stretched over a flexibly lashed framework of wood, plus pieces of bone for ribs. These were amazingly ingenious contrivances and made exceedingly good sea boats, except that if they were in the water more than 48 hours they became waterlogged and the hides softened and parted from the ribs. If an Eskimo was caught in a storm and blown out to sea, his kayak was likely to dissolve under him.

In winter they wore tailored skin clothing, usually with the fur left on. Their footgear was an improved moccasin called *mukluks,* which had sole and sidepieces in one section and, except for the rubber boot, are the only form of footgear so far devised which will keep out snow water.

They made some pottery which, while unfired because of the shortage of wood, was adequate for boiling food. They had some crude basketry, but their real skills were concentrated in bone and stone working.

On the long winter nights they carved delightful little figures of men and animals in ivory. They had no metal, but in the late period, when drift iron washed in occasionally, they made good use of it and worked it into knives and axes.

The Eskimos, since they lived in territory which the white men did not covet, have been less affected by white settlement than any other aboriginal group, and in many regions still live much as they did when Columbus landed.

(2) The climate of the Barren Ground, which included interior Canada from Hudson Bay to the Rockies, was almost as severe as that of the Eskimo territory, and the food situation was even more precarious. The people subsisted largely on fresh-water fishing. They also hunted snowshoe rabbits and caribou, which moved in tremendous herds in this Arctic waste, migrating with the seasons. If the hunters succeeded in catching up with a caribou herd they could kill enough meat for several months' supply. If they failed to do this, they had to live on short rations.

This was a highly nomadic culture. In summer they traveled by bark or skin canoe, in winter by snowshoe or toboggan, a strip of bark with forward end curled up. Houses were conical skin tents or lean-to huts.

In spite of the severity of the climate and the poverty of the culture, the social organization was more complicated than that of the Eskimo. They had a genuine band organization, groups who habitually lived and hunted together and who were controlled by chiefs, with a tendency for the chieftainship to become hereditary. Although there were no group religious ceremonies, shamans performed magic rites and healing rituals. The idea of the individual guardian, a supernatural being with whom one could establish personal relations through a dream vision, was important here. By keeping certain taboos and making certain sacrifices to one's guardian, one could secure needed help in hunting and fighting.

(3) The Northeast Woodlands comprised Eastern Canada, extending north to the tundra, and the Eastern United States from the Atlantic to the Great Plains and as far south as Virginia.

The Indians of this region had longer and closer contact with whites than those of any of the other groups. The early colonists would have starved to death if the tribes of the eastern seaboard had not introduced them to local crops and techniques for cultivating them. It was helpful also for the whites that the diseases which the first explorers had brought with them had decimated the villages along the coast to such an extent that abandoned fields and deserted village sites could be taken over by the colonists. If the tribes had been in full strength, settlement would have been much more difficult.

At the time of the discovery this region was populated by a great

variety of tribes, most of which had a loosely organized clan system with
tribal chiefs. The territory in most areas was heavily forested, and non-
migratory game was plentiful, so that hunting was good all year. Most of
the tribes were farmers as well as hunters, although they tended their
fields only at planting and harvest and followed the game at other seasons. One of the striking features of this area was that the Algonkian
tribes, from Labrador to Virginia, had a system of private ownership of
land, which was rare in aboriginal America. Each family had its own
designated hunting and fishing places. If another group wished to hunt
or fish in this territory, they could lease the forest and fishing rights tem-

BULL HEAD WAR CLUB, IROQUOIS

porarily. Land was never sold, however, so that when the whites offered
the Indians payment for their lands, the aborigines thought that they
were paying for hunting rights and became indignant when the whites
tried to take over the lands and drive the Indians away.

The Northeast Woodlands were occupied by so many diverse tribes
that it would be impossible to describe them all. The one which had
most influence on the colonists was the Iroquois. The League of the
Iroquois was a force to be reckoned with in the early days, and its pattern of confederacy may have influenced the formation of the American
confederation of colonies.

Centered in the New York and eastern Great Lakes area, the Iroquois represented a degree of cultural advancement beyond that of their
surrounding Algonkian neighbors. To be sure, they shared many similar
traits of culture with these; yet they were unique in at least two important respects, the extent of their agriculture and their political sophistication. They are interesting to us also because of the role they played as
a political power in our own colonial and revolutionary history.

The principal tribes known to us as Iroquois were the Five Nations
of the League, or the Confederacy. These were, from east to west, the
Mohawk, Oneida, Onandaga, Cayuga, and Seneca, all located in what
is now New York State. Other tribes of the Iroquoian linguistic family,

however, were the Huron and Neutrals, north of Lake Huron and Lake Erie respectively, and the Erie and Conestoga and others in the Ohio and Pennsylvania area. The Hurons were traditional enemies of the Five Nations, and their enmity was reinforced through their coming under the influence of the French at a very early period, while the tribes of the Five Nations fell strongly under British influence.

The Neutrals were so called because, although their territory lay between that of the emergent League of the Iroquois and that of the League's chief enemies, the Huron, neither of the belligerents engaged in war with this small tribe. The Neutrals were able to maintain their neutrality because they held the only good flint quarries in the vicinity and traded flints to both sides. Neither group dared to attack them because they knew that this would bring the other side to the defense of the little tribe and the quarries. The Neutrals occupied a position much like that of Sweden in the late war, until the Iroquois began to acquire firearms and swords from the Dutch and English and no longer needed flints. Then they attacked the Neutrals and conquered them.

In family and social organization the Iroquois were distinct from their Algonkian neighbors, being matrilineally organized, whereas their neighbors were predominantly of patrilineal orientation. The families of a group of sisters, or of cousins related in the female line, lived together in what were known as "long-houses." These were of bark construction, containing a number of compartments for the individual families. In authority over the families in a long-house was the matriarch, the eldest woman of the lineage, often the mother or grandmother of the women heads of the individual families. Such an extended household, or perhaps two or three of such households, constituted a lineage, and one or more of such lineages constituted the matrilineal clan. The number of clans of the Iroquois differed with the tribes, but in all cases the clans cut across several tribes. The clans were exogamous, so that a member of any one clan would not marry one of the same clan, either in his own tribe or in a different tribe. Members of the same clan were regarded as close blood relatives, no matter how near or remote, or indeed, fictitious, the actual relationship may have been. Blood relationship ties outside of one's own matrilineal clan were of less importance and were regarded as dissolved with the passage of a few generations.

In this fashion the matrilineal clans and the tribes furnished a crisscrossing basis of social organization. The tribes were local and linguistic units, living in different parts of the Iroquois area and speaking different languages or dialects, while the clans cut across these and functioned as extended kinship and social solidarity units.

Agriculture was carried on principally by the women under the direction of the matriarch of each lineage or clan. Work parties were organized as bees, announcements being sent out in advance to all the women of a lineage or clan by the matriarch. The work was done co-operatively on jointly held land, and the produce was divided among the member families. The work-bees were often occasions for social good times as well as for labor. This pattern was taken over by the pioneer settlers of the United States. The men's business among the Iroquois was primarily hunting, politics, and warfare, all of which involved extensive travel, leaving the women with the sedentary occupations.

The League of the Iroquois represents an interesting type of political development. Its origin is somewhat obscured by the passage of time and fanciful embroidery in legend, yet the main outlines remain clear. It probably began sometime in the last half of the 15th century or very early in the 16th century, or, as the Iroquois still say, "about three life-spans before the coming of the white man." Its instigators come down to us in legend as Hiawatha (Hayonhwatha) and Deganawida, two visionaries who, after overcoming many obstacles, finally won acceptance for their ideas. The Iroquoian tribes at that time were in a state of feuding and warfare with each other as well as with non-Iroquoian neighbors. The League was to be a League of Peace to abolish warfare. The Onondaga were the most difficult to bring into the League and finally capitulated only with the stipulation that they should hold the highest office in the League.

A political code or constitution was evolved, consisting of articles and laws covering every contingency envisioned by the founders. It was

STONE PIPE, TENNESSEE

passed on by word of mouth until recorded in modern times. It represented an interesting mixture of political sophistication and primitive naiveté. It was envisioned that the League should embrace not only the founding tribes, but that "The Great Peace" should be spread to all surrounding tribes as well so that there could be an end to warfare. Yet the founding tribes were unwilling to give up their political prerogatives within the League, and wished to bring in other tribes only as subordinate to themselves. What began as an instrument to end war, and what was known as "The Great Peace," evolved into an instrument of conquest which became the terror of all surrounding peoples. The following is an example from the Articles of the Constitution which specifies how peace shall be spread to neighboring tribes:

> *When the proposition to establish the Great Peace is made to a foreign nation it shall be done in mutual council. The nation is to be persuaded by reason and urged to come into the Great Peace. If the Five Nations fail . . . after a third council . . . the war captain of the Five Nations shall address the head chief of the rebellious nation and request him three times to accept the Great Peace. If refusal steadfastly follows the war captain shall let a bunch of white lake shells fall from his outstretched hand and shall bound quickly forward and club the offending chief to death. War shall thereby be declared and the war captain shall have his men at his back to support him in any emergency. War shall continue until won by the Five Nations . . . Then shall the Five Nations seek to establish the Great Peace by a conquest of the rebellious nation.*

> *When peace shall have been established by the termination of the war . . . then the war captain shall cause all weapons of war to be taken from the nation. Then shall the Great Peace be established and the nation shall observe all the rules of the Great Peace for all time to come.*

> *Whenever a foreign nation is conquered, their own system of internal government may continue so far as is consistent but they must cease all strife with other nations.[1]*

The men who constituted the original council of the League numbered fifty, and represented several tribes. Their names became the titles of fifty offices. Forty-nine of these have become perpetual offices to be filled by representatives to the council, and they survive to the present day. The fiftieth office, that of Deganawida, was to remain unfilled, since there could never be another worthy of so exalted a name. The offices are hereditary within certain noble matrilineages, but within the noble lineage the particular incumbent is elected by the women of the lineage.

---

[1] Arthur C. Parker: *The Constitution of the Five Nations* (New York State Museum Bulletin, No. 184). Albany, 1916.

In case of poor conduct in office, the women reserve the power to depose or "remove the antlers from" any man whom they have sent as the representative of their clan and tribe to the council. An elaborate ritual was evolved for the conduct of political business, for conducting mourning rites for officers upon their death, and for installation of new officers to replace them.

As happened in other cases in aboriginal history, the outlawing of internal warfare forced intertribal strife into a more civilized form—the ball game. Lacrosse was played with great seriousness by the tribes of the League. It is probably not an accident that confederacies and inter-tribal or inter-town ball games seem to go hand-in-hand in aboriginal America (see below, p. 612). Games were prepared for as war was prepared for: by both training and supernatural means. It is the Iroquoian ball game which is the ancestor of lacrosse as we know it. The Iroquoian game differed from the games of tribes of the Southeast and Midwest in the type of racquet used and in certain other details. The regulation racquet used in this sport today is of the Iroquoian type.

The League of the Iroquois was a political power to be reckoned with by the American colonists and by the British and American governments. At the time of the Revolutionary War a portion of the Iroquois, principally the Oneidas, were persuaded by Reverend Samuel Kirkland, a missionary to the Oneidas, to remain neutral. Most of the remainder, however, sided with the British, knowing full well that they would lose their lands and independence should the colonists be victorious. The power of the League was finally broken when General Sullivan, in 1779, was sent by Washington with orders to eliminate this source of British strength. Sullivan's method was to burn the villages and fields rather than to engage the Iroquois in direct battle. The amount of food destroyed at that time is indicative of the extent of the Iroquoian agriculture. The record of this expedition describes the destruction of 160,000 bushels of corn, together with a vast quantity of vegetables of every kind, as well as innumerable apple trees, of which there were 1500 in one orchard. With their villages and food destroyed, the power of the Iroquois was at an end. Many of them fled to Canada, while others remained to make peace later with the Colonies. From that date to the present, the President of the United States has been known as *Ranadagaryas*, "The Destroyer of the Settlements."

The religion of the Iroquois is also of interest to us. Out of a varied assortment of magical beliefs and practices there evolved, probably in the fairly late prehistoric period, the nucleus of what has become a religion of considerable beauty and dignity. This received further stimulus and new codification by a Seneca prophet known as *Ganyadaiyo*, or "Handsome Lake," during the severe crisis period which followed in

the wake of the American Revolution. In this form it survives to the
present. The principal themes which recur in the ritual of this religion
are the theme of thankfulness to the Creator and to the various members
of the astral and agricultural pantheon for the blessings bestowed by
them, and the theme of affirmation that these blessings and the status
quo should endure forever. In the prayers which were offered at each of
the religious festivals of the ceremonial year, and in fact at any communal gathering, these ideas were reiterated, while "Our Mother the
Earth," "Our Elder Brother the Sun," "Our Grandmother the Moon,"
"Our Grandfathers the Thunderers" and above all the Creator were addressed and thanked. In these prayers the blessings were enumerated,
beginning with those in the sea and those near the surface of the ground,
and then the higher bushes, the trees, the things in the air, and so on
upward.

The Iroquois today live on half a dozen reservations in New York
State, two reservations in lower Ontario, one in Quebec, one in Wis-
consin, and one in Oklahoma. Many have drifted to the cities, and the
Mohawks in particular have become noted for the ease with which they

SHELL GORGET, TENNESSEE

have taken to structural steel work at high altitudes. This latter adaptation to modern conditions is of some interest in view of the fact that an early Colonial historian noted with amazement the absence of fear which the Iroquois had at high altitudes and the abandon with which they would walk the roofbeam of a house or barn in construction.

STONE DISC, MISSISSIPPI

The League of the Iroquois survives both in Canada and in New York State. It is recognized by the United States Government and is the political organ with which they still deal. In Canada, where the Canadian Government has instituted an elective council, it is no longer recognized as the organ of political representation. The League therefore has more or less gone underground there, where it survives primarily with religious rather than political functions.

The Iroquois played an important role in our history. Today, although most of us know little of them, we continue to use the names which they have bestowed upon towns, cities, and countries. Canada is an Iroquoian word meaning "the settlement." Schenectady means "on the other side of the trees." The name, however, was applied by the Iroquois to Albany and not to Schenectady. An extensive pine forest once existed between these two cities. Other names known by any resident of New York State are those of the cities of Canajoharie, "a washed basin," named for a whirlpool in the rocks, and Skaneatales, "long lake." These are only a sample; a map of the state contains many more.

(4) The Southeast Woodlands included the territory of the Southern United States from the Atlantic coast to the edge of the Plains, with the exception of the Seminoles in Southern Florida who had an aberrant culture which will not be discussed in this volume. The Southeast culture is frequently underestimated because it was destroyed early in the historic period, but it was probably the richest and most complex north of Mexico.

The archaic people of this region were seed-gatherers. River mussels were their chief protein food and they left great shell heaps of these undelectable fish behind them, indicating that they lived in one place for considerable periods. There was a gradual emergence of plant agriculture: amaranth, gourds, sunflowers (for seeds), and tobacco. None of these crops was desirable as a staple, but they served to develop techniques of farming, so that, when the corn-beans-squash complex was introduced from Mexico about the beginning of the Christian era, it was taken over rapidly, with the subsequent advance in population and culture which these crops have always brought.

By 1300 A.D. the region had a large and relatively stable population with a high development in all the arts. The people did exceedingly fine stone-working and made pottery in a great variety of forms with painted decoration. They also made many objects of copper. Above all, they were excellent farmers. Accounts of early visitors mention cultivated fields several miles square.

The people lived in houses of timber and stucco: a frame of cypress poles filled with a mixture of clay and Spanish moss, the whole of which was whitewashed. Early visitors also commented on the cleanliness of the towns, not an ordinary characteristic of Indian villages. The towns were usually built around an open square, with a temple pyramid at one end and a council house at the other. Priests officiated constantly in the temples and kept the sacred fire going day and night. Among the Natchez in Mississippi there was a priest-king, descended from the Sun God, reminiscent of the priest-kings of the Old World civilization of the Near East, and the only instance of this office in North America.

The temples were built on huge earth sub-structures which undoubtedly derive from the ceremonial pyramids of Mexico. These people built a retaining wall for the pyramid and then filled it in as the Mexicans did, although they used earth or wood rather than stone. From time to time the mound would be renovated by adding an extra layer; sometimes this was done seven or eight times. The Cahokia mound in East St. Louis, made in this way, is one of the largest primitive structures in the world.

There was an important cult of the dead in this culture and also elaborate group rituals, the most interesting being an annual purification

ceremony called the *busk*. This was held when the young corn was ripe
enough to eat on the ear. At this time all the houses were cleaned and
whitewashed, all debts were paid, and house fires were extinguished
and rekindled from the eternal fire in the temple. Everyone took a ceremonial bath and then danced in the square in new clothes.

The social and political organization in this region was particularly
interesting. The unit was the town. Within the town were a series of
matrilineal clans, each clan occupying its own particular district in the
town and having its special place on the town square when the members
assembled for games and ceremonies. The clans were divided into two
groups, Reds and Whites, with the clans in each group ranked in a
social hierarchy. The leading clan of the Red moiety provided the war

POTTERY JAR, MISSISSIPPI

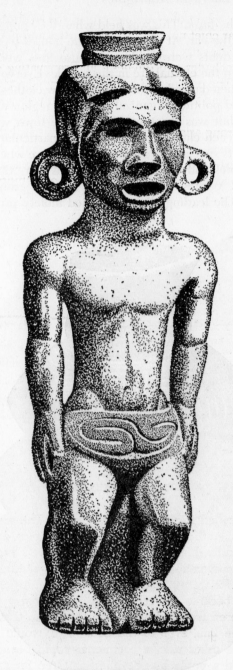

EFFIGY PIPE, HOPEWELL

chief of the village, while the leading clan of the Whites provided the peace chief. The war chief not only led war parties and planned defense, but also organized all sorts of communal activities: landclearing, repairs to fortifications (stockades and ditches), and renovating of the temple and council house. The peace chief was a judiciary who settled disputes, prevented quarrels, and ran the legislature, which was made up of clan chiefs.

There was a strong aristocratic pattern, with a great deal of authority vested in the chiefs. This reached its highest point among the Natchez, who had an extraordinary social system. There was a small, aristocratic group in which there were three grades of nobility and a large

EFFIGY PIPE, HOPEWELL

commoner group, called stinkards by the French. The aristocrats were divided into the Suns (the highest nobility), the nobles, and the honorable persons. An individual from any of these levels had to marry a stinkard. If it were a woman of the Sun group, her children would take her own rank, but if it were a man of the Sun group, his children would drop one step and become nobles. His son would marry an honorable, and the son's children would drop another notch, so that by the third generation the male line, even of the Great Sun, would have become commoners. On the other side, a commoner could become an honorable person or even a noble by providing children for sacrifice at the death of one of the nobles.

There was a high development of human sacrifice in this culture, and prisoner torture as well. When a noble died, the wife or husband, who was a commoner, would be sacrificed and buried with the noble. This was done as painlessly as possible by administering three large balls of ground tobacco by way of anesthetic and then strangling the individual.

The most important political feature of this region was the confederacies. All the so-called tribes in the Southeast were actually confederacies of towns and, as usually happens, the organization of these confederacies was a direct projection of the political organization of the individual towns. The confederacies were divided into Red and White moieties, with all towns ascribed to either one or the other. Town chiefs formed the tribal council, and, again, at the head of the tribe were a war chief from a Red town and a peace chief from a White town.

Rivalry between towns was taken care of by competitive sports, specifically a form of lacrosse played with two sticks and a stitched leather ball. The American confederacies seem to have realized that it was not enough to develop techniques for settling disputes between their component members. Members needed an opportunity to work off their hostilities in harmless action. There is an almost exact correlation in the distribution in America of confederacies and of organized inter-community ball games. Whether these games were the various forms of lacrosse played in the eastern United States or the more elaborate and ceremonial basketball-like games played in Middle America, they had certain features in common. In preparing for them, the magic used by the contenders seems to have been essentially the same as war magic. The winning community gained heavy profits as a result of the wagers placed on their team, or by formalized rights to loot. In the Southeast one might say that the towns waged lacrosse against each other. The inter-town games began with the same sort of ritual which preceded setting out on war parties. If a town was defeated by its antagonist four times running, it had to shift over to the moiety of the winning town; that is, if the defeated town were a White town, it had to become Red.

The Southeastern culture began to decline about the time of the De Soto expedition in 1540. It is probable that new diseases introduced by the whites swept over the Indian settlements with epidemic violence, When the whites actually began to encroach on the territory, the Indians made an attempt to live as farmers among their white neighbors. However, their lands were too prosperous, and when, in 1839, gold was discovered in Georgia, the fate of the Southeast tribes was sealed. In the mad rush for gold the Indians were gathered up and, in violation of all treaties, packed off to Oklahoma. The gold deposits proved to be small and unprofitable, but by the time this fact was discovered, there were no Indian settlements left in the Southeast.

(5) The Great Plains extended from the Woodlands to the Rockies south to the Mexican border and north to the sub-Arctic forests and Barren Ground. This territory in early times was the center for the big game hunters, the Folsom-Yuman culture. Later, the marginal Southeastern people began pushing into the Plains, following along the river valleys. They brought agriculture with them, and, though all the hunting people were not converted to it, they nevertheless became dependent upon it. The hunters roamed the high plains in the summer after game and in the winter retired to the agricultural settlements along the river valleys, or went south to Mexico and lived with the eastern Pueblos.

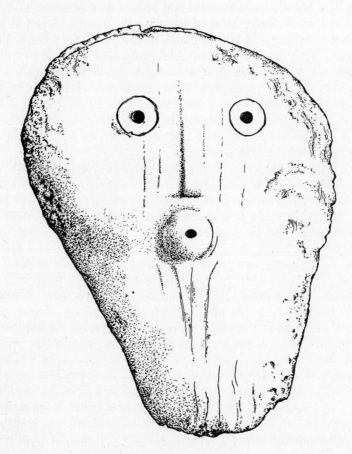

SHELL MASK, TENNESSEE

Along the Missouri drainage there was a curious relationship between the hunting tribes and the agricultural people. Although they were normally at war, a truce was established at the time when the goldenrod was in bloom. The hunting tribes came freely to the villages of the settled tribes, bringing skins and dried meat to trade for corn. At this time the enemies would get together, boast of their fights, and count coup. But as soon as the goldenrod went to seed, the hunters gathered up their share of the trade and went back to the hills, and, from then until next season's goldenrod, the members of the two groups would kill each other on sight.

The river valley people lived in villages surrounded by cornfields, and fortified with ditches and stockades. They built earth lodges, which were large permanent dwellings in which a group of families lived together. The Mandan and Hidatsa had houses 80 feet across and 30 feet high at the smoke hole. Most of the time the people stayed in the villages, but in spring and fall they took to the plains for some hunting of their own. They used light, portable equipment for these expeditions and camped out in conical skin tents. A crude vehicle called a *dog travois* was used for transport. This was a pair of poles which were lashed to the sides of the dog, sometimes with a breast strap and belly band. A netted frame was strung between the poles and baggage of all sorts was lashed to this. The baggage which couldn't be put on the travois was carried by the women.

With the introduction of the horse, things changed rapidly on the Plains. This had been a marginal area, made up of people from the poorer edge of the eastern agricultural area plus a few nomadic hunting tribes. The horse was a new animal on this continent, since the original American horse had become extinct along with the mammoth and the sloth. The first horses were brought here by Cortez, who landed in Tabasco in the spring of 1519 with eighteen mounts. Any of these which survived were undoubtedly eaten by the starving Spaniards. Cortez brought nearly a thousand horses from Spain on his next expedition, and De Soto landed in Florida in 1539 with about a hundred of them.

By the middle of the 1600's there were wild horses working well up in the Plains, probably Spanish escapees from the Southwest. The Plains were an ideal grazing ground, and reproduction was rapid. The Indians went into a state of wild excitement and began to catch or steal horses as their main sport. By the middle of the 1700's practically every Plains Indian had a mount. The coming of the horse made possible for the first time really effective exploitation of the buffalo herds. The combination of a practically unlimited food supply, and a transport animal which made possible the enrichment of a nomadic pattern of life, made the Plains the center of a sort of gold rush, with tribes from all sides tumbling into the region. The settled people, who had been living along the river valley, found that hunting expeditions were more profitable, as well as more fun, than hoeing corn, so that agriculture steadily deteriorated.

The mobile equipment which had been developed on a small scale with dog transport was now expanded, and a new, highly mobile culture characterized by extreme development of war patterns emerged. Tents became large and commodious. The framework was made of four main poles, with about twenty smaller poles arranged in a circle. Over this was stretched a cover of buffalo skins dressed to a gleaming whiteness and decorated with paint and quill work. Twenty hunters could sleep in one tent, ranged around the central fire on their fur robes, with their clothing and weapons dangling from the tent poles.

Nomadic cultures are usually believed to be casual and disorganized. However, the Plains Indian band moved with as much discipline and accuracy as a troop of United States Cavalry. There was a definite pattern of travel. Women, children, and pack animals were put in the center, with the old men as advance and rear guard. The young men rode around the group and acted as a screen of scouts against enemies.

The actual movement and the setting up of camp was taken care of by the women. Horses were packed with the same objects in the same way, so that if a particular awl or a spare pair of moccasins was needed on the way, the women knew exactly where to lay their hands on it without delay. When the group reached the camp site selected by the scouts, the chief of the band rode to the point where his teepee was going to be set up. Then automatically the other families took their positions like squads in a company bivouac. The Plains Indian camp was essentially a village which was lifted up bodily and set down at a distance of twenty or thirty miles with everything in the same order. The wives worked in teams to set up the tepees and unpack the goods. In less than an hour from the time the chief stopped on his spot the tents would be set up and fires kindled.

There were no natural barriers in the Plains, and consequently the tribes were constantly coming into conflict with one another. Also, horses are a most tempting form of loot, since the booty provides its own means of escape. So war and horse-thieving became the great preoccupation of the men of the Plains. The Plains Indians were probably the best individual fighters the world has ever seen. The men were organized into a series of societies much like fraternities, and competed with each other for war honors and in wife stealing, which was a regular pattern of the Plains Indian.

Along with taking war honors went an extreme desire for supernatural help. This was the region of the vision quest. Spirits appeared to the men in dreams or visions, offering them counsel on warfare and hunting. Not just the adolescents fasted for visions; so did the warriors who felt their powers waning and desired to go out to acquire more. The northern tribes indulged in fasting and masochistic practices which would induce the supernatural to take pity on them and give them help. The Shoshonian tribes in the south, however, went to the supernatural beings and demanded powers, if they felt worthy of receiving them. The powers were used by young men, primarily for success in war. The Plains cultures in general had no place for old men. The ideal pattern was that a man would be a great warrior, steal hundreds of horses, have many wives, and then, in full strength, be killed. Good men who had the misfortune to live to old age gave up their former way of life and became gentle, kindly advisors. Bad men, when they were too old to go on war parties, became magicians.

The ritual life of the Plains focused on one great ceremony, the Sun dance. This was a time when all the tribes assembled. They came bringing their provisions, and camped, each band in its regular place, in a great tribal camp circle which sometimes was as much as a mile across. A special Sun dance lodge was erected, a big earth lodge of the type these people had lived in before they became nomadic. An altar was set up, and the various dancers sought power by long-continued dancing and self-torture. Most of the Plains dancing was directed toward putting the individual into a hypnotic state in which he heard voices and saw visions.

These mounted Plains warriors, in their feather war-bonnets, were the Indians who harassed the wagon trains and were immortalized in the boys' adventure stories and Western movies. The Indians of the Plains were the last of the aborigines to be conquered and brought under control by the whites, and they managed to give the United States Cavalry a stiff fight.

(6) The Rocky Mountain Plateau extended from Utah and Colorado north almost to the Canadian line. This was one of the simplest cultures in North America, a direct derivative of the old seed-gathering base. These people had no permanent dwellings. Their houses consisted of a flimsy wooden framework filled with grass and brush. They made no pottery but wove good baskets which they used for everything: storing, carrying and winnowing seeds, and for cooking by the stone boiling method (dropping hot stones into a basket of water). They ground their seeds on soapstone metates. Clothing was minimal, and made of bark. They went barefoot all year, but in winter the men wound their legs with strips of fur while the women contented themselves with hemp leggings.

The social unit was an extended family group of vague content: usually an old couple with adult children and their families. There were no rigid rules of residence in marriage. The newly-weds moved in with whichever set of in-laws had the best food supply in their territory. There were no chiefs and no formal political organization. Such power and control as existed were vested in the old people and the medicine men, who practiced mainly as healers of disease. The religion was char- *Religion* acterized by the vision quest and an extreme fear of ghosts.

(7) The Southwest area included New Mexico and Arizona, extending north into parts of Colorado and Utah. It was distinguished from the Rocky Mountain Plateau more by its richer culture than by its climate. This is one of the most studied and best known areas of the United States archeologically, for the dry climate has preserved perishable materials which have disintegrated in other cultures, and tree-ring dating has made possible more accurate time sequences than are available in other regions. All this tends to make the culture look richer than it actually was.

The earliest people in the Southwest were seed-gatherers and small game hunters, with intrusion of the Folsom-Yuman peoples on the east. This early base divided into two main lines of evolution: in the east

POTTERY JAR, PUEBLO, NEW MEXICO

East
West

were the Basket-Makers, who developed into the Anasazi cultures; on the west were the Cochise, who developed into the Mogollon and Hohokam.

The earliest recognizable sites of the Basket-Maker culture date from about 200 A.D. These people had no pottery but made execellent baskets of the coiled type. They also did twined weaving on a hanging warp without a loom. The open sites suggest that they lived in simple brush shelters much like those of the historic Plateau people. They lacked the bow, but used javelins with spearthrowers in the way their ancestors had for about a thousand years.

Beans
supplemented
meal

About 700 A.D. beans were introduced into the Southwest, with a tremendously stimulating effect on the culture. Corn and squashes were old crops, but the people had to obtain the necessary protein from wild game, which was not plentiful. Consequently, when beans came in and provided a good supply of protein food, the ceiling on population was lifted. For the next 200 years the Southwestern Indians went through a rapid development of culture. In 700 A.D. they were simple village-dwellers living in semi-subterranean pit-houses or caves, with scanty

POTTERY BOWL, HOHOKAM

agriculture and very little equipment of any kind. Within 200 years
they were building permanent houses above ground of timber and
adobe; the bow and arrow supplanted the *atlatl;* and they developed
great skill in all the arts, particularly pottery and weaving. They spread
out and increased their territory, and also traded over long distances.

later

The high period of Anasazi culture was 1050 to 1300. This was
the time when the great communal structures and cliff dwellings were
built. One of the largest of these "apartment" houses was Pueblo Bonito,
which was started in 919 A.D. but not completed until 1067 or later. It
covered three acres of ground, and it is estimated that it could have
housed 1200 people. These pueblos were built around a central court.
The outer walls were sheer and windowless, making an impregnable fort
against enemies without siege machinery. The main building was on three
sides of the court and was terraced back from a one-story level in front
to four stories in the rear. The outer rooms were living quarters, while
the inside, unlighted rooms were used for storage. In the central plaza
were the *kivas.* These were subterranean rooms built much like the old
pit-houses but used for religious ceremonies and clubhouses for the
men. Religion traditionally clings to old forms, so the pit-house was retained as a kiva long after it had been abandoned as a dwelling house.
The cliff dwellings were really villages built in great high caves protected by massive sandstone overhangs, which provided excellent shelter
and a natural defense against enemies. The Cliff Palace at Mesa Verde
had 200 rooms and 23 kivas.

Community living had a far-reaching effect on the Pueblos. A small
family group living alone must produce for itself anything it uses, but
in these unit-houses there was an immediate trend toward specialization.
The person skilled at a particular craft concentrated on that, played with
his techniques and developed new forms, and exchanged his work with
other specialists. The elaborate ritual life which has become the outstanding feature of Southwestern culture began to develop at this time.
Kivas were enlarged, faced with stone work, and decorated with sacred
paintings. Ceremonials became more and more elaborate.

Specialization
due to
group living

The decline of this great period was probably brought about by a
combination of drought and soil exhaustion. We know that there was a
dry period between 1276 and 1299. Also, while desert soils are rich, they
are not inexhaustible. In this region the fields had produced well for
such a long period that the people had become anchored to the territory
by permanent structures and such elaborate equipment that they had
ceased to have mobility, and clung to their fields long after production
had dwindled. At any rate, this high culture seems to have collapsed
after 1300. The cliff dwellings and great pueblos were abandoned. The
survivors apparently moved southward.

The retreat may have been speeded up by the arrival of the ancestors of the Navajo Indians, a Nadene-speaking people who were pushing
down from the north. The present Pueblo peoples speak languages of
several different linguistic stocks, which suggests that there were repeated invasions into their territory by simpler out-lying tribes who later
took on their patterns and were absorbed. The Pueblos retreated to
what is their present territory, where they survive as the Hopi and Zuni
to the west, and in the east are scattered along the Rio Grande.

The Pueblos had a strong clan organization which was usually
matrilineal. Each clan had its own quarter of the village and its own
kiva. Political control was in the hands of the elders, with two functionaries, a war chief who organized war parties and directed the activities
of the young men, and a *cacique* (a term taken over from the Spanish).
Nowadays the war chief takes care of practical matters, repairs of public
buildings, and organization of ceremonies, while the cacique is so holy
that he stays completely in the background.

Religion centered around rain and crops. The sun and the corn
maidens were the main deities, but there were innumerable lesser gods
representing classes of beings rather than individuals. The dancers at
rituals wore masks designed to represent these spirits, or *Kachinas,* as
they are called. Kachina dolls were made for the children as playthings,
but were also used to acquaint the young with the attributes of the numerous spirits.

The year was divided into two seasons: the winter season when the
gods were believed to be in the pueblo, and the summer season when
the gods retreated to the mountains. At the change of season, in the fall,

PAINTING, NORTHERN ARIZONA

the gods returned with much ceremony. The men of the village, masked and dressed to impersonate the gods, came into the village, danced, and then went into the kivas. In due course they emerged as men again, so that it was apparent that the gods were still in the kiva. The entire win-

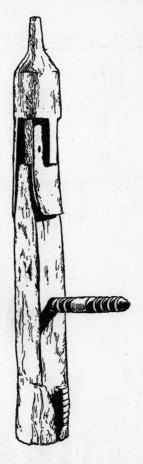

WAR GOD, ZUNI

ter was devoted to a round of ceremonies, in which the gods passed from kiva to kiva.

The Navajo were a Nadene-speaking people who originally lived in the Rocky Mountain Plateau as a nomadic hunting group. Between 1200 and 1300 A.D. they began to drift southward, attracted by the prosperity and high culture of the Pueblos. They settled in southern Colorado and northern New Mexico and took over most of the arts of their neighbors, agriculture, pottery making, and weaving, and also borrowed

KACHINA, HOPI

used and even art, they began to learn something and strive to live, the men
set the such habit coming of the Inca so they... was settled in southern Colo-
rado and northern New Mexico and took up almost all the parts of all the
dwellings, agriculture, pottery making, and weaving, and also borrowed

a good deal of ceremonial paraphernalia. However, they preferred the individual house and never built communal structures in Pueblo style. After the Spanish introduced sheep they became heavily pastoral, as they still are. They had never been enthusiastic agriculturalists. The Navajo word for corn literally means "enemy food," which is evidence that they got it first from the Pueblos, with whom they fought. Also, since they took over the lands which were already worn out, they never got beyond cultivating small patches near their settlements.

All during the time of the Spanish occupation of the Southwest, from the middle 1600's through the Mexican War, the Navajo made trouble for the Pueblos to the south, who were not as good fighters as they. They made raids at harvest time, ran off flocks, and kidnapped women and children. These depredations brought them into sharp conflict with the American forces after the Mexican War. In 1863 Colonel "Kit" Carson invaded their territory, and finally subdued them by killing off so many of their sheep that the people had no means of support. The Navajo were rounded up and carried off into captivity until 1867.

Being realistic, like most of the Nadene people, they settled down after their defeat, herded sheep, and developed their arts and crafts. They raised blanket-making to a fine art and also took up the craft of silver-working, which they learned from Mexican captives. The elimination of war, the development of pastoral resources, and the money income from blankets and silver left the Navajo with a certain amount of spare time, which was taken up by a progressive development of ceremonialism. These ceremonies were directed, not toward crops, as the Pueblo ceremonies were, but toward healing. They became a society of hypochondriacs. If a Navajo felt sick, his whole kin group would chip in to get him a magical cure. To accomplish this healing, the medicine man made, first of all, an elaborate design on the ground by dribbling colored sand between the palms of his hands. Designs were colorful and intricate and based on mythological references. The individual to be healed was placed on the design and an endless series of songs were sung, in the course of which the design was destroyed, point by point.

The Navajo have been successful in maintaining their tribal identity and in resisting white control of their culture. This resulted largely, of course, from the fact that their territory is too poor to be coveted by whites. They have bred tremendously. At a recent count there were 50,000 of them, as opposed to 7,300 in 1867. However, at the present time they have overbred their resources and are on the verge of starvation.

The early Cochise culture in Arizona split off into two distinct lines because of climate differences in the region. The people who settled in the western part of the state, which is desert country, became the Hohokam, while in the eastern plateau, which had a high altitude and more rainfall, lived the Mogollon. The two groups, originally of the same stock, evolved two quite different patterns of life.

The beginnings of Hohokam culture can be traced to about 300 B.C., at which time they were already using pottery and the bow, raising corn, and living in pit-houses. The archeological record for the Hohokam is less complete than for the Anasazi cultures because they lived in open settlements and because they practiced cremation.

In this dry territory any sort of large-scale agriculture was impossible without regular irrigation. Therefore, this region became the only place in North America where systematic irrigation was practiced. By 700 A.D. the Hohokam had devised a system of irrigation ditches which they continued to enlarge and improve up to 1400. Canals were as much as thirty feet wide and ten feet deep, and covered an aggregate length of 150 miles. When one considers that this engineering feat was accomplished by a people with only crude stone and wooden tools, it is truly remarkable. There must have been some centralized authority who directed the work, since it served many settlements. The canals had to be continually serviced, as they were constantly silting up and requiring additional labor.

Between 600 and 900 there was a strong Mexican influence in this territory. This brought an unusual development of carving in stone, bone, and shell. Cotton was introduced from the south, as were ball courts, in which a game somewhat like basketball was played in Mexican fashion with a rubber ball.

Somewhere between 1100 and 1400 there was an invasion of the region by what is known as the Salado culture, which had strong Anasazi influence. Instead of fighting it out, these two people settled down amicably and lived together, with very little diffusion of culture, however. Archeological evidence shows the houses and pottery of the two distinct groups existing in the same settlements at the same time. This is puzzling and most unusual, but some clue may be found in the existence of the ball courts for intergroup sports which, as has been pointed out, served as a technique for working off hostility and as a safety valve to prevent wars. Also, the cooperation needed to build and maintain the irrigation system would be impossible in a group which indulged in inter-tribal warfare. It may also be that the Hohokam were ferocious enough, when they did fight, to discourage attack. They were the ancestors of the modern Pima, Yuma, and Papago, famous fighters who defended their territory against the warlike Apache as well as against the whites.

The territory of the Mogollon had just enough rainfall so that it was possible to raise corn without irrigation. Lacking the incentive which spurred the Hohokam to inter-tribal cooperation and industry, the Mogollon scraped by in meager fashion doing little to develop their semi-arid land. Their chief craft was pottery-making, the so-called *Mimbres* wares of the Mogollon being among the best of the Southwestern styles. These prehistoric peoples were eventually absorbed by the Anasazi. In historic times their territory was occupied by wandering groups of Nadene Apache. (The name Mogollon derives from the Mogollon Mountains, which in turn were named for Juan Ignacio Flores Mogollon, an early governor of New Mexico.)

(8) The California area extended from the Rockies to the Pacific Coast, and north roughly to what is now the California border. It was a region in which the old seed-gathering, small game-hunting culture was given an opportunity to reach the limit of its basic potentialities, as the region was geographically isolated by mountain and desert. The fine climate apparently discouraged initiative. The California Indians had no

POTTERY BOWL, MIMBRES

agriculture, no pottery, and no weaving. They hunted small game and, if they were near the coast, fished, but their main staple was acorns. These nuts are bitter, since they contain tannic acid, and are usually considered inedible, but the Indians pounded the hulled nuts into a coarse meal which they piled into a hole scooped in the sand. Over this they poured hot water which leached out the acid and left a tasteless but nutritious meal, from which acorn mush was made.

The Channel Island group made a peculiar kind of plank canoe, but elsewhere, when the Californians took to the water, it was on a sort of raft called a *balsa,* a cigar-shaped bundle of reeds wrapped with bajuna vines, on which they rode astride much as modern vacationers at California beaches ride rubber animals.

Clothing was minimal, and houses were flimsy affairs made of a light framework of sticks covered with thatch or bark. However, each village had one well-built house, the dance house. This was a semi-subterranean circular lodge, apparently a descendant of the pit-house. It was entered through a smokehole or side tunnel and served as a men's clubhouse and ceremonial center. On the occasional frosty nights the whole village used it as a dormitory. They would build a fire in the middle of the floor, keep it roaring until the place was thoroughly heated, then put out the fire, close the smokehole, and bed down for the night. If they had headaches in the morning, they attributed them to the work of evil spirits.

Arts and crafts were at a low mark, with the exception of basketry, in which these people excelled. Apparently they expended all their aesthetic cravings on this one art. The Hupa made a globular basket with bird feathers caught into the weaving, so that the entire basket was covered with a thick, velvet-like nap of vari-colored iridescent feathers. Ceremonial robes were also made from soft feathers fastened to a netted base, somewhat suggestive of Polynesian feather cloaks.

In social organization, the pattern was that of small tribes. The largest political unit was the village, usually a unilateral kin group. There were neither chiefs nor councils. However, there was an extensive trade and exchange of baskets, shells, and deer skins. In northern California trade became so extensive that a regular currency was developed, based on dentalium shells which were fished from the Puget Sound area and traded over the region.

The tribes were exceedingly localized and spoke a diversity of languages, each valley having its own dialect. California was a sort of cultural *cul de sac* into which small groups drifted, settled down, and lost all memory of where they had come from. It became a mosaic of tribes which stayed self-contained in their own territory. The Californians had an elaborate creation myth, but each tribe believed that the world had been created in its own territory. Each tribesman could stand in the center of his own valley and point out to his children where the Creator had made everything, point by point. Each tribe regarded its own territory as the center of the world and had little desire to wander outside of it.

When the Creator had finished making the world and everything in it, the animals turned upon him and killed him. He became a dead deity, a literary figure who did not require placation or prayer. Religious attention could therefore be devoted to the more immediate spirits who controlled hunting and good luck of one sort and another. Featured in most of the stories and legends of this region is Coyote, the trickster, who held the place in California folklore that Brer Rabbit does in the

Belief

Storytelling

WOODEN RATTLE, HAIDA

IVORY "SOUL CATCHER"

Uncle Remus stories: he was the wily, clever one who always got the best of the deal.

Boys were initiated into manhood in a series of elaborately costumed ceremonies. The bull roarer was an important part of this ritual, one of the few instances in which this instrument appears in North America. Sorcery was important here and was used for social control, particularly in trading patterns. The threat of malevolent magic was an effective spur to delinquent debtors.

Funerals, among those families who could afford to honor their dead, were fairly elaborate. The body was exhumed for the formal ceremony, which took place when the family had collected enough surplus for the event. A scaffold was set up and the body or bodies placed upon it. Then the framework would be hung with as many baskets, blankets, and ornaments as the family had been able to assemble. The fire was then kindled and everything went up in smoke, an example of ostentatious waste reminiscent of Northwest Coast *potlatches.*

(9) The Northwest Coast area extended along the British Columbian coast from Northern California to Southern Alaska. Although it was well to the north, the warm Japanese current gave it a mild climate and the heavy rainfall produced a temperate jungle of hemlock, spruce, and cedar. This region was unique in that it is the only place in the world which produced a really high culture without the development of either agriculture or domestic animal husbandry. This was made possible by the abundant food supply. Salmon ran in the many streams in the spring; the sea teemed with halibut, cod, and herring; elk, deer, and bear roamed the forests, and the forest undergrowth was rich in berries and edible greens. These people had no need to undertake the laborious work of clearing and planting.

They made no pottery, for wood was so plentiful that it was used for everything. They even cooked in wooden boxes by the stone boiling method. They were expert wood carvers, and both their utensils and their ceremonial objects were of high aesthetic quality. Their wood carving achieved its most spectacular display in the huge totem poles which are characteristic of this culture. They made baskets and also wove on the true loom, using shredded cedar bark sometimes mixed with mountain goat wool or even dog hair. Clothing was simple. They wore robes and capes but no foot gear. In rainy weather, which was about half the time in that country, they donned broad rain hats woven of straw, the only aborigines to use hats except as ceremonial headdress.

Houses were large wooden rectangular structures made by fastening split plants to a framework of upright posts. In the north the planks were put on vertically and the roof was gabled. In the south they built with horizontal planks and a shed roof. The houses were large and were occupied by several families of the same lineage: the house chief and his unmarried children, his daughters and their husbands and children, perhaps a younger brother or nephew and his family, and usually a few odd relatives and a slave or two. One of the largest of the prehistoric Kwakiutl houses was 520 feet long and 60 feet wide. The main house posts, and sometimes the corner posts, were elaborately carved in heraldic designs which embodied the family history and the crest of the lineage. These totem pole house posts were often as much as 60 feet

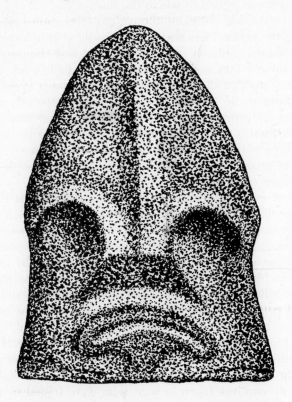

PECKED STONE PILE DRIVER, KWAKIUTL

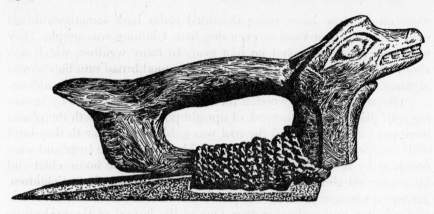

HAND ADZE, KWAKIUTL

high, rising well above the roof. Single totem poles were set up also, often as grave posts which told in narrative symbolism the history of the family or some legend to which the lineage had special rights.

Villages were laid out along the water's edge, with houses, one row deep, facing the water. Piers and canoe runs were built along the beach. During the summer salmon runs, the hunting, and the harvest seasons, the village moved into encampments close to their work, where they lived in flimsy wooden shacks and labored from dawn to dark. The men fished and hunted; the women dried and smoked the fish and meat on racks built in the camps. Women and children picked berries and dried them for winter. By the time the cold weather arrived, the storerooms were piled high with wooden boxes stuffed with food, some dried, some put down in grease. With provisions assured, the people could turn their energies to other matters.

The most extreme manifestation of this culture was the *potlatch*. This was an elaborately staged competitive feast at which wealth was ceremonially displayed, distributed, and frequently destroyed as a symbol of conspicuous waste. This was a society of distinct social gradation, and the only way to achieve power and prestige was by giving a potlatch. House chiefs who had given potlatches were the nobles of the village. The village was the chief political unit, organized along clan lines. Social prestige was not fixed, however, and had to be constantly maintained. The commoners attached to the household of a noble worked for him in order to raise the status of their household. If any one of them could acquire enough wealth to give a potlatch of his own, he could rise to noble status. At the bottom of the social scale were the slaves, usually captives taken in war, who were forced to work in the chief's household until they were ransomed by their own people.

The potlatch undoubtedly originated in a ceremony designed to attract labor for the extensive task of building the great houses and erecting totem poles. Later, however, it became a form of competition and a means of establishing the position of groups in the tribal hierarchy. Although there was some inter-tribal warfare and considerable plundering, the potlatch drew off inter-village rivalry and served as a substitute for war. A chief would invite the chief of a group, with whom he was competing, to a potlatch feast. The guest arrived with all his followers and his household, and they were feasted and entertained at a ceremony which went on for days or weeks. Gifts were distributed according to rank in an elaborate ritual. In the early days gifts consisted of blankets, carved bowls and boxes, goat horn spoons, and even slaves. After contact with the whites, wash boilers, sewing machines, phonographs, and such things were included among the gifts. In addition to such real property, these people also recognized another kind of property. Special rights to certain songs and dances, religious society memberships, and crests could be sold, pawned, or given away at a potlatch.

In addition to the gifts, property was destroyed. The host would tell his servants to build up the fire, and they would break up a canoe and use it for firewood, pile on blankets, and pour on fish oil, a prized commodity in this group, to make the fire blaze up. The guests were

PAINTED MASK, KWAKIUTL

not supposed to move back from the fire and frequently singed their clothing at these displays. The chief who was the recipient of all this had to accept everything with no show of emotion, but he and his household slipped down in the social scale until he could give a return potlatch at which he offered his rival as much as he had received plus 100 per cent interest. If he could make it more than 100 per cent he could really shame his competitor, who went way down in the social scale after such an insult.

The financing of these competitive orgies required the establishment of loans and interest rates. In a society which had no mechanized economy and no form of investment except loans and gifts, the potlatch pattern resulted in an inflation of credit in which the outstanding property of a single individual might exceed the total wealth of the tribe. In order to keep the system working, a sort of banknote, called copper, was devised. This was a copper plate which started out with a normal value of from ten to twenty dollars, depending on how good a piece it was. Each time it was used in a gift exchange, however, it increased in value 100 per cent—soaked up credit, so to speak, until there were certain coppers which were worth as much as $15,000. Thus the potlatch became a form of investment, with cycles of giving and receiving and with interest mounting and social prestige going up and down.

PAINTED MASK, KWAKIUTL

Credit was stable, however, as the social status of the borrower was at stake and this was a culture in which one's social standing was of supreme importance.

It may appear that the long occupancy of the Indian tribes had left little imprint on the present culture of North America, which is predominantly North European in origin. With the exception of many local crops, most of which have now been incorporated into world agriculture, and the sharing of knowledge of techniques for dealing with a new territory which the aborigines offered the early settlers, the Indian population appears to have made little contribution in the north. However, it may be significant that the pattern of confederacy which was widespread on the North American continent has rarely emerged elsewhere. Confederacies, as opposed to empires, are characterized by the importance attached to individual initiative and freedom of choice. It is at least interesting to speculate that the establishment of the confederacy which became the United States of America may have had its roots in aboriginal patterns, and that the tradition of democracy and individual freedom flourished with special vigor in the land which the proud and independent Indian had prepared for us.

Chapter XLI

High Cultures of the South

THE HIGH CIVILIZATIONS of the New World all arose south of the Rio Grande. Although all the Indian migrants came from the north, the northern tribes never became civilized in the strict sense of the word, which implies the ability to build and live in cities. Even the Indians of the Southeast and Southwest, who achieved the highest culture, remained villagers and farmers.

The region below the Rio Grande must have been settled several thousand years later than the north, for it would have taken the migrants that long to make their way southward, generation by generation. The reason the southern people outdistanced those of the north was that they acquired, early in their settlement of the region, a basic crop upon which a large population could be built. Corn (maize), the great American staple, was domesticated first in this region. Some authorities hold that the wild plant (of which no trace has ever been found) came from the highlands of Guatemala; others make a case for its development on the plains of Paraguay. In either case, it was a southern plant. Beans, peppers, potatoes, tomatoes, peanuts, and other important food crops were also domesticated first in the south and diffused later to the northern groups.

The high cultures of the south succumbed inevitably to the Spaniards, for the assumptions of European superiority had a sound basis in European military power. The rapid and overwhelming victories of the Conquistadores may be summed up in Hillaire Belloc's couplet:

> *Whatever happens we have got*
> *The Maxim gun and they have not.*

However, these cultures were too populous and too brilliant to be completely absorbed or contained by a foreign power. In all Latin America, culture complexes are arising which are not European in pattern. The

old Indian cultures, as well as the old Indian physical type, are reas-
serting themselves throughout the highland regions from Mexico south.

In Mexico two types of cultures arose in early times: the plateau
cultures of the Valley of Mexico and the lowland cultures along the
coast in Central America. Although a continuous series of cultures
emerged in the South, this volume will touch only on the three outstanding ones: the Mayan civilization, which was the most splendid outgrowth of the lowland area; the Aztec civilization, which was the high
point of the plateau culture; and the great civilization of the Incas,
which flourished on the west coast of South America at the time of the
Conquest. These three cultures represented quite different ways of life
and lay so far apart that they were scarcely aware of each other's existence, although much of the learning of the Mayas was diffused into the
Aztec culture.

The ancient Mayas occupied what are now the states of Yucatan,
Campeche, British Honduras, and most of Guatemala, a territory of some
125,000 square miles. They were isolated from the rest of the Mexican
Peninsula, being surrounded on three sides by water (the Mexicans

PORPHYRY MASK, MAYA

SCULPTURED MARBLE VASE, MAYA

were never navigators) and on the fourth by the lofty Cordillera Mountains. The unique civilization of the Mayas was developed without influence from outside sources and was due to the native genius of the Mayan peoples and the rich and fertile environment in which they were fortunate enough to live.

The economy of the civilization was based upon maize, but the region was also rich in everything needed for a high civilization. Beans, squash, chili, tomatoes, sweet potatoes, cacao, alligator pears, and tobacco were raised in addition to maize. Food was seasoned with vanilla and allspice. Cotton was woven into cloth and gourds were used for utensils. The forest provided a variety of fine woods, and the local limestone was one of the finest building materials in pre-Columbian America. It was easily quarried, hardened on exposure, and turned into lime when burned. There were also, throughout the region, beds of gravel which made a natural lime cement. All the materials for a durable stone and mortar masonry were at hand, and the Maya developed a unique stone architecture which was the finest, at least from an aesthetic standpoint, in the New World. Although they never discovered the use of the keystone arch, they built fabulous structures using the corbeled stone roof-vaults. The great ceremonial centers such as Chichen Itza, Uxmal, and Peten are of breathtaking beauty even in their ruined state.

Mayan sculpture ranks among the great art of all time. The Mayan temples are a maze of delicate and intricate carving depicting gods with their attributes, religious rituals, and kingly triumphs, as well as stylized birds, flowers, and serpents. The Old Empire city of Palenque was probably the early center for this amazingly beautiful craft, as much of the sculpture and moulded stucco work found there dates back to the middle of the 7th century. The great limestone cover of the sarcophagus discovered in 1952 in the Temple of Inscriptions at Palenque compares with the finest of the low-relief sculptures of ancient Egypt.

At the time of the Conquest, Mayan civilization was in a state of decline. The people were living in villages or in the shells of their great cities. Old Empire cities such as Palenque had been long deserted and lost in the teeming jungle growth. It was not until early in the 19th century that archeologists cleared the brush from the crumbling beauty of the long dead cities and discovered how great this civilization had been.

The Mayas were not only the finest sculptors and architects of the New World; they were also the greatest scientists and the group who came closest to developing a consistent system of writing. The Mayas employed an ideographic writing in which characters or signs were used

STONE BALL COURT MARKER, HONDURAS

as conventionalized symbols for ideas. Although the Mayan civilization
was in decline at the time of the Conquest, scientific knowledge and the
art of writing survived in the priesthood and the ruling class and were
still going forward. If they had had more time they would undoubtedly
have developed a more flexible and expressive system of writing. However, as their first act of occupation, the Spanish Conquistadores made
a point of stamping out learning and its bearers, so that the small group
of intellectuals who carried this knowledge was promptly eliminated
after the Conquest. Diego de Landa, archbishop of Yucatan, in 1562 collected and burned in the plaza at Merida hundreds of books of history,

RECUMBENT ANTHROPOMORPH, MEXICO

astronomy, and mathematics. The only volumes which survived were a
few which were sent back to Europe as curiosities. From these, scholars,
after years of study, eventually deciphered the graphic system of Mayan
writing.

The Dresden Codex, the most important of the surviving books, is
a mathematical and astronomical treatise in which the periods of revolution of the various planets, and the times of eclipses, lunar and solar,
have been worked out in a sort of long-range almanac. These calculations demonstrate that the Mayas at the time of the Conquest were
vastly better astronomers than any in Europe and as competent mathematicians. They had also devised a cumbersome but extraordinarily accurate calendar in which, by using several different systems of notation

simultaneously, they could place any date exactly within the period of the Calendar Round, which covered 52 years of 365 days each, or 18,980 days. The Aztecs, Mixtecs, and Zapotecs, who borrowed their respective calendars from the Mayas, made use of these 52 × 365 day-periods, which the Aztec called the "year bundle." However, they were never able to calculate beyond this 52-year cycle and achieve long-range dating as the Mayas did. The Mayas, as is shown by the inscriptions on the monuments, were aware of the exact length of the solar year. They were thus capable of extended calculations in which the position of a certain day could be worked out from their initial starting point.

Unfortunately for the Mayas, intellectual and aesthetic development were not linked with correspondingly high achievements in political and military science. However, the collapse of the Old Empire, which occurred during the 9th century, was due less to foreign aggression than to internal economic causes. The culture had concentrated on the arts and sciences to such a degree that these aspects had become over-elaborated, while the economic and agricultural system was neglected and finally became unable to provide for the increasing needs of a growing population. In the 12th century the Empire was invaded by wandering groups of Toltec people who, under the impact of the expanding Aztec Empire, forced their way south into Mayan territory. They came first as mercenaries, much as the Goths penetrated the Roman Empire.

The weakened Empire succumbed to the invaders, but the foreign conquerors who remained in the region were absorbed by the superior culture. About 1000 there was a renaissance of Mayan culture and from that time until 1400 the New Empire flourished, centered chiefly in the Yucatan. During this period the great cities of Chichen Itza and Uxmal were built. These were ceremonial centers and not cities in the Old World sense. However, the Mayas were never able to achieve a strong centralized government. Their Empire was never a united kingdom, but rather a group of cities ruled by its own hereditary line of priest-kings. They formed a few short-lived and loosely organized confederacies. This ancient civilization had fallen into decline long before the Spaniards arrived.

The Aztecs, who occupied the valley of Mexico when Cortez arrived in 1519, were themselves new to civilization. They were a Nahuan tribe who settled on a marshy island in Lake Texcoco in the 13th century and established the city of Tenochtitlan, the site of the present city of Mexico. Because of their inhospitable and inaccessible location, they were protected from invasion and their civilization gradually advanced in population and culture. Under their fourth king, Itzcoatl (1427–1440), they formed an alliance with two other city states, Texcoco and

AZTEC POTTERY DESIGN

Tlacopan. This tripartite confederacy warred against the other Nahuan peoples and expanded until it had established an empire which extended from coast to coast and dominated most of central Mexico.

The Aztec Empire was a plunder empire much like that of Assyria in the Old World. Its rulers achieved wealth and power from loot and tribute, but did little to organize or assimilate the subject tribes. Since the Aztecs lived by war it was natural for them to build a strong military system. All able-bodied men were trained for war and liable to military service. Wars were frequent but not ordinarily of long duration. The principal Aztec weapons were heavy javelins thrown with a spear thrower, bows and arrows, and wooden swords, along the edge of which sharp flakes of obsidian were inserted. It is reported that an Aztec warrior could pierce Spanish armor with a javelin thrust and decapitate a horse with his wooden sword. The common soldier fought naked except for a loin cloth, but war leaders wore corselets of quilted cotton soaked in brine to make them resistant, and helmets carved of wood in animal likenesses. Great lords went to battle wearing cuirasses of gold plates,

THALOC, GOD OF RAIN, AZTEC

over which were draped colorful mantles of featherwork. Battles were more ceremonial than bloody, since the object was to capture the foe, not to kill him. A warrior did not receive acclaim for killing men in battle. The coveted military honors of knighthood went to those who brought captives back to the capital to be sacrificed on the altars of the gods. Huitzilopochtli, the God of War, was the highest deity in the pantheon. To keep him strong so that he would make his followers victorious in battle, it was necessary to offer the hearts of many military captives, and the higher in rank the victim was, the greater the power the god received. The necessity for sacrificial victims led to war, and war led to sacrifice, in an ever-extending cycle.

Tenochtitlan at the time of the Conquest was a large and beautiful city built on islands in Lake Texcoco. Socially and governmentally it was a typically Indian tribal town, but its size and wealth gave it the

QUETZALCOATL, GOD OF LEARNING, AZTEC

aspect of a capital city of a great empire. The city had few streets, but was crisscrossed by canals with portable bridges. Along the edges of the island were the "floating gardens" diligently cultivated by the peasants, who paddled their produce to town in tiny dugouts. The houses of the aristocrats were one-story dwellings built around a courtyard bright with flowers and shrubbery. On pyramids high above the city rose the great temples, before which were the plazas where the thrilled populace gathered for the bloody rituals of sacrifice performed on the temple steps. The society was aristocratic, and the life of the upper classes was luxurious and elaborate. The political base was the exogamous clan; a group of clans comprised the tribe. The tribal council, which was the chief governing body, was made up of representatives from each tribe chosen on a basis of merit.

The judiciary was well-developed, and crime was rigorously punished. Anti-social acts, graft, venality in office, and drunkenness, except among the old who had retired from active life, were serious offenses. Theft might have been a simple matter in this wealthy society where doors were never locked, if it had not been regarded as an unforgivable offense which carried the death penalty when detected. The state took care of the people and no one had to steal because of hunger. Corn patches were planted along the roadside for the use of the needy. In case of famine military campaigns were inaugurated so that additional supplies could be exacted as tribute and distributed to the people. The Aztecs also had a unique institution of voluntary slavery which acted as a sort of poor relief.

TEXTILE DESIGNS, AZTEC

There were several different types of slavery in Aztec society. Military captives were sometimes enslaved, but for the most part they were dedicated to the sacrificial knife of the priests. Poor families, if they had more children than they could conveniently support, sometimes sold a child or two into slavery. Criminals, instead of being imprisoned, were sentenced to serve as slaves for a given length of time. They were usually handed over to the person against whom their offense was committed, for justice here was based on restitution to the injured individual rather than revenge on the wrong-doer. There was also the system of voluntary slavery. A landless man who was unable to support himself could give himself away as a slave so that he would be taken care of. Profligates who had dissipated their means by high living or gambling could become slaves until they could recoup their fortunes. Handsome young women from poor families would sometimes go into voluntary slavery for a time in order to accumulate the finery necessary to set themselves up as prostitutes. Slavery was not too exacting. A slave could marry, control his family, and own and accumulate property. There were

TEXTILE DESIGNS, AZTEC

even slaves who had slaves of their own. Children born in slavery were free. No one who had been a slave was eligible for tribal office but, with this exception, voluntary slavery was not a great social disgrace.

Children were educated at home by the parents. At fifteen, boys were sent to a school maintained by the clan, called a "house of youth." There they were grounded in citizenship, war, history, and religious observances. The important temples also conducted schools called *calmecacs* for training in priestcraft. Parents frequently presented their sons to the calmecac in infancy. The training was rigorous and complicated. Boys were taught writing, a hieroglyphic system like that of the Mayas and used primarily for law and business records. They were also required to memorize the long series of mnemonic chants in which the mythology and literature of the Aztec religion were preserved. Those who continued in the school and went into the priesthood were also initiated into the organization of the pageantry and ritual of the religious ceremonies. Fasting and self-torture were also a part of this regime. The highest offices in the temples were awarded to those who had distinguished themselves in the calmecac schools.

The Spaniards justified the conquest and looting of the Aztec Empire by insisting it was their Christian duty to wipe out the leaders of a heathen nation which sacrificed men to its vile gods. To the Aztecs, the sacrifices were an expression of true religious feeling. The gods required to be strengthened, and nothing was more nutritive than the human heart, which the priest offered the god, still dripping from the body on the stone altars. The victims suffered none of the torture and humiliation which the Spanish Inquisition was meting out to heretics at this time. Many of the captives who were dedicated to the gods were treated

POTTERY DESIGN, CHICHIMEC, PRE-AZTEC

CLAY TIGER GOD, ZAPOTEC

with honor, given luxurious quarters with handmaidens to attend them, and feasted and regaled. The ceremonial death executed before crowds of thrilled spectators frequently brought religious ecstasy to the victim also, for death on the altar insured his entry into the highest heaven. Even the knowledge that his body would be thrown down the steps and carried off to form a ceremonial feast was not a humiliation, for the flesh was consumed in the belief that the eaters were establishing a closer union with the god himself. It was a religious concept not unlike that of the Christian communion, except that the Aztecs were painfully literal about it.

The Indian civilizations, with their vast treasures of gold, were predestined prey for the greed and zeal of the Spanish aggressors. However, the swift capitulation of the powerful Aztec Empire to Cortez, who arrived with a force of 450 men and 18 horses, was due to a combination of factors which operated in favor of the Spaniards.

MURAL, BONAMPAK

First was the initial confusion as to who Cortez was and what he wanted. Throughout Mexico there persisted the legend of Quetzalcoatl, the Plumed Serpent, a Toltec god who had in ancient times descended from heaven to live on earth as a king and bring art and wisdom to the people. When he was driven away by a more powerful god, he fled over the ocean in a boat of serpent skins, promising to return to bring a golden age to his people. Quetzalcoatl was sometimes represented as a bearded white man, and the belief that Cortez might be the reincarnated god paralyzed the will of the Aztec warriors. Cortez entered the capital unchallenged.

He promptly seized Montezuma as a hostage, but even this act of aggression merely terrified the people and failed to crystallize resistance. Cortez was permitted to leave for the coast, leaving his lieutenant Alvarado in charge. The people closed the markets and kept to their houses, but when the feast of Huitzilopochtli was to be celebrated they assembled in the square for this important ritual. Alvarado interpreted this as a military assemblage, and at his order the worshippers were slaughtered, men, women, and children. This roused the city to violent action, but too late.

The great weakness of the empire soon became apparent. The conquered peoples had been held in line by force and obliged to pay tribute, but had never been incorporated into the Empire and consequently felt no loyalty. Many of the subject tribes were easily persuaded to join the beleaguered troops of Alvarado. Even those who identified themselves with the Aztec state were reluctant to take up arms at this time, for it was harvest season and the loss of their crops seemed a greater calamity than the depredations of the invaders. The Aztec warriors were no match for men with guns, and their patterns of ceremonial warfare were of little avail against the realistic tactics of the Spaniards. Once aroused, they fought with stern and hopeless courage, but treachery, plagues, and bloody losses brought the nation to its knees.

In South America the great civilization arose in the Andean Highlands. The populating of South America is an archeological puzzle, for the Isthmian region, even at the present time, is an almost impenetrable

CLAY BOTTLE, NAZCA

jungle, while the coastal waters, particularly on the Pacific side, are difficult for navigation; there are adverse winds and no good harbors, because the jungle grows down to the sea. But somehow the migrants got
through this inhospitable territory and fanned out over the continent.
At the time of the Conquistadores the tropical forests of the Amazon
were peopled by savage tribes who lived in thatched huts; the men
hunted and fished and the women cultivated patches of corn, peanuts,
and manioc. The pampas of Argentina and the plains of Patagonia were

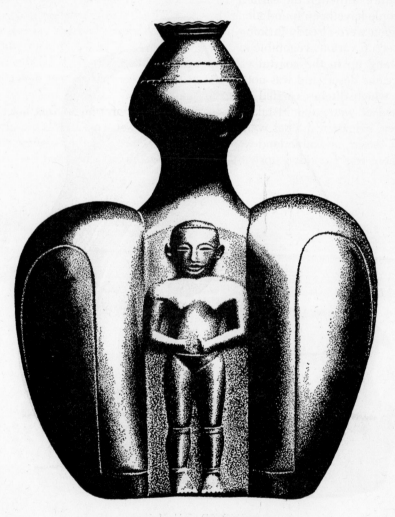

GOLD FLASK, COLOMBIA

occupied by hunting and seed-gathering nomads. Only in the Andean region was there advanced civilization, with city living and high technological, political, and religious achievements.

The Andean region is so high in elevation that it would seem an unfavorable place for the development of a great civilization. However, the Indians of the high Andes have a tremendous lung capacity and a greater concentration of red corpuscles in the blood stream, so that they are able to carry more oxygen and can do heavy work at an altitude at which the average European becomes dizzy and turns blue.

It is believed that the plateau was the starting point for Andean culture, although the earliest evidences of the settlement of agricultural people have been found along the coast. The first migrants in the coastal region were already farming people who settled in the river valleys and lived on various vegetable and root crops and fish. Independent cultures sprang up in the coastal valleys. Back from the stream beds the land became desert and was not arable. A system of irrigation was developed in which ditches carried the river water out to the limit to which the head of water would take it. To prevent evaporation in this hot, dry area, irrigation ditches were roofed over. The settlements were built on the desert, as arable land was too precious to be used for dwelling sites. There was a sudden upswing of culture in this region about 1000 B.C.,

MOCHICA JAR

when the coastal farmers acquired corn and beans to supplement their root crops.

The next great cultural upswing took place in the 3rd or 4th century in the northern coastal valleys, and was known as the Mochica. In this period the craftsmanship reached great heights, particularly pottery and weaving. The Mochica made jars in the forms of sculptured heads so realistic that they can properly be called portraiture. Their painted pottery shows scenes of daily life, mythology, and battle scenes which give a fine picture of the culture. They were apparently a warlike people whose expansion was based on military conquest.

The next great period, about 1000 A.D., was the Tihuanaco, named for the great ceremonial center, the ruins of which lie on the southern shore of Lake Titicaca in Bolivia. This empire extended over Bolivia and Peru. It is difficult to see how this region, which has poor, stony soil and an elevation of 14,000 feet, was able to support a population with the surplus time and energy to build structures such as those at Tihuanaco. In the plateau north of the center there are pyramids of cobblestones forty feet high. These are not ceremonial pyramids but merely stones removed in the clearing of the fields and stacked in great heaps.

The Tihuanacan skill in handling large stones was remarkable. They erected huge monolithic gateways, each hewn from a single piece of stone and elaborately but rather unimaginatively carved with a series of figures which were obviously copied from textile designs. How such a monument, weighing from sixty to seventy tons, was transported for

PAINTED CLAY BOWL

GOLD TUMBLER, ICA VALLEY

several miles, as it must have been, remains a mystery. These people did not even have the wood for making skids and levers.

Apparently one of the early discoveries in this region, which came into full use in the Tihuanaco period but characterized all the later Andean cultures, was the ability to organize and direct mass labor. A series of empires, apparently developed by conquest, spread throughout the plateau and gradually incorporated the coastal valleys. One of the most important of these was the Chimu, which arose about 1300 A.D. and represented a partial re-emergence of Mochica, modified by Tihuanaco. Like the Mochica, this was a period characterized by fine craftsmanship, particularly evidenced in the pottery, which was made in striking and beautiful animal effigies. The Chimu were city dwellers who built large city units of two types: the ceremonial centers of the Tihuanaco type and also big, true cities of the Old World type, which were residential and military centers. The population was large and well-organized, and land was systematically irrigated so that every available acre was under cultivation.

The famous Inca Empire (1438 to 1532) was the last and greatest of these. The term Inca refers to the ruling tribe of the Empire and also was the name taken by the hereditary king. The Inca ruling group achieved power by profiting from the techniques of recruiting and applying mass labor which had already been developed. The Inca were originally a small Quechua clan living in a Peruvian valley of the pla-

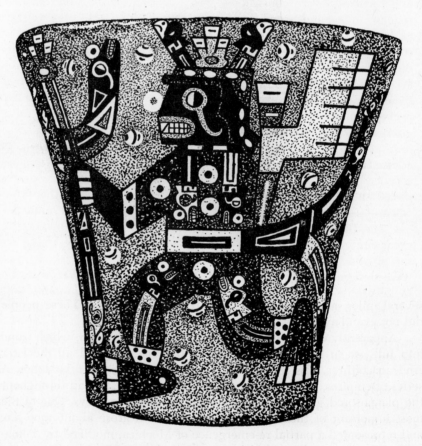

CEREMONIAL URN, SOUTH COAST PERU

teau. The valley was only 10,000 feet in elevation, so that corn, potatoes, and other crops could be raised profitably. However, most of the land was so steep that terraced agriculture was necessary. These terraces rose, one above the other, for thousands of feet, with occasional gutters faced with stone cut through to carry off the heaviest rainfall. Water from springs was diverted to trickle down from terrace to terrace. These terraces were so well planned and solidly constructed that their outlines are still discernible on the hillsides. The people had worked out the altitudes at which various crops would thrive and also knew about fertilization. All human and animal excrement was saved to use on the fields. Although they did not have the plow, this Andean horticulture was comparable to the terraced, carefully fertilized fields of the Chinese or Japanese.

The Incas were remarkable engineers and builders. Their temples and fortresses were constructed from great blocks of stone, cut in irregular angles and ground and adjusted until they fitted together with perfect accuracy. No mortar was used. This was earthquake country, in which walls of squared stones would have toppled at the first tremor, but even now, nearly 500 years after they were placed there, these stones are so perfectly joined that a knife blade cannot be inserted between them. Inca buildings give an effect of massed brute strength which is overwhelming. In the days of the Empire, representatives of foreign groups whom the Inca were attempting to bring in would be taken out to inspect the great fortress at Sacsahuaman. The massive strength of the edifice frequently impressed the ambassadors to such an extent that they acceded to Inca demands without a struggle. This fortress was completed shortly before the arrival of the Spaniards, so that this type of construction was by no means a lost art at the time of the Conquest.

The Incas also understood the need for rapid communication in a great empire and built better roads than any people before them, with the possible exception of the Romans. Roads were narrow, since they were designed for runners, not wheeled vehicles. But they were built to be usable in all weather in difficult terrain, over mountains, across canyons and rushing torrents. At intervals along the way were post houses in which couriers always waited to take over a message from a preceding runner. It was possible to send a message from Cuzco to Quito, a distance of 1300 miles, by this method.

The Incas incorporated the neighboring tribes into the Empire by a steady process of expansion, generation by generation, peaceable when possible, for the Incas had no delight in war for its own sake. Finally, their territory included all the Andean plateau and coast culture complex, extending northward into Columbia and southward over Bolivia and Chile. To the west lived the Aymara Indians of the lowlands, a

INCA CUP

savage group whom the Incas never conquered, although they managed
to establish occasional trading posts there.

The Inca Empire was an early and extreme example of a totalitarian
state knit together by lines of command which kept every phase of life
under complete control. Land, mineral wealth, and herds (llama and
alpaca) were the property of the state and were administered by the
state in exchange for levies of labor. The land was divided into three
parts: one for the Incas (the ruling class), one for the temple, and the
third and largest portion for the people. The people's land was assigned
by families and was reapportioned each year. If there was a new baby in
the family another strip of land was added; if there was a death, the
holding was reduced. Each newly-married couple was provided with a
house and land and two sets of new clothes. An order would go out that
on a certain day public marriages would be made. All the young unmarried people would be brought together into a prefectural center and
given a few hours to get acquainted, although frequently betrothals were
already arranged between the couples. Marriages were arranged by the
State.

When certain districts became overpopulated, a section of the population would be drawn off by regular draft and moved to unoccupied
land in another part of the Empire. Care was taken, however, to move
these people to districts where the general climate, altitude, and vegetation was similar to those in the region which they had left. This system, which was known as the *mitamae,* was also used to keep conquered

groups under control. After a province had been added to the kingdom, about half the population would be gathered up and sent to a region about a hundred miles away. Another displaced group, who did not speak the local language, would be moved into the vacated territory. In this way the Incas were able to break up the older cultures of the conquered people and impose Inca culture upon them, so that within a few generations they were completely assimilated.

The population was divided into groups of ten families, with one man acting as representative for the group. He was held personally responsible for the conduct of his group, much like the corporal of a squad. Five of the groups of ten would be organized under another leader, and two of these groups of fifty would be subject to a centurion. Five centurions would be subject to a chief, and two chiefs to a general, who thus headed a thousand families. Four vice-roys controlled the four sections of the Empire, which extended in the four directions from the capitol at Cuzco. Heads of the various political divisions were forbidden to have direct relations with one another. Business was routed through channels up to superiors and down again. At the top of the scale was the Inca himself, who was a divine descendant of the sun. From time to time the Inca traveled through the land in a magnificent and ceremonial tour of inspection.

INCA BOWL

There was no destitution in the Inca State. In case of famine or crop failure, the people would be provided from the public granaries. The flocks of llama and alpaca belonged to the Inca. Once a year they were rounded up, and the wool was plucked, rather than cut, and distributed to families to be spun into thread. The thread was collected and reissued for dyeing. The dyed thread was collected and distributed to expert weavers to be made into cloth. Weaving was developed to an extraordinary extent, many of the textiles comparing favorably with the

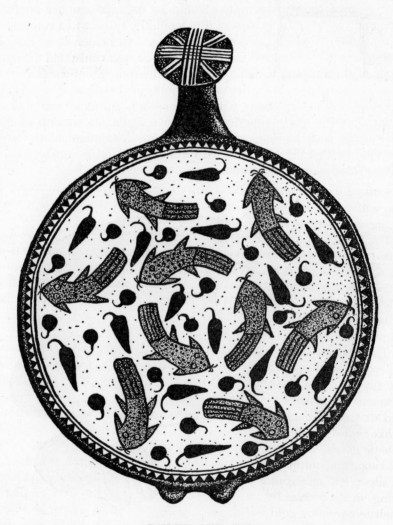

PAINTED DISH, INCA

INCA WALL NEAR CUZCO

best work of the Chinese or 16th century Europeans. A straight weaving frame without even a thrown spindle was used, but it was manipulated with uncanny manual skill.

The tremendous amount of accounting which a system of this sort entailed was handled by curious string records called *quipus*. These were dangling cords in which knots of various sorts were tied to represent various transactions. It was a kind of shorthand which depended partly on memory. The quipu could not be read accurately by anyone but the man who had made it, but the quipu makers were able to handle involved long-range transactions with this type of record.

There was a special group of men who were drafted as youths for the personal service of the emperor. The *Yanacuna,* as they were called, were supported by the state and assigned to various duties. The finest artists and craftsmen came from this group. The Inca apparently recognized that a populace completely directed and conditioned to constant ant-like industry would not have the imagination or initiative to produce aesthetic goods. This group was selected and trained to supply this need. The Yanacuna smiths were particularly skillful. They worked with copper, silver, and gold, but had no iron. They used both smelting and hammering, made bronze by mixing copper and tin, and also made plated vessels by applying gold leaf to silver and silver leaf to copper and hammering it in. Gold poured into the capitol. The palace walls were decorated with gold friezes; the Inca ate from a solid gold service; during public ceremonials, the entire plaza of Cuzco was roped off by a chain made with solid gold links. In the Temple of the Sun there was a golden garden in which trees, flowers, and birds were all made of gold and a life-sized golden shepherd tended a herd of golden llamas. Butterflies and other insects, made of delicate gold filigree so light and perfectly balanced that they floated through the air, hovered over the golden flowers.

Roughly corresponding to the Yanacuna was a special group of young women called the *Allacuna.* They were selected at the age of eight or nine and put into a sort of nunnery. Some became priestesses, some became imperial concubines, and some were given as wives to favored Yanacuna or nobles. These girls were also trained as fine weavers who prepared the beautiful textiles used in the palace of the Inca.

The ruling group was recruited from the hereditary nobles of the conquered tribes. These young men were sent to school in Cuzco, the capital. The ablest ones were chosen for administrative posts in the capital, and the others were sent to govern outlying provinces. The Incaship was a hereditary office, the heir being the eldest son of the reigning Inca by his eldest sister. Contrary to popular beliefs about inbreeding, it should be noted that six generations of this type of marriage produced a line of highly able and intelligent rulers.

Inca conquests were as systematic and well-organized as those of the German army. There were regular levies in preparation for foreign wars. Before a territory was invaded, the Inca built roads leading to it, established forts to fall back on, and accumulated supplies. Spies were sent out to bring back information on the country to be invaded. Attempts were made to stir up some sort of local revolt in the country to be attacked so that the defense would be disunited and in confusion. Conquered groups were given easy terms if they submitted. Occasionally this was accomplished without war.

The Inca Empire was probably the most successful totalitarian state the world has ever seen. Unfortunately for the Inca, and perhaps for history, the Spaniards arrived at a time when a break in the united front had just occurred. The father of Atahualpa, the last Inca, had married a Quito wife as well as his regular sister-wife. Some of the northern tribes, not yet completely fused into the Empire, recognized the Quito son as king, and this revolt was in progress when the Spaniards arrived. Pizarro got a foothold in the country by offering the aid of his men as mercenaries to help Atahualpa put down this revolt. As soon as the northern groups had been defeated, the Spanish, already entrenched in the capital, captured Atahualpa and murdered him and most of his nobles.

The great defect of totalitarianism, wherever it is found, soon became evident here. When people are accustomed to taking orders and never thinking for themselves, their initiative is destroyed and they are easy prey for any leader who takes command. The Spaniards were thus able to dominate the Inca group in a way which would have been impossible if the people had not been already so thoroughly regimented.

The Spanish, as usual, introduced a period of incredibly short-sighted exploitation. As they were primarily interested in gold, they failed to maintain the irrigation canals and aqueducts on which the economy of the country depended. Epidemics and excessive levies of forced labor in the mines further decimated the population. In the first years of the Spanish occupation the population of the Empire dropped to less than half of what it had been. The science and learning of the Inca was lost with the elimination of the upper classes, but the village pattern which was the base on which the Empire was built survives among the Andean Indians. They have been gradually increasing in number and consequently the culture which develops here will be built on a strong Indian base.

Conclusion

This chapter is a lecture delivered by Dr. Linton on June 3, 1948, the final lecture in that academic year in the course from which this book developed. It is a clear statement of the principles which animate this book, and we have therefore, except for slight mechanical changes, reprinted it verbatim.

As I TOLD YOU last time, I have been unable to cover the American cultures in the latter part of the course with anything like the completeness that I wanted to, and have had to skip over to what really should have been led up to more gradually, what appears to be the present situation in our society and perhaps the immediate future.

I remember on one occasion I attended a talk by Archibald Mac-Leish, who made the comment that, "Our period is unique for the great number of middle-aged individuals who have a knowledge of the future and are eager to share that knowledge with others." I do not wish to be included in that category. I do not have a knowledge of the future.

The only thing, however, that the anthropologist can say is that following the ordinary techniques of extrapolation—the term means sighting along in the direction in which things are now moving from a comfortable distance, so that you can see what the trends have been—there are at least certain things which we can say it is highly improbable will happen any time in the immediate future, while there are other things that it seems highly probable will happen.

In order to give you a little of this background, I will go back and recapitulate two or three things very briefly. You remember that as far back as the first semester, I spoke of the great and small mutations that took place in culture. I said that the general pattern of cultural growth appeared to be not a uniform, continuous progress, in which each stage was a little better than the one before, and so on, but that actually culture growth has proceeded by a process somewhat like that of biological mutation. It also is preceded, of course, by the small, cumulative changes. Just as in biology, you have, side by side, small variations in selection, and mutations due to some freak of the genes. You have an extreme change taking place in form, and taking place in such a way that it will be hereditary, can become fixed.

661

Now, then, in the history of human culture there have been three basic mutations. The first one was the use of tools, fire, and language. The second, which came only some six thousand to seven thousand years ago, was the discovery of how to raise food, which immediately brought in its train a whole series of social and technological advances, such things as, on the technological side, the smelting of metals, the working of metals, the development of the wheel, the plow and loom, the basic mechanisms, the invention of writing; the development on the social side of city life, of kingship, drilled armies. In other words, within a thousand years after this second mutation, the basic patterns of civilization, as we ordinarily think of it, of the culture stream which originated in Southwestern Asia, and which is directly ancestral to our own civilization, were established, and survived with very little change down until about 1800.

Because we are close to this series of cultures—despite Mr. Toynbee, who has apparently no culture perspective whatever—we see the minor differences in them as being of supreme importance. As a matter of fact, the so-called rise and fall of the civilizations in this particular line, which include all the great civilizations except possibly that of India, which is marginal in certain respects, actually only affected the surface of the culture. You will remember that I told you that Indian culture is partly of Southeastern Asiatic origin rather than Southwestern. The changes in official religion by which, let us say, the local baal of a Palestinian village later became a Roman deity, and then a Christian saint, and is now a Mohammedan saint—I don't know what he will be after the new state of Israel is established, but I will bet he will still be around—these changes are only superficial.

Throughout the marvelous age of the Renaissance just as throughout the Dark Ages, while kings came and went, and scholarship rose or degenerated, the peasant with his ox went right on plowing the land, raising the same sort of crops that his ancestors had raised for the last three or four thousand years, carrying on the same sort of hand industries. In the cities, when they reasserted themselves, again and again you found the same patterns which went back to Sumer repeated; the pattern of the organized hand craftsmen, who were not only manufacturers, but also salesmen, the guild type of craft organization in which the main idea was fine craftsmanship, plus equitable distribution of opportunity.

Even the technology remains strikingly the same. There were a few minor changes that came in. For instance, when this civilization took form, it was dependent on bronze as its principal metal, and later this gave place to iron, with a sort of proletarianization of metal-using, because iron was cheap and abundant, and bronze had been scarce and expensive. You had the earlier, more complex types of writing, which required professionals in all the regions outside China, giving place to another proletarian device, the alphabet, which made possible a much more universal literacy, a few things of this sort. During this period, the culture had changed only slightly, and it had reached an effective adjustment between the technology, the patterns of economic distribution, and social forms, the sort of adjustment which can only be achieved by long experimentation.

Since the late 1700's, the third great mutation in human culture has really gotten under way. The fact that we are in the middle of a mutation is very confusing to scholars who do not have this sense of culture depth, who don't know what has happened before. For instance, you have such gentlemen as my friend, Dr. William F. Ogburn, of the University of Chicago, taking the chart of the patents in the United States Patent Office, and showing that they have increased at such and such a rate per year, and then projecting this for a thousand years, by which time presumably everybody in the world will be making five or six patents a year, as an individual.

Well, as a matter of fact, we know that this is highly improbable. We are in a period now of very rapid change, probably not past the middle of the working out of this third mutation. I will come back to this in just a moment. The third mutation itself consisted in certain basic inventions, certain new basic inventions, of which two were perhaps the most important, that lay at the root of the whole pattern of change, I would say.

First of all was the discovery of how to get power from heat. The ancients knew how to use power. As a matter of fact, as we excavate the sites of the classical period, particularly of the Roman period, we find that there were very few fundamental mechanical appliances, such things as gears and belting, and so on, for the transmission and use of power, that the classical people didn't know. But the only source of power which they had, aside from animal and human power, and to a lesser extent, wind power, was water power.

This discovery of how to get power from heat, first from the steam engine, later with the internal combustion engine, and now with the jets, and so forth, which is passing over into atomic energy, was basic. It is interesting to note that still all the plans to use atomic energy are to utilize the heat that is generated in this way. It is the use of the heat that is still basic in our power production.

Next to this heat discovery, making it possible to use power machinery anywhere that you could get fuel, was the discovery of the scientific method. Now, this is in itself an invention. You will be told repeatedly that the Greeks were the ones who discovered the scientific method.

They discovered or developed it only to a very limited degree, and not in the terms in which we now think of science. The Greek scientist, whenever he came to an impasse, fell back upon philosophy and pure reason, not recognizing that when you are dealing with multiple phenomena, operating in configurations, the logical results are by no means always the correct results. You can see some beautiful examples of this in the social sciences, or, let us say, in classical economics, where logical developments have been carried to a point which bear only the faintest relation to reality.

The Greeks believed in the infallibility of the human mind, and this was the last resort to which any question that could not be settled otherwise could be referred. During the dominance of the Christian Church, the great age of faith and epidemics which intervened between the fall of the Roman Empire and the Renaissance, the Church, for the support of its own authority, kept pounding away on the fallibility of the human mind, and it managed to get the European population pretty well convinced of the fact.

Then, when the authority of the Church, which it had sought to substitute for reason as the final test of the validity of any conclusions, when the authority of the church could no longer be maintained, Europeans cast about for other infallible things that they could refer to, to put checks on their ideas, and evolved the pattern of experiment in the modern sense. The Greeks experimented, but having tried a thing once and having gotten a result that looked fairly good to them, they quit there. The essence of the scientific method is that you try an experiment, you record the results as accurately as possible, and you use, wherever possible, mechanical means of recording, because the scientist realizes at present that one of the easiest things in the world is for a man to fool himself, if he wants to get a certain outcome. He must watch himself constantly. The results of the experiment and the techniques are announced and published, whereupon a dozen different men who are working in this field promptly try the experiment and see whether they get the same results or not, and so on. It is by this method of rigidly controlled experiment, building up bit by bit, establishing one point after another as a frontier, a solid frontier, a fortified post, you might say, in which to move forward into the unknown, that most of the gains in our basic knowledge have been made.

Combined with this shift in techniques has also gone, since Classical times, a very decided shift in attitude. Although the Greeks were moving toward modern science and its technical application, there was a block in their case based on value judgments. They felt that gentlemen did not work; in fact, gentlemen did not do anything practical. The Greek gentleman went down to the market place and spent the day standing around talking politics, while his slave was shopping, and then he came home, and another slave gave him a good rubdown, another slave cooked his dinner, and so forth. But gentlemen didn't do anything.

I am reminded of that great American classic, "Archie and Mehitabel." I don't know whether any of you have read it or not. It is an interview with one of the ancient pharoahs, in which the pharoah said that the boys of the settee set were far too aristocratic to have any purpose, that they spent their time gadding about, or having pyramids sent home to try on. The Greeks did not indulge in pyramids, but they didn't like to apply their philosophic knowledge to anything practical. On the rare occasions when they did, it was definitely felt that the philosopher, mathematician, or what not, had been guilty of unethical practice.

Many of you have probably read the story of the siege of Syracuse, in Sicily, which had a large Roman army on the outside, and Archimedes on the inside. Largely as a result of the activities of Archimedes, the city stood off a siege of over two years, because he devised all sorts of interesting little apparatus to annoy the Romans, such things as a setup of parabolic mirrors, with which he focused the sunlight on the Roman fleet that was lying at anchor in the harbor and set it on fire, various machines that were used for casting projectiles, and so on. He simply scared the life out of the Romans, who were a bunch of ignorant savages anyway at this point. But Plutarch, writing 600 years later, nevertheless feels it necessary to apologize for Archimedes having made practical use of his mathematical formulae, and so on, that he had worked on, and he says that the philosopher had made these machines, not of his own free will, but because the King of Syracuse had requested him to build these machines as a demonstration of the clear laws of mathematics and mechanics which, in this way, could be explained to persons of lower minds, who could not perceive the truths in the abstract.

In other words, it would be on a par with saying that the manufacture of a 16 inch gun was done to illustrate the laws of ballistics realistically. Well, the Europeans got over this during the Dark Ages. With the collapse of the upper class, there also went the idea that you should not interest yourself in practical matters. In fact, during the Dark Ages, they had to be exceedingly practical to keep alive, most of the time. It is interesting to note that the mechanical foundations of modern culture were really laid during this period, which all those people who were trained in the scholastic discipline regard as being one of the low points in the West. As a matter of fact, more mechanical improvements were made during the Dark Ages than during the whole Greek and Roman Classical period. They were hard up. They had to devise methods for doing the same things as well and much more cheaply, with much less expenditure of energy and materials.

You had, for instance, the heavy Romanesque architecture giving place to the Gothic, which required much less labor and much less material, but also required a much better knowledge of the qualities of stone, of the interaction of stresses, and so on, much more scientific building.

Well, finally, as I say, there was a gradual build-up here, beginning in the Dark Ages, increasing through the Renaissance, and with the modern period, the third mutation getting definitely under way in perhaps the middle 1700's, since which time it has proceeded with a steady acceleration.

Now, there is one other thing which characterizes all periods of rapid culture growth, and that is that groups seem to be interested in one thing at a time. Culture growth is practically always disharmonic. The inventors, and so on, are like chickens. If you ever fed chickens, you know that you throw a handful of corn over in this corner of the pen, and they all bolt for that. Long before that is consumed, you throw a handful of corn in the other corner of the pen, and they all bolt for that. Societies get interested in one thing at a time. In this mutation, so far, the interest has been almost entirely in mechanical improvements. Now, this is perfectly normal, but it is reflected in a rather curious attitude. A few years ago I saw a sign advertising a new lubricating oil, and the only thing they had to say about it was that it was the first new lubricating oil developed in twenty years. That was the only thing on the board to advertise it. At the same time that you expect to sell things simply because they are new, mechanical appliances, and so on, you have the sort of Congressional investigations that are now under way. In other words, in this disharmony, we have on the one side a steady pushing forward of the mechanical and technological developments, with extreme willingness to accept new things; while, at the same time, until very recently, practically no attempts have been made to bring the rest of the cultural equipment, the reorganization of the social structure, the reorganization of distribution, and so on, up to time and into harmony with the progress that has already been made.

Now, one of the things that has gone on here, without our realizing it, is that due to the new technology, and the new science, there has been a subtle but very real change in the actual values. By this, I am not speaking of morals or anything of that sort, but of the things that are worth having in our society, a change which has gone on without most people realizing it or understanding what is happening, a change which must parallel what took place with the development of agriculture when, for the first time, land ceased to be something that you chased deer over, and became something which could be individually owned, and, in fact, used to exclude other people from achieving a livelihood.

In this new pattern that is emerging, you have the old values steadily diminishing. In the first place, the value of real goods has gone down, is going down steadily. This is masked nicely by the fact that there is more and more gold in the world, and countries still use it as a yardstick for measuring their money. There is also inflation, so that although a dollar looks like a dollar, it only buys 33 cents of what it bought in 1938, and so forth. But actually, in terms of basic value, the amount of materials, labor, and so forth, that are required to produce goods, the value of goods is going down steadily. With your mass production methods, particularly with the increasing mechanization of the assembly line, you can turn out tremendous quantities of goods at a very small relative cost.

A good picture of this is to contrast the actual value in materials and labor required of a modern rayon dress, shall we say, with the dress of the present wearer's grandmother's. The great-grandmother was probably a peasant woman who wore a dress made from wool raised on the sheep on the farm, clipped, spun, dyed, woven, made up, and so forth. Think of it in sheer terms of calories and man-hours, the contrast between the two. As a matter of fact, we are already in a position where, in the mechanized countries—and all countries will be mechanized before very long—our main problem ordinarily is not one of producing enough, but one of overproduction actually. However, this is not based on the elimination of need, but is based on the fact that we don't have the techniques for getting the goods around. Our distribution techniques are still, shall we say, 18th century, except for high-pressure advertising, which is not exactly meeting the problem, while our production techniques are 20th century. One of the things that our immediate ancestors collected and hoarded, real goods, has lost much of its value. Also, the real value of land has diminished. Again, all these things are masked by the inflationary trends. But actually, land, while it is desirable if you expect a runaway inflation, nevertheless, is not something that does you much good at the present time as an investment, because it cannot be hidden; it is too subject to taxation.

Also, I may say, with the development of modern farming techniques, and so forth, much of the marginal land is certainly going to become valuable only for tree growing or some other long-range, slow-return investment. I am told by one of my agronomist friends that, given the application of full modern techniques, you can raise all the food normally required for the population of the United States on the area of the State of Kansas. I think this is probably true, but these techniques have not spread. I may say that one of the nice little problems that comes in here is that as you mechanize your land more and more, your people and your farmers drift off it. As agriculture gets on a factory basis, the next question is, How do you get your population to breed? City populations have never been able to reproduce themselves. The country people provide the raw population, the country yokels, who come in and are transformed into city slickers, in the same way that they provide all the other raw materials that go to the upkeep of the city. If you cut out your rural population, you will have to resort to some new devices, as yet uninvented, or at least untried, in order to keep your population up. You have another thing that is happening here, and that is the passing of those adjustments that have been made in the West to the new conditions, through the exploitation of foreign, unmechanized markets; in other words, the passing of the conditions upon which capitalism, as we ordinarily understand it, has been built. For the last 200 years, Europe, and to a lesser extent America, have lived by selling their skills, they being the first people who were in the vanguard of the mechanical revolution, the first ones who were able to step up their per capita production. They have met the fundamental problems of readjustment by producing in excess, and then marketing this excess in other countries that were not yet mechanized. In this way, they were able to keep pretty much the outward forms of the old system working.

At the present time, these unmechanized markets are going to go very rapidly, or are gone. No technique has been devised so far to really prevent the diffusion of valuable scientific and technological knowledge. The attempt is being made now with the Iron Curtain, and so forth. Of course, if you were really thoroughgoing in modern warfare, since in modern warfare every new gadget may conceivably be of use, the logical conclusion is for no country to let anybody else find out what is being invented or discovered here. The result would be a very simple paralysis of progress.

But anyway, this business of mechanization is going on apace. Most people do not realize, for instance, that the largest and most modern steel mill in the world is in India. Even with the internal confusion in China, in the last two or three years before the World War broke out, and after the Japanese episode, as we call it, after the Japanese had begun their attempt to conquer China, China was exporting more manufactured goods than it was importing. Japan, before the war, was able to manufacture and sell in Lancashire in England a cotton shirt of the quality that was produced in Lancashire, cheaper than they could make it in Lancashire. In other words, the good old days when the West could exploit the world, and had all this outlet for its surplus capital, and so on, are about gone.

So that most of the things which we thought of and have been brought to think of as being of extreme value actually are being quietly undermined, are no longer as much worth having as they were. But, the thing that is emerging as being most valuable is the assured job. This is the thing that is most important to have at the present time. And the best job of all is, of course, the government job, as long as you belong to the party that is in power. I am very much interested in this contract that has just been signed by the Auto Workers, in which, instead of having a flat dollar rate, so many cents an hour, the scale is going to vary relative to the cost of living. This is the sort of thing that has been done in government jobs in various places, not the United States, because the United States has very decidedly still not come to that adjustment.

The man who has the government job, as long as his party is in power, can't be fired. He usually gets pretty liberal allowances for retirement, vacations, and what not; and therefore, this is the thing that is worth having. Even in those large organized industries which now *big business* approach governmental status in everything except the absence of control over them by the population which they exploit, the assured job is also highly important. If you look at this, if you look at the more recent social, and political developments in these terms, you will see that after all, both your Communist and Fascist movements represent small organized groups which have grabbed the government jobs, which are the things most worth having under the circumstances.

This movement is exactly parallel to what happened at the time of the Roman collapse, when various mobsters, with their gangs—"familia" was the Latin name for them—moved out and took over sections of land with the peasants on them, which were the most valuable things under the current circumstances. In the same way, you have your one party, so-called totalitarian groups, moving in and taking over the government control and government jobs.

Now, then, the question is, What happens from here on? We can go on pushing the present trends of technological development and of endless increase of production, without making changes anywhere else, until we finally reach a state of stasis, and then of collapse, the sort of thing that we came very close to in the 1929 panic.

We know that there is going to be a world-wide diffusion of techniques and mechanization, which means that all countries, or at least all politically organized groups of countries, such as Benelux, all customs unions, and so on, are going to have to reorganize their industry and their distributive and governmental techniques in terms of production for internal consumption with, at most, a 50–50 exchange on foreign trade. That is, one country will simply not be in a position to exploit another through superior skills.

It means that there will be no new markets, and to a considerable extent, no new natural resources. However, these natural resources will be developed internally through new technological advances, and various *ersatz* products, the sort of thing that nylon is. We have got a pretty clear map, I would say now, of what the future world situation is going to be on that. We also may look forward to the end of free competition, even within the units. This is an unpopular fact, but it is a fact. More and more in the United States—and elsewhere also—small industry, small factories, are being either absorbed by the big boys, or are being organized into associations, and so forth, which have extinguished real competition. The trend, therefore, can go in two ways at this point. Either you can move toward the socialized state, or toward an oligarchy of great companies, which have entirely ceased to be competitive, and which control the government instead of the government controlling them. You can't tell which way this is going to go.

As regards socialization, I would say that we can view both the earlier Nazi and the present Communist and more recent British experiments in socialization as the first attempts to really grapple with this problem. And as first attempts, all of them are clumsy. The essential problem here is down to what size productive or marketing unit your direct governmental control can function efficiently.

Obviously, when the farmer has to sign six papers in order to kill his pig in the fall, you have long since passed the point of diminishing returns. What we still need to find out, and probably only will find out by experiment—let us hope that other countries can do quite a bit of experimenting for us—is what industries have to be controlled by the government, and how far down the line in size we must go, in order to insure at the same time efficient operation and a fair distribution of the products.

Now, there is another trend, looked at from the individual angle, which is very strong here, and this is the trend for lessened social mobility and toward the emergence here in the United States of a class system. You can see this taking shape steadily. You have, for instance, the emergence of hereditary skilled craft groups, suggestive in this respect of the Indian caste organization. You may remember that a short time ago one of the midwestern carpenters' unions was sued for passing a regulation that only the sons of carpenters would be taken as apprentices. This was declared illegal, but does not prevent the thing from operating in practice. Most of the skilled handcrafts at the present time are largely hereditary, even in the United States. And with this, of course, a class system is emerging.

In industry, there has been a somewhat countertrend of despecialization, that is, in the big industries, less and less requirement for skilled craftsmen, and more of the "tightening nut No. 39" sort of thing on the assembly line. But the thing that is required here is more and more managerial skill and technical skill. There is an excellent probability for the emergence of a distinct managerial class.

It is very interesting to note that in Russia, where the new aristocracy is being organized on this basis, the Russians, starting with the good intentions of most revolutionaries, have now wound up with a situation in which there is free education to the end of high school. Then, there are not only heavy fees to be paid for the university, but for the first two years of the university, there are no fellowships or other aids to students. For the last two years, they can get financial aid. But this means that the only people who can go on from the high school level, which is the level of education required to make good factory foremen, the only ones who can go on are those whose families are in a position to pay the university fees. The only people in Russia who are in such a position are the specialists of one sort and another, and the party members. And in order to be specialists, you have to have university training. Therefore, you can see the emergence here by a device as unobtrusive as the one party ballot box, shall we say, a new aristocracy, and a new mechanism for retaining their aristocracy.

I may say that the American patterns of vertical mobility could be maintained perfectly well in the face of this present change, whether the ownership of industries becomes socialistic or oligarchic, by certain very simple devices. However, I have found that these devices usually are not greeted with enthusiasm by the people who make the most noise about maintaining the good old American patterns.

The first device would be a 100 per cent inheritance tax, so that everybody would, theoretically, at least, start from scratch. The second would be unlimited, but selectively applied educational opportunities. This is something which we approach in our state universities at the present time, but it should be carried even further, so that any man who had the intrinsic ability for high training and specialization, management, and so on, could get it, irrespective of what his family had been or where he had started in the social scale. Perhaps third, to complete the picture, would be the most effective device employed by the Catholic Church to assure itself of constant new blood from below, that is, the combination of celibacy of the clergy, plus a rule that no illegitimate child can become a member of the clergy. This immediately rules out family successions. There are certain exceptions to this, as with the Medici Popes, and so forth, but in general the rule has been pretty well maintained.

A combination of the first two of these, plus hopefully the third, would assure the maintenance of patterns of vertical mobility, and with this, of a really homogeneous society. No strong class lines could emerge, because each individual, who, through his own abilities, rose to a position in the ruling group, would not be tied to relatives in the lower social levels, you see, and the various backgrounds of the members of the upper group would help them to keep in touch with the people.

There is very little probability that any such technique will be put into play. We are, however, faced by a necessity for maintaining our present democratic patterns and institutions, imperfect as they are, for as long as we can. We must realize that at the present time any one party system which manages to get into power in a modern state and introduce the police state of the sort which the Russians developed first, and the Nazis then elaborated and improved, any group that is able to get into power in a modern nation and to stay in for the few months required to anchor themselves in this way, is practically impossible to get rid of. It is one thing that all anthropologists recognize. There is a direct correlation between the military techniques at any particular time and the degree of despotism on the part of the ruling group.

In societies in which the average man or the average community has an excellent opportunity for successful revolt, in which he is, as a fighting unit, practically on a par with the trained soldier, you find either democratic institutions or else a touching solicitude on the part of the ruling group for the well-being of the governed. I may say that this was the beginning of American democracy. Given the tactics of 1776, and a squirrel rifle over the fireplace, you don't have to bother much about despotism on the part of the ruling group.

To achieve an equivalent situation at the present time, there would have to be a tank in every garage. As things stand now, the weight is all on the side of the professional soldier and of the government that can buy his services and provide him with the highly technical and elaborate equipment that he needs. If democracy slips at this point, she is gone for a long time to come. We might as well recognize that fact. There is always a terrible temptation to turn over your control to one strong and able man, because he gets things done. He doesn't produce committees to investigate un-American activities, and so forth, usually. The first man to set up a dictatorship is usually a pretty able man; he has to be. The trouble is that we have never devised any mechanisms for keeping on getting good ones after the first, and I don't know that they can actually be devised. But in spite of this temptation, and in spite of the bungling which is characteristic of all democratic governments, it is the one system which retains sufficient flexibility so that it has the possibility of adjusting to changing conditions without periodic revolutions and destruction and the general inconvenience that these cause.

I am not at all optimistic about our ability to maintain democracy, but neither am I pessimistic about the sort of thing that is going on at the present time. After all, I went through World War I, and I remember the great upswing of religious fervor which brought us Prohibition, and a more highly organized variety of crimes than the United States had ever seen. I remember the red hunts that were organized at the close of World War I, which bear striking resemblance to the sort of thing that is being carried on now.

Well, in summary, I do not claim to know what is going to happen, but we can be fairly sure of this, that in due course of time, a successful *modus vivendi* is going to be worked out, in which the advantages of modern science and modern technology will be combined with social systems which are really adjusted to them, and which work. Some of the most important advances that are being made at the present time are, I believe, those which are coming from the studies of personality and culture. That is, for the first time we are beginning to get some insight into what is really human nature, and how it is shaped. So that while adjusting forms, and so on, to the machine at one end, we are more and more learning how we may operate to adjust human beings to this system, at the other end. By this, I do not mean making them better on assembly lines. The man tightening nut No. 36 on the Ford assembly line was, after all, as even engineers recognize, a transitory phenomenon. As the machines got better, more and more men came off the assembly line, until you got a situation such as the factory in Milwaukee which, with a crew of eleven men, was able to make all the automobile frames in the United States. It turned over to war manufacturing, during the war, but I imagine they are getting it readjusted. All the men did here was to sort of walk up and down the assembly line, and if anything got stuck, replace the broken part. or what not. This is the sort of thing that is going to go on.

Well, the best we can say is that human beings are tough, and that they always have succeeded in readjusting.

The atom bomb raises interesting possibilities in this connection, but I doubt even if our occasional two-headed descendants, after thorough irradiation of the northern hemispheres, will differ very much from ourselves. They may have split personalities of a very different sort. But the main line of scientific development now is actually not in the development of more machines and more atomic fission, and so on, but a steadily advancing understanding of human beings, of what can be done with them; and with this, more and more possibility for developing techniques by which we can produce well-adjusted and satisfied populations.

However, the great difficulty in this work, and in the social sciences in general, is that it tends to bring out points which are not greeted with enthusiasm by those in power. In the totalitarian state, there is no use for either the social scientist or the psychologist, except as a pure technician, providing superior methods for producing the particular results that the party in power wants and finds to their own advantage. The trend, at the present time, outside of a few favored areas, is certainly toward the suppression of both. If we now go into a totalitarian phase—the beginnings of which are quite possible—I anticipate that those scientists who are interested now in human studies will go the way of the Greek philosophers, that they will be among the first victims of regimentation. However, the Greek philosophers left behind them a fair amount of knowledge that had been acquired. They were able to start a number of things, so that when the bonds of Church and State were once more relaxed, after a few thousand years, people were able to pick up and carry on from there. The hope of the modern worker in the social sciences is that during this period of really surprising freedom—because periods of freedom are rare in world history—we may be able to get far enough ahead to lay a solid platform from which the workers in the next civilization can go on.

Bibliography

CHAPTER I

CLELLAND, H. F.: *Our Primitive Ancestors.* New York: Coward-McCann; 1928.
HOOTON, E. A.: *Man's Poor Relations.* New York: Doubleday & Company; 1942.
————: *Up From the Apes.* Revised edition. New York: The Macmillan Co.; 1946.
HOWELLS, W. W.: *Mankind So Far.* New York: Doubleday & Company; 1944.
LE GROS CLARK, W. E.: *History of the Primates: An Introduction to the Study of Fossil Man.* London: British Museum Guide; 1949.
SIMPSON, G. G.: *The Meaning of Evolution.* New Haven: Yale University Press; 1950.
WEIDENREICH, F.: *Apes, Giants, and Men.* Chicago: University of Chicago Press; 1946.
WHITE, A. T.: *Men Before Adam.* New York: Random House; 1942.
YERKES, R. M., and A. W.: *The Great Apes: A Study of Anthropoid Life.* New Haven: Yale University Press; 1929.
ZUCKERMAN, S.: *The Social Life of Monkeys and Apes.* New York: Harcourt, Brace & Co.; 1932.

CHAPTER II

DALY, R. A.: *The Changing World of the Ice Age.* New Haven: Yale University Press; 1934.
FLINT, R. F.: *Glacial Geology and the Pleistocene Epoch.* New York: John Wiley & Sons; 1947.
WRIGHT, W. B.: *The Quaternary Ice Age.* London: The Macmillan Co.; 1914.
ZEUNER, F. E.: *Dating the Past.* Revised edition. London: Methuen & Co.; 1950.

CHAPTER III

ASHLEY-MONTAGU, M. F.: *An Introduction to Physical Anthropology.* Springfield, Illinois: C. C. Thomas; 1945.
BOYD, W. C.: *Genetics and the Races of Man.* Boston: Little, Brown & Co.; 1950.
COON, C. S.: *The Races of Europe.* New York: The Macmillan Co.; 1948.
————, GARN, S. M., and BIRDSELL, J. B.: *Races: A Study of the Problems of Race Formation in Man.* Springfield, Illinois: C. C. Thomas; 1950.
COUNT, E. W., editor: *This Is Race.* New York: Henry Schuman; 1950.
HOOTON, E. A.: *Up From the Apes.* Revised edition. New York: The Macmillan Co.; 1946.
HOWELLS, W. W.: *Mankind So Far.* New York: Doubleday & Company; 1944.

CHAPTER IV

BENEDICT, R.: *Patterns of Culture*. New York: Houghton Mifflin Co.; 1934.
ERICKSON, E. H.: *Childhood and Society*. New York: W. W. Norton & Company; 1950.
GILLIN, J., editor: *For a Science of Social Man*. New York: The Macmillan Co.; 1954.
GOLDENWEISER, A.: *History, Psychology and Culture*. New York: Alfred A. Knopf; 1933.
HARING, D. G.: *Personal Character and Cultural Milieu: A Collection of Readings*. Revised edition. Syracuse: Syracuse University Press; 1949.
HONIGMANN, J. J.: *Culture and Personality*. New York: Harper & Brothers; 1954.
KARDINER, A.: *The Individual and His Society*. New York: Columbia University Press; 1939.
————: *The Psychological Frontiers of Society*. New York: Columbia University Press; 1946.
KLUCKHOHN, C., and MURRAY, H. A.: *Personality in Nature, Society, and Culture*. New York: Alfred A. Knopf; 1948.
LINTON, R.: *The Study of Man*. New York: Appleton-Century-Crofts; 1936.
————: *The Cultural Background of Personality*. New York: Appleton-Century-Crofts; 1945.
LOWIE, R. H.: *Primitive Society*. New York: Boni and Liveright; 1920.
————: *Social Organization*. New York: Rinehart & Company; 1948.
MURDOCK, G. P.: *Social Structure*. New York: The Macmillan Co.; 1949.
NEWCOMB, T. M., and HARTLEY, E. L.: *Readings in Social Psychology*. New York: Henry Holt & Co.; 1947.
SAPIR, E.: *Selected Writings of Edward Sapir in Language, Culture, and Personality*. Edited by D. G. Mandelbaum. Berkeley: University of California Press; 1949.
SARGENT, S. S., and SMITH, M. W.; editors: *Culture and Personality*. New York: Viking Fund Publications; 1949.
SPIER, L.; HALLOWELL, A. I.; and NEWMAN, S. S.; editors: *Language, Culture, and Personality: Essays in Memory of Edward Sapir*. Menasha, Wisconsin: Sapir Memorial Fund; 1941.
WHITING, J. W. M., and CHILD, I. L.: *Child Training and Personality: A Cross-Cultural Study*. New Haven: Yale University Press; 1953.
YOUNG, K.: *Sociology*. New York: American Book Company; 1942.

CHAPTER V

BARNETT, H. G.: *Innovation: The Basis of Cultural Change*. New York: McGraw-Hill Book Co.; 1953.
DIXON, R. B.: *The Building of Cultures*. London: Charles Scribner's Sons; 1928.
FIRTH, R.: *Elements of Social Organization*. London: Watts & Co.; 1951.
GILFILLAN, S. C.: *The Sociology of Invention*. Chicago: Follett Publishing Company; 1935.
HODGEN, M. T.: *Change and History*. New York: Viking Fund Publication No. 18; 1952.
LINTON, R., editor: *Acculturation in Seven American Indian Tribes*. New York: Appleton-Century-Crofts; 1940.

————, editor: *The Science of Man in the World Crisis.* New York: Columbia University Press; 1945.

MALINOWSKI, B.: *The Dynamics of Culture Change.* New Haven: Yale University Press; 1945.

MUMFORD, L.: *The Condition of Man.* New York: Harcourt, Brace & Co.; 1944.

OGBURN, W. F.: *Social Change.* New York: B. W. Huebsch; 1923.

REDFIELD, R.; LINTON, R.; and HERSKOVITS, M. J.: "Memorandum on the Study of Acculturation." *American Anthropologist;* Vol. XXXVIII (1936); pp. 149–52.

CHAPTER VI

CHILDE, V. G.: *Man Makes Himself.* New York: Oxford University Press; 1939.

————: *Social Evolution.* London: Watts & Co.; 1951.

CLARK, G.: *From Savagery to Civilization.* London: Cobbett Press; 1946.

CHAPTER VII

ELLIS, H. H.: *Flint Working Techniques of the American Indians.* Columbus, Ohio; 1940.

KNOWLES, SIR F. H. S.: *Stone Workers' Progress: A Study of Stone Implements in the Pitt Rivers Museum.* Oxford: Pitt Rivers Museum of Oxford University Occasional Papers on Technology No. 6; 1953.

WATSON, W.: *Flint Implements: An Account of Stone Age Techniques and Cultures.* London: British Museum Guide; 1950.

CHAPTER VIII

ANDERSON, E.: *Plants, Man, and Life.* Boston: Little, Brown & Co.; 1952.

BRUNNER, E. DE S.; SANDER, I. T.; and ENSMINGER, D.: *Farmers of the World.* New York: Columbia University Press; 1945.

CURWEN, E. C., and HATT, G.: *Plough and Pasture: The Early History of Farming.* New York: Henry Schuman; 1953.

JANSEN, L. B.: *Man's Foods.* Champaign, Illinois: Garrard Press; 1953.

MANGELSDORF, P. C., and REEVES, R. C.: *The Origin of Indian Corn and Its Relatives.* Austin: Texas Agricultural Experimental Station, Bulletin No. 574; May, 1939.

SAUER, C. O.: *Agricultural Origins and Dispersals.* New York: American Geographical Society; 1952.

VAVILOV, N. I.: *Studies on the Origin of Cultivated Plants.* Leningrad: Bulletin of Applied Botany and Plant Breeding; Vol. XVI; 1926.

————: *The Origin, Variation, Immunity, and Breeding of Cultivated Plants.* Translated by K. Starr Chester. Waltham, Mass.: Chronica Botanica Co.; 1951.

CHAPTER IX

Story of Writing. Achievement of Civilization Series No. 1.

COGHLAN, H. H.: *Notes on the Prehistoric Metallurgy of Copper and Bronze in the Old World.* Oxford: Pitt Rivers Museum of Oxford University Occasional Papers on Technology No. 4; 1951.

CURWEN, E. C., and HATT, G.: *Plough and Pasture: The Early History of Farming.* New York: Henry Schuman; 1953.

DIRINGER, D.: *The Alphabet: A Key to the History of Mankind.* New York: Philosophical Library; 1948.

FORBES, R. J.: *Metallurgy in Antiquity.* Leiden: E. J. Brill; 1950.

KROEBER, A. L.: *Anthropology.* Revised edition. New York: Harcourt, Brace & Co.; 1948.

MASON, W. A.: *A History of the Art of Writing.* New York: The Macmillan Co.; 1920.

MOORHOUSE, A. C.: *Writing and the Alphabet.* London: Cobbett Press; 1946.

————: *The Triumph of the Alphabet: A History of Writing.* New York: Henry Schuman; 1953.

RICKARD, T. A.: *Man and Metals.* Vols. I and II. New York: Whittlesey House; 1932.

ROSENTHAL, E.: *Pottery and Ceramics.* Harmondsworth: Pelican Books; 1949.

SAYCE, R. U.: *Primitive Arts and Crafts.* Cambridge: The University Press; 1933.

CHAPTER X

LOWIE, R. H.: *The Origin of the State.* New York: Harcourt, Brace & Co.; 1927.

MAINE, H. S.: *Ancient Law.* Third American edition. New York: Henry Holt & Co.; 1873.

OPPENHEIMER, F.: *The State.* Indianapolis: The Bobbs-Merrill Company; 1914.

REDFIELD, R.: *The Folk Culture of Yucatan.* Chicago: University of Chicago Press, 1941.

SEAGLE, W.: *The Quest for Law.* New York: Alfred A. Knopf; 1941.

CHAPTER XI

BRAIDWOOD, R. J.: *Prehistoric Men.* Chicago: Chicago Natural History Museum Popular Series: Anthropology, No. 37; 1948.

BRODRICK, A. H.: *Early Man: A Survey of Human Origins.* St. Albans: Mayflower Press, Hutchinson's Scientific and Technical Publications; 1948.

BURKITT, M. C.: *The Old Stone Age: A Study of Paleolithic Times.* Second edition. Cambridge: The University Press; 1949.

CHILDE, V. G.: *Man Makes Himself.* London: Watts & Co.; 1937.

HOEBEL, A. E.: *Man in the Primitive World.* New York: McGraw-Hill Book Co.; 1949.

LEAKEY, L. S. B.: *Adam's Ancestors.* London: Methuen and Co.; 1934.

MacCURDY, G. G.: *Human Origins: A Manual of Prehistory.* Vols. I and II. New York: Appleton-Century-Crofts; 1924.

OAKLEY, K. P.: *Man the Tool Maker.* London: British Museum Guide; 1949.

CHAPTER XII

BERNDT, R. and C.: *The First Australians.* Sydney: Ure Smith Publication; 1952.

BOGORAS, V. G.: *The Chukchee.* New York: American Museum of Natural History, Memoirs, 11; 1904–09.

ELKIN, A. P.: *The Australian Aborigines.* Sydney: Angus and Robertson; 1938.

JOCHELSON, W.: *The Peoples of Asiatic Russia.* New York: American Museum of Natural History; 1928.

MAN, E. H.: *On the Aboriginal Inhabitants of the Andaman Islands.* London: Trübner & Co.; [preface dated 1883].

MURDOCK, G. P.: *Our Primitive Contemporaries.* New York: The Macmillan Co.; 1935.

RADCLIFFE-BROWN, A. R.: *The Andaman Islanders.* Cambridge: The University Press; 1933.

SCHAPERA, I.: *The Khoisan Peoples of South Africa.* London: G. Routledge & Sons; 1930.

SCHEBESTA, P.: *Among Congo Pygmies.* London: Hutchinson & Co.; 1933.

SELIGMANN, C. G., and B. Z.: *The Veddas.* Cambridge: The University Press; 1911.

SKEAT, W. W., and BLAGDEN, C. O.: *Pagan Races of the Malay Peninsula.* 2 volumes. London: The Macmillan Co.; 1906.

CHAPTER XIII

BUCK, SIR P. H.: *The Coming of the Maori.* Nelson, N.Z.: Cawthron Institute of Scientific Research; 1925.

————: *Vikings of the Sunrise.* New York: Frederick A. Stokes Co.; 1938.

DUFF, R.: *The Moa-Hunter Period of Maori Culture.* Wellington, N.Z.: Department of Internal Affairs; 1950.

LINTON, R.: *The Archeology of the Marquesas Islands.* Hawaii: B. P. Bishop Museum Bulletin, No. 23; 1925.

MOVIUS, H. L., JR.: *Early Man and Pleistocene Stratigraphy in Southern and Eastern Asia.* Cambridge: Papers of the Peabody Museum, Harvard University, Vol. XIX, No. 3; 1944.

RIESENFELD, A.: *The Megalithic Culture of Melanesia.* Leiden: E. J. Brill; 1950.

CHAPTER XIV

BURROWS, E. G.: *Western Polynesia: A Study in Cultural Differentiation.* Gothenburg: Ethnographic Museum; Ethnographic Series 7; 1938.

CODRINGTON, R. H.: *The Melanesians.* Oxford: Clarendon Press; 1891.

COON, C. S., and ANDREWS, J. M., IV: *Studies in the Anthropology of Oceania and Asia.* Cambridge: Papers of the Peabody Museum, Harvard University, Vol. XX; 1943.

DEACON, A. B.: *Malekula: A Vanishing People in the New Hebrides.* London: G. Routledge & Sons; 1934.

FIRTH, R.: *We, the Tikopia.* London: G. Allen & Unwin; 1936.

————: *Primitive Economics of the New Zealand Maori.* New York: E. P. Dutton & Co.; 1929.

GOODENOUGH, W. H.: *Kin and Community on Truk.* New Haven: Yale University Publications in Anthropology, No. 46; 1951.

KRIEGER, H. W.: *Island Peoples of the Western Pacific, Micronesia, and Polynesia.* Washington: Smithsonian Institution, War Background Studies No. 16; Sept., 1943.

LINTON, R.: *The Material Culture of the Marquesas Islands.* Hawaii: Memoirs of the B. P. Bishop Museum, Vol. VIII, No. 5; 1923.

————: *The Tanala, a Hill Tribe of Madagascar.* Chicago: Field Museum of Natural History, Anthropological Series, Publication No. 317, Vol. XXII; 1933.

LINTON, R.; WINGERT, P.; and D'HARNONCOURT, R.: *Arts of the South Seas.*
New York: Museum of Modern Art; Simon and Schuster; 1946.

MALINOWSKI, B.: *Argonauts of the Western Pacific.* New York: E. P. Dutton
& Co.; 1932.

————: *Coral Gardens and Their Magic.* London: G. Allen & Unwin; 1935.

MEAD, M.: *From the South Seas.* New York: William Morrow & Co.; 1939.

OLIVER, D.: *The Pacific Islands.* Cambridge: Harvard University Press; 1951.

RIVERS, W. H. R.: *History of Melanesian Society.* Cambridge: The University
Press; 1914.

SPOEHR, A.: *Majuro: A Village in the Marshall Islands.* Chicago: Chicago
Natural History Museum; 1949.

WHITING, J. W. M.; *On Becoming a Kwoma.* New Haven: Yale University
Press; 1941.

WILLIAMS, F. E.: *Papuans of the Trans-Fly.* Oxford: Clarendon Press; 1936.

CHAPTER XV

BARTON, R. F.: *The Kalingas.* Chicago: University of Chicago Press; 1949.

BRIGGS, L. P.: *The Ancient Khmer Empire.* Philadelphia: Transactions of the
American Philosophical Society; 1951.

COLE, F. C.: *The Peoples of Malaysia.* New York: D. Van Nostrand Co.;
1945.

COVARRUBIAS, M.: *The Island of Bali.* New York: Alfred A. Knopf; 1937.

DOBBY, E. H. G.: *Southeast Asia.* New York: John Wiley & Sons; 1950.

DU BOIS, C.: *The People of Alor.* Minneapolis: University of Minnesota Press;
1944.

FIRTH, R.: *Malay Fishermen: Their Peasant Economy.* London: Kegan Paul,
Trench, Trubner & Co.; 1946.

HEINE-GELDERN, R.: "Prehistoric Research in the Netherlands Indies." In
Science and Scientists in the Netherlands Indies. Edited by Pieter Honig
and Frans Verdoorn. New York: 1945.

KENNEDY, J.: *The Ageless Indies.* New York: The John Day Co.; 1942.

KROM, N. J.: *Borabudur: Archeological Description.* The Hague: M. Nijhoff;
1927.

PERRY, W. J.: *The Megalithic Culture of Indonesia.* London: Longmans,
Green & Co.; 1918.

TER HAAR, B.: *Adat Law in Indonesia.* Translated. New York: Institute of
Pacific Relations; 1948.

WINSTEDT, R.: *The Malays: A Cultural History.* London: Routledge & Kegan
Paul; 1950.

CHAPTER XVI

BRAIDWOOD, R. J.: *The Near East and the Foundations of Civilization.* Eu-
gene, Oregon: Oregon State System of Higher Education; 1952.

CHILDE, V. G.: *New Light on the Most Ancient East.* Revised edition. London: Routledge & Kegan Paul; 1952.

DAVISON, D.: *The Story of Prehistoric Civilizations.* London: Watts & Co.;
1951.

FRANKFORT, H.: *The Birth of Civilization in the Near East.* London: Williams
& Norgate; 1951.

PERKINS, A. L.: *The Comparative Archeology of Early Mesopotamia.* Chicago: Studies in Ancient Oriental Civilizations, No. 25; 1949.

CHAPTER XVII

CHILDE, V. G.: *The Dawn of European Civilization*. Fourth edition. New York: Alfred A. Knopf; 1948.
————: *Prehistoric Migrations in Europe*. Oslo: H. Aschehough & Co.; 1950.
DAVISON, D.: *The Story of Prehistoric Civilizations*. London: Watts & Co.; 1951.
HAWKES, C. F. C.: *The Prehistoric Foundations of Europe: To the Mycenean Age*. London: Methuen & Co.; 1940.
PEAKE, H., and FLEURE, H. J.: *The Corridors of Time Series*. Vols. I—IX. New Haven: Yale University Press; 1926–36.

CHAPTER XVIII

CHILDE, V. G.: *The Bronze Age*. Cambridge: The University Press; 1930.
————: *The Dawn of European Civilization*. Fourth edition. New York: Alfred A. Knopf; 1948.
————: *Prehistoric Migrations in Europe*. Oslo: H. Aschehough & Co.; 1950.
CLARK, J. G. D.: *Prehistoric Europe: The Economic Basis*. New York: The Philosophical Library; 1952.
DAVISON, D.: *The Story of Prehistoric Civilizations*. London: Watts & Co.; 1951.
HAWKES, C. F. C.: *The Prehistoric Foundations of Europe: To the Mycenean Age*. London: Methuen & Co.; 1940.

- CHAPTER XIX

CHILDE, V. G.: *The Aryans: A Study of Indo-European Origins*. London: Kegan Paul, Trench, Trubner & Co.; 1926.
HUDSON, A. E.: *Kazak Social Structure*. New Haven: Yale University Press; 1938.
JOCHELSON, W.: *The Peoples of Asiatic Russia*. New York: American Museum of Natural History; 1928.
KELLER, A. G.: *Homeric Society*. New York: Longmans, Green & Co.; 1902.
LAMB, H.: *Genghis Khan, Emperor of All Men*. New York: Penguin Books; no date.

CHAPTER XX

The Cambridge Ancient History. 12 volumes. Cambridge: The University Press; 1923–29.
BAIKIE, J.: *The Life of the Ancient East*. New York: The Macmillan Co.; 1923.
GLUECK, N.: *The Other Side of the Jordan*. New Haven: American Schools of Oriental Research; 1940.
MUSIL, A.: *The Manners and Customs of the Rawala Bedouin*. New York: Czech Academy of Sciences and Arts; 1928.
O'LEARY, DE L.: *Arabia Before Muhammed*. London: Kegan Paul, Trench, Trubner & Co.; 1927.
PATAI, R.: *Man and Temple*. New York: Thomas Nelson & Sons; 1947.
SWAYNE, H. G. C.: *Seventeen Trips Through Somaliland*. London: R. Ward; 1900.
WOOLLEY, SIR L.: *Abraham: Recent Discoveries and Hebrew Origins*. New York: Charles Scribner's Sons; 1936.

CHAPTER XXI

BREASTED, J. H.: *Ancient Times, A History of the Early World*. Boston: Ginn
& Co.; 1916.
CARLETON, P.: *Buried Empire*. New York: E. P. Dutton & Co.; 1939.
CHILDE, V. G.: *New Light on the Most Ancient East*. Revised edition. Lon-
don: Routledge & Kegan Paul; 1952.
DAVISON, D.: *The Story of Prehistoric Civilizations*. London: Watts & Co.;
1951.
DELAPORTE, L.: *Mesopotamia: The Babylonian and Assyrian Civilization*.
New York: Alfred A. Knopf; 1925.
FRANKFORT, H.: *The Birth of Civilization in the Near East*. London: Williams
& Norgate; 1951.
WOOLLEY, C. L.: *The Sumerians*. Oxford: Clarendon Press; 1928.
————: *Ur of the Chaldees*. New York: Charles Scribner's Sons; 1930.

CHAPTER XXII

ALBRIGHT, W. F.: *The Archeology of Palestine*. Harmondsworth: Pelican
Books; 1949.
CHILDE, V. G.: *New Light on the Most Ancient East*. Revised edition. Lon-
don: Routledge & Kegan Paul; 1952.
DOUGHERTY, R. P.: *The Sealand of Ancient Arabia*. New Haven: Yale Uni-
versity Press; Yale Oriental Series: Researches, Vol. XIX; 1932.
GURNEY, O. R.: *The Hittites*. Harmondsworth: Pelican Books; 1952.
MORET, A., and DAVY, G.: *From Tribe to Empire*. New York: Alfred A.
Knopf; 1926.
OLMSTEAD, A. T.: *History of Assyria*. New York: Charles Scribner's Sons;
1923.
————: *History of the Persian Empire (Achaemenid Period)*. Chicago: Uni-
versity of Chicago Press; 1948.

CHAPTER XXIII

EVANS, SIR A.: *The Palace of Minos at Knossos*. 4 volumes. London: Macmil-
lan & Co.; 1921–35.
HOMER: *The Iliad*. Translated by W. H. D. Rouse. New York: New American
Library of World Literature (Mentor Classics); 1950.
————: *The Odyssey*. Translated by W. H. D. Rouse. New York: New Ameri-
can Library of World Literature (Mentor Classics); 1950.
PENDLEBURY, J. D. S.: *The Archeology of Crete*. London: Methuen & Co.;
1939.
PLATO: *The Works of Plato*. Selected and edited by Erwin Edman. New
York: Modern Library; 1930.
PLUTARCH: *The Lives of the Noble Grecians and Romans*. Translated by John
Dryden. New York: The Modern Library; 1932.

CHAPTER XXIV

BLÜMNER, H.: *The Home Life of the Ancient Greeks*. Translated by Alice
Zimmern. New York: Funk and Wagnalls Co.; no date.
DURANT, W.: *The Life of Greece*. New York: Simon and Schuster; 1939.
GLOVER, T. R.: *The Ancient World: A Beginning*. New York: The Macmillan
Co.; 1935.

HALL, H. R.: *The Civilization of Greece in the Bronze Age.* London: Methuen & Co.; 1928.

HERODOTUS: *The History of Herodotus.* Translated by G. Rawlinson. New York: Tudor Publishing Co.; 1932.

HYDE, W. W.: *Ancient Greek Mariners.* New York: Oxford University Press; 1947.

PLATO: *The Works of Plato.* Selected and edited by Erwin Edman. New York: The Modern Library; 1930.

PLUTARCH: *The Lives of the Noble Grecians and Romans.* Translated by John Dryden. New York: The Modern Library; 1932.

ROSTOVTZEFF, M. I.: *Out of the Past of Greece and Rome.* New Haven: Yale University Press; 1932.

CHAPTER XXV

GREEN, A. S.: *History of the Irish State to 1014.* London: Macmillan & Co.; 1925.

JACOBSTHAL, P.: *Early Celtic Art.* Oxford: Clarendon Press; 1944.

TACITUS: *The Complete Works of Tacitus.* Translated by A. J. Church and W. J. Brodribb. New York: The Modern Library; 1942.

THUCYDIDES: *The Complete Writings of Thucydides.* Translated by Crawley. New York: The Modern Library; 1934.

CHAPTER XXVI

BARROW, R. H.: *Slavery in the Roman Empire.* London: Methuen & Co.; 1928.

CARCOPINO, J.: *Daily Life in Ancient Rome.* Translated by E. O. Lorimer. New Haven: Yale University Press; 1940.

DURANT, W.: *Caesar and Christ.* New York: Simon and Schuster; 1944.

GIBBON, E.: *The Decline and Fall of the Roman Empire.* 2 volumes. New York: The Modern Library; 1932.

RANDALL-MACIVER, D.: *The Etruscans.* Oxford: Clarendon Press; 1927.

————: *Italy Before the Romans.* Oxford: Clarendon Press; 1928.

CHAPTER XXVII

BROCKELMANN, C.: *History of the Islamic Peoples.* Translated by J. Carmichael and M. Perlmann. New York: G. P. Putnam's Sons; 1947.

COON, C. S.: *Caravan: The Story of the Middle East.* New York: Henry Holt & Co.; 1951.

DIENER, B.: *Imperial Byzantium.* Translated by E. and C. Paul. Boston: Little, Brown & Co.; 1938.

HELL, J.: *The Arab Civilization.* Translated by S. K. Bukhsh. Cambridge: W. Heffer and Sons; 1925.

HITTI, P. K.: *The History of the Arabs.* Third edition, revised. London: Macmillan & Co.; 1943.

LINDSAY, J.: *Byzantium into Europe.* London: The Bodley Head; 1952.

RUNCIMAN, S.: *Byzantine Civilization.* London: Edward Arnold and Co.; 1936.

YOUNG, T. C., editor: *Near Eastern Culture and Society.* Princeton: Princeton University Press; 1951.

CHAPTER XXVIII

BURKITT, M. C.: *South Africa's Past in Stone and Paint.* Cambridge: The University Press; 1928.

CATON-THOMPSON, G.: *The Zimbabwe Culture: Ruins and Reactions.* Oxford: Clarendon Press; 1931.

CLARK, J. G. D.: *The Prehistoric Cultures of the Horn of Africa.* London; 1953.

HAMBLY, W. D.: *Source Book for African Anthropology.* Parts I and II. Chicago: Field Museum of Natural History, Anthropological Series, Publication No. 394, Vol. XXVI; 1937.

GOODWIN, A. J. H., and VAN RIET LOWE, C.: *The Stone Age Cultures of South Africa.* Capetown: Annals of the South African Museum, Vol. XXVII; 1929.

LEAKEY, L. S. B.: *Stone Age Cultures of Kenya Colony.* Cambridge: The University Press; 1931.

————: *Stone Age Africa.* London: Oxford University Press; 1936.

————, editor: *Proceedings of the Pan-African Congress on Prehistory, 1947.* New York: 1949.

POND, A. W.; CHAPUIS, L.; ROMER, A. S.; and BAKER, F. C.: *Prehistoric Habitation Sites in the Sahara and North Africa.* Beloit, Wisconsin: Logan Museum Bulletin No. 5; 1938.

D'UCEL, J.: *Berber Arts: An Introduction.* Norman, Oklahoma: University of Oklahoma Press; 1932.

WULSIN, F. R.: *Prehistoric Archeology of Northwest Africa.* Cambridge: Papers of the Peabody Museum, Harvard University; Vol. 19, No. 1; 1941.

CHAPTER XXIX

BAUMGARTEL, E. J.: *The Cultures of Prehistoric Egypt.* Oxford: Oxford University Press; 1947.

BREASTED, J. H.: *A History of Egypt from the Earliest Times to the Persian Conquest.* New York: Charles Scribner's Sons; 1905.

BUDGE, E. W.: *A Short History of the Egyptian People.* London: J. M. Dent & Sons; 1914.

CARTER, H., and MACE, A. C.: *The Tomb of Tut-Ankh-Amen.* London: Cassell & Co.; 1923.

CHILDE, V. G.: *New Light on the Most Ancient East.* Revised edition. London: Routledge & Kegan Paul; 1952.

EDWARDS, J. E. S.: *The Pyramids of Egypt.* Harmondsworth: Penguin Books; 1947.

HAYES, W. C.: *The Scepter of Egypt.* New York: Harper and Brothers; 1953.

HUZAYYIN, S. A. S.: *The Place of Egypt in Prehistory: A Correlated Study of Climates and Cultures in the Old World.* Cairo: Memoires de l'Institut Egypte, Vol. 43; 1941.

MANCHIP-WHITE, J. E.: *Ancient Egypt.* New York: Thomas Y. Crowell Co.; no date.

MURRAY, M. A.: *The Splendour that Was Egypt.* New York: Philosophical Library; 1949.

PETRIE, W. M. F.: *Prehistoric Egypt.* London: British School of Archeology in Egypt; 1920.

SELIGMAN, C. G.: *Egypt and Negro Africa: A Study in Divine Kingship.* London: George Routledge and Sons; 1934.

TABOUIS, G. R.: *The Private Life of Tutankhamen.* New York: The McBride Company; 1930.

WADDELL, L. A.: *Egyptian Civilization: Its Sumerian Origin and Real Chronology.* London: Luzac & Co.; 1930.

WILSON, J. A.: *The Burden of Egypt.* Chicago: University of Chicago Press; 1951.

CHAPTER XXX

CHILD, G. M.: *Umbundu Kinship and Character.* London: Oxford University Press; 1949.

COLSON, C., and GLUCKMAN, M. (editors): *Seven Tribes of British Central Africa.* London: Oxford University Press; 1951.

CULWICK, A. T., and G. M.: *Ubena of the Rivers.* London: G. Allen & Unwin; 1935.

DELAFOSSE, M.: *The Negroes of Africa.* Translated by F. Fligelman. Washington, D.C.: The Association Publishers; 1931.

DOKE, C. M.: *The Lambas of Northern Rhodesia.* London: G. G. Harrap & Co.; 1931.

EVANS-PRITCHARD, E. E.: *Witchcraft, Oracles and Magic among the Azande.* Oxford: Clarendon Press; 1937.

————: *The Nuer.* Oxford: Clarendon Press; 1940.

FORTES, M.: *The Dynamics of Clanship Among the Tallensi.* London: Oxford University Press; 1945.

————: *The Web of Kinship Among the Tallensi.* London: Oxford University Press; 1949.

FORTES, M., and EVANS-PRITCHARD, E. E.: *African Political Systems.* London: Oxford University Press; 1940.

HUNTER, M.: *Reaction to Conquest.* London: Oxford University Press; 1936.

JUNOD, H. P.: *The Vathonga.* Cambridge: Deighton, Bell & Co.; 1935.

KABERRY, P.: *Women of the Grassfields: A Study of the Economic Position of Women in Bamenda, British Cameroons.* London: H. M. Stationery Office, for the Colonial Office; 1952.

KENYATTA, J.: *Facing Mount Kenya.* London: Secker & Warburg; 1938.

KRIGE, J. D., and E. J.: *A Realm of a Rain Queen: A Study of Lovedu Society.* New York: Oxford University Press; 1943.

LUTTIG, H. G.: *The Religious System and Social Organization of the Herrero.* Utrecht: Kemink en zoon n.v.; 1934.

MEEK, C. K.: *The Northern Tribes of Nigeria.* 2 volumes. London: Oxford University Press; 1925.

NADEL, S. F.: *The Nuba.* London: Oxford University Press; 1942.

RADCLIFFE-BROWN, A. R., and FORDE, D., editors: *African Systems of Kinship and Marriage.* London: Oxford University Press; 1950.

REY, C. F.: *The Real Abyssinia.* Third edition. Philadelphia: J. B. Lippincott Co.; no date.

RICHARDS, A. I.: *Land, Labour and Diet in Northern Rhodesia.* Second impression. London: Oxford University Press; 1951.

RODD, F. R.: *People of the Veil.* London: Macmillan & Co.; 1926.

SCHAPERA, I.: *The Khoisan Peoples of South Africa.* London: G. Routledge
& Sons; 1930.
————: *A Handbook of Tswana Law and Custom.* London: Oxford University Press; 1938.
————, editor: *The Bantu Speaking Tribes of South Africa.* London:
G. Routledge & Sons; 1937.
SCHWAB, G.: *Tribes of the Liberian Hinterland.* Cambridge: Papers of the
Peabody Museum, Harvard University; Vol. 31; 1947.
SMITH, E. W., and DALE, W. M.: The Ila-Speaking Peoples of Northern
Rhodesia. London: Macmillan & Co.; 1920.
TALBOT, P. A.: *Peoples of Southern Nigeria.* 4 volumes. London: Oxford
University Press; 1926.
WAGNER, G.: *The Changing Family among the Bantu Kavirondo.* London:
Memoranda of the International African Institute; No. 18; 1939.
WEEKS, J. H.: *Among the Primitive Bakongo.* London: Seeley, Service &
Co.; 1914.
WILSON, M. H.: *Good Company.* London: Oxford University Press; 1951.
WILSON-HAFFENDEN, J. R.: *The Red Men of Nigeria.* London: Seeley, Service & Co.; 1930.
WINGERT, P.: *The Sculpture of Negro Africa.* New York: Columbia University Press; 1950.

CHAPTER XXXI

HADFIELD, H.: *Traits of Divine Kingship in Africa.* London: Watts & Co.;
1949.
HERSKOVITS, M. J.: *Dahomey, an Ancient West African Kingdom.* Vols. I
and II. New York: J. J. Augustin, Inc., Publishers; 1938.
KUPER, H.: *An African Aristocracy.* London: Oxford University Press; 1947.
MAIR, L. P.: *An African People in the 20th Century.* London: G. Routledge
& Sons; 1934.
MEEK, C. K.: *A Sudanese Kingdom.* London: Kegan Paul, Trench, Trubner
& Co.; 1931.
MURDOCK, G. P.: *Our Primitive Contemporaries.* New York: The Macmillan
Co.; 1934.
NADEL, S. F.: *A Black Byzantium.* London: Oxford University Press; 1942.
RATTRAY, R. S.: *The Ashanti.* Oxford: Clarendon Press; 1923.
ROSCOE, J.: *The Baganda.* London: Macmillan & Co.; 1911.

CHAPTER XXXII

BARNETT, L. D.: *Antiquities of India.* London: P. L. Warner; 1913.
CHILDE, V. G.: *New Light on the Most Ancient East.* Revised edition. London: Routledge & Kegan Paul; 1952.
MARSHALL, J., editor: *Mohenjo Daru and the Indus Civilization.* London:
A. Probsthain; 1931.
MACKAY, E.: *Early Indus Civilizations.* Revised edition. London: Luzac and
Co.; 1948.
MITRA, P.: *Prehistoric India.* Revised edition. Calcutta: University of Calcutta; 1927.
MOVIUS, H. L., JR.: *Early Man and the Pleistocene Stratigraphy in Southern and Eastern Asia.* Cambridge: Papers of the Peabody Museum,
Harvard University; Vol. 19, No. 3; 1944.

————: *Lower Paleolithic Cultures of Southern and Eastern Asia.* Philadelphia: Transactions of the American Philosophical Society, Vol. 38, No. 4; 1949.

PIGGOTT, S.: *Prehistoric India.* Harmondsworth: Pelican Books; 1950.

PRABHAVANANDA, S.: *Vedic Religion and Philosophy.* Editorial supervision by P. H. Houston. Mylapore, Madras: Sri Ramakrisna Math; 1950.

SEN, G. E.: *The Pageant of India's History.* New York: Longmans, Green & Co.; 1948. Vol. I.

TERRA, H. DE, and PATERSON, T. T.: *Studies on the Ice Age in India and Associated Human Cultures.* Washington: Carnegie Institution of Washington Publication No. 493; 1939.

WHEELER, R. E. M.: *Five Thousand Years of Pakistan.* London: C. Johnson; 1950.

CHAPTER XXXIII

GROUSSET, R.: *The Civilization of India.* Translated by C. A. Phillips. New York: Tudor Publishing Co.; 1939.

HAWKRIDGE, E.: *Indian Gods and Kings: The Story of a Living Past.* Boston: Houghton Mifflin Co.; 1935.

HUTTON, J. H.: *Caste in India.* Cambridge: The University Press; 1946.

MORGAN, K. W., editor: *The Religion of the Hindus.* New York: The Ronald Press Company; 1953.

RICE, S.: *Hindu Customs and Their Origins.* London: G. Allen and Unwin; 1937.

RIVERS, W. H. R.: *The Todas.* London: Macmillan & Co.; 1906.

SEN, G. E.: *The Pageant of India's History.* New York: Longmans, Green & Co.; 1948. Vol. I.

SENART, E.: *Caste in India.* Translated by E. D. Ross. London: Methuen & Co.; 1930.

SWANATHA, S. V. V.: *Racial Synthesis in Hindu Culture.* London: Kegan Paul, Trench, Trubner & Co.; 1928.

CHAPTER XXXIV

DAVIDS, C. A. R.: *Sakya; or Buddhist Origins.* London: Kegan Paul, Trench, Trubner & Co.; 1931.

RADH-KRISHNAN, S.: *Gautama, the Buddha.* London: Oxford University Press; 1938.

THOMAS, E. J.: *The Life of Buddha as Legend and History.* London: Kegan Paul, Trench, Trubner & Co.; 1927.

CHAPTER XXXV

ARCHER, J. C.: *The Sikhs: A Study in Comparative Religion.* Princeton: Princeton University Press; 1946.

CROOKE, W.: *The Natives of Northern India.* London: A. Constable & Co.; 1907.

ELWIN, V.: *The Baiga.* London: J. Murray; 1939.

HUTTON, J. H.: *Caste in India.* Cambridge: The University Press; 1946.

MORGAN, K. W., editor: *The Religion of the Hindus.* New York: The Ronald Press Company; 1953.

SEN, G. E.: *The Pageant of India's History.* Vol. I. New York: Longmans, Green & Co.; 1948.

SENART, E.: *Caste in India.* Translated by E. D. Ross. London: Methuen & Co.; 1930.

CHAPTER XXXVI

ANDERSSEN, J. G.: *Children of the Yellow Earth.* New York: 1934.
———: *Researches in the Prehistory of the Chinese.* Stockholm: Bulletin of the Museum of Far Eastern Antiquities No. 15; 1943.
CHI LI: *The Formation of the Chinese People.* Cambridge: The University Press; 1928.
CREEL, H. G.: *The Birth of China.* New York: The John Day Co.; 1937.
———: *Studies in Early Chinese History.* (First Series). Washington: American Council of Learned Societies Studies in Chinese and Related Civilizations, No. 3; 1938.
CRESSEY, G. B.: *China's Geographic Foundations.* New York: McGraw-Hill Book Co.; 1934.
MOVIUS, H. L., JR.: *Early Man and the Pleistocene Stratigraphy in Southern and Eastern Asia.* Cambridge: Papers of the Peabody Museum, Harvard University, Vol. 19, No. 3; 1944.
———: *Lower Paleolithic Cultures of Southern and Eastern Asia.* Philadelphia: Transactions of the American Philosophical Society, Vol. 38, No. 4; 1949.
WHITE, W. C.: *The Bone Culture of Ancient China.* Toronto: University of Toronto Press, Museum Studies No. 4; 1945.
WU, G. D.: *Prehistoric Pottery in China.* London: Kegan Paul, Trench, Trubner & Co.; 1938.

CHAPTER XXXVII

BUXTON, L. H. D.: *China, the Land and the People.* Oxford: Clarendon Press; 1929.
———: *The Peoples of Asia.* New York: Alfred A. Knopf; 1925.
CREEL, H. G.: *Sinism, A Study of the Evolution of the Chinese World View.* Chicago: The Open Court Publishing Co.; 1929.
FUNG, Y. L.: *A Short History of Chinese Philosophy.* Edited by Derk Bodde. New York: The Macmillan Co.; 1948.
GOODRICH, K. C.: *A Short History of the Chinese People.* Revised edition. New York: Harper & Brothers; 1951.
DE GROOT, J. J. M.: *The Religion of the Chinese.* New York: The Macmillan Co.; 1910.
LATOURETTE, K. S.: *The Chinese: Their History and Culture.* New York: The Macmillan Co.; 1934.
PAN KU: *History of the Former Han Dynasty.* Translated by Homer H. Dubs. Baltimore: The Waverly Press; 1938.
WALKER, R. L.: *The Multi-State System of Ancient China.* Hamden, Connecticut: The Shoestring Press; 1953.
WILHELM, R.: *A Short History of Chinese Civilization.* Translated by J. Joshua. New York: The Viking Press; 1929.
WILLIAMS, S. W.: *The Middle Kingdom.* Revised edition. Vols. I and II. New York: Charles Scribner's Sons; 1883.
WITTFOGEL, K. A., and FÊNG CHIA-SHÊNG: *History of Chinese Society: Liao (907–1125).* Transactions of the American Philosophical Society, Vol. 36, 1946. New York: Distributed by The Macmillan Co.; 1949.

CHAPTER XXXVIII

CHIANG MONLIN: *Tides from the West*. New Haven: Yale University Press; 1947.

FEI, H. T.: *Peasant Life in China*. London: Kegan Paul, Trench, Trubner & Co.; 1947.

FRIED, M. H.: *The Fabric of Chinese Society*. New York: Frederick A. Praeger; 1953.

HSU, F. L. K.: *Under the Ancestors' Shadow*. Routledge & Kegan Paul; 1949.

———: *Americans and Chinese: Two Ways of Life*. New York: Henry Schuman; 1953.

KULP, D. H.: *Country Life in Southern China*. New York: Teachers College, Columbia University; 1925.

LANG, O.: *Chinese Family and Society*. New Haven: Yale University Press; 1946.

LAUFER, B.: *Jade*. Chicago: Field Museum of Natural History, Anthropological Series, Publication No. 154, Vol. X; 1912.

LEONG, Y. K., and TAO, L. K.: *Village and Town Life in China*. London: 1915.

MORSE, H. B.: *The Gilds of China*. London: Longmans, Green & Co.; 1909.

SIREN, O.: *A History of Early Chinese Painting*. London: The Medici Society; 1933.

YANG, M. C.: *A Chinese Village*. London: Kegan Paul, Trench, Trubner & Co.; 1948.

CHAPTER XXXIX

EMBREE, J.: *The Japanese Nation: A Social Survey*. New York: Rinehart & Co.; 1945.

GROOT, G. J.: *The Prehistory of Japan*. Edited by B. S. Kraus. New York: Columbia University Press; 1951.

HEARN, L.: *Japan: An Attempt at Interpretation*. New York: The Macmillan Co.; 1904.

LATOURETTE, K. S.: *The History of Japan*. New York: The Macmillan Co.; 1947.

MUNRO, N. G.: *Prehistoric Japan*. Yokohama; 1911.

NORBECK, E.: *Takashima*. Salt Lake City: University of Utah Press; 1954.

REISCHAUER, E. O.: *Japan, Past and Present*. Revised edition. New York· Alfred A. Knopf; 1953.

SANSOM, G. B.: *Japan: A Short Cultural History*. Revised edition. New York: Appleton-Century-Crofts; 1943.

TAKEKOSHI, Y.: *The Economic Aspects of the History of the Civilization of Japan*. Vols. I, II, & III. New York: The Macmillan Co.; 1930.

CHAPTER XL

BIRKET-SMITH, K.: *The Eskimos*. New York: E. P. Dutton & Co.; 1936.

CATLIN, G.: *North American Indians*. 2 volumes. London: Chatto and Windus; no date.

CODERE, H.: *Fighting with Property*. New York: J. J. Augustin, Inc., Publishers; 1950.

COLLIER, J.: *The Indians of the Americas*. New York: W. W. Norton & Company; 1947.

CURTIS, E. S.: *The North American Indian.* Second revised edition. 20 volumes. Norwood, Mass.: The Plimpton Press; 1907–30.

DALE, E. E.: *The Indians of the Southwest.* Norman, Oklahoma: University of Oklahoma Press; 1949.

EGGAN, F.: *The Social Organization of the Western Pueblos.* Chicago: University of Chicago Press; 1950.

GRINNELL, G. B.: *The Cheyenne Indians.* 2 volumes. New Haven: Yale University Press; 1923.

HODGE, F. W., editor: *Handbook of the American Indians North of Mexico.* Washington: Smithsonian Institution, Bureau of American Ethnology Bulletin No. 30, Parts I and II; 1907.

JENESS, D.: *Indians of Canada.* Ottawa: National Museum of Canada, Bulletin No. 65; 1932.

KENTON, E., editor: *The Indians of North America.* 2 volumes. New York: Harcourt, Brace & Co.; 1927.

KINIETZ, W. V.: *The Indians of the Western Great Lakes, 1615–1760.* Ann Arbor: University of Michigan Press; 1940.

KLUCKHOHN, C., and LEIGHTON, D.: *The Navaho.* Cambridge: Harvard University Press; 1946.

KROEBER, A. L.: *Cultural and Natural Areas of Native North America.* Berkeley: University of California Press; 1949.

———: *Handbook of the Indians of California.* Berkeley: California Book Co.; 1953. (Bureau of American Ethnology Bulletin No. 78, 1925.)

LOWIE, R. H.: *The Crow Indians.* New York: Rinehart & Company; 1935.

MACGOWAN, K.: *Early Man in the New World.* New York: The Macmillan Co.; 1950.

MARTIN, P. S.; QUIMBY, G. I.; and COLLIER, D.: *Indians Before Columbus.* Chicago: University of Chicago Press; 1947.

MORGAN, L. H.: *The League of the Ho-Dé-No-Sau-Nee or Iroquois.* H. M. Lloyd, editor. 2 volumes. New York: 1901.

MURDOCK, G. P.: *Our Primitive Contemporaries.* New York: The Macmillan Co.; 1934.

OPLER, M. E.: *An Apache Life-Way.* Chicago: University of Chicago Press; 1941.

OSGOOD, C.: *Ingalik Material Culture.* New Haven: Yale University Publications in Anthropology, No. 22; 1940.

PARKMAN, S., JR.: *The Oregon Trail.* New York: Caxton House; no date.

PARSONS, E. C.: *The Pueblo of Jemez.* New Haven: Yale University Press; 1925.

RASMUSSEN, K.: *The People of the Polar North.* Edited by G. Herring. Philadelphia: J. B. Lippincott Co.; 1908.

———: *The Netsilik Eskimo.* Copenhagen: Report on the Fifth Thule Expedition, 1921–24. VIII, No. 1 and 2; 1931.

RITCHIE, W. A.: *The Pre-Iroquoian Occupations of New York State.* Rochester: Rochester Museum Memoir No. 1; 1944.

SELLARDS, E. H.: *Early Man in North America.* Austin, Texas: University of Texas Press; 1952.

SPECK, F. G.: *Naskapi.* Norman, Oklahoma: University of Oklahoma Press; 1935.

SPIER, L.: *Yuman Tribes of the Gila River.* Chicago: University of Chicago Press; 1933.

STERN, J.: *The Rubber-Ball Games of the Americas*. New York: J. J. Augustin, Inc., Publisher; 1948.

SWANTON, J. R.: *Indian Tribes of the Lower Mississippi Valley and the Adjacent Coast of the Gulf of Mexico*. Washington: Smithsonian Institution, Bureau of American Ethnology Bulletin No. 43; 1911.

————: *The Indians of the Southeastern United States*. Washington: Smithsonian Institution, Bureau of American Ethnology Bulletin No. 137; 1946.

————: *The Indian Tribes of North America*. Washington: Smithsonian Institution, Bureau of American Ethnology Bulletin No. 145; 1952.

UNDERHILL, R. M.: *Red Man's America*. Chicago: University of Chicago Press; 1953.

WISSLER, C.: *The American Indian*. Third edition. New York: Oxford University Press; 1938.

WORMINGTON, H. M.: *Prehistoric Indians of the Southwest*. Denver: Colorado Museum of Natural History, Popular Series No. 7; 1947.

————: *Ancient Man in North America*. Third edition, revised. Denver: Colorado Museum of Natural History, Popular Series No. 4; 1949.

ZEISBERGER, D.: *History of the North American Indians*. Edited by A. B. Hulbert and W. N. Schwarze. Columbus: Ohio State Archeological and Historical Society; no date.

CHAPTER XLI

BENNETT, W. C., and BIRD, J. B.: *Andean Culture History*. New York: American Museum of Natural History, Handbook Series No. 15; 1949.

BENNETT, W. C., and ZINGG, R. M.: *The Tarahumara*. Chicago: University of Chicago Press; 1935.

COLLIER, J.: *The Indians of the Americas*. New York: W. W. Norton & Co.; 1947.

GANN, T., and THOMPSON, J. E.: *History of the Mayas*. New York: Charles Scribner's Sons; 1931.

HAY, C. L., and others: *The Maya and Their Neighbors*. New York: Appleton-Century-Crofts; 1940.

JOYCE, T. A.: *South American Archeology*. New York: G. P. Putnam's Sons; 1912.

KARSTEN, R.: *A Totalitarian State of the Past*. Helsingfors: Societas Scientarum Fennica; Commentationes Humanarum Litterarum XVI; 1949.

KELEMAN, P.: *Medieval American Art*. 2 volumes. New York: The Macmillan Co.; 1943.

MARKHAM, C. R.: *The Incas of Peru*. London: Smith, Elder & Co.; 1910.

MEANS, P. A.: *Ancient Civilizations of the Andes*. New York: Charles Scribner's Sons; 1931.

MONGE, C.: *Acclimatization in the Andes*. Translated by D. F. Brown. Baltimore: Johns Hopkins University Press; 1948.

MORELY, S. G.: *The Ancient Maya*. Stanford, California: Stanford University Press; 1946.

MURDOCK, G. P.: *Our Primitive Contemporaries*. New York: The Macmillan Co.; 1935.

PARSONS, E. C.: *Mitla, Town of Souls*. Chicago: University of Chicago Press; 1936.

SPINDEN, H. J.: *Ancient Civilizations of Mexico and Central America*. Third

edition. New York: American Museum of Natural History, Handbook
Series No. 3; 1928.

STEWARD, J. H., editor: *Handbook of South American Indians*. Washington:
Smithsonian Institution, Bureau of American Ethnology Bulletin No.
143; 1949. Vols. I—VI.

TAX, S., editor: *Heritage of Conquest*. Glencoe, Illinois: The Free Press;
1952.

THOMPSON, J. E.: *Mexico Before Cortez*. New York: Charles Scribner's Sons;
1933.

VAILLANT, G. C.: *Aztecs of Mexico*. New York: Doubleday & Company;
1941.

Index

i

A NOTE ON THE

T Y P E

IN WHICH THIS BOOK IS SET

THE TEXT of this book is set in Caledonia, a Linotype face that belongs to the family of printing types called "modern face" by printers—a term used to mark the change in style of type-letters that occurred about 1800. Caledonia borders on the general design of Scotch Modern, but is more freely drawn than that letter.

The book was composed, printed, and bound by KINGSPORT PRESS, INC., Kingsport, Tenn. The illustrations were reproduced by CAPPER ENGRAVING CO., INC., Knoxville, Tenn. The paper was manufactured by S. D. WARREN COMPANY, Boston, Mass.